STUDIES IN CHRISTIAN HISTORY AND THOUGHT

Enlightenment, Ecumenism, Evangel

Theological Themes and Thinkers 1550–2000

STUDIES IN CHRISTIAN HISTORY AND THOUGHT

A full listing of all titles in this series appears at the close of this book

STUDIES IN CHRISTIAN HISTORY AND THOUGHT

Enlightenment, Ecumenism, Evangel

Theological Themes and Thinkers 1550–2000

Alan P. F. Sell

Wipf & Stock
PUBLISHERS
Eugene, Oregon

Wipf and Stock Publishers
199 W 8th Ave, Suite 3
Eugene, OR 97401

Enlightenment, Ecumenism, Evangel
Theological Themes and Thinkers 1550–2000
By Sell, Alan P. F.

ISBN: 1-59752-744-0
Publication date 6/6/2006
Previously published by Paternoster, 2005

This Edition Published by Wipf and Stock Publishers
by arrangement with Paternoster

PATERNOSTER

Paternoster
9 Holdom Avenue
Bletchley
Milton Keyes, MK1 1QR
Great Britain

STUDIES IN CHRISTIAN HISTORY AND THOUGHT

Series Preface

This series complements the specialist series of *Studies in Evangelical History and Thought* and *Studies in Baptist History and Thought* for which Paternoster is becoming increasingly well known by offering works that cover the wider field of Christian history and thought. It encompasses accounts of Christian witness at various periods, studies of individual Christians and movements, and works which concern the relations of church and society through history, and the history of Christian thought.

The series includes monographs, revised dissertations and theses, and collections of papers by individuals and groups. As well as 'free standing' volumes, works on particular running themes are being commissioned; authors will be engaged for these from around the world and from a variety of Christian traditions.

A high academic standard combined with lively writing will commend the volumes in this series both to scholars and to a wider readership.

Series Editors

To
Hugo

Contents

Preface xi

Acknowledgements xvii

Chapter 1
Puritans, Platonists and Powicke 1

Chapter 2
John Gratton, A Quaker Star 46

Chapter 3
Some Theological Aspects of the English Enlightenment Calmly Consider'd 70

Chapter 4
The Gospel its own Witness: Deism, Thomas Paine and Andrew Fuller 111

Chapter 5
From Worms to Sunbeams: The Dilution of Calvinism in English Congregationalism 144

Chapter 6
'Change and Decay' or 'Onward Still, and Upward'? Reflections on the Development of Doctrine 166

Chapter 7
The Perennial Peril of Pantheism 205

Chapter 8
Some Reformed Reflections on Spirituality 221

Chapter 9
Reformed Theology in Britain in the Twentieth Century: A Bibliographical Survey 245

Chapter 10
The Alliance in Dialogue, 1970–2002: Retrospect and Reflections 260

Chapter 11
The Holy Spirit and Ecumenism: Some Catholic Ruminations of a Reformed Theologian **281**

Chapter 12
Nicknames, Labels and Slogans in Christian History and Thought **299**

Chapter 13
May We Still Glory in the Cross? **377**

Index of Persons **401**

General Index **414**

Preface

'Idleness is the great inlet to the most destructive vices.'[1]

In the course of an untitled lecture delivered in Balliol College, Oxford, in May 1947, F. M. Powicke, the son of F. J. Powicke from whom the first paper in this collection sets out, declared that the historian

> has a duty to the past. He should not forget the services rendered by an old order of things, whether it was embodied in a class of society or in a system of beliefs, in the days of its strength. He should not be too sure that forgotten values have lost their worth, still less that they never had any worth to lose.[2]

I stumbled across this quotation recently as I was pondering the fact that my first academic article was published about forty years ago. As I reflected upon my scribblings in the light of Powicke's remark, it seemed to me not only that I could endorse his words in so far as my historical interests are concerned, but that I could extend them to my related interests in philosophy and theology. For highly important though philosophical analysis be (and would it were employed more rigorously by some theologians), those philosophers who are not simply content to abstract the ideas of their predecessors as if they were sitting next to them in the Senior Common Room, are aware of the importance of the historical context of writings if philosophers of the past are to be understood in the way they intended. (I am well aware that some postmodernists declare that authorial intention for ever eludes us; I do not believe it, and were it true they would have no grounds for becoming agitated, as some of them do, if the rest of us fail, whether for conceptual, terminological or grammatical reasons, to grasp their meaning.) An added dimension comes into view when we apply Powicke's words to theologians, for they ought to have an interest in hearing the voice of the faithful through the ages if only as a caution against the temptation (to which a few seem to succumb) to invent theologies *de novo* with each new morning—an implicit denial of the providence of God, and an arrogant refusal to adjust their sights in relation to the wisdom of believing forebears.

In my academic life I have not found it easy to honour the inter-disciplinary boundaries which, partly on grounds of increased

---

[1] Joseph Priestley, *Theological and Miscellaneous Works*, ed. J. T. Rutt (1817–31), Bristol: Thoemmes Press, 1999, XXIV, p. 340.

[2] F. M. Powicke, *Three Lectures given in the Hall of Balliol College, Oxford in May 1947*, London: Oxford University Press, 1947, p. 21.

specialization, have been erected over the past century. This is because my running concern through what may appear, at first sight to be a miscellany of writings, is encapsulated in the following composite question: What is the heart of the Christian Gospel and what is its most appropriate mode of expression (theology); how may we most satisfactorily articulate it—especially in face of intellectual challenges to it (philosophy of religion/apologetics); what happens on the ground when Christians take their beliefs seriously (history); and how may we best heal the inner-Christian divisions which our history has bequeathed to us (ecumenism)? Let me break this question down into its component parts.

The question of the heart of the Christian Gospel and its most appropriate mode of expression has been with me throughout. I found it an existential as well as an intellectual necessity to try to order my thoughts on Calvinism and Arminianism and on theological liberalism and conservatism. Hence my early books on those subjects;[3] hence also the studies I have made of P. T. Forsyth who, of all twentieth-century theologians, seems to me to have struck most deeply to the heart of the Gospel,[4] and my attempt at a 'devotional systematics' for ministers and church members which would remind them of the heritage of Christian testimony, enliven doctrine with warmth and offer substance to devotions.[5]

But what of the intellectual challenges to the Gospel? These have motivated my studies of theologico-philosophical relations especially from the seventeenth century to the present day. I have reviewed the philosophical contribution of those who were excluded on religious grounds from the English universities,[6] and examined relations between Christian and secular philosophy from 1875 to 1980;[7] I have provided 'mini-resurrections' for a number of apologists, many of them sadly neglected;[8] I have investigated a number of those who have countered, or

---

[3] *The Great Debate: Calvinism, Arminianism and Salvation* (1982), Eugene, OR: Wipf & Stock, 1998; *Theology in Turmoil. The Roots, Course and Significance of the Conservative-Liberal Debate in Modern Theology* (1983), Eugene, OR: Wipf & Stock, 1998.

[4] See the papers in *Testimony and Tradition. Studies in Reformed and Dissenting Thought*, Aldershot: Ashgate, 2005.

[5] *God Our Father*; *Christ Our Saviour*; *The Spirit Our Life*, Shippensburg, PA: Ragged Edge Press, 2000.

[6] *Philosophy, Dissent and Nonconformity 1689-1920*, Cambridge: James Clarke, 2004.

[7] *The Philosophy of Religion 1875-1980*, (1988), Bristol: Thoemmes Press, 1996.

[8] For example, *Robert Mackintosh, Theologian of Integrity*, Bern Peter Lang, 1977; *Defending and Declaring the Faith: Some Scottish Examples 1860-1920*, Exeter: Paternoster Press and Colorado Springs: Helmers & Howard, 1988.

at least been ambivalent towards, Christian claims;[9] and my own attempt to enquire into which philosophical and theological issues need to be addressed before we offer an intellectual commendation of the Christian faith (that is, it is a second-order enquiry, a prolegomenon to apologetics, not an apologetic as such—a tiny minority of more somnolent reviewers notwithstanding) has resulted in a further trilogy.[10]

What happens on the ground when Christians take their beliefs seriously? Sometimes, sadly, they divide from one another. I have attempted a number of studies which trace doctrinal changes and the secessions which sometimes ensue. *Church Planting. A Study of Westmorland Nonconformity*,[11] ostensibly a local church history, is in fact an account of how the several Nonconformist traditions became established in, or in the case of the Baptists, Methodists and Quakers, found their way to, what was a relatively remote part of the country, and how their histories were to some extent shaped by doctrinal debates. Again, I have discussed the way in which most of those eighteenth-century English Presbyterians who did not become Congregationalists during that century had become Unitarian by the end of it. Although I do not accept some of their conclusions, I have considerable affection for such Presbyterian divines as Henry Grove, John Taylor, Samuel Bourn, Richard Price and others in the eighteenth century whose personal integrity and concern for Scripture prompted them to swim against the orthodox tide.[12] At the other end of the Dissenting spectrum, the 'hyper' tradition of Calvinism has also interested me, as witness my short study of a self-taught Strict Baptist pastor who left more than enough writings for us to catch the drift of his sometimes idiosyncratic thought.[13]

I may in passing note that while I have from time to time discussed such prominent theologians as Barth, Bultmann, Tillich and others, and have written frequently on the Reformed tradition, I have felt a special vocation to enquire what the English theological heritage has to offer. I have done this mostly because of its intrinsic value, but also because my wanderings far and wide have yielded evidence that while the names of

---

[9] Especially John Stuart Mill. See *Mill on God. The Pervasiveness and Elusiveness of Mill's Religious Thought*, Aldershot: Ashgate, 2004, and *Mill on God: Contemporary Responses to Three Essays on Religion*, Bristol: Thoemmes Press, 1997.

[10] *Philosophical Idealism and Christian Belief*, Cardiff: University of Wales Press and New York: St. Martin's Press, 1995; *John Locke and the Eighteenth-Century Divines*, Cardiff: University of Wales Press, 1997; *Confessing and Commending the Faith: Christian Witness and Apologetic Method*, Cardiff: University of Wales Press, 2002.

[11] (1986), Eugene, OR: Wipf & Stock, 1998.

[12] *Dissenting Thought and the Life of the Churches. Studies in a Christian Tradition*, Lewiston, NY: Edwin Mellen, 1990; *Testimony and Tradition*. I find that two of my titles include the term 'integrity'.

[13] *Alfred Dye, Minister of the Gospel*, London: Fauconberg Press, 1974.

the Germans and Swiss are on the lips and in the writings of many, the English tradition is surprisingly little known—in some cases even to the English themselves.[14] One could, for example, illustrate the major themes of systematic theology from the history of eighteenth-century English Dissent: trinitarianism/unitarianism, high/low Christology; Augustinianism/Pelagianism; Calvinism/Arminianism; enthusiasm/rationalism; paedobaptism/believer baptism; the several church orders; sundry millenarianisms; the eternity/non-eternity of punishment—they are all there, each with their pamphleteering advocates. The bibliography offered in chapter 9 is intended to show something of the variety of theological writing within one British Christian tradition during the twentieth century.

So to the ecumenical emphasis in my work. On the one hand I am persuaded that God has called out one Church; on the other hand I have sought to face up to the fact that the unity which Christians by grace have in Christ, far from being fully manifested by them is too often grievously obscured. Christian disunity at the Lord's table is the most appalling example of this tragic failure. Hence my pursuit of the ecumenical cause, my abhorrence of the sectarian spirit from whencesoever it comes, and my utter failure to understand those who take to themselves either the label 'evangelical' or the label 'catholic' whilst setting their faces against those Christians with whom they do not agree. The evangel is not that God has called isolated individual souls who then coalesce around their favoured doctrines, brandishing them against all opponents, it is that he has called out one people; and to be truly catholic is to understand that all who by grace are in Christ are one body, and to live accordingly. This is not to capitulate to the idea that an ecumenism into which Christians tumble simply because nobody believes anything in particular will suffice. On the contrary, I have not been slow to represent the Reformed family, not least its Congregational branch, in ecumenical circles, believing as I do that we have been given an understanding of catholicity and of church order which is of great value for the whole Church.[15] But it

---

[14] On more than one occasion Reformed theologians from elsewhere in the world have expressed surprise that there is an English, as distinct from a Scottish, Reformed tradition.

[15] It is an understanding of the Church for which I hope that, like some of my Separatist forebears, I would be prepared to die (I hope with equal fervour that I shall not have to). *Saints: Visible, Orderly and Catholic. The Congregational Idea of the Church*, Geneva: World Alliance of Reformed Churches and Allison Park, PA: Pickwick Publications, 1986; *A Reformed, Evangelical, Catholic Theology. The Contrbution of the World Alliance of Reformed Churches 1875-1982*, (1991), Eugene, OR: Wipf & Stock, 1998; and papers in *Dissenting Thought*; *Aspects of Christian* Integrity, (1990), Eugene, OR: Wipf & Stock, 1998; *Commemorations. Studies in Christian Thought and History*, (1993), Eugene, OR: Wipf & Stock, 1998; *Testimony and Tradition.*

is seriously to question all who claim to be of Christ's one Church whilst refusing communion to some of those whom he has joined together.

It is not blatant self-indulgence on my part to offer the above scribbler's record. Rather, it is a way of introducing the present volume. For having gathered the papers in this volume together, six of which have been specially written for it, I find that all the categories described above are, to a greater or lesser extent, represented herein. Thus chapters 1 to 4 and 7 concern the stances of some of those—Puritans, Cambridge Platonists, Quakers and critics of deism and pantheism who, from the second half of the sixteenth century to the end of the nineteenth, sought to articulate the Gospel in the intellectual environment in which they had been set. Far from having antiquarian interest only, I strive to show that the underlying concerns are of continuing relevance in ecumenical discussion, and that some present-day ways of assessing the Enlightenment are, to put it mildly, unsubtle. Chapter 5 traces some aspects of doctrinal change over four-and-a-half centuries in one Christian tradition, while in chapter 6 the question of doctrinal development is more thematically treated. Chapter 8, on spirituality, echoes some of the earlier concerns of the Separatists, Cambridge Platonists and Quakers, but casts them in the current context in which spirituality is, for many, the 'in' thing and one is repeatedly told that one is on a journey (though the distinction is frequently not drawn between the journey of seekers towards faith, and the journey of the saints within the faith). Chapter 9, a bibliographical survey of Reformed theology in twentieth-century Britain, is designed to indicate something of the range of interest within one ecclesiastical tradition. Chapters 10 and 11 concern the ways in which the Gospel to be articulated is shared in ecumenical circles with special reference to those neuralgic issues such as the nature of the Church, the ministry and the sacraments over which Christians divide (though, as earlier chapters suggest, there are underlying philosophical presuppositions to such discussions which, unfortunately, seldom surface in ecumenical discussion). Chapter 12, a plea for careful discrimination in theological writing and argument and a caution against sectarianism, concerns such current themes as contextual theology and inclusivism in relation to church membership and discipline, ethics and the Trinity. Finally, in chapter 13 I attempt to go to the root of the matter. I suggest that we may and must glory in the Cross, and that if the Cross is not central to our theology, we have sold the pass.

As I look back over the past decades, I become increasingly grateful for the wisdom of those who suggested to me in the 1950s that the place to go for a comprehensive and ecumenically-staffed theological education was the University of Manchester. It was a privilege to sit at the feet of H. H. Rowley, T. W. Manson, E. Gordon Rupp, S. G. F. Brandon and, among the younger teachers, Ronald Preston, then pioneering the study of Christian Ethics in this country, and John Heywood Thomas, then at the beginning of his career and already an authority on Kierkegaard and Tillich. Of those named only the last is still with us but, in this the centenary year of Manchester's Faculty of Theology I salute them all—and their junior colleagues too. It was an intellectually bracing place to be, and the fact that to this day I sometimes find myself saying, 'Now I know what Professor X meant' suggests to me that our contemporary scrutineers of higher education who go in quest of 'measurable outcomes' at the end of twelve-weeks of modular 'input' have somehow failed to grasp what the theological disciplines are about. Nor shall I ever forget the frosty look I received from a managerial person to whom I gently explained that in theology we have no final evidence whether or not the material has 'taken' until after the students are dead.

As before, though not as a matter of form, I should like to express my deepest gratitude to my wife, Karen, whose support of all my endeavours, and whose willingness to restart her own career on a number of occasions as a consequence of my movements, has always been wholehearted. On previous occasions I have dedicated books to her, and she knows that in a real sense they are all hers. On this occasion, however, I greet Hugo, who has but recently arrived, and who could not, therefore, be listed with our other grandchildren at the front of *Confessing and Commending the Faith*. He may at present feel inclined to chew upon this book—literally. I trust that in due course his chewing on it will be metaphorical.

Alan P. F. Sell
Milton Keynes

Acknowledgements

The author and publisher are grateful to those named for permission to reprint the following papers:

'Some theological aspects of the English Enlightenment calmly consider'd', *Eighteenth-Century Thought*, II, 2004: James G. Buickerood, editor, forthcoming.

'*The Gospel its own Witness*: deism, Thomas Paine and Andrew Fuller', in R. Glenn Wooden, Timothy R. Ashley and Robert S. Wilson, eds, *You will be my Witnesses. A Festschrift in Honor of the Reverend Dr. Allison A. Trites on the Occasion of his Retirement*, Macon, GA: Mercer University Press, 2003: Marc Jolley, Mercer University Press, pp. 188-229.

'From worms to sunbeams: the dilution of Calvinism in English Congregationalism', *Journal of the United Reformed Church History Society*, VII no. 4, May 2004: Professor Clyde Binfield, editor, pp. 253-74.

'Some Reformed reflections on spirituality', *Reformed Review*, LVI no. 2, Winter 2002/2003: Dr. Robert E. Van Voorst, editor, pp. 139-61.

'Reformed theology in twentieth-century Britain: a bibliographical survey', *Studies in Reformed Theology*, IX, 2004: Professor A. van de Beek, editor, forthcoming.

'The Alliance in Dialogue, 1970-2002: retrospect and reflections', *Reformed World*, LIII no. 4, December 2003: Dr. Odair Pedroso Mateus, Theological Secretary, World Alliance of Reformed Churches, pp. 210-28.

'The Holy Spirit and ecumenism: some catholic ruminations of a Reformed theologian', in Adelbert Denaux, ed., *The Holy Spirit and Ecumenism*, Leuven: Peeters, 2004: Paul Peeters, publisher, pp. 75-92.

Abbreviation:

ODNB *Oxford Dictionary of National Biography*

The cover illustration of The Memorial Hall, London (1875), erected to commemorate the ejected ministers of 1662, is reproduced by kind permission of the Trustees of The Congregational Library, London.

CHAPTER 1

Puritans, Platonists and Powicke

Frederick James Powicke was born at Kidderminster on 20 July 1854 and, as befits a son of that town, he became an authority on Richard Baxter.[1] He was educated for the Congregational ministry at Spring Hill College, Birmingham, under the principalship of David Worthington Simon, whose biography he later wrote.[2] Two pastorates followed: the first at Alnwick, Northumberland (1879-1886), the second at Hatherlow, Cheshire (1886-1916). During the latter ministry he published a characteristically accurate and comprehensive centenary history of the Cheshire Congregational Union, the chair of which he occupied on two occasions.[3]

Powicke was a hard-working member of the Lancashire Independent College Committee; for forty years he served as secretary of the Stockport and District Ministers' Fraternal; and, following his retirement from Hatherlow and his removal to Stockport, where he was a deacon at Heaton Moor church, he was a valued member of the board of governors of the John Rylands Library, Manchester. Powicke did not seek outward show or wordly success, and he was content to minister in small spheres whilst concurrently devoting himself to scholarship. At heart Powicke was a prime example of that now increasingly rare phenomenon, the scholar pastor. In his case both terms should be accorded equal emphasis. He loved his people, he was devoted to scholarship. He was 'a man of beautiful spirit with a shrewd judgment of men and affairs; he exercised a wide ministry of personal counsel and comfort'.[4]

---

[1] See his two-part *magnum opus*, *A Life of the Reverend Richard Baxter 1615-1691* [*sic*, but actually 1661), London: Jonathan Cape, 1924; *The Reverend Richard Baxter under the Cross, 1662-1691*, London: Jonathan Cape, 1927; also a number of papers in *The Bulletin of the John Rylands Library*.

[2] See *David Worthington Simon*, London: Hodder and Stoughton, 1912. Spring Hill College was the predecessor of Mansfield College, Oxford, for which see Elaine Kaye, *Mansfield College, Oxford: Its Origin, History and Significance*, Oxford: Oxford University Press, 1996.

[3] See *A History of the Cheshire County Union of Congregational Churches*, Manchester: Thomas Griffiths, 1907.

[4] K[enneth] L. P[arry], obituary of Powicke in *The Congregational Year Book*, London: Congregational Union of England and Wales, 1937, p. 705.

Through Spring Hill College Powicke secured the MA (London), and for his book on Norris he earned the PhD of the University of Rostock, Germany.[5] For his contributions to scholarship he was awarded the Honorary DD of Glasgow University in 1929. Powicke married Martha Collyer (1845-1935). They had four daughters and two sons, of whom one, William Alfred,[6] followed his father into the Congregational ministry, while the other, Frederick Maurice, became Regius Professor of Modern History at Oxford University. Powicke himself died on 7 December 1935, and was buried in the family grave at Hatherlow.

In addition to the works already mentioned, Powicke focused upon a bevy of radical Puritan Separatists and a group of contemplative Platonists, with occasional sidelong glances at the Quakers. I wish to suggest that these disparate groups are in fact united by a common thread of experimentalism derived from their openness towards the 'light'. More interesting than that, however, are their differing understandings of the light, the different directions in which their grasp of the light took them, and the legacy which, accordingly, they have left to present-day theological and ecumenical debate. Setting out from a study of Powicke's works I shall hope in what follows to make good these claims. Before proceeding further I must emphasize the fact that Powicke did not set out to produce an exhaustive study of the Cambridge Platonists. He informs us that he has never

> read carefully the whole of what they wrote—the whole of Cudworth's *Intellectual System of the Universe* for example, of the whole of More's philosophical works and his dissertations on the Apocalypse. I could get no spiritual nutriment out of these, and it was spiritual nutriment that I had been told to look for.[7]

The following list will introduce the main writers to be considered; it will set the chronological boundaries of the discussion; and it will make

---

[5] F. J. Powicke, *A Dissertation on John Norris of Bemerton* (hereinafter *JN*), London: George Philip, [1894].

[6] William Alfred Powicke (1880-1950), who trained for the ministry at Mansfield College, was MA of Glasgow and Oxford Universities. Of a scholarly disposition, he devoted himself to the cure of souls. Of him it was said, 'Perhaps his best contribution was made in country churches, for with a fundamental love of learning he combined simple tastes and a discerning sympathy with humble people.' See his obituary, *The Congregational Year Book*, 1951, p. 519.

[7] F. J. Powicke, *The Cambridge Platonists. A Study* (hereinafter *CP*), London: Dent, 1926, p. vi. Powicke informs us (ibid., p. v) that 'Many years ago an old and learned friend drew my attention to the Cambridge Platonists. He seemed quite unaware of the fact that, in some of their best characteristics, they foreshadowed himself.' This 'old and learned friend', whom I suspect to have been Powicke's theological college principal, D. W. Simon, advised him to focus on Norris as being more important than had hitherto been recognized. Hence Powicke's doctoral theme.

plain the importance of Cambridge University in the story. The first four names are those of radical Puritan Separatists (of whom Browne later returned to the Church of England, while Barrow and Greenwood were executed at Tyburn[8]); the six following are the most prominent of the Cambridge Platonists, four of whom were members of Emmanuel College at a time when its strong reputation for Calvinistic Puritanism (which never took it as far as Presbyterianism, still less Separatism) was being diluted in a Latitudinarian direction—not least by the Cambridge Platonists themselves.

Robert Browne (c.1550-1633); Corpus Christi College, Cambridge
Henry Barrow (c.1550-1593); Clare Hall, Cambridge
John Greenwood (c.1560-1593); Corpus Christi College, Cambridge
John Robinson (c.1576-1625); possibly at Corpus Christi College[9]
Benjamin Whichcote (1609-1683); Emmanuel College, Cambridge
Peter Sterry (1613-1672); Emmanuel College
Henry More (1614-1687); Christ's College, Cambridge
Ralph Cudworth (1617-1688); Emmanuel College
John Smith (1618-1652); Emmanuel College
Nathaniel Culverwel (1619-1651); Emmanuel College

The 'odd man out' as to generation and education is John Norris (1657-1711) of Exeter College, Oxford, and Fellow of All Souls, who, in almost complete isolation (though with contact through letters with both More and Cudworth's daughter, Damaris), carried a Platonist line of thought into the eighteenth century.[10] Powicke neatly placed Norris *vis à vis* the Cambridge men thus:

> [Norris was] an Oxford man, a Fellow of All Souls, a High Churchman, a pronounced Tory—a contrast, in short, to the Cambridge men in many respects. He admired Henry More, but not exactly for what was best in him. He made much of the Platonic doctrine of ideas, but not so much in Plato's way as in that of the eccentric Malebranche (1638-1713), whose almost solitary English disciple he was proud to

---

[8] See Alan P. F. Sell, *Commemorations. Studies in Christian Thought and History*, Calgary: University of Calgary Press and Cardiff: University of Wales Press, 1993, ch. 4.

[9] Powicke states that he was. See his *John Robinson (1575?-1625)*, London: Hodder and Stoughton, [1920), pp. xi, 5-6. However, Alexander Gordon, in his article on Robinson in the *Dictionary of National Biography*, refers to puzzles surrounding three contemporary John Robinsons, but concludes that the pastor to the Pilgrims probably studied at Cambridge during the last decade of the sixteenth century. In this he is followed by *The Oxford Dictionary of the Christian Church*. Of more recent writers, R. Tudur Jones opts for Corpus Christi College without qualification. See *John Robinson's Congregationalism*, London: The Congregational Memorial Hall Trust, 1987, p. 3.

[10] This was so much in my mind on one occasion that I inadvertently described Norris as a *Cambridge* Platonist. See *Commemorations*, p. 160.

> be. Norris the moralist, as revealed in his sermons, is a tonic; but Norris the metaphysician, as revealed in his *Theory of the Ideal and Intelligible World*, is a fantastic.[11]

It is fair to say that apart from the doctrine of the Church, Powicke's concern with the Separatists is largely historical. Evincing considerable skills of detection and of historical judgement, he undertakes the intricate task of sifting such evidence as there is with a view to providing as full and clear an account as possible of the life and work of Browne, Barrow, Greenwood and Robinson.[12] But my concern is to show how and why, notwithstanding a general intellectual environment they broadly shared, the Separatists and the Cambridge Platonists diverged from one another on ecclesiologial questions. This divergence is alluded to by Powicke, and it can be inferred from his writings at many points, but he does not major on it. Since the Cambridge Platonists and Norris covered a wider range of thought than the Separatist pamphleteers as treated by Powicke,[13] whose principal doctrinal interest was ecclesiological, I shall proceed thematically, taking my cue from the former and introducing the latter as appropriate. Powicke's references to Baxter and to the Quakers will likewise be referred to *en passant*.

---

[11] *CP*, p. v. Richard Acworth cites Powicke as one who finds Norris separated from the Cambridge Platonists principally 'by his uncritical following of Malebranche'. According to Acworth, Norris 'was in reality a notably more modern thinker than they. Where the Cambridge Platonists were strongly influenced by the vitalism and occultism of the Renaissance, Norris belonged to a newer age' in repudiating Platonic theories of pre-existent souls and the existence of ethereal or lucid bodies, and endorsing 'an essentially mechanistic view of the material world'. See R. Acworth, *The Philosophy of John Norris of Bemerton (1657-1712)*, Hildesheim: Georg Olms, 1979, p. 286. From none of which, however, does it follow that Norris could not be what he was, namely, a channel through whom Platonically-influenced philosophical theology passed down to the eighteenth century. Those who live 'between the times' frequently develop the ability to echo the past, to adjust to the present, and sometimes even to anticipate the future. For Norris's sources see Flora Isabel MacKinnon, *The Philosophy of John Norris of Bemerton*, Baltimore: Psychological Review Publications, I no. 2, October 1910. Neither in the case of *CP* nor *JN* does Powicke provide references for all of his quotations. I have supplied these as far as possible, providing also the references to *CP* and *JN*. Where I quote without reference to *CP* and *JN*, I do so in my own right.

[12] See *Henry Barrow, Separatist (1550?-1593) and the Exiled Church of Amsterdam*, London: James Clarke, 1900; *Robert Browne, Pioneer of Modern Congregationalism*, London: Congregational Union of England and Wales, 1910; *John Robinson*.

[13] The first volume of Robinson's *Works* comprises fifty-seven essays on a wide range of theological and moral topics, most of which fall outside Powicke's purview. See *The Works of John Robinson, Pastor of the Pilgrim Fathers. With a memoir and Annotations by Robert Ashton, Secretary of the Congregational Board, London*, 3 vols, London: John Snow, 1851.

I

We shall do well first to reflect a little further on the Cambridge Platonists' Puritan inheritance and its partial dilution at their hands. Powicke attributes this dilution to a number of factors: an anti-Puritan reaction was prompted by Archbishop Laud, who appointed a number of moderate divines to headships of Cambridge colleges; the irenic and well-attended preaching of Lancelot Andrewes of Pembroke College, among others, helped to undermine more hard-line interpretations of doctrine; the teaching of theology departed from doctrinal scholasticism more rapidly in Cambridge than at Oxford, and was not unconnected with the increasing space given in the curriculum to Plato and Platonism.[14]

It is clear that as compared with their High Church older contemporaries, John Hales and William Chillingworth, whose commitment to free enquiry in religious matters made them in that respect harbingers of the Cambridge Platonists, the latter were on the Puritan side. But this statement requires immediate qualification because, with the exception of Culverwel whose commitment to Calvinistic predestinarian teaching betokened 'arrested development' in Powicke's opinion, the Cambridge Platonists balked at predestination, whilst in other respects variously maintaining the Calvinist line or, at least, not repudiating it or confessing Arminianism—though Powicke thinks that Whichcote (who, when challenged, denied having read any of Arminius's writings) was closer to the Arminians' five points than to the Calvinists' reply to them at the Synod of Dort.[15] This surmise notwithstanding of Cudworth, Powicke writes, 'his Puritanism, like that of Whichcote, was far more a matter of ethical temper, or even political sympathy, than theological agreement. Certainly he did not hold the Calvinistic creed'.[16]

Again, while in his writings Sterry accorded a central place to Christ and the Trinity, in his metaphysics the sovereignty of God loomed so large as to yield the conclusion that there are no secondary causes, and that the will of God is the sole will: the human will is from eternity

---

[14] These are the main points from *CP*, pp. 3-13.

[15] *CP*, 25. The points advanced by the Arminians in 1610 were: (1) God's decrees of election and reprobation are conditional upon foreknown faith, or lack of it. (2) Christ died for all, though believers only enjoy forgiveness. (3) Regeneration by the Holy Spirit is necessary to salvation. (4) Grace is resistible. (5) The final perseverance of the saints can be neither denied nor positively asserted. For the entire dispute, see Alan P. F. Sell, *The Great Debate. Calvinism, Arminianism and Salvation*, (1982), Eugene, OR: Wipf & Stock, 1998, ch. 1. John C. English has suggested that, Culverwel excepted, an Arminian interpretation of the way in which grace operates was 'implicit' and 'muted' in the writings of the Cambridge Platonists. See 'The Cambridge Platonists in Wesley's "Christian Library"', *Proceedings of the Wesley Historical Society*, XXXVI, October 1968, 165.

[16] *CP*, 110.

predetermined in the divine understanding.[17] They reverenced the Bible; they were content with the Apostles Creed provided that they could bring their interpretations to bear upon it; they were loyal to the Church of England as a divinely ordained institution,[18] though they were temperamentally disinclined to seek high ecclesiastical office. As we shall see, they varied in the degree to which they were inclined to tolerate Separatists and, later, Quakers; but to a man they opposed the claims of Rome. For their general geniality and openness the Latitudinarians were abused by the more fanatical Puritans as 'people that have revived the abominable principles of the old *Gnosticks*', those 'long since extirpated Hereticks'. To them the Latitudinarian, to use 'the long Nick-name; which they have taught their tongues to pronounce as roundly as if it were shorter than it is, by four or five syllables', was a 'gentleman of a wide swallow'.[19] Some more discriminating men, too, were somewhat disquieted by their Platonist offspring. Anthony Tuckney, for example, Whichcote's Puritan tutor at Emmanuel, remembered Whichcote even in his student days as 'somewhat cloudy and obscure in your expressions'.[20]

Before passing from the theme of Puritanism, of which the Separatists were radical exemplars, a little more must be said regarding the Cambridge Platonists' rejection of Protestant scholasticism and Calvinistic predestination.[21] Powicke illustrates the pitfall of scholasticism by reference to John Smith. Against those who are over-confidently sure of their acceptance by God on account of their doctrinal orthodoxy, Smith declares, 'God respects not a bold, confident, and audacious faith that is big with nothing but its own presumptions';[22] and he cautions against 'our dogmata and notions about Justification [which] may puff us up in

[17] *CP*, p. 181, referring to P. Sterry, *A Discourse of the Freedom of the Will*, London: John Starkey, 1675, pp. 63ff.

[18] Though following the Restoration of the monarchy in 1660, Cudworth was under a cloud for having previously favoured the Nonconformists, his verses congratulatory of Charles II notwithstanding. See Gilbert Burnet, *History of My Own Times*, 1724-34, Appendix, p. 464.

[19] So the description of [Edward Fowler], *Principles and Practices of certain Moderate Divines in the Church of England, (greatly misunderstood) Truly Represented and Defended...*, London: Lodowick Lloyd, 1670, pp. 7-10.

[20] Letter of Tuckney to Whichcote, quoted by John Tulloch, *Rational Theology and Christian Philosophy in England in the Seventeenth Century*, Edinburgh: Blackwood, 1872, II, p. 51.

[21] We may note in passing that the Quakers, no less than the Cambridge Platonists, opposed predestinarian teaching. See especially Robert Barclay, *An Apology for the True Christian Divinity*, (1678), Glasgow: R. Barclay Murdoch, 1886, pp. 106-112—a section of which the evangelical Arminian, John Wesley, thought highly.

[22] *CP*, 104, quoting John Smith's *Discourse of Legal and Evangelical Righteousness*, in his *Select Discourses*, London: Rivingtons and Cochran, 3rd edn, 1821, p. 354.

far higher and goodlier conceits of ourselves than God hath of us...'[23] As for the scholastic systematizers who value assent to their own doctrinal scheme above concern for holy living, Smith observes that 'We have many grave and reverend idolaters that worship truth only in the image of their own wits...'[24] Again,

> to seek our divinity merely in books and writings, is to seek the living among the dead: we do but in vain seek God many times in these, where his truth often is not so much enshrined as entombed; no...seek for God within thine own soul; he is best discerned, as Plotinus phraseth it, by an intellectual touch of him.[25]

Smith sums up his case thus: 'The knowledge of divinity that appears in systems and models is but a poor wan light; but the powerful energy of divine knowledge displays itself in purified souls...'[26] That John Norris had taken this lesson to heart is clear from his sermon on the theme of the law's not being made void through faith, in which, says Powicke, he 'indignantly brushed aside the "empty notional way of preaching up the Doctrine of Faith in Christ," and laid it down that "*he* preaches Christ best that insists most upon the necessity of obedience to his commands; and *he* makes the best Christians that makes the best men...'[27] At this point the anti-'notions' protest of the Quakers comes to mind.

The importance which Powicke attached to this line of thought cannot be over-estimated. Having set down Smith's position he allows himself an application of the point, albeit for a different reason, to his own times. Indeed, it is difficult not to believe that he is speaking for himself:

> Our danger may arise not so much from barren orthodoxy, or speculative dogmatism, as from a state of unsettling doubt. We have claimed our freedom to think, but claimed it at a great and, as some of us may have found, a very painful cost. We welcomed the critic with a light heart. We handed over to him our sacred treasures...we said, take them all, put them all to the test... But...how few of our early treasures has he seemed to return unscathed; how even the best things, even God Himself and Christ and the soul and the whole spiritual world, have seemed at times to be dissolving away; how cold and dark has seemed the loneliness when we have felt, perhaps, that we could not even pray![28]

---

[23] Ibid., p. 105, quoting Smith's *Discourse*, ch. 4.

[24] Ibid., quoting Smith's *Select Discourses*, p. 11.

[25] Partially quoted in *CP*, p. 108, from Smith, *Select Discourses*, p. 5.

[26] Smith, *Of the True Way*, p. 5.

[27] *JN*, pp. 21-22, quoting Norris's *A Discourse shewing That the Law is not made void through Faith*, in his *Practical Discourses upon several Divine Subjects*, London: S. Manship, 1693, III, p. 158.

[28] *CP*, pp. 106-7.

The remedy, he continues, is not to revile reason as a deceiver, to succumb to despair of ever walking in the light, or to 'clasp the hand of any plausible guide who cries with an air of authority: "This is the way, walk ye in it."' Still less should we so elevate the critical understanding as to think that it alone can solve the doubts it has created; for

> there is a better way—at least so far as spiritual truth is concerned. Of such truth the critical understanding can never do more than touch the form, the shell, the husk. Its essence abides; and waits to enter by a lowlier door. There *is* a faith—a faith in God, in Christ, in the soul, in the great realities of which these are the centre—there is a faith which comes of self-control: the self-control which binds us firmly to the primal duties, the simple virtues, the clear behests of conscience.[29]

Compatibly with this, Powicke concludes a note appended to his chapter on Smith with Plotinus's words, 'Divinity is not so well perceived by a subtle wit as by a purified sense.'[30] The ecclesiological implications of this stance, especially as they might bear upon such matters as credal or confessional assent and church membership, are not far to seek; but it was the Separatists and their heirs who pressed them in relation to church order, as we shall see.

As for the Cambridge Platonists' aversion to predestination (Culverwel excepted), Powicke explains that since Calvinism was 'the ruling creed' at Cambridge, those who were thought to deviate from it at any point were immediately suspect. He reminds us both that Whichcote was hurt when Tuckney accused him of undue familiarity with Socinian and Arminian works, and that the Arminian Puritan, John Goodwin, dedicated his *Redemption Redeemed* to Whichcote. The Cambridge Platonists felt acutely the tension occasioned by the apparently clear biblical teaching concerning the *decretum absolutum* on the one hand, and the equally biblical (and Platonic) insistence upon the fact that God is light and the fountain of all goodness.[31] Cudworth could not conceive that God would from eternity condemn persons 'to eternal torments without fault or conscious sin of their own', and in his doctoral disputation of 1653 he defended the thesis, *boni et mali rationes eternas et immutabiles*.[32] Indeed, as early as his BD thesis of 1644 Cudworth had upheld the eternity and immutability of morality against the perceived threat from Calvinism; and John Passmore does well to emphasize the fact that Cudworth did this seven years before Hobbes published *Leviathan*, which some have

---

[29] Ibid., p. 107.
[30] Ibid., p. 109.
[31] Ibid., pp. 35-6; cf. pp. 56-7.
[32] Ibid., p. 111.

supposed prompted Cudworth's defence of morality.[33] For his part, Henry More had learned Calvinism from his father, mother and tutor. His parents, he informs us, were 'great Calvinists, but withal pious and good ones'. Nevertheless, he 'could not swallow that hard doctrine concerning fate'.[34] Norris, too, gradually thought his way out of predestinarian theory: as witness his early *Tractate* against the *Decretum Absolutum* (1682).[35]

In reflecting on the anti-Calvinistic stance of the Cambridge Platonists Powicke notes that while they rightly deplored the negative emphasis given by many Calvinists to reprobation—'to just that side which was most dishonouring to God and...demoralising to its advocates',

> There is...a spring of mighty moral energy—to which the Cambridge men did scant justice—in realising that God is *the* Initiating Agent from first to last in the process of salvation; and that the human part is merely receptive, is an unstinted readiness to let God work. Examples of this were before their eyes even in Cambridge.[36]

Not surprisingly, he observes that 'Calvinism is usually spoken of by Norris and the Cambridge men as if it meant little more than' predestination.[37]

Once again, ecclesiological implications flow from Powicke's remarks. For if the Cambridge Platonists' elevation of things spiritual and repudiation of the merely 'notional' could provide the basis of a critique of outward confessional subscription, their neglect of the positive side of predestination placed them apart from the Separatists and later Congregationalists for whom the Church comprised only the saints elect, gathered and covenanted.[38] To this subject we shall return in due course.

---

[33] See J. Passmore, *Ralph Cudworth. An Interpretation*, (1951), Bristol: Thoemmes Press, 1990, p. 11. Cudworth's BD thesis was entitled, 'Dantur boni et mali rationes aeternae et indispensabiles'.

[34] Ibid., p. 170; cf. H. More, 'Prefatio Generalissima,' prefixed to his *Opera Omnia*, 1679, p. v.

[35] See *JN*, p. 4.

[36] *CP*, p. 37.

[37] *JN*, p. 129. The same restricted understanding permeates the writings of John Stuart Mill, among many others. See Alan P. F. Sell, *Mill on God. The Pervasiveness and Elusiveness of Mill's Religious Thought*, Aldershot: Ashgate, 2004, ch. 4.

[38] See Powicke's remark on Cromwell and the Independents in 'English Congregationalism in its greatness and decline (1592-1770),' in Albert Peel, ed., *Essays Congregational and Catholic*, London: Congregational Union of England and Wales, [1931], p. 286.

II

Having set the Cambridge Platonists and Norris against the background of their Puritan inheritance, we may turn next to their general characteristics as thinkers, and then to their primary beliefs and objectives.

Powicke aptly brands them philosophical divines:

> Philosophers simply—in the sense of mere searchers after truth in general—they were not. Their chief concern was the highest truth, truth religious and moral; and *that* was not a mere *quaesitum*—it was something given, something already within reach. But they were philosophic divines...inasmuch as they maintained that religious truth can never contradict other truth, can never contradict itself—can, in short, never be other than rational in its source, its nature, its relations, its results. We have here the key to their whole theory and practice.[39]

We shall have more to say concerning their theory. As to their practice, Whichcote deftly indicates the way in which this—not least where it concerns the manner of argument—should be modelled upon God's dealings with us:

> God applies to our faculties, and deals with us, by reason and argument. Let us learn of God to deal with one another in meekness, calmness, and reason, and so represent God.[40]

Despite their differences of emphasis and temperament, Powicke was not wide of the mark in describing their general intellectual stance thus:

> Love of Plato and the Platonists; reverence for reason; the use of Reason as a handmaid of Christian faith; rejection of Calvinism [i.e. double predestination]; the assertion of 'Morals' as a necessary outcome of religion; attachment to the Church of England, and indifference towards public affairs.[41]

But it is necessary to say a little more about Plato and the Platonists, not by way of denying the affection in which the Cambridge divines and Norris held them—they did wish to return the Church to 'her old loving Nurse the Platonick philosophy'[42]—but in order to take note of the qualifications which Powicke elsewhere introduces. He questions how much More knew of Proclus and Plotinus; he notes that Cudworth alone

---

[39] *CP*, pp. 27-8.

[40] *CP*, p. 38, quoting Whichcote's *Moral and Religious Aphorisms: Collected from the Manuscript Papers of the Reverend and Learned Doctor Whichcote*, Norwich: Fr. Burges, 1703, no. 572.

[41] *JN*, p. 126.

[42] S.P. (possibly Simon Patrick), *A Brief Account of the New Sect of Latitude-men: Together with some Reflections upon the New Philosophy*, London, 1662, p. 24.

borrowed significantly from Platonism, especially in his account of the Trinity and his theory of the mundane soul. 'But', he continues, 'these things hardly touched the core of their thought. They were its mere trimmings. What they held to be vital for faith and life, came to them from a higher Teacher—though it was good to catch the echo of his voice in the Platonists.'[43] As John Smith said, the Christian's participation in the divine nature is, 'by the Platonist's leave'[44] exclusively the gift of Christ. More particularly, Powicke finds them both like and unlike their Platonist predecessors.

While noting that the Cambridge Platonists uncritically disregarded the gap of six hundred years, and the intellectual decay, which separated Plato from Plotinus, Powicke concludes that this did not adversely obstruct 'their mainly practical purpose'.[45] Like the neo-Platonists the Cambridge divines held to the immutability of moral principles; they respected science and all the activities of reason; opposing the carnal to the spiritual, they believed that spiritual things are spiritually discerned, and when discerned the resulting experience is trustworthy; they upheld the link between spiritual discernment and right living, and *vice versa.* Although John Smith, and to a lesser extent Whichcote, echo the neo-Platonic teaching that sin is pure negation, they do not agree with Plotinus that it can be banished by 'a course of discipline'; and if they sometimes speak of the transcendent God as being entirely beyond our epistemological grasp, they believe it possible 'to obtain a real knowledge of God and Fellowship with Him in the way of moral obedience; and not simply in the way of an ecstacy, unattainable save to one here and there at rare moments'.[46] Further, they elevate the love of God in a way the neo-Platonists did not,[47] and against Plotinus's idea of the human ascent to God through a series of emanations, they extol Christ as the one mediator between God and the soul. As Henry W. Clark put it, 'when they came to actual dealing with religion...it was not at all a Neo-Platonic contents-bill that they displayed, and it was for the most part to tolerably orthodox views of doctrine that they settled down'.[48] Clark concludes:

---

[43] *CP*, p. 194.

[44] J. Smith, *Of the True Way or Method of attaining Divine Knowledge*, in *Select Discourses*, p. 24.

[45] *CP*, p. 18, n. 1.

[46] *CP*, p. 20. We may here recall that to say that we may have a true apprehension of God though not a full comprehension of him was a running theme among the Puritans.

[47] Powicke does not expand upon this contrast. However, for the way in which neo-Platonists thought of love, see Placid Spearritt, 'Love among the Platonists', *The Downside Review*, XCII, April 1974, pp. 92-101.

[48] Henry W. Clark, *Liberal Orthodoxy. A Historical Survey*, London: Chapman and Hall, 1914, p. 45. Clark (1869-1949) was, like Powicke, a Congregational minister. He trained at Hackney College, London, under Alfred Cave (not, *contra* his *Year Book* entry,

> In the end, the Cambridge Platonists, standing face to face with religious problems, borrowed from Neo-Platonism's armoury little more than a conviction that philosophy must be religion's servant; borrowed from a purer Platonism a conviction of the divineness of human reason; and added a last conviction that Christianity, fitting easily as it did with its pronouncements into the moulds which divine-human reason had ready, was the natural thing for man to believe.[49]

Turning now to the main positions of the Cambridge Platonists and Norris, we shall consider first reason, then the Bible, then their strong emphasis upon morality. Powicke's discriminating discussion of the divines makes plain the fact that while there are clear family resemblances between them, there are also some interesting differences of emphasis. Thus, for example, while both Whichcote and Smith valued the natural evidences of religious truth, its reasonableness, and its necessary relation to godly living, Smith, 'dwelt more on the inwardness of religion, on the spirit of Christ as the living spring of Evangelical righteousness, on the mystic union with God which is the effect of obedience, and is the surest pledge of immortality'.[50] As Smith said, 'There is an inward beauty, life, and loveliness in divine truth, which cannot be known but only when it is digested into life and practice.'[51] Nevertheless, both Whichcote and Smith were in broad epistemological agreement. Smith could without difficulty have endorsed Whichcote's words:

> God hath set up two lights to enlighten us in our way: the light of reason, which is the light of his creation; and the light of Scripture, which is after-revelation from him. Let us make use of these two lights; and suffer neither to be put out.[52]

Smith amplifies the point in his discourse, 'The Excellency and Nobleness of True Religion', which Powicke proceeds to summarize. Reason, says Smith, is 'a light flowing from the fountain and Father of

---

under P. T. Forsyth, who did not arrive there until 1901). In 1890 he became assistant minister at George Square, Greenock, but almost immediately was injured in a railway accident and confined to bed for three years, and robbed of nine years' active service in all. In 1899 he became the first minister of Woking Congregational Church, where he remained for five years. He then turned to teaching and writing, and for his scholarly contribution St. Andrews University honoured him with its DD. See *The Congregational Year Book*, 1950, p. 508.

[49] Ibid., 46. We may here note the view of C. A. Staudenbaur that Whichcote was neither a Platonist in any significant sense nor a philosopher, and that chronology prohibits his customary appellation, 'the father of the Cambridge Platonists'. See 'Platonists, theosophy, and immaterialism. Recent views of the Cambridge Platonists', *Journal of the History of Ideas*, XXXV no. 1, January-March 1974, pp. 158-162.

[50] *CP*, p. 96.

[51] Smith, *Select Discourses*, p. 11.

[52] Whichcote, *Aphorisms*, no. 109.

lights' (an unquestioned presupposition this, on which later divines would not so justifiably be able to rest). The function of reason is

> to enable man to work out of himself all those notions of God which are the true Groundwork of Love and Obedience to God and conformity to Him... But since Man's fall from God, the inward virtue and vigour of Reason is much abated[53]... Therefore, besides the truth of natural inscription, God hath provided the truth of Divine revelation, which issues forth from His own free will, and clearly discovers the way of our return to God from Whom we have fallen. And this truth...the Scripture is wont to set forth under the name of grace, as proceeding merely from the free bounty and overflowings of the divine love... But, besides this outward revelation of God's will to men, there is also an inward impression of it on their minds and spirits, which is, in a more special manner, attributed to God. We cannot see Divine things but in a Divine light...[54]

We may observe in passing that Calvin's 'two books'—nature and Scripture—through which God speaks to human beings are there in Smith's, as in Whichcote's remarks,[55] as also are the ideas of the disruption by sin of human-divine communication, the necessity and nature of grace, and the inner witness of the Holy Spirit.[56]

Wherein lies the Platonism? I offer two answers. The first is that of Norris, who both traces the lineage of his ideal system and makes it clear that his views were confirmed by, rather than derived from, others:

> [W]ere we not otherwise prepossess't in favour of the vulgar Philosophy, what would be more familiar and obvious than to conclude that we see all things in *God*? This is a Notion which I very early alighted upon by *Natural Parturiency* of my own mind, before I had consulted with any Authors that might imbue me with it. But afterwards I met with some that confirmed me in it. For it is a Notion very frequently touched upon by *Platonists*—by *Plotinus*, *Proclus*, by *Marsilius Ficinus*, by *St. Austin*, by the late French philosopher *Du Hamel*, in his book '*De Mene Humana*'—and is sometimes glanced at by *Aquinas* himself; but by none that I know so copiously, so purposely, and so dextrously managed as by the incomparable

53 Cf. Clark's poetic phrase: 'human reason was the divine reason working its way along valley-roads where cramping hills blocked out the infinite view'. *Liberal Orthodoxy*, p. 30. The upshot is that the image of God in human beings, though defaced, is not entirely obliterated.

54 *CP*, pp. 98-99, quoting J. Smith, *The Excellency and Nobleness of True Religion*, in *Select Discourses*, pp. 411-12.

55 Cf. also H. More, *An Explanation of the Grand Mystery of Godliness*, London: J. Flesher, 1660, pp. 3, 32-3.

56 See further, J. Calvin, *Institutes of the Christian Religion*, Bk. I.

> Monsieur *Malebranche*, who, I think, has established the truth of it beyond all cavil or exception, as well as reasonable doubting.[57]

Powicke quotes Norris in summary of the latter's general position:

> The essential point is this, and this only, 'that as God contains in Himself, after an intelligible manner, the perfections of all Beings, both actual and possible, and by these intelligible perfections, or ideas, knows the essence of all things,'...so God is also our true light—enabling us to see His works 'by the perfections of their Creator, even by those very ideas whereby they were made.'[58]

The second answer is Powicke's perfectly proper one to the effect that the Platonism is epitomized in the conception of reason as the highest faculty in human beings, which answers to what is highest in God: 'Man's grandest privilege and most serious duty is to escape the mere shows of life; it is to rise by means of discriminating intellectual effort and purifying moral discipline, from the confused to the clear, from that which seems to that which is.'[59] Hence, when the Cambridge divines spoke, after Proverbs 20:27, of reason as the 'candle of the Lord', they were thinking of reason 'not so much as the *light* as the eye of the soul, an organ of intellectual apprehension, derived from God, and godlike':[60]

> [W]e may say that to the Cambridge Platonists reason, while undoubtedly 'the candle of the Lord', was but a candle, not a searchlight. Moreover, the candle is lit by God: 'The Spirit of a Man is the Candle of the Lord; Lighted by God, and Lighting us to God.'[61]

For the present we may note an epistemological tension in the minds of at least some of the Cambridge Platonists and Norris. Once again, Culverwel epitomizes it. Powicke rightly points out that Culverwel, good Calvinist and one-sided Augustinian that he was, makes much of the noetic effects of sin (unlike More, who, in the wake of Origen, attributed

[57] *JN*, pp. 181-2, quoting J. Norris, *Reason and Religion: or. The Grounds and Measures of Devotion, Consider'd from the Nature of God and the Nature of Man*, London: S. Manship, 1693, pp. 185-6.

[58] *JN*, p. 74, quoting J. Norris, *An Essay towards the Theory of the Ideal or Intelligible World*, London: S. Manship, 1704, II, pp. 512-13.

[59] *CP*, p. 22.

[60] Ibid., p. 23.

[61] Alan P. F. Sell, *Confessing and Commending the Faith. Historic Witness and Apologetic Method*, Cardiff: University of Wales Press, 2002, p. 263, quoting Whichcote, *Aphorisms*, no. 916. See further, J. D. Roberts, Sr., *From Puritanism to Platonism in Seventeenth-Century England*, The Hague: Martinus Nijhof, 1968, ch. 5. For the use of the Proverbs text from patristic authors onwards, and with special reference to Whichcote, see Robert A. Greene, 'Whichcote, the candle of the Lord, and synderesis', *Journal of the History of Ideas*, LII no. 4, October-December 1991, pp. 617-644.

sin to the lapse of pre-existent souls[62]), but nevertheless thinks that reason is God's gift which lightens every person, and that it is still competent to yield a 'certain' light. But, Powicke continues, when Culverwel comes to faith and revelation he has no compunction about opposing revealed truths to those of reason on the ground that God, in his unconditional grace, has willed to improve the 'naturals' of some, but not of others. In other words, says Powicke, 'God's grace is arbitrary'; and he permits himself the following surmise:

> that one who started with so high a conception of the inner light should come to assert that, in matters of fundamental morality, the 'candle of the Lord' might actually be darkness, must have been to Cudworth, with a stern fight for immutable moral laws against Hobbes on his hands, nothing less than betrayal.[63]

Whichcote, to whom religion was a 'seed of a deiform nature', was more typical of the Cambridge Platonists in remarking with respect to humanity at large and not to the elect only, 'To go against reason is to go against God... Reason is the Divine governor of man's life; it is the very voice of God.'[64] In this connection, Powicke elsewhere remarks, the moderate Puritan, Richard Baxter, 'stands nearer to the Cambridge Platonists, especially Benjamin Whichcote, than to any other of his

---

[62] See H. More, *The Immortality of the Soul*, 1659, pp. 240-5. Cf. Nicholas Tyacke, *Aspects of English Protestantism c.1530-1700*, Manchester: Manchester University Press, 2001, p. 295. Though, for example, Cudworth believed that our souls would ever be rising up to the true knowledge of God 'did we not *detain it*, and hold it down, *in unrighteousness*'; Smith quoted Socrates to the effect that 'It is not lawful for any impure nature to touch divinity'; and Norris held that God 'enlightens us *Efficiently* by his Spirit, assisting our intellectual Faculties, and purging our Hearts from those Lusts and Prejudices which darken and pervert our apprehensions of things'. See, respectively, Cudworth's Dedication to *A Discourse on John, chap. ii. Vers. 3, 4, preached before the Honourable House of Commons, at Westminster, March 31, 1647*, in R. Cudworth, *The True Intellectual System of the Universe*, London: J. F. Dove, 1820, IV, p. 293; Smith's *Of the Existence and Nature of God*, in *Select Discourses*, p. 160 (cf. *CP*, p. 103); and Norris's *An Essay towards the Theory of the Ideal or Intelligible World*, II, p. 510 (cf. *JN*, p. 74).

[63] *CP*, p. 149. Perhaps, therefore, we should qualify Sarah Hutton's claim that 'Like his fellow Platonists, Culverwell was a divine who resisted the stern Calvinist establishment of his College.' See her article on Culverwell in Andrew Pyle, ed., *Dictionary of Seventeenth-Century British Philosophers*, Bristol: Thoemmes Press, 2000, p. 228. It would seem more accurate to say that the struggle between Calvinism and Platonism was more intense in Culverwel than in the others, and that this sometimes led him into inconsistencies peculiar to himself.

[64] *CP*, p. 23, quoting Whichcote, *Aphorisms*, no. 76.

contemporaries'.[65] In evidence of this he quotes from Baxter's *The Reasons of the Christian Religion*:

> God hath made Reason essential to our nature; it is not our *weakness* but our essential excellency, and his image in our nature... If God would have us know without reason, he would not have made us reasonable creatures... Faith is an act, or species of knowledge: it is so far from being contrary to reason that it is but an act of clear elevated reason. It is not an act of immediate intuition of God, or of Jesus Christ himself, but a knowledge of the truth by the divine evidence of its certainty.[66]

For his part, Norris related the reasonable to the moral: God 'will not forcibly determine us to good, because He has made us free, so neither does he require anything from us but what is good and consistent with Reason, because He has made us Rational'.[67] Small wonder that to Smith the rationalist was one who rested upon the reason and understanding alone, divorcing the perception of the common principles of virtue and goodness from the practice of them.[68]

On all of which Powicke remarks, 'the distinction and the offence of the Cambridge men was, not that they exercised or even commended reason more than others, but only that they made it the ultimate authority'.[69] This leads him to point out that while the scholastic approach came to mean the unquestioning acceptance of doctrines, the original formulating of the doctrines was an intensely rational exercise. But when, gradually, questions were raised about Aristotelian presuppositions and the authority of the Church, 'by the use of reason came the emancipation of reason'.[70] The impetus in this direction as far as the Cambridge divines and Norris were concerned was the conviction that since reason is divine and since God is free, reason ought also to be free. J. H. Muirhead was not without justification in declaring that to the Cambridge men 'freedom and rationality were not two different things, but one and the same'.[71]

---

[65] Powicke, *Reverend Richard Baxter under the Cross*, p. 238. In a note, Powicke says that when in London Baxter sometimes went to hear Whichcote preach, and seems to have known him.

[66] Ibid., pp. 238-9. Though I have elsewhere tentatively suggested that in his deference to empirical evidence, Baxter was not as resolutely intuitionist as the Cambridge Platonists. See Sell, *Confessing and Commending the Faith*, pp. 262-4.

[67] *JN*, p. 128, quoting 'The Christian Law asserted and Vindicated', in *A Collection of Miscellanies,* Oxford: John Crosley, 1687, p. 225.

[68] *CP*, p. 98.

[69] Ibid., pp. 23-24.

[70] Ibid., p. 24.

[71] J. H. Muirhead, *The Platonic Tradition*, in *Anglo-Saxon Philosophy*, London: Allen and Unwin, 1931, p. 63.

Not indeed that reason *qua* free and spiritual sanctioned enthusiastic license. Whichcote was as terse as any: 'Enthusiastic Doctrines—good things strained out of their Wits. Among Christians, those, that present to be *Inspired*, seem to be Mad: among Turks, those, that are Mad, are thought to be Inspired.'[72] For all Henry More's ecstatic extravagances,[73] he defined 'enthusiasm' as 'a full, but false, persuasion in a Man that he is inspir'd'[74]—a condition which he was sometimes quick to detect and rebuke in Quakers. Other Cambridge Platonists (though not the more tolerant Cudworth) followed suit. No doubt More's attitude was to some extent prompted by his disappointment that his favourite student, Lady Conway, had gone over to the Friends. However that may be, his *Discourse of Enthusiasm* makes his complaint against them sufficiently clear. He ranked them with the oft-despised Familists (though on other occasions More could hold them up as an example to other Christians), and did not like their name which, as he understood it,[75] derived from their habit of taking their quakings 'to be an infallible sign that they are inactuated by the Spirit of God'.[76] They are, sadly, 'deluded souls'—indeed, they are 'the most Melancholy Sect that ever was yet in the world'.[77] This brings us to the crux of the matter. To the Quakers, the light was a supernatural gift distinct from their own reason; to More and the Cambridge Platonists it was God-bestowed reason as such. In 1656, for example, Fox had argued against the Independent John Owen that the light was not a natural light, but 'divine and spiritual from Christ the divine and spiritual man'.[78]

This claim appears regularly in Quaker writings, but it is perhaps expressed most pertinently from our point of view by Robert Barclay, for he was early Quakerism's systematic theologian *par excellence*, and he

---

[72] Whichcote, *Aphorisms*, in E. T. Campagnac, *The Cambridge Platonists*, Oxford: Clarendon Press, 1901, p. 75.

[73] See Robert Crocker, 'Mysticism and enthusiasm in Henry More', in Sarah Hutton, ed., *Henry More (1614-1687). Tercentenary Studies*, Dordrecht: Kluwer, 1990, pp. 137-155; Robert Crocker, 'The role of illuminism in the thought of Henry More', in G. A. J. Rogers, J. M. Vienne and Y. C. Zarka, eds., *The Cambridge Platonists in Philosophical Context. Politics, Metaphysics and Religion*, Dordrecht: Kluwer, 1997, pp. 129-44.

[74] H. More, *A Collection of Several Philosophical Writings of Dr. Henry More*, London, 4th edn., 1712, p. 2.

[75] Though, according to George Fox, Justice Gervase Bennet of Derby 'first called us Quakers because we bid them tremble at the word of God'. G. Fox, *The Journal of George Fox*, ed. John L. Nickalls, (1952), London: Religious Society of Friends, 1975, p. 58.

[76] *CP*, p. 166, quoting H. More, *Enthusiasmus Triumphatus; or, A Brief Discourse of the Nature, Causes, Kinds, and Cure of Enthusiasm*, in H. More, *A Collection of Philosophical Writings of Dr. Henry More*, London: Joseph Downing, 1712, p. 18.

[77] More, *Enthusiasmus Triumphatus*, pp. 18-19.

[78] G. Fox, *Journal of George Fox*, p. 274. See further, Sell, *Commemorations*, pp. 70-72.

was directly challenged by Norris. Barclay makes it clear that when he speaks of the light which lightens every man he is not referring to natural light, but to

> a spiritual, heavenly, and invisible principle, in which God, as Father, Son, and spirit dwells; a measure of which divine and glorious life is in all men as a seed, which of its own nature draws, invites, and inclines to God; and this we call vehiculum Dei, or the spiritual body of Christ...but we are far from ever having said that Christ is thus formed in all men, Or in the wicked.[79]

Moreover, '*we understand not this divine principle to be any part of man's nature, nor yet to be any relics of any good which Adam lost by his fall ...* '.[80]

Like Fox, Barclay could not see how our natural conscience or reason could be the light, for both are subject to corruption. Hence his conviction that

> we do distinguish betwixt the certain knowledge of God, and the uncertain; betwixt the spiritual knowledge, and the literal; the saving-heart knowledge, and the soaring, airy-head knowledge. The last, we confess, may be divers ways obtained; but the first by no other way than the inward immediate manifestation and revelation of God's Spirit, shining in and upon the heart, enlightening and opening the understanding.[81]

This position was reaffirmed by the Yearly Meeting of the Religious Society of Friends in 1879.[82] On it the Quaker Edward Grubb commented:

> The Quakers had recovered the Divine immanence, but they tried vainly to express it in the terms of dualism... The Light they had rediscovered they must make wholly human and natural, or else wholly Divine and spiritual. The former alternative landed them in the conclusion that man needed no saving grace of God; and from this they recoiled in horror. They found themselves, therefore, shut up to the other alternative...[83]

---

[79] R. Barclay, *An Apology for the True Christian Divinity as the same is held forth and preached by the people, in scorn, called Quakers*, etc., 14th edn., 1886, pp. 96, 100.

[80] Ibid., p. 101.

[81] Ibid., p 12.

[82] See *Christian Faith and Practice in the Experience of the Society of Friends*, (1959), London: Religious Society of Friends, 1998, no. 170.

[83] E. Grubb, 'The Society of Friends', in W. B. Selbie, ed., *Evangelical Christianity. Its History and Witness*, London: Hodder and Stoughton, [1911], p. 201. W. R. Inge thought that the Quakers would have benefited from intellectual contact with the Cambridge Platonists, but they were intellectually isolated. See his *The Church in the World*, London: Longmans, Green, 1927, p. 78. John Punshon considers that with

To Norris, however, who argued that there was 'no medium between God and the creature', Barclay's *vehiculum Dei* was 'gross' and 'material'.[84] Norris similarly took exception to the explanation of the Quaker, George Keith, that human beings are not illumined by 'the Godhead itself, but [by] a certain middle nature, substance, or being, betwixt the Godhead and mankind'.[85] Norris further disagreed with what he took to be the Quaker restriction of the light to moral and spiritual truths, and to their recourse to it as a means of interpreting the Bible: 'I do not appropriate this Divine Light to Moral or Spiritual things, but extend it as far as all Truth, yea, as far as all that is Intelligible...'.[86] Norris was keen to reveal the epistemological gap between his position and that of the Quakers because some had understood him to be at one with the Quakers' doctrine of the inward light.[87]

Nothing which has been said concerning the objections of the Cambridge Platonists and Norris to enthusiasm should delude us into thinking that they were coldly cerebral logic choppers. Of none of them was this true, of More least of all. Cudworth, for example, had no difficulty in treating the House of Commons to the following eulogy: 'O Divine love! The sweet harmony of souls! The music of angels! The source of true happiness! The pure quintessence of heaven...'[88]

III

In the opinion of the Cambridge Platonists, human reason had nothing to fear from the new science of Bacon and others. Indeed, both More and Cudworth were Fellows of the Royal Society. The Cambridge divines

---

respect to claims to illumination understood as more secure than reason and sensation, Barclay 'bequeathed to Friends a highly unstable metaphysics' because 'any tests for the genuineness of such claims must fail because they belong to the same category of outward knowledge that Barclay was attacking'. See *Reasons for Hope. The Faith and Future of the Friends Church*, Richmond, IN: Friends United Press, 2001, p. 239.

[84] See J. Norris, *Two Treatises concerning the Divine Light*, 1692. The second of these is addressed to Barclay. For Powicke's summary of them see *JN*, pp. 189-192. See further on Barclay on the light, Sell, *Commemorations*, ch. 6, especially p. 160 n; and ch. 2 below.

[85] G. Keith, *The Way to the City of God*, p. 130, quoted by J. Norris, *Two Treatises*, p. 11.

[86] *JN*, pp. 146-7, quoting Norris's Appendix to *Reflections upon the Conduct of Human Life* London: S. Manship, 1691, pp. 184-5.

[87] See J. Norris, *Treatises upon Several Subjects*, London: S. Manship, 1698, p. 202. That a latter-day Quaker likewise regrets the turn which Barclay took is clear from Edward Grubb's remarks in *Quaker Thought and History*, London: Swarthmore Press, 1925, pp. 30-1.

[88] R. Cudworth, *Sermon before the Honourable House of Commons*, in *The Works of Ralph Cudworth, D.D.*, Oxford: D. A. Talboys, 1829, IV, p. 335.

regarded Bacon's appeal to sensible experience as a welcome relief from Aristotelian abstractions and, since Bacon kept his science in a separate compartment from his Bible, they had nothing to fear on that score. 'Bacon', wrote Powicke, 'honoured theology as the Jews honoured the Holy of holies. He thought it too sacred to enter.'[89] Tulloch was not wide of the mark in saying of the new experimentalism that the Cambridge Platonists 'were so far in hearty affinity with this and all other forward tendencies of the time, although their own speculative impulse came from a different quarter and followed a different method'.[90] Norris, however, seems to have been more sceptical on this point, and he enters something of a minority report on the ground of reason's inability to understand very much of the natural order:

> *We have seen but a few of God's works*...and we *understand* yet *fewer*. There are almost an infinite number of things which we never so much as *thought* of, and of *most* things we conceive very *darkly* and *uncertainly*, and there is not *one* thing from the greatest to the *least*, which we do or can understand *thoroughly*.[91]

But if Bacon was perceived as unthreatening, the same was not the case with Hobbes. On the contrary, some[92] of the Cambridge divines thought it imperative that the naturalism of Hobbes be stoutly opposed. Hobbes so distinguished divinity, which he took on trust, from philosophy that deliverances of the latter could be at utter variance with the former without vitiating religious faith. Clearly, to one of Cudworth's persuasion, this could only be anathema. Hobbes is clearly in Cudworth's sights in *The True Intellectual System*, though the author declines to name him, preferring to speak of 'a modern philosopher', 'a modern writer', 'a modern atheistical pretender'.[93] Passmore neatly summarizes the situation thus:

> Hobbes symbolized five things: atheism, materialism, determinism, individualism and ethical relativism. Cudworth was a theist, a dualist, a libertarian, who believed in the organic theory of the State and in eternal and immutable morality. Both accepted the atomic theory of the body, both rejected the scholastic 'faculties', and there were certain other coincidences of doctrine, but on the vital philosophical issues there could be no compromise.[94]

---

[89] *CP*, p. 26.

[90] Tulloch, *Rational Theology*, II, p. 24.

[91] Norris, *Reflections on the Conduct of Human Life*, pp. 114-15.

[92] Powicke notes that Whichcote and Smith do not mention Hobbes, and that More's references to him are mild. See *CP*, p. 122.

[93] See *CP*, p. 123, n.

[94] Passmore, *Ralph Cudworth*, p. 12. Remarking on the mutual compliments which Hobbes and More paid each other, Powicke suggests that More 'seems never to have

In Powicke's opinion, the case against materialism has seldom been put more cogently than by Cudworth, and this despite the fact that, 'If he did not exactly beat the bush without starting the hare, he beat up the dust as well to such an extent that the hare, when started, could hardly be seen.'[95] The allusion here is to Cudworth's method of piling up authorities in his own favour; as Powicke further says, 'His arguments are not new. They are as old as Plato and as modern as Martineau.'[96] Passmore supplied the reason for this methodological rummaging: 'Cudworth's scholarship is not mere pedantry: it is a deliberate protest against the modern emphasis upon originality and innovation.'[97] Accordingly, Tulloch's contention that both Cudworth and More 'are only to be understood in the light of Hobbes's theories'[98] was rightly called into question by Clark, though for the wrong reason, namely, that 'the Platonists represent, not a reaction, but a new and independent start'.[99] In fact they represent and perpetuate what they regarded as a perennial tradition: as Clark himself averred six lines earlier, 'their message would in its main outlines have been the same even though Hobbes had not been known'.[100] Again, those Cambridge Platonists who dealt with him 'came *to* Hobbes as they did their work, rather than started *from* him to do it...'.[101]

The relations of the Platonists and Norris to Descartes is of particular interest. Powicke finds[102] that whereas Bacon kept faith and science in

---

realised the bottomless gulf which divided Hobbes' system of thought from his own'. See *CP*, p. 123.

[95] *CP*, p. 123.

[96] Ibid.

[97] Passmore, *Ralph Cudworth*, p. 14. The point seems to be lost on W. R. Inge in *The Platonic Tradition in English Religious Thought*, London: Longmans, Green, 1926, p. 58: 'it was unnecessary, in opposing Hobbes, to go back to Democritus'.

[98] Tulloch, *Rational Theology*, II, p. 30. Tulloch is followed by Samuel I. Mintz, *The Hunting of Leviathan. Seventeenth-Century Reactions to the Materialism and Moral Philosophy of Thomas Hobbes*, Cambridge: Cambridge University Press, 1962, opening of the otherwise helpful ch. 5. On his previous page Tulloch reveals himself as aware of Cudworth's BD dissertation of 1644 in which, seven years before the appearance of *Leviathan*, the lines of his thought were laid.

[99] Clark, *Liberal Orthodoxy*, p. 35.

[100] Ibid.

[101] Ibid.

[102] *CP*, 27. In keeping with his quest of spiritual sustenance, Powicke does not delve in detail into the relations between Cudworth and Descartes. See, however, L. Gysi, *Platonism and Cartesianism in the Philosophy of Ralph Cudworth*, Bern: H. Lang, 1962; J. E. Saveson, 'Differing reactions to Descartes among the Cambridge Platonists', *Journal of the History of Ideas*, XXI no. 4, October 1960, pp. 560-7; Danton B. Sailor, 'Cudworth and Descartes', *Journal of the History of Ideas*, XXIII no. 1, January-March 1962, pp. 133-140. Sailor concludes (p. 140) that 'Cudworth's rejection of Cartesianism was comprehensive.'

separate compartments, Descartes, in the dedication of his *Meditations*, held that it was philosophy's task to treat the existence of God and the nature of the soul. In so far as the Cambridge Platonists upheld the harmony of reason and faith, they sided with Descartes, but this did not imply complete agreement with him. For example, More's intellectual pilgrimage took him from early eulogizing of Descartes to ever increasing recourse to the Bible—especially to its prophetic and apocalyptic portions[103]—so that he could say that even concerning matters demonstrable by natural reason, the Bible provided greater certainty. Eventually, in his enthusiasm to defend revealed religion by recourse to supernatural 'evidences' as supplied by the occult, astrology and witchcraft, he turned against the 'clear and cool intellectualism' of Descartes.[104] In particular, he repudiated Descartes's doctrine of animal automatism, and charged Descartes with losing the spirit-matter distinction, hence aiding and abetting materialism.[105] The degree of More's emphasis upon more sensationalist forms of mysticism distanced him from the other Cambridge Platonists, and landed him in a 'subjectivism which was not very different from that enthusiasm which he so decried in others'.[106]

For a quite different reason, Norris was critical of Descartes. He objected to what he understood as Descartes's view that all truth is positively ordained by God. Though Descartes was a 'great man', this was a 'most monstrous' doctrine, for it was a denial of the absoluteness, necessity and eternity of truth. Powicke states the heart of his case thus: 'Truth, as dependent on God's free decree, is necessarily contingent; may, therefore, be truth only for a time; may, "like *almanacks*, be outdated".'[107] A further point of difference between Descartes and Norris

[103] See further, C. Webster, 'Henry More and Descartes: Some new sources', *The British Journal for the History of Science*, IV.iv.16, December 1969, pp. 359-77. In *Reverend Richard Baxter under the Cross*, pp. 160-1, Powicke recounts More's hostility to Baxter's 'modest agnostic attitude to the Apocalypse'.

[104] See *CP*, 156-9. Powicke cites the Letter to the Reader in More's *Divine Dialogues* (1668) as indicative of More's reaction against Descartes.

[105] See H. More, *Manual of Metaphysics, or Enchiridium Metaphysicum*, London, 1671. See further, C. Webster, 'Henry More and Descartes: Some new sources', and Alan Gabbey, 'Philosophia Cartesiana Triumphata: Henry More (1646-1671)', in Thomas M. Lennon, John M. Nicholas and John W. Davis, eds., *Problems of Cartesianism*, Kingston and Montreal: McGill-Queens University Press, 1982, pp. 171-250.

[106] *CP*, 159. For 'Descartes' influence on John Smith, Cambridge Platonist', see J. E. Saveson, *Journal of the History of Ideas*, XX no. 2, April 1959, pp. 258-63.

[107] *JN*, p. 47, quoting Norris, *An Essay towards the Theory of the Ideal or Intelligible World*, I, p. 344. Powicke (*CP*, pp. 119-20) finds the same criticism of Descartes in Cudworth's philosophy, and quotes James Martineau, *Types of Ethical Theory*, Oxford: Clarendon Press, 3rd edn revised, 1891, II, p. 416 in support. However, John Passmore (*Ralph Cudworth*, pp. 8-11), criticises J. H. Muirhead (*The Platonic Tradition*, p. 26) for

concerns the way in which we come to know God. Norris contends that no idea of God is necessary to represent him to us, for nothing can bring him nearer to the soul than he already is; indeed, no idea could represent him. This being so, Descartes's argument fails because 'it all proceeds upon the false, though common, Supposition, that we perceive God, as we do other things, by an Idea that is really distinct from him; and, indeed, that the idea of God is one of his *Effects*'.[108] None of Norris's objections to Descartes require him to deny a fundamental point of agreement between them, namely that they are dualists. Norris, like Descartes, thinks in terms of the natural and the ideal, or spiritual, world.[109] Indeed, Norris insists that the existence of the latter is more certain than that of the former, negatively, because we cannot show *a priori* that the sensible world was not a 'necessary emanation' from its cause; and positively, because metaphysical intuitions are certain and their conclusions more demonstrable than those of sensation, and because rational evidence is superior to sensible as affording 'the best ground of Certainty or Criterion of Truth'.[110]

The relations between the Cambridge Platonists and Norris on the one hand, and Locke on the other, are, if anything, even more intriguing than their likeness and unlikeness to Descartes. At first glance the parties may appear to be poles apart. For example, John Smith's view that 'all Humane Knowledge hath not its rise from Sense',[111] and Henry More's denial that the human mind is '*a Table book in which nothing is writ*', and his affirmation that there is 'an active and *actuall Knowledge* in a man'[112] are diametrically opposed by Locke.[113] Again, Locke found much with which to find fault in Norris's position.[114] In particular, Locke

---

taking Cudworth's rebuke of the Cartesians for their 'mechanically-atheistic humour' as the final general word of the Cambridge Platonists as a whole on Descartes (whereas in fact it was a particular complaint concerning Descartes's theory of animal mechanism). In justification of his criticism, Passmore specifies the following points of agreement between Cudworth and Descartes: they both subscribed to the doctrine of clear and distinct perceptions; they believed that the atomic theory provided the best foundation for theism; that mind and body are distinct substances; and that sensation is 'confused thought'.

[108] *JN*, pp. 63-4, quoting Norris, *An Essay towards the Theory of the Ideal or Intelligible World*, II, p. 292.

[109] *JN*, p. 38.

[110] *JN*, pp. 47-8. Powicke quotes Norris, *An Essay towards the Theory of the Ideal or Intelligible World*, I, p. 194.

[111] J. Smith, *Of the Immortality of the Soul*, in Select *Discourses*, ch. 3.

[112] H. More, *An Antidote against Atheism*, London: Roger Daniel, 1653, p. 13.

[113] See further, G. A. J. Rogers, 'Locke, Newton and the Cambridge Platonists on innate ideas', *Journal of the History of Ideas*, XL, 1979, 191-205.

[114] See further, Charlotte Johnson, 'Locke's *Examination of Malebranche* and John Norris', *Journal of the History of Ideas*, XIX no. 4, October 1958, pp. 551-8; Alan P. F.

regards Norris's assertion that we have a distinct idea of God as sheer presumption. But Norris is at pains to point out that he, too, is opposed to non-figurative talk of 'Mental Impressions, or Characters, written upon the mind.' He is committed to something nearly analogous to innate ideas, however, namely, to the view that God 'exhibit[s] some particular Truths of the Ideal world more early, more clearly, and more constantly to the view of the Soul than others, that by these she may be the better directed to the good and Reasonable Life, as animals by sensitive Instincts and Inclinations are to the good sense'.[115]

On this question, as on others, Culverwel emerges as the odd man out. Referring to what he calls 'connate' ideas, Culverwel declares that we bring none of them with us into the world. From birth, we have the capacity for knowledge, but the 'candle of the Lord' is lit then, and not before.[116] As Tulloch puts it, 'the capacity or faculty of knowledge is from within—the content is from without'.[117] Culverwel's modification apart, it is not difficult to discern the motive underlying the stance taken generally by the Cambridge Platonists and Norris on this question: the view that ideas were derived from sensible objects, and the denial that they were spiritual realities, could lead only to materialistic atheism; and such atheism, they agreed, must stoutly be resisted.

As for Norris's view (confirmed for him by Malebranche) that we see all things in God, Locke presses this to the point of pantheism—with some justification, judges Powicke: 'What is this better than what those say who make God to be nothing but the universe, though it be covered under unintelligible expressions of simplicity and variety, at the same time, in the essence of God?'[118] To the charge of pantheism we shall return. For the present we may utter a word cautionary against the too ready labelling of thinkers. Locke's sensationalism, and his wounding remark that Norris produced 'Platonic gibberish' notwithstanding,[119] the former could nevertheless write,

---

Sell, *John Locke and the Eighteenth-Century Divines*, Cardiff: University of Wales Press, 1997, p. 19.

[115] *JN*, p. 80, quoting J. Norris, *Cursory Reflections upon a Book call'd, an Essay concerning Human Understanding*, 1692, p. 21. See further on Locke and Norris, John Hoyles, *The Waning of the Renaissance 1640-1740*, The Hague: Martinus Nijhof, 1971, pp. 105-9.

[116] N. Culverwel, *An Elegant and Learned Discourse of the Light of Nature*, London: T.R. and E.M. for John Rothwell, 1652, ch. 11.

[117] Tulloch, *Rational Theology*, p. 421.

[118] *JN*, p. 82. Powicke quotes J. Locke, *Remarks upon some of Mr. Norris's books—wherein he asserts P. Malebranche's opinion of our seeing all things in God*, 1693; see Sell, *John Locke and the Eighteenth-Century Divines*, p. 19.

[119] See *JN*, p. 37.

> *Reason* is natural *Revelation*, whereby the eternal Father of Light, and Fountain of all Knowledge and Fountain of all Knowledge communicates to Mankind that portion of Truth, which he has laid within the reach of their natural Faculties: *Revelation* is natural *Reason* enlarged by a new set of Discoveries communicated by GOD immediately, which *Reason* vouches the Truth of, by the Testimony and Proofs it gives, that they come from God. So that he that takes away *Reason*, to make way for *Revelation* puts out the light of both, and does much what the same, as if he would perswade a Man to put out his Eyes the better to receive the remote Light of an invisible Star by a Telescope.[120]

Powicke was not without justification in detecting 'the voice—nay, in part, even the words of Whichcote and Smith and Culverwel'[121] in Locke's definitions. But, as he also (almost certainly ruefully) observed, whereas to the Cambridge Platonists 'Reason was a divine light, or the organ of a Divine Spirit...in the prevailing thought of the eighteenth century, it became another name for common sense.'[122]

IV

Of the reverence which the Cambridge Platonists and Norris showed towards the Bible there can be no question. As Rosalie Colie properly pointed out, they 'relied principally upon the authority of Scripture for their truth'.[123] They adverted to it in their sermons, of course, but they did not write tracts or treatises upon it. It is not difficult, however, to gather their references to Scripture, and when this is done we see that here as elsewhere they manifest certain differences of emphasis.

Powicke summarizes their general position: the Cambridge Platonists could not hold that Scripture was more divine than 'natural light', for God was equally the fountain of both. Scripture confirms what is given naturally, clarifies matters concerning immortality and the last things at which Plato stopped short, and reveals God's 'surpassing love'.[124] They were suspicious of 'determinations beyond Scripture' which, wrote Whichcote, have 'enlarged faith, but lessened charity, and multiplied divisions'.[125] On the other hand, they did not agree with Tuckney that propositions were true simply because they were to be found in the Bible. It is not that Tuckney repudiated reason, but he subordinated it to the

---

120 Powicke quotes this, unreferenced, *CP*, p. 199. I have recourse to Locke's *An Essay concerning Human Understanding*, IV.xix.4, ed. Peter H. Nidditch, Oxford: Clarendon Press, (1995), 1997.

121 *CP*, p. 199.

122 *CP*, p. 213.

123 R. Colie, *Light and Enlightenment*, Cambridge: Cambridge University Press, 1957, p. 2.

124 *CP*, pp. 31-2.

125 *CP*, p. 41, quoting Whichcote, *Aphorisms*, no. 981.

biblical text. Whichcote, on the other hand, gave greater prominence to reason: 'The reason of a man's mind must be satisfied; no man can think against it.'[126] This position Whichcote represented as being in accord with the Reformation principle regarding the right of private judgment.[127] The following are among Whichcote's words which Powicke selects to reinforce the point:

> If you let go scripture in the sense to which the context leads, and if you let go the true and impartial proposals, and dictates of sober reason; then do we open the door to all manner of delusion and imposture, and shall be carried we do not know whither... [S]cripture, as it is a matter of faith, is not a single text, but all the scripture...for the scripture is to be read as a man would read a letter from a friend, in which he doth only look after what was his friend's mind and meaning, not what he can put upon the words.[128]

This calls to mind the approach to the Bible adopted by Locke, whose method was to read the New Testament epistles right through at least once so as to grasp the general sense, before dwelling upon particular portions; and whose practice influenced a number of subsequent divines:

> I continued to read the same Epistle over and over, and over again, till I came to discover, as it appeared to me, what was the Drift and Aim of it, and by what Steps and Arguments *St. Paul* prosecuted his purpose.[129]

Once again, Culverwel differs from other Cambridge Platonists. Powicke quotes his description of the Bible as, 'Those sacred and heavenly volumes that are strung together as so many pearls, and make a bracelet for the spouse to wear upon her hands continually.'[130] Faith, instructed by the Bible, takes precedence over reason where reason is blind: 'For this is the voice of Nature itself, that whatever God reveals must needs be true; and this common principle is the bottom and

---

[126] *CP*, 59

[127] Though, as Philip Watson has insisted, 'There could hardly be any more perverse caricature of Luther's whose intention than to say that the main plank of his reforming platform was the assertion of the "right of private judgement".' He goes on to explain that Luther's challenge to Rome was not in the interests of his own private judgment, but it something to which he was propelled by the Word of God. In face of the undeniable fact of diverse interpretations of that Word, Luther contended that those doctrines are true which set forth the glory of God alone. See *Let God be God! An Interpretation of the Theology of Martin Luther*, London: Epworth Press, 1947, pp. 13-14.

[128] *CP*, p. 78, quoting B. Whichcote, *The Works of the Learned Benjamin Whichcote, D.D.*, Abderdeen: J. Chalmers, 1751, III, p. 117; II, p. 245.

[129] J. Locke, *A Paraphrase and Notes on the Epistles of St. Paul*, ed. Arthur W. Wainwright, Oxford: Clarendon Press, 1987, I, p. 110. See further Sell, *John Locke and the Eighteenth-Century Divines*, ch. 3.

[130] *CP*, p. 143.

foundation of all faith to build upon.'[131] On this Powicke offers the cautionary reflection:

> if you plead the word of God for something which does violence not merely to the primitive intuitions of natural conscience, but, still more, to the highest intuitions of a purified Christian conscience, you cancel the meaning and purpose of all revelation. Texts, many or few, may be in its favour; but it is not texts which can seal the Divinity of a fact or doctrine: it is agreement with the clear truth of Christ—and of this truth Reason, quickened and guided by the spirit of God, is the only possible judge. Hence it is that Calvinism as expounded by Culverwel, and much else adduced in the name of Scripture, have had to go.[132]

He further points out that this is not that rationalism which seeks to preclude faith; on the contrary, he accepts that religion usually begins with acts of faith. But 'such *implicit acts of faith* are, at the same time, *implicit acts of the reason*. Unless they were, experience would not justify them. Because they *are*, they may be vindicated by conscious thought.'[133] Powicke concludes that because of his conviction that the 'candle of the Lord' may actually be darkness, needing the Bible for its replacement, Culverwel strayed from his teacher Whichcote, and also from Smith and Cudworth—even to the point of betrayal.

In a different way, Henry More ended at a certain distance from other Cambridge Platonists as far as the Bible was concerned. We have already noted the increased attention he paid to it as his disenchantment with Descartes increased. It remains only to add that he eventually reached the point of saying that Scripture yields greater certainty even regarding things demonstrable by natural reason. Powicke quotes him as saying that the Scriptures 'rightly and completely understood' surpass 'the clearest fountain of philosophy'. He even regrets that he had not reached this conclusion earlier, for it would 'in greatest part have extinguished that so ardent desire of philosophising which seized me when I was very young'.[134]

In the Epilogue to his study of the Cambridge Platonists, Powicke shows how the Cambridge Platonists stand at the threshhold of a deluge of apologetic endeavours. For if it be affirmed that the Bible must be received as the Word of God, the question will be raised,

---

131 Ibid.

132 For the way in which this dilution worked out in Powicke's own tradition, see ch. 5 below. In Powicke's words we have the gist of a Christocentric-pneumatic, reasonable doctrine of authority which it was not to his purpose here to work out in detail. It is a position which befits one nurtured by the 'believing liberalism' of D. W. Simon.

133 *CP*, p. 146.

134 *CP*, p. 157.

> 'How do you know that the Scriptures are the Word of God?'; and, when the answer came, 'They are proved to be such by prophecies fulfilled and miracles performed as well as by intrinsic marks of truth,' immediately the whole wide field of controversy about evidences was opened—controversy in which the combatants lost themselves in noise and smoke. Nor could the battle be decided until it came to be seen and acknowledged: (a) that too much had been handed over to natural light in the first instance, or, in other words, that there had been ascribed to it not a little which was derived from Scripture; (b) that the chief end of Scripture was to record a revelation growing more and more to its perfect day in Christ;[135] and (c) that the acceptance of this depends not on miracles and prophecies but on that witness of the spirit which is given in the experience of a humble and obedient heart. But *that* lay beyond the orbit of eighteenth-century thought...[136]

With these remarks, and because of its relevance to the ecclesiological question to be raised shortly, we may note Powicke's account of the non-subscribing, mostly Presbyterian, 'Arians' of the eighteenth century, who, at Salters' Hall in 1719, took 'with unqualified seriousness, the traditional Protestant principle that the Bible, and the Bible only, must determine the form of a doctrine, the Trinity included'.[137] In other words, by failing to see that a concept may be present in a text even if a term is not, they became what might be termed (anachronistically) fundamentalist literalists in reverse, holding that because a term, 'the Trinity' is *not* in the Bible, we will not affirm it.[138] Also with a view to what follows, and with respect to those other devotees of the light, the Quakers, we may note the judgment of one of their own authors. Too many Friends, 'not merely the wilder section such as poor James Naylor and his associates, but even the calm and intellectual Robert Barclay...attached a somewhat subordinate position, not only to the authority of the Holy Scriptures, but also to the importance of the Incarnation and the *historic* Christ'.[139]

V

Especially in view of their emphasis upon the immutability of morality, the judgement of Henry Clark to the effect that there is not 'any injustice in saying that it was the intellectual aspect of religion as related to philosophy, not the moral and spiritual impulses it might impart, that

---

[135] A judgment which turns upon the idea of progressive revelation, popular in Powicke's day but since challenged by many biblical scholars—especially by those who seek to hold traditional theology at a distance when examining biblical texts.

[136] *CP*, p. 205.

[137] Powicke, 'English Congregationalism in its greatness and decline', p. 305.

[138] See further, Alan P. F. Sell, *Dissenting Thought and the Life of the Churches. Studies in an English Tradition*, Lewiston, NY: Edwin Mellen Press, 1990, ch. 5.

[139] William Tallack, 'The "Cambridge Platonists" and Quakerism', *The Friends' Quarterly Examiner*, XIII, 1889, p. 190.

captivated [the Cambridge Platonists] most'[140] must be regarded as a gross and uncharacteristic lapse on the part of a generally careful scholar. In fact, against naturalism, and in opposition to theories grounded in self-interest, the Cambridge Platonists staunchly defended the view that moral principals are eternal, and that they are known by intuition. Faced as they were by doctrinal disputes and sundry sectarianisms, they sought a platform of unity in widely approved moral theory and practice. As to theory, Tulloch rightly observed that 'They sought to bring every truth or doctrine to the test of the Christian reason, and to estimate it by a moral standard—in other words, by its tendency to exalt or degrade our conceptions of the divine.'[141] As to exhortations to practice, the writings of the divines are replete with them. Thus, Whichcote declares that '*Religion* must be the *Frame* of our Minds, and the *Rule* of our Lives.[142] Again, 'the first Act of Religion is to *know* what is True of God; the second Act is to *Express* it in our lives'.[143] In fact, wrote Smith, 'Divine truth is better understood, as it unfolds itself in the purity of men's hearts and lives, than in all those subtile niceties into which curious wits may lay it forth.'[144] Directly relating this insight to religious faith he explains that 'The righteousness of faith is that powerful attractive which by a strong and divine sympathy draws down the virtue of heaven into the souls of men, which strongly and forcibly moves the souls of good men into a conjunction with that divine goodness by which it lives and grows.[145] Smith underlines the point that evangelical righteousness is not a 'doctrine wrapt up in ink and paper [but] *vitalis scientia*, a living impression made upon the soul and spirit'.[146]

As for Cudworth, Powicke affirms with reference to his *Treatise on Immutable Morality* that while 'All the Cambridge men...put morals first...Cudworth gives them the first place with special emphasis.'[147] 'He is the best Christian', wrote Cudworth, 'whose heart beats with the purest pulse towards heaven; not he, whose head spinneth out the finest cobwebs.'[148] Nor was he anything but disapproving of Puritan religious hypocrisy: 'He is a true Christian indeed, not only he that is book-taught, but he, that is God-taught... Ink and paper can never make us Christians...can never form Christ, or any true notions of spiritual things,

---

[140] Clark, *Liberal Orthodoxy*, p. 47.

[141] Tulloch, *Rational Theology*, II, p. 41.

[142] Whichcote, *Aphorisms*, no. 315.

[143] *CP*, p. 83, quoting Whichcote, *Aphorisms*, no. 219. Cf. *CP*, p. 33.

[144] Smith, *Select Discourses*, p. 11.

[145] *CP*, p. 43, quoting J. Smith, *Discourse on Legal and Evangelical Righteousness*, in *Select Discourses*, p. 359.

[146] Smith, *Discourse on Legal and Evangelical Righteousness*, p. 349.

[147] *CP*, p. 118.

[148] R. Cudworth, *Works*, IV, p. 297.

in our hearts.'[149] But Cudworth did not intend that his insistence upon genuine Christianity should in any way undermine the view he urged so strongly against Hobbes, namely, that while God presides over all, morality belongs to the *natural* order—which prompted Passmore to point out that once Cudworth's epistemology is shown to fail his ethics

> can be interpreted in terms wholly secular... Only if morality is somehow ontologically dependent upon God—as it is, of course, in the Calvinistic ethics Cudworth so bitterly opposed—can ethics be retained as a theological preserve.[150]

For his part, Norris denounced antinomians who think that by reason of Christ's satisfaction, believers are excused from duty and obedience; those who equate religion with the holding of orthodox opinions; and the 'Solafidians' who teach that since the merits of Christ alone prevail, the Christian is required to do nothing—a view which is 'against all *Logic* and common sense'.[151] Far from its being abrogated, the divine Law is sharpened by the Gospel which reveals love as the all-inclusive virtue.[152]

This section on morality may fittingly be concluded by reference to Richard Baxter who, as presented by Powicke, is both like and unlike the Cambridge Platonists and Norris. On the one hand, according to Baxter, 'Christianity did not need to do more than sharpen the vision of truths already revealed, and reinforce them by opening up fresh springs of moral power. Which was precisely the teaching of Benjamin Whichcote and John Smith', and it explains Baxter's recourse to heathen moralists when demonstrating 'the natural and universal grounds of religious faith and moral obligation'.[153] On the other hand, Baxter is unlike them in thinking of faith as a duty, 'an obligation which must be obeyed because God wills it, not because faith is the natural and necessary means of relating the soul to "God and his Christ"'.[154] In other words the moral claims of the Gospel are to be heeded because they are commanded, not because they are the 'fruits of a life in One with whom the Christian is in vital fellowship'.[155] Hence Baxter's detestation of antinomianism, and hence Powicke's conclusion:

> If Baxter had been more of a mystic and possessed a deeper sympathy with Paul's mystic experience of life in Christ, he would have been a far wiser critic of so-called

[149] R. Cudworth, *Sermon before the Honourable House of Commons*, in *Works*, IV, p. 297.

[150] Passmore, *Ralph Cudworth*, pp. 88-9.

[151] *JN*, p. 130, quoting 'The Christian law asserted and vindicated', in *A Collection of Miscellanies*, Oxford: John Crosley, 1687, p. 215.

[152] Note the echo of Malebranche. Cf. *JN*, pp. 16, 141.

[153] Powicke, *Richard Baxter under the Cross*, pp. 247, 241.

[154] Powicke, *A Life of the Reverend Richard Baxter*, p. 241.

[155] Ibid., p. 241.

Antinomians like Mrs Hutchinson and Sir Harry Vane and Peter Sterry and the Quakers. As it was, the predominantly intellectual cast of his spirituality made him 'hard-grained'[156] towards such as these—to his own serious loss.

VI

Although Henry Clark was open to question regarding the Cambridge Platonists' concern for morality, he was unquestionably correct in asserting that 'they laid no rough hands on any Christian doctrine in such wise as to leave it, after their handling of it, unrecognisable by those who loved it...'.[157] Turning now to that other group which engaged Powicke's interest, the radical Puritan Separatists, I wish to show that their way of understanding the things of the Spirit, especially in relation to the nature and order of the Church distanced them both from the Cambridge Platonists and Norris, and from the Quakers.

In the context of their time, the Separatists had stern things to say about the Church of England. To them it was an impure Church because of its intended (and legally supported) comprehensiveness. It allowed to the monarch an authority in Church affairs which belonged to Christ alone, and, especially in connection with the undisciplined reception of communicants at the Lord's table, it violated the principle that the Church comprises believers, the regenerate.[158] These negative positions, on which it is not necessary to expatiate further, derived from clearly expressed positive ecclesiological principles for which Barrow, Greenwood and others were prepared to die, and did die. These may briefly be stated in their own words.

First, writing from the Fleet prison in 1589 or 1590, Henry Barrow takes his stand on the Bible as the supreme rule of faith and order: 'I have not desired to speak in the words taught by human wisdom, but in the words taught of the Holy Ghost.'[159]

---

[156] Ibid., p. 242.

[157] Clark, *Liberal Orthodoxy*, p. 60.

[158] See further, Alan P. F. Sell, *Saints: Visible, Orderly and Catholic. The Congregational Idea of the Church*, Geneva: World Alliance of Reformed Churches and Allison Park, PA: Pickwick Publications, 1986; *Commemorations*, ch. 4; and *Testimony and Tradition. Studies in Reformed and Dissenting Thought*, Aldershot: Ashgate, 2005, ch. 11.

[159] Powicke refers to this and Barrow's other ecclesiological points in *Henry Barrow*, ch. 2. I draw my quotations from Leland H. Carlson, ed., *The Writings of Henry Barrow 1587-1590*, London: Allen and Unwin, 1962. The present quotation is from *A Brief Discoverie of the False Church*, in Carlson, ed., *Writings of Henry Barrow*, p. 266. I have modernized the spelling.

Powicke proceeds to record Barrow's conviction that far from being a matter of private judgement, the interpretation of Scripture is rightly done as believers are illumined by the Holy Spirit. We thus find Barrow

> neither striking against the rocks of popery, nor falling upon the shelves and quicksands of Anabaptistry. He did not, like the former, add tradition to Scripture; nor, like the latter (as he supposed), make Scripture subordinate to the inner light.[160]

Secondly, from Scripture we learn that the true Church comprises faithful people who are separated from the world (and by implication from the Church of England, into which 'the world' has crept), and gathered under Christ their sole Head:

> The true planted and rightly established Church of Christ is a company of faithful people—separated from the unbelievers and heathen of the land—gathered in the name of Christ, whom they truly worship and readily obey as their only King, priest, and Prophet, and joined together as members of one body, ordered and governed by such officers and laws as Christ, in His last will and testament, hath thereunto ordained...[161]

Thirdly, although there were few Separatist communities when Barrow wrote, and little opportunity for free fellowship between them, he did not in principle rule out wider fraternal relations. However,

> Synods and councils were not instituted to pluck away the power, or to execute the public duties of the Church, but to instruct, stir up, and confirm them in their duties; to help them to decide controversies; to show them the rules of God's Word, and not to break them or make new...[162]

In all of this we have the gist of the position advanced not only by Barrow himself, but also by Browne, Greenwood, Robinson and others.[163]

---

[160] Powicke, *Henry Barrow*, p. 93.

[161] Ibid., quoting Barrow's letter of 1588 to the Presbyterian Thomas Cartwright and others.

[162] Ibid., p. 125, quoting H. Barrow, *A Plaine Refutation of Mr. George Giffarde's Reproachful Booke*, 1590-91, for which see, Leland H. Carlson, ed., *The Writings of Henry Barrow 1590-1591*, London: Allen and Unwin, 1966, p.151. See further, Patrick Collinson, 'Separation in and out of the Church: The consistency of Barrow and Greenwood', *Journal of the United Reformed Church History Society*, V no. 5, November 1994, pp. 239-58.

[163] For the general situation, see Stephen Brachlow, *The Communion of Saints*, Oxford: Oxford University Press, 1988. For Browne, see especially B. R. White, *The English Separatist Tradition from the Marian Martyrs to the Pilgrim Fathers*, London: Oxford University Press, 1971, ch. 3; Diane Willen, 'Robert Browne and the dilemma of religious dissent', *Journal of the United Reformed Church History Society*, II no. 6,

It is a position which has human responsiveness to a divine command at its heart. As Powicke put it,

> we miss the whole inwardness of the matter if we fail to see that the attitude of the Early Separatists was that of Luther—'So help me God I can *do* no other.' It became forces upon them as a *duty* to separate. There was no thought, or talk, of clutching at a right to do as they liked. Duty was the word—a duty imposed by Christ himself, as they believed, because otherwise his holy will could not be done... Obedience was the condition of blessing.[164]

For institutional, temperamental, doctrinal and philosophical reasons it was not a position which could be adopted by the Cambridge Platonists and Norris. Institutionally, as beneficiaries of the idea of the Church as a divinely ordained body,[165] officially linked with the state and coterminous with it, they were generally content with the arrangements governing the Church of England. As Alexander Mackennal put it,

> The Puritan [and in this respect the Cambridge Platonists were Puritans] looked on the church as a national institution; all Englishmen who heard the word of God and accepted the sacraments were members of the English church. The Separatists affirmed that not hearing only, but believing and obeying the word, made a man a Christian; any society of spiritual men, but only such a society, was a church of Christ.[166]

Temperamentally, the Cambridge divines and Norris did not see themselves as ecclesiastical statesmen, still less, reformers. Equally temperamentally, they set their faces against sectarianism. 'I am above all sects whatsoever as sects', declared Henry More, 'for I am a true and free Christian...'.[167] This explains why their objection to religious toleration was not of the ordinary sort. That is to say, it did not spring from a desire to enforce conformity upon those whose consciences rebelled against the prevailing ecclesiastical norm. On the contrary, it arose from the conviction that differences over the interpretation of doctrines did not justify separation. In his sermon on 'The unity of the Church maintained

October 1980, pp. 166-75. For Robinson, see Stephen Brachlow, 'John Robinson and the lure of Separatism', *Church History*, L, 1981, pp. 288-301.

[164] F. J. Powicke, 'Historic Congregationalism in Britain', *Proceedings of the Third International Congregational Council*, London: Congregational Union of England and Wales, 1908, p. 262.

[165] See, e.g., *JN*, p. 14. For Powicke's account of historic 'minority reports' on this matter from Montanism onwards, see *Henry Barrow*, pp. xiv-xvi.

[166] A. Mackennal, *The Story of the English Separatists*, London: Congregational Union of England and Wales, 1893, p. 20. Powicke dedicated his *Henry Barrow* to Mackennal. For Mackennal (1835-1904) see *ODNB*.

[167] Preface to *Reply to Eugenius Philalethes*, quoted by Tulloch, *Rational Theology*, p. 339.

by sincere Christians', Whichcote declared that 'They who agree in the main, but differ in other particulars, ought nevertheless to hold together as if they were in all things agreed; *to walk by the same rule, to mind the same things.*'[168] 'There should be but one division', he continued, 'the Church and the world'[169]—exactly the point urged by the Separatists, though how different their practical response to it. As Tulloch epitomized the Platonists' view: 'The Church subsists in communion of spirit, not in coincidence of doctrine.'[170]

Doctrinally, since the Cambridge Platonists repudiated the received Calvinistic view of predestination, they were not so inclined as were the Separatists to distinguish between the once- and the twice-born, or to make the distinction between those who are, in Paul's phrase, 'in Christ', and those who are not, integral to their ecclesiology. In Powicke's opinion, 'There is indeed a spring of mighty moral energy—to which the Cambridge men did scant justice—in realising that God is *the* Initiating Agent from first to last in the process of salvation.'[171] *A fortiori* the Cambridge divines did not envisage locally covenanted gatherings of the saints as became the norm in Congregationalism.[172] In this connection, the remark of C. C. J. Webb is of interest:

> although in the Greek philosophical schools, especially in the Platonic and the Stoic, a very high ethical teaching was to be found, yet there remained even in these a certain discrepancy between theology and ethics owing to the fact that their doctrine of God was reached primarily by means of contemplation of and reflexion upon the order of the world, and not by way of an experience of a covenant-relation with him, as in the theology of Israel.[173]

Thus, whereas Powicke rightly applauds the Cambridge Platonists for understanding reason as being more than logic, and quotes Whichcote as saying that 'Nothing is the *true improvement* of our Rational Faculties, but the Exercise of the several *Virtues* of Sobriety, Modesty, Gentleness, Humility, Obedience to God, and Charity to men',[174] it must be said that there is a strain of individualism running through their writings which, coupled with their contentment with an hierarchical church structure,[175]

---

[168] Whichcote, *Works*, II, p. 22.

[169] Ibid., p. 26. Cf. *CP*, p. 64.

[170] Tulloch, *Rational Theology*, p. 458.

[171] *CP*, p. 37.

[172] Though there was a marked reduction in the number of local covenants entered into by the 1840s. See further, Sell, *Dissenting Thought and the Life of the Churches*, ch. 1.

[173] C. C. J. Webb, *A Century of Anglican Theology and Other Lectures*, Oxford: Blackwell, 1923, p. 80.

[174] *CP*, p. 47, quoting Whichcote, *Aphorisms*, no. 541.

[175] Of Norris, Powicke writes, 'he never ceased to manifest an undue deference to rank and authority. But it should be remembered, by way of excuse [there writes a Dissenter],

precludes the concept of the church gathered in covenant community, *corporately* seeking the mind of Christ, *corporately* building one another up in faith and practice, and *corporately* exercising church discipline.[176] In this last connection, for example, Barrow contended that 'The whole Church also, even every peculiar congregation, hath power in itself to censure not only any doctrine delivered, but the person of any member or minister of the same congregation.'[177] It must, however, be said that the Cambridge Platonists and Norris were much less vitriolic in their opposition to the Separatists than was Richard Baxter, on whose tract, *The Cure of Church-Divisions*, Powicke comments thus:

> It was not pleasant for Separatists...to hear themselves spoken of as 'weak Christians'; and exhorted to prove themselves 'strong' by practising communion with the parish churches... [Baxter's] self-complacent attendance on the Church-services; his laudation of the liturgy; his extolling of Ministers as *juro divino* rulers of the Church, and of the sovereign civil power at its *jure divino* head; his decrying of the people's rule in the Church, under Christ, as sheer democracy; and his denunciation of Christ-governed congregations, outside the limits of a state-church, as organized expressions of self-will, pride, etc.—all this (they said) simply showed that he had much to learn in the way of truth as well as love.[178]

---

that in his view rank and authority were Divine Facts, institutions ordained of God.' See *JN*, p. 14. It is noteworthy that when John Wesley, who strongly maintained that believers were obliged to use the means of grace, abridged John Smith's writings he omitted a sentence which opened the door to individualism. Smith wrote, 'As sincere and reall Christians grow up towards true perfection, the lesse need have they of Positive precepts or Externall helps.' See J. Smith, *Select Discourses*, p. 160; cf. J. Wesley, *A Christian Library*, Bristol: Felix Farley, 1749-1755, vol. XIX, p. 279. See further, John C. English, 'The Cambridge Platonists in Wesley's *Christian Library*', *Proceedings of the Wesley Historical Society*, XXXVI, October 1968, 161-8.

[176] In his discussion of Douglas Hedley's *Coleridge, Philosophy and Religion: AIDS TO REFLECTION and the Mirror of the Spirit*, Cambridge: Cambridge University Press, 2000, Leslie Armour adverts to an Anglican attitude, namely, that of Jeremy Taylor, which appears to be distinct from that of the Cambridge Platonists: 'He was the ultimate "broad church" divine, and the basis of his theology was that one could trust human beings to weigh their own evidences. As much as Coleridge, he wanted people to reflect on their own inner experiences, but he clearly wanted this to take place in a community of shared experiences [so far the Separatists], and it was because of his belief that everyone has a place in the continuum of human experience that he believed that the church must be broad enough for all [at which point the Separatists beg to differ].' See the review in *British Journal for the History of Philosophy*, X no. 3, 2002, p. 473.

[177] Powicke, *Henry Barrow*, pp. 103-4; cf. *The Writings of Henry Barrow 1590-1591*, pp. 138-40.

[178] Powicke, *Reverend Richard Baxter under the Cross*, pp. 200-01. We may note in passing that the Quakers' repudiation of an official and paid ministry was a factor in prompting Baxter's obsessive conviction that Quaker antics were fomented by the Pope

Philosophically, a tension arises in the thought of the Cambridge Platonists which does not seem to be present, at least to the same degree, in the Separatists, or in their contemporary Dissenters and Quakers. On the one hand they turn their faces against pantheism; on the other hand, given their emphasis upon human-divine communion as natural, it is difficult for them always to avoid the charge that they have so blurred the Creator-creature distinction as to have blunted the edge of the Gospel.

Certainly it was not difficult to find seventeenth-century theologians who took a radically different position to that of the Cambridge divines. The Fall, they contended, had provoked God's withdrawal from human beings; apart from sovereign electing grace they were utterly lost. Scripture alone, the Word of God written under the inspiration of the Holy Spirit, was the only revelation to yield light. Hence, as Powicke reminds us, the 'strenuous endeavours of orthodoxy to prove that, if men like Plato and Aristotle did not get the truth in their writings from Adam, then it must have come to them somehow from the Hebrew Scriptures'.[179] In illustration of the point Powicke cites the Independent, Theophilus Gale (1628-1678), who

> was really attracted by Plato: his Puritan soul was often thrilled with admiration and delight by the noble heathen's truth and love of truth. He would fain have owned some direct operation of God in Plato, some inspiration of the Spirit. But his theology stepped in. Plato was not a Jew; therefore, outside the sphere of God's personal action: so there was nothing for it but to show that he must have 'borrowed' from that sphere by roundabout ways: which Gale tried to do in two bulky volumes whereon he spent the best years of his life.[180]

We may note in passing that just as echoes of Platonism are found in present-day theological writing, so too are echoes of Gale, as when Donald Bloesch declares that Platonism and neo-Platonism 'from my

---

so that 'sober Protestants', tiring of the excesses of individualism, would find their way back to the catholicity of Rome. See Powicke, *A Life of the Reverend Richard Baxter*, pp. 252-4. It should be remembered that the Quakers' refusal to take oaths meant that they did not formally abjure papal authority. This caused some to suspect them—whether genuinely or as a matter of policy—of being covert Romanists. Even so level-headed a person as John Locke did not modify his earlier anti-toleration views to the extent of advocation of toleration for Roman Catholics, largely because the latter were understood to give allegiance to a foreign power. See further, Sell, *John Locke and the Eighteenth-Century Divines*, ch. 5, and pp. 327-9, nn. 20-21.

[179] *CP*, p. 28.

[180] *CP*, pp. 28-9. The bulky volumes are Gale's *The Court of the Gentiles*. For Gale see *ODNB*.

point of view stand in diametrical opposition to the insights and affirmations of biblical faith'.[181]

But our main purpose is to enquire how far the Cambridge Platonists and Norris blurred the Creator-creature distinction in a pantheistic way. This is what they were frequently charged with; this is what they repudiated (though Powicke concluded that Sterry's idea of personality was 'the quintessence of vagueness; and quite powerless to hold him back from that gulf of Pantheism into which he certainly had no wish to fall'[182]); but in so far as there is any justice in the charge, this is a further point of distinction between themselves and the Separatists.

The tendency towards pantheism can find expression in a number of ways. Epistemologically, it may be seen in Cudworth's insistence (as construed by Powicke) that 'Mind in God and mind in man are the same.'[183] Cudworth propounds the idea of plastic nature, which is the divine reason 'immersed and plunged into matter and, as it were, fuddled in it and confounded with it'.[184] At this posited fuddling and confounding, some saw warning lights. In attempting to meet such a challenge, Norris explains that 'the Ideas whereby we understand are Divine Ideas'.[185] Ontologically, and as a debt he owes to Malebranche, Norris can say that 'Being itself is the cause of all particular beings, for all particular beings are what they are by partaking of Being itself...'[186] He can even think of God as 'Being in general.'[187] On this Powicke remarks, that 'the Malebranchean hypothesis—unreservedly accepted by Norris—looks toward Pantheism, and marks a point more than half way on the road from Descartes to Spinoza'.[188] Yet Norris could also describe a theory not dissimilar to Spinoza's as 'that stupid conceit of taking the world for God';[189] and he was alive to the difficulty of accounting for the imperfections of the phenomenal order if all things exist in God. The upshot is that Norris's account of the way in which God and the world are related leaves something to be desired. Indeed, he candidly admits that he

---

[181] D. G. Bloesch, *God the Almighty: Power, Wisdom, Holiness, Love*, Carlisle: Paternoster Press, 1995, p. 16.

[182] *CP*, p. 180.

[183] *CP*, p. 117.

[184] R. Cudworth, *The True Intellectual System*, I, p, 337.

[185] J. Norris, *Ideal World*, II, p. 426.

[186] *JN*, p. 84, paraphrasing J. Norris, *Reason and Religion*, pp. 26-7.

[187] *JN*, p. 182, referring to Norris, *Reason and Religion*, p. 43.

[188] *JN*, p. 86.

[189] Norris, *An Essay towards the Theory of the Ideal or Intelligible World*, I, p. 176. Cf. Acworth, *The Philosophy of John Norris of Bemerton*, p. 286: Norris 'never shared the tendency of the Cambridge school to deify nature'.

cannot explain 'how an Idea purely Spiritual can represent *body*'.[190] Ethically, as we have seen, the Cambridge Platonists and Norris acknowledged the disruptive effect of sin upon the divine-human relationships, but they did not make the disjunction as absolute as did those Puritans to whom humanity was utterly depraved. To put the point in my own way: we might say that they understood, rightly, that the divine image was defaced but not utterly obliterated.[191] It would thus seem that their account of ethics—above all, perhaps, Cudworth's stout defence of human moral freedom—was more favourable to the maintenance of the Creator-creature distinction than was their epistemology.

VII

This study F. J. Powicke's writings on the Cambridge Platonists and the radical Puritan Separatists, and of his passing comments upon the Quakers and Richard Baxter, is almost finished. What are the main findings?

First, that although superficially distinct in their thought forms, and sometimes poles apart from one another in their self-estimations, our subjects all upheld the importance of spiritual experience, they all had things to say about the 'light', and none of them is entirely free of Platonist influence: to all of them the world of reality is more than the phenomenal world. On the basis of these shared interests they rang a diversity of changes.

Secondly, there is something attractive in all of those studied. It is difficult not to admire the equable spirit of the Cambridge Platonists in those dangerous and religiously divided times. It is hard not to agree that some of their spirituality is as lofty as it is orthodox. Thus, for example, John Smith writes that the enlightened mind cannot but

---

[190] Norris, *An Essay towards the Theory of the Ideal or Intelligible World*, I, p. 296. See further, MacKinnon, *The Philosophy of John Norris of Bemerton*, pp. 90ff. In *Quaker Thought and History*, p. 41, Edward Grubb perhaps goes too far in saying that Norris 'got well over the border that divides essential Christianity from Pantheism'. It seems more accurate to say that he floundered on the border. J. H. Muirhead would seem to agree: 'By insisting on the distinction between the ideal and natural order [Norris] escaped from the impiety of making the created and contingent a part of the Creator. But to assign them a being independent of Him and beyond His control was equally repugnant to one who was committed to the entire dependence of the creature upon the Creator so that "God may be all and in all". In the doctrine of degrees of being and of the union in all reality of the potential and the actual, he had himself provided a clue to the solution of this difficulty. It is all the more regrettable that he failed to follow it out in a reinterpretation of the nature of All-Being as at once immanent and transcendent, at once appearing in and always breaking through the limits of the finite.' See *The Platonic Tradition*, p. 107.

[191] See further, Sell, *Confessing and Commending the Faith*, pp. 66-8, 320-21.

> behold itself everywhere in the midst of that glorious unbounded Being who is indivisibly everywhere. A good man finds every place he treads upon holy ground; to him the world is God's temple; he is ready to say with Jacob, 'How dreadful is this place! This is none other but the house of God.[192]

At the same time, we may feel the need to balance this emphasis with that of the Quakers, to whom the historic Christ was, through the Spirit, so powerful a presence.[193] As for the Separatists, the determination of their leaders to stand for their grasp of God's Word even to the death is as inspiring as it is admirable. Their objective of a Church comprising saints covenanted and gathered under the sole Lordship of Christ is a standing challenge to those who would have the Church bow to other lords, take too much colouring from the society in which it is set, and entrust its ordering to selected persons. On these points Powicke was particularly clear:

> the Church of Christ cannot be restricted to a priestly caste; nor extended to a mixed unsifted multitude of the baptized, or orthodox, or superficially devout. Facts are sometimes narrow; but to state a fact is not narrowness... [A] Christian Church *must* consist of Christians...[194]

As for Baxter, his concern for good church order and for as wide a Christian fellowship as possible is laudable, even if at times it prompted undue harshness against those who saw things differently (though the constantly reiterated complaint of the Quakers that all paid ministers were 'hierling priests' was, no doubt, tiresome; and there is much more in Baxter that is wholly admirable than has been brought into view here).

While fully welcoming and valuing these positive features, the subjects of this enquiry also prompt concern at certain points. Thus, as we have seen, the Cambridge Platonists and Norris do at times veer in the direction of pantheism, with the resulting threat to that Creator-creature distinction apart from which the terms of the Gospel become meaningless. This is a danger which percolates down the centuries, taking various forms in post-Hegelian idealism,[195] process thought, and the like. More fundamentally still, the Cambridge Platonists and Norris, writing when it was still possible to make the assumptions of Christendom and before the challenges of deism, Hume, Kant and others, were able to posit the natural divine-

---

[192] J. Smith *The Excellency and Nobleness of True Religion*, in *Select Discourses*, pp. 467-8.

[193] For an example of such a Quaker see ch. 2 below.

[194] F. J. Powicke, *The Inevitableness of the Congregational Principle*, London: Congregational Union of England and Wales, [1910], pp. 9, 22.

[195] See further, Alan P. F. Sell, *Philosophical Idealism and Christian Belief*, Cardiff: University of Wales Press and New York: St. Martin's Press, 1995; and ch. 7 below.

human mental relationship and the reality of the spiritual world as axiomatic in a way which can no longer be done.[196] As Tulloch remarked,

> Advocates of Reason, they yet never asked themselves plainly what is reason, and how rational and irrational ideas are to be distinguished, not merely in the sphere of religion, but of speculation. Their Rationalism was adequate to sift the notional dogmatism of the popular religion, and the vagaries of Quakerism and other enthusiasms; but it failed to reach the sources of their own thought, or to clear their own speculative vision.[197]

The ambivalence we have detected in their writings constitutes evidence of this. At the same time, I cannot forbear to remark, How easy such hindsight judgements are. The fact remains that even as they wrote, the deists were dipping their quills in the ink with anti-supernaturalistic intent.[198]

Where the Quakers are concerned, Barclay's concept of a light above reason, which acts for specific purposes, stands at a considerable remove from the Platonist and Norrisian understanding of the light, and seems to drive a wedge between natural reason and the supernatural illumination of the human mind which is difficult to justify psychologically, even if the latter be admitted as a possibility. While I cannot pursue the point here, an examination of the course of Quaker thought would reveal that once the biblically-grounded thought and language of Fox, Barclay and others met the challenge of rationalism, some were tempted to appeal, individualistically, and against the original Quaker understanding of the 'children of the light' as a covenant people,[199] to the light within *apart from* the Word, with results which seem at a far remove from traditional Christianity. This was precisely the danger perceived by many Puritans, to whom the holding together of Spirit and Word was of fundamental importance. Said Richard Sibbes, 'The breath of the Spirit in us is suitable to the Spirit's breathing in the Scriptures; the same Spirit doth no breathe contrary motions.'[200] All of this throws into relief the question how far developments of doctrine may be said to be legitimate or illegitimate.[201]

---

[196] See Clark, *Liberal Orthodoxy*, pp. 61-4.

[197] Tulloch, *Rational Theology*, p. 483.

[198] See further, ch. 3 below.

[199] Cf. Punshon, *Reasons for Hope*, p. 111.

[200] *The Complete Works of Richard Sibbes, D.D.*, ed. A. B. Groshart, (1862-4), Edinburgh: Banner of Truth Trust, 1977, V, p. 427. For a valuable survey of the Puritan mind in relation to the Holy Spirit and human reason, see Geoffrey F. Nuttall, *The Holy Spirit in Puritan Faith and Experience*, (1946), Chicago: University of Chicago Press, 1991.

[201] For which question see further, ch. 6 below.

I come finally to those of the Separatist/Congregational tradition, for these are Powicke's people, and on them I make three points. First, there is little doubt that at their best these Dissenters understood that the Church, God's calling, is catholic, and that to be a member of the Church catholic is to be a member of the church local: it is to be an enrolled and locally anchored saint; to be engrafted into the Vine is to be visibly related to all the branches. One cannot be a Christian 'in general':

> We have here a conception of Catholic unity far more sublime than any based on uniformity. It expresses, indeed, the only real unity; and just to say that it is not inconsistent with the Congregational idea would be saying too little. Rather it lies at the very heart of the Congregational idea.[202]

This point was not lost on the Anglican scholar, A. E. J. Rawlinson:

> It is in a sense no small paradox that the point of view which in one way most nearly approaches that of Catholicism, though in another it differs from it most widely, is that of Congregational Independency. Both are at one in conceiving the Church as primarily a mystical and religious entity, eternal in the heavens, a spiritual communion of the elect people of God, which is of a higher order than space or time; and both agree in conceiving the assemblage of Christian people for worship as a manifestation visibly on earth of this invisible or ideal Church—*ubi tres ibi ecclesia.*[203]

But sometimes through historical circumstance—the Separatists and the Dissenters of the period 1660-1689 were, strictly, outside the law—and sometimes through human perversity, what has aptly been called 'granular Independency' has manifested itself. Powicke, for example, notes that in the first half of the eighteenth century

> many an orthodox Church died of its own orthodoxy—an orthodoxy so dry and sapless that it starved the highest impulses of the soul and only fed its self-righteousness, its malice, and its pride... Each Church stood in isolation—withering often on its own feet. No vivid sense of contact with a living Head, no glow of fellowship with the Church Catholic or even with neighbouring Churches, no missionary ardour.[204]

It is to be noted that Powicke does not make a universal claim here: there were more hopeful stirrings; and his contemporary, A. J. Grieve, declared that

---

[202] Powicke, 'Historic Congregationalism in Britain', p. 263.

[203] A. E. J. Rawlinson, 'The principle of authority', in B. H. Streeter, ed., *Foundations. A Statement of Christian Belief in terms of Modern Thought by Seven Oxford Men*, London: Macmillan, (1912), 1922, pp. 393-4.

[204] Powicke, 'English Congregationalism in its greatness and decline' p. 309.

> It is a libel to say that the local churches had no dealings with one another. It is one of the divine paradoxes that separatism and catholicity meet in the Congregational way. We stand for the fullest possible association of the freest possible units.[205]

But there was no smoke without fire; and with the individualism we detected in the Cambridge Platonists and Norris in mind, we can only admit that not all those of the Congregational way have risen to the comprehensiveness of Alexander Mackennal's catholic vision:

> Nothing seems clearer to me—I say this, remembering the exaggerated individualism into which the churches have been betrayed by the necessity of maintaining the demand for personal repentance, personal faith and personal obedience in order to personal salvation—nothing in the Apostolic writings is clearer than that the '*full grown man*,' of whom St. Paul speaks, is completed humanity. '*The measure of the stature of the fulness of Christ*,' to which, in '*the unity of the faith and of the knowledge of the Son of God*' we are to attain, is the measure of the body of Christ, not of the individual believer. The crowning blessedness of the Christian life is, that the blessings conferred on every trusting soul are added top and swallowed up in the endless benediction of redeemed humanity.[206]

Secondly, the witness of the Separatist/Congregational tradition to the need of the Church to govern its life under its sole Lord, Jesus Christ, whose will is made known by the Spirit through the Word discerned in the fellowship, is of great and ecumenical importance, and it led to an ecclesiology significantly different from that of the Cambridge Platonists. But in this connection, too, there is a shadow side to the story. In *Savoy* we read,

> we acknowledge the inward illumination of the Spirit of God to be necessary for the saving understanding of such things as are revealed in the Word; and that there are some circumstances concerning the Worship of God and the Government of the Church, common to humane actions and Societies, which are to be ordered by the Light of Nature and Christian prudence, according to the general Rules of the Word, which are always to be observed.[207]

We can almost hear the Cambridge Platonists and Norris saying 'Amen' to the last clause here. Indeed, A. G. Matthews remarked with some

---

[205] A. J. Grieve, 'The Congregational tradition', an address given at Carrs Lane Congregational Church. Birmingham, 1 June 1948, quoted by Charles E. Surman [his son-in-law], *Alexander James Grieve 1874-1952*, Manchester: Lancashire Independent College, 1953, p. 47.

[206] A. Mackennal, 'The witness of Congregationalism', in D. Macfadyen ed., *Constructive Congregational Ideals*, London: H. R. Allenson, [1902], pp. 148-9.

[207] A. G. Matthews, ed., *The Savoy Declaration of Faith and Order 1658*, London: Independent Press, 1959, p. 77 (= I.vi).

justification that 'in the mid-years of the 17th century [Congregationalism] attained a fullness of spiritual and intellectual stature that has never belonged to it at any other time, before or since'.[208] But as time passed, and as the fluid denominational tendencies of the seventeenth and eighteenth centuries began, in part under the impetus of sundry doctrinal disputes, in part under the necessity of organizing for mission at home and abroad, to harden into the denominational organizations with which we are familiar, the mystical aspect of the polity was all but shelved in favour of an ultra-Protestant recourse to the letter of Scripture, as first one and then another of the denominations sought to show that its polity alone represented that of the true Church, and that those bodies which did not share it were to that extent defective.[209] In this cause, more or less staunch Calvinists, and others in the evangelical line, approached Scripture in the same 'proto-fundamentalist' way as their 'Arian' opponents, to whom reference has already been made. With none of this was Powicke in sympathy: 'the notion that any office, or type of government, was necessary to the *being* of a Church is a heresy not found in the New Testament'.[210] Nor was Powicke slow to specify John Owen, Congregationalism's greatest seventeenth-century theologian, as being the primary culprit in this matter: 'that everything connected with worship or church government as well as doctrine must be sanctioned by Scripture, was for Owen an absolutely binding rule', and with him Puritan reverence for Scripture 'was carried to the point of bibliolatry'.[211] This is ironic in view of the statement just quoted from the *Savoy Declaration*, in the preparation of which Owen was the leading light.

Thirdly, the Separatist/Congregational tradition has, no less than other Christian traditions, been influenced in many ways by the cultural context in which it has lived. For example, by the end of the nineteenth century many of the old doctrinal certainties had been undermined,[212] some

---

[208] A. G. Matthews, 'The Seventeenth Century', in *Congregationalism Through the Centuries*, London: Independent Press, 1937, p. 51.

[209] A delightful example, this, of the pot calling the kettle black; for these same people would rebuke those who took the identical stance on behalf of Rome or Canterbury. See further on restorationism, ch. 6 below.

[210] Powicke, *The Inevitableness of the Congregational Principle*, p. 8.

[211] Powicke, 'English Congregationalism in its greatness and decline', p. 299. He cites in evidence Owen's pamphlet, *Of the Divine Original, Authority, Self-Evidencing Light, and Power of the Scriptures: with an Answer to that Inquiry, How do we know the Scriptures to be the Word of God*, in *The Works of John Owen*, ed. William H. Goold, (1850-53), London: Banner of Truth Trust, 1968, XVI, pp. 295-343. He further notes that this was a cause of friction between Owen and Baxter. For the development of the Congregational Way between 1640 and 1660 the authoritative account remains Geoffrey F. Nuttall's *Visible Saints*, (1957), Oswestry: Quinta Press, 2001.

[212] See further ch. 5 below.

churches were becoming alive to the needs of society as never before, and were organizing programmes to meet the needs of those around them. But some, Powicke among them, feared that certain fundamentals were at risk:

> to me there seems no real hope for our churches unless they can be persuaded to realize what they stand for—and to stand for it. We may live on, and even multiply, as respectable social clubs, or preaching stations, or centres of activity more or less philanthropic. We may succeed in reviving and intensifying a vigorous denominational sentiment. We may applaud our ancestors, and build their tombs, and repeat their watchwords. But if we do not regain the essence of their faith, and grasp it as the mainspring of our life, and apply it with undoubting sincerity in the practice of our churches both individually and collectively—when we come together in church meeting or in congregational assembly—we have lost our *raison d'être*.[213]

Yet in his own practice, Powicke shows how insidious 'alien' influences can be, for elsewhere he writes,

> It is...to the good that Baptism is not now confined to the children of believing parents—one or both. For that is a change due to escape from the Calvinistic conception of a limited covenant—a covenant for the elect only—to the conception of a grace, which is in covenant, or saving relation, to all mankind.[214]

It is difficult not to think that Powicke here jettisons a primary plank in the platform of his forebears who, in understanding paedobaptism as properly observed within the covenanted fellowship, had both logic and theology on their side. Apart from the doctrine of covenant the case for the baptism of infants surely falls, and we are left with a service of dedication, a rite of passage or a naming ceremony.

VII

Among the many questions posed by this enquiry are three which, I believe, have continuing ecumenical importance: Where is the locus of authority for the Church: is it in the Bible, the light, the ecclesiastical institution, or in one of the possible permutations of these? How are we to understand the relationship between the Holy Spirit, the light of reason, the Bible, the ecclesial fellowship and the societal context? Even more fundamentally: How may we most appropriately think of the divine-human relationship as it bears upon epistemology, ethics and theology?

---

213 Quoted by A. Peel, *Inevitable Congregationalism*, London: Independent Press, 1937, p. 57.

214 F. J. Powicke, 'The Congregational Churches', in Selbie, ed., *Evangelical Christianity, its History and Witness*, p. 105.

Over the past thirty years numerous inter-confessional dialogues, whether local, regional, national or international have taken place.[215] Not surprisingly, many of these have concentrated upon such historically neuralgic matters as Church, ministry and sacraments. But positions adopted by dialogue partners on these issues turn upon answers given to the questions I have just posed, yet those questions seldom surface in the context of dialogue. It may be that deeper analysis of these questions would so place the overtly neuralgic points in perspective that we should see more clearly how to remove the road blocks which preclude the Church from manifesting the unity it has already been given in Christ. Of course, seeing how to do it is one thing, doing it is another. The doing will only occur as Christians on all sides prayerfully and gratefully reappropriate the Gospel of redemption which is the only ground of their unity.[216]

F. J. Powicke had ecclesiology in mind when he invoked Plato; and with what he says this study may fittingly conclude:

> Plato can teach us that ideas have hard work to gain anything like a perfect embodiment in time; and that it is the *highest* ideas which take longest to subdue to themselves the intractable [raw material] of nature and human nature. But still the ideas are the *real* things, and they are *eternal*.[217]

---

[215] For an account of the dialogue activity of one tradition, the Reformed, see below ch. 10 below.

[216] For further thoughts in this vein, see ch. 11 below.

[217] Powicke, *The Inevitableness of the Congregational Principle*, p. 16. The words within the brackets are my translation of the Greek term used by Powicke.

CHAPTER 2

John Gratton, A Quaker Star

Lest it be thought that the title of this chapter represents an attempt to 'hype up' 'that ancient servant of Christ', John Gratton, after the manner of the twenty-first century media, let it clearly be understood that the allusion is to the title page of Gratton's *Journal*, which carries the following quotation from Daniel 12:3-4:

> Many shall run to and fro, and Knowledge shall be increased; and they that be wise shall shine as the Brightness of the Firmament; and they that turn many to Righteousness, as the Stars forever and ever.[1]

It would have been almost equally appropriate to have chosen the title, 'To and fro with John Gratton', for he was tireless in travels the objective of which was to proclaim the Gospel and have many turned to righteousness by the convincing Spirit of God. Indeed, the title conferred upon him by Spencer T. Hall, 'the Quaker apostle of the Peak', restricts rather than adequately specifies his geographical range, which encompassed many parts of England and Wales, with excursions to Scotland and Ireland too. But to have focused on the 'tos and fros' would have obscured the prior, and very important, spiritual 'ups and downs' through which Gratton passed before he found peace with Christ, which occupy one third of his *Journal*.

John Gratton is by no means the best known Quaker of his period, but he is a particularly engaging one. Of his *Journal*, W. C. Braithwaite remarked, 'There are few books with more of the pith of Quakerism in them than the *Journal* of John Gratton.'[2] Highly respected by most, loved by many, Gratton is especially interesting because of his carefully nuanced thought. His story has been told in a number of places, but most accounts do little, if anything, more than summarize his *Journal*.[3] I here

[1] The *Journal* was first published in 1720. I used the edition of 1805: Stanford, NY: Daniel Lawrence.

[2] W. C. Braithwaite, *The Second Period of Quakerism*, (1919), 2nd edn., Cambridge: Cambridge University Press, 1961, p. 370.

[3] See, for example, William Evans and Thomas Evans, eds., *Piety Promoted, in a Collection of Dying Sayings of many of the People called Quakers, with A Brief Account of some of their Labours in the Gospel, and Sufferings for the Same*, Philadelphia:

attempt to place Gratton more firmly in his ecclesiastical and intellectual context, referring to his *Journal*, but also drawing upon his other writings. By so doing I hope to bring to the fore both Quaker distinctives and the principles and presuppositions they shared with other Christians. Prompted by Gratton's life and witness, I shall conclude with a few reflections on the current religious situation.

I

Some biographical remarks will introduce John Gratton and, more importantly, will acquaint us with his spiritual struggle, which entailed his progressing through a number of Christian traditions before he landed happily among the Friends.

Neither the date nor the place of Gratton's birth is certain, and about both his *Journal* is silent. The biographers give us the choice of 1641 or 1642 for his birth, while his place of birth is variously said to be Tideswell and Bonsall, both villages in Derbyshire. He refers to Tideswell as 'the place where I spent all my time', and this village appears in a list of places where, following his preaching, a number of his family members came into the light. But the original *Dictionary of National Biography*, playing for safety, has him 'probably born not far from Chesterfield'—a description which applies to both villages and suffices us.

Since Gratton minded his father's sheep and used Latin against some of his clerical opponents, the inference is drawn that his father was a farmer who could afford to send his son to the grammar school. Gratton could also cite Augustine and earlier Church fathers, though this should not be taken as necessarily implying that he was well versed in their writings. Even Robert Barclay, early Quakerism's theologian *par excellence*, was accused by his erstwhile companion, George Keith, of obtaining his patristic quotations at second hand.[4]

Like many others—George Fox and John Bunyan spring at once to mind—Gratton knew spiritual strife from an early age. When he was ten or eleven years old,

---

Friends' Book Store, 1854, II, pp. 143-5; Spencer T. Hall, 'John Gratton, the Quaker preacher', *The Reliquary*, July 1860, pp. 21-29; Frances Ann Budge, *Annals of the Early Friends. A Series of Biographical Sketches*, London: Samuel Harris, 1886, reprinted from *The Friends' Quarterly Examiner*, V, 1871, pp. 351-61; Emily Manners, *John Gratton. A Derbyshire 'Quaker' Preacher and Prophet of the XVIIth Century*, Heanor, Derbyshire: W. Baker, 1922, reprinted from *The Friend*, 16 September 1921, pp. 603-4 and 23 September 1921, pp. 618-19.

[4] See Alan P. F. Sell, *Commemorations. Studies in Christian Thought and History*, (1993), Eugene, OR: Wipf & Stock, 1998, pp. 147-8.

> the Lord visited me with the light of his Son, and gave me to see my vain life and way I lived in; being much given to play amongst vain boys, and took great delight in playing at cards, shooting at butts, and ringing of bells, for which I was reproved; and I came to see that vain sports and pleasures were displeasing to the Lord...[5]

But he did not yet know the Lord experimentally, and so 'followed hireling priests, Presbyterians, &c. Yet was uneasy among them all'.[6] In 1656 we find him praying that God 'would shew me who were his people that worshipped him aright, according to his will'.[7] Gratton's concerns were twofold. First, 'I was not satisfied with their doctrine of election and reprobation, which put me in deep trouble, and I was sometimes very near concluding, that I was a reprobate...yet I believed, that men who were in Christ were elected, but men out of Christ are out of the way to God...'[8] Secondly, the response he received from the Presbyterians to whom he laid bare his soul did not satisfy him. They told him that 'the best of God's children had all along their failings', and that he should 'sit down contented, before I was washed and cleansed from my sins'.[9] In this condition he felt it would have been hypocritical to join in singing the Psalms.

Since Gratton supplies no names in the *Journal* entries so far quoted, it is interesting to speculate upon whom these Presbyterians and the '&c' might have been. It is conceivable that Gratton had some contact with the Dissenters in Chesterfield, where the vicar was John Billingsley, and the curate was James Ford. The former favoured the Presbyterian polity, the latter the Congregationalist. This prompts the reminder that not until the nineteenth century are we concerned with denominations in the modern institutional sense. In the seventeenth and eighteenth centuries ministers would frequently move between the various ecclesistical traditions, and in Chesterfield the pattern developed for some years of concurrent Presbyterian and Congregational ministers. Billingsley had become vicar in 1653; dates for Ford are not known, but he is said to have died of consumption before the age of thirty.[10] In January 1654/5 Billingsley and

---

[5] J. Gratton, *A Journal of the Life of that Ancient Servant of Christ, John Gratton, giving an Account of his Exercises when Young, and how he came to the Knowledge of the Truth, and was thereby raised up to Preach the Gospel; As also of his Labours, Trials and Sufferings for the same*, (herinafter *Jnl*), p. 31.

[6] *Jnl*, p. 32.

[7] Ibid., pp. 34-5.

[8] Ibid., p. 35. Cf. the doctrinal position of Robert Barclay and the Cambridge Platonists (except Culverwel), in ch. 1 above.

[9] Ibid., p. 36.

[10] For Billingsley (1625-1683) see *ODNB*; A. G. Matthews, *Calamy Revised*, (1934), Oxford: Clarendon Press, 1988, pp. 53-4; Douglas W. Robson, *Origins and History of Elder Yard Chapel, Chesterfield*, Chesterfield: n.p., 1924, p. 13. On being forced to leave

others disputed with the Quaker, James Naylor, at Chesterfield.[11] In this connection he published *The Grand Quaker prov'd a Gross Liar* (1656), a pamphlet which drew a response from George Fox: *The Great Mystery of the Great Whore Unfolded...* (1659).

A younger Presbyterian whom Gratton almost certainly knew by reputation in his early years and later in person was William Bagshaw, who was to become 'the Apostle of the Peak'. Bagshaw was ordained on 1 January 1650/1 by presbyters in Chesterfield. He had been born at Litton in the parish of Tideswell, and had been baptized in Tideswell Parish Church on 19 January 1627/8.[12] Yet another was John Oldfield, a Presbyterian, born near Chesterfield, who had settled as Rector of Carsington, about twelve miles from Tideswell, in 1649.[13] Gratton knew him, as we shall see.

Quite apart from his doctrinal and spiritual scruples, what finally broke Gratton's relations with the Presbyterians was the response of the latter to the Act of Uniformity of 1662. By this Act all ministers of religion and schoolmasters were required to give their 'unfeigned assent and consent' to the Book of Common Prayer, and to use it only in the conduct of public worship.[14] Nearly two thousand ministers, of whom the majority were of Presbyterian persuasion, including Billingsley, Bagshaw and Oldfield, refused to bend their consciences to an Act which assumed the monarch and Parliament's right to determine the worship of the Church.[15] 'Whereupon', writes Gratton,

> it came into my mind to search the Scriptures, to see whether those the Lord sent forth to preach the Gospel, in the demonstration of the Spirit, could be silent at man's command, though they were men in authority that forbid them... For I believed, that if God had sent them, and set them up, then man ought not to pull them down...[16]

Chesterfield by the provision of the Five Mile Act of 1665, Billingsley removed to Mansfield. However, he came secretly to preach in Chesterfield every fortnight. Night-time travel in order to escape detection ruined his health and he died, aged 59.

[11] See Immanuel Bourne, *A Defence of the Scriptures*, London, 1656.

[12] For Bagshaw (1627/8- 1702) see *ODNB*; Alexander Gordon, ed., *Freedom After Ejection. A Review (1690-1692) of Presbyterian and Congregational Nonconformity in England and Wales*, Manchester: Manchester University Press, 1917, p. 204; A. G. Matthews, *Calamy Revised*, p. 22; John M. Brentnall, *William Bagshawe, The Apostle of the Peak*, London: The Banner of Truth Trust, 1970.

[13] For Oldfield see Matthews, *Calamy Revised*, p. 373.

[14] For this and other relevant Acts see Henry Gee and William John Hardy, *Documents Illustrative of English Church History*, London: Macmillan, 1896.

[15] For the general situation see further Sell, *Commemorations*, ch. 5.

[16] *Jnl*, p. 39.

Gratton took the matter up with his local Dissenting 'priest', who answered that, like Paul at Rome, he continued to preach at his own hired house; 'but', says Gratton, 'that did not satisfy me, for Paul was a prisoner, and they were not. Had they staid till they had been pulled out, and put in prison, then they had done like men that trusted in God...'.[17]

We may surmise that Gratton would have been no better pleased than was John Bunyan, another radical Puritan searcher of the Scriptures, by those who trimmed their doctrinal positions in order to avoid ejection. Bunyan had expected that John Fowler, who had been a Presbyterian chaplain during the interregnum and later became Bishop of Gloucester, would suffer ejection in 1662. When Fowler remained in post, Bunyan branded him a 'weathercock spirit'. Later, when the imprisoned Bunyan received Fowler's book on holiness, he composed one of his more contentious tracts, in which he argued that Fowler's work 'more vilifieth Jesus Christ than many of the Quakers themselves'. This, in turn, prompted a tract, allegedly by Fowler's curate, entitled, *Dirt wiped off, or a manifest discovery of the gross ignorance, erroneous, and most unchristian spirit of one John Bunyan, Lay Reader in Bedford.*[18]

Gratton was no more pleased by what followed the ejection of the Presbyterians:

> But then the Presbyterians being not only removed out of their pulpit, but out of my heart also; then the Episcopal Priests came in their white surplices, and read common prayers, with long composed sermons, and other stuff, that we had nothing of in the Holy Scriptures... I met with nothing at all of any life or power of God in them.[19]

He was particularly disgusted by an 'old Presbyterian' who, having conformed, 'swallowed down that, which before he had vomited up'.[20] So Gratton left their 'dead forms'. He 'did not join with them, but separated myself, or rather was separated from them by the Lord: blessed be his name for ever...'.[21]

The Presbyterians feature in the story once more, fifteen years later. Under the Declaration of Indulgence of 1672 the Presbyterians obtained a barn at Ashford in the Water, some four miles from Monyash where Gratton was by then living. One day in 1677 Gratton was in the vicinity when he saw what was to him a disturbingly large crowd leaving a Presbyterian meeting. The word of the Lord came to him to attend the

---

[17] Ibid., p. 42.

[18] The unimproving tale is recounted by F. J. Powicke, *The Reverend Richard Baxter under the Cross (1662-1691)*, London: Jonathan Cape, 1927, pp. 56-7.

[19] *Jnl*, p. 44.

[20] Ibid., p. 45.

[21] Ibid., p. 46.

meeting, which he did. '[W]hen the priest had done (whose name was Oldfield, whom I knew) I then desired the privilege of the gospel...' He prophesied the swift demise of that assembly, which occurred a few weeks later; but for his pains he was violently set upon and ejected. '[T]he priest looked pale', he continues, 'though I charged him with false doctrine; when I was out, I declared against their priests and worship, but none answered me in defence of their way...' The discomfited Presbyterians 'fled and got into holes in those suffering times'.[22] Bagshaw's biographer points out that 'No appeal could be made to the authorities owing to the illegal nature of such meetings.'[23]

Returning to young Gratton's spiritual quest, we find that he continued working his way through the available ecclesiastical options. He heard good reports of some Dissenters who met in private houses,

> some of whom were called Independents, some Presbyterians, and some Anabaptists. So I found some of this mixed multitude believed that God had elected a certain number to be saved, and had reprobated all the rest; others of them held forth free grace; some held baptizing infants in water; some said, nay, none ought to be baptized in water till they believe; some baptized not at all...[24]

Sadly,

> the Lord to my comfort I met not among them; nor could I see the power of God upon them; but pride abounded, slandering one another, foolish jesting, vain talking, fashioning themselves according to the customs of the world; and conforming many of them so far as to go one while to their own meeting, and another while to the steeple-house; and all upon one day, though they had much to say against steeple-house worship.[25]

Gratton next journeyed to Chesterfield to seek out the Independents. But they were 'dead professors, and dry trees, not bringing forth fruit'. In particular they were blurring the biblical distinction between the 'the children of God, and the children of the wicked one'[26] by not insisting on the new birth. (To the extent that Gratton's judgement is accurate, the Independents were in breach of their covenant polity and of their ecclesiology prefigured by the Separatists which insisted that the Church comprises Christians.)[27] As a result,

---

[22] Ibid., pp. 152-3.

[23] Brentnall, *William Bagshawe*, p. 72.

[24] *Jnl*, pp. 47-8.

[25] Ibid., p. 48.

[26] Ibid., pp. 49-50.

[27] See ch. 1 above.

> I got no true peace with God among them, nor enjoyment of the Lord in my poor soul. Whereupon I left them, and all churches and people, and continued alone, like one who had no mate or companion.[28]

Shortly afterwards, in 1664, Gratton had his first encounter with some Quakers, but on that occasion he was more disturbed than comforted. On leaving them his way took him, in sorrowful mood, through a dark wood where he had a vision of 'the people called Quakers, a poor, despised, low sort of people'. He perceived that they endured more sufferings than any other group of believers, and as he went on 'I knew my countenance was altered'.[29] It was borne in upon him that he must forsake the world utterly. Following a meeting with the sectaries Reeve and Muggleton, to which I shall return, he was more confused than ever, to the point of rejoicing if he heard evil reports of the Quakers.

In 1668 Gratton removed to Monyash, where he was to remain until April 1707. Here he made contact with the Anabaptists, concluding that 'they came nearest to the Scriptures of any I had yet tried'.[30] In the Episcopal Returns of 1669, these Anabaptists are given as located at Bakewell, 'Att the house of Ralph Humbleton sometimes at great Longstone at the house of Robert Clarke sometimes at the house of John Gratton of Moniash.' About thirty in number, their 'Qualitie' is 'Of the meaner sort of common people', and their 'Heads and Teachers' are 'John Wilson, a Taylor, George Horton of Blackwell-Ditch, Shoomaker, John Jackson of Pattowhill, Husbandman, one Ainsworth out of Leicestershire, & one King, a Taylor.'[31]

During his sojourn among the Anabaptists, Gratton came near to offering himself for baptism, but on hearing the explanation that water baptism was a sign of dying to sin and rising again to new life, he refrained on the ground that since he was not free from sin, and hence not dead, he could not be buried, and therefore could not rise again: 'if I should go and be buried under water, as though I were dead, I should dissemble and lie, or deal falsely both with God and man'.[32] A leading Anabaptist sought to persuade Gratton that many more unfit that he had been baptized, but 'I said, that was nothing to me, I durst not.'[33] Presumably not sharing his scruples, his sister was baptized. As far as Gratton could see, the Anabaptists professed to be dead to sin, but actually lived in it, and did not manifest the power and Spirit of God. He

---

[28] *Jnl*, p. 51.

[29] Ibid., p. 56.

[30] Ibid., p. 65.

[31] See George Lyon Turner, *Original Records of Early Nonconformity under Persecution and Indulgence*, London: T. Fisher Unwin, 1911, I, p. 53.

[32] *Jnl*, p. 65.

[33] Ibid., p. 66.

remained with them for a while, however, and on one occasion asked to address the gathering. It was explained to him that it was not their normal practice to allow the unbaptized to speak, but since he appeared to be an honest man, they would make an exception:

> So I turned me to the meeting, and spake so that tears ran down; I admired my condition I was then in, for I was like a bottle uncorked, and the power of the spirit flowed in me, and when it stopped I ceased to speak.[34]

On the following Sunday he attended the meeting at Humphry Chapman's house, where news that the Second Conventicle Act of 1670 was to be enforced was received. This Act reaffirmed and reinforced its predecessor of 1664, which provided that if five or more persons over the age of sixteen, other than members of the same household, met for religious purposes, they were liable to be fined. Gratton was concerned that the leading Anabaptists, a preacher among them, did not wish to suffer by hosting meetings. In the midst of the ensuing discussion about what should be done, Gratton became convinced that these were not the people of God, for they did not stand in God's power, so he left them, 'and went no more to join with them in worship'.[35] He did, however, resolve to lead a holy life, though this resolution by itself brought him no peace.

In the meantime, on 24 June 1669, Gratton had married Ann.[36] She was a member of the Church of England, who tried, without avail, to persuade Gratton to join her at worship: 'we disputed oft, till we both wept, and my sorrow was great'.[37] Gratton's spiritual quest continued. At a widow's house at Over Haddon he declined to open the meeting with prayer when asked to do so by the Independent preacher from London, because the Lord alone, not men, can exhort people to pray; but after the preacher had done, Gratton, as it were, out-prayed him, and all were amazed. At last, at harvest-time 1671 he had the experience which changed his life. The Holy Spirit appeared to him:

> Oh! Then I was glad, and my soul was filled with joy, because I had met with the Lord, who I knew was sufficient to teach me all things, and gave me to see, that my sins would be remitted and forgiven in and thro' Jesus Christ! And Christ Jesus was now become my light, and my salvation, and living faith sprung in me; for I felt power and strength to believe. And then I saw and felt what true faith was, and also

---

[34] Ibid., p. 69.

[35] Ibid., p. 70.

[36] She died on 4 October 1707. They had a number of children. 'The Derbyshire & Nottinghamshire Quarterly Meeting Births and Marriages Digests' list the following: John (b. 4 April 1670), Joseph (b. 30 October, 1671), Phebe (b. 16 July 1675) and Josiah (b. 10 September 1676).

[37] *Jnl*, p. 75.

> saw, that I never had true living faith before then; this was the free gift of God, for it sprung up in his power, and stands in it.[38]

Here are the classical ingredients of the evangelical conversion experience: the presence of Christ through the Holy Spirit bringing forgiveness and bestowing peace and joy; granting new life and power; and all of this as a free gift. Of critical importance for Gratton's soon-to-be-prominent position among the Quakers is his identification of the light with Jesus Christ. This light is supernaturally bestowed. It is neither the natural light of the Cambridge Platonists,[39] nor the undifferentiated light sought by some, then as now, within themselves.

Where, finally, should Gratton find his Christian fellowship? In the course of earnest prayer, 'the Lord made known unto me, that the people called Quakers are his people above all other people'.[40] Accordingly, he sought for Quakers, there being none at Monyash. He found some at widow Farney's house at Exton (*sic.* more probably Elton), and became persuaded that he must throw his lot in with the Friends. This decision was not without its consequences:

> my poor wife was sore grieved that I went among Friends...and the people of our town began to rage, some disputed with me, some cursed me, as I heard, some pleaded for me, some derided and mocked me, calling after me, Quaker, Quaker...[41]

Undeterred, Gratton 'went cheerfully to Friends meetings, and was edified and comforted'.[42] He spoke at meetings, he began to visit other counties and, in 1672, in fulfilment of a word from the Lord which he had already received, his wife was convinced.

II

It is no part of my purpose to describe Gratton's preaching tours in detail. Rather, I wish to turn to a number of themes, some of which have continuing importance. First, what of Gratton's relations with the authorities of Church and state? Although Gratton's *Journal* does not record the facts, we should not forget that at the time of his joining the Quakers that body was suffering greatly in some areas, not least in parts of Derbyshire. The Bishop of Lichfield excommunicated sixty-six Quakers in 1668, many of whom were imprisoned; two years later, John Sykes and his son Samuel were unsuccessfully pursued by Christopher

---

[38] Ibid., p. 77.
[39] See further, ch, 1 above.
[40] *Jnl*, p. 82.
[41] Ibid., p. 88.
[42] Ibid., p. 94.

Lawson, 'Priest' of Bakewell, for tithes amounting to 4s and 6d respectively, and were gaoled; in 1670 five Matlock families had lost goods to the value of £100 3s. 10d. for failure to pay fines for holding meetings—which they continued to hold. In Derbyshire as a whole goods to the value of £310 18s. were forfeited in 1670.[43]

One of the standing complaints of Quakers against the clergy of the Church of England was that they were 'hireling priests' reliant upon tithes for their living. This jibe irritated not only post-1662 incumbents, but also, for example, the ejected Puritan Richard Baxter.[44] Gratton's most articulate opponent on this question was the Reverend W. Wilson of Monyash. In response to a third letter from Gratton on the subject of tithes, Wilson published *The Clergy's Legal Right to Tythes Asserted in a Dispute between a Clergy-man and a Quaker* (1702). In answer to Gratton's charge that the clergy profess to sow spiritual things whilst being very keen to harvest carnal ones, Wilson declares that what he teaches is 'agreeable to the Holy Scriptures. We do not pretend to an Infallible Light within us, and tell them that what we deliver in the Name of the Lord, they must receive it as a Divine Truth.'[45]

Gratton's published response is predictable. He opposes tithes because the ministers of God are not to seek carnal things—especially money. They are called to preach lovingly in the power of the Holy Spirit, and to trust God to meet all their needs: 'on Him alone, who is God over all, his People depend'.[46] Whereas God's ministers are called and equipped from above, in Wilson's Church the uncalled can work miracles, 'For is it not a Miraculous Work, with a few drops of Water, and a few formal Prayers, for a Man to make a Infant a Child of God, a Member of Christ, and an Inheritor of the Kingdom of Heaven?'[47] Moreover, Jesus never commanded anyone to pay tithes. On the contrary, the apostles preached without financial recompense. In stark contrast, Gratton knows some today 'who manifested themselves to minister for Hire, and filthy Lucre'.[48] Free-will offerings of the people are the prescribed way—in which connection Gratton invokes the support of Tertullian, Cyprian and

---

[43] For the examples given in this paragraph I am indebted to Thomas Davidson, 'Early Quakerism in the Peak', *The Friend*, LXXX no. 49, 1907, p. 385.

[44] See F. J. Powicke, *A Life of the Reverend Richard Baxter*, London: Jonathan Cape, 1924, p. 252.

[45] W. W[ilson], *The Clergy's Legal Right to Tythes Asserted in a Dispute between a Clergy-man and a Quaker*, London: Rob. Clavel, 1701, pp. 91-2.

[46] J. Gratton, *The Clergy-Man's Pretence of Divine Right to Tithes, Examined and Refuted. Being a Full Answer to W.W's Fourth Letter, in his Book, Intituled, The Clergy's Legal Right to Tithes Asserted. To which he hath also annexed A Justification of the Divine Right, Erroneously so called*, London: T. Sowle, 1703, p. iii.

[47] Ibid., p. 6.

[48] Ibid., p. 20.

others. He then chronicles the history of tithing with a view to showing that we do not have to do what is not forbidden by Scripture—which could include going to Mass—but to follow what Christ has taught. Tithing is against the law of Christ, and was introduced by the Pope. 'Gospel ministers', he insists, 'ought to be content with Gospel-Maintenance.'[49] Gratton proceeds to answer a number of charges levelled against Quakers, including William Penn, and makes it clear that Quakers agree that the magistracy is an ordinance of God, and that they 'declare it to be our Faith and Duty to yield Quiet, Peaceable subjection to the Queen, and all in Authority under her...'.[50] He concludes with the following exhortation:

> Now, Friend *William*, Consider of all these things coolly, in Lowliness of Mind; and think not thy self too High, Great and Mighty, to be inform'd by a *Peter* or a *John*, though Ignorant and Unlearned Men, in Humane Arts and Languages; yet have been with *Jesus*, and laid down all to follow him, and do his will; unto whom he promised, that they should know of his doctrine.[51]

In a Postscript Gratton addresses a number of doctrinal and other points, one of which, in which he accuses the clergyman of adoptionism, is particularly interesting:

> as to thy words, of *Christ being a Man, Only by taking Humane Nature of the Virgin* Mary; Where findest thou this term, *Only*? I refuse such Unscriptural, Ignorant and Unlearned Questions; and might ask thee, What was he before Mary was, seeing he was before *Abraham* was?

It is not surprising that, in view of his teaching and his actions, Gratton should from time to time fall foul of the law. Not, indeed, that the law was always strictly enforced against the Quakers. For example, the Quaker meetings at Baslow were flourishing, though Hugh Masland and George Ellis were taken to Derby gaol. On one occasion informers reported them to Justice Ayre of Highlow, and sought a warrant to distrain their goods:

> But he was displeased and sharp with them, and bid them look to themselves; for if he found that they did forswear themselves, and that he ever catched them in a lie, or to that effect, he would have their ears; by which they were so daunted, that they went away and let it fall, and troubled us no more.[52]

On another occasion, Wilson, the 'high priest' of Bakewell, encouraged opposition to the Monyash Quakers, but the high constable, George Dale,

---

[49] Ibid., p. 45.
[50] Ibid., p. 62.
[51] Ibid., p. 76.
[52] *Jnl*, p. 123.

'a loving, friendly, moderate man', was on their side. When a trained soldier-*cum*-informer fired his musket one day, it exploded in his hands, nearly killing him. He came to regard this as a punishment for his maltreatment of Quakers: 'so he troubled us no more'.[53] Gratton was not always so fortunate, and in 1680 he began a prison sentence in Derby which lasted for five-and-a-half years. One gaoler was strict, another allowed him a certain liberty—not least that of visiting his dying son, John. When two 'priests', Wilson and Fern, met at the Tideswell Inn, the former told the latter that Gratton was in prison: 'I am glad of it, said Fern', and Gratton comments, 'These are the hirelings that shew their envious spirit, who spare not the flock of Christ!'[54] In1683 Gratton wrote a letter of encouragement to the London Yearly Meeting, 'Written in Derby gaol, where I am a prisoner for the truth's sake...'[55] As time went on, and to the annoyance of the 'priests', Gratton was allowed home for varying periods of time. He addressed passers by from his prison window; he took the gaoler's son to London and placed him in work with a Quaker, George Watts; on being released to attend the funeral of Robert Meller at Whitehough, Staffordshire, in 1684, informers were foiled when the justices refused to order the distraint of his goods on the ground that he was a prisoner;[56] and he lost no opportunity of declaring the truth to some 'Papists' who were his prison companions. He was grateful that

> This prison was made easy to me, and things went well at home with my dear wife and family; and though she was a tender woman, yet she was enabled (through mercy!) to keep markets, to carry on our business for a livelihood; she also came sometimes to see me in prison, though it was sixteen miles, which was hard for her in the winter season.[57]

The case of John Gratton provides one among many instances of the way in which the laws imposed against Dissenters were applied with varying degrees of rigour.[58]

In 1686 Gratton was 'set at liberty by King James the second'.[59] After spending sometime at home, he set off on his evangelistic tours once more. He visited such Quaker strongholds as Kendal and Sedbergh; he

---

[53] Ibid., pp. 127-8.

[54] Ibid., p. 167.

[55] Ibid., pp. 167-71.

[56] This incident is also recounted by A. G. Matthews, *The Congregational Churches of Staffordshire*, London: Congregational Union of England and Wales, [1924], pp. 81-2.

[57] *Jnl*, p. 196.

[58] For further examples, see M. R. Watts, *The Dissenters. From the Reformation to the French Revolution*, Oxford: Clarendon Press, 1978, ch. 3; Sell, *Commemorations*, pp. 131-4; and for a particular county, Sell, *Church Planting. A Study of Westmorland Nonconformity*, (1986), Eugene, OR: Wipf & Stock, 1998, ch. 2.

[59] *Jnl*, p. 197.

toured Scotland,[60] following up his visit with an epistle to all Friends there;[61] and he paid an extended visit to Ireland.[62]

It was characteristic of John Gratton to view all matters in biblical and theological perspective. It therefore comes as no surprise that in 1683, from prison, he published *The Prisoners Vindication with A Sober Expostulation and Reprehension of Persecutors*. He tells how he was apprehended and taken to Derby gaol, 'a very strange way to convince me of an Error, if I be in any',[63] on account of his blasphemy and heresy. He was accused of being 'The Ringleader of a Factious People'.[64] His wife appealed to the archdeacon to no avail. Gratton was told that he would be released if only he recanted. This he refused to do because it would be wrong to conform to the worship of the priests of the nation, and because the way he worships is the true way to worship God. His captors, he continues, are acting against the command of Christ, for if he, Gratton, is truly a tare he should be left among the wheat until harvest. Again, while Christ whipped buyers and sellers out of the temple, 'yet we never read that he whipt any in'[65] and imprisoned and fined them if they would not come. Those who persecute Gratton align themselves with those who persecuted Christ.

There follows a catalogue of biblical characters who were persecuted for conscience's sake, and throughout Gratton insists that he is not a heretic, and is a peaceable man. Nor is he a schismatic as charged, for he enjoins no separation from the truth. On the contrary, 'its those that serve not our Lord Jesus Christ, but their own Bellys, who by good Words and fair Speeches deceive the Hearts of the Simple'[66] who are the true disturbers of Christ's flock. All his trials notwithstanding, Gratton concludes by expressing his conviction that 'God, even our God, will over all Exalt his own Name and Truth, to the Joy of all the Upright-hearted'.[67]

In all of this, Gratton represents many who, according to their light, have been willing, at some personal cost, to stand for God when Caesar

---

[60] His visit to Aberdeen is recorded in the MS records of the Aberdeen Yearly Meeting: 'Dear John Gratton (an ancient and worthy friend) with his honest companion Thomas Aldam were at Aberdeen Quarterly Meeting in the Sixth Month.' See William F. Miller, 'Stranger Friends Visiting Scotland, 1650-1797', *Journal of the Friends Historical Society*, XII, 1915, p. 143.

[61] *Jnl*, pp. 208-14,

[62] Ibid., pp. 214-20.

[63] J. Gratton, *The Prisoners Vindication with A Sober Expostulation and Reprehension of Persecutors*, London: Andrew Sowle, 1683, p. 3.

[64] Ibid., p. 4.

[65] Ibid., p. 10.

[66] Ibid., p. 31.

[67] Ibid., p. 32.

makes demands to which refusal is deemed by the faithful to be the only proper response.

III

Having seen in general terms how John Gratton's spiritual and ecclesiastical pilgrimage prompted him to take a stand against authorities ecclesiastical and civic, we may now turn in more detail to the doctrinal themes which motivated him. The topics for consideration are the Church and the sacraments, and church discipline.

In the opinion of the present-day Quaker theologian, John Punshon, 'Quakerism, with its seventeenth-century background, possesses a strong doctrine of the Church.'[68] By way of illustration we may turn to the first entry in the Minute Book of Monyash Monthly Meeting. The entries are from 1672 to 1735, and the first is written and signed by John Gratton:

> This booke was bought the 21 day of the 12 month, 1672. The prise was 0-2-10, and is for the use of the church and people of god, called by his grace, and gathered and knit together by and in his spirit of light, life, and loue, in which wee now meett and asemble together to wait upon and worship the god and father of our lord Jesus Crist, who freely hath guien unto euery one of us a measure of the holy ghost, by which wee come and are in measure comn unto the true knowledg of the mynd and will of god, tho wee are a poore, unworthy, and dispised people, scattered amongst the rocky mountains and derk ualleys of the hy peak Country; and were many of us conuinced of gods light, way, and truth in this same year abouesaid. Glory, glory, glory, to the lord god of Jsaraell, who keeps Couenant, an his mercys endure for euer. Praises to his name for euer, saith the soulle of one of the poorest and unworthyest of his little remnant.—J.G.[69]

At a number of points one hears echoes of Separatist/Congregationalist ecclesiology in this statement.[70] The emphasis is upon the Church as originating in God's calling out of his people and gathering them into a covenant body. The initiative lies with God, who freely and graciously enlightens those whom he calls. This work of grace is, moreover, construed in resolutely trinitarian terms.

John Gratton had a good deal to say on the sacraments or, to be more precise, he had a few clear points which he reiterated. When he left the Monyash Anabaptists they were, he writes,

---

[68] John Punshon, *Reasons for Hope. The Faith and Future of the Friends Church*, Richmond, IN: Friends United Press, 2001, p. 19.

[69] Reprinted in *Journal of the Friends Historical Society*, III no. 3, July 1906, pp. 82-3; also, with spelling modernized, in T. Davidson, 'Early Quakerism in the Peak', p. 386.

[70] For the Separatist and later Congregational ecclesiologies see ch. 1 above.

> displeased with me, when they saw there was no hopes of my return unto them, and often disputed with me...but the Lord had opened my understanding, and also the holy scriptures to me. And I wrote a little book...[71]

This 'little book', in which the author describes himself as a 'well-wisher of the Anabaptists', is entitled, *John Baptist's decreasing and Christ's Increasing Witnessed: Being a Treatise concerning Baptism In the Type and Baptism in the Mystery* (1674).

In the Preface 'To the Friendly Unprejudiced Reader', Gratton says that the Presbyterians, by denying baptism to the infants of unbelieving parents, make 'the Child a Sufferer for the Sin of the Father's Unbelief, which God hath said, shall never be'.[72] (The Presbyterians, of course, would have supposed that they were honouring their understanding of infant baptism as appropriate in the case of children of the covenant.) If the Episcopalians are correct in their doctrine of baptismal regeneration, he continues, 'What farther need of a Saviour?'[73] Baptists restrict baptism to believers, but Gratton finds no scriptural commandment to this effect.

Positively, he contends that

> They that are baptised into Christ, have put on Christ, live in him, and are One Spirit with, or in him; and are all united by One Spiritit [*sic*] into One Body, and are Members of his Body, of his Flesh and of his Bones, and of his fulness receive Grace for Grace; and know One Lord, One Faith, One Baptism; and are One in him, and he in them; and so are come into the *Alpha* and *Omega*, the Beginning and the End, the First and the last; He, whose Name is called *The Word of God*, by which all things were made in heaven and in Earth; to him be Glory for ever.

Baptism in the Spirit alone suffices. But what of those who remind us that Jesus himself was baptized? Gratton replies that Christ has fulfilled the law and the outward observances, and that Christians are no longer under law, but under grace (an entry point here for those who might wish to accuse seventeenth-century Quakers of being antinomians). John the Baptist's baptism was but a type of that baptism in the Spirit which was to come. In so far as the apostles baptized people, they did it in condescention to John's baptism, and they did not do it in the name of the Trinity. So, urging Baptists to return from their Babylonian captivity, he cries,

---

[71] *Jnl*, pp. 112-13.

[72] J. Gratton, *John Baptist's Decreasing and Christ's Increasing Witnessed*, London: T. Sowle, 1696, p. iv.

[73] Ibid., p. v.

> Prop as hard as you can, and take ye altogether, ye Water-Baptists, of all sorts, and work never so hard with both Hands, your *Babel*-buildings will all fall, and great will be the Fall thereof.[74]

No apostles ever cried out,

> Water-Baptism is the Door; for Christ Jesus said, I am the Door, by ME, mark, not Me and Water, not Me and John, but BY ME, if any man enter in, he shall be saved (Oh he is of himself sufficient) and shall go in and out and find pasture.[75]

Again, the apostles never called baptism an initiating ordinance, and Christ never commanded its observance. Paul said he was sent not to baptize but to preach the Gospel—'But say you, *Paul means* NOT ONLY: Oh Friends! Would you have this hole to creep out at?'[76] To those who say that Philip baptized the eunuch, Gratton replies that Philip did this at Peter's command, and all had not yet been revealed to Peter. The true baptism 'is with the Holy Ghost and Fire'.[77] In answer to the Baptist point that water baptism signifies dying and rising with Christ, Gratton declares that that such dying and rising is the work of the Spirit, not of water. 'So', he concludes,

> we own *John* in his Place and Time, but we own the *Bridegroom* above *John*, although *John* was his Friend, and did what was commanded, but thought not much to give him place who had commanded him.[78]

There follows an expression of love to all Friends, but chiefly to Anabaptists, for whom he has written this work. He ascribes glory to God, and appeals to all to turn to the Lord. In his *Journal* he notes that the Baptists never replied to him in print, though he received and answered some private letters from them on the subject.[79]

The two dominical sacraments are the subject of Gratton's pamphlet, *A Treatise concerning Baptism and the Lord's Supper* (1695). This is written against the background of his conviction that religious divisions are attributable to the fact wicked ministers have 'gone away from God, Christ, the Holy Ghost, and are gone into the Kingdom of Satan, and live in sin all their Days...'.[80] He reiterates his position regarding the baptism of John the Baptist, observing that that baptism left those who underwent

---

74 Ibid., p. 30.
75 Ibid., p. 36.
76 Ibid., p. 38.
77 Ibid., p. 45.
78 Ibid., p. 58.
79 *Jnl*, p. 113.
80 J. Gratton, *A Treatise concerning Baptism and the Lord's Supper*, London: T. Sowle, 1695, p. iv.

it 'short of power, and of the Holy Spirit also; but Christ's Baptism impowered them to be Witnesses after they had it...'.[81] The true baptism is that in which we die to sin; it is a spiritual matter. As for the Lord's Supper, Gratton roots this in the Jewish Passover, and takes the injunction to keep it 'till he come' to be redundant now that Christ has come and lives in true believers.[82]

Like the Separatists and others of the Dissenting sort, the Quakers were concerned that those who professed Christ should manifest a 'godly walk' consistent with that profession. When they did not, church discipline hove into view. It is quite conceivable that members sometimes enjoyed 'policing the saints' too much; but at their best they understood that the objectives of such discipline were the glory of God, the integrity of the Church, and the restoration of offenders. It would seem that John Gratton was involved in an exemplary case of church discipline. Thomas Wolrich (or Woolrich) of Whitehough had, by his actions, brought his family into disrepute. In a letter of 1684 addressed to the meeting at Whitehough he confessed his waywardness and repented of his behaviour. To this three leaders replied in the following terms (I quote the letter in full in order to underline the intensely pastoral and practical, rather than legalistic, attitude of the respondents):

> We are glad of thy submission & owning of thy condemnation for thy disobedience to thy father and the just occasions of offence thou hast given against the truth & lovers of it; in hopes of a goodly sorrow in thee, which will work repentance not to be repented of. And we tenderly advise thee to be carefull for the time to come; and also counsell thee in the love of God to consider seriously the complaints people have made against thee, for wronging them in thy dealings, and wherein thou art conscious to thyselfe of any wrong done to any man that thou make sattisfaction and if any complaint should be made against thee for any new matter, we counsell thee to decline that way of obtaining certifficates thou hath formerly used; and take some honest friend, or friends, and goe to the partty accusing and speak face to face before the friend or friends. And our further advice to thee is, to be truly obedient to thy parents, true to thine owne soule, just to all men, and have a tender regard to the Truth, which advice if thou put in practice will answer our travaill & labour of love and the benefitt thereof will be thine owne, and God shall have the praise, this from thy friends
> William Gibson
> John Gratton

---

[81] Ibid., p. 8.

[82] George Keith, who left the Quakers after 1689, countered the sacramental position of Gratton and others, though without mentioning Gratton in his text, in *The Arguments of the Quakers, More particularly, of George Whitehead, William Penn, Robert Barclay, John Gratton, George Fox, Humphry Norton, And my own, Against Baptism and the Supper Examined and Refuted. Also Some clear Proofs from Scripture; shewing that they are Institutions of Christ under the Gospel...*, London 1698.

Roger Haydock[83]

To those in the Reformed and Dissenting traditions the characteristic marks, or notes, of the Church which, when visible, assure us that we are looking at the true Church, are that the Word is faithfully preached, the sacraments rightly administered and discipline rightly exercised. We have so far seen that the Quakers, as exemplified by John Gratton, paid much heed to the sacraments spiritually conceived, and that they sought to maintain godly discipline under the Gospel. But what, finally, of the proclamation of the Word and the place of the Bible? This question must be considered in relation to the concept of light, and we shall thereby be led to our conclusion.

IV

There seems no doubt that in connection with the divine presence and communication Gratton, like other early Quakers, regards the terms light, Christ and the Spirit as being synonymous. Thus, for example, in his 'Epistle to Friends' of 1673 he exhorts them to 'keep in the light of which you were convinced, and by which you are converted and turned to the Lord'; on the next page he writes, 'had not the Lord come to visit us, we had been in slavery even till now'; and on the next page he beseeches them to fear the Lord so that 'your hearts will be clean habitations for his holy spirit to dwell in'.[84] Positively, Gratton holds that the light which enlightens everyone is Christ; negatively, he implicitly denies that it is the natural conscience of which Paul speaks in Romans 1.[85] Barbour and Roberts concur: 'The Light, a metaphor which suggests a searchlight into a well or a candle in a dark closet and not man's own mental power, is not to be distinguished in early Quaker experience from Christ or the Spirit within men.'[86] This was a position to which Richard Baxter, for example, took exception. He held that all in the world of nature were by nature

[83] Leek MSS, Crosfield Collection, MS Vol. 330, pp. 150-51, at Friends Library, London. John Gratton was, together with Roger Haydock, a witness to a 1688 statement resolving differences between William Ffallowfield and Humphry Woolrich. George Fox was also concerned in this dispute. For this statement and Fox's response see *Journal of the Friends Historical Society*, VI no. 1, January 1909, p. 16. Gratton was also involved in the case of John Scanfield, who fell into debt. See *Journal of the Friends Historical Society*, V no. 4, October 1908, p. 180.

[84] *Jnl*, pp. 110-12.

[85] Cf. Corey Beals, 'Review of Rosemary Moore's *The Light in their Consciences*', in *Quaker Religious Thought*, nos. 99-100, April 2003, pp. 51-2.

[86] Hugh Barbour and Arthur O. Roberts, eds., *Early Quaker Writings 1650-1700*, Grand Rapids: Eerdmans, 1973, p. 22.

enlightened by the natural light; but those who came into the world of grace received the light of supernatural revelation.[87]

A problem arises when people differ over the deliverances of the light. The problem may be illustrated by reference to Gratton's dealings with Ludovic Muggleton. It was in 1666 that a young man, a seeker like Gratton, told Gratton of a book which affirmed that God had spoken audibly to John Reeve and directed him to Muggleton, who should be his mouthpiece, as Moses was to Aaron. The message proclaimed was that those whom Muggleton and Reeve blessed were blessed, and those whom they cursed were cursed to all eternity.[88] Gratton was ready to believe this at the time; he saw the book in Chesterfield, afterwards bought it, and then spent a further five shillings on other books by Muggleton. But God brought him to see that Muggleton's writings 'were clearly opposite to the Holy Scriptures in many respects'.[89] The Muggletonians had no worship, they did not study the Bible, preach or pray—all of this Gratton discovered for himself at widow Carter's house.[90]

The significance of this incident is clearly that Gratton was not inclined to dissociate the Spirit from the Word, and was ready to judge Muggleton's subjective assurance by the Scriptures. In 1671, by which time Gratton was a convinced Quaker, he attended a meeting at Tideswell during which a Baptist woman was convinced. Her husband was a Muggletonian, and he wrote to his leader to request that Gratton be cursed, 'Upon which Muggleton, by letter, sent me his curse, the words of which were not worth mentioning; but in answer gave him to understand, I mattered it not.'[91]

Three years later Gratton met Muggleton in person. Together with Robert Barclay, than whom there was no more powerful Quaker advocate of the light,[92] Patrick Levingstone (*sic* : Livingstone) and William Hague, Gratton called upon Muggleton in London. Gratton, who had so recently exchanged letters with Muggleton, and been cursed by him, asked his companions not to disclose his name. But on coming into the room, Muggleton asked, 'Is any of you John Gratton?' to which Barclay replied, 'art thou a prophet, and needest thou to ask?' On hearing the accent, Muggleton said, 'You are a Scotchmen, and I will have nothing to

---

87 See R. Baxter, *The Quaker's Catechism*, 1655, p. 7. See further Geoffrey F. Nuttall, *The Holy Spirit in Puritan Faith and Experience*, (1946), Chicago: University of Chicago Press, 1991, ch. 10.

88 See further on the Muggletonians, Christopher Hill, Barry Reay and William Lamont, *The World of the Muggletonians*, London: Temple Smith, 1983.

89 *Jnl*, p. 61.

90 Ibid., p. 62.

91 Ibid., p. 95.

92 See ch. 1 above; R. Barclay, *An Apology of the True Christian Divinity*, Glasgow: R. Barclay Murdoch, 1886, pp. 77-138; Sell, *Commemorations*, ch. 6.

do with you; for I was lately cheated by a Scotchman, one John Swinton.'[93] It appears that Swinton, thinking that Muggleton was a poor man, had given him half a guinea, but had then denounced him as a false prophet, whereupon he was cursed. Gratton proceeded to press Muggleton as to his authority. He said it had come from (the late) John Reeve. Gratton continued, 'Dost think it would not be a credulous thing for me to venture my eternal salvation upon the bare word of a man? To this he answered, You must, if ever you be saved.'[94] The conversation rambled on, with Muggleton cursing Livingstone and saying to Gratton (his identity still undisclosed) that if he was careful he would do well. This did nothing to increase Gratton's confidence in Muggleton as a reliable witness, since he had so recently been cursed by him.

If the Bible was sometimes appealed to discredit the unworthy, it could also be resorted to in defence of the Quakers. The 'priest' of Baslow, having declared that there was no revelation at the present time, and that no man currently had the spirit of God in him, issued a challenge to Gratton. He gave him a book written in Greek, and said that if Gratton had the spirit of God he would be able to read it. Gratton turned to his Bible and read Paul's passage concerning the diverse gifts of the spirit, contending that 'The spirit of God is given to all, but not to all alike.'[95]

One of the charges against the Quakers—a charge repeated by Baxter[96]—was that they paid little attention to the historic Jesus, and especially to the Cross, whilst over-emphasizing the Christ within. That nothing was further from Barclay's intention is clear from his declaration that

> *We do not...intend any ways to lessen or derogate from the atonement and sacrifice of Jesus Christ*; but on the contrary do magnify and exalt it. For as we believe all those things to have been certainly transacted which are recorded in the holy scriptures concerning the *birth, life, miracles, sufferings, resurrection, and ascension of Christ*; so we do also believe that it is the duty of every one to believe it to whom it pleases God to reveal the same, and to bring them the knowledge of it...[97]

But there was no smoke without fire; and as the years passed some Quakers came to rely upon their inward light as if it were dissociated from Christ and as if they were not accountable to the Bible.

---

93 *Jnl*, p. 130

94 Ibid., p. 131.

95 Ibid., p. 124.

96 R. Baxter, *The Quakers Catechism*, London: A.M. for Thomas Underhill, 1655, p. 30.

97 Barclay, *Apology*, p. 99.

V

With this we come to the continuing importance of the story of John Gratton. We have seen him standing against the authorities on biblical grounds. We have heard him proclaiming his faith in biblical terms and defending his doctrinal positions by reference to Scripture. Indeed, it was the Spirit-illuminated Scripture which gave him the message he so faithfully preached against all odds. We have seen, too, his loyalty to the covenant fellowship of believers. But if Spirit, Word and fellowship are sundered, what then?

Let it at once be admitted that the Quakers are by no means alone in having been exercised by the question of the Spirit-Bible-fellowship relation. To take one example from twentieth-century Congregationalism, the liberal scholar, C. J. Cadoux reproved Hubert Cunliffe-Jones for his account of *The Authority of the Biblical Revelation* because of its pro-Barthian emphasis upon the Word of revelation. In Cadoux's view the options were either literalistic fundamentalism or the adoption of the methods of modern biblical criticism and the ultimacy of the inner light. Cunliffe-Jones explains that he has no intention of denying the importance of the inner light, for by it we ascertain truth and acknowledge authority. But he denies that the inner light is the ultimate authority, not least because of the relativism that would ensue if each made his own light ultimate. His contention is that beyond the inner light is the authority of Christ under which we stand.[98]

Clearly, Cadoux did not propound his views apart from Scripture, still less in ignorance of it: he was a considerable biblical scholar; but some, including some Quakers, who tread the mystic path have distanced themselves from the Bible (and perhaps some nowadays would not think of themselves as mystics in any traditional sense). From the 'Introduction' to a recent survey of 'non-theist' Friends, we learn that 'probably around 30% [of British members and attenders] will characterize themselves as Agnostic or Atheist...' and there are 'many others whose beliefs would not be recognizable by traditional Christians'.[99] Not surprisingly, some non-Quaker ecumenical Christians wonder how to respond to such a situation. It is not difficult to imagine what John Gratton would have thought about it all. More seriously, the question of the development of doctrine is clamantly raised.[100] As for the dimension of spirituality implicit in all of this, we now learn from the

---

[98] See C. J. Cadoux, 'Scripture and theology', *Congregational Quarterly*, XXV, 1947, pp.21-6; H. Cunliffe-Jones, 'Christian theology for the twentieth century', *Congregational Quarterly*, pp. 127-32.

[99] David Rush, 'They too are Quakers. A survey of 199 Nontheist Friends', *The Woodbrooke Journal*, no. 11, Winter 2002/3, p. 4.

[100] See further, ch. 5 below.

director of Britain's Living Spirituality Network that whereas ecumenism is for many 'dusty and irrelevant', 'spirituality is a word whose time has come'. She continues:

> Our work is founded on the belief that spirituality is a vital part of the humanity we all share: it is that in each of us which seeks for meaning beyond the material.[101]

No doubt such undifferentiated spirituality, even in some cases post-religious spirituality,[102] need not take an introspective, even an egocentric turn, but there are many indications that it can do so. In this respect it is a product of what is frequently branded 'Enlightenment individualism'.[103] This yields such commonplace injunctions as 'Find yourself' and 'Do your own thing'. There is a strong strand within historic Quakerism, not to mention the Reformed tradition, which would insist that such 'self help' approaches to spirituality can even become 'works' which obscure the prevenience of God's grace. As John Punshon has said of the Quakers, 'Convincement was wholly the gift of God, not something procured by spiritual discipline.'[104]

The present-day elasticity of the term 'spirituality' is by no means altogether novel. At the Leicester Conference of 1877, the

---

[101] Beverley McAinish, 'Why we have moved on from ecumenism', *The Sunday Citizen* (Milton Keynes), 26 October 2003, p. 8. The Living Spirituality Network is based at Milton Keynes. For a different understanding of spirituality see ch. 8 below.

[102] Cf. an unattributed item in *Christian Century*, 15 November 2003, p. 6: '[William] James could well have coined the oft-quoted contemporary mantra, "I'm spiritual, but not religious", biased as he was against corporate and cognitive forms of faith.'

[103] On which theme see further, ch. 3 below.

[104] Punshon, *Reasons for Hope*, p. 66. In this connection it is interesting to note that Corey Beals has regretted that while the Quaker Rosemary Moore 'does not explicitly *exclude* the possibility of divine activity in and through these early Quakers, neither does she explicitly *include* such a possibility'. See his review of Moore's *The Light in their Consciences*, p. 53. Moore does not deny that her account is naturalistic, but justifies it thus: 'I was attempting to write a book that would be acceptable in academic circles, and it is a fact—unfortunate if you like—that God has to be left out of academic discourse... However...I think that naturalistic and divine explanations of events are not mutually exclusive, but merely two ways of looking at the same events.' *Quaker Religious Thought*, April 2003, p. 64. First, it is possible to query Moore's 'fact'. No doubt in some rarified, intellectually sectarian, positivistic circles of fifty years ago the attitude expressed was entertained. But much water has since flowed under the verificationist bridge, and in many academic circles, not least philosophical, religious claims are the subject of intense debate. Equally, in intellectual history as currently practised the contextualizing of thought is widely held to be desirable, and when, as is frequently the case, the context is religious, this fact is given due consideration. Secondly, whatever latter-day sceptics may make of it, the early Quakers were persuaded that God had called them, God equipped them, God upheld them, and God gave them something to proclaim. We have not finished with them if we bracket such convictions.

Congregational minister, J. Allanson Picton, presented a paper entitled, 'The relations of theology to religion', in which he argued that religious feeling is largely independent of any object which inspires it, and that it provides a basis upon which those of many views may unite. To this Principal D. W. Simon replied,

> Is it a matter of indifference whether I conceive my God as a bundle of rags—will it have the same effect on my spiritual life as if I conceived Him as the One who revealed Himself in Jesus Christ in Judaea?... [T]he history of religion is, I affirm, opposed to this indifference of the object which we present for the sake of stimulating the religious life...[105]

It is for reasons such as this that I remain persuaded that, as far as Christians are concerned, it is only as our several personal 'intimations' are construed in relation to the Bible discerned by the Spirit within the covenant fellowship (with reference as appropriate to the heritage of Christian witness) that we are spared the eccentricities of an individualistic mystical Muggleton and the prejudices of an equally individualistic biblical fundamentalist. Which is another way of saying that the ecclesiology of those in the traditions of Separatism, Dissent[106] and early Quakerism, far from having exhausted its practical usefulness, is worth commending to Christians of other stripes.

Two sentences of the Congregational theologian, Robert Mackintosh, will bring this study to its conclusion. In the first he issues a challenge of perennial relevance:

> A passage from anxiety into peace which does not issue in a dedicated life is spurious Christianity, be its alarms never so terrifying, be its joys never so hectic.[107]

Undeniably, John Gratton stands as one whose appropriation of Christ's peace was rooted in his experience of the Christ of the Bible. This experience, far from cocooning his person and numbing his motives, urged him to testify to the light against all odds. In 1707 the Grattons left Monyash for the home of their daughter Phebe Bateman at Farnsfield,

---

[105] Quoted by F. J. Powicke, *David Worthington Simon*, London: Hodder and Stoughton, 1912, pp. 99-100. For the Leicester Conference see John W. Grant, *Free Churchmanship in England 1870-1940*, London: Independent Press, n.d., pp. 90-6; Mark D. Johnson, *The Dissolution of Dissent, 1850-1918*, New York: Garland, 1987, ch. 2.

[106] See further ch. 1 above; Alan P. F. Sell, *Saints: Visible, Orderly and Catholic. The Congregational Idea of the Church*, Geneva: World Alliance of Reformed Churches and Allison Park, PA: Pickwick Publications, 1986.

[107] R. Mackintosh, 'The genius of Congregationalism', in A. Peel, ed., *Essays Congregational and Catholic*, London: Congregational Union of England and Wales, [1931], p. 117.

Nottinghamshire. Ann died on 4 October of that year. Gratton died, aged sixty-nine, on 9 January 1712. In testimonies prefixed to his *Journal* he is said to have 'preached the gospel of life and salvation freely'; he 'sought not to be applauded by men'; 'his imprisonment and loss of goods for his testimony for Truth, he bore with a great deal of patience'; and 'He had great openings; was sound in doctrine, and skilful in hitting the mark.'[108]

In Mackintosh's immediately following sentence there resides a challenge of particular relevance to the early years of the twenty-first century:

> [W]hat is harder perhaps for our generation to grant—the Christianity which has no concern with guilt, and no recognition of Christ who is our Lord as being also our Saviour, is a miserably mutilated thing.[109]

Gratton would surely have agreed. I therefore think that while he would probably have appreciated the kindly testimonies to his life and witness which Friends offered following his death, he would have been much more concerned that the prayer with which the Cheshire Friends concluded their testimony be answered:

> The Lord God Almighty raise up and send forth many more such faithful labourers into his harvest, that the scattered may be gathered, and the dispersed brought home to the fold of safety, where they may be prepared, with the Redeemed of the Lord, to give unto him, and unto the Lamb that sits upon the throne, the glory, honor, and high praises that is his due, and our duty to render him, even world without end. Amen.[110]

---

[108] See *Jnl*, pp. x, xii, xv, xix.

[109] R. Mackintosh, 'The genius of Congregationalism', p. 117. See further, ch. 13 below.

[110] *Jnl*, pp. xvi-xvii.

CHAPTER 3

Some Theological Aspects of the English Enlightenment Calmly Consider'd

It is a paradox that on occasion discussions of the Enlightenment generate more heat than light. The most cursory glance at the writings of some present-day theologians will amply demonstrate the point. We are advised, to the point of boredom, that 'the Enlightenment project is over'. Sadly, most of those who chant the mantra decline to explain that the 'project' was, or by what means an entire intellectual movement can be brought to a halt and how we may determine that it is in fact extinct. They tend not to differentiate between the several Enlightenments—the English, the Scottish, the French, the German—to which current scholarship regularly draws our attention; and they frequently supply little evidence of having read any Enlightenment texts. In some cases the Enlightenment serves merely as the diving-board from which they launch themselves into the myriad (sometimes murky) pools of postmodernism.

These tendencies are particularly disturbing when they surface in handbooks and dictionaries which may be expected to have a long shelf life, and which will be consulted in good faith by many general readers and students who may not have access to reliable correctives. In this way inadequate judgements and even blatant errors can be passed down the generations, and that not only in student essays but even in the writings of scholars under pressure to publish.

Lest by now some readers of my uncharacteristically polemical introduction may be thinking that this essay would be more appropriately entitled, in good eighteenth-century fashion, 'The Knockers Knock'd', I shall offer a few disconcerting illustrations.

The article on 'The Enlightenment' in the *Blackwell Encyclopedia of Modern Christian Thought* is by the volume's editor, Alister E. McGrath. He makes many valuable points, and introduces a number of appropriate qualifications—not least that the Enlightenment is multi-faceted; but amongst these are to be found some assertions which cause the eyebrows to rise. Thus, we are informed that 'The Enlightenment criticism of traditional Christianity was based upon the principle of the omnicompetence of human reason.'[1] This may apply to some of those of the English deistic tendency (they were too disparate to be a 'school' or even a 'party'),[2] but it needs to be balanced by the consideration that the Cambridge Platonists,[3] Calvinists like John Gill, evangelical Arminians like John Wesley, and even the most 'advanced' eighteenth-century English Dissenters were united in the belief that reason is God-given, as, indeed, was the father of the English Enlightenment, John Locke.[4] Again, McGrath declares that 'the Enlightenment was not prepared to accept [the resurrection of Jesus] as a historical event'.[5] But, as we shall see, both the broad-minded Presbyterian, Henry Grove, and the (eventually) ardent Unitarian Joseph Priestley wrote at length in defence of the resurrection as an actual historical occurrence.

McGrath's anti-Enlightenment denunciations are not confined to his *Dictionary*. Elsewhere he asserts that 'A pervasive and characteristic feature of Enlightenment thought' is that 'Supplementation of this faculty [i.e. reason] by external sources (such as divine revelation) was regarded as not merely unnecessary but as a potential threat to the autonomy of human reason.' He repeats the point later, claiming that any appeal to revelation 'was unacceptable to the Enlightenment, which saw in it an irrational appeal to superstition and authority (in the pejorative sense of the term)'.[6] Passing over the unargued disjunction of reason, 'the candle of the Lord', from revelation, we shall see that even the most rational of the English rational divines upheld special revelation (as did Locke, the 'father of the English Enlightenment') and, especially in the case of Priestley, were deeply offended by any suggestion that they were deists.

In yet another book McGrath welcomes the 'tidal wave of dissent rising against the Enlightenment' and, verging upon the hysterical, asks, 'Who wanted anything to do with an intellectually dubious movement, which had given rise to the Nazi holocaust and the Stalinist purges?'[7] Even the least skilled in logic may suspect that a few steps in the argument are here omitted, and that what we have is an empty emotional denunciation. It was in rebuttal of talk of this kind that Donald MacKinnon, than whom no twentieth-century philosopher agonized more

---

1 A. E. McGrath, 'Enlightenment', in A. E. McGrath, ed., *The Blackwell Encyclopedia of Modern Christian Thought*, Oxford: Blackwell, 1993, p. 152.

2 See further, ch. 4 below.

3 For whom see ch. 1 above.

4 See further, Alan P. F. Sell, *John Locke and the Eighteenth-Century Divines*, Cardiff: University of Wales Press, 1997, ch. 3.

5 McGrath, 'Enlightenment', p. 155.

6 A. E. McGrath, *The Genesis of Doctrine. A Study in the Foundations of Doctrinal Criticism*, Oxford: Blackwell, 1990, pp. 140, 184-5.

7 A. E. McGrath, *The Renewal of Anglicanism*, London: SPCK, 1993, pp. 110, 17.

deeply over man's inhumanity to man, declared, 'in our tormented century, it is from declared enemies of the Enlightenment that Nazi and Fascist ideologues found some of their readiest and most eloquent Christian recruits'.[8]

The above remarks notwithstanding, I have no intention of falling into the opposite trap of contending that the Enlightenment was all sweetness and light. My excuse for parodying John Wesley's title, *Predestination Calmly Consider'd*, is that I wish to focus attention upon the adverb. In other words, I plead for discrimination and balance in a field which is much more intricate and interesting than either blanket denunciations or commendations would suggest. I shall seek to show in true straight-up-the-middle English fashion that, as far as theology is concerned, the English Enlightenment was in some ways a blessing, in others a bane. I shall focus my attention upon texts written by representatives of Old Dissent, whose opinions occupy the continuum from high—even hyper—Calvinism at one end to Unitarianism at the other, with sidelong glances as appropriate at Anglican divines and Arminians of the Evangelical Revival. In particular, I hope to make good the following claims: (a) that in England the Enlightenment emphasis upon the right of private judgement and the conscientious moral critique of doctrine was beneficial to theology and preferable to wanton submission to arbitrary authorities whether ecclesiastical or biblicist; (b) that their doctrinal divergences notwithstanding, English Enlightenment divines held to the sufficiency of Scripture and urged the necessity of special revelation; (c) that in homiletic practice divines of all stripes evince a considerable likeness of style and content; (d) that the English Enlightenment gave a boost to older notions concerning the right of private judgment, and that these, accruing from the Revival as much as from the rational divines, were to have an adverse effect upon ecclesiology; and (e) that when the final balance sheet is drawn up, latter day blanket denunciations of the Enlightenment are seen to be unsubtle and even anachronistic.

Into the antecedents of the English Enlightenment I cannot here delve,[9] though I endorse Roy Porter's finding that

---

[8] D. M. MacKinnon, unpublished typescript Comments on Colin Gunton, 'Knowledge and culture: towards an epistemology of the contcrete', in Hugh Montefiore, ed., *The Gospel and Contemporary Culture*, London: Mowbray, 1992, pp. 84-102. The Comments were prepared for the consultation on 'The Gospel and Our Culture', held at Swanwick, Derbyshire, 11-17 July 1992, at which Gunton delivered his paper.

[9] For contrasting emphases on this matter see, for example, J. G. A. Pocock, 'Post-Puritan England and the problem of the Enlightenment', in P. Zagorin, ed., *Culture and Politics from Puritanism to the Enlightenment*, Berkeley: University of California Press, 1980, ch. 4; Mark Goldie, 'John Locke and Anglican Royalism', *Political Studies*, XXXI, 1983, pp. 61-85.

> The simple fact is that Enlightenment goals—like criticism, sensibility or faith in progress—throve in England *within* piety. There was no need to overthrow religion itself, because there was no pope, no inquisition, no Jesuits, no monopolistic priesthood with a stranglehold on children through education and on families through confession... [I]n England almost alone, the realization of Enlightenment hopes was not thwarted at every turn by the existing order of state and society.[10]

As to the socio-intellectual context of the English Enlightenment, I equally briefly advert to the following factors. First, the prevailing fear of civil strife, which was fostered by keen memories of the sectarian rivalry and Civil War of the preceding century, prompted many eighteenth-century thinkers to seek a reasonable foundation on which a more or less harmonious society could be built. The endurance of the Toleration Act of 1689 was not a foregone conclusion; some resented its enactment, while others, having in mind the restriction of its benefits to orthodox Protestant Dissenters (that is, not to Roman Catholics, Unitarians and atheists) felt that it did not go far enough. The Sacheverell riots of 1715 and the Birmingham riots of 1791 stand like book-ends at either end of the century, and had the Schism Bill become law in 1714 (the fact of its failure owing to the death of Queen Anne on 1 August, the day she was due to sign it, being construed as a signal providence in the eyes of many Dissenters) some of the Dissenters' recently-granted rights in education would have been clawed back.[11]

Secondly, developments in scientific method had a considerable impact upon intellectual thought in general. The Aristotelian quest of final causes was largely abandoned by scientists not, in most cases, because they no longer believed in purposive creation, but because they became persuaded that it was not the business of science to pursue such teleological considerations by deductive arguments. Rather, they must devote themselves to observation and experiment, to the framing and testing of hypotheses: in short, to empirical procedures. In all of this the most prominent catalyst was Isaac Newton. When this approach coincided with continuing commitment to the Cartesian body-soul dualism, it was,

---

[10] R. Porter, 'The Enlightenment in England', in R. Porter and Miklulás Teich, *The Enlightenment in National Context*, Cambridge: Cambridge University Press, 1981, pp. 6-7.

[11] For Henry Sacheverell (1674?-1724), the High Church Tory, see *ODNB*; G. S. Holmes, *The Trial of Dr Sacheverell*, London: Eyre Methuen, 1973. For the Birmingham riots, see David L. Wykes, '"A finished monster of the true Birmingham breed": Birmingham, Unitarians and the 1791 Priestley Riots', in Alan P. F. Sell, ed., *Protestant Nonconformists and the West Midlands of England*, Keele: Keele University Press, 1996, pp. 43-69. It is said that the Independent Thomas Bradbury, known to Queen Anne as 'bold Bradbury', delivered a sermon following her death on 2 Kings 9:34: 'Go, see now this accursed woman, and bury her: for she is a king's daughter.' The reference is to Jezebel.

for some, but a short step to the conclusion that scientific knowledge is normative in so far as it is concerned with what actually is, whereas matters spiritual are purely speculative if not entirely groundless.

Thirdly, flowing down from the Middle Ages through such writers as Grotius and Pufendorf, both of whom were read in the English universities and Dissenting academies,[12] was the emphasis upon natural rights, which mingled with the Cartesian epistemological commitment to the *individual's* clear and distinct ideas. The English divines were not alone in drawing on this heritage in their explication of the right of conscientious private judgement. Not, indeed, that this particular right was an Enlightenment discovery: rather, it was a legacy of the Renaissance. Thus, for example, even though he sat loose to natural rights where property was concerned on the ground that everything we have is on trust from God, Grotius's contemporary, the 'ever-memorable' John Hales (1585-1656), declared that 'they that come and tell you what you are to believe, what you are to do, and tell you not why, they are not physicians, but leeches; and if you so take things at their hands, you are not like men but like beasts'.[13] That many eighteenth-century English divines eschewed any likeness to beasts, and were strongly disinclined unthinkingly to bend their necks to presumed authorities will now become clear.[14]

I

On 8 November 1733 the Presbyterian Henry Grove, the broad-minded tutor at the Dissenting academy in Taunton, delivered a charge at the ordination of Farnham Haskoll. His address, *A short and easy Rule of Conduct for Ministers of the Gospel*, comprises an exposition of 2 Timothy 2:15, 'Study to shew thyself approved unto God.'[15] In it Grove remarks:

---

[12] See for the academies, Alan P. F. Sell, *Philosophy, Dissent and Nonconformity 1689-1920*, Cambridge: James Clarke, 2004. For the differences between Grotius and Pufendorf, and for the divergent Medieval and Renaissance readings of Aristotle, see Richard Tuck, *Natural Rights Theories. Their Origin and Development*, Cambridge: Cambridge University Press, 1979.

[13] J. Hales, *Of Enquiry and Private Judgment in Religion*, in *The Works of the Ever Memorable Mr. John Hales*, ed. D. Dalrymple, Glasgow, 1765, III, p. 150.

[14] As Charles Gray Shaw pointed out long ago, 'This conflict between reason-rights and tradition-authority...recalled the ancient Sophist contrast between *phusis* and *nomos*, the exact reiteration of which may be found in Cudworth's *Treatise concerning Eternal and Immutable Morality*, 1678.' See 'The Enlightenment', *Encyclopaedia of Religion and Ethics*, ed. James Hastings, Edinburgh: T. & T. Clark, (1912), 1937, V, p. 310.

[15] See *The Works of the Reverend and Learned Mr. Henry Grove, of Taunton. Containing All the Sermons, Discourses, and Tracts published in his Life-Time*, (1747),

> It is, indeed, the right of every man to use the faculties which God hath given him, and, as far as he is capable, and has opportunity for it, to see with his own eyes, to search the Scriptures, to try notions and spirits, and having proved all things, then to hold fast to that which is good, which sometimes cannot be known to be good before trial. This is every man's birthright, as a man, and much more every Christian's; and being their right, must in a greater or lesser degree, according to the diversity of their capacities and circumstances, be their duty too.[16]

Fifty years on, Joseph Priestley, who repudiated his family's strict Calvinism as a youth and proceeded *via* Arminianism to Unitarianism,[17] was, as we might expect, in entire sympathy with his highly-regarded predecessor. In Part Two of his *Institutes of Natural and Revealed Religion* (1763) he declares that

> we ought to be very far from relinquishing our reason, when we come to consider the subject of revelation... It is only by the help of that faculty which we call *reason*, that we can distinguish between any two systems of religion that may be proposed to us.... Let us, therefore, upon all occasions, call to our aid that power which God has given us to be the guide of life, and especially in matters of so great importance to us as those certainly are which relate to the will of God, what he requires of us, and what we have to expect from him.[18]

Priestley returns to this theme on a number of occasions. Urging the professors of Christianity to use their reason 'in matters of religion, or where the Scriptures are concerned', he explains that 'They both of them proceed from the same God and Father of us all... They cannot, therefore, be contrary to one another, but must mutually illustrate and enforce one another.' Those who decry human reason and require its abandonment in matters of religion are to be distrusted: 'A Popish priest would require nothing more than this, to make you believe the doctrine of transubstantiation...'[19] In 1771 Priestley reassures an anonymous pamphleteer that 'though I believe many things on the authority of

reprinted as *Henry Grove: Ethical and Theological Writings*, with an Introduction by Alan P. F. Sell, Bristol: Thoemmes Press, 2000, IV, pp. 145-89. The Introduction is reprinted in Alan P. F. Sell, *Testimony and Tradition: Studies in Reformed and Dissenting Thought*, Aldershot: Ashgate, 2005, ch. 5. For Grove (1684-1738) see also Alan P. F. Sell, *Dissenting Thought and the Life of the Churches. Studies in an English Tradition*, Lewiston, NY: Edwin Mellen Press, 1990, ch. 6, and *Philosophy, Dissent and Nonconformity*, *passim*; *ODNB*.

[16] Grove, *Works*, IV, p. 165. I have discussed eighteenth-century attitudes towards reason in *John Locke and the Eighteenth-Century Divines*, ch. 3.

[17] See *The Theological and Miscellaneous Works of Joseph Priestley*, ed. J. T. Rutt, (1817-32), reprinted Bristol: Thoemmes Press, 1999, I, pt. 1, pp. 21-2. Cf. Priestley, XIX, pp. 264-5. For Priestley (1733-1804) see *ODNB*.

[18] Priestley, *The Theological and Miscellaneous Works*, II, p. 117.

[19] Ibid., p. 384.

revelation, which could never be discovered by human reason; yet still I can believe no farther concerning them than the inspired writers explain them, by giving me ideas of them';[20] and in 1785 we find him preaching to Birmingham Dissenters on *The Importance of Free Enquiry in Matters of Religion*.[21]

I have deliberately set out from liberal theologians from either end of the eighteenth century by way of suggesting that although they exalt human reason, where religion is concerned they habitually think of it in close relation to the Bible. I shall return to this point shortly, but first there are three further points concerning reason to be made.

First, it would be a serious error to suppose that more liberal divines alone placed a premium on reason. A number of orthodox divines upheld the right of private judgement no less ardently than their liberal counterparts. For example, the evangelical Calvinist Baptist, Caleb Evans opened the confession of faith he prepared for his ordination service with these words:

> The right of private judgment, especially in matters of religion, I apprehend is the undoubted and unalienable privilege of every rational intelligent creature. It is a privilege I claim for myself, and for the use of which I am accountable only to God; and it is a privilege which I think everyone *ought* to exercise, and has a right *fully* and *freely* to enjoy.[22]

Later in his statement Evans refers to the current fashion of decrying the compositon and delivery of such confessions on the ground that they invade Christian liberty. He affirms that those who adopt this attitude in fact have their own confession which they willingly defend; and that what they object to is the creed of the Reformation. Hence,

> it is I think very evident that a minister's giving a confession of his faith previous to his ordination, is so far from interfering with the right of private judgment, notwithstanding all the florid declamations to the contrary, that it is rather on the

[20] Ibid., XXI, p. 18.

[21] Ibid., XV, pp. 70-82.

[22] *A Charge and Sermon, together with an Introductory Discourse, and Confession of Faith, delivered at the Ordination of the Rev. Mr. Caleb Evans, August 18, 1767, in Broad-mead, Bristol*, Bristol: S. Farley, 1767, p. 14. For Evans (1737-91) see Stephen A. Swaine, *Faithful Men; or, Memorials of Bristol Baptist College, and some of its most Distinguished Alumni*, London: Alexander, 1884; Norman Moon, *Education for Ministry: Bristol Baptist College 1679-1979*, Bristol: Bristol Baptist College, 1979, pp. 114-15, and *passim*.

> other hand a necessary *consequence* of the natural exercise of this right, betwixt a minister and the people to whom he is called to minister.[23]

If the notion of the right of private judgement was in the air before the Enlightenment, it outlived the eighteenth century too. Thus in 1808 we find the evangelical Congregational ordinand, John Bruce, giving the reasons why he wished to minister among the Dissenters rather than within the established Church in good eighteenth-century order. They are:

> the right of private judgment and liberty of conscience with regard to religious sentiment and duty; [and only then] the supremacy of Christ as the only Head of his Church; and the sufficiency of the Holy Scriptures as the only rule of faith and practice... I also esteem their mode of worship and administration of the ordinances of the new Testament, more consistent with the simplicity of the Gospel, and the practice of primitive churches, than those which are adopted in the national establishment.[24]

Evangelical divines appealed to reason in a variety of ways,[25] but few were as rationalist in method as some of the high Calvinists. The point is

---

[23] *A Charge*, p. 17. Interestingly or, according to theological taste, ominously, by 1790 Priestley could refer to the ordination candidate's confession of faith as being something 'which was formerly required', but now certain questions are put to the ordinand 'which lead him to give as much as he thinks proper of his views of christianity and the ministry of it, and the motives and maxims of his own conduct, for the instruction of the audience'. See *A View of Revealed Religion; A Sermon Preached at the Ordination of The Rev. William Field of Warwick, July 12, 1790 by Joseph Priestley LL.D., F.R.S. With a Charge Delivered at the same Time by the Rev. Thomas Belsham*, Birmingham, 1790, Preface, p. vi. Two observations are called for: 1. It had been a long-standing Presbyterian practice to address such questions to ordinands, as we shall see in the case of Thomas Hadfield. 2. The ordinand's confession of faith may be heard to this day in some churches in the line of Old Dissent (though such confessions are frequently less determinedly theological and more jolly than their eighteenth-century counterparts).

[24] *Discourses delivered at the Solemn Separation of the Rev. John Bruce to the Pastoral Office over The Congregational Church assembling in St. James-Street, Newport, Isle of Wight, On the Twenty-fifth of May 1808, By The Rev. John Pye-Smith, D.D. Homerton. Rev. Samuel Bruce, Wakefield, Rev. James Bennett, Romsey. To which is added, A Sermon preached in the Evening of the same Day, by the Rev. Robert Winter, London*, 1808, p. 10. I have used this, and other, examples of Congregational ordination confessions in a paper devoted specifically to 'Confessing the Faith in English Congregationalism'. See my *Dissenting Thought and the Life of the Churches*, ch. 1. In the present essay I place a few of these examples in their broader intellectual and ecclesiastical context. For Bruce (1782-1874) see *The Congregational Year Book*, 1876, p. 319.

[25] I have referred briefly to a few of these in *John Locke and the Eighteenth-Century Divines*, p. 70, *Confessing and Commending the Faith: Historic Witness and Apologetic*

easily made by reference to the most significant such theologian of his period, the Baptist John Gill.[26] Gill published prolifically, but his most substantial work is the *Complete Body of Doctrinal and Practical Divinity: Or A System of Evangelical Truths Deduced from the Sacred Scriptures*. As frequently happens in the case of eighteenth-century titles which offer an alternative, the clue to what is going on is in the latter part. In this case it is the phrase, *Evangelical Truths Deduced from the Sacred Scriptures*. Negatively, this suggests that Gill has no expectation of finding truths other than evangelical ones in the Bible; positively it indicates his commitment to a form of Cartesian rationalism, whereby in *a priori* fashion he sets out from an axiom and deduces truths therefrom with copious reference to biblical texts. From literally dozens of possible illustrations I select Gill's chapter on the sovereignty of God's will.

Gill has already proved God's existence to his own satisfaction, proposing eight arguments including those from universal consent, the light of nature, the works of creation, the fulfilment of prophecy and miracles, and he has argued for the Bible as the source of authoritative propositional truth. He proceeds to discuss the nature and attributes of God, among them God's will. Drawing upon biblical texts, Gill 'proves' that there is a will in God which is both secret and revealed in God's law and in the Gospel. The objects of his will are his own glory, and all other things, both good and evil. His will is essential to him; it is eternal, immutable, always efficacious; it has no cause out of himself and hence it is not conditional; it is free and sovereign, as is shown in creation, providence, and in things sacred. He concludes, 'But though the will of God is sovereign, it always acts wisely: some sovereign princes will things rashly and foolishly; but God wills nothing contrary to his perfections of wisdom, justice, holiness, &c...'[27] In a word, Gill supplies a classic example of a Calvinistic deductive system of divinity.

Method, Cardiff: University of Wales Press, 2002, p. 230, and *Philosophy, Dissent and Nonconformity*, pp. 92-4, 97. For specific references to Baptists, see Frank Louis Maudlin, 'Truth, heritage, and eighteenth-century English Baptists', *Baptist Quarterly*, XXXV no. 5, January 1994, pp. 211-28.

[26] For Gill see *ODNB*; Alan P. F. Sell, *The Great Debate: Calvinism, Arminianism and Salvation*, (1982), Eugene, OR: Wipf & Stock, 1998, p. 127 and *passim*; Walter Wilson, *The History and Antiquities of Dissenting Churches and Meeting-Houses in London, Westminster, and Southwark*, London: W. Button, 1808-12, IV, pp. 213-225; J. A. Jones, *Bunhill Memorials*, London: James Paul, 1849, pp. 60-3. Timothy George, 'John Gill', in Timothy George and David S. Dockery, eds., *Baptist Theologians*, Nashville: Broadman Press, 1990, ch. 4; George M. Ella, *John Gill and the Cause of God and Truth*, Eggleston, Co. Durham: Go Publications, 1995; Michael A. G. Haykin, ed., *The Life and Thought of John Gill (1697-1771). A Tercentennial Celebration*, Leiden: Brill, 1997.

[27] J. Gill, *Complete Body of Doctrinal and Practical Divinity*, (1767), reprinted from the 1839 edn, Grand Rapids: Baker Book House, 1978, I, p. 112.

Secondly, 'reason' is frequently used by the Dissenting divines and others in a broader sense than Gill's rationalistic deductions would suggest. Indeed, in his opening chapter in which he argues for God's existence, Gill himself is a child of his age in that the largest space is devoted to a cosmological argument. This argument came into its own during the eighteenth century, and it recurs not only in doctrinal and apologetic treatises and polemical pamphlets, but also in the confessions of faith delivered by ordinands, and this whether they are high Calvinists, liberal Arians or out and out Unitarians.

By way of illustrating the change of intellectual key we may note first the general drift of the thirty-six page confession of faith delivered by the Congregational Calvinist, Thomas Bradbury, at his ordination in 1707. He first resolves to uphold the Scriptures: 'To this Law and Testimony I *profess to bring every opinion.*' God's self-revelation 'includes both his Eternal Unity, and a Trinity of Persons'. God has made the world and rules it; he 'made a Covenant with our first Parents', who sinned and broke it. With true Calvinist particularism he continues, '*I believe that God resolved to glorify himself by redeeming some of the lost Race.*' God '*did from Eternity PREDESTINATE some to the Adoption of Children by Jesus Christ... This Election was free, and it will have a certain Issue. I believe* that the Remnant are saved according to the Election of GRACE, not for the Works *which they should afterwards do*, but according to his own Purpose and Grace, before the World began.' Salvation could be brought only by a Mediator between God and man, and he is 'the Man Christ Jesus'. Jesus is divine; he is a teacher from God, a priest for ever, and king of the saints. He was crucified, buried and raised, and is now ascended. He is the universal judge. Those who are predestinated are called and justified freely by God's grace: '*I believe that we lay hold on this Mercy by* FAITH, and that it is not of our selves, but a gift of God.' Those who are adopted by grace may sin and 'have their Iniquities visited by stripes', but they cannot finally fall [the doctrine of the perseverance of the saints]. Christ is to be worshipped, and the sacraments and prayer are to be honoured. Finally, '*The Christian, at his Death, enters upon two Blessings, a Complete Purity, and a satisfying Enjoyment.*' The righteous shall be raised at the last day, while the wicked 'shall be punish'd with Everlasting Destruction'.[28]

---

[28] *A Confession of Faith, at the Publick Ordination of Thomas Bradbury, London, July the Tenth 1707. With an Exhortation to Minister and People by Mr. John Shower*, 1707. For Bradbury (1677-1759) see *ODNB*; Wilson, *The History and Antiquities of Dissenting Churches*, III, pp. 450-2, 504-35; Jones, ed., *Bunhill Memorials*, pp. 10-13. Born in Wakefield, Bradbury trained for the ministry under Timothy Jollie at Attercliffe. He served as a supply minister and as an assistant from 1697 until his ordination ten years later. He was buried at Bunhill.

It would seem that 'Bold' Bradbury's doctrinal views, unlike those of some others, did not become more progressive with the passage of the years, for in his funeral oration for Bradbury, Thomas Hill praised him for '*useful Pieces* which he published *against the enemies* of God and their Country, who were endeavoured to revive and propagate the *destructive Notions* of the *Arians* and *Pelagians*, and the *inslaving Doctrines* of *Passive Obedience* and *Non-Resistance*'.[29]

With all of this may be contrasted the ordination answers and experience of the Presbyterian, Thomas Hadfield, trained at Findern under Ebenezer Latham and ordained at Peckham in 1726. On being asked to '*confess those Truths which you believe and desire to preach unto others*', in a way which could not be more different from that of Bradbury, he strikes the note of the 'cosmological' eighteenth-century, adding ontological considerations for good measure:

> As the Being and Existence of GOD is the Foundation of all Religion, I am abundantly persuaded, *That there is a* GOD. When I seriously consider the visible Constitution of nature; for Instance, the Number, Magnitude, Distances, Motion and Uses of the Heavenly Bodies: When I survey this Earth, and reflect upon its Figure, Gravity, with regard to the Fountain of Light and Heat...[and so on for a further twenty-four lines]... I am hereupon fully convinced, that from all Eternity there must have existed a Being of absolute Perfection, whose Existence is necessary and uncaused, and which it must be a Contradiction to suppose not to exist.... THIS Supreme Cause, of whose Necessary Eternal Existence there is such cogent and irrefragable Proof, I therefore believe must essentially and immutably be the infinite Power, Wisdom, Goodness, Truth, Righteousness, Excellence and Perfection... A Truth, that is demonstrable not only from Effects and constant Experience, but from *prior* Evidence; such as arises from the Perfection of One absolutely Necessary and Self-Existent Being.[30]

Only after five pages does Hadfield come to God's revelation in the Bible, and thence to Calvinistic doctrine.

We may note in passing a further distinction between Hadfield and Bradbury. Whereas the latter retained his staunch Calvinism to the end, Hadfield's views, on what Samuel Chandler called 'some of the abstruser

---

[29] *A Sermon Occasioned by the Death of the Reverend Mr. Thomas Bradbury, who departed this life September 9 1759, in the 82nd Year of his Age: Preached at New-Court on Lord's-Day Afternoon, Sept. 16. And Published at the Request of the Church. By Thomas Hill,* London, 1759, p. 35.

[30] *Ordination to the Ministry, an entrusting Men with the Gospel. A Sermon Preach'd at the Ordination of Thomas Hadfield, M.D. At Peckham in the Country of Surrey, October XIX, MDCCXXVI. By Joseph Hill. With Dr. Hadfield's Confession of Faith, and his Answers to the Questions then propos'd to him by the Reverend Mr. John Beaumont. To which is Added, The Charge given by the Reverend Mr. Thomas Reynolds*, London, 1717, pp. 41-2, 43-4.

Points of Religion', altered towards the end of his relatively short life.[31] Chandler continued,

> I am well assured this alteration did not proceed from Fickleness and Levity of Temper, or a Love of Novelty, but from the full Persuasion and maturest Conviction of his Judgment and Conscience... An Alteration of Sentiments in such Circumstances, must I think create a real Esteem for his Memory, even amongst such of you, should there be any such, to whom such Alteration might not be altogether so agreeable.[32]

It would seem that here we have diplomatic code descriptive of one who tended in an Arian direction. Interestingly, however, Chandler also quotes Hadfield's rule of life for the 'Safety and Comfort' of his bereft congregation, and I reproduce this by way of showing that 'coldly cerebral' is not the only description which may be applied to eighteenth-century ministers who proceeded with integrity to love God with all their mind:

> I will keep my heart with all Diligence. I will make God my End, my Chief End in all my Actions, and in all my Enjoyments. I will carefully observe, attend to, and regard every Suggestion of my Conscience, and the good Spirit of God, whom I implore to be my continual Light and Guide. My Bible shall be my daily Study and Rule, for therein do I find great Delight. Oh, how I love thy Law! Secret Prayer I love, and am refreshed in. Never, whilst I am able to pray, will I omit or neglect it. He is no true Christian who hath no secret Converse with God. I will prize my Sabbaths, those delightful Days to renewed Souls. I hope I have found them so. I will speak Evil unnecessarily of no Man. That I may be cheerful, good tempered, affable and patient, I will endeavour always to walk closely with God, and to keep a good Conscience, thus to have fair Weather always within. When I lie down, it shall be with explicit Meditations on God, that awakening I may still be with him.[33]

For a Congregational example we may turn to John Notcutt, whose confession of 1735 begins:

---

[31] For an account of doctrinal change in eighteenth-century English Presbyterianism see Sell, *Dissenting Thought and the Life of the Churches*, ch. 5; for doctrinal change in English Congregationalism see, ch. 5 below.

[32] *Death the Wages of Sin, and eternal life the Gift of God by Christ Represented in a Sermon Preached at Peckham in Surrey, March 8, 1741. On Occasion of the Death of the late Reverend Thomas Hadfield, M.D., Who died February 21, 1741, in the 46th Year of his Age. By Samuel Chandler*, London, 1741, pp. 60-1. Hadfield was baptized at Chesterfield on 9 October 1701. He attended Chesterfield Grammar School, was apprenticed to a shoemaker, and then became medically qualified. He succeeded Chandler at Peckham. His tutor, Latham, also an M.D., was, like Henry Grove, a tutor of the open-minded sort.

[33] Ibid., pp. 61-2.

> When I take a Survey of this visible Creation, and seriously reflect on the several Objects which therein do continually offer themselves to our View, I cannot suppose this World, and the Things therein contained, to be independent; since nothing can cause itself to exist. I must therefore conclude, that there is one supreme Being, who is independent, and upon whom all Things do depend for their Existence: And this great Being is GOD.[34]

Notcutt exemplifies the fact that it was not always Presbyterians who became Socinians, for, his confessional commitment to the federal theology and particular redemption notwithstanding, he turned in that direction, left the ministry *circa* 1750, went into business in Ipswich, and died in 1778.

There is no need to supply further detailed examples of Congregational confessional statements. Suffice it to say that Thomas Gibbons launched forth from the fact that 'The Light of Nature fully convinces me, that there is a GOD';[35] John Angus argued that '*As something now is, and as nothing* can create itself, it is evident that something must have existed from all Eternity; and it is as certain that some one at least in the Circle of Beings must be uncaused...';[36] even the staunchly evangelical and Calvinistic James Rooker could confess that 'The Light of Nature fully convinces me, that there is a GOD.'[37]

---

[34] *A Sermon Preached at the Ordination of the Reverend Mr. John Notcutt, at the Meeting-House in Green-Street, Cambridge, on July 22, 1735 by William Ford. With the Charge then given him by Revd. Mr. Tobias Wildboar; and Mr. Notcutt's Confession of his FAITH*, 1735, p. 25.

[35] *A Sermon preached at the Ordination of the Reverend Mr. Thomas Gibbons, October 27, 1743. At Haberdasher's Hall, London. By John Guyse, D.D. Together with an Introductory Discourse by Richard Rawlin. Mr. Gibbons's Confession of Faith. And an Exhortation to him by Thomas Hall*, London, 1743, p. 19. For Gibbons (1720-85) see *ODNB*; Wilson, *The History and Antiquities of Dissenting Churches*, III, pp. 178-83; Jones, *Bunhill Memorials*, pp. 55-6.

[36] *A Sermon at the Ordination of the Reverend John Angus, October 26, 1748. At the Meeting at Bishop-Stortford, By John Guyse, D.D. Together with an Introductory Discourse by Thomas Gibbons; Mr. Angus's Confession of Faith; and a Charge delivered by Samuel Price*, 1748, p. 20. For Angus (1724-1801) see *ODNB*.

[37] *Mr. Hayward's Introductory Discourse at the Ordination of Mr. Rooker*, 1751, p. 15. For Rooker (1728/9-1780) see Sell, *Dissenting Thought and the Life of the Churches*, ch. 11. The statement of Alan Saunders is thus incredible: 'For the Calvinist, God is so infinitely removed from humankind that knowledge of him is inaccessible to human reason.' See his 'The state as highwayman: from candour to rights', in Knud Haakonssen, ed., *Enlightenment and Religion: Rational Dissent in Eighteenth-Century Britain*, Cambridge: Cambridge University Press, 1996, p. 250. This is not to deny that some divines, John Ellis among them, regarded reason as redundant where matters of religion were concerned (and rebuked Locke for thinking otherwise) and had recourse solely to revelation. But the majority was of another mind. See J. Ellis, *Some Brief Considerations upon Mr. Locke's Hypothesis, That the Knowledge of God Is Attainable by Ideas of*

Although 'natural theology' style ordination confessions continue into the nineteenth century, it is only proper to point out that under the influence of the Evangelical Revival, with its emphasis upon Gospel proclamation to the ends of the earth, different notes are sounded from about 1770 onwards. Indeed, in that year John Fell was ordained at Thaxted. His confession of faith starts not from theism, but from 'the scriptures of the Old and New Testament' as the 'inspired and holy word of God'. He does not use the term 'predestination', and declares not that God has called some, but 'a great multitude of our race to be redeemed, renewed, and raised to eternal life and blessedness...'. Further, 'I am sensible that the gospel is to be "preached unto every creature", that "the children of God, who are scattered abroad" among all nations, may be gathered from the world into separate societies...'.[38] On leaving Thaxted in 1787 he became tutor at Homerton Academy, but his appointment was terminated in 1797. It is said that his rigidity distressed the students, his orthodoxy offended some supporters, his republicanism others. All of which, no doubt, lies behind the title and contents of the funeral sermon preached on his death by Henry Hunter. Under the rubric, *The Intellectual and Moral Difference between Man and Man*, he declares, with a seasoning of astronomical imagery:

> Mr. Fell, it is well known, was a firm and strenuous assertor of the peculiar doctrines of Christianity. I will not apply to him the quaint epithets of Orthodox, or Calvinist, terms which, in the estimation of some, imply all that is silly and foolish, and of others, all that is venerable and dignified... Our friend was John Fell, the intelligent, pious, zealous, liberal-minded [a disputed point this], bible Christian. He was too great to be the echo of a shibboleth; he was not destined to be the last expiring spark in the tail of a comet, but to be himself a star of the first magnitude, with satellites, and belts, and rings surrounding him,—I feel myself falling into my own nothingness, and I hurry to my expiring friend... Speaking of the doctrine of the atonement, to a bosom friend, 'I can conceive', said he, 'no resting-point between believing this and believing nothing.'[39]

Reflexion. Wherein it is Demonstrated, upon his own principles, That the Knowledge of God Is Not Attainable by Ideas of Reflexion..., London: J. Watts, 1743, and, *The Knowledge of Divine Things from Revelation...*, 1743. See the references to Ellis in Sell, *John Locke and the Eighteenth-Century Divines*.

[38] *An Introductory Discourse by John Angus, Mr. Fell's Confession of Faith; a Charge by Thomas Davidson; and a Sermon by Thomas Towle B.D. all delivered at the Ordination of the Rev. Mr. John Fell, In Thaxted, Essex, October 24th 1770*, 1770, pp. 9, 11, 16. For Fell (1735-97) see *ODNB*; Jones, *Bunhill Memorials*, p. 46.

[39] *The Intellectual and Moral Difference between Man and Man: A Sermon, preached at The Old Jewry, Sept. 24th, 1797, on occasion of the Death of the Reverend John Fell, formerly of Thaxted in Essex, lately of Homerton in Middlesex. By Henry Hunter, DD, Minister of The Scots Church, London Wall*, London, 1798, pp. 47-8.

If natural theology is silently set in its place in Fell's confession, in Sir Harry Trelawney's it, among other things, is strongly denounced in what is most graciously described as a minority report. He takes a swipe at the Latinate curriculum through which he had passed at Christ Church, Oxford; he laments the fact that 'Our seminaries are under the direction of heathen authors' with the result that 'pulpits are filled with the same stuff—Divinity I dare not call it. A moral essay on the dignity of man, and the beauty of virtue, is all that can be expected from such heathen-taught gentlemen.' The Triune God is set aside, the covenant of redemption forgotten or denied. Instead,

> Natural religion is esteemed the foundation of revealed, as if God had left man to himself, for two thousand years, to try his skill at making a scheme of divinity... What I intend by all this unusual preliminary is an apology for not beginning my confession with some account of what I have discovered by dint of reason. I know nothing naturally but sin—Truth I can receive only from the Scriptures.[40]

Such uncharacteristic tirades apart, the weight of evidence lies in favour of the view that the employment of reason to sustain the theistic position was taken for granted by most of the eighteenth-century Dissenting divines, no matter what their theological or 'denominational'[41] stripe (and, of course, they were not alone in this).

Thirdly, although great heed was paid to the right of private judgement and the appropriate use of reason, there was widespread recognition of the limits of reason on the part of eighteenth-century divines, and by no means all of it was as extremely expressed as Trelawney's view that the only thing he knew naturally was sin. The Puritan John Mason articulated a view frequently to be found among his contemporaries when he wrote, 'We may truly conceive of God, though we cannot fully conceive of Him. We may have right apprehensions of Him, though not an exact

---

[40] *A Sermon at the Ordination of the Rev. Sir Harry Trelawney, Baronet and A.B. (late of Christ Church, Oxford) To the Pastoral Office in the Church of CHRIST, in WEST LOOE, CORNWALL, Preached at SOUTHAMPTON, April 22, 1777. By Edward Ashburner, A.M.,* [1777], pp. 26-7. Something of an ecclesiastical rolling stone, Trelawney (matriculated 1773, aged 17, d. 1834) was raised an Anglican, joined the Methodists, then the Congregationalists, finally returning to the Church of England as a Vicar in Cornwall from 1791.

[41] I place this work in inverted commas as a caution against the supposition that the 'three denominations'—Presbyterian, Congregational and Baptist—were denominations in the modern sense of centrally-organized churchly bodies. The latter are the invention of the nineteenth century. In the eighteenth century there was a good deal of fluidity. The academies frequently trained students of mixed ecclesiastical views; ministers moved fairly frequently from one tradition to another, sometimes because their views changed, sometimes because those of their church members did.

comprehension of Him.'[42] This idea was endorsed by Locke, whose influence upon eighteenth-century divines was considerable (both positively and negatively), in such a remark as the following:

> There being many Things, wherein we have very imperfect Notions, or none at all; and other Things, of whose past, present, or future Existence, by the natural Use of our Faculties, we can have no Knowledge at all; these, as being beyond the Discovery of our natural Faculties, and above *Reason*, are, when revealed, *the proper Matter of Faith.*[43]

Many others, Anglicans and Dissenters alike, concurred. Joseph Butler, for example, has a sermon 'Upon the ignorance of man' the gist of which is that because 'The wisest and most knowing cannot comprehend the works of God, the methods and designs of his providence in the creation and government of the world', we should employ ourselves most appropriately were we to '*Fear God and keep his commandments; for this is the whole concern of man.*'[44] John Norris seems strongly in the line of Locke[45] in arguing that

> the incomprehensibility of a thing is no argument against the belief of it, and, therefore, in the believing of a thing, the proper work of my Reason is not to consider whether it be incomprehensible. But when a thing is proposed to me as from God, all that my Reason has to do in this case is seriously, soberly, diligently, impartially, and, I add, humbly to examine whether it comes with the true Credentials of His authority, and has Him for its real author or no. This is all that Reason has to do in this matter, and when she has done this, she is to rise from the seat of judgment, and resign it to Faith, which either gives or refuses her assent, *not* as the thing proposed is comprehensible or not-comprehensible; but as it is either revealed or *not* revealed.[46]

To all of which William Law adds the consideration that it is not simply that reason's reach is limited; it is also that natural reason is weakened by sin:

> Granting that all matters of religion, must be agreeable to *right*, *unprejudiced* reason; yet this could be no ground for receiving nothing in religion, but what

[42] John Mason, *Select Remains*, reprinted as *Mason's Sayings*, Sheffield: Zoar Publications, c.1974, p. 2. For Mason (1646?-94) see *Alumni Cantabrigienses*.

[43] J. Locke, *An Essay Concerning Human Understanding*, ed. Peter H. Nidditch, Oxford: Clarendon Press, 1975, IV.xviii.7.

[44] J. Butler, *Fifteen Sermons Preached at the Rolls Chapel*, ed. W. R. Matthews, London: G. Bell, 1953, pp. 232, 242.

[45] See Locke, *An Essay Concerning Human Understanding*, IV.xviii.8.

[46] J. Norris, *An Account of Reason and Faith*, London: S. Manship, 1697, pp. 294-5. For Norris see ch. 1 above.

> *human* reason could prove to be necessary; for *human* reason is no more *right unprejudiced* reason, than a sinner is *sinless*, or a man an *angel*.[47]

Since their views have been so frequently caricatured as coldly and exclusively rational, it is of particular importance to observe that the rational Dissenters were in complete accord with the above-mentioned authors on this point. Priestley, for example, points out that

> The mind of man will never be able to contemplate the being, perfections and providence of God, without meeting with inexplicable difficulties... But notwithstanding this, we may know enough of the Divine Being, and of his moral government, to make us much better and happier beings than we could be without such knowledge; and even the consideration of the insuperable difficulties referred to above is not without its use, as it tends to impress the mind with sentiments of reverence, humility and submission.[48]

But whether they think more of the human epistemic condition, or of the noetic effects of sin, all the divines concur that God has not left himself without a witness, and that in the Bible he has spoken definitively. There is not, however, the same measure of agreement as to what he has actually said, as we shall now proceed to discover.

II

It may be appropriate at this point to utter a caution against reading the eighteenth-century English divines anachronistically. In unitedly maintaining the sufficiency of Scripture, they were neither the late nineteenth-century liberals who, in the wake of the more desiccating versions of higher criticism were denounced by P. T. Forsyth: 'Too many are occupied in throwing over precious cargo; they are lightening the ship even of its fuel';[49] nor were they reacting against modern biblical criticism in the way that latter-day fundamentalists did. As to the first point, they had no doubt that the Bible contained a written revelation from God which was religiously necessary to confirm or supplement his revelation in nature. Thus, to invoke Priestley again on the ground that he might be supposed by some to have had least truck with special revelation,

---

[47] *The Life and Works of William Law*, (1762), Bristol: Thoemmes Press, 2000, II, p. 137.

[48] Priestley, *The Theological and Miscellaneous Works*, II, p. xx.

[49] P. T. Forsyth, *The Principle of Authority*, (1913), London: Independent Press, 1952, p. 261. See further on the rise and reception of modern biblical criticism, Alan P. F. Sell, *Theology in Turmoil: The Roots, Course and Significance of the Conservative-Liberal Debate in Modern Theology*, (1983), Eugene, OR: Wipf & Stock, 1998, ch. 2.

> Whether...we consider the precepts of religion, that is, the rules of a virtuous and happy life, the authority requisite to enforce the observance of them, the motives by which they are enforced, or the evidence of their truth, revealed religion has unspeakably the advantage of natural; and therefore so far is the scheme of revelation from being improbable *à priori*, that it must appear such as a wise and good Being...would adopt in preference to any other; being the best adapted to gain his end.[50]

The significance of this is that it underlines the characteristic stance of the Rational Dissenters, namely, that natural religion will not suffice, and this in turn explains Priestley's anxiety not to be mistaken for a deist. Priestley's older contemporary, the Arian Presbyterian, John Taylor of Norwich, added the following considerations:

> Nature and Reason, in their pure and most perfect State, may be sufficient to direct in the Way of Duty, yet when Nature is corrupted, and Reason obscured, or almost quite extinguished, they are by no means sufficient to restore and recover themselves to Knowledge and Obedience of the Truth; because they themselves, are sick and disabled. But it was the primary Intention of Revelation to restore and preserve the Knowledge of God and of his Will in a corrupt and degenerate World.

At the same time, Taylor continues, 'We should always interpret Scripture in a Sense consistent with the Laws of natural Religion; or with the known Perfections of God, and the Notions of Right and Wrong, Good and Evil, which are discoverable in the Works of Creation, and in the present Constitution of Things.'[51]

As to the second point, the divines were not biblical literalists holding a 'crude' dictation theory of the plenary inspiration of the Bible. Lest the more orthodox divines might be suspected of doing precisely this, we may heed the crystal-clear denial of the redoubtable John Gill: 'when we say that the Scriptures are the word of God...we do not mean that it was spoken with an articulate voice by him; or written by the finger of God...'. The Bible is, however, 'the same as if it was written by himself...especially since the penmen were directed, dictated and inspired

---

[50] Priestley, *The Theological and Miscellaneous Works*, XVI, p. 35. Thus, to cite one example from many, in his generally illuminating study of Erskine of Linlathen, Don Horrocks's reference to English eighteenth-century thought is too sweeping: 'The eighteenth century...mindful of the religious extremism of the previous century, and encouraged by the Deists, experienced a general reaction of dissatisfaction and scepticism concerning any approach to religious authority involving special revelation.' See his *Laws of the Spiritual Order. Innovation and Reconstruction in the Soteriology of Thomas Erskine of Linlathen*, Carlisle: Paternoster Press, 2004, p. 138.

[51] J. Taylor, *A Scheme of Scripture Divinity*, 1762, pp. 2, 6. For Taylor (1694-1761) see *ODNB*; Sell, *Dissenting Thought and the Life of the Churches*, ch. 7, and *Philosophy, Dissent and Nonconformity*; G. T. Eddy, *Dr. Taylor of Norwich: Wesley's Arch-heretic*, Peterborough: Epworth Press, 2003.

by himself...'.[52] This, as we saw, is the foundation upon which Gill erected his system of divinity. As for the rational divines, Martin Fitzpatrick has well said that they 'inherited the Protestant attachment to the scriptures as the sole source of religious truth, but if they were to a degree primitivists, they were certainly not fundamentalist'.[53]

Orthodox and rational divines alike agreed with Gill that by the sufficiency of the Scriptures is meant that 'they answer the ends and purposes for which they were written. As, *for doctrine, for reproof, for correction, and for instruction in righteousness*, 2 Tim. iii.16'.[54] For these purposes the Bible is authoritative. Accordingly, Kant's claim that the characteristic feature of Enlightenment man is that he has shunned external authority requires qualification.[55] As far as the eighteenth-century English divines were concerned, the vast majority of them upheld the authority of Scripture, however much they might resist particular interpretations of it, especially if attempts were made to impose these by ecclesiastical authority.

Positively, they regarded it as their right and duty to approach the Bible with their rational antennae as finely tuned as possible. Hence Samuel Bourn's conviction, shared by many, regarding 'every Man's *Right* to inquire into the Sense of the Bible, and his *Obligation* to profess according to his sentiments'.[56] But what might such enquiry entail? In his sermon delivered at the ordination of his nephew, Thomas Amory, and William Cornish, Henry Grove offers some answers. The faithful minister

> may have his favourite opinions which he never thoroughly tried by the standard of scripture; he may have taken things too much upon trust, and substituted the interpretations of scripture by fallible men in the room of the scripture doctrines themselves. Hath he *searched the scriptures diligently*, and that he might have *the mind of Christ* in them? Hath he laid aside all prejudice, as far as the weakness of human nature in this state of imperfection will admit of it? Hath he proceeded with the same care, and in the same method, in order to come at the right meaning of the *inspired scriptures*, that are used in settling the sense of other authors, especially those that are *antient*, *viz*. Considering the occasion, scope and connection of the discourse, comparing one part with another, making plainer and more numerous passages the rule by which to understand those that are more obscure, and fewer...?[57]

---

[52] Gill, *Complete Body of Doctrinal and Practical Divinity*, I, p. 16.

[53] M. Fitzpatrick, 'Toleration and truth', *Enlightenment and Dissent*, I, 1982, p. 4.

[54] Gill, *Complete Body of Doctrinal and Practical Divinity*, I, p. 28.

[55] See Kant's essay, 'What is Enlightenment?', (1784), trans. Mary C. Smith, at www.columbia.edu/acis/ets/CCREAD/etscc/kant.html

[56] [S. Bourn], *A Dialogue between a Baptist and a Churchman*, 1739, p. 122.

[57] Grove, *Ethical and Theological Writings*, I, p. 520.

Underlying all of this is a governing principle, a strategic motive, a theological interest and a pastoral concern. The governing principle is concisely expressed in one of the two theses which Samuel Clarke defended when supplicating for the degree of Doctor of Divinity of the University of Cambridge: 'No Article of the Christian Faith, delivered in the Holy Scriptures, is Disagreeable to Right Reason.'[58] Henry Grove articulated the strategic motive thus: 'Honest men that think for themselves, will value you the more for doing what they themselves have done, though the consequence should be your differing from them in some opinions...'.[59] The theological interest is that 'Christ is the glorious subject of the Gospel revelation'.[60] The pastoral concern is summed up by Priestley thus: 'In Christian assemblies, the Scriptures...are constantly read and explained... It is in consequence of being in a habit of attending to these things, at least on one day in seven, ...that...those things which relate to our well-being hereafter, are not forgotten.'[61]

The more liberal divines were especially eager to draw the distinction between the individual's duty to adopt a reasoned approach towards Scripture understood as sufficient, and the alleged duty of subscription to credal statements devised by others, however authoritative they might be said to be. If we subscribe to such statements, however venerable, we may simply be imbibing the errors of others. Thus, Samuel Bourn writes,

> we never defend Reason in Opposition to *Revelation*; we always own its Insufficiency—but we justify the Use of Reason, in distinguishing a Revelation of God from the Doctrines of Men, and in finding out the true Sense of that Revelation.[62]

Henry Grove cautions against man-made creeds and confessions thus:

> That we may be cautious how we advance any doctrines, without examining whether they are a part of the true *original scheme* of Christianity, let us consider, that while we tie ourselves down to any *human Creeds* and *Confessions*, and *Catechisms*, it is very possible that some part of what we are building upon the common *foundation* may be only *hay and stubble*, not, what we take it for, *gold and silver*...[63]

Samuel Bourn was as blunt as ever:

> It has been the antient Practise for Church Bigots, and Orthodox Zealots to make many Fundamentals in Religion, many Conditions of Salvation, which God never

---

[58] B. Hoadly, ed., *The Works of Samuel Clarke*, 1738, I, p. xvi.

[59] Grove, *Ethical and Theological Writings*, IV, p. 213.

[60] Grove, *Ethical and Theological Writings*, I, p. 528.

[61] Priestley, *The Theological and Miscellaneous Works*, XV, p. 34.

[62] [S. Bourn], *Dialogue between a Baptist and a Churchman*, p. 35.

[63] Grove, *Ethical and Theological Writings*, I, p. 522.

> made so; and then to miscall, curse, excommunicate and damn those who do not believe and submit to them... [W]e *hope* this Anti-Christian Spirit will not haunt the Christian Church much longer...[64]

What incensed John Taylor was that, Reformation having been achieved, Protestants themselves were now requiring subscription to imposed confessional schemes; and he had a name for it:

> Protestant Popery; which, though in some respects better than Romish, is yet more inconsistent, because it renounceth infallibility, and yet imposeth and persecuteth as if infallible;...[and] permitteth the Scriptures to be read, but not understood; or, which is all one, to be understood only in the sense of schemes formed and established by men.[65]

Henry Grove further wondered

> why we must not receive *the Doctrine of Christ* from *Christ himself...* Or why it is thought a necessary qualification in a Minister of the Gospel to understand (at least) the *Original Language*, in which the writings of the *New Testament* were pened, if, in studying these writings, he is tied up to one particular System of Notions...[66]

To all of which Priestley added the consideration that

> to be a Dissenter...is to bear our testimony against the authority and imposition of men in matters of religion, and also against the many abuses and corruptions in Christian doctrine, discipline, and worship, which had their source in the antichristian church of Rome, and which yet remain in our established church.[67]

Priestley was thus firmly in the line of Samuel Bourn, who had earlier remarked that to impose religious tests 'Is to give up *Scripture-sufficiency*, it is to return back into the Tenets of Popery....'[68]

III

What did the divines find when they took their own advice and went straight to Scripture? 'Material for much polemical pamphleteering' is

---

[64] S. Bourn, *The True Christian Way of striving for the Faith of the Gospel. A Sermon preached to a Congregation of protestant Dissenters, Ministers, and Private Christians, at their Yearly Meeting at Dudley in Worcestershire. On May 23rd 1738, being Whitsun-Tuesday*, London: J. Robinson, 1738, p. 9.

[65] J. Taylor, *A Defence of the Common Rights of Christians; and of the Sufficiency and Perfection of Scripture, without the aid of Human Schemes, Creeds, Confessions, &c.*, (1737), London: The British and Foreign Unitarian Association, 1839, p. 14.

[66] Grove, *Ethical and Theological Writings*, IV, p. 166.

[67] Priestley, *The Theological and Miscellaneous Works*, XV, pp. 25-6.

[68] Bourn, *The True Christian Way*, p. 109.

one possible answer. But let us proceed ever calmly, and consider the doctrine of the Trinity, which caused a theological problem to many, and the doctrines of predestination, sin and atonement which, as articulated by the orthodox, seemed to liberal divines to require a determined moral critique.

I am well aware that the doctrine of the Trinity had been discussed in many circles from the Reformation onwards. In England, however, a fresh flurry of activity arose around the doctrine in the 1690s, and further life was injected into the debate by the appearance of Samuel Clarke's *The Scripture Doctrine of the Trinity* (1712).[69] It is also the case that the writings of Locke, which were studied in the Dissenting academies and known to many of the Dissenting divines, reveal their author as less than bold where the affirmation of the Trinity is concerned. This, in fact, puts it mildly: Locke nowhere denied the doctrine, but brought much suspicion upon himself by not confessing it openly. Into this matter I have enquired in some detail elsewhere.[70] In Dissenting circles the ripples from the Salters' Hall conference of 1719 were still being felt, though since the majority of the non-subscribers to the doctrine of the Trinity afterwards published a tract in which they affirmed the doctrine, it was

---

[69] See further T. C. Pfizenmaier, *The Trinitarian Theology of Dr. Samuel Clarke*, Leiden: Brill, 1997.

[70] See Sell, *John Locke and the Eighteenth-Century Divines*, ch. 6. I note that in *'Nice and Hot Disputes' : The Doctrine of the Trinity in the Seventeenth Century*, London: T. & T. Clark, 2003, p. 163, Philip Dixon reveals himself as somewhat less than a careful critic. With reference to Locke's affirmation of the phrase, 'Jesus is the Messiah' as the indispensable minimum of belief, Dixon says that 'Sell tries to construe this slogan as "a portmanteau claim rather than a minimalist one".' 'Tries' is a weasel word here: I think I show this rather clearly, and from Locke's own mouth (pp. 188-9), and Dixon offers no refutation of my stance. I remind him of the reply Locke himself made to his swashbuckling critic, John Edwards: he 'does not observe the difference there is between what is necessary to be believed by every man to make him a christian, and what is required to be believed by every christian' (p. 188). Dixon proceeds to say why it is that I seek to exonerate Locke from the charge of being anti-trinitarian (actually, I do not: I simply say that it cannot be affirmed with complete assurance that he was a Socinian), and brushes aside what is but one of four possible reasons for Locke's reticence, the cumulative effect of which is not inconsiderable, and one of which concerns the sufficiency of Scripture. Dixon continues, 'Even Sell is driven to acknowledge' that Locke never denied the doctrine of the Trinity but never affirmed it; but this form of words suggests reluctance on my part, whereas this is precisely what I was seeking to establish. Finally, in a note, Dixon says, 'Sell claims to find trinitarian speech patterns in *The Reasonableness* but does not display them.' I refer him to the head of my chapter where, from the *Vindication* of *The Reasonableness*, an example of such patterns is placarded (p. 185). It is not my normal custom to reply to critics who *argue* for conclusions other than my own. In this instance, however, I judge that I have been sufficiently misrepresented to justify this attempt to set the record straight.

clear that what they really objected to was credal subscription, and this for a number of reasons, among them the following:

> We saw *no* Reason to think, That a *Declaration* in *other Words* than those of *Scripture*, would serve the Cause of *Peace* and *Truth*; but rather be the Occasion of *greater Confusions* and *Disorders*.[71]

In a word, we are returned to the doctrine of the sufficiency of Scripture (and how frequently the titles of eighteenth-century tomes and tracts begin with the words 'The Scripture Doctrine of...'); and enough has been said to indicate that in venturing into the trinitarian debate the eighteenth-century divines were well aware that they were handling a live—even a potentially dangerous—issue.[72]

As we might expect, Samuel Bourn had his views on the Trinity. His aversion to subscription notwithstanding, he regarded it as 'a *principal Doctrine* of the Gospel; it is also a *plain*, intelligible Doctrine'. He went on to explain that 'if we give up any Points relating to this Doctrine, it is only *Human Explications* of it; and we give them up only because, either wholly Incomprehensible to us, or utterly indefensible by us'.[73] Elsewhere, however, Bourn was more explicit:

> I hold Jesus Christ to be God, or a God... But I can't bring myself to believe in his *Supreme Deity*, because I believe in the same supreme Deity of God the Father; and it appears to me a plain contradiction to say there are two persons or Beings who are both of 'em *Supreme* or *most High* God; and I never yet had Faith eno' to believe two contradictory Propositions.[74]

Not surprisingly, the high Calvinist John Gill smelled the burning rubber of Arianism at this point: 'I take [the anonymous author, Bourn] to be a *Heathen*, and not a *Christian*... since he gives strong intimation of

---

71 *An Authentick Account of Several Things Done and agreed upon by the Dissenting Ministers Lately assembled at Salters-Hall*, London: John Clark, 1719, p. 25. See further on Salters' Hall and related issues, Sell, *Dissenting Thought and the Life of the Churches*, ch. 5; Alexander Gordon, *Addresses Biographical and Historical*, London: Lindsey Press, 1922, ch. 5; F. J. Powicke, 'The Salters' Hall controversy', *Transactions of the Congregational Historical Society*, VII, no. 2, 1916, pp. 110-24; Roger Thomas in C. G. Bolam *et al.*, eds, *The English Presbyterians*, London: Allen and Unwin, 1968, pp. 151-74, and 'The non-subscription controversy amongst Dissenters in 1719: The Salters' Hall debate', *The Journal of Ecclesiastical History*, IV, 1953, pp. 162-86.

72 Apart from anything else, to deny the Trinity was to go against the law of the land.

73 Bourn, *The True Christian Way*, p. 21.

74 [S. Bourn], *A Dialogue between a Baptist and a Churchman*, p. 11.

his belief of a supreme and subordinate Deity....'[75] Gill had already published *A Treatise on the Doctrine of the Trinity* (1731), he returned to the theme with *The Doctrine of the Trinity Stated and Vindicated* (1752), and in his major *Body of Divinity* he sought in his deductive way to 'prove' the doctrine from Scripture once again:

> Having proved the unity of the divine Being...my next work will be to prove that there is a plurality in the Godhead; or, that there are more persons than one, and that these are neither more nor fewer than three; or, that there is a Trinity of Persons in the unity of the divine essence.[76]

Where the Trinity was concerned, Gill felt it incumbent upon him to fight on more than one front. He not only rebutted the Arians, he turned upon the Congregationalist, Thomas Ridgley, accusing him (not entirely fairly) of having denied the doctrine of the eternal generation of the Son—a sure way, thought Gill, of undermining the Trinity.[77]

Unlike Gill, when John Taylor turned to the Scriptures he did not find orthodox Trinitarianism at all. In fact, he did not find a host of terms:

> Entity, Trin-Unity, Quoddity, Quiddity, Formalities, Essentialities, Primalities, Consubstantiality, necessary Emanation, hypostatical Union, mutual Circumplexion, a Trinity of Modes, Communication of Properties, Oeconomical, Co-essential, Co-equal, Co-eternal. These, Christians, are barbarous Sounds, unknown to the pure and divine Mouth of thy Saviour, and the inspired Voice of his Apostles, whereby the Principles of Religion, in themselves noble and heavenly, simple and plain to every Capacity, have been worked into pompous Nonsense and profound Darkness.[78]

---

[75] J. Gill, *An Answer to the Birmingham Dialogue-Writer Upon the following subjects: The Divinity of Christ, Election, Original Sin, Free Will, Irresistible Grace, Imputed Righteousness, Perseverance, and Baptism*, 1739, p. 6.

[76] Gill, *A Complete Body of Doctrinal and Practical Divinity*, I, p. 187.

[77] See J. Gill, *Sermons and Tracts*, (1814), Choteau, MT: Old Paths Gospel Press, 1997, VI, p. 219. For Ridgley (c.1667-1734) see *ODNB*; Wilson, *History and Antiquities*, II, pp. 72-82; Jones, *Bunhill Memorials*, pp. 230-2; Sell, *Philosophy, Dissent and Nonconformity*. For his chapter on eternal generation see Gill's *A Body of Divinity: Wherein the Doctrines of the Christian Religion are Explained and Defended. Being the Substance of Several Lectures on the Assembly's Larger Catechism*, (1731), New York: Robert Carter, 1855, I, pp. 160-6. His case is that the biblical texts advanced in support of eternal generation in fact refer to Christ as God-man, Mediator. He insists that he intends to uphold the orthodox doctrine of the Trinity. Ridgley is on my list of divines who merit a mini-resurrection, see my forthcoming *Hinterland Theology: Some Reformed and Disseting Adjustments*, Carlisle: Paternoster, also in this series.

[78] J. Taylor, *A Narrative of Mr. Joseph Rawson's Case: or, An Account of several Occurrences relating to the Affair of his being excluded from Communion with the*

One is tempted, however anachronistically, to think that at this point Taylor is a mirror-image of latter-day fundamentalists, for whereas they might say, 'It's in the Book and therefore we must believe it', he is affirming with equal confidence 'It's not in the Book and therefore we are not bound to it.' Interestingly, at this point Gill, frequently regarded as a Puritan 'throw-back' emerges as the more 'advanced' philosopher, for he understands that a concept may be scriptural even if particular terms are not to be found in the Bible: 'Words and phrases, though not literally expressed in Scripture, yet if what is meant by them is to be found there, they may be lawfully made use of; as some respecting the doctrine of the Trinity....'[79] None of which impressed Priestley who, by the end of the century was openly defending Unitarianism on the basis of the sufficiency of Scripture:

> There is no subject on which the Scriptures are so clear and emphatical as they are on this. The worship of one God, and that one God the maker of all things... The doctrine of the strict Unity of God was considered as the most fundamental principle of all religion, by the whole body of the *Jews*, in our Saviour's time... [W]hile the *Father*, the *Son* and the *Holy Spirit*, separately considered, are each of them maintained to be true and very God, without the least deficiency of any one attribute of divinity, they cannot, in common sense or common arithmetic, make less than three gods.[80]

But if more liberal divines had intellectual difficulties with the orthodox doctrine of the Trinity, they were in many cases filled with righteous indignation by the perceived slight upon God's love and justice resulting from received doctrines of predestination, original sin and atonement. Hence their earnest moral critique, to which I now turn.[81]

The question how far the doctrine of predestination as promulgated in the eighteenth-century was in accord with that of Calvin himself cannot here detain us.[82] What we do need to notice, however, is that during the eighteenth century the moral protest against the doctrine was lodged from more than one direction, notably from the 'Arian' Presbyterians and from the evangelical Arminians, of whom John Wesley was the chief. In order to make clear what the liberals and Wesley were reacting against we may once again invoke John Gill, a distinguished representative of the high Calvinist breed.

Congregational Church in Nottingham. With a Prefatory Discourse in Defence of the Common Rights of Christians, London: M. Ferrier, 2nd edn, 1742, p. 13.

[79] Gill, *A Complete Body of Doctrinal and Practical Divinity*, I, p. xv.

[80] Priestley, *The Theological and Miscellaneous Works*, XVI, pp. 479-80.

[81] For the contribution of eighteenth-century English Dissenters to moral philosophy, see Sell, *Philosophy, Dissent and Nonconformity*, ch. 3.

[82] See further ch. 12, below.

Having set out from the claim that Christ is 'God's first and chief elect',[83] Gill turns to the rest of humanity. He readily grants that we are in no position to say that particular individuals are elect or repropbate, and we should ever remember that 'no man, be he ever so vile, is out of the reach of powerful efficacious grace'.[84] Election

> is to be understood as the choice of certain persons by God, from all eternity, to grace and glory; it is an act by which men are chosen of God's good will and pleasure, before the world was, to holiness and happiness, to salvation by Christ, to partake of his glory, and to enjoy eternal life, as the free gift of God through him... [85]

All of this having been fully discussed, Gill, in biblicist-*cum*-rationalist fashion, then says, 'I shall prove that there is a non-election, or rejection of some of the sons of men, when others were chosen; and, indeed, from the election of some, may fairly be inferred, the non-election of others.'[86] He further explains that by preterition is meant God's passing by of some; by pre-damnation is meant 'God's appointment, or pre-ordination of men to condemnation for sin'.[87] In all of this 'The efficient cause is God; it is the Lord, that makes all things for his own glory',[88] and the 'moving cause' is 'the good pleasure of his will'.[89]

With many aspects of this doctrine more liberal divines found themselves in disagreement, but with none more so than the decree of reprobation. Samuel Bourn was not one to conceal his policy in such matters:

> I think I ought to acknowledge that there are Doctrines which I am not able to defend; and therefore I give them up: They appear to me...inconsistent with Gospel *Declarations*... A very good Account may be, and has been given of the many Texts which speak of *Predestination* and *Election*; without drawing in a Scheme so dishonourable to God.[90]

In less rumbustious style, Henry Grove, never a willing controversialist (he was not present at Salters' Hall), advanced a number of considerations against the received doctrine. First, it reflects adversely on the character of God:

---

[83] Gill, *A Complete Body of Doctrinal and Practical Divinity*, I, p. 253.

[84] Ibid., p. 254.

[85] Ibid., p. 258.

[86] Ibid., p. 277.

[87] Ibid., p. 279.

[88] Ibid., p. 281.

[89] Ibid., p. 282.

[90] Bourn, *The True Christian Way*, p. 20.

> The *love* of God [so it is said]...is his making choice of some to be the objects of his munificence, while others, and they the vastly greater number, are left destitute of all power to emerge out of that miserable condition into which they are fallen through no fault of their own. Is there not too much reason to say, that this notion of the *love* of God to man is utterly unworthy of him? What does the Deity discover by such a *love* (if it must be called by that name) but *uncontrolable power*... Yes, it may be said, he shews his *goodness* too to his *elect*. Tell me how, if in all that he does for them he hath no direct regard to their happiness, but determines their happiness rather than misery, just to shew his *arbitrary* will and pleasure, not from any pleasure he hath in beneficent actions as such?[91]

Secondly, the unacceptable arbitrariness in the predestinarian doctrine whereby the final destinies of individuals are secured before the beginning of time destroys the notion of moral good and evil, thereby leading to immoral living,

> for, if once a man believes that all actions alike are indifferent, as to any moral good or evil that is in them, any praise or blame they deserve, there can be no room for *conscience*... *Again*, if all things...are in pursuance of absolute decrees, it is certain that men are not *free agents*; and if men are not *free*, so as to have a *power* to do good or evil, they cannot be *obliged* to do the one, and to forbear the other; nor can anything they do be properly good or evil, in a *moral sense*, being the pure effect of necessity.[92]

Thirdly, there is the pastoral consideration that if a person who believes in the absolute decrees is 'of a temper naturally timerous', questions his election and accuses himself of lack of faith,

> It is to no purpose to tell him, that he must not give way to such thoughts...this is a very strange way of administering comfort to a sorrowful spirit, and instead of freeing such a one from his melancholy, only sinks him the deeper in it. While others of a more robust and sanguine complection...gladly lay hold of the handle afforded them by these notions, and draw this conclusion...that, since God acts out of mere *sovereignty*, and not from any regard to the *reason* and *fitness* of things...therefore whatsoever sins they have committed...they have none to answer for...than which there cannot be a more fatal delusion.[93]

From the evangelical Arminian side came Wesley's tract, *Predestination Calmly Considered* (1752). The doctrine had been causing puzzlement in Wesleyan circles, but John Gill was especially in Wesley's

---

91 Grove, *Ethical and Theological Writings*, IV, p. 101; cf p. 219 n.

92 Ibid., pp. 216-17, n. Cf. Priestley, *The Theological and Miscellaneous Works*, XIII, p. 446.

93 Grove, *Ethical and Theological Writings*, III, pp. 26-7.

sights.[94] Wesley does not deny that in the Bible believers are called the elect, or that there is a class of reprobate persons. What he strongly objects to is the idea that there is unconditional election, for this implies unconditional reprobation; and this he could tolerate no more than could the liberal divines, to whom, on other matters, he was so stoutly opposed. He threw down the gauntlet before Gill thus:

> Find out any election which does not imply reprobation, and I will gladly agree to it. But reprobation I can never agree to while I believe the Scripture to be of God; as being utterly irreconcilable to the whole scope and tenor both of the Old and the New Testaments.[95]

Never one to resist a challenge, Gill took up his pen against Wesley's 'harangue', and plied the Arminian with a great variety of biblical evidence in support of the Calvinistic understanding of predestination. His general point is that

> There is nothing comes by chance to God, nothing done without his knowledge, nor without his will or permission, and nothing without his determination; every thing, even the most minute thing, respecting his creatures, and what is done in this world in all periods and ages of time, is by his appointment...[96]

His particular complaint against Wesley is that while the latter states that 'election is a divine appointment of *some men* to eternal happiness', and refers to this as an eternal decree, he then proceeds to contend that the election is conditional. This Gill strongly denies:

> it is true, indeed, that they who are real believers, are the elect of God; but then the reason why they are the elect of God is not because they are believers, but they become believers because they are the elect of God; their faith is not the cause or condition of their election, but their election is the cause of their faith...[97]

---

[94] It would take us too far afield to launch a blow by blow account of this intricate debate. Reference may be had to Sell, *The Great Debate*, ch. 3; and to Herbert Boyd McGonigle, *Sufficient Saving Grace. John Wesley's Evangelical Arminianism*, Carlisle: Paternoster Press, 2001, ch. 8. The latter is among the most competent doctoral theses it has been my privilege to examine. For a pro-Gill account see George M. Ella, *John Gill*, ch. 11.

[95] J. Wesley, *The Works of the Rev. John Wesley M.A.*, ed. T. Jackson, London, 3rd edn. 1872, X, p. 211.

[96] Gill, *Sermons and Tracts*, V, p. 103.

[97] Ibid., pp. 108-9.

For good measure, Gill draws Wesley's attention to Article VII [in fact, XVII] of the Church of England, to which Wesley had subscribed, which clearly states the doctrine of predestination.[98]

If the liberal divines were concerned by the way in which, as they saw it, the doctrine of predestination slighted God's love and justice, they were no less appalled by the doctrine of original sin and its implications for the doctrine of the atonement.

We may once again take our bearings from John Gill's system. He staunchly upholds the doctrine of original sin: 'The sin, fall, and ruin of man were of himself. It was not through ignorance and want of knowledge that Adam fell....'[99] But fall Adam did, and his guilt is imputed to all his descendants. Hence 'the corruption of nature derived unto [Adam's posterity] from him; by which is meant the general depravity of mankind, of all the individuals of human nature, and of all the powers and faculties of the soul, and members of the body'.[100]

Against this standard Calvinistic view, the Presbyterian John Taylor famously and vigorously protested in his treatise (note the first three words of the title), *The Scripture-Doctrine of Original Sin* (1740). He finds that the consequences of Adam's transgression are referred to on only five occasions in the Bible, and he subjects each instance to close examination, concluding thus:

> THE Sum of all that we have found is this: That upon the Sin of Adam God subjected him and his Posterity to Sorrow, Labour and Death; from which Death we are delivered, and are restored to Life at the Resurrection, by the Grace of God having Respect to the Righteousness and Obedience of Christ. And furthermore, That God in Christ hath bestowed upon us Mercy and Gifts, Privileges and Advantages, both in this and a future World, abundantly beyond the reversing of any Evils we are subject to in Consequence of Adam's Sin.[101]

Noticeably absent from this conclusion is any reference to the imputation of Adam's guilt. Indeed, the suggestion of such imputation was precisely what Taylor found abhorrent, and in an Appendix he sets down his moral objections to the doctrine of original sin:

> Is it not highly injurious to the God of our Nature, whose Hands have fashioned and formed us, to believe our Nature is originally corrupted, and in the worst Sense of Corruption too?... Doth not the Doctrine of *Original Sin* teach you to transfer your

---

[98] Gill's reply is *The Doctrine of Predestination Stated and Set in the Scripture-Light, In Opposition to Mr. Wesley's Predestination Calmly Consider'd*, London: G. Keith, 1752. By a slip, he directs Wesley to Article VII, not to XVII.

[99] Gill, *A Complete Body of Doctrinal and Practical Divinity*, I, p. 457.

[100] Ibid., p. 470.

[101] J. Taylor, *The Scripture-Doctrine of Original Sin Proposed to Free and Candid Examination*, London: J. Wilson, 1740, p. 63.

> Wickedness and Sin to a wrong Cause? Whereas in Truth you ought to blame or condemn *yourself alone* for any wicked Lusts, which prevail in your Heart, any evil Habits you have contracted, any sinful Actions you commit, you lay the whole upon *Adam*.... What can be more destructive of Virtue than to have a Notion that you must, in some Degree or other, be necessarily vicious? And hath not the common Doctrine of *Original Sin* a manifest Tendency to propagate such a Notion?... Is not this Doctrine hurtful to the Power of Godliness, not only as it filleth Mens Heads with frightful Chimeras, and loads their Consciences with the heaviest Fetters of Error, but also as it diverts their Thoughts from the heavenly and substantial Truths of Religion?[102]

Not surprisingly, Taylor's stout defence of individual responsibility under God did not go unchallenged. In a pamphlet entitled, *The Doctrine of Original Sin* (1757), John Wesley charged him with overthrowing the foundations of scriptural Christianity, while from across the Atlantic Jonathan Edwards charged Taylor with overlooking, in individualistic fashion, human solidarity, and argued that unless original sin be posited we cannot explain how every individual, as a matter of fact, freely chooses what is evil.[103] None of this moved Priestley, who in 1791 summarized the moral protest (in a no less *a priori* way than Gill asserted the opposite) thus: 'We may receive harm by means of one person, and benefit by means of another; but no sin of the former, or righteousness of the latter, can be considered as ours, in the eye of an equitable and just God.'[104]

Priestley's reference to imputed righteousness brings us to a final illustration, the atonement. Here Gill is at his most circular: human beings are corrupt and 'The necessity of redemption by Christ, and of regeneration by the Spirit of Christ, shows that men must be in a corrupt state.'[105] From this state they cannot rescue themselves, but God, whose love is everlasting, has provided redemption through Christ his Son. With his own blood he has voluntarily paid the price for our sins:

> Now this price is paid into the hands of God, whose justice is offended, whose law is broken, and who is the lawgiver, that is able to save and to destroy; and against whom all sin is committed; and who will not clear the guilty, unless his justice is satisfied; for he is the judge of all the earth who will do right; wherefore Christ is said to redeem men unto God by his blood. The price of redemption, which is the

---

[102] Ibid., pp. 249, 250-1, 253-4.

[103] J. Edwards, *The Great Christian Doctrine of original Sin Defended*, in *The Works of Jonathan Edwards* (1834), reprinted Edinburgh: Banner of Truth Trust, 1974, I, pp. 146-233. See further, David Weddle, 'Jonathan Edwards on men and trees, and the problem of human solidarity', *Harvard Theological Review*, XVII, 1974, especially pp. 155-75; Sell, *Dissenting Thought and the Life of the Churches*, pp. 245-9.

[104] Priestley, *The Theological and Miscellaneous Works*, II, p. 389.

[105] Gill, *A Complete Body of Doctrinal and Practical Divinity*, I, p. 471.

> blood of Christ, was paid unto God, whereby redemption from vindictive justice was obtained...[106]

The great transaction done, God's justice is satisfied, the redeemed are adopted as children of God, the elect are sanctified and everlastingly saved, and God is glorified.

Time and again Priestley rises up in rebuttal of this Anselmic, satisfaction, doctrine of the atonement. 'The general tenor of Scripture by no means favours it', he declares, 'for the Scriptures every where represent men to be entitled to the favour of God solely on account of their personal moral qualifications. The doctrine of *satisfaction for sin* clashes with those absolute and unlimited declarations of God's free mercy to sincere penitents, which the Scriptures every where abound with....'[107] Positively, Priestley writes,

> To die, as Christ did, in the glorious cause of truth and virtue; to die, as he did, in order to shew us an example of patiently suffering death for our religion, and the good of mankind, and in firm hope of a resurrection to a future and eternal life; to die, as he did, in express attestation of his own divine mission, by his manifest resurrection from the dead, and as the fullest proof of that doctrine, by means of which sinners are continually reconciled unto God, was a noble sacrifice indeed.[108]

It takes little imagination to think up such orthodox polemical titles as *Emaciated Exemplarism Exploded*; and while I have not discovered such a title, the sentiments indicated were widely touted in opposition to Priestley's views. Undeterred, Priestley was not slow to emphasize the practical implications of his position:

> We who profess what we wish to be considered as *rational christianity*, have least of all any just cause for a deficiency in that tempter, and a want of those good works, which our religion requires. We, depending on the free mercy of God to the penitent, reject the idea of being saved by any righteousness that is not our own. We believe that no man can obey the laws of God for another, or suffer the punishment due to the crimes of another; and we disclaim any belief of any thing whatever standing in the place of moral virtue. We believe the gospel both to contain a sufficient rule of life, and also sufficient motives to the observance of it.[109]

---

106 Ibid., II, pp. 9-10.

107 Priestley, *The Theological and Miscellaneous Works*, VII, p. 291; cf. pp. 398, 476.

108 Ibid., VII, p. 398. Cf. pp. 207, 294.

109 *A View of Revealed Religion; A Sermon preached at the Ordination of The Rev. William Field of Warwick, July 12, 1790 by Joseph Priestley LL.D., F.R.S. With a Charge Delivered at the same Time by the Rev. Thomas Belsham*, Birmingham 1790, pp. 36-7.

Here is set one of the significant problems for subsequent theology: How may we deny that we are saved by our own righteousness whilst at the same time repudiating the punishment of one person for another's sins—and all of this in the context of a view of human solidarity?

Enough has been said to indicate the way in which more rational divines lodged intellectual and moral objections to the positions adopted by high Calvinists who were, in their own way, equally rationalistic. Before offering some concluding reflections on the English Enlightenment as a whole, there is one further topic which, in the interests of accuracy and balance, must be addressed.

IV

Since many divines of all theological stripes entered with such gusto into doctrinal polemics, and issued such a considerable number of books and pamphlets, it is easy to overlook the fact that most of them, as far as we can tell, studiously avoided controversial points in their sermons. Thomas Wright Hill, who had been raised in the Old Meeting, Kidderminster, described the congregation as comprising a mixture of Calvinists, Arminians and Arians. Benjamin Fawcett, a pupil of Philip Doddridge and an Arian, ministered there from 1745 to 1780. Of him Hill writes that 'he managed so far to conceal his opinions as to be very popular with his hearers, a large chapel being crowded at all the Sabbath-day services'.[110] Hunsworth, who quotes these words, finds it incredible that Fawcett would be able to conceal his beliefs from his intelligent hearers. But if it would be cynical to suppose that Fawcett trimmed in order to protect his stipend, it is by no means impossible to believe that he simply followed widespread practice in not introducing controversial topics into the pulpit. He may even have thought that such matters should not be church-dividing.

The advice which John Withers gave Micaijah Towgood, a Presbyterian high Arian,[111] at his ordination was followed by many:

---

[110] Quoted by George Hunsworth, *Baxter's Nonconformist Descendants; or Memorials of the Old Meeting Congregational Church Kidderminster*, Kidderminster: Edward Parry, 1874, p. 41. For Fawcett (1715-80) see *ODNB*.

[111] By a high Arian I mean one who thought it appropriate to offer worship to Jesus Christ. The Arian Presbyterian, Richard Price, for example, did not think it fitting to do this. For Towgood (1700-92) see *ODNB*; James Manning, *A Sketch of the Life and Writings of the Rev. Micaijah Towgood*, 1792; Anon., *Observations on the Rev. James Manning's Sketch of the Life and Writings of the Rev. Micaijah Towgood*, 1792; Jerom Murch, *A History of the Presbyterian and General Baptist Churches in the West of England*, 1835, pp. 432-7; Sell, *Dissenting Thought and the Life of the Churches*, ch. 7.

> As for the *Matter* of your Sermons, I conceive the weighty Matters of the Gospel Repentance towards God, and Faith in the Lord Jesus Christ, ought principally to be insisted on. Your Business is not to fill Mens heads with nice and useless Speculations, but to influence their Hearts with the Love of Piety and Vertue, and to enamour them of these divine and Godlike Graces by which they may resemble the glorious Author of their Beings. Not to make Men subtil Disputants, but exact and holy Walkers.... What little Advantage hath the Protestant Interest gain'd by those eager fierce Disputes which have been set on Foot, concerning the Divine Counsels and Decrees, which some have marshall'd up with as much Exactness as if they had been Privy-Counsellors to the Almighty.... We should insist upon the great and weighty *Matters of the Law, Faith, Judgment* and *Mercy*; not the *Annise, Mint* and *Cummin*, that grew in our own Gardens.[112]

It would seem that Towgood heeded the advice, for his biographer later wrote that 'The main scope and tenor of his preaching was practical. He led not his flock for nourishment, to the dry and barren hills of cold and unedifying speculation.'[113]

Joseph Priestley likewise declared that 'it has always been my opinion, and my practice has been agreeable to it, to keep all subjects of religious controversy, as much as possible, out of the pulpit...'.[114] He clearly knew himself well enough to include the qualification, because on occasion he found it quite impossible to hold his tongue. Thus, for example, on undertaking the pastorate of the New Meeting, Birmingham, one of whose previous ministers was Samuel Bourn, to whom Priestley pays warm tribute, he delivered a sermon of John 17:16 in which he managed to denounce the doctrinal corruption of the Christian ages, notably those of the Roman Church (antichrist), uphold the unity of God, repudiate the worship of Christ, and advocate Unitarianism.[115]

The inability of preachers to resist an homiletic rebuke was not confined to the more liberal divines. In his sermon on *The Doctrine of Grace cleared from the Charge of Licentiousness*, John Gill charges Arminians first with immorality and then with doctrinal error:

> Who are they that walk abroad in the fields on Lord's-days? Who are they that frequent taverns and public houses, when they should be attending the house of

---

[112] *A Charge given to Mr. Micaijah Towgood, at his Ordination in Moreton Hampstead, Devon, August 21. 1722. By John Withers*, 1723, pp. 19-20.

[113] Manning, *A Sketch*, pp. 92-3. Manning further reminds us of important doctrinal differences within the broadly liberal party: '[Towgood's] religious opinions were as opposite to those of Dr. Priestley, as those of Mr. Whitefield and Mr. Wesley; but this did not prevent his entertaining a very high opinion of his abilities and integrity' (p. 128). Towgood differed from Priestley *inter alia* on the materiality of the soul, its sleep between death and the resurrection, the pre-existence of the Logos and the liberty of moral agents.

[114] Priestley, *The Theological and Miscellaneous Works*, XV, p. 23.

[115] Ibid., XV, pp. 31-45; cf. p. 81.

> God? Are these the men who are commonly called Calvinists, the asserters of the doctrine of grace? Should the examination be strictly made, the above persons will be found, if not to a man, yet by far the greater part, Arminians, if capable of giving any account of their sentiments... Who are the deniers of Christ's person, of his proper deity and equality with the Father, of his plenary satisfaction and expiatory sacrifice, of his imputed righteousness, and the efficacy of his blood? The deniers of these things are the men that turn the grace of God into lasciviousness; either by asserting it to be a licentious doctrine; or by treating the doctrine of special grace in a wanton and ludicrous manner, scoffing at it, and lampooning it; or, by making the doctrine of grace universal, extending it equally alike to all mankind, and thereby harden and encourage men in sin.[116]

For all his pulpit pugilism, Priestley, like other liberal divines, regularly tackled the great subjects. Like Henry Grove before him, whose *Works* include three substantial consecutive sermons on the resurrection,[117] Priestley, no less than the high Calvinist John Gill,[118] regularly returned to this theme,[119] and also to those of the second coming, final judgment[120] and heaven.[121] Indeed, although he believed that 'From the light of nature we are able to make out a tolerable system of natural religion, as far as it respects the *duty of men* in this life',[122] it was the deliverances of revelation, supremely those concerning the future state, that most sharply distinguished Christianity from deism—a distinction upon which Priestley was determined to insist.[123]

A further point to which divines of all theological persuasions devoted great attention was the necessity that religious profession go hand in hand with uprightness of life. Said Henry Grove, 'Christianity *is a system composed of two other systems*, one, *of things to be* believed, *the* other *of things to be done; and between these* two *there is such a perfect harmony* [that] *to a serious and judicious mind it must appear to be* a frame of Religion put together by a divine hand.'[124] At the ordination of Isaac Smithson, John Taylor declared that 'any Knowledge, or Persuasion, merely speculative, how exact or excellent soever in itself, will be of little

---

[116] Gill, *Sermons and Tracts*, II, pp. 72-3.

[117] Grove, *Ethical and Theological Writings*, I, pp. 361-465.

[118] Gill has two substantial sermons on the resurrection in *Sermons and Tracts*, VI, pp. 1-69.

[119] See, for example, Priestley, *The Theological and Miscellaneous Works*, XVI, pp. 287-311.

[120] See, for example, ibid., XV, pp. 82; 472-3.

[121] See, for example, ibid., XV, pp. 32, 413, 452.

[122] Ibid., II, p. 341.

[123] See ibid., XVII, p. 99.

[124] Grove, *Ethical and Theological Writings*, I, pp. 493-4.

Significancy to any of us, especially to a Minister, if it is not worked upon the heart; and reduced to Practice'.[125]

On the death in 1743 of the Congregational minister, John Hubbard, John Guyse said that Hubbard had embraced 'that Scheme of Evangelical Doctrines, which are commonly known by the Name of *Calvinistick*', but immediately went on to point out that 'his heart seem'd most earnestly set upon reducing all his Principles to *Experience* and *Practice*, in himself and others. For *this* he laboured *zealously* in the pulpit....'[126] Of the Baptist, Bernard Foskett, Caleb Evans wrote,

> His religious principles, which were those commonly called *Calvinistical*, he ever maintained with a steady christian zeal. But though he was strenuous for what he apprehended to be the truth; yet he was fond of no extreme. While he strongly asserted the honours of free grace, he earnestly contended for the necessity of good works; preaching duty as well as privilege, and recommending holiness as the only way to happiness.[127]

James Scott, the Presbyterian/Congregationalist, who was among others called from Scotland to the north of England with a view to dispelling the 'cloud of Socinian darkness' in that region, and who later became the first principal of Heckmondwike Academy, was said by Jonathan Toothill, his pupil, to be one who

> preached the Doctrines of original Sin, and redemption by Christ—of...the necessity of the Spirit's operations in renewing the Soul—of Perseverance in holiness to everlasting life. He also insisted largely upon the *necessity* and *end* of good works, and was not only *careful to maintain* them in preaching, but in practice.[128]

---

[125] *A Sermon and Charge, delivered, the Former by the Revd. Mr. Milner of Yarmouth; the Other by the Revd. Mr. Taylor of Norwich. At the Ordination of the Revd. Mr. Smithson, at Harlestone in Norfolk, Nov. 11, 1755*, London: J. Waugh, 1755, p. 34.

[126] J. Guyse, *A Sermon Occasion'd by the much lamented Death Of the Reverend and Learned Mr. John Hubbard, Who departed this Life July 13, 1743, in the Fifty-first Year of his Age*, London: John Oswald, 2nd edn. [1743], pp. 31-2. Hubbard (1692-1743) was theological tutor at Homerton from 1740.

[127] C. Evans, *Elijah's Exclamation. A Sermon Occasioned by the Death of The Rev. Hugh Evans, M.A. Who departed this Life, March 28, 1781, In the 69th Year of his Age*, Bristol: W. Pine, [1781], pp. 25-6 n. For Foskett (1685-1758) see *Bristol Baptist College. 250 Years 1697-1929*, published by the College, [1929], pp. 17-19; Moon, *Education for Ministry*; Roger Hayden, 'The contribution of Bernard Foskett', in William H. Brackney, Paul S. Fiddes and John H. Y. Briggs, eds., *Pilgrim Pathways. Essays in Baptist History in Honor of B. R. White*, Macon: Mercer University Press, 1999, pp. 189-206; Sell, *Philosophy, Dissent and Nonconformity*, 42-3, 82, 102.

[128] J. Toothill, *The Foundation of the dying Christian's Triumph, in the prospect of Nature's Dissolution. A Sermon, Preached, Feb. 2, 1783, at Heckmondwike in Yorkshire;*

Finally, we shall do well to note the great emphasis placed by divines of all persuasions upon the life of devotion. John Gill, for example, has a winsome sermon on *The Presence of God, What it is, and the Means by which it may be Enjoyed*, and another in which he instructs his hearers in the art of prayer.[129] Henry Grove has two sermons and two essays on prayer,[130] while Samuel Bourn, however much he enjoyed an intellectual fight—especially if there were Baptists to be teased—nevertheless paid considerable attention to catechetics (he devised his own catechisms)[131] and to fostering the devotional like of his flock.[132] In the latter connection he published a book of prayers in which he had regard to all age-groups and to the several stations in life of his church members.

In a few lines in his Amory-Cornish ordination charge the peaceable Henry Grove sums up the doctrinal, ethical and practical stance of many of his peers and successors:

> We the Ministers of Christ are under special obligations to seek his honour and interest, in regard we are the *messengers of Christ...* And what is our message, but *to beseech sinners in Christ's stead, to be reconciled unto God?...* To promote the Religion of the blessed Jesus both in the knowledge and practice of it...? To explain the method of reconciliation, and the blessings and terms of the Gospel covenant? To persuade those who make a profession of Christianity, to live agreeably to their profession?...[and] to assist them in acquiring all those divine virtues and qualifications which are necessary to prepare them for a part in the heavenly felicity? This is what we are to endeavour with the greatest fervency and application of mind. Not to teach men how to *dispute* and *wrangle*, but to *live well*; ...to gain them to Christ, and to the love of eternal goodness. We must not *preach ourselves, but Christ Jesus our Lord.*[133]

On Occasion of the Death of the Rev. Mr. James Scott, Late Pastor of the Church, and Tutor to an Academy at that Place, Huddersfield: J. Brook, 1783, p. 28. For Scott (1710-83) see K. W. Wadsworth, *Yorkshire United Independent College*, London: Independent Press, 1954, pp. 34-55.

[129] Gill, *Sermons and Tracts*, III, pp. 247-263; IV, pp. 257-284.

[130] Grove, *Ethical and Theological Writings*, II, pp. 159-291.

[131] See S. Bourn, *Religious Education Begun and Carried on in Three Catechisms*, 1748.

[132] See S. Bourn, *The Young Christian's Prayer Book. Dedicated to the Young People in Birmingham and Coseley*, 1733, and The *Christian Family Prayer Book: Or Family Prayers for morning and Evening, with a Variety of Occasional Forms: Prefaced with a Discourse Representing the Reasonableness, Beauty, Pleasure, and Usefulness of Family Religion*, 4th corrected edn, 1770. See also his *Twenty Sermons on the most Serious and Practical Subjects of the Christian Religion. Fitted for the Use of Private Families*, 2nd edn, 1757.

[133] Grove, *Ethical and Theological Writings*, I, pp. 514-15.

V

Although I have drawn upon a few only of the many Dissenting divines who published tracts, books and sermons in England during the eighteenth century, the selection has been representative and, I believe, sufficient to allow some 'calm' conclusions to be drawn regarding the Enlightenment in its English dress.

As promised, I have adduced evidence to show that divines of all doctrinal persuasions within Old Dissent brought reason to bear upon matters of faith. Gill represented those who constructed a biblical-rationalist system on the basis of doctrinal truths held *a priori*, though with *a posteriori* adhesions. Others, more directly in the wake of Locke, breathed the cosmological air of the eighteenth century, and this not only in their more formal writings, but also in sermons and ordination confessions. They all proceeded with deference to the right of private judgment and the sufficiency of Scripture, and all of them allowed an important place to special revelation. Where they differed was in their interpretations of Scripture. The more liberal divines brought biblical and ethical considerations to bear upon such received doctrines as the Trinity, predestination and original sin, the terms in which the latter two were expressed being regarded as slighting God's love and justice and eradicating human responsibility. It has also become clear that, polemical contexts apart, for the most part (Priestley being a somewhat irrepressible exception in this connection—though he applauded the policy) divines of all persuasions covered a range of doctrines in their preaching, and were equally concerned to draw out the practical implications of belief, and to nurture their flocks in Christian teaching and devotional practice.

On two matters, announced at the outset, I have yet to comment. First, I declared that the English Enlightenment gave a boost to older notions concerning the right of private judgment, and that these, accruing from the Revival as much as from the rational divines, were to have an adverse effect on ecclesiology. As to the older notions: it is sometimes said that these derive especially from the Reformation. The argument is that Luther made it possible for every individual to have direct recourse to God and to the Bible. However, it seems to me that in the intellectual context then prevailing, accessibility to Scripture in the language of the people was a product of the Renaissance, and that Luther's primary concern was not so much the individual's right of private judgment ('shall it be lawful for every fantastical spirit to teach what himself listeth?', asked Luther[134]), as the right of God, so to speak, freely to

[134] M. Luther, *Commentary on St. Paul's Epistle to the Galatians*, London: James Clarke, 1953, p. 41. It should not be forgotten that the Reformation doctrine of the priesthood of all believers concerns not the priesthood of every individual conceived as a solitary atom, but the priesthood of all the believers together: it is a corporate concept.

address his people through the Word, regardless of the ecclesiastical apparatus. Hence P. T. Forsyth's pungent remarks:

> Salvation is personal, but it is not individual... What did the Reformation stand for? Not for religious individualism. But I hear someone asking in the back of his mind, Was not the Reformation the charter of private judgment and individual independence? It was nothing of the kind. It was the charter of personal direct faith and its freedom. What the Reformation did was to turn religion from being a thing mainly institutional into a thing mainly personal. The reformers were as strong as their opponents about the necessity of the Church for the soul—though as its home, not its master. They were not individualists. Individualism is fatal to faith. It was the backbone of the rationalism and atheism of the French Revolution. The Reformation stands for personal religion and social religion and not for religious individualism.[135]

It cannot, however, be denied that the personal was tilted in the direction of the individualistic during the English Enlightenment. This tilting, as we shall see, did not come from one side alone.

On the one hand, I wish to side with all those of the English Enlightenment who lodged a moral protest against *expressions of* Christian doctrine which turned God into a tyrant or human beings into automata. This is an Enlightenment gift of which, as processed through the work of such nineteenth-century writers as Thomas Erskine of Linlathen and John McLeod Campbell in Scotland and S. T. Coleridge and F. D. Maurice in England, we today—and not least the wanton Enlightenment-bashers—are the beneficiaries. If sometimes heated theological skirmishes are the price to be paid to secure this benefit, it is a price worth paying. While my own preference is for orthodox doctrine purged, as it can be, of grotesque adhesions and informed by modern biblical scholarship, it is at least an open question how the eternal scales will settle if in one pan are placed orthodox doctrines formally and hypocritcally assented to, and in the other, (unharmful[136]) heterodox views achieved and embraced with integrity.

On the other hand, it must be said that during the English Enlightenment the personal recourse to God encouraged and facilitated by the Reformation could and sometimes did take an individualistic turn. It is important to recognize that more than the liberal and rational divines were implicated in this. Indeed, in terms of long-term adverse ecclesiological consequences it is exceedingly difficult to say whether more damage was done by the privatizing liberals or the privatizing

---

[135] P. T. Forsyth, *The Work of Christ*, (1910), London: Independent Press, 1958, pp. 119-20.

[136] I supply the adjective by way of cautioning against the popular view that 'It does not matter what you believe so long as you are sincere.' We have seen too many sincere tyrants to fall for that sort of sentimentalism.

evangelicals. If the former emphasized the individual's conscientious judgment, the latter emphasized the individual's personal experience as evidential of God's activity within. Here we have a harbinger of Romanticism, and the most casual glance at John Wesley's sermons will make the point. Thus, for example, Wesley contends that true religion lies in 'the hidden man of the heart'. He continues:

> A man may be orthodox in every point; he may not only espouse right opinions, but zealously defend them against all opposers; he may think justly concerning the incarnation of our Lord, concerning the ever-blessed Trinity, and every other doctrine contained in the oracles of God; he may assent to all the three creeds...and yet it is possible he may have no religion at all, no more than a Jew, Turk, or Pagan.[137]

What is required is repentance and a casting of oneself upon the Saviour Jesus Christ, the Lamb of God who takes away the sins of the world. Those who do this receive the spirit of adoption; they are raised to a new birth by the Spirit; the new birth alone, and not the performance of religious duties, avails.[138]

The ecclesiological impact? Well, just as liberal individualists may land in fellowships comprising those whose beliefs range from liberal Christian through theist to Buddhist and further (all of which raises the question of the permissible degree of doctrinal tolerance within the Church), so those who came to make the entry to the Church turn upon a personal experience of conversion diluted the traditional emphasis upon the covenant people of God which had been the ecclesiological mainstay of Old Dissent in all its forms, and ushered into the churches those who had been saved if not always baptized. It is not difficult, for example, to show that during the rapid post-Revival expansion of English Congregationalism during the nineteenth-century the number of local church covenants declined whilst the number of chapels dramatically increased.[139] Not surprisingly, church meeting, the primary plank of local church polity was a related casualty. When the English Congregational minister and scholar, F. J. Powicke, reflected on the Evangelical Revival he declared with some justification that it 'would have worked out far better for the future of religion in England if a reasonable response to the light of truth represented by the maligned Arian movement, could have

---

137 J. Wesley, *Sermons on Several Occasions. First Series*, London: Epworth Press, 1946, p. 75.

138 Ibid., pp. 173, 520, 526.

139 See Sell, *Dissenting Thought and the Life of the Churches*, ch. 1, especially pp. 64-7.

been conjoined with a reasonable respect for tradition as represented by a true orthodoxy'.[140]

Coming down to our own time, Margaret Canovan has observed that 'One of the main aspects of the current return to the Enlightenment is...the rise of much less sociological and more individualistic ways of thinking';[141] and with reference to the churches the Canadian sociologist, Reginald Bibby, has stated the obvious: 'Religious groups...have frequently catered to individualism, providing Canadians with an array of items in response to what amounts to consumer demand.'[142] That consumerism is not necessarily tied to contemporary materialism is, however, clear from the following remark of Priestley:

> Dissenters in London, having no connexion with their minister, except in the character of a *preacher*, come at length to attend to nothing but his eloquence and delivery; and if these are not sufficient to keep them attached to any place, they go for their *entertainment* (for it deserves no other name) elsewhere...[143]

At which point one is tempted to agree with the Preacher: 'there is nothing new under the sun'.[144] The warning of F. J. Powicke's teacher, D. W. Simon, is still very much to the point: 'Two principles, condition sound, healthy, vigorous progress, namely, the individual or independent, and the organic or corporate. If either is exaggerated, the ultimate result is stagnation....'[145]

Finally, if the English Enlightenment as seen in the writings of the divines of Old Dissent was neither an unmitigated curse nor an unmixed blessing, how can we explain the blanket denunciations from which I set out?[146] The answer may lie in one or both of the following possible explanations. It may be that those perpetrating the denunciations have been blinded by the truly anti-religious motivations of some, especially

---

[140] F. J. Powicke, 'English Congregationalism in its greatness and decline (1592-1770)', in A. Peel, ed., *Essays Congregational and Catholic issued in Commemoration of the Centenary of the Congregational Union of England and Wales*, London: Congregational Union of England and Wales, [1931], p. 209. For Powicke see ch. 1 above.

[141] M. Canovan, 'Reason recycled: the Enlightenment today', *Enlightenment and Dissent*, IX, 1990, p. 11.

[142] Quoted in *Canada Lutheran*, V, March 1990, p. 27.

[143] Priestley, *The Theological and Miscellaneous Works*, XV, p. 54.

[144] Ecclesiastes 1:9.

[145] Quoted by F. J. Powicke in his *David Worthington Simon*, London: Hodder and Stoughton, 1912, p. 278.

[146] Knud Haakonssen finds Peter Gay's interpretation of the Enlightenment as 'the rise of modern paganism' influential but one-sided. See Haakonssen, ed., *Enlightenment and Religion*, p. 1, where the reference is to P. Gay, *The Enlightenment: An Interpretation*, New York: Vintage, 1966.

French, Enlightenment thinkers, and have misread the part for the whole; and/or they may be reading back into the preceding century the products of nineteenth-century positivism, atheism and agnosticism with their attack on the supernatural, and the post-Darwinian denial of final causes. What is clear is that even if particular cases of anti-religious Enlightenment polemics can be found (and, truth to tell, they are not in short supply), this only serves to strengthen my case which is that the *English* Enlightenment, and hence Enlightenment thought as a whole, is too varied and too interesting to be either utterly denounced or uncritically lauded. The moral is that in those who explore this intriguing and multi-faceted intellectual territory 'calmness' is *de rigueur*.

CHAPTER 4

The Gospel its own Witness: Deism, Thomas Paine and Andrew Fuller

Andrew Fuller (1754–1815) is widely and rightly remembered as a prominent founder and first secretary—the 'ropeholder'—of the Baptist Missionary Society (f. 1792).[1] Historical theologians and students of eighteenth-century thought may recall him as one who, in *The Gospel Worthy of All Acceptation* (1785)—a work written under the influence of Jonathan Edwards—repudiated the hyper-Calvinism of those who contended that since salvation was for the elect alone there could be no general offers of the Gospel. Fuller's ground for upholding the free offer is summarized in the sub-title of his book: *The duty of sinners to believe in Jesus Christ*.[2] But there is another aspect of Fuller's work which is not so frequently recalled, or, if recalled, is not discussed in any detail.[3] The pastor whose only formal education was at the village school in Soham, and whose life was spent in ministry there and, from 1782, at Kettering,

---

[1] See Brian Stanley, *The History of the Baptist Missionary Society 1792-1992*, Edinburgh: T. & T. Clark, 1992, *passim*.

[2] For the context of this complicated and thorny issue see Alan P. F. Sell, *The Great Debate. Calvinism, Arminianism and Salvation*, (1982), reprinted Eugene, OR: Wipf and Stock 1998, chs. 2 and 3.

[3] This is true whether we consider modern students of Fuller or of Paine. As to the former, an exception is E. F. Clipsham, 'Andrew Fuller and Fullerism: a study in evangelical Calvinism. Fuller as a theologian,' *Baptist Quarterly*, XX no. 6, April 1964, pp. 271-274. Phil Roberts declines to consider Fuller's anti-deistic and anti-Socinian works because 'they were not primarily theological treatises but attempts to demonstrate the ethical superiority of Calvinism versus Socinianism and Deism'. See 'Andrew Fuller', in Timothy George and David S. Dockery, eds., *Baptist Theologians*, Nashville, TN: Broadman Press, 1990, p. 138 n. 36. But in the eighteenth century that was an intensely theological business! In any case, as we shall see, Fuller makes many specifically theological points in his anti-deist tract. For his anti-Socinian writings see Alan P. F. Sell, *Testimony and Tradition: Studies in Reformed and Dissenting Thought*, Aldershot: Ashgate, 2005, ch. 6. As to the latter, Fuller's name is not indexed in Samuel Edwards, *Rebel! A Biography of Thomas Paine*, New York: Praeger Publishers, 1974; A. J. Ayer, *Thomas Paine*, London: Secker & Warburg, 1988; Mark Philp, *Paine*, Oxford: Oxford University Press, 1989; Edward H. Davidson and William J. Scheick, *Paine, Scripture and Authority*, Bethlehem, PA: Lehigh University Press, 1994; Jack Fruchtman, Jr., *Thomas Paine Apostle of Freedom*, New York: Four Walls Eight Windows, 1994.

was also a dogged controversialist. He published rebuttals of Socinianism, Sandemanianism, universalism and deism.[4] It is with the last that we are here concerned. In 1799 Fuller published *The Gospel its own Witness* in reply to Thomas Paine's two-part work, *The Age of Reason* (1794, 1795). A more pungent opponent Fuller could scarcely have had, as we shall see. But first we must adjust our sights to the complicated phenomenon of deism.

I

It cannot be denied that in some quarters the deists have received a bad press. The erstwhile Anglican, Leslie Stephen (1832–1904), declared that 'The deist writings are but shabby and shrivelled little octavos, generally anonymous, such as lurk in the corners of dusty shelves, and seem to be the predestined prey of moths.'[5] While there are undoubtedly anonymous deist tracts, there are also the substantial contributions of Collins, Tindal, Toland and, supremely, Paine, all of which are studied to this day. For his part, the Congregational theologian A. M. Fairbairn (1838–1912) was as lofty as ever: the deists, he informs us, were 'irrepressible men like Toland, men of mediocre culture and ability like Anthony Collins, vulgar men like Chubb, irritated and disagreeable men like Matthew Tindal, who conformed that he might enjoy his Oxford fellowship and wrote anonymously that he might relieve his conscience'.[6] We need not comment on this *ad hominem* outburst. Finally, in our own time, and without reference to the stated desire of many deists to assist the unlettered to discriminate between truth and superstitious error, Gordon Rupp described the deists as 'a self-conscious elite, and, with the exception of Thomas Chubb, the tallow chandler of Salisbury, upper class; aristocrats like Shaftesbury and Bolingbroke, and the landed gentleman Anthony Collins, dons like Wollaston, Woolston and Tindal, and the medical man, Thomas Morgan'.[7] (We might, however, note that Thomas Morgan, 'a poor lad in a farmer's house', was given a free

---

4 See now Michael A. G. Haykin, ed., *'At the Pure Fountain of Thy Word': Andrew Fuller as an Apologist*, Carlisle: Paternoster Press, 2004, especially Tom J. Nettles, 'Christianity Pure and Simple: Andrew Fuller's Contest with Socinianism', pp. 139-173, Michael A. G. Haykin, 'Andrew Fuller and the Sandemanian Controversy', pp. 223-236, Barry Howson, 'Andrew Fuller and Universalism', pp. 174-202, and Michael A. G. Haykin, '"The Oracles of God": Andrew Fuller's Response to Deism', pp. 122-138.

5 L. Stephen, *History of English Thought in the Eighteenth Centuy,* (1876), New York: Harcourt, Brace & World, 1962, I, p. 72.

6 Quoted by Robert Mackintosh, 'Apologetics,' *Encyclopaedia Britannica,* 11th edn., 1910–1911, p. 191.

7 Gordon Rupp, *Religion in England, 1688-1791,* Oxford: Clarendon Press, 1986, p. 277.

education by the Dissenting minister, John Moore.[8]) Chubb—and here we encounter the difficulty of pin-pointing deists—was in some ways closer to the non-deist Samuel Clarke, the moderate Anglican Arian, than Shaftesbury and Bolingbroke were to deism. All of which underlines the fact that the deists did not constitute anything so precise as a school of thought, or even a clearly-defined movement. Rather, they were writers who in a general way imbibed prevalent scepticism regarding some of the claims of orthodox Christianity, revelation, Christian 'evidences' as generally conceived, the authority of the Church, and the probity of the priesthood, whilst being unlike one another on many points of detail. We should also be alive to the fact that in that nick-naming age less than careful pamphleteers might apply 'deist' as a term of abuse to those whose doctrinal views they ardently repudiated. Thus, for example, in his *View of the Principal Deistical Writers* (1757) John Leland lumps Hobbes and Hume together with others more generally regarded as deists.[9]

One frequently-alleged point of agreement must be completely disavowed: the best-known late-seventeenth and eighteenth-century deists were *not* united in the belief that God, having created the world, then retreated from it and left it to its own devices, remaining transcendent above it. On the contrary, their major point was that God was the God of the natural order, which testified to his power and wisdom. While some of the earlier deists allowed a supernatural revelation provided it were sanctioned by reason, later writers, notably Tindal, declared supernatural revelation redundant. To put the point otherwise, while it may be argued that deism paved the way for modern naturalism and secularism, its representatives of the period which concerns us were deeply attached to the notion that God is to be known in the book of nature: they were not opposed to religion as such, however much some of them deplored some of its manifestations and intellectual commitments;[10] and they did not wish to be mistaken for atheists.

It is true that Samuel Clarke (1675–1729) describes one species of deist who 'pretend to believe in the existence of an Eternal, Infinite, Independent, Intelligent Being; and, to avoid the name Epicurean Atheist, teach also that this Supreme Being made the World: Though at the same time they agree with the Epicureans in this, that they fancy God does *not at all concern* himself in the *government* of the World, nor has any regard

---

[8] So Leslie Stephen, 'Thomas Morgan,' *DNB*.

[9] For the usage of 'deism' see, for example, Frank E. Manuel, *The Eighteenth Century Confronts the Gods*, Cambridge, MA: Harvard University Press, 1959; Robert E. Sullivan, *John Toland and the Deist Controversy*, Cambridge, MA: Harvard University Press, 1982, ch. 7.

[10] For a lucid discussion of this point see further Peter Byrne, *Natural Religion and the Nature of Religion*, London: Routledge, 1989.

to, or care of, what is done therein.'[11] This position, Clarke insists, 'leads necessarily and by unavoidable consequence, to *plain Atheism*',[12] because if God has no regard to what is done in the world, 'it will follow that he is not an Omnipresent, All-powerful, Intelligent and Wise Being; and consequently, that he Is not at all'.[13] But Clarke's allusions at this point are to classical sources, not to his contemporaries.

It is also true that by the nineteenth century, when a number of related terms were being more precisely defined, the disputed view came to be known as deism. Thus, for example, one standard encyclopedia of the period defines 'deism' as 'that view of God, which, as against atheism, recognizes his real existence; as against pantheism, his distinctness from the world; and, as opposed to theism, represents him not merely as transcendent above the world, and distinct from it, but also as separate, in the sense, that, having once created the world, he is not immanent in it as its providential ruler and guide, but allows it to pursue an independent course'. But the author immediately and properly adds, 'This philosophical definition is, however, of recent date.'[14] On this matter the erudite Robert Flint may have the last word, and lead us to our next point: He refers to the 'historical application' of 'deism' to the English deists, pointing out that it is wrong to 'represent them as having denied that God was present and active in the laws of nature. This is erroneous and unfair. One or two of them may have done so, but certainly what as a body they denied was merely [Flint's 'merely' makes the denial seem less significant than it is] that God worked otherwise than through natural laws.'[15]

---

11 Samuel Clarke, *A Discourse concerning the Unchangeable Obligations of Natural Religion, and the Truth and Certainty of the Christian Revelation,* London: W. Botham, 1706, p. 19. Clarke found three other varieties of deist: 1. Those who believe in the being and providence of God, in God's governing power in the natural order, but who deny that God is concerned with the morally good or evil actions of human beings: 'these things depending, as they imagine, merely on the arbitrary constitution of humane Laws' (pp. 26-27). 2. Those who believe in God's providence and moral governance, but who are prejudiced against the idea of immortality (p. 32). 3. Those who believe in providence, moral government and immortality, but who do so only so far as the light of natural reason permits, and without appealing to divine revelation (p. 37).

12 Ibid., p. 23.

13 Ibid., p. 24.

14 G. V. Lechler, 'Deism', in Philip Schaff and Samuel Macauley Jackson, *A Religious Encyclopedia: or Dictionary, etc.,* (1882), New York: Funk & Wagnels, 3rd edn. 1894, p. 621 (b). Peter Byrne reiterates the point in 'Deism', in Alister E. McGrath, *The Blackwell Encyclopedia of Modern Christian Thought,* Oxford: Blackwell, 1993, p. 103.

15 Robert Flint, *Anti-Theistic Theories,* Edinburgh: William Blackwood, 6th edn. 1899, p. 443.

II

We are now in a position briefly to characterize, in chronological order of representative works, some of the main lines of deism as it flowed down to Paine and Fuller. In attempting this intricate task we should have in mind the following contextual points. First, behind the appeal of a number of eighteenth-century deists to reason and natural revelation there lay the memory of the previous century's civil strife and religious unrest—some of it occasioned by the appeals of sectaries to special revelations. The deists desired no repetition of this. Equally, many of them were at best cool towards the 'enthusiasm' of the Evangelical Revival, whose beginnings the later deists witnessed. Thirdly, now that the Toleration Act of 1689 had, for all its limitations, legalized Christian traditions other than that of the Church of England there was no one ecclesiastical authority to which appeal on religious questions could be made. This posed the question, again with regard to societal coherence, whether natural religion might provide common ground—even universally agreed common ground—(analogous to the generalizations of science which the 'new' scientists were drawing from their observations of the world's phenomena) on which those of many doctrinal persuasions might stand. None of which prevented critics of deism from alleging that deists sought a wider toleration than was currently available (Roman Catholics, Jews and unitarians not enjoying the benefits of 1689) only in order to subvert the state by ruining the established Church. That this was the desire of atheists, deists, fanatics and the 'spawn of jesuits' (note the imprecision of scurrility) was precisely the view of the anonymous author of a polemical tract of 1705, *An Essay upon Government, Wherein the Republican Schemes reviv'd by Mr. Lock, Dr. Blackal &c. are fairly consider'd and refuted.* Two years later the nonjuror, Charles Leslie (1650–1722) accused Tindal and Collins of espousing Locke's moderately progressive views on toleration for the same purpose.[16] With these considerations and cautions in mind we may turn to the deists themselves.[17]

While we cannot here delve into the continental hinterland of English deism, or trace the intellectual indebtedness of particular deists in detail, we may say in general terms that there were many currents in the intellectual air they breathed. From Francis Bacon (1561–1626) there flowed a strong current of scientific empiricism. It was the task of the scientist, he maintained, not to seek final causes, but to proceed inductively from known facts. While he distinguished between knowledge

---

[16] See [Charles Leslie], *The Second Part of the Wolf Stript of his Shepherds Cloathing*, London, 1707, p. 3.

[17] I have provided a brief general sketch of deism in *Dissenting Thought and the Life of the Churches. Studies in an English Tradition*, Lewiston, NY: Edwin Mellen, 1990, ch. 2.

and faith, natural philosophy and theology—especially with respect to their terms of reference—he did not, as some of his opponents contended, repudiate the idea of a final cause. On the contrary, at the beginning of his celebrated essay 'Of Atheism' he famously declared,

> I had rather beleeve all the Fables in the *Legend,* and the *Talmud,* and the *Alcoran,* then that this universall Frame, is without a Minde. And therefore, God never wrought Miracle, to convince *Atheisme,* because his Ordinary Works convince it. It is true, that a little Philosophy inclineth Mans Minde to *Atheisme*; But depth in Philosophy, bringeth Mens Mindes about to *Religion:* For while the Minde of Man, looketh upon Second Causes Scattered, it may sometimes rest in them, and goe no further: But when it beholdeth the Chaine of them, Confederate and Linked together, it must needs flie to *Providence,* and *Deitie.*[18]

With this conclusion, as with Bacon's method and his denunciation of 'scandalous priests',[19] many deists were in general accord.

From Thomas Hobbes (1588–1679) some deists learned that no revelation could run contrary to reason, and from him, too, some of them imbibed anti-clerical iconoclasm. But from the concluding chapters of *Leviathan* (1651), with their anti-Roman Catholic strictures against purgatory, transubstantiation and the like, those of a sceptical turn of mind could also learn to challenge doctrines traditionally received as scriptural—the incorporeality of spirits, for example—on the ground that they are not taught in the Bible. This is consistent, on the one hand, with Hobbes's strictures upon 'the vain philosophy of Aristotle' with its talk of separated essences, and on the other with his staunch materialism, according to which '(...the *universe,* that is, the whole mass of things that are), is corporeal, that is to say, body...that which is not body, is no part of the universe...'.[20]

By exalting reason as the 'candle of the Lord'—lit by God and receiving God's light—even the very differently-tempered Cambridge Platonists, stalwart upholders of the interdependence of reason and faith, whose prominent representative Benjamin Whichcote (1609–83) lamented the way in which 'Bacon, Hobbes, Puritans and Prelatists, agreed in treating philosophy and theology as things wholly different in kind',[21] opened the way to deistic constructions of their phrase with which they

18 F. Bacon, *The Essayes or Counsels, Civill and Morall,* London, 1625, pp. 90-91.

19 Ibid., p. 94.

20 T. Hobbes, *Leviathan,* in William Molesworth, ed., *The English Works of Thomas Hobbes of Malmesbury,* London: J. Bohn, 1839, III, pp. 674, 672.

21 Quoted by W. R. Inge, *The Platonic Tradition in English Religious Thought,* London: Longmans, 1926, p. 48. See further on the Cambridge Platonists, ch. 1 above.

themselves would not have been in sympathy.[22] Note, for example, the terms in which Toland described reason: 'Reason is not less from God than Revelation; 'tis the Candle, the Guide, the Judg he has lodg'd within every Man that cometh into this World'.[23]

Notwithstanding what I have just said concerning empiricism and the inductive method, the 'grandfather of English deism',[24] Herbert of Cherbury (1583–1648), rested on five *innate* principles, namely, that God exists; that he is to be worshipped; that we honour him by the practice of virtue; that repentance is obligatory upon human beings; and that we are liable to *post mortem* reward and punishment. The validity of these *a priori* principles is immediately known independently of revelation (which Herbert did not repudiate, but did not need); they are universal and certain. He inveighed against those clerics who, for their own unscrupulous ends, had obscured these fundamental principles. Herbert's views are found in his *De Veritate* (1624) and his posthumous *De Religione* (1663). D. P. Walker has pointed out that the 1645 edition of the former work tightens the five principles—now described as a perfect circle from which nothing may be subtracted and to which nothing may be added—in such a way as to make it more difficult to regard them as a foundation on which might be erected a Christian superstructure.[25] Later deists for the most part imbibed Herbert's five principles but generally, in empiricist fashion, construed them in an *a posteriori* manner as deliverances of experience.

To Herbert's list of five principles Charles Blount (1645–93), in *The Oracles of Reason* (1693), adds two more: God 'governs the World by Providence'; and 'our Worship consists in Prayer to him and Praise to him'.[26] He prefixes his points with a clear definition: 'Natural Religion is the Belief we have of an Eternal Intellectual Being, and of the Duty which

---

22 I have elsewhere suggested that there is a clearer line to the deists *via* the 'ever memorable' Oxford Latitudinarian author John Hales (1584–1656) than *via* the Cambridge Platonists, for Hales allowed reason to be the arbiter between truth and falsehood. See his *Of Enquiry and Private Judgment in Religion,* in *The Works of the Ever Memorable Mr. John Hales of Eaton,* Glasgow: Robert and Andrew Foulis, 1765, III, pp. 141-166; Alan P. F. Sell, 'Platonists (ancient and modern) and the Gospel', *Irish Theological Quarterly,* XLIV no. 3, 1977, pp. 161-162.

23 John Toland, *Christianity Not Mysterious: or, A Treatise Shewing that there is Nothing in the Gospel Contrary to Reason, nor Above It: and That no Christian Doctrine can be properly call'd a Mystery,* London: S. Buckley, 1696, p. 146.

24 Though Peter Byrne has drawn attention to elements in Herbert's thought which distance him from subsequent Enlightenment thinkers. See his *Natural Religion and the Nature of Religion,* ch. 2. See also R. D. Bedford, *The Defence of Truth,* Manchester: Manchester University Press, 1979; David A. Pailin, 'Herbert of Cherbury and the deists', *Expository Times,* XCIV, 1983, pp. 196-200.

25 D. P. Walker, *The Ancient Theology,* London: Duckworth, 1972, p. 167.

26 C. Blount, *The Oracles of Reason,* London, 1693, pp. 195-6.

we owe him, manifested to us by our Reason, without Revelation or positive Law.'[27] He ridicules clerics for their myopia, and seeks to undermine the credibility of biblical miracles. His reiterated appeal is to the morality or otherwise of believing that such and such is the case. By this criterion deists could include pre- and non-Christians among the faithful—a degree of ecumenism to which more conservative divines were by no means open. In a section entitled, 'A Summary Account of the Deist's Religion', Blount discusses the manner of worshipping God, and declares that proper worship is 'Not by a Mediator; for, first it is unnecessary; *Miserecordia Dei* being *sufficiens justitiae suae*. 2ly, God must appoint this Mediator, and so was really reconciled to the World before. And 3ly, a Mediator derogates from the infinite mercy of God, equally as an Image doth from his *Spiritualitie* and *Infinitie*.'[28] With some justice Blount has come to be regarded as a forerunner of English free thought.[29]

In 1696 *Christianity Not Mysterious* was published by John Toland (1670–1722).[30] His argument is summed up in the continuation of his title: *Showing that there is nothing in the Gospel contrary to Reason nor above it, and that no Christian doctrine can properly be call'd a Mystery.* Here we have a clear rationalistic line, the phrase 'nor above it' ruling our any appeal to supernatural revelation. He hopes that Christians will not be offended by him when he endeavours 'to confirm and elucidate Revelation... I hope to make it appear, that the Use of Reason is not so dangerous in Religion as it is commonly represented...'.[31] He seeks to show that when the Bible is brought to the bar of reason, insofar at it is vindicated, secure faith in its deliverances is justifiable. If the doctrines of the Gospel are the word of God they cannot be contrary to reason,[32] and they certainly cannot be certified by appealing to mystery, since there is nothing above reason in the Gospel.[33] In Toland's view, 'Reason is the only Foundation of all Certitude...'.[34]

---

27 Ibid., p. 195.

28 Ibid., p. 89.

29 See further, J. A. Redwood, 'Charles Blount (1654–93), Deism, and English Free Thought', *Journal of the History of Ideas,* XXXV, 1974, pp. 490-495.

30 For Toland see R. E. Sullivan, *John Toland and the Deist Controversy*; S. H. Daniel, *John Toland: His Methods, Manners and Mind,* Kingston and Montreal, Ontario: McGill-Queen's University Press, 1984.

31 Toland, *Christianity Not Mysterious,* p. viii.

32 Ibid., p. 23.

33 Ibid., p. 67.

34 Ibid., p. 6.

With Anthony Collins (1676–1729)[35] the presuppositions of deism, namely, that human beings are free to employ their reason, and that they are competent to discover truth for themselves (an implicit check upon the authoritarian imposition of beliefs), are brought to the fore. His *Discourse of Freethinking occasioned by the Rise and Growth of a Sect called Freethinkers* appeared in 1713. He here contends that those who decline to assent to self-evident truth manifest a 'distemper'd State of Mind', and are prey to 'the Dictates of artificial designing men or crack-brain'd Enthusiasts'.[36] He proceeds on the basis of the following definition: 'By Free-Thinking then I mean, The Use of the Understanding, in endeavouring to find out the meaning of any Proposition whatsoever, in considering the nature of the Evidence for or against it, and in judging of it according to the seeming Force or Weakness of the Evidence.'[37] Among the matters upon which people have the right to think freely—the denials of the enemies of free thought notwithstanding—are, 'the Nature and Attributes of the Eternal Being or God, of the Truth and Authority of Books esteem'd Sacred, and of the Sense and meaning of those Books; or, in one word, of Religious Questions'.[38] He feels that great benefits will accrue to society if only people will employ their reason in the way he recommends. By way of encouragement he holds before his readers a galaxy of those he claims as freethinkers, from Socrates, 'the divinest Man that ever appear'd in the heathen World',[39] through Erasmus and others, to Locke.[40]

In his *Discourse of the Grounds and Reasons of the Christian Religion* (1724), Collins asks, 'Of what use is it to consult *reason* and *Scripture* at all, as any means of information, if we are not, upon conviction, to follow their dictates? And what *principles* of religion are men to *profess* (which all say must be) *openly,* and act upon, but those, whereof they are convinc'd?'[41] He charges clergymen with the duty of integrity: 'they cannot act more effectually against the design of their own profession, than either by being silent as to the discoveries they make, or by preaching and writing contrary to their own light...'.[42] Collins pioneers a sceptical approach to the alleged facts of the Bible, and implies that if

---

35 For Collins see James O'Higgins, *Anthony Collins. The Man and his Works,* The Hague: Martinus Nijhof, 1970.

36 A. Collins, *A Discourse of Free-Thinking, occasion'd by the Rise and Growth of a Sect call'd Free-Thinkers*, London, 1713, p. 4.

37 Ibid., p. 5.

38 Ibid., p. 32.

39 Ibid., p. 123.

40 Ibid., p. 177.

41 A. Collins, *A Discourse of the Grounds and Reasons of the Christian Religion,* London, 1724, p. xiv.

42 Ibid.

Scripture is unreliable, apologetic arguments based on the appeal to the fulfilment of prophecy are seriously weakened. Indeed, appealing to the scholarship (though not to the ecclesiastical loyalty) of Hugo Grotius, he concludes that Old Testament prophecies were not fulfilled by Christ. Indeed, 'these *proofs* taken out of the *Old,* and urg'd in the *New* Testament, being sometimes, either not to be found in the *Old*, or not urg'd in the *New*, according to the literal and obvious sense, which they seem to bear in their suppos'd places in the *Old,* and therefore not proofs according to scholastick rules...'[43] they are patient of allegorical interpretation only. In Part Two he argues that in his *Essay towards restoring the True Text of the Old Testament* (1722) the now deposed Anglican Arian divine William Whiston (1667–1752),[44] who wishes to show that the text of the Old Testament is 'the very same now that it ever has been from the utmost antiquity', undercuts his own argument by adverting to the corruptions of the text and to the inconsistencies between it and that of the New Testament.[45]

Thomas Woolston (1669–1733), in his *Six Discourses on the Miracles of our Saviour* (1727–30), reveals his agreement with Collins as to the alleged evidential value of prophecy. He believes that the controversy over that issue 'will end in the absolute Demonstration of Jesus's *Messiahship* from Prophecy, which is the only way to prove him to be the Messiah'.[46] But the method of proof requires that the prophecies be construed not literally, but allegorically, after the manner of the early Fathers; and this despite the fact that 'this way does not please our ecclesiastical *Writers* in the Controversy'.[47] Woolston now follows up, like Blount before him, with an analogous attack upon apologetic arguments which assume the evidential value of biblical miracles. To his own satisfaction he finds that the accounts of fifteen miracles are deficient and incredible, but he does not, on this account, wish to deny the Messiahship of Jesus. But miracles, no less than prophecies must be interpreted allegorically, after the manner of the early Fathers. He finds that some of the miracles recorded in the gospels never took place, but are 'prophetical and parabolical Narratives of what will be mysteriously and more wonderfully done by him'.[48] Indeed, to construe the miracles literally is to 'imply Improbabilities and Incredibilities, and the grossest Absurdities, very dishonourable to the name of Christ'.[49] His first

---

43 Ibid., 39.

44 Whiston joined the General Baptists in 1747.

45 A. Collins, *A Discourse,* pp. 270-271.

46 T. Woolston, *A Discourse on the Miracles of our Saviour, in View of the Present Controversy between Infidels and Apostates,* 5th edn., London, 1728, p. 1.

47 Ibid., p. 2.

48 Ibid., p. 3.

49 Ibid., pp. 19-20.

Discourse ends with the following bold statement: 'The History of *Jesus's* Life, is an emblematical Representation of his spiritual Life in the Soul of Man; and his Miracles are Figures of his mysterious Operations. The four Gospels are in no Part a literal Story, but a system of mystical Philosophy or Theology.'[50] He sustains this position through his discourses, and in the sixth, devoted to showing that the resurrection of Jesus is a 'monstrous and incredible Miracle',[51] he argues that when Jesus appealed to his own works and miracles as a testimony to his authority, he 'did not properly and ultimately refer to those done in the *Flesh,* but to those mystical ones he would do in the *Spirit,* of which those done in the Flesh are but mere Types and Shadows'.[52] He concludes by emphasizing that all he has done has been for 'the Demonstration of the messiahship of our Spiritual Jesus...'.[53]

In 1730 Matthew Tindal (1656–1733), who claimed his place among the 'True Christian Deists', published the work which, by common consent, most adequately sets forth the principles of deism. His title, *Christianity as Old as the Creation, or the Gospel a Republication of the Religion of Nature,* precisely announces his theme. By 'natural religion' Tindal means 'the Belief of the Existence of a God, and the Sense and Practice of those Duties which result from the Knowledge we, by our Reason, have of him and his perfections; and of ourselves, and our own Imperfections; and of the relation we stand in to him and our Fellow-Creatures; so that the *Religion of Nature* takes in every thing that is founded on the Reason and Nature of things'.[54] 'True Religion' is thus 'a constant Disposition of Mind to do all the Good we can; and thereby render ourselves acceptable to God in answering the End of his Creation.'[55]

Tindal argues that God treats all alike in the sense of endowing everybody with the capacity to discern and pursue the path of duty. His will is immanent throughout the created order (so far is Tindal from the allegedly 'deist' view that God, having set the cosmic process going, has retreated from it). It is 'the reason of things, or the relation they have to each other' which 'teaches us our Duty in all cases whatever'.[56] Supernatural revelation and appeals to the miraculous are thus redundant: he argues 'That the Religion of Nature is absolutely perfect; and that

---

50 Ibid., p. 65.

51 Woolston, *A Sixth Discourse*, 1729, p. 5.

52 Ibid., p. 51. So some miracles at least were done in the flesh? Woolston does not seem here to be at his most logical.

53 Ibid., p. 71.

54 M. Tindal, *Christianity as Old as the Creation,* 3rd edn, London, 1732, p. 11.

55 Ibid., p. 18.

56 Ibid., p. 16.

external Revelation can neither add to, not take from its perfection.'[57] We do not need an incarnate Lord, or an atoning work at the Cross. What Jesus does is simply to republish the religion of nature.

Since 'God requires nothing for his own sake',[58] and since the law of nature is clear, 'Religion, even in relation to the Worship of God, as it is a reasonable Service, [cannot] be any thing, but what necessarily flows from the consideration of God, and the creatures.'[59] As for our moral duty, no supernatural revelation of it could improve upon the revelation of it in nature, because only commands perceived to be reasonable are obligatory, and such perception is within the sphere of natural religion.[60] For 'Whatever is confus'd and perplex'd, can never come from the clear Fountain of all Knowledge, nor that which is obscure, from the Father of inexhaustible Light; and as far as you suppose God's Laws are not plain to any part of Mankind, so far you derogate from the Perfection of those Laws, and the Wisdom and Goodness of the divine Legislator.'[61] Hence, 'were there an instituted Religion which differs from That of Nature, its Precepts must be arbitrary, as not founded on the Nature and Reason of Things, but depending on meer Will and Pleasure; otherwise it would be the same with Natural Religion'.[62]

Tindal proceeds to show how his argument for the clarity of the natural revelation of God's law counters superstition, and how it applies to the whole of religion: 'natural and reveal'd Religion can't differ: Because whatever Reason shows to be worthy of having God for its Author, must belong to Natural Religion; and whatever Reason tells us is unworthy of having God for its Author, can never belong to the True Reveal'd Religion'.[63]

Towards the end of his work there appears Tindal's appeal: if only people believed 'that all, who were equally sincere, were equally acceptable to God', and if they were 'wholly bent against Immorality, discoverable by the Light of Nature', there would come, 'in the Scripture-Phrase, *a new Heaven and a new Earth*'.[64] (At which we may imagine that those divines for whom sin was a reality and atoning grace an urgent necessity uttered the eighteenth-century equivalent of 'In your dreams!')

Thomas Chubb (1679–1747), who had been a semi-Arian of the Clarkeian kind, gradually veered towards deism and, in 1731, published *A*

---

57 Ibid., p. 49.
58 Ibid.
59 Ibid., p. 53.
60 Ibid., p. 59.
61 Ibid., p. 91.
62 Ibid., p. 99.
63 Ibid., p. 197.
64 Ibid., p. 374.

Discourse concerning Reason. He sets out to show, as his subtitle indicates, that *Reason is, or that it ought to be, a sufficient guide in matters of Religion*. In *The True Gospel of Jesus Christ Asserted* (1738), he follows Tindal in holding that supernatural revelation is unnecessary and, under attack, published further works in defence of his view that religion is founded on nature. He believes that moral living renders us acceptable to God, that repentance for sin is rewarded by God's mercy, and that all will be judged. He is, however, sceptical of a number of portions of Scripture, and thinks, for example, that Christ's resurrection in no way proves his divinity. In his *Discourse on Miracles* (1741) he argues that the biblical miracles do no more than offer a 'probable proof' of a revelation.

Thomas Morgan (d. 1743), though an Independent minister at Burton, Somerset, was ordained at Frome in 1716 by the Presbyterian, John Bowder. He became heterodox, and was dismissed from his church in the early 1720s. He turned to medicine, became a freethinker, and eventually described himself as a Christian deist. He wrote tracts against Athanasian Christology, against Chubb's early works, against enthusiasm, and in defence of the Quaker apologist, Robert Barclay. Assailed from many sides, he was ever ready to respond. In *The Moral Philosopher* (1737, with replies to Leland and Chapman in 1739, to Leland and Lowman in 1740, and a final volume, *Physico-Theology* in 1741) he sets out from the principle that whether doctrines have been conveyed by reason, immediate personal revelation from God, or authentic testimony from originally enlightened and supernaturally assisted persons, the proof of the religion nonetheless turns upon 'the moral Truth, Reasonableness and Fitness of the Doctrines themselves, as appearing to the Understanding, upon a fair, impartial Consideration and Judgment of Reason'.[65] Morgan divorces the Old from the New Testament, severely criticizes the former, and repudiates the latter's teaching on the atonement—a corruption, he thought, of Jewish sacrificial ideas. The nub of his case is that 'None of the Doctrines of Revelation...can be fundamental or necessary, because mistakes in such a Case are easily made, and may be unavoidable; nay, no Man can be certain that he understands the true, determinate Sense of the Holy Ghost, or the inspired Writers, concerning...fundamental Truths and Doctrines, which are delivered in ambiguous Terms, and cloth'd with Expressions capable of very different Constructions.'[66]

Over one further name we need not long delay. In 1742 Henry Dodwell the Younger (d. 1784) anonymously published *Christianity not Founded on Argument*. He contends that reason is redundant where questions of faith are concerned; that the faithful are best advised not to

---

65 T. Morgan, *The Moral Philosopher*, London, 1738, p. x.

66 Ibid., pp. 17-18.

question what they believe, but simply to welcome the immediate communications of the Holy Spirit. Some Christians welcomed this as leaving the way open for faith; but Philip Doddridge, in his *Answer to a Late Pamphlet* (1743), and John Leland both in his *A View of the Principal Deistical Writers* and in his 1744 *Remarks* specifically directed against Dodwell's tract, construed it, correctly in the opinion of most scholars, as an ironic expossure to ridicule of the stated views in order that the superiority of reason would clearly be seen.

III

If anything, the responses to deism are even more diverse in content than deism itself. They are also exceedingly numerous: Tindal's *Christianity as old as the Creation* alone provoked more than thirty replies. Our selection of responses to deism as a whole is simply designed to show something of the flavour of the authors concerned, and to place Andrew Fuller's reply to Paine in context.

In 1641, during his first Kidderminster ministry the Reformed pastor *par excellence,* Richard Baxter (1615–91), underwent a period of doubt. This prompted him (in Cartesian fashion) 'to dig to the very foundations, and seriously to examine the reasons of Christianity, and to give a hearing to all that could be said against it, so that my faith might be indeed my own'.[67] As a result of this enquiry 'the being and attributes of God were so clear to me that he was to my intellect what the sun is to my eye'. Accordingly, atheism was ruled out, and then Baxter saw that 'there is no other religion in the world which can stand competition with Christianity... [M]ere Deism, which is the most plausible competitor, is so turned out of almost all the whole world as if Nature made its own confession that without a mediator it cannot come to God...'.[68] Although in the seventeenth century 'deism' was often used synonymously with 'theism', the reference to nature suggests that Baxter has natural religion in mind. He does not go into a detailed critique of deism, but in the reference to the deists' bypassing of the need of a mediator Baxter announces what will be a common refrain in many orthodox critiques of deism, namely, that the deists do not take the full measure of humanity's sinful plight and, accordingly, they do not see the need for the saving remedy but are, on the contrary, over-optimistic that people will behave reasonably, seek the good of others and prize benevolence. This we might label as primarily a religious response to deism, whereas the response of

---

67 R. Baxter, *The Autobiography of Richard Baxter,* (abridged), London: Dent, 1931, pp. 26-27.

68 Ibid., p. 27.

Joseph Butler, for example, is, as we shall see, more philosophical in character.

The position of Baxter's contemporary John Locke (1632–1704) with respect to deism has been much discussed.[69] The way in which Locke's friend Anthony Collins added Locke to his honour roll of freethinkers tempted some hostile critics into making Locke guilty by association; but not even the most vociferous of his intellectual foes branded Locke a deist—a not insignificant fact in that nicknaming age when numerous epithets lay to hand. Unlike Toland, for example, Locke did not deny that there are truths of revelation which are above reason, and Leland complimented Locke on having shown, 'with great clearness and force, the usefulness of divine revelation, for setting the great principles of the law of nature, and the important duties of religion and morality in a strong and convincing light, and enforcing them with the most powerful motives...'.[70] Locke's apologetic work, *The Reasonableness of Christianity as Delivered in the Scriptures* (1695), was directed against the deists. In a letter to his supporter, Samuel Bold, reproduced in the Preface to his *Second Vindication* (1697) of *The Reasonableness,* Locke expressed the hope that his results will be helpful

> especially to those, who thought either that there was no need of revelation at all, or that the revelation of our Saviour required the belief of such articles for salvation, which the settled notions, and their way of reasoning in some, and want of understanding in others, made possible to them. Upon these two topics the objections seemed to turn, which were with most assurance made by deists against christianity; but against christianity misunderstood.[71]

His own position is clear: 'A great many things we have been bred up in the belief of from our Cradles...we take for obvious Truths, and easily demonstrable; without considering how long we might have been in doubt or ignorance of them, had Revelation been silent.'[72] As for natural religion, it provides insufficient incentives for facing the hardships of the virtuous life, its view of immortality is too vague to serve as a moral sanction, and it has no word for sinners who are incapable of fulfilling its perfect moral law. We may therefore endorse J. C. Biddle's apt conclusion: 'although Toland and later Deists drew heavily upon his philosophy, Locke seems not to have been an intentional party to their

---

69 See, for example, Alan P. F. Sell, *John Locke and the Eighteenth-Century Divines,* Cardiff: University of Wales Press, 1997, pp. 78-82, 205-213, and *passim.*

70 J. Leland, *A View of the Principal Deistical Writers*, London, B. Dod, 1754, p. 18.

71 J. Locke, *The Works of John Locke in Ten Volumes,* 11th edn., London: W. Otrige, 1812, VII, p. 188.

72 John Locke, *The Reasonableness of Religion,* 1695, pp. 277-278.

emphasis upon reason and natural religion. Rather, as an opponent of the Deists and a defender of revelation, he sought a simple, moral Christianity based on faith.'[73]

Samuel Clarke makes a number of anti-deist points. First, that 'almost all the Things that are said wisely and truly by modern Deists, are plainly borrowed from that Revelation, which they refuse to embrace'.[74] Indeed, to have had to discover our duty without the aid of revealed light would have been 'like groping for an unknown way in the obscure Twilight'.[75] Secondly, 'the Rewards and Punishments of another World, the great Motives of Religion, cannot be so *powerfully inforced,* to the influencing the Lives and Practice of all sorts of Men, by one who shall undertake to demonstrate the reality of them by abstract Reason and Arguments...'.[76] Thirdly, in answer to the objection (raised, for example, by Blount) that the revelation of God's Son is not known equally by all nations, Clarke retorts that, similarly, the obligations of natural religion are not universally acknowledged. Nevertheless, as the benefits of the redeeming work of Christ encompass those who lived before his birth, it cannot be proved 'but that the same benefit may likewise extend it self forwards to those who never heard of his appearance, tho' they lived after it'.[77] But at the heart of Clarke's plea is the religious point we noted earlier in Baxter's brief remarks: 'There was plainly wanting a *Divine Revelation,* to recover Mankind out of their universal corruption and degeneracy', to make plain how God should be worshipped, to show what expiation was necessary for sins, and how the 'Authority, Honour, and Dignity of [God's] Laws might be effectually vindicated'; and to give people full assurance of the truth of the great motives of religion, namely, the rewards and punishments of a future state.[78]

Richard Bentley (1662–1742), Benjamin Hoadly and William Whiston were among others who rose to the bait of Collins's *A Discourse of Free-*

---

73 John C. Biddle, 'Locke's critique of innate principles and Toland's deism', *Journal of the History of Ideas,* XXXVII no. 3, 1976, p. 422. It is an exaggeration to imply that all later deists drew heavily on Locke. Toland and Tindal were most heavily indebted to him. At the end of the eighteenth century and beyond we may still find writers on the one hand invoking Locke's aid against the deists, and on the other hand declaring the Locke has subverted divine revelation. The former are exemplified by Uzal Ogden (1744–1822), rector of Trinity Church, Newark, New Jersey, whose *Antidote to Deism*, 2 vols, Newark, 1795, is a two-volume critique of Paine's *The Age of Reason.* For an example of the latter see *Principles of Nature,* London, 1819, by the deist Elihu Palmer (1764–1806).

74 Clarke, *A Discourse concerning the Unchangeable Obligations of Natural Religion*, p. 254.

75 Ibid.

76 Ibid., p. 257.

77 Ibid., pp. 321-322.

78 Ibid., pp. 241-244.

Thinking. Bentley complained that the Freethinkers' definition of 'freethinking' meant simply to '*Think and Judge as you find;* which every Inhabitant of *Bedlam* practises every day'. In fact '*Free* with them has no relation at all to outward Impediment or Inhibition...but means an inward Promptness and Forwardness to decide about Matters beyond the reach of their Studies, in *opposition* to the rest of mankind.'[79] In the following year Thomas Halyburton (1674–1712), professor of divinity at St Andrews, published, *Natural Religion Insufficient and Revealed Necessary to Man's Happiness,* in which he brought Calvinistic orthodoxy to bear upon the views of Herbert and Blount.

From the side of English Dissent, Isaac Watts (1674–1748) rose up against deism. In 1722 he wrote *A Caveat against Infidelity,* though the tract was not published until 1729. By that time he could hold it back no longer, for 'deism and infidelity [have] made such violent efforts, of late, in this nation'. They have managed 'to draw some from the faith of the blessed gospel, and to stagger others in their unbelief...'.[80] His case is that we cannot hope for the favour of God, or for life eternal, unless we seek them by God's appointed means, namely, through the one mediator, Jesus Christ. While ignorance of the Gospel is not as such a crime, and while those who have never heard the Good News are not culpable, the deists are wilful unbelievers: having seen the light, they reject it. It will not do to say that sincerity in holding opinions is more important than the truth of the opinions, for the Gospel does not ask for sincerity, but '*faith in Jesus Christ,* or trust in the mercy of God through Jesus the Mediator'.[81] *The Strength and Weakness of Human Reason* (1731) is a refutation of the deists' claim that '*human reason, without any revelation from heaven, is sufficient to guide and conduct mankind in a way of religion, to the favour of God, and future blessedness*'.[82] The truth rather is that apart from God's supernatural revelation in Christ humanity is lost. In *The Redeemer and the Sanctifier* (1736) Watts argues, against the deists, that Christ came to do more than restore the religion of nature: he inculcated new doctrines concerning himself, and called for obedience to himself. Watts takes his stand against all who would pare down Christianity by excising references to Christ's propitiation and the sanctifying work of the Holy Spirit: 'Have we any good and sufficient Reason', he expostulates, 'to subdue the Words of *Christ* and his Apostles down to the Meaning and Sense of infidels...?'[83] There followed *Self-love*

---

79 R. Bentley, *Remarks upon a late Discourse of Freethinking,* London: Morphew, 2nd edn, 1713, pp. 10-11.

80 I. Watts, *The Works of the Rev. Isaac Watts, D.D.*, Leeds: Edward Baines, 1800, II, p. 552.

81 Ibid., p. 571.

82 Ibid., III, p. 9.

83 I. Watts, *The Redeemer and the Sanctifier,* London: J. Oswald, 1736, p. 12.

and Virtue Reconciled only by Religion (1739) in which he contends that 'the only Effectual Obligation of mankind to practise Virtue, depends on the Existence and Will of God'.[84] While reason can discover 'the general rules of virtue, and the chief boundaries of good and evil', the sense of obligation is lacking apart from 'the supposition of a God'.[85] Finally, in *The Ruin and Recovery of mankind* (1740), he insists that because human beings are in the line of sinful Adam, their reason is depraved. Accordingly, they require the supplement and correction provided by God's revelation in Christ, the Saviour. Watts looks for the time when 'The deist will have no longer cause to triumph in the assurance of his attacks against Scripture....'[86]

In 1733 the Nonconformist divine John Leland (1691–1756) published *An Answer to a late Book intituled Christianity as Old as the Creation.* Against Tindal he claims to have shown

> that whatever human Reason may be suppos'd absolutely speaking to be capable of, if carried to the utmost possible Improvement, yet taking Mankind as they are, if left to themselves they wou'd be greatly at a Loss in many Things which it is of great Importance to us to know; that even with respect to those Principles and Duties of the Law of Nature, that seem capable of the clearest Proof to right Reason, yet Men have been under great Darkness and Uncertainty, where they have been left meerly to their own unassisted Reason.

Over and above the principles and duties of the law of nature, there are other matters which unaided human reason could not grasp, for example,

> the Methods God will take with his offending Creatures that have transgress'd his Law; whether and how far and upon what Terms he will pardon their Iniquities; whether he will reward even their imperfect Obedience, and what kind of Reward he will confer... It were therefore greatly to be wish'd that God wou'd give us an express Revelation of his Will on these heads; and if he has done so, we ought to accept it with great Thankfulness, and with a deep Sense of our Obligations to the divine Goodness.[87]

Such a revelation, declares Leland, has been provided.

In addition to *A View of the Principal Deistical Writers* (1754), in which Bolingbroke looms large, Leland published a further two-volume anti-deist work in 1764, the burden of which is expressed in its title, *The Advantage and Necessity of the Christian Revelation, shewn from the State of Religion in the Antient Heathen World: especially with respect to the Knowledge and Worship of the One True God: a Rule of Moral Duty:*

---

84 Watts, *Works,* II, p. 355.

85 Ibid., p. 368.

86 Ibid., III, p. 370.

87 J. Leland, *An Answer to a Late Book,* Dublin: S. Powell, 1733, pp. 204-206.

and a State of Future Rewards and Punishments. To which is prefixed, a Preliminary Discourse on Natural and Revealed Religion. Here, once more, he reiterates his point concerning the necessity of supernatural revelation.

A distinctly different approach (and style) is found in *The Case of Reason, or Natural Religion Fairly and Fully Stated* (1731) by the spiritual writer William Law (1686–1761). In his opinion prevailing infidelity finds its support in natural religion, and he sets out to counter Latitudinarianism in general and Matthew Tindal in particular. Reason, declares Law, is incompetent either for the defence or for the refutation of Christianity. Utterly distinct from revelation, reason is in no position to judge its deliverances. Rather, we have a faculty of spiritual intuition, and it is this which conveys to us the truth of revelation. Here is a religious response to deism which does not rely upon the accusation of missing doctrines (notably sin and the atonement), but elevates what can only be described as a mystical epistemology that bypasses reason and therefore cannot in the end engage directly with the deists' mode of argument.

Engaging with the deists' mode of argument was exactly what Joseph Butler (1692–1752) did in *The Analogy of Religion to the Constitution and Course of Nature* (1736).[88] Judicious, fair and balanced, Butler allows as much as he can to the deists, and then shows that the parameters of their method have forced them to omit matters of importance. Thus, for example, he grants that Christianity is 'a republication, and external institution, of natural or essential religion...intended to promote natural piety and virtue', but adds that Christianity also contains 'an account of a dispensation of things not discoverable by reason'. Hence, 'though natural religion is the foundation and principal part of Christianity, it is not in any sense the whole of it'.[89] We see at once that Butler is assuming with the deists (in a way which would be impossible to us today) that all right-minded persons agree that God is the author of the cosmos. He also holds that the doctrines of natural religion are probable. It is crucial to his case against the deists that he can make this out, for his argument is that if the doctrines upon which the deists rely are probable only, then the deists are in no different case from orthodox believers who, relying upon revealed truth, cannot claim absolute epistemological certainty—not least because of the element of mystery in the deepest theological claims, and the fact that in this life we are on probation and have to make moral judgements in circumstances which are not always clear.[90] Hence the objections the deists wish to lodge against claims to revealed truth can be

---

88 He says as much himself. See *The Analogy of Religion*, (1736), London: Ward, Lock, n.d., p. 192.

89 Ibid., 110.

90 Ibid., p. 72.

lodged with equivalent force against their claims made on the basis of natural religion.[91]

Between the writings of Law and Butler there appeared *Scripture Vindicated* (1732) by the Anglican theologian Daniel Waterland (1683–1740). He here invokes Locke against Tindal's *Christianity as Old as the Creation,* and seeks to defend the Old Testament—not least the doctrine of the Fall—from the deist's attack. As an example of more popular opposition from one who clearly felt that his congregation needed to be warned against deism (and who resorts to *ad hominem* tactics rather than to reasoned argumentation) we may turn to the Presbyterian minister Josiah Owen (1711?–55). In a sermon of 1735 he declared that 'Most of the Objections of Deists center in this, that they mistake the Traditions of men, for the Doctrines of God; they charge those Chimera's upon the Almighty, that have no Existence, but in the Brains of Persons, who perhaps of all Others, are the most Superficial,—next to themselves... [T]hese Objections don't affect true Christianity.'[92] Two years later there appeared the first volume of *The Divine Legation of Moses* (1737–41) by William Warburton (1698–1779), Bishop of Gloucester. It must be said that his approach was novel—even eccentric. He argued that the doctrine of future rewards and punishments is essential to the moral endeavour of human beings. However, no such doctrine is found in the Old Testament—an *absence* which he explained by invoking divine revelation, which the deists denied. Perhaps not surprisingly Leslie Stephen described Warburton as 'the rather knock-kneed giant of theology, whose swashing blows, if too apt to fall upon his allies, represented at least a rough intellectual vigour'.[93] Warburton also accused Collins of dishonouring the name of Locke by making it appear that Locke was on his side.[94]

From time to time the eighteenth-century evangelicals, whether Calvinist or Arminian, delivered themselves of opinions hostile to deism. Three illustrations must suffice. In the midst of a debate on the question

---

[91] For a lucid and thorough account of Butler's philosophy of religion see Terence Penelhum, *Butler,* London: Routledge, 1985. See also David Brown, 'Butler and deism' and Basil Mitchell, 'Butler as a Christian apologist', in Christopher Cunliffe, ed., *Joseph Butler's Moral and Religious Thought,* Oxford: Clarendon Press, 1992, pp. 7-28 and 97-116.

[92] [Josiah Owen], *The Difficulties and Discouragements that attend the Dissenting Ministry, With the most Proper Methods to Remove Them; Impartially Consider'd, in a Sermon Preach'd to a Congregation of Protestant Dissenters*, 1735, p. 38. For Owen see *ODNB*; but cf. Sell, *Dissenting Thought and the Life of the Churches,* pp. 301-302, regarding Owen's elusive movements.

[93] Stephen, *History of English Thought in the Eighteenth Century,* I, 72.

[94] W. Warburton, *The Works of the Right Reverend William Warburton, D.D.,* 12 vols., London: Luke Hansard, 1811, I, pp. 161-162.

whether the cause of evangelism would be helped or hinderd by the preservation of the Welsh language, Griffith Jones, Llanddowror, (1683–1761), upheld the cause of Welsh, among his reasons being the fact that there are 'some advantages peculiar to the Welsh tongue favourable to religion, as being perhaps the chastest in all Europe. Its books and writings are free from the deadly venom of Atheism, Deism, Infidelity, Arianism, Popery, lewd plays, immodest romances, and love intrigues.'[95] At Carmarthen on 5 May 1748 Solomon Harris was put up to dispute with the Calvinistic evangelist Howel Harris (1714–73). Solomon Harris, an Arian, said that 'reason was enough to lead us on if it be followed, and when it was objected, that then a Mahomedan was in as good a way as a Christian he said it was not enough without the help of divine revelation. When we objected to this and said as the first was Deism, this was throwing away the Holy Spirit, he then owned we must have the assistance of the Blessed Spirit.'[96] Finally John Wesley (1703–91) was not fooled by Dodwell's *Christianity not founded on Argument*. He construed the author's objective as being 'to render the whole of the Christian Institution both odious and contemptible'.[97] Again, in a letter to Mary Bishop of 7 February 1788 he declared 'Nothing in the Christian system is of greater consequence than the doctrine of Atonement. It is properly the distinguishing point between Deism and Christianity.'[98] With this we return to the heart of the religious case against deism.

By the time Wesley wrote the deist controversy was largely exhausted, and in 1790 Edmund Burke asked of the deists, 'Who, born within the last forty years, has read one word of Collins, and Toland, and Tindal, and Chubb, and Morgan, and that whole race who called themselves Freethinkers? Who now reads Bolingbroke? Whoever read him through? Ask the booksellers of London what is become of all these lights of the world.'[99] He received his answer four years later when his intellectual opponent Thomas Paine revived the debate by publishing the first part of *The Age of Reason*. Many read Paine—not least Andrew Fuller.

---

95 David Jones, *Life and Times of Griffith Jones*, London: SPCK, 1902, p. 96.

96 H. Harris, *Howell Harris's Visits to Pembrokeshire*, transcribed by Tom Beynon, Aberystwyth: Cambrian News Press, 1966, p.149.

97 J. Wesley, *The Works of the Rev. John Wesley*, ed. T. Jackson, 14 vols., 1829–1831, VIII, p. 14.

98 J. Wesley, *The Letters of the Rev. John Wesley, M.A.*, ed. John Telford, London: Epworth Press, 1931, VI, p. 297.

99 E. Burke, *Reflections on the Revolution in France, and on the Proceedings in certain Societies in London relative to that Event*, 1790, in *The Works of the Right Honourable Edmund Burke*, London: F. and C. Rivington, 1823, V, pp. 170-171.

IV

This is not the place for a detailed account of the colourful career of Thomas Paine (1737–1809). Suffice it to say that after a diversity of positions in England he adopted Benjamin Franklin's suggestion and went to North America in 1774. He became an editor, gaining prominence for his opposition to slavery, and his advocacy of American independence. Returning to England in 1787, he published the first part of *The Rights of Man* in 1791. This was a reply to Burke's anti-revolutionary *Reflections on the Revolution in France*. The second part was published in 1792, whereupon Paine was forced to flee to France, whose revolutionaries he supported. Then came the first part of *The Age of Reason* (1794), with the second part, written whilst he was in gaol, following in 1795. A number of factors motivated him in sending forth this two-part blast. He was dismayed by the way in which so many clerics were opposed to societal change and supported the forces of reaction. But, like other erstwhile supporters of the French Revolution, he did not approve of the way things were working out. As he wrote in the Preface to the second part of *The Age of Reason,* 'The intolerant spirit of Church persecutions had transferred itself into politics.'[100] He was almost as concerned by the drift towards atheism (opposition to which, he thought, had been a factor in his being imprisoned) as by those clerics who, in his view, wilfully held people under a cloud of superstition. In 1802 he returned to America, where he remained until his death.

A few lines into Part One, Paine announces his *credo*: 'I believe in one God, and no more; and I hope for happiness beyond this life. I believe in the equality of man, and I believe that religious duties consist in doing justice, loving mercy, and endeavouring to make our fellow-creatures happy.' (p. 1) He appeals for intellectual integrity, believing that 'it is impossible to calculate the moral mischief...that mental lying has produced in society'. (p. 2) In particular, the action of those priests who subscribe to what they do not believe is destructive of morality. Paine echoes Herbert[101] in understanding revelation to be an immediate communication from God to man—hence 'It is a contradiction in terms and ideas to call anything a revelation that comes to us at second hand, either verbally or in writing.' (p. 3) This is the root of Paine's critique of clerical and scriptural authority. No more than Thomas the disciple of Jesus will he take the resurrection on trust from others, though he does think it probable that Jesus existed and was crucified. In good deist fashion he proceeds to adduce difficulties arising in the Old Testament,

---

[100] T. Paine, *The Age of Reason,* London: Watts, 1938, p. 60. The page references in brackets refer to this edition.

[101] See Lord Herbert of Cherbury, *De Veritate,* tr. H. Carre, Bristol: Bristol University Press, 1936, p. 308.

especially those concerning prophecy and then, turning to the New Testament, he declares, 'Had it been the object or intention of Jesus Christ to establish a new religion, he would undoubtedly have written the system himself, or *procured it to be* written in his lifetime. But there is no publication extant authenticated with his name.' (p. 17). The four gospels and Acts are anecdotal, Revelation is an enigma, and it is as probable that the epistles are forgeries as that they are genuine.

Not, indeed, that there is no revelation: 'The Word of God is the creation we behold; and it is in *this word*, which no human invention can counterfeit or alter, that God speaketh universally to man.' (p. 23). Indeed (here is Paine's ecumenical motive), 'It is only in the creation that all our ideas and conceptions of a *word of God* can unite', (p. 24), for this word 'preaches to all nations and to all worlds'. (p. 24). In creation we see God's power and wisdom. Accordingly, if we wish to know what God is we must 'search not the book called the Scripture, which any human mind might make, but the Scripture called the Creation'. (p. 25)

The only way by which we come to God is that of reason. By contrast, the Christian system of faith 'appears to me as a species of Atheism; a sort of religious denial of God. It professes to believe in a man rather than in God.' (p. 28) A devotee of Newton, greatly influenced by scientific intelligence concerning the immensity of the cosmos, Paine argues that science is 'the study of the works of God, and of the power and wisdom of God in his works, and is the true theology'. By contrast, theology as generally conceived is 'the study of human opinions and of human fancies *concerning* God'. (p. 28) In a particularly striking paragraph he summarizes many of his objections:

> Putting them aside as a matter of distinct consideration, the outrage offered to the moral justice of God by supposing him to make the innocent suffer for the guilty, and the loose morality and low contrivance of supposing him to change himself into the shape of a man in order to make an excuse to himself for not executing his supposed sentence on Adam...it is certain that what is called the Christian system of faith, including in it the whimsical account of the creation, the strange story of Eve, the snake, and the apple, the amphibious idea of the man-god, the corporeal idea of the death of a god, the mythological idea of a family of gods, and the Christian system of arithmetic that three are one, and one is three, all are irreconcilable, not only to the divine gift of reason that God hath given to man, but to the knowledge that man gains of the power and wisdom of God, by the aid of the sciences, and by studying the structure of the universe that God has made. (pp. 35-36)

Paine then lambasts the Church for its persecution of scientists, and for the foolish way in which it builds on untruths. Small wonder that Christian parents are ashamed to teach their children the principles of Christianity: 'the Christian story of God the Father putting his son to death, or employing people to do it (for that is the plain language of the story), cannot be told by a parent to a child; and to tell him that it was done to make mankind happier and better is making the story still worse, as if mankind could be improved by the example of murder; and to tell him that all this is a mystery is only making an excuse for the incredibility of it.' (pp. 41-42) Then comes his punch line: 'How different is this from the pure and simple profession of Deism! The true Deist has but one Deity; and his religion consists in contemplating the power, wisdom, and benignity of the Deity in his works, and in endeavouring to imitate him in everything moral, scientific, and mechanical.' (p. 41) Paine proceeds to lament the unscientific way in which, against modern knowledge concerning the plurality of worlds, Christianity adheres to belief in one world only. There follows a critique of the ideas of mystery, miracle and prophecy, all of which 'are appendages that belong to fabulous and not to true religion'. (p. 52) Part One concludes with a summary of his main points: the idea of a word of God printed, written or spoken is inconsistent; creation is God's word; our moral duty is to imitate the moral goodness and beneficence of God; and (while he does not elaborate the point) it is more probable that he will continue to exist after death than that he should have existed in the first place. The one point on which all nations are agreed is that there is a God, and 'Adam, if ever there was such a man, was created a Deist.' (p. 59)

When Paine wrote Part One of *The Age of Reason* he did not have a Bible to hand. This incovenience was repaired by the time he wrote the second part (a mixed blessing indeed, according to many of his critics). We need not follow him in detail. Suffice it to say that he trawls through the Scriptures pointing to inconsistencies, and repudiating the prophetic and the miraculous. At the end of his Old Testament expedition he says, 'I have now gone through the Bible, as a man would go through a wood with an axe on his shoulder, and fell trees. Here they lie; and the priests, if they can, may replant them. They may, perhaps, stick them in the ground, but they will never make them grow.' (p. 127) He proceeds to employ similar tactics to the New Testament. Since the latter is founded upon Old Testament prophecies, and since these are worthless, the New Testament falls too. Paine is not concerned with the existence or non-existence of its characters, but he is entirely opposed to 'the fable of Jesus Christ...and the wild and visionary doctrine raised thereon...'. (p. 128) He makes merry with the genealogies of the infancy narratives, and regards the Virgin Birth as fantastic: 'Were any girl that is now with child to say, and even to swear it, that she was gotten with child by a ghost, and that an angel told her so, would she be believed? Certainly she would not. Why then are we to believe the same thing of another whom we never saw, told by nobody knows whom, nor when, nor where?' (p. 133) He finally reiterates his position on revelation, pointing out that while to the

Almighty all things are possible, no supernatural revelation has been given, and thus are prevented 'the imposition of one man upon another, and...the wicked use of pretended revelation'. (p. 160) He underlines his main point thus: 'I totally disbelieve that the Almighty ever did communicate anything to man, by any mode of speech, in any language, or by any kind of vision, or appearance, or by any means which our senses are capable of receiving, otherwise than by the universal display of himself in the works of the creation, and by that repugnance we feel in ourselves to bad actions, and disposition to good ones'. (p. 160) Deism teaches us 'all that is necessary or proper to be known. The creation is the Bible of the deist.' (p. 164) As for Christianity, 'Of all the systems of religion that ever were invented there is none more derogatory to the Almighty, more unedifying to man, more repugnant to reason, and more contradictory in itself, than this thing called Christianity.' (p. 165)

V

The full title of Andrew Fuller's reply to Paine[102] is, *The Gospel its own Witness; or The Holy Nature and Divine Harmony of the Christian Religion contrasted with the Immorality and Absurdity of Deism.* In his Preface he points out that 'The peaceful nature of Christianity does not require that we should make peace with its adversaries... On the contrary, we are required to make use of those weapons of the divine warfare with which we are furnished.' (p. 1)[103] Following a passing reference to Paine's begging of the question in his title, and to the fact that if Christianity be of God none of its enemies can overthrow it, he gets down to business. He agrees with all who hold that reason is the common ground upon which believers and unbelievers must stand in order to decide their contests; but he regrets the way in which so few antagonists have used the weapon fairly: 'On the contrary, they are driven to substitute dark insinuation, low wit, profane ridicule, and gross abuse.' (p. 4) In this regard Paine is linked with such other culprits as Shaftesbury, Tindal, Morgan, Bolingbroke, Voltaire, Hume and Gibbon. Fuller has no intention of engaging the deists at every point. Rather, he will focus upon one relatively neglected issue: 'The *internal evidence* which Christianity possesses, particularly in respect of its holy nature and divine harmony.'

---

[102] In the course of his tract Fuller lodges objections also to the views of Shaftesbury, Hume and Bolingbroke. But his remarks are all part of his general case against deism which was provoked by Paine. For this reason, and also because, as pointed out earlier, Shaftesbury and Bolingbroke—and still more Hume—do not represent the main line of deist thought (blurred though that is) I shall not here delve into their works in order to assess Fuller's criticisms of them.

[103] The page references in brackets are to the first volume of *The Complete Works of the Rev. Andrew Fuller,* 5 vols, London: William Ball, 1837.

(p. 4) While agreeing that 'the Scriptures having been conveyed to us through the medium of man, the work must necessarily, in some respects, have been humanized; yet there may be sufficient marks of divinity upon it to render it evident, to every candid mind, that it is of God.' (p. 5) The witness of Scripture—for example, to the creation—is endorsed by the created order itself. But when Paine elevates nature above Scripture on the ground that the latter is a disputed collection of texts while 'No Deist can doubt whether the works of nature be God's works', Fuller retorts that atheists dispute the latter proposition; and Christians might as well say 'No Christian doubts the truth of Scripture: the one proves just as much as the other.' (p. 6) Fuller's strategy is to show that Christianity is self-authenticating in that it is the only religion which inspires the love of God and man, endues those who embrace it with 'a principle of justice, meekness, chastity, and goodness, and even gives a tone to the morals of society at large'. (pp. 6-7) He hopes to demonstrate that Christianity is 'in harmony with itself, correspondent with observation and experience, and consistent with the clearest dictates of sober reason...'. (p. 7) His final introductory point is that the Christianity he defends is that of the New Testament, not that of popish superstition or of national establishments, both of which corruptions merely furnish weapons to unbelievers.

Fuller's primary claim against the deists is that while professing belief in God they overlook his moral character—presumably because 'a *holy* God is not suited to their inclinations'. (p. 11) This holy God is to be worshipped. Now Paine believes that our religious duty 'consists in "doing justice, loving mercy"—and what? I thought to be sure he was going to add "walking humbly with God." But I was mistaken. Mr. Paine supplies the place of walking humbly with God, by adding *"and endeavouring to make our fellow-creatures happy."*' (p. 14) Paine is offended by the idea of walking humbly with God; he ridicules the practice. He will not consider himself 'an outcast, a beggar, or a worm', he has no need of a mediator, and he regards 'redemption as a fable'. Yet 'To admit a God, and yet refuse to worship him, is a modern and inconsistent practice.' (p. 15) The inevitable conclusion is that 'Modern unbelievers are Deists in theory, Pagans in inclination, and Atheists in practice.' (p. 17)

Holiness and spirituality inform the Christian standard of morality, and direct us first to love God and then one another. The Bible's precepts 'aim directly at the heart'. (p. 19) But deism's God takes no cognizance of the heart, and elevates love of self as the highest moral objective. While not disparaging the light of nature on which deists rely, this light in the end only leaves the sinner without excuse: it does not 'afford him any well-grounded hope of forgiveness, or answer his difficulties concerning the account which something within him says he must hereafter give of his present conduct'. (p. 23) Neither does it recover the sinner, nor 'render the *whole will* of our Creator evident, and that in the most *advantageous manner*'. (p. 25) The deists have no standard of morality above their own inclinations, but Christians have God's will and heart revealed in Jesus Christ.

Fuller next considers the motives to moral living. While some deists admit the doctrine of a future life, 'the greatest truth, if dissevered from other truths of equal importance, will be divested of its energy'. (p. 29) Among such truths is that concerning rewards and punishments—a truth repudiated by many deists, who find it easier to contemplate 'the hope of happiness beyond this life' than the thought of giving an account of the manner in which they have lived on earth: this latter prospect, says Paine, would 'render him "the slave of terror".' (p. 33)

To the deists' charge that Christianity has been the mother of persecution and war, Fuller replies that such evils predate Christianity; that those who ordinarily perpetrate them are not real Christians; that many courts of Christian princes have been composed more of deists than of serious Christians; and that unbelievers themselves have no remedy for the wickedness of which they complain. Against Paine's claim that 'men, by becoming Deists, would "live more consistently and morally than by any other system"', Fuller contends that it is better to be inconsistently good than uniformly wicked, while as for morality, 'if Mr. Paine could coin a new system of morals, from which the love of God should be excluded, and intemperance, incontinency, pride, profane swearing, cursing, lying, and hypocrisy, exalted to the rank of virtues, he might very probably make good his assertion'. (p. 43) Moreover, if the Bible is as immoral a book as Paine says it is, how has it managed to reclaim so many from immorality? 'How is it, also, that to say of a man, He rejects the Bible, is nearly the same thing, in the account of people in general, as to say, He is a man of a dissolute life?' (p. 43) Indeed, 'The morality, such as it is, which is found among Deists, amounts to nothing more than a little exterior decorum. The criminality of *intention* is expressly disowned.' (p. 45) There follows a catalogue of the hypocrisies of deists. By contrast, Christianity produces good effects in those who believe it, and these permeate society. Fuller gives instances of non-Christian societies, ancient and modern, which indulge in practices of which he disapproves, and he challenges the deists to produce, if they can, a cause other than Christianity for the higher moral calibre of Christian societies. Even the nobler moral characteristics of the deists themselves accrue from the Christian society in which they have been reared: 'So long as they reside among people whose ideas of right and wrong are formed by the morality of the gospel, they must, unless they wish to be stigmatized as profligates, behave with some degree of decorum.' (p. 65)

Deists, claims Fuller, espouse a shallow view of human happiness. Christians find that 'all natural pleasure, when weighed against the hopes and joys of the gospel, will be found wanting'. (p. 68) Indeed, 'Who but Christians can contemplate the loss of all present enjoyments with satisfaction?' (p. 68) Furthermore, as sinners whose souls are depraved human beings stand in need of mercy. The Gospel alone can meet this need, and those who overcome are those who believe that Jesus is the Son of God. As for society, its evils are caused not so much by ignorance as by depravity, and its hope lies in the espousal of Christian principles. But the charge is that Christianity has been tried and found wanting—to which Fuller replies: 'That [Christianity] has not been, as yet, sufficient to banish unjust wars from the earth is true; and it were more than wonderful if it had, seeing it has never yet been cordially embraced by the majority, nor perhaps by the preponderating part of any nation.' (pp. 76-77) Nevertheless, 'the kingdoms of this world shall become the kingdoms of our Lord and of his Christ'. (p. 77)

In Part Two of his work Fuller seeks to show that the harmony of the Christian religion is an evidence of its divinity. He first addresses Paine's charge that the biblical prophecies are poetic statements unfulfilled in history. Where Paine says that the prophecies are 'a book of falsehoods', Fuller cites examples—not least Jesus's prediction of the fall of Jerusalem—as counter evidence. Secondly, he argues that Scripture harmonizes with the dictates of an enlightened conscience. Nominal Christians and deists shrink from seeing their own vices portrayed in the Bible, but the Bible does more than this: it makes clear that the root cause of all evil is human depravity, and in terms of this, the persecutions and wars which are laid at the door of Christianity are entirely explicable. As for the style of the Bible, whereas Paine 'is pleased to censure the writings of Isaiah as "bombast, beneath the genius of a schoolboy"', (p. 94) the Bible's literary merits outclass all other writings. Moreover, the spirit in which the Bible is written is one of reverence—the writers when recording history see in it the hand of God, for example; and so it is with prophecy and miracles. Even the alleged inconsistencies of Scripture witness to its truthfulness: it is not a contradiction-free work of imposture. Whereas those who approach Scripture with a candid mind are conscious of its authority, it is not surprising that the prejudiced Paine finds otherwise, for 'If men choose delusion, God also will choose to give them up to it.' Hence, 'if such a scorner had found wisdom, the Scriptures themselves had not been fulfilled.' (p. 101)

Paine agrees that we are created by God, that we sin against God, and that we may be called to account for our conduct, but he objects strongly to the notion of a mediator between humanity and God. Fuller's reply is that 'it is less *humbling* for an offender to be pardoned at his own request than through the interpositon of a third person'; secondly that 'forgiveness without a mediator...provided less for the *honour* of the offended'; thirdly, 'To exercise pardon without a mediator would be fixing no such *stigma upon the evil of the offence* as is done by a contrary mode of proceeding'; and finally, 'To bestow pardon without a mediator would be treating the offence as *private,*...an affair which does not affect the well-being of society.' (pp. 102-103) The only one qualified to be a mediator is one who is in no way implicated in the offence, namely, Jesus Christ. Paine protests that 'The doctrine of Redemption has for its basis an idea of pecuniary justice, and not that of moral justice.' But Fuller explains that the pecuniary language concerning our being bought with a price is not to be taken literally, and 'As sin is not a pecuniary, but a moral debt, so the atonement for it is not a pecuniary, but a moral ransom.' (p. 111) It should be noted, first, that while deists and Socinians think of grace in terms of God's liberality, and set aside the idea of satisfaction, 'Free grace, according to Paul, requires a *propitiation,* even the shedding of the Saviour's *blood,* as a medium through which it may be honourably communicated.' (pp. 112-113) Secondly, forgiveness is thereby bestowed while God's displeasure at sin and regard for righteousness are maintained. Thirdly, God's righteousness 'continues to be manifested in the acceptance of believers through his name'. (p. 113) Fourthly, all other spiritual blessings are freely communicated on the same ground. As a final retort to Paine's abhorrence at the innocent suffering for the guilty, Fuller declares, 'The truth is, the atonement of Christ affords a display of justice on too large a scale, and on too humbling a principle, to approve itself to a contracted, selfish, and haughty mind.' (p. 116) [So there!]

Finally, Fuller addresses Paine's charge that while science now thinks in terms of a vast cosmos, the Christian religion focuses upon one world only, namely ours. He seeks to show that 'there is nothing in the Scripture doctrine of redemption which is inconsistent with the modern opinion of the magnitude of creation'. (p. 119) It is true, he agrees, that the Scriptures do not teach that there are many worlds, but they do not deny it either. The Bible is not a textbook of astronomy or geography: 'The great object of revelation is to instruct us in the things which pertain to our everlasting peace; and as to other things...they are only touched on in an incidental manner, as the mention of them might be necessary to higher purposes.' (p. 121) The Christian doctrine of redemption is strengthened rather than weakened by recognition of the vastness of the universe, for '*The mediation of Christ is represented in Scripture as bringing the whole creation into union with the church or people of God*.' (p. 125) It is by revelation alone that we discover things of which human beings would never, by themselves, have conceived.

Fuller's work concludes with brief addresses to deists, Jews and Christians. He urges deists to consider what they owe to their Christian inheritance, and warns them that although some of them when faced by death may, like Hume and Paine, 'brave it out', 'For one unbeliever that maintains his courage, many might be produced whose hearts have failed them, and who have trembled for the consequences of their infidelity.' (p. 138) Conversely, there is no single instance of a Christian who was troubled at death '*for having been a Christian*'. (p. 138) He therefore expresses his earnest desire for their salvation, reminds them that 'The door of mercy is not yet shut', and warns them that 'to be crushed to atoms by falling rocks, or buried in oblivion at the bottom of mountains, were rather to be chosen than an exposure to the wrath of the Lamb.' (p. 140)[104]

VI

In this chapter we have been introduced to some of the varieties of English deism, and to a number of varied responses to it. In particular, we have recounted the arguments of Paine and his opponent Fuller. How successful was Fuller, and, two hundred years on, how far can his performance guide us in our Christian apologetics today?

Fuller and Paine agree that God is known in his works. They are at one with Butler and all the rest in believing that there is well nigh universal consent that there is a God. This assumption is by no means as open to us as it was to them. Neither, in the wake of Hume's demolition of the cosmological argument for God's existence,[105] and of Mill's devastating articulation of nature's red-in-tooth-and-claw-ness,[106] can we presuppose as they all did that in the book of creation the word of God is plain for all to see.

As for Paine's denial of supernatural revelation, he was, we recall, anxious to preclude the imposition of belief by one person upon another, and to rule out the wicked use of revelation. While not denying that God could reveal himself in speech and writing if he so chose, Paine contended that he never had done so, but had only revealed himself immediately to the individual. For this view Paine presents no argument, and Fuller does not challenge him directly on the point. Instead, Fuller offers an assertion which, interestingly, is the obverse of Butler's. Where

---

104 Fuller likewise urges Jews to receive the Gospel and flee the wrath to come. He urges the Christians to be sincere, to embrace vital, practical Christianity, to cultivate a good understanding among themselves, and not to fear the onslaughts of infidels.

105 D. Hume, *Dialogues concerning Natural Religion,* ed. Norman Kemp Smith, Oxford: Clarendon Press, 1935, Part IX, pp. 231-236.

106 J. S. Mill, *Three Essays on Religion,* London: Longmans, 1885, p. 28. For contemporary responses to Mill see Alan P. F. Sell, ed., *Mill and Religion,* Bristol: Thoemmes Press, 1997; see also idem, *Mill on God: The Pervasiveness and Elusiveness of Mill's Religious Thought*, Aldershot: Ashgate, 2004.

Butler cautioned the deists that their case against supernatural revelation could be turned against their own claims made on the basis of natural religion, Fuller declares that the 'sacred writings may contain such *internal* evidence of their being what they profess to be as that it might, with equal reason, be doubted whether the world was created by the power of God, as whether they were written by the inspiration of his Spirit...'.[107]

Fuller and Paine agree that reason is the common ground upon which intellectual 'contests' may be settled. Two points should be made here. First, Butler, as we saw, agreed with this policy, and of all the opponents of deism he was the most faithful in adhering to it, and the most gracious in applying it. But by restricting himself to rationalist ground, he was, as he realized, unable to introduce many of the Christian considerations to which he himself was committed. This raises the question of starting-points in Christian apologetics: how far ought we to accept the argumentative parameters of our intellectual opponents, whether deists then or latter-day positivists now? Perhaps the most pressing question as we reflect upon the dusty path we have travelled is, 'How far can Christian apologetics proceed without invoking the supernatural?' This is a question to which few clear answers have been given of late. On the other hand, the question 'Is it possible to make God so "wholly other" that he might as well not exist at all?' has received one answer in the death of God theologians, some of them erstwhile disciples of Barth.

Secondly, in fact Fuller appeals to considerations—notably the saving work of Christ—which fall outside rationalistic confines. In particular, like Baxter, Clarke and Wesley before him, Fuller is apprised of the realities of a holy God, a sinful humanity, and the need of a mediator between them. Paine will not have this; and Fuller, in replying that the fact of the innocent suffering for the guilty 'is seen every day, in every part of the world',[108] does not do as much as he might have done to draw the sting of the hoary deist view that the angry God punished the innocent Son. Fuller might have invoked Paul's words at this point: 'God was in Christ reconciling the world to himself' (2 Cor. 5:19);[109] and allowed trinitarian considerations to remind him that no wedge must be driven between the Father and the Son, and that the work of redemption is the work of all the persons of the Trinity. Be that as it may, the general question arising for apologetic method today is, What are the implications of W. P. Paterson's verdict upon deism, namely, that 'it makes upon God

---

107 Fuller, *Works,* I, p. 5.

108 Ibid., p. 114.

109 It might appear that that minority of radical feminists who accuse the Father of child-battering the Son are doing the deist's work in our own time—and overlooking Paul into the bargain.

a claim which is too small in view of human needs, and also too small in view of the magnaminity of God'?[110]

Fuller correctly charges Paine and all deists with overlooking God's moral character as holy, and he has a strong point in emphasizing the way in which the quest of holiness and spirituality illuminates the Christian moral standard and motivates moral practice. Paine's omissions, Fuller contends, give him no right to the moral high ground. But Fuller's attempted demonstration of the moral superiority of Christianity, and of its influence for good upon society, is one which can easily be turned around by sceptics who, like Collins, can produce their own lists of moral exemplars; and it certainly requires careful handling in the pluralist society of which we are increasingly consciously a part. It may be more obvious to us than it was to Fuller that people can lead morally good lives whilst believing non-Christian—even fantastic—doctrines, or no doctrines at all.[111] We recall his claim that Christianity is 'the only religion in the world' which inspires love to God and man.[112] This throws into relief the question of truth, which Fuller's method of adverting to the moral influence of Christianity sidesteps—despite the fact that he constantly presupposes the truth of such propositions as that 'Jesus is the only Mediator'. The question, 'What is the epistemological status of such a claim?', is not answered by a demonstration (even if it were possible) that Christians lead morally better lives than everybody else.

Fuller's reply to Paine's charge concerning the evils allegedly perpetrated by Christianity is cogent, though we should no doubt wish to revise his adverse interpretation of some pre- and non-Christian societies. But we cannot rest content with his response to Paine's attacks on prophecy and miracles. In fact, from our side of modern biblical criticism, we cannot be satisfied with either of their positions, nor with the allegorizing proposal of Blount, Collins and Woolston. They pit text against text in a way which is now precluded by modern biblical scholarship (though it is still practised by some Christians—and by their secular opponents too[113]). But the question how prophecy and miracles

---

110 W. P. Paterson, *The Rule of Faith,* London: Hodder & Stoughton, 1912, p 320.

111 The attitude of Joseph Barber (1727–1810), who became a tutor at Hoxton Independent Academy, is representative of many evangelical Christians of the time. He refers to those who say that 'we are to have charity for all sorts of Heretics; to have charity for Jews, Deists, Atheists, &c. i.e. we are to believe, they may be very good men, and may be saved, notwithstanding any erroneous principles they have imbibed. But the Gospel knows nothing of this sort of charity.' See his *Sermons on Regeneration,* 1770, p. 16.

112 Fuller, *Works,* I, p. 6.

113 In the very week in which I began to write this paper Ludovic Kennedy, broadcaster, writer, atheist and scourge of Christian fuzziness published an article entitled, 'How can the resurrection be a metaphor?' He accuses a number of modern

are to be construed is still open, as is the question of their place in apologetics: how far can or do they constitute evidence of a kind likely to convince a sceptic? Related to this is Fuller's conviction that the Bible is self-authenticating. But it was not so understood by Paine. How, then, would Fuller demonstrate the fact to Paine? He offers no adequate arguments at this point. Certainly his appeal to the fine style of the Bible is weak (a) because not every portion of the biblical texts is elevated in style—remember the 'begats'; and (b) because to appear to rely upon the kind of assumption in the title of a celebrated collection of purple passages, *The Bible Designed to be Read as Literature,* can be a wonderful way of missing the main point of the Bible, which is a means of divine revelation and not a resource book for aesthetes or elocutionists. When Fuller further argues that the Bible's reliability is shown by the fact that its historical narratives are written by those who see the hand of God in history we may feel that he speaks the truth, but this will not commend the Scriptures to any who do not first believe; they are more likely to accuse the biblical writers of special pleading.

As for Fuller's parting shot concerning the deist's need to flee the wrath of the Lamb: in the absence of a considerable amount of interpretation this is more likely to challenge the godly than to move genial secularists at the beginning of the third millennium. On the other hand, insofar as the deists stood against untoward authoritarianisms whether biblicist or ecclesiastical, and for honest religion, and a moral deity, they, for all their one-sidedness, elevated concerns to which not all Christians have yet paid heed.

Fuller thought that the Gospel witnessed to its own truth, and that those who believed it in turn leavened society for good. What can we say today concerning the apologetic value (if any) of Christian witness? In order to answer this question we shall need first to scrutinize the concept of witness. Where better to start than with the writings of Dr Allison Trites?[114]

---

theologians—Tillich, Cupitt and others—of substituting belief in myth for belief in fact. The starting-point of his article? Paine's demolition of the Virgin Birth! See *The Observer*, 17 January 1999, p. 28. One hundred years ago the pages of *The Freethinker* were rehearsing the same, tired, argument. See Jim Herrick, *Vision and Realism. A Hundred Years of The Freethinker,* London: G. W. Foote, 1982, p. 24 and *passim*.

[114] What, I think, we cannot say is, 'A plague on apologetics: let us give ourselves to witness!' For not the least important part of witnessing is honestly (which includes being agnostic where necessary) addressing the pressing questions which are posed to Christian faith. Nor do all of the questions come from outside the fellowship of the Church. I suspect that more of these questions remain unarticulated within Christian congregations (perhaps because the puzzled feel guilty about their doubts, or think that they would be slapped down or deemed deficient by the godly) than we realize. See further, Alan P. F. Sell, *Confessing and Commending the Faith: Christian Witness and Apologetic Method*, Cardiff: University of Wales Press, 2002.

CHAPTER 5

From Worms to Sunbeams: The Dilution of Calvinism in English Congregationalism[1]

Let us begin with hymn 67 from Isaac Watts's collection:

> Great God! How infinite art thou!
> What worthless worms are we!
> Let the whole race of creatures bow,
> And pay their praise to thee.

Lest the saints are suffering from short term memory loss, and have forgotten their lowly status by the end of the hymn, Watts repeats the verse without alteration there. Again, in his paraphrase of Psalm 8 we find the following words in verse three:

> When I survey the stars,
> And all their shining forms,
> Lord, what is man, that worthless thing,
> Akin to dust and worms.[2]

There they are again: worms—even though, be it gently said in deference to our greatest hymn writer, that Watts himself has slithered them in; they are not in Psalm 8.

By the time Isaac Watts was in full flow worms were conventional not only in hymns but elsewhere too. If you were being received as a Congregational church member in Cockermouth from 1651 onwards, you would have been invited to sign, or place your cross under, the covenant of 2 October of that year which begins,

> We poor worms, lost in Adam, being by the grace of God through the Spirit, called to be saints, conceiving it to be our duty to observe gospel ordinances, for the future do agree together to walk as a people whom the Lord hath chosen.[3]

---

1 The Annual Lecture of The Association of Denominational Historical Societies and Cognate Libraries, delivered at Dr Williams's Library, London, Thursday 30 October 2003.

2 The hymn and the paraphrase are in *The Psalms and Hymns of the Rev. Isaac Watts, D.D.*, new edn., London: Caxton Press, n.d.. The hymn is in Book Two.

You would also have been expected to 'give in your experience'; that is, to come before Church Meeting and tell the saints what God had done for your soul. This exercise typically entailed the rehearsal of one's sinful state prior to the intervention of saving grace, and it frequently included an account of a harrowing and protracted period of soul-searching seasoned with fears as to one's eternal destination should one fail to wake one morning. As Samuel Rix told the Church Meeting at Denton, Norfolk, on 3 June 1709:

> I had such apprehensions of the Wrath of God due for Sin, and of the Continual danger I was in, as I have often, in the evening, Pray'd that I might not be in Hell the next morning. That I might be spar'd, at least one night more. Now I Saw the Hypocrisie and Wickedness of my Heart more than ever before. Now I was under the Spirit of Bondage, and Walked in Darkness and Saw no light for many Months more.[4]

True, Mr Rix stops short of calling himself a worm, but he manifests all the characteristics of others who did not hesitate to apply the label to themselves.

It would be churlish on my part to overlook the fact that those of us in the Reformed tradition do not have all the worminess to ourselves. It was perfectly possible for a person to be an Arminian worm, as witness Henry Alline, the American Congregationalist who did so much to stir the Atlantic Baptists into revival. At the beginning of 1781 he writes a long poem in his diary, in the course of which he entreats God thus:

> Take me O God into thy heavenly care
> And lead a worm thy goodness to declare.[5]

By the middle of the nineteenth century the liturgical days of the lowly worm were numbered as far as the larger Nonconformist bodies were concerned, though it continued its burrowings in the more introspective soil tilled by some Strict Baptists, some of whom used William Wileman's

---

3 See W. Lewis, *History of the Congregational Church, Cockermouth*, n.p., 1870, p. 6. In *The Ejected of 1662 in Cumberland & Westmorland*, Manchester: Manchester University Press, 1911, I, p. 686, Benjamin Nightingale quotes the circumstances of the founding of the church from the *Church Book*, but does not reproduce the covenant into which 'the seven poor unworthy ones' entered.

4 'Mr. Samll. Rix his experience given in to the church June the 3d 1709', *Transactions of the Congregational Historical Society*, XIV no. 2, November 1941, p. 96.

5 James Beverley and Barry Moody, eds., *The Journal of Henry Alline*, Hantsport, Nova Scotia: Lancelot Press for Acadia Divinity College, 1982, p. 138. Cf. George Edward Levy, *The Baptists of the Maritime Provinces 1753–1946*, Saint John, New Brunswick: Barnes-Hopkins, 1946, pp. 22-25.

Hymns for the Sunday School, the eleventh edition of which appeared in 1900. Ominously, the collection contains thirteen hymns on death, one of which begins,

Death, in a thousand dreadful forms,
Sweeps down our mortal, sinful race;
The grave, corruption, earth, and worms,
Shortly must be our dwelling place.[6]

Already in 1889 R. W. Dale had felt entitled to say of the evangelicals at large that perhaps most of them

> would shrink from the severer statements of the Calvinistic and Augustinian theology concerning the corruption of human nature. They would probably shrink from saying with the great bishop of Hippo, that even the virtues of the unregenerate are only splendid sins. Nor am I quite sure that their real conception of human nature, apart from the life of God given in the new birth, would find its most natural expression in the words of Paul: 'In me, that is, in my flesh, dwelleth no good thing.' But they hold firmly the substance of the great truth that, 'Except a man be born anew he cannot see the kingdom of God.'[7]

Not surprisingly, as we move into the twentieth century we find ourelves in an almost entirely worm-free zone. The hymns sung by most children are distinctly jollier than those collected by Mr Wileman. Three hundred years on from the Cockermouth covenant the children at Worplesdon Congregational Church, like thousands of others, were not regretting that they were worms, but resolving that they would be sunbeams. In the immortal words of Nellie Talbot, set to the lilting music of Edwin Othello Excell (1851–1921), the son of a German Reformed pastor who died whilst accompanying Gypsy Smith on an evangelistic tour, and whose singing prowess prompted the awe-filled compliment, 'That man has swallowed a brass band', the children sang,

Jesus wants me for a sunbeam....
I'll be a sunbeam for him.

It would seem at first sight that, psychologically, we have here two very different mindsets: one humble, sometimes to the point of morbidity; the other cheerful, sometimes to the point of presumption. And so it is. But there is more to it than that. In either case the primary motivation is doctrinal. My suggestion in this chapter is that especially during the

---

6 W. Wileman, *Hymns for the Sunday School*, London: W. Wileman, 1900, no. 313.

7 R. W. Dale, *The Old Evangelicalism and the New*, London: Hodder and Stoughton, 1889, p. 42.

hundred years to 1930 a significant dilution of Calvinism occurred within English Congregationalism which explains the widespread transition, at least in that tradition, from worms to sunbeams. On the face of it, it is a transition which turns upon the doctrine of humanity. I shall argue that in fact it reaches to the heart of the doctrine of the triune God.

But let us go step by step. The first question is, What was it that was diluted? In two words the answer is 'scholastic Calvinism'.[8] This term has been so wantonly bandied about that it is necessary to unpack it at the outset. Historically, 'scholasticism' refers to the method of argument employed by the medieval Schoolmen from Anselm to William of Ockham. Typically, according to this method, a thesis would be stated, objections to it would be discussed, and these would be answered by appeal, variously, to Scripture, Church tradition and the deliverances of reason. Clarity of definition and precision of argument were the goals, and these are worthy goals indeed.[9] However, the process could be, and frequently was, strung out to encompass ever more refined deductions, until Erasmus was moved to protest that the whole enterprise of multiplying distinctions was boring and useless. For his part, while Calvin welcomed the scholastics' desire to achieve precise statement and clear thinking, he too protested against what he perceived as their undue commitment to intellectual subtleties: 'I abhor contentions about words, with which the church is harassed to no purpose',[10] he declared. Notwithstanding the hesitations of Calvin and others, scholastic methods, especially as modified by Peter Ramus, flowed into English Puritanism, and were adopted in the universities and in the earliest Dissenting academies. By now Calvinism itself was beginning to be subjected to codification and to ever more refined systematization. To the charge of undue logic-chopping was added opposition to perceived attempts to impose particular interpretations of doctrine upon the saints. This was the complaint of such eighteenth-century Presbyterian 'Arian' divines as John Taylor and Samuel Bourn. As if echoing Milton's remark that 'New Presbyter is but old Priest writ large', they feared that having rid themselves of Roman popery, a Protestant popery was now being advocated by those who wished to impose their confessions of faith or their doctrinal systems upon others. In the interest of the principle of the

---

8 For a variety of views on scholasticism see Willem J. Van Asselt and Eef Dekker, eds, *Reformation and Scholasticism: An Ecumenical Enterprise*, Grand Rapids, MI: Baker, 2001.

9 It is difficult to suppress the unsanctified thought that we would have been spared some of the more turgid tracts of present-day theology had their authors caught a dose of scholasticism in this sense.

10 J. Calvin, *Institutes of the Christian Religion*, ed. John T. McNeill, trans. and indexed, Ford Lewis Battles, 2 vols, Philadelphia: Westminster Press, 1960, II.ii.7.

sufficiency of Scripture and the right of all to bring their consciences to bear upon it, Taylor expostulated,

> Who were the first Reformers? Or who were any Synods or Assemblies of Divines, that they DARED to model Christian Faith into their own invented Forms, and impose it upon the Minds of Men, in their own devised Terms and Expressions? Hath *Christ* given Authority to *all* his Ministers, to the End of the World, to new-mould his Doctrines by the rules of *Human Learning*, whenever they think fit?[11]

Samuel Bourn of Coseley and Birmingham[12] was likewise convinced that to impose Trinitarianism

> Is to give up *Scripture-sufficiency*, it is to return back to the tenets of Popery... If we pay that Regard to any Body of Men, tho' the most learned Assembly in the World, which is due to *Christ* only, we make a *Christ* of these Men; they are our Rabbi.[13]

It comes as no surprise to realize that what Taylor and Bourn had especially clearly within their sights was the Westminster Confession of 1647, in which federal, or covenant, theology took one of its classical shapes. Whereas Bullinger, Calvin and others accorded primacy to the covenant of grace, this is a Calvinism informed by that federal theology which was taught (in various permutations) by such theologians as Ursinus, Gomarus, Witsius and Cocceius on the continent, by the Scot, Robert Rollock, and by the Englishmen, William Perkins and William Ames.[14] As received at Westminster the teaching is that

---

11 J. Taylor, *A Further Defence of the Common Rights of Christians, and of the Sufficiency of Scripture, without the Aid of Human Schemes, Creeds, Confessions &c.*, 1738, p. 33. See further, Alan P. F. Sell, *Dissenting Thought and the Life of the Churches. Studies in an English Tradition*, Lewiston, NY: Edwin Mellen Press, 1990, ch. 7; G. T. Eddy, *Dr. Taylor of Norwich: Wesley's Arch-heretic*, Peterborough: Epworth Press, 2003.

12 Thus described in order not to confuse him with his father and son, both Samuel and both ministers.

13 S. Bourn, *The True Christian Way of Striving for the Faith of the Gospel*, 1738, p. 23. See further, Sell, *Dissenting Thought*, ch. 7.

14 While agreeing and, in view of differing intellectual environments, finding it not at all surprising, that there are points of development/divergence as between Calvin and later Calvinists, I do not side with those who wish to drive too firm a wedge between Calvin and his successors. For the latter position see, for example, Holmes Rolston III, *John Calvin Versus the Westminster Confession*, Richmond, VA: John Knox Press, 1972; R. T. Kendall, *Calvin and English Calvinism*, (1979), Carlisle: Paternoster Press, 1997. For adverse criticisms of these see, for example, Paul Helm, *Calvin and the Calvinists*, Edinburgh: Banner of Truth Trust, 1982; G. Michael Thomas, 'Calvin and English Calvinism: a review article', *Scottish Bulletin of Evangelical Theology*, XVI no. 2, Autumn 1998, pp. 111-127.

> The first covenant made with man was a covenant of works, wherein life was promised to Adam, and in him to his posterity, upon condition of perfect and personal obedience.
>
> Man by his fall having made himself incapable of life by that covenant, the Lord was pleased to make a second, commonly called the Covenant of Grace: whereby he freely offereth unto sinners life and salvation by Jesus Christ, requiring of them faith in him, that they may be saved; and promising to give unto *those that are ordained unto life* his Holy Spirit, to make them willing and able to believe.[15]

The phrase 'those that are ordained unto life' refers directly to the doctrine of God's eternal decree. According to this, before the foundation of the world God predestined some who are fallen in Adam to be elect in Christ; others 'for the glory of his sovereign power' he passes by, having ordained them 'to dishonour and wrath for their sin, to the praise of his glorious justice'.[16]

That the Congregationalists and Particular Baptists rested largely upon the *Westminster Confession* in preparing their *Savoy Declaration of Faith and Order* (1658) and *Second London Confession* (1677) is well known. But the former introduced a number of significant modifications, among them a completely new chapter XX, 'Of the Gospel, and of the extent of

---

[15] *Westminster Confession*, VII, ii, iii, my italics; cf. *Savoy Declaration of Faith and Order*, VII, ii. iii. On federal theology see further, Alan P. F. Sell, *The Great Debate. Calvinism, Arminianism and Salvation*, (1982), Eugene, OR: Wipf & Stock, 1998, pp. 35-42, 111-13. James B. Torrance is among a number of theologians who have argued that federal theologians abused the concept of covenant and lost the Gospel by construing covenant in contractual terms. See his papers, 'Covenant or contract? A study of the theological background of worship in seventeenth-century Scotland', *Scottish Journal of Theology*, XXIII no. 1, February 1970, pp. 51-76; 'Calvin and Puritanism in England and Scotland—some basic concepts in the development of "federal theology"', in *Calvinus Reformator. His Contribution to Theology, Church and Society*, Potchefstroom: Potchefstroom University for Christian Higher Education, 1982, pp. 264-286; 'Strengths and weaknesses of the Westminster theology', in Alasdair I. C. Heron, ed., *The Westminster Confession in the Church Today*, Edinburgh: Saint Andrew Press, 1982, pp. 40-53. Criticisms of Torrance's position have been advanced by David B. McWilliams, 'The covenant theology of the *Westminster Confession of Faith* and recent criticism', *Westminster Theological Journal*, LIII, 1991, pp. 109-124; Donald MacLeod, 'Covenant theology', in Nigel M. deS. Cameron, *et al.*, *Dictionary of Scottish Church History and Theology*, Edinburgh: T. & T. Clark, 1993, pp. 217-18; Richard A. Muller, 'The covenant of works and the stability of divine law in seventeenth-century Reformed orthodoxy: a study in the theology of Herman Witsius and Wilhelmus à Brakel', *Calvin Theological Journal*, XXIX no. 1, April 1994, pp. 75-101. For a Reformed Old Testament scholar's argument that Reformed theologians have 'fastened upon a *secondary* biblical theme and elevated it to preeminence', see John H. Stek, '"Covenant" overload in Reformed theology,' *Calvin Theological Journal*, XXIX no. 1, April 1994, pp. 12-41.

[16] *Westminster* and *Savoy*, ch. III.

the Grace thereof'. Though still federal in tone, it does declare that in all ages the preaching of the Gospel has been heard, and that under it people have, by the Spirit, been quickened into newness of life. We seem to have here an evangelical note missing from *Westminster*, and a caution against that hyper-Calvinism which was already on the horizon, which would restrict the Gospel offer to the elect, since they alone could respond to it: this in opposition to what was perceived as Arminian synergism (in our own time lambasted as decisionism).

Among Congregationalists who adopted the hyper-Calvinist position was Joseph Hussey (1659–1726) the erstwhile Presbyterian, who followed the Congregational polity during his Cambridge pastorate. In 1707 he published what has become a classic statement of this position, *God's Operations of Grace but no Offers of Grace*. However, hyper-Calvinism never became characteristic of Congregationalism as a whole. None was more critical of it than its erstwhile supporter, Matthias Maurice (1684–1738), who published *The Modern Question* in 1737. He here argued that it was the duty of hearers of the Word to receive the promises of the Gospel and believe in Christ. A year after his death his tract, *The Modern Question Affirm'd and Prov'd* was published. His position was restated, and a Preface by the well-known London minister, Thomas Bradbury, helped to ensure that the controversy spread to London, where the Baptists John Gill and John Brine came out for the opposition, while in 1735 the Congregationalist Abraham Taylor published a work in support: *The Modern Question concerning Repentance and Faith Examined*. Taylor's book was later to make a favourable impression upon the Baptist Andrew Fuller, the 'ropeholder' of the Baptist Missionary Society.[17]

A central position was similarly adopted by Thomas Ridgley (1677?–1734), tutor at Moorfields Academy and a heavyweight systematician in both senses of the word. In 1731 he published his *Body of Divinity*, an exposition of the *Westminster Larger Catechism*. According to his nineteenth-century editor, John M. Wilson, although Ridgley exceeds other comparable writers in 'freedom from the trappings of system and technicality and metaphysics', he 'still wears, if not the full uniform, at least the badge and the collar of scholasticism'.[18] Be that as it may, Ridgley shows himself fully aware of the hostages to fortune offered by some versions of Calvinism, and he earnestly seeks to limit the damage at a number of crucial points. Thus, for example, while upholding the doctrine of double predestination, he makes it clear that

---

17 See further Sell, *The Great Debate*, pp. 78-9, 128 n. 80.

18 J. M. Wilson, 'Editor's Introduction' to T. Ridgley, *A Body of Divinity*, New York: Robert Carter, 1855, I, p. xiv.

> I cannot approve of any thing advanced by [supralapsarians], which seems to represent God as purposing to create man, and then to suffer him, as a means by which he designed to demonstrate the glory of his vindictive justice. This notion has given occasion to many to entertain rooted prejudices against the doctrine of predestination, as though that doctrine necessarily involved in it the supposition, that God made man to damn him.[19]

As to those who are passed by, Ridgley expostulates,

> God forbid that any one should think that there is a positive act affirmed in these words, as though God infused hardness into the hearts of any. The meaning only is this, that he determined to deny heart-softening grace to that part of mankind whom he had not foreordained to eternal life.[20]

Some of us may feel that that in itself is a sufficient deprivation; but my point is that Ridgeley was aware of the bad press which scholastic Calvinism could attract, and he strove to draw the sting of criticism. This in itself entailed a softening of the hardest of Calvinistic lines.

When we come to our next landmark, Edward Williams (1750–1813), we are in a significantly different world. We are on our side of the Evangelical Revival. *The Modern Question* had done its work. As early as 1747 Philip Doddridge, a supporter of Matthias Maurice, was putting the case for world mission at a meeting in Norfolk. It would take us too far afield to describe the difficulties which High Calvinists placed in the path of those who sought to go into all the world with the Gospel, or to document the influence on the wider tribe of Dissenters of the Baptist Andrew Fuller's book, *The Gospel Worthy of all Acceptation* (1785). Suffice it to say that the evangelical Calvinists were generally united in the view that Jesus commanded his followers to go to the ends of the earth with the Good News, and that hyper-Calvinism Calvinism simply would not preach. This, of course, was more than a matter of homiletic pragmatism; it entailed a moral protest against the kind of God scholastic Calvinism was deemed to portray. As we shall see, nothing did more to modify the doctrine than this moral protest; nothing did more to modify—even in some instances to swamp—the Congregational polity than the influx of the newly converted.

It fell to Edward Williams, successively minister at Ross-on-Wye, minister and tutor at Oswestry, minister at Carrs Lane, Birmingham, and principal at Rotherham whilst pastoring the Masboro' church, to articulate a form of Calvinism which accommodated both the doctrinal heritage and the evangelistic and missionary vocation. This he did in two influential works: *An Essay on the Equity of Divine Government and the*

---

19 Ridgley, *A Body of Divinity*, I, p. 269.

20 Ibid., p. 296.

Sovereignty of Divine Grace (1809) and *A Defence of Modern Calvinism* (1812). Greatly influenced by Hugo Grotius's emphasis upon God as moral governor, Williams stoutly opposed the hyper-Calvinistic distortion that the non-elect acted sinfully because they were predestined so to do; this, he insisted, was a slight upon the goodness of the creator-God. In the wake of Jonathan Edwards he contended that human beings are free agents accountable to God for their actions; hence the reprobate have none but themselves to blame for their final state. Worst of all is any 'endeavour to set up our own obedience instead of the righteousness of Christ'. This 'is rebellion against the authority of God and undervaluing his wisdom and grace. None deserve condemnation more than those who reject the only remedy....'[21] On the other hand, those who respond to the call of the Gospel are those who were foreordained to do so. The call, however, is universal:

> In a word, Jesus Christ, in the plan of DIVINE GOVERNMENT, is the appointed 'Saviour of all men'; but, in the plan of DIVINE SOVEREIGNTY, with an infallible and further *specialty* of intention, 'of those that believe' through gracious influence, in virtue of Christ's suretyship as well as His merits.[22]

A number of other Congregationalists followed in Williams's wake, among the most significant of whom was Ralph Wardlaw. In *The Extent of the Atonement* (1830), he reiterated the view that Christ's atonement was sufficient for all, but efficient only in the case of the elect. In this somewhat unstable way Williams and others sought to uphold the sovereignty of electing grace, human responsibility for sin, and the legitimacy of evangelism and mission. As ever, there were time-lags in the reception of newer, more moderate ideas. Of John Pye Smith, for example, John Stoughton wrote that he was 'a studious maintainer of Augustinianism, after the Calvinistic type, walking in the steps of Owen and Thomas Goodwin rather than those of John Howe or Richard Baxter'.[23] But what came to be known as Moderate Calvinism soon prevailed among Congregationalists, as witness the *Declaration of Faith* which they promulgated on establishing the Congregational Union of England and Wales.

On 8 May 1832 a meeting of Congregationalists in London resolved to form the Congregational Union of England and Wales. At the same meeting the draft of a *Declaration of Faith*, prepared by George Redford of Angel Street, Worcester, was read and sent to the churches for their

---

21 *The Works of the Rev. Edward Williams*, ed. Evan Davies, London: James Nisbet, 1862, IV, p. 216.

22 Ibid., I, p. 133.

23 J. Stoughton, *Reminiscences of Congregationalism Fifty Years Ago*, London: Hodder and Stoughton, 1881, p. 12.

consideration. Joseph Turnbull, the Union's secretary, sent an accompanying letter of 4 June 1832, in which he made it clear that the *Declaration* had not been drawn up so much for the benefit of Congregationalists, as for the information of those who were accusing them of being Socinians or Methodists. He further pointed out that since the *Savoy Declaration* was scarce and obsolete a new initiative was needed. A very slightly revised version of the *Declaration* was unanimously adopted on 10 May 1833, and it was printed in every edition of *The Congregational Year Book* from 1858 to 1918.[24]

Clearly by now nervous of any imputation of scholasticism, the 'Preliminary Notes' to the document explain that 'It is not intended to present a scholastic or critical confession of faith, but merely such a statement as any intelligent member of the body might offer, as containing its leading principles.' It is also underlined that subscription is not in view, and that 'the most perfect liberty of conscience' is upheld. Under the heading 'Principles of Religion' there is a reference to the covenant of grace, but not to that of works. We are informed that the Congregationalists believe that 'before the foundation of the world [God] designed to redeem fallen man', and that 'all who will be saved were the objects of God's eternal and electing love, and were given by an act of Divine sovereignty to the Son of God'; but there is no reference to preterition, and the term 'predestination' is conspicuous by its absence. They do, however, believe that at the final judgment God will 'send away the wicked into "everlasting punishment"'. In the list of 'Principles of Church Order and Discipline' *Savoy* is closely followed in that the Church is said to be a voluntary society of true believers, meeting under its only Head, Jesus Christ, untrammelled by the state. But they add the important phrase the Church is obliged 'to perpetuate and propagate the Gospel in the world'. We are in the period of modern missionary advance.

But we are also in the period of increasing unease with Calvinism as traditionally received. While some viewed the modifications of Calvinism with real concern—among them Richard Winter Hamilton, who demanded of the Union secretary, Algernon Wells, that 'The full-blooded dogma of the old school must be revived'[25]—the majority were content

---

24 See further, Albert Peel, *These Hundred Years. A History of the Congregational Union of England and Wales, 1831–1931*, London: Congregational Union of England and Wales, 1931; Sell, *Dissenting Thought*, 51-3, and *Saints: Visible, Orderly and Catholic. The Congregational Idea of the Church*, Geneva: World Alliance of Reformed Churches and Allison Park, PA: Pickwick Publications, 1986, pp. 67-70.

25 Quoted by J. Stoughton, *Reminiscences*, p. 53. Stoughton says of him that 'His thoughts gulped out like liquid from a large full bottle with a tiny neck', p. 55. Lest it be thought that ministers alone could set the doctrinal clock back, we should note, for example, that in the very year, 1831, in which the *Declaration* was promulgated, James

that, in the interests of propagating the Gospel, the more angular features of Calvinism were rapidly being smoothed away, and they would have accepted the verdict of the American Congregationalist, Williston Walker, that the *Declaration* was 'a sweet spirited statement of which the English churches have no cause to be ashamed'.[26] When, at the centenary of the Congregational Union, Robert Mackintosh reviewed the *Declaration* he noted what he called 'A most staggering statement' in it, namely, the opinion of the framers that 'there is no minister or church among them that would deny any one' of the doctrinal or ecclesiastical principles expressed in it. 'How unlike present-day conditions!', exclaims Mackintosh.[27] Certainly, if the *Declaration* marked a softening of Calvinism, the general Congregational mind-set a century on represented a significant dilution of it.

At this point it will be helpful to enumerate some of the causes of the dilution. First, confidence in lingering scholasticism quickly declined. This decline was by no means confined to England. Of Solomon Stoddard, Perry Miller declared that

> His sermons were outstanding in his day for the decision with which he swept away the paraphernalia of theology and logic...and he was the first minister in New England openly to advocate the preaching of Hell-fire and brimstone in order to frighten men into conversion.[28]

We may feel it to be less than an altogether preferable transition to go from the frying pan of scholastic logic into the fire of hell. In England some managed the situation in a less inflammatory way: they simply accentuated the positive and were silent on the less palatable aspects of their inherited tradition. Thus, for example, although James Matthews, the first minister of the Congregational church at Totteridge/Whetstone was 'a rigid Calvinist', he was at the same time 'The sincerest of the sincere, the mildest of preachers, himself an example to the wholesale dealers in

---

Davies left his Totteridge/Whetstone pastorate for Haverhill because of 'the introduction of Antinomianism amongst some of the leading and most influential members of the Congregation'. Believing this to be 'a perpetual and pernicious heresy', Davies resigned. See Harry E. Hill, *The History of Christ Church at Whetstone*, privately published, [1988], p. 8.

[26] W. Walker, *The Creeds and Platforms of Congregationalism*, (1893), Boston: Pilgrim Press, 1960, p. 546.

[27] R. Mackintosh, 'The genius of Congregationalism', in A. Peel, ed., *Essays Congregational and Catholic*, London: Congregational Union of England and Wales, [1931], p. 111.

[28] P. Miller, 'Solomon Stoddard', *Harvard Theological Review*, XXXIV, 1941, p. 317.

brimstone.'[29] Of William Jay of Bath it was written that in his opinion 'the Calvinistic system...was a thing to be held, not formally preached'.[30] Even better known is John Angell James of Carrs Lane, Birmingham, whose colleague and eventual successor, R. W. Dale, writes as follows:

> He said to me one day, with great energy—raising his arm and clenching his hand as he said it—'I hold the doctrines of Calvinism with a firm grasp!' 'But,' said I, 'you never preach about them.' 'Well,' he replied—with the *naïveté* which was one of the chief charms of his character—'you know that there is not much about them in the Bible.'... Bees are said to have a very ingenious way of dealing with a fellow-citizen who happens to die in the hive; they leave the dead body where it lies, but seal up the cell with wax. Our modern Calvinists treat Calvinistic doctrine very much in the same way. The doctrine is allowed to remain in their creed undisturbed; but, to keep their creed quite sweet and wholesome, the cell in which their Calvinism lies is hermetically sealed.[31]

Others, however, were still trying to repair what they could of the old paths. Prominent among these was George Payne, who in 1836 sought to draw the sting of doctrinal criticisms of Calvinism. This he did as a Moderate Calvinist in the line of Edward Williams and his friend Ralph Wardlaw. Bolstering his comment with a quotation from Williams he asks

> Why...should a positive determination, on the part of God, to save some of the human family, be supposed to imply of necessity a counter and positive determination not to save the other members of the family? Not to save men, is not to act—it is just doing nothing.[32]

---

[29] H. E. Hill quoting Charles Matthews, minister's son and comedian, in *The History of Christ Church at Whetstone*, p. 2.

[30] Letter of Henry V. D. Johns to the Rev. R. Bolton, quoted in George Redford and John Angell James, eds., *The Autobiography of William Jay*, (1854), Edinburgh: Banner of Truth Trust, 1954, p. 221.

[31] R. W. Dale, 'On some present aspects of theological thought among Congregationalists', *Congregationalist*, VI, January 1877, pp. 5-6.

[32] G. Payne, *Lectures on Divine Sovereignty, Election, the Atonement, Justification, and Regeneration*, 3rd edn., London: John Gladding, 1846, p. 41. Note the echo of Ridgley's explanation of a century earlier. Although in this chapter I am concerned with English Congregationalism, I cannot forbear to note the way in which one Scottish Congregational minister sought to be 'all things to all men' by fluctuating doctrinally between his morning and evening services. Alexander Begg of Fraserburgh died in 1840, and was succeeded by Archibald Duff, whose son, the professor of the same name, recalled that his father's predecessor 'had been wont to preach in the morning service—where the well-to-do folk attended—the high old-fashioned notion that God loved and saves through Jesus only a selected few of us poor human folk whilst in the evening service—where the masses attended—Mr. Begg told out freely and grandly the unlimited love of the great "Jesus" heart of the Creator.' Duff resolved to preach in the

Increasingly, however, many came to believe that a God deemed omniscient could hardly fail to foresee that if he positively elected some, others would be passed by, and that to do nothing about them seemed more than a little un-grace-ful. It must also be said that Payne and others were clearly struggling to make the best of a bad job, for there is surely a distinction between doing nothing and, to recall Calvin's own words, determining to devote some to destruction.[33] Small wonder that D. W. Simon called Moderate Calvinism 'Calvinism with its teeth filed but not drawn.'[34] There was particular concern among many in the nineteenth century over the fate of deceased infants. At the same time we must heed the testimony of Robert Halley, that in Payne 'we have an instance of one of the straitest sect of our religion among the most free and evangelical in the application of the truth to the wants, the responsibilities, and the consciences of all men'.[35]

In all of this what is happening is that a moral critique of scholasticism is winning the day.[36] The contrast is easily drawn. In 1741 the Congregationalist Joseph Hart inveighed against the 'old Arminian errors' of John Wesley. Hart agrees with Wesley that 'Many things that happen are inconsistent with one's natural notions of justice and mercy', but he turns the words against his Arminian rival: 'How', he asks, 'can any man presume to say that the doctrine of predestination cannot be true, only because it disagrees with our reason, and contradicts our natural conceptions of justice and mercy?'[37] Here Hart seems concerned above all else to guard God's omnipotence—a besetting sin of Calvinists thought another Congregationalist, Robert Mackintosh who, in 1908 declared,

---

latter style at both services, but Church Meeting decided that 'God's heart was of the smaller size.' A secession followed, with Duff and others constituting Manse Street Church. See [Robert Duthie], *A Northern Light. The Story of Mid Street Congregational Church in Fraserburgh*, Banff: Banffshire Journal, 1947, pp. 15-16.

33 Calvin, *Institutes*, III.xxi.7

34 Quoted by F. J. Powicke, *David Worthington Simon*, London: Hodder and Stoughton, 1912, p. 264.

35 R. Halley, 'Opening Address' to the Congregational Union, *Congregational Year Book*, 1856, p. 12. In this connection we may note that Payne was by no means as hostile as some to the American revivalist Charles G. Finney's *Lectures on Revivals of Religion*, 1835.

36 For the philosophical roots of this critique among Dissenters see Alan P. F. Sell, *Philosophy, Dissent and Nonconformity,1689–1920*, Cambridge: James Clarke, 2003, ch. 3.

37 Quoted in Thomas Wright, *Joseph Hart*, London: Farncombe, 1910, p. 10. Hart's tract is *The Unreasonableness of Religion. Being Remarks and Animadversions on Mr. John Wesley's Sermon on Romans viii. 32*, London, 1741.

> The eternal odium of Calvinism—I had almost said the eternal infamy of Calvinism—is...its determination that whatever comes of morality, or of God's character, it shall make sure of God's omnipotence. Now—if we must choose—is not that the less true and less Christian alternative?[38]

But, secondly, it is not only that scholastic Calvinism suffered erosion from within because of its unpreachability and its perceived slighting of God's character; it was undermined from without by what the Methodist John Scott Lidgett called in his book of that title, *The Victorian Transformation of Theology*. The transformation consisted in the turn to the concept of the Fatherhood of God. I cannot pursue this theme further, except to say that in some hands this became an unduly sentimentalized idea, to the extent that Dale lamented that 'God's authority does not impress us as it should. We find it hard to make men feel—whatever they may say—that sin is an awful offence, because committed against him.'[39] In a word, the need of the corrective ultimately supplied by P. T. Forsyth was becoming urgent, namely, that God's love is holy love.

Thirdly, the onset of Social Gospel ideas created a climate inimical to hyper-Calvinism at least, but it also fostered a humanitarian-cum-Pelagian attitude in some which failed to hold together grace and works as the fruit of grace, and even encouraged them to think that by their efforts they were bringing in the Kingdom of God—as if the Kingdom is not always God's gift.

Fourthly, sizeable tracts of nineteenth-century thought became increasingly individualistic. At the risk of one's personal safety, one might gently suggest that from one point of view the Evangelical Revival was Enlightenment individualism gone pious. With which observation I return to the hint dropped earlier that the Revival promoted among Congregationalists at least the view that the way into the Church is by the route of conversion. The new birth is necessary. One of the results of this was that from about 1830 the covenant ecclesiology of traditional Congregationalism tailed off, and with it attendance at Church Meeting and, in many instances, commitment to baptism. Hence Robert Mackintosh's wry protest: 'the Church's tradition is anti-individualist. Infant baptism is the great rock of offence to the triumphant revival.'[40]

---

38 R. Mackintosh, 'Recent philosophy and Christian doctrine', *Proceedings of the Third International Congregational Council*, London: Congregational Union of England and Wales, 1908, p. 82.

39 Dale, 'On some present aspects of theological thought among Congregationalists', p. 7.

40 R. Mackintosh, *The Insufficiency of Revivalism as a Religious System*, bound with *Essays Towards a New Theology*, Glasgow: Maclehose, 1889, p. 27. Cf. his 'The genius of Congregationalism', 118. For this sadly neglected theologian see Alan P. F.

Hence also Dale's remark that evangelicalism was 'satisfied with fellowship of an accidental and precarious kind. It cared nothing for the idea of the Church as the august society of saints. It was the ally of Individualism.'[41] Not, indeed, that those on the liberal wing of theology were deprived of ways of being individualists. The *Rivulet* controversy surrounding the hymns of T. T. Lynch, and attitudes expressed at the Leicester Conference of 1877 from which the Congregational Union felt overwhelmingly bound to distance itself in the interests of its stance as genuinely evangelical, amply demonstrate the point,[42] as does Julie Jephson's pride in the fact that Congregationalism was the most democratic and undoctrinal of all Christian Churches, in which believing in the spirit of such doctrines as the Incarnation and the Atonement sufficed.[43]

Coupled with this exaltation of freedom of thought was a pronounced hostility to the doctrine of predestination construed as deterministic. There is, as ever, no smoke without fire, and it is not difficult to find examples of Calvinistic teaching which bear a markedly deterministic stamp, and this not only in popular writing and sermons. Augustus Toplady, for example, whose *Works* were published in 1825, rhetorically asked, 'what is Calvinism, but a scriptural expansion of the philosophic principle of necessity?' He welcomed the fact that this was so, and even teased the Unitarian Joseph Priestley for being on the way to Calvinism because of his commitment to philosophical necessity: 'I think', said Toplady, 'you have admitted a Trojan horse into your gates.'[44] From the other side, Dale protested that Calvinism denied the freedom of the

---

Sell, *Robert Mackintosh, Theologian of Integrity*, Bern: Peter Lang, 1977. On the converted influx to Dissent see A. Peel, *These Hundred Years*, pp.

22-3. For an interesting parallel from another part of the Reformed family, we may note that it was not liberal theology but revivalism which so tempered the 'Dortness' of the eastern branch of the Dutch Reformed Church in America as to lead it into the American denominational mainstream. See Firth Haring Fabend, *Zion on the Hudson: Dutch New York and New Jersey in the Age of Revivals*, Piscataway, NJ: Rutgers University Press, 2000.

41 Dale, *The Old Evangelicalism and the New*, p. 17; cf. p. 31; also his *A Manual of Congregational Principles*, London: Hodder and Stoughton, 1884, p. 177, and *Essays and Addresses*, London: Hodder and Stoughton, 1899, p. 209. For a later argument to the same effect see H. F. Lovell Cocks, *The Nonconformist Conscience*, London: Independent Press, 1943, pp. 84-87.

42 On these matters see further Mark D. Johnson, *The Dissolution of Dissent, 1850–1918*, New York: Garland, 1987; and on the Leicester Conference see Mark Hopkins, *Nonconformity's Romantic Generation: Evangelical and Liberal Theologies in Victorian England*, Carlisle: Paternoster Press, 2004, pp. 85-121.

43 See Julie Jephson, *Christian Democracy*, London: T. Fisher Unwin, 1902.

44 A. M. Toplady, *The Works of Augustus M. Toplady*, London, 1825, VI, pp. 240-42, 291.

human will and branded necessarian philosophy 'Calvinism without God'.[45] Although I cannot develop the point in detail here, I am bound to point out that both Toplady and Dale are misguided on this matter. Predestination is a religious doctrine. It arises when Paul, retrospectively, realizes that he has not come to his new life under his own steam, as it were. Undoubtedly confusion arises when predestination is equated with philosophical necessity; undoubtedly when that happens human freedom is under threat. But neither of these circumstances need arise, and neither represents genuine Calvinism. The fact is that while most Calvinists have been determinists in philosophy, a significant number have been libertarians; yet all could affirm predestination.[46]

I do not overlook the fact that sociological factors also played a part in diluting scholastic Calvinism. I have already implied that this was one consequence of the sweeping in to the fold of the 'saved' under the influence of the Revival. But, as Dale noted as early as 1877, the ministry and theological leadership were affected, too, as men, some of them Arminians, entered the ministry from Wales, Scotland and Ireland, and from Presbyterianism and Methodism.[47] But my main point is that to a large extent scholastic Calvinism was diluted from within as the moral protest against untoward doctrine took hold, and as a result, too, of the accession of the newly-converted. Moreover, all of this was set in train before the higher criticism and evolutionary thought, or such alien doctrines as agnosticism and positivism, hove into view to any significant degree.

Eustace Rogers Conder described the upshot as concisely as anyone: 'The old theology did not perish under the assault of a rival system... It expired because an atmosphere had been created in which it could not breathe.'[48] Or, as Dale put it,

> 'Moderate Calvinism' was Calvinism in decay. The old Calvinistic phrases, the old Calvinistic definitions, were still on the lips of the Independents when George III

---

45 Dale, 'On some present aspects of theological thought among Congregationalists', p. 6.

46 For a classic discussion of this point see William Cunningham, *The Reformers and the Theology of the Reformation*, (1862), London: Banner of Truth Trust, 1967, 471-524; Sell, *The Great Debate*, ch. 1.

47 Dale, 'On some present aspects of theological thought among Congregationalists', p. 3.

48 E. R. Conder, 'What have the churches gained and lost in spiritual influence through the changes which have taken place in recent years in doctrinal beliefs?', *Proceedings of the International Congregational Council, London 1891*, London: James Clarke, 1891, p. 196.

> died; but in the spirit and tendency of their theology they were Calvinists no longer.[49]

By 1879 Dale felt able to report that 'Mr. Spurgeon stands alone among the modern leaders of Evangelical Nonconformists in his fidelity to the older Calvinistic creed';[50] and, speaking for himself, he declared 'Like the rest of the world, I have given up Calvinism.'[51]

But I have already noted Dale's concern at the loss of a sense of what H. H. Farmer later called 'the Godness of God'. Conder had similar qualms:

> Grant that our forefathers were too apt to substitute anatomical preparations of truth for its living presence. They loved to dangle before you the skeleton of the Gospel till all its joints rattled, when what you needed was the tone of her comforting voice, a Divine smile on her countenance, the warm grasp of her helping hand. But let us not forget that the anatomist's knife lays bare nothing but what is essential to life, health, and beauty. And the higher the life, the more complex the system in which it is embodied. Creatures which can be cut to bits or turned inside out, and live on all the same, are of a very low type. To the highest, the loss of a single vertebra would be death. The 'plan of salvation' is not the 'Glad Tidings'; the philosophy of religion is not religion; the most logical scheme of doctrine which Theology will ever frame will not take the place of the living word, by which souls are born again, and purified in obeying truth. No! But nevertheless, a religious life strong in feeling and action, but intellectually feeble; a faith which is firm and simple as Trust, but as Belief is unintelligent, hazy, unable to distinguish doctrine from doctrine or truth from error;—these are not worthy of the disciples of [Christ]... Nor is it in such characteristics that we can trace the features of the Church of the Future.[52]

Conder went on to argue that 'The old Theology was not overthrown by argument' but 'by the expansive force of love. The breaking point of the strain was the restriction it laid on an honest offer of salvation to all.' He further surmised that Calvinists had got hold of the wrong end of 'the great problem of human salvation, in beginning with the eternal decrees of God, and the eternal covenant between the Father and the Son, instead of busying themselves with the end put into their hands by the Saviour's command—"Go ye into all the world, and preach the Gospel to every creature"'.[53]

---

[49] R. W. Dale, *History of English Congregationalism*, London: Hodder and Stoughton, 1907, p. 588

[50] R. W. Dale, *The Evangelical Revival and Other Sermons*, London: Hodder and Stoughton, 1880, p. 21.

[51] Ibid., p. 195.

[52] E. R. Conder, 'The decay of theology', *The Congregational Year Book*, 1874, pp. 70-71.

[53] Ibid., p. 72.

One generation on, Walter F. Adeney, principal of Lancashire Independent College, was disinclined to concede any advantage to Calvinism. In a manner which is suggestive of heat rather than light, or even of scholarly accuracy and fairness, he, in typical liberal-evangelical fashion, attributes the demise of Calvinism to the new humanitarian temper flowing down from Rousseau and the French Revolution. By contrast, Calvinism, 'While prostrating itself before the awful Majesty of God...had no pity for man'[54]—a statement, surely, requiring qualification. Robert Burns, John McLeod Campbell and Thomas Erskine of Linlathen all contributed to the idea of redemption as spiritual rather than as mere deliverance from punishment; while F. D. Maurice, Robertson of Brighton and the Congregationalist Baldwin Brown made the doctrine of God's Fatherhood central to theology, displacing that of his sovereignty. Utterly repudiated, Adeney declares, is any idea that God's sovereignty is independent of morality, as if God were 'a sort of Sultan acting with pure caprice in choosing one for everlasting bliss, and relegating another to everlasting torment, on the Turk's plea that he "has a right to do as he will with his own"'.[55]

Here, once again, is the equation of predestination with determinism and, as I have suggested, it is an unscholarly if understandable union: understandable because Calvinists like Toplady and others did make the link themselves; and many had been spiritually wounded by such teaching, among them three of Congregationalism's most distinguished theologians of the early years of the twentieth century: A. M. Fairbairn (who found a 'larger and nobler' theology on the continent than that in which he had been nurtured in Scotland); Robert Mackintosh (who regarded himself as a refugee who fled from the Calvinism of the Free Church of Scotland to the freer air of Congregationalism); and A. E. Garvie (who, when asked why in *The Christian Belief in God* he had not taken notice of Karl Barth replied, 'Having given so much toil of mind and travail of soul to escape from Calvinism, I have no mind to return to its bondage').[56] Garvie further declared,

> I do not envy the man who to-day can avow himself as a Calvinist, since it was this type of theology which not only turned my mind for a time away from the ministry, but almost drove me into entire unbelief. Does God elect some to salvation and

---

54 W. F. Adeney, *A Century's Progress in Religious Life and Thought*, London: James Clarke, 1901, p. 122.

55 Ibid., p. 130.

56 See A. M. Fairbairn, 'Experience in theology: a chapter of autobiography', *The Contemporary Review*, XCI, January–June 1907, p. 567; Robert Mackintosh, 'The genius of Congregationalism', p. 105; A. E. Garvie, *Revelation Through History and Experience. A Study of the Historical Basis of the Revelation of the Godhead*, London: Ivor Nicholson and Watson, 1934, p. xii.

> predestinate others to damnation? Does He give His Spirit only to the elect, and withhold His Spirit from others? Does he use the devil as His agent to secure their damnation? Does He, to ensure the salvation of the elect, and them alone, make His grace irresistable, and provide for the perseverance of the saints? Did God decree the Fall? Unless a man accepts these propositions, he is mistaken in calling himself a Calvinist.[57]

But by the time—1934—that Garvie wrote those words changes were afoot in English Congregationalism. The emphases of P. T. Forsyth,[58] the sometimes cordial but frequently muted reception given to Karl Barth,[59] and a general feeling that World War I had shattered the optimism of a liberal theology which had led to a sentimentalized understanding of God which could not sustain the saints in the evil hour[60]—all of these factors and others explain the letter of 12 March 1939 which was sent to all Congregational ministers. It was drafted by Bernard Lord Manning, revised by Nathaniel Micklem and John Whale, and signed in addition by H. F. Lovell Cocks, John Marsh, Hubert Cunliffe-Jones, W. A. Whitehouse, Daniel Jenkins, J. D. Jones, E. J. Price and John Short. It was a call to a deeper understanding of the Church as utterly dependent upon the Gospel of God's free grace, and this as transmitted especially through the Reformed tradition. Some of the signatories and their associates were labelled the 'Genevan' Congregationalists. Not the least sign of the influence of this group was the formation of the Church Order Group and a renewed concern for worship marked by freedom within order. Reverence before the holy God, realism concerning human sinfulness, and a joyous celebration of God's eternal, redeeming, love—these were the notes now being sounded.[61] A coupling, one might almost say, of the worm with the sunbeam.

---

[57] Garvie, *Revelation Through History*, p. 161. It is interesting to note in passing the eagerness with which some liberal theologians strove to palliate the so-called 'hard sayings' of the Gospels, and their disinclination to accord the benefit of the doubt to, or even in some cases to bring careful exegesis to bear upon, the 'harder sayings' of Calvinism.

[58] For a discussion of these see Alan P. F. Sell, *Testimony and Tradition. Studies in Reformed and Dissenting Thought*, Aldershot: Ashgate, 2005, ch. 7, and 'P. T. Forsyth: theologian for a new millennium?', in Alan P. F. Sell, ed., *P. T. Forsyth. Theologian for a New Millennium*, London: United Reformed Church, 2000, ch. 9.

[59] See further, Alan P. F. Sell, 'The theological contribution of Protestant Nonconformists in the twentieth century: some soundings', in Alan P. F. Sell and Anthony R. Cross, eds., *Protestant Nonconformity in the Twentieth Century*, Carlisle: Paternoster Press, 2003, pp. 42-46.

[60] See further, Alan P. F. Sell, *Theology in Turmoil. The Roots, Course and Significance of the Conservative–Liberal Debate in Modern Theology*, 1986, Eugene, OR: Wipf & Stock, 1998, chs. 5 and 6.

[61] See further, Sell, *Testimony and Tradition*, ch. 2.

There I might have left it. But from our present vantage point I should like to pose two questions. First, can it be that the worm is turning? Just over a year ago I came across a hymn in *Celebration Hymnal*, one of the books in use at The Church of Christ the Cornerstone, Milton Keynes, which contains a stanza beginning thus:

> If I were a wiggly worm
> I'd thank you, Lord, that I could squirm.

This worm, be it noted, is significantly different from his hymnological ancestors. He is not a lowly creature struggling against the miry clay; he is a feel-good worm who cheerfully wiggles across the golden sands of a package holiday. To be like him is not to be humbled, but to be ever so happy. The moral is, As your doctrine is, so will your worship be.

But this raises the second question: how is it with our doctrine? You will have realized that I have been concerned throughout with the dilution of Calvinism as it received scholastic shape in the *Westminster Confession* and the derivative but amended *Savoy Declaration*. The discussion of election and predestination from John Owen, through Thomas Ridgley, Edward Williams, Ralph Wardlaw, George Payne, and on into the early decades of the twentieth century all took place within that context. But what if the context were not the most helpful? Understandably enough, creeds and confessions are always creatures of their age.[62] It is not difficult to see why, in face of what they took to be untenable views of Church authority, our forebears opened their confessions with strong statements on the authority of Scripture. We can understand how, under the impress of Enlightenment rationalism, this later emerged as the biblical inerrancy doctrine of Old Princeton as represented by the Hodges, Warfield and Machen. But the more immediate effect of this way of opening the *Confession* was to inculcate the view that the first affirmations to be made concern a book rather than the triune God. Indeed, the eight lines on the triune God are shelved until we have been through ten paragraphs upon the Bible and two on the general attributes of God. The work of Christ is delayed until chapter 8, and the doctrine of the Holy Spirit to chapter 10, where it is treated rather inadequately, because the Spirit is conceived largely as the one who applies the things of Christ to us, and not, for example, as our intercessor or the bond of our union with Christ.[63] The charge is not that the authors and most of their

---

62 For further discussion of this point see Alan P. F. Sell, *Aspects of Christian Integrity*, Calgary: University of Calgary Press and Louisville, KY: Westminster/John Knox, 1990, ch. 4, and *Confessing and Commending the Faith. Historic Witness and Apologetic Method*, Cardiff: University of Wales Press, 2002, pp. 27-29.

63 See the strictures of Torrance, 'Strengths and weaknesses of Westminster theology', p. 53.

theological heirs were not trinitarian: the proliferation of tracts against Socinians and Unitarians testifies to the strength of trinitarian conviction if not always to the graciousness of the elect. The point is that in what one might call their in-house teaching and catechetical instruction the *Westminster Confession* and its Congregational and Baptist successors fostered a pattern of study and reflection in which the grace of God the holy Trinity did not assume primacy, and in which convictions concerning God's sovereign power were inadequately balanced by those concerning his grace and mercy.

Despite this, however, the Congregationalists of the eighteenth century, largely because of their polity in which the giving in of experience had a conserving effect, and their hymns, remained orthodox while most Presbyterians took another direction.[64] But by the nineteenth century, in preaching and theological writing, the Trinity had slipped into the background. This fact was deeply regretted by Principal David Worthington Simon in his address to the friends of Yorkshire United Independent College, Bradford, in September 1897. He spoke of the general doctrinal downgrade, and in particular of the fate which had befallen the Trinity, 'the foundation doctrine of the Christian doctrinal system'. Whenever this doctrine has been forgotten, ignored or denied, he continued, 'the system of Christian truth has crumbled to pieces'.[65]

It seems to me that Simon here issues a challenge of perennial importance to trinitarian churches,[66] and what he says has to do with more than systematic theology. I believe that in the claim that on the ground of the Son's finished work the Father calls out by the Spirit a people for his praise and service, we have the heart of our Gospel, the trinitarian foundation of our doctrine, the root of our church polity, and the source of our abiding hope. If this is so, then if we do not continually and openly rehearse the Good News of the sovereign grace of the triune God, Father, Son and Holy Spirit, we shall lose our grip on Gospel, doctrine and ecclesiology. Were that to happen, even the most arid tracts of Calvinist scholasticism would seem like oases as compared with the theological and liturgical desert we should by then have entered.

I conclude with a word from E. R. Conder, uttered in 1891, which is a cautionary as it is challenging:

> Our churches have gained in breadth, catholicity, elasticity, activity, sympathy with the temporal as well as the spiritual need and woe of our neighbours, of our

---

64 See further Sell, *Dissenting Thought*, chs 1 and 5.

65 Quoted by Powicke, *David Worthington Simon*, p. 219. Cf. Simon's paper, 'The present direction of theological thought in the Congregational churches of Great Britain', *Proceedings of the International Congregational Council, London 1891*, pp. 76-80; Stoughton, *Reminiscences*, pp. 76-7.

66 Thus no aspersions are here cast against those who are Unitarian by conviction.

nation, of the world. But in personal spiritual life—*q.d.*, in faith, prayer, fervour, unworldly simplicity, intense religious conviction, stern loyalty to truth and conscience, self-denial, the life of conscious relation to things unseen and eternal, and living communion with our Saviour and our Father by the mighty indwelling Spirit; glad as I should be to believe it, I dare not assert that we surpass—I doubt if we equal—the Christians whose characters were shaped and toughened by a severer creed in a more wintry social, civil, moral, and religious climate.[67]

67 E. R. Conder, 'What have the churches gained and lost?', p. 198.

CHAPTER 6

'Change and Decay' or 'Onward Still, and Upward'? Reflections on the Development of Doctrine

From New Testament times to the present day the question of the permissible degree of doctrinal tolerance within the Church has been raised and debated, sometimes heatedly. The challenge has sometimes been posed by those deemed heretical, whether in fourth-century Alexandria, eighteenth-century Scotland or nineteenth-century America. Excommunications, secessions and even death (remember Servetus) have followed the authoritative declaration that commitment to such and such a doctrinal position places the protagonist beyond the ecclesiastical pale. What might be called the doctrinal policing of the saints—an activity sometimes more, sometimes less, harsh—has been justified in terms, variously, of honouring the truth, upholding the Bible, being faithful to Church Tradition, preserving the peace of the Church or the harmony of Church and state. In the name of freedom under the Holy Spirit,[1] or of fidelity to Scripture—albeit Scripture interpreted otherwise than by the majority—intellectually adventurous Christian pilgrims of integrity (albeit sometimes with a tinge of perversity) have pushed the boundaries of ecclesiastically tolerable belief. Today the question of the permissible degree of doctrinal tolerance is frequently raised in inter-confessional dialogue where the worst fate suffered by participants is most likely to be jet-lag. But the question is nonetheless important for that. P. T. Forsyth declared that 'There must surely be in every positive religion some point where it may so change as to lose its identity and become another religion.'[2] But how is the point to be specified; by whom; and on what authority?

I have long felt that a careful analysis of the concept of doctrinal development is a pressing need in Christian circles. Experience of international ecumenical dialogue over more than two decades has persuaded me that some of the 'talking past' one another which

---

1 P. T. Forsyth's cautionary word comes to mind: 'The freaks ascribed to the Spirit arrest far more attention than the frost which settles on the Word.' See *Faith, Freedom and the Future*, (1912), London: Independent Press, 1955, p. 41.

2 P. T. Forsyth, *The Principle of Authority in Relation to Certainty, Sanctity and Society*, (1913), London: Independent Press, 1952, p. 219.

undoubtedly occurs in dialogue sessions is directly attributable to the fact that one party tacitly assumes that certain doctrinal developments are legitimate, while the other does not. Participants then stand by their articulated positions without investigating the validity or otherwise of the assumptions upon which they rest, and thus ecclesiological progress is inhibited if not arrested altogether. To illustrate the point in brief, admittedly crude, terms: a Roman Catholic theologian may wish to argue that ordination is a sacrament in which a special power (*potestas*) is conferred upon the candidate such that he (for such persons are all male), having been received into the priestly ranks, will be able to administer valid or regular sacraments. A Protestant theologian might in reply point out that the concept of *potestas* in the sense intended by the dialogue partner was unknown before the Middle Ages. The former then appeals to Church Tradition (capital 'T'), the latter to the Bible. The result is a stalemate which can be broken only by the achievement of a degree of *rapprochement* on the underlying assumptions which both theologians are making regarding doctrinal development. But, to repeat, the analysis of those assumptions all too infrequently occurs.[3]

Partly because to indicate a lacuna without attempting to fill it might suggest laziness or a failure of nerve, but principally because of the importance of the issue, I shall attempt an analysis of 'development'. I shall then, in turn, discuss the fact, the impetus towards, the authority for, and the adjudication and implications of, doctrinal change. I shall conclude by suggesting that while the Christian witness is not well served by haziness of proclamation, undue preoccupation with ecclesiastically-approved doctrinal formulae can lead to a 'Pelagian' cerebralism which prompts us to forget that the Christian evangel primarily concerns a saving *act*, that Christianity is a Way, not a doctrinal system, and that the gate to the pilgrim pathway is opened by God's sovereign grace to which we respond by a faith which is both truly ours and also a gift, and not by assent to a set of prescribed dogmas by whomsoever authorized.

I

Building upon the *Oxford English Dictionary* definition of 'development' we can say that any *x* may be said to have undergone development when it has been brought, or come, 'to active or visible state, or to maturity'; or when it has unfolded or been revealed or made progress or become 'fuller or bigger or more elaborate or systematic'. Thus human development concerns matters physical, psychological and,

---

[3] Though for some post-Vatican II Roman Catholic reflections on the matter see Nicholas Lash, ed., *Doctrinal Development and Christian Unity*, London: Sheed and Ward, 1967.

where character is concerned, moral and even spiritual. Within this broad framework we may speak, for example, of the development of muscles, of the intellect, of affections, of the moral sense, of the divine–human relationship. We may speak of the development of talents and of skills. Where skills are concerned, I note that a new profession has 'developed' in higher education; for at the time of writing this paragraph London's City University is advertizing for a Lecturer in Educational Development who will 'play a leading role in the teaching and development of academic staff'.[4] The nature of the envisaged 'development' is not further specified. We may, however, presume that the appointee will not be asked to break current law by developing academic staff from scratch by cloning the ablest scholars, or to alter the personalities of colleagues by the application of drugs or of sinister brainwashing techniques.[5]

Again, we speak of the development of systems, whether intellectual as in philosophy and theology, or procedural as in law or industrial production. Other animals develop too, a fact of which anyone who has studied zoology or heard Sunday School lessons about caterpillars and butterflies will be fully aware. As to things inanimate, we speak of rural, urban and land development; of the development of photographs and of musical themes; and, in the natural world, of storms.

What is common to all of the above is that something—material, ability, process, circumstance—is given in relation to which change occurs. Many, but not all, people pass through all the stages of human development from embryo to old age; given particular circumstances and encouragements the mind and character of a person will normally develop; with the growing complexity of socio-political life, legal systems will develop in the sense of changing to meet new circumstances; given the requisite knowledge, skills and raw materials, industrial processes will develop; the development of town and countryside is incessant; from given materials photographs are developed; in relation to theoretical skill and aesthetic insight musical themes are developed.

However, not all change is welcome. If muscles can develop, so can boils and cancers. We speak metaphorically of deformed characters, of bad law, of inhuman processes. If, in the hey-day of theological liberalism of the more optimistic/sentimental kind, a church in Cambridge could display a poster proclaiming David Livingstone's slogan, 'I will go anywhere if only it be forward' (on seeing which a friend of Bernard

---

4 *The Times Higher Education Supplement*, 28 May 2004, p. 51.

5 As I write this sentence I recall a former student of mine, much given to unwitting ambiguity of expression, who proclaimed on his course assessment form, 'Professor Sell does not always understand what I saying to him.' He was quite innocent of the fact that one of the oldest tricks in the philosophy teacher's book is that of construing an ambiguous utterance in the way least likely to be intended by the speaker, with a view to encouraging clarity and precision on the latter's part.

Lord Manning's said, 'I should like to write underneath *And so say all of us (signed) the Gadarene Swine*'),[6] today, as Margaret Canovan has properly observed, 'It is...clearer to us... , in the shadow of nuclear weapons, that there is no necessary connection between progress in the sense of having more knowledge, and progress in the sense of behaving better.'[7] Developed photographs may be technically competent but pornographic, musical themes banal or tasteless. We speak of rural decline and urban blight. In every case judgements are being expressed on the way in which what has been given has 'turned out' or been abused, exploited, tarnished, disfigured.

There are thus raised the questions of the validity of the judgements and the authority and reliability of those making them. These questions are raised not only when judgements are originally made, but also when they are, over time, revised. Such revisions can work in either direction. Something originally deemed an undesirable development can come to be regarded later as of worth. For example, many were horrified when, owing to pressing housing needs at the end of World War II, clusters of prefabricated dwellings sprung up all over the land. Architects and aesthetes far and wide were highly critical of them. But although these 'prefabs' were intended to have a life of twenty years only, some still survive and are now highly prized by the heritage industry. Conversely, something at first deemed to be a desirable development can come to be regarded as a disaster. Thus, many of the high-rise tower blocks created during the 1960s to replace the 'prefabs', though at first lauded as the last word in affordable housing, proved to be socially counter-productive, became subject to vandalism, and have long since been bulldozed out of existence.

All of the points noted—and they could be 'developed' further—apply to the consideration of the development of doctrine, as I shall now seek to show.[8]

---

6 See B. L. Manning, *Essays in Orthodox Dissent*, (1939), London: Independent Press, 1953, p. 140.

7 M. Canovan, 'Two concepts of liberty—eighteenth-century style', *The Price-Priestley Newsletter*, No. 2, 1978, p. 39.

8 In what follows I am concerned only with the Christian religion. I do not deny that other faiths also have discussions concerning the development of doctrine. Among Muslim scholars, for example, the doctrine of *Jihad* is currently under discussion from this point of view. Moreover, the phrase 'development of doctrine' is used outside the sphere of religion altogether. The United States has a Military Joint and Service Doctrine Development Program which is concerned with 'strategic, operational and technical doctrine'. See www.mpri.com/site/net_jointdocdev.html

II

It would be difficult to deny that the way doctrines are articulated has changed over time. We do not find it easy to sing some hymns from the past—or indeed from the present—not so much because of archaic language as because we no longer believe exactly what, or in the way, our forebears did or some of our contemporaries do. Hymns which suggest that the God of all grace could not be gracious and merciful unless or until Jesus died, or which speak of our bringing in the Kingdom as if the Kingdom were not God's gift, do not fall easily from our lips.[9] In most of the circles with which I am most familiar sermons which treated the congregation to fifty-five minutes of sin and the threat of hell and five minutes of the Gospel would not be very welcome.[10] Clearly, in speaking of 'doctrinal change' I am here referring to what is believed and to how it is formulated. I leave open for the moment the question whether or not a complete body of teaching has existed from the beginning, aspects of which become apparent to believers only after a lapse of time—even of centuries.

In the sense now under review, doctrine has been developing from the earliest days of the Church. Christians should not be surprised at this for with reference to God the Holy Spirit Jesus said, 'He will take what is mine and make it known to you.'[11] This implies a learning process and a growth in understanding on the part of the disciples. In his address on this Johannine text delivered to the International Congregational Council in 1920, J. D. Jones of Richmond Hill Church, Bournemouth, entered the following important caveat:

> while our Lord's word here contemplated growth and development, it also suggests the limits within which such growth and development must always proceed. It is an ever enlarging knowledge of Christ the Spirit gives. The Truth He reveals has been all the while implicit, resident in Christ. In Him dwelleth all the fulness of the Godhead; in Him are all the treasures of wisdom and knowledge hidden. What the Spirit does is to take of this infinite 'treasure' and turn it into the current coin of our thought and worship. The Spirit does not, so to speak, invent new truth. He works

---

9 See further Alan P. F. Sell, *Confessing and Commending the Faith. Christian Witness and Apologetic Method*, Cardiff: University of Wales Press, 2002, pp. 126-128. For a discussion of the sense in which Christians subscribe to the *same* faith through the ages see pp. 69-79.

10 I suspect that a sermon on any theme which lasted for one hour would not be very welcome in some quarters; and if any present-day preacher were to sit down to catch his breath after the first hour of his sermon before proceeding to the next, as John Angell James was wont to do in the nineteenth century, some members of the congregation would be more inclined to throw oranges at him than pass them to him as in James's case.

11 John 16:14.

> ever within the sphere of Christ and the result of His work is to make Christ more glorious, more wonderful, more Divine.[12]

Jones further pointed out that within the New Testament itself the understanding and articulation of Christian teaching underwent development:

> There was a vast difference between the Peter who at the suggestion of death cried, 'God forbid, this shall never be unto Thee,' and the Peter who could preach that it was through death God exalted Christ to be a Prince and a Saviour... There is a very considerable difference between the Paul who wrote the letter to the Thessalonians and the Paul who wrote the letters to the Ephesians... The story of the disciples is that of men who grew in their understanding of the truth as it is in Jesus, and whose growing understanding carried with it a certain amount of re-statement, as their own epistles testify.[13]

To this much more might be added. For example, the variety of the titles accorded to Jesus are indicative of the way in which, in relation to diverse contexts, views of his person and work were being formed; and *pace* Paul's earlier opinion, Christian eschatology—and Paul himself—had to come to terms with a less-than-imminent Parousia. Jones sums matters up by declaring that 'The ceaseless revealing of the Spirit involves the necessity of continuous re-statement.'[14] No doubt, provided that we allow the Spirit to address the Church through a diversity of persons and contexts.

From the many possible illustrations of change in doctrinal interpretation and articulation which might be drawn from extra-biblical sources I shall mention three from the history of English Dissent. First, there is that 'dilution' of Calvinism in English Congregationalism, to which I have drawn attention in a previous chapter.[15] This is by no means unconnected with the moral critique of doctrinal statements which was stimulated by the English Enlightenment.[16] Secondly, it is undeniable that a doctrinal sea-change has occurred between the seventeenth-century Quaker John Gratton's broadly evangelical doctrine and that of those

---

12 J. D. Jones, 'The doctrine of development', *Proceedings of the International Congregational Council*, New York: National Council of the Congregational Churches of the United States, 1921, p. 60. I fear that the final clause here, though oratorically rhythmic as one might expect from a Welshman, is theologically dubious. But the main point stands. For Jones (1865–1942) see *The Congregational Year Book*, 1943, p. 417; Arthur Porritt, *J. D. Jones of Bournemouth*, London: Independent Press, 1942.

13 Jones, 'The doctrine of development', pp. 60-61.

14 Ibid., p. 62.

15 See ch. 5 above.

16 See ch. 3 above.

present-day Friends who identify themselves as non-theistic.[17] This, it would appear, results from a disjoining of Spirit from Scripture, and the construal of the former in a privatized manner[18]—a conclusion confirmed by the Quaker scholar, John Punshon, who writes of early Quaker experience that 'It was not an experience of an undifferentiated ultimate; it was an experience of the God of the Christian scriptures.'[19] Arthur O. Roberts concurs. He reminds us that Robert Barclay 'posited a harmony among inward revelation, Scripture, and right reason within the context of a covenant people collectively sensitive to the voice of Christ.'[20] Thirdly, I have elsewhere referred to the course taken by eighteenth-century Presbyterians. By the end of that century those who had not become Congregationalists had almost entirely become unitarian in doctrine, some of them having passed through Arianism and Socinianism *en route*.[21] I now wish to note the chasm between even that position and views entertained by some within present-day Unitarianism. A stage on the journey is represented by the following description of J. H. Muirhead:

> Under [James Martineau's] leadership Unitarianism had recently been emancipated from belief in the miraculous element in Christian doctrine, including the resurrection and the authenticity of the Messianic claims as we have them in the Fourth Gospel. Jesus of Nazareth was a fellow man and an elder brother, only knowing the mind of the common Father more intimately and profoundly than any other before or since, and in that sense the captain of our salvation. To be worthy followers constituted man's highest task, believing *with* him rather than *in* him. Religion was to be directed *by* Jesus rather than *to* Jesus.[22]

---

17 See ch. 2 above.

18 W. R. Inge writes that 'The crumbling of traditional theology has left the foundations of Quakerism untouched.' If this were true, it could only be because those foundations are defined in terms of undifferentiated mysticism. See his *The Church in the World*, London: Longmans, Green, 1927, p. 57.

19 J. Punshon, *Reasons for Hope. The Faith and Future of the Friends Church*, Richmond, IN: Friends United Press, 2001, p. 103.

20 A. O. Roberts, 'John Punshon's *Reasons for Hope*... A Review', *Quaker Religious Thought*, nos. 99 and 100, April 2003, p. 11. Edward Grubb attributed Quaker doctrinal reduction to the fact that from the beginning of the eighteenth century to the middle of the nineteenth 'The idea came to prevail that all the teaching that was required would be supernaturally supplied, and no adequate steps were taken to make provision for it.' See his paper, 'The Society of Friends', in W. B. Selbie, ed., *Evangelical Christianity, Its History and Witness*, London: Hodder and Stoughton, [1911], p. 203.

21 See Alan P. F. Sell, *Dissenting Thought and the Life of the Churches. Studies in an English Tradition*, Lewiston, NY: Edwin Mellen Press, 1990, ch. 5.

22 J. H. Muirhead, *Reflections by a Journeyman in Philosophy on the Movements of Thought and Practice in his Time*, London: Allen & Unwin, 1942, pp. 64-65. For Martineau (1805–1900) see W. J. Mander and Alan P. F. Sell, eds., *Dictionary of Nineteenth-Century British Philosophers*, Briston: Thoemmes Press, 2002; Alan P. F.

Such trends notwithstanding, in 1928 the Unitarian scholar, S. H. Mellone, could expect widespread agreement within his denomination that 'The very essence of the Unitarian gospel...is the Fatherhood of God.'[23] Today, however, some within the Unitarian fold describe themselves as atheists, agnostics or humanists.[24]

III

As already hinted, a variety of stimuli may prompt changes in the way doctrine is articulated. As soon as the infant Church carried the Gospel into Hellenistic culture doctrine had to be freshly interpreted in order to engage with the thought forms of that culture. The qualification of the term *logos* by the words 'made flesh' is a classic example of the rebaptism of terms for proclamatory purposes. Again, the confrontation of those within the Church deemed heretical required the clarification and defence of doctrine. Through this process, for example, the biblical clues regarding the Trinity were, over time, elucidated in relation to the experience of those who had been called by the Father to follow the Son in the power of the Spirit.

Contextual factors of one kind or another seem always to be involved in cases of doctrinal change: whether the state of the Church, as at the time of the Reformation; the perception of the need to offer a moral critique of doctrine as during the English Enlightenment; or the modern ecumenical movement as fostering the restatement of ecclesiological positions as a prelude to inner- or trans-confessional union.[25]

By way of illustrating contextual factors in doctrinal reformulation in a little more detail, I shall now refer to two nineteenth-century developments in ecclesiology: those of the Mercersburg theologians and the restorationists of the Disciples of Christ. I select these because in the

---

Sell, *Commemorations. Studies in Christian Thought and History*, Calgary: University of Calgary Press and Cardiff: University of Wales Press, 1993; reprinted Eugene, OR: Wipf & Sdtrock, 1998, chs. 1 and 10.

23 S. H. Mellone, *Back to Realities: A Way out of the Present Chaos in Religion*, London: Constable, 1928, p. 90. For Mellone (1869-1956) see Mander and Sell, eds., *Dictionary of Nineteenth-Century British Philosophers*; Alan P. F. Sell, *Philosophy, Dissent and Nonconformity 1689–1920*, Cambridge: James Clarke, 2004; Andrew M. Hill, 'Too soon forgotten: Sydney Herbert Mellone, 1869–1956', in Leonard Smith, ed., *Unitarian to the Core: Unitarian College, Manchester, 1854–2004*, Manchester: Carnegie Publishing for the Unitarian College, 2004, ch. 5.

24 So George Chryssides, *The Elements of Unitarianism*, Shaftesbury: Element Books, 1998, p. 106.

25 See, for example, Alan P. F. Sell, *Testimony and Tradition. Studies in Reformed and Dissenting Thought*, Aldershot: Ashgate, 2005, ch. 12, for an account of the process by which the Congregational Union of England and Wales became the Congregational Church in England and Wales.

midst of the rise of modern historiography, one of the consequences of which was that increased attention was paid to the *theory* of doctrinal development, these two movements represent significantly different responses to their contexts. Moreover, they represent tendencies which are not dormant in ecumenical discussion to this day.

With more than a little indebtedness to the organic thrust of that blend of Romantic post-Hegelian idealism with Scottish common sense realism which Frederick A. Rauch (1806–1841) expounded whilst at the Mercersburg Seminary of the German Reformed Church, the erstwhile Presbyterian John Williamson Nevin (1803–66) and the distinguished church historian Philip Schaff (1819–93) developed what came to be known as the Mercersburg theology. They did this in response to a number of contextual stimuli.[26]

First, in Nevin's view the German Reformed Church was imbibing too much of the spirit of that individualistic evangelicalism associated supremely with the name of C. G. Finney, whose use of the 'new measures'—the anxious bench and the like—for fostering revival Nevin abominated:

> If Finneyism and Winebrennerism, the anxious bench, revival machinery, solemn tricks for effect, decision displays at the bidding of the preacher, genuflections and prostrations in the aisle or around the altar, noise and disorder, extravagance and rant, and encouragement ministered to all fanatical impressions: if these things, and things in the same line indefinitely, have no connection in fact with true serious religion and the cause of revivals, but tend only to bring them into discredit, let the fact be openly proclaimed.[27]

Nevin proceeded openly to proclaim the fact with a zeal which any evangelist might envy. In particular, he argued that

> The spirit of the Anxious Bench is at war with the spirit of the Catechism. ...[W]here the system of the Catechism prevails great account is made of the Church, and all reliance placed upon the means of grace comprehended in its constitution as all-sufficient under God for the accomplishment of its own

26 For the philosophical background to Mercersburg theology, see Linden Jay DeBie, 'German Idealism in Protestant Orthodoxy: The Mercersburg Movement, 1840–1860', unpublished doctoral dissertation, McGill University, 1987; William DiPuccio, 'Nevin's idealistic philosophy', in Sam Hamstra, Jr., and Arie J. Griffioen, *Reformed Confessionalism in Nineteenth-Century America*, Lanham, MD: Scarecrow Press, 1995, pp. 43-67. Some of DiPuccio's assertions, for example, those regarding Bacon and Howe, are open to question. For the general history of Mercersburg theology see J. H. Nichols, *The Mercersburg Theology*, New York: Oxford University Press, 1966.

27 J. W. Nevin, *The Anxious Bench*, (1843), 2nd edn. 1844, reprinted in Charles Yrigoyen, Jr., and George H. Bricker, eds., *Catholic and Reformed. Selected Theological Writings of John Williamson Nevin*, Pittsburgh, PA: Pickwick Press, 1978, p. 30.

purposes. The means are felt to be something more than the devices of human ingenuity... Due regard is had to the idea of the Church as something more than a bare abstraction, the conception of an aggregate of parts mechanically brought together. It is apprehended rather as an organic life springing perpetually from the same ground, and identical with itself at every point.[28]

Secondly, Nevin, influenced by the writings of Neander, regarded this drift as symptomatic of a deeper malaise which prompted many Protestants to embrace the ahistorical view that nothing except apostasy occurred in Church history from the end of the New Testament to the Reformation. In a word, they lost the idea of the catholicity of the Church at all times and in every place:

Whatever differences there may be between the first ages and those that followed, it is still plain enough that the course of things was from the very start *towards* that order at least, which afterwards prevailed; that this later order therefore stands bound by true historical connection with what went before; and that Protestantism accordingly, as a still more advanced period in the general movement of history, holds a living relation to the first period only through the medium of the second, and is just as little a copy of the one as it is of the other.[29]

Nevin, we note in passing, is no restorationist.

Thirdly, Nevin inveighed against what he called 'the sect plague' with its ahistorical individualism:

Their common watchword is: The Bible and Private Judgment! But in no case do they show themselves true to its demands.... What sect in reality allows the Bible and Private Judgment to rule its faith? Is it not notorious that every one of them has a scheme of notions already at hand, a certain system of opinion and practice, which is made to underlie all this boasted freedom in the use of the Bible, leading private judgment along by the nose, and forcing the divine text always to speak in its own way?[30]

Nevin therefore charges that 'The sect habit, as such, is constitutionally unfree. All true emancipation in religion begins only when the power of this habit has been broken, and the sense of a true catholic Christianity is brought to reign in its place.'[31] Philip Schaff was in general agreement with Nevin on this, though he expressed himself more temperately. Neither the sects nor rationalism were 'the work of Satan only', but

---

28 Ibid., pp. 101, 110-111.

29 J. W. Nevin, 'Early Christianity', reprinted from *The Mercersburg Review*, 1851, in Yrigoyen, Jr., and Bricker, eds., *Catholic and Reformed,* p. 197.

30 J. W. Nevin, 'The sect system', reprinted from *The Mercersburg Review*, 1849, in Yrigoyen, Jr., and Bricker, eds., *Catholic and Reformed*, p. 140; cf 'Early Christianity', in *Catholic and Reformed*, p. 244.

31 Nevin, 'The sect system', p. 143.

having made their protest they should return to the larger fold so that their isolated insights would take their place within the organism of Christian truth.[32]

Nevin further complained against the sects that, under rationalistic influence and committed to the right of private judgment, they had transmogrified the Lord's Supper into a memorial meal, failing to regard it as a celebration of the true presence of Christ. In his view,

> the sacramental doctrine of the primitive Reformed Church stands inseparably connected with the idea of an inward living union between believers and Christ, in virtue of which they are incorporated into his very nature, and made to subsist with him by the power of a common life. ...[Hence, the Lord's Supper] is not simply an occasion, by which the soul of the believer may be excited to pious feelings and desires; but it embodies the actual presence of the grace it represents in its own constitution: and this grace is not simply the promise of God on which we are encouraged to rely, but the very life of the Lord Jesus Christ himself.[33]

Running strongly through the writings of Nevin is the view that the Church is an organism: 'the living and life-giving body of Jesus Christ'.[34] Because Christianity is real and organic, it must be historical. Schaff strongly endorsed this position. As Klaus Penzel properly reminds us, Schaff's view

> faithfully mirrored Schleiermacher's 'Protestant view' of the Christian church 'as a whole that is capable of motion, progress and development, with the single restriction without which Christianity would collapse...namely, that such progress is nothing but a better understanding and a more perfect appropriation of what is found in Christ.'[35]

---

32 P. Schaff, *The Principle of Protestantism*, eds. Bard Thompson and George H. Bricker, Philadelphia, PA: United Church Press, 1964, p. 165. See further, John B. Payne, 'Schaff and Nevin, colleagues at Mercersburg: The Church question', *Church History*, LXI no. 2, June 1992, pp. 169-190.

33 J. W. Nevin, *The Mystical Presence and Other Writings on the Eucharist*, eds. Bard Thompson and George H. Bricker, Philadelphia, PA: United Church Press, 1966, pp. 31, 33-4. See further, Lawrence S. Stepelvich, 'Eucharistic theory: Hegelianism and Mercersburg theology', *The New Mercersburg Review*, no. 20, Autumn 1996, pp. 3-16.

34 Nevin, *The Mystical Presence and Other Writings on the Eucharist*, p. 24. It should not be supposed that Nevin's views were endorsed by all in the German Reformed Church. On the contrary, his erstwhile defender, J. H. A. Bomberger, for example, because his staunchest opponent. See Sell, *Commemorations*, ch. 11.

35 K. Penzel, *Philip Schaff: Historian and Ambassador of the Universal Church*, Macon, GA: Mercer University Press, 1991, pp. xliii-xliv. Penzel quotes F. D. E. Schleiermacher, *Die christliche Sitte nach den Grundsätzen der evangelischen Kirche im Zusammenhang dargestellt*, ed. L. Jonas, in *Sämmtliche Werke*, sec. 1, vol. 12, 2nd ed., Berlin 1884, p. 72.

Indeed, Schaff went so far as to declare that 'The recognition of God in history is the first principle of all sound philosophy of history'.[36] Under the providential hand of God the empirical Church is the ideal Church as anchored in history, ever developing until the ideal is attained and its potential fully reached. The reference to the divine providence is of crucial importance, for although some theologians found in Darwinism and its harbingers a treasure trove of metaphors allegedly applicable to the onward march of history construed as the outworking of God's purposes; and although post-Hegelian immanentism provided fertile soil for this intellectual move,[37] it would be a serious mistake to align Mercersburg's understanding of organism with Darwinism—least of all with that evolutionary optimism to which Herbert Spencer, among others, was so deeply committed, and which in its ethical ramifications was scuppered by F. H. Bradley who observed that, as distinct from evolutionism, for Darwinism 'the true idea is the idea which prevails...without any regard for its character. And this must surely leave us in the end with no criterion at all.'[38]

On the question of organism, Schaff was no less an Hegelian than F. A. Rauch. With indebtedness to his teacher, F. C. Baur, and also to Schelling's positing of three ages of Church history which are identified successively with Peter, Paul and John, he thinks in terms of three ages of Church history: the age of the ancient Church, the Church of the Middle Ages and the Church of the Reformation.[39] He finds that in different permutations objectivity and subjectivity characterize the three ages. In the first objectivity and subjectivity are held in balance; in the second, objectivity (leading to authoritarianism) takes precedence, while in the third subjectivity (with its peril of licence) is disproportionally emphasized. Pitfalls notwithstanding, it is of the nature of an organism such as the Church that 'What is untrue and imperfect in an earlier stage

---

[36] Quoted by H. W. Bowden, *Church History in the Age of Science*, Chapel Hill, NC: University of North Carolina Press, 1971, p. 52. See further the unpublished doctoral dissertations of Theodore L. Trost, Jr, 'Philip Schaff's Concept of the Church' (University of Edinburgh, 1958), and George H. Shriver 'Philip Schaff's Concept of Organic Historiography' (Duke University, 1960).

[37] See further, Alan P. F. Sell, *Theology in Turmoil. The Roots, Course and Significance of the Conservative–Liberal Debate in Modern Theology*, (1986), Eugene, OR: Wipf & Stock, 1998, chs. 1, 3.

[38] F. H. Bradley, *Essays on Truth and Reality*, Oxford: Clarendon Press, 1914, pp. 322-323.

[39] See P. Schaff, *History of the Apostolic Church with a General Introduction to Church History*, (1854), in Yrigoyen, Jr., and Bricker, eds., *Reformed and Catholic*, pp. 149-313, especially pp. 198-211. See further, K. Penzel, 'The Reformation goes West: The notion of historical development in the thought of Philip Schaff', *Journal of Religion*, LXII, July 1982, pp. 219-241.

is done away by that which follows; what is true and essential is preserved, and made the living germ of further development.'[40]

Turning now to our second nineteenth-century ecclesiological illustration, we find that, much more indebted to Locke and Scottish common sense realism than to Hegelianism, the leaders of the Disciples of Christ had no such confidence in organic development.[41] Beset by frontier lawlessness and a *mélange* of competing denominations,[42] and motivated by a desire to make a common witness to the Gospel alongside other Christians, they sought to go back to basics. They resorted to the New Testament, convinced that there they would find *the* pattern of churchly life which they could then reproduce in their own context, and which all true Christians would happily adopt. In a word, they adopted a restorationist stance. This is epitomized in the *Declaration and Address* which Thomas Campbell (1763–1854), the Irish Seceder Presbyterian who arrived in the Pennsylvania in 1807, had ready for publication in 1809, the year in which his son Alexander (1788–1866) joined him in America. Thomas Campbell's *Address*, explanatory of the *Declaration*, includes thirteen propositions of which the first reads as follows:

> That the Church of Christ upon earth is essentially, intentionally, and constitutionally one, consisting of all those in every place that profess faith in Christ and obedience to Him in all things according to the scriptures, and that manifest the same by their tempers and conduct, and of none else, as none else can be truly and properly called Christians.

The second proposition declares that 'there ought to be no schisms, no uncharitable divisions' among 'particular and distinct societies' of Christians; while the third insists that nothing 'be admitted as of divine obligation in their church constitution and managements, but what is expressly enjoined by the authority of our Lord Jesus Christ and His Apostles upon the New Testament Church, either in expressed terms, or by approved precedent'.[43] As Alexander Campbell succinctly put it, 'We

---

40 Schaff, *History of the Apostolic Church*, p. 169.

41 See Winfred Ernest Garrison, *Alexander Campbell's Theology: Its Sources and Historical Setting*, St. Louis: Christian Publishing, 1900; Lynn A. McMillon, 'Alexander Campbell's early exposure to Scottish restorationism', *Restoration Quarterly*, XXX nos.2 and 3, 1988, pp. 105-110; Michael Casey, 'The origins of the hermeneutics of the Churches of Christ. Part One: The Reformed Tradition; Part Two: The Philosophical Background', *Restoration Quarterly*, XXXI nos. 2 and 4, 1989, pp. 75-91, 193-206.

42 William Warren Sweet states that in Pennsylvania in 1776 there were 403 particular churches representative of eleven denominations. See his *Religion in Colonial America*, New York: Charles Scribner's Sons, 1942, p. 163.

43 T. Campbell, *Declaration and Address*, (1809), reprinted in David M. Thompson, ed., *Stating the Gospel. Formulations and Declarations of Faith from the Heritage of the United Reformed Church*, Edinburgh: T. & T. Clark, 1990, pp. 135-136.

take the Bible, the whole Bible, and nothing but the Bible, as the foundation of all Christian union and communion.'[44]

We should note the strong affirmation of the given unity of the Church. 'Jesus', wrote Alexander Campbell, 'in the new creation, by his Spirit sent down from heaven after his glorification, did, by a positive, direct, and immediate agency create one congregation, one mystical or spiritual body...'.[45] But we should also be aware that the Campbells did not, after the fashion of more recent ecumenists, work for the uniting of the many Christian parties by which they were surrounded: 'I have no idea of seeing, nor wish to see, the sects unite in one grand army', wrote Alexander Campbell: 'For this the Saviour did not pray. It is only the *disciples dispersed among them* that reason and benevolence would call out of them....'[46] Hence the Disciples' aspiration was that once the beliefs and practices of the earliest Christianity were restored, true Christians of hitherto diverse allegiance would join them. We should also underline the fact that the Campbells, no less than Nevin and Schaff, abominated the sectarian spirit, notwithstanding that Nevin regarded the Campellites as among the tribe of sectaries to whom he was opposed. His objection to the Campbellites was what he deemed to be their ahistorical rationalism—and Campbell certainly believed that the world was now bereft of genuine Christianity.[47]

It would seem that there were two principal sources of tension in the Disciples' articulated positions. First, under the impress of modern biblical criticism, those who became known as the Christian Church (Disciples of Christ) came to think more in terms of general ecumenism than of restorationism, while others, who continue as the Churches of Christ, emphasized restorationism and became ever more sectarian in attitude and practice. Secondly, Alexander Campbell's commitment to the idea of human progress, when blended with his restorationism, persuaded him that once the union of all true Christians had been achieved the millennium would dawn. This ahistorical looking fore and aft, so to speak, proved difficult for some to grasp, and the problem was

---

[44] A. Campbell, *The Christian System in Reference to the Union of Christians, and a Restoration of Primitive Christianity, as Plead in the Current Reformation*, (1839), Nashville, TN: Gospel Advocate, reprint of 2nd edn, 1970, p. xvii.

[45] Ibid., p. 150.

[46] A. Campbell, *The Christian Baptist*, II, 1825, p. 85.

[47] Nevin, 'The sect system', pp. 162-164. Cf. A. Campbell, *Millenial Harbinger*, 3, 2 January 1832, p. 6. For a brief discussion of similarities and differences, see W. Clark Gilpin, 'The doctrine of the Church in the thought of Alexander Campbell and John W. Nevin', *Mid-Stream*, XIX no. 4, October 1980, pp. 417-427.

exacerbated when Campbell's prominent co-leader, Barton W. Stone, espoused an apocalypicism which insisted that the new age was now.[48]

The general charge which Nevin levelled against the sects, namely, that in fact they brought their own philosophico-theological preconceptions to bear upon the Bible seems undeniable. In the case of the Disciples, Nevin charged Alexander Campbell with propagating what was,

> in its best view Judaism... Christianity is no such outward statute-book of things to be believed and things to be done. It is 'the law of life in Christ Jesus.' It is a new constitution of grace and truth starting in Christ's *person*, and perpetuating itself in this form, as a most real historical fact, by the Church. The difference between this conception and the other...is very great; and we only wish that Mr. Campbell, and many others, could be led to revolve it solemnly and earnestly in their minds.'[49]

It was under the influence of Bacon, Locke and the Scottish common sense thinkers that Campbell and others, taking the inductive way, were led to regard the Bible as a repository of reproducable facts. This went hand in hand with a view of revelation which some present-day scholars of the Churches of Christ tradition have repudiated: 'Hardline patternism approaches Scripture as a revelation of propositional truths rather than of the heart of the Father.'[50] Nothing could be further from Nevin's post-Hegelian Romantic doctrine of the Church as an organism. While it is no doubt easier to see what is happening with hindsight—especially standing as we now do on our side of modern biblical criticism, and having learned that there is a measure of interpretation in every announcement of a 'fact'—I cannot resist the conclusion that the following assertion of Alexander Campbell is but a forlorn 'if only...':

---

[48] The literature on this restorationist movement (it was not the only one, of course: the [Plymouth] Brethren are another) is vast. Reliable introductions include Richard T. Hughes, *The Churches of Christ*, Westport, CT: Praeger, 2001. This book includes a helpful bibliographical essay.

[49] Nevin, 'The sect system', p. 153.

[50] Russ Dudrey, 'Restorationist hermeneutics among the Churches of Christ: Why are we at an impasse?', *Restoration Quarterly*, XXX no. 1, 1988, p. 41. It must, however, be said that Campbell was less than consistent in the application of his hermeneutical principles—especially as regards scriptural silences, which he sometimes construed as offering no justification for a particular practice, at other times as permitting liberty of opinion or action. See further Woody Woodrow, 'The silence of Scripture and the Restoraton movement', *Restoration Quarterly*, XXVIII, 1985–86, pp. 27-39.

> Were all students of the Bible taught to apply the same rules of interpretation to its pages, there would be a greater uniformity in opinion and sentiment, than ever resulted from the simple adoption of any written creed.[51]

Underlying this statement is Campbell's commitment to the principle of the sole sufficiency of Scripture: '*We choose to speak of Bible things by Bible words*, because we are always suspicious that if the word is not in the Bible the idea which it represents is not there....'[52] This, which is exactly the stance adopted by the eighteenth-century Arians with respect to the Trinity and Christology,[53] only goes to show how diverse are the interpretations which shelter under the umbrella of the sole sufficiency of Scripture.

We have thus seen that at a time when the question of historical method was coming to the fore, the Mercersburg theologians offered one kind of response to the doctrine of the Church, the restorationists a radically different one; and both responses presuppose different understandings of doctrinal development. For the former the Church is an organism which, under the Spirit and in union with Christ, develops through time; for the latter the true order of the Church is given in the Bible and, in face of general apostasy, it must be and can be restored. For both the promptings of the prevailing religious context were similar in kind, but the extra-biblical philosophical lenses through which they viewed Scripture were significantly different. Hence whilst equally concerned with the doctrine of the Church, they were far from mutual ecclesiological harmony.

I by no means suggest that the Disciples were the first to follow the restorationist path. The English Separatists, prompted by their aversion to the untoward ecclesiological pretensions of the state and the perceived indiscipline of the Church of England, turned to the Bible for the true Church order, and sought to implement it.[54] Contemporaneously with the American Disciples, the Irish Presbyterian, Thomas Witherow, having dismissed prelacy and independency, concluded that it was 'beyond all reasonable doubt' that Presbyterianism '*comes nearest to the model of apostolic times*'.[55] He did, however, concede that no 'Church on earth is *in everything* an exact model of the pattern presented in the primitive age'—not least because the apostles were 'vested with extraordinary powers, which have been handed down to no successors'.[56] We may

---

51 A. Campbell, *Christianity Restored*, Bethany, VA: M'Vey and Ewing, 1835, p. 15.

52 Campbell, *The Christian System*, p. 103.

53 See further ch. 3 above.

54 See further, ch. 1 above.

55 See T. Witherow, *The Apostolic Church: Which Is It?* (1856), Publications Committee of the Free Presbyterian Church of Scotland, 1967, p. 76.

56 Ibid., p. 72.

further note, with some relief, Witherow's view that 'There is such a thing as being a Presbyterian without being a Christian, as it is possible to be a Christian without being a Presbyterian.'[57] It must in fairness be granted that the Separatists were writing long before modern biblical criticism had done its work, and the frontier Disciples and Witherow had some excuse, for they were, as we might say, living between the times on this issue. But we cannot so easily absolve William P. Breed, whose 1880 defence of Presbyterian order included the *ad hominem* affirmation that 'no intelligent Bible student needs to be informed that...an eldership existed in the Church, at least from the time when that Church was held in Egyptian bondage. Out of the burning bush came the command, "Go, call the elders."'[58] We can but take of our shoes...

By 1908 the Congregationalist F. J. Powicke[59] felt able to remind the International Congregational Council that

> we have long since ceased to vaunt the divine right of our own church order as if it, and it only, reflected the pattern delivered in the New Testament. We think Browne, Barrow, Robinson and other early advocates of that position were mistaken in seeking a New Testament pattern at all.... We have learnt that the types of church government, or administration, discernible in the New Testament were not uniform, but varied according to the genius of place and people; and this fact does not trouble us because, realizing the character of Christianity as a Gospel of the spirit, it is just what we should expect.[60]

It would seem that in his characterization of Christianity as 'a Gospel of the spirit' Powicke leans too far in the pneumatic direction. For from the fact that there is no one pattern of church order prescribed for all time in the New Testament we need not, and I think we should not, tacitly infer that there is no guidance there at all in the matter of polity. If there can be a restorationist legalism, there can also be a tyranny of mutually contradictory spiritual 'insights', and both can be equally disruptive of churchly fellowship. Freedom within order is a not altogether unattainable objective, and it turns upon the willingness of the Church to seek the mind of Christ by the Spirit through the Scriptures within the catholic fellowship. But this leads us towards our next question: How are doctrinal changes to be evaluated?

---

57 Ibid., p. 91.

58 W. P. Breed in *The Catholic Presbyterian*, III, 1880, p. 47.

59 For whom see ch. 1 above.

60 F. J. Powicke, 'Historic Congregationalism in Britain', *Proceedings of the Third International Congregational Council*, London: Congregational Union of England and Wales, 1908, p. 266. Cf. Powicke's 'The Congregational churches', in Selbie, ed., *Evangelical Christianity*, pp. 108-109.

IV

I shall seek to answer this question by reference to three divines who gave considerable thought to it and, within a period of about fifty years, produced interestingly different responses to it. They are the Unitarian Joseph Priestley (1733–1804), the Congregationalist Robert Vaughan (1795–1868) and the Anglican-turned Roman Catholic John Henry Newman (1801–90). That changes in any field may be for the better or for the worse is clear. As Bertrand Russell quizzically observed,

> Organic life, we are told, has developed gradually from the protozoon to the philosopher, and this development, we are assured, is indubitably an advance. Unfortunately it is the philosopher, not the protozoon, who gives us this assurance, and we can have no security that the impartial outsider would agree with the philosopher's self-complacent assumption.[61]

The pressing question is thus, How are judgements as to the worth or otherwise of changes—in our case, of doctrinal changes—arrived at; by whom; and on what authority?

To Joseph Priestley, whose prodigious industry yielded charts of biography and history, history is a matter of a process occurring within time. With reference to his biographical chart he declared, 'Time is continually suggested to us...under the idea of a *river*, flowing uniformly on, without beginning or end.'[62] Moreover, the historical process presupposes freedom to develop. Indeed, 'It is an universal maxim, that the more liberty is given to every thing which is in a state of growth, the more perfect it will become; and when it is grown to its full size, the more amply will it repay its wise parent for the indulgence given to it in its infant state.'[63]

However, this general view of historical process is complicated (some might say subverted) in Priestley's writings by an *a priori* theological position concerning the providence of God and the faith once delivered to the saints. Thus, on the one hand, Priestley grants that Christianity—its

---

61 B. Russell, *Mysticism and Logic*, London: Allen and Unwin, 11th impression 1959, p. 106..

62 J. Priestley, *The Theological and Miscellaneous Works of Joseph Priestley*, ed., J. T. Rutt, (1817–32), Bristol: Thoemmes Press, 1999, XXV, p. 476. There is a considerable literature on Priestley. Initial pursuit may be made *via ODNB* and John W. Yolton, John Valdimir Price and John Stephens, eds., *Dictionary of Eighteenth-Century British Philosophers*, Bristol: Thoemmes Press, 1999. See also Robert E. Schofield, *The Enlightenment of Joseph Priestley. A Study of his Life and Work from 1733 to 1773*, University Park, PA: Pennsylvania State University Press, 1997.

63 J. Priestley, *An Essay on the Principles of Civil Government, and on the Nature of Political, Civil and Religious Liberty*, in *The Theological and Miscellaneous Works*, XXII, p. 123.

doctrines, sacramental practices and ecclesial polities—have been corrupted through the ages, and this theme weighed heavily upon him. He treats it briefly in 'A preliminary discourse concerning the spirit of Christianity, and the corruption of it by false notions of religion' (1770),[64] and at great length in *An History of the Corruptions of Christianity* (1782). The latter, originally intended as the concluding section of his *Institutes of Natural and Revealed Religion*, outgrew that already lengthy treatise and was published separately, and dedicated to Priestley's friend Theophilus Lindsey. On the other hand, there is an overarching divine providence which gave the uncorrupted Gospel in the first place, an optimism that the corruptions are progressively being removed, and a millennial hope which presupposes a dramatic conclusion to God's purposes. In a word, Priestley's idea of historical development is crucially qualified by his conviction that 'every thing which I deem to be a *corruption of Christianity* has been a departure from the original scheme, or an *innovation*...and no part of the original scheme'.[65] Hence (as if in a pre-emptive strike against some later theological modernists and liberals) he insists that 'it is not a *progressive religion*, but a *progressive reformation* of a corrupted religion, that is pleaded for'.[66] Priestley's spring-cleaning of Christianity's house is motivated by a desire to bring to light the original plan. He is no unprincipled iconoclast. On the contrary, he genuinely feels that when doctrinal and ecclesial lumber is removed, rational persons will be drawn to Christianity as it really is. There is thus a restorationism at work here which is far broader than one concerned primarily with the doctrine of the Church, as in the case of the Campbells and their co-religionists. At the point where the pure Gospel, once given, is concerned there is necessarily, as far as Priestley is concerned, arrested development.[67]

---

64 J. Priestley, Prefixed to *A Free Address to Protestant Dissenters on the Subject of Church Discipline*, 1770, in *The Theological and Miscellaneous Works,* XXI, pp. 374-387.

65 J. Priestley, *An History of the Corruption of Christianity*, in *The Theological and Miscellaneous Works,* V, p. 8.

66 Ibid., p. 503. Margaret Canovan's statement that for Priestley 'the past represented the gradual education from mankind from error to truth, under the beneficent guidance of Providence' thus needs to be qualified by the realization that, where doctrine was concerned, Priestley sought a *recovery* of truth once given but subsequently obscured, not a progress towards truth as if it had never been given. See her 'Two concepts of liberty—eighteenth-century style', *The Price-Priestley Newsletter*, II, 1978, p. 33.

67 It is, therefore, misleading on the part of H. John McLachlan to say that for Priestley 'Christanity was a *developing* phenomenon ...'. It would be truer to say that in Priestley's opinion what developed in Christianity was a bowdlerized version of the real thing. See H. J. McLachlan, 'Joseph Priestley and the study of history', *Transactions of the Unitarian Historical Society*, XIX no. 4, April 1990, p. 260. See also the stimulating paper by Martin Fitzpatrick, '"Through the glass of history": some reflections on

What, to Priestley, was the pure Gospel? Here is his answer:

> The great outline of it is, that the Universal Parent of mankind commissioned Jesus Christ to invite men to the practice of virtue, by the assurance of his mercy to the penitent, and of his purpose to raise to immortal life and happiness all the virtuous and the good, but to inflict an adequate punishment on the wicked. In proof of this he wrought many miracles, and after a public execution he rose again from the dead. He also directed that proselytes should be admitted by *baptism*, and that his disciples should eat bread and drink wine in commemoration of his death.[68]

He continues: 'Here is nothing that any person could imagine would lead to much subtle speculation, at least such as could excite much animosity.'[69] But, through the ingress of corruptions—largely through the entanglement of the pristine message with 'the established opinions of the heathen world, and especially the philosophical part of it'[70]—that is exactly what has happened, as our Lord predicted that it would.

As already hinted, Priestley's catalogue of corruptions embraces the doctrinal and the practical, but of central importance are those regarding the person and work of Christ and the Trinity. It is not to my purpose here to display all the evidence he adduces for his doctrinal claims, still less to enter into debate with him on the positions he reaches (in 'a very incomplete and thoroughly one-sided way' according to Philip Schaff[71]). My objective is simply to show how he understands doctrinal development—and its limits. Thus, a brief reference to a handful of doctrines will sufficiently indicate the nature of his concern.

Priestley sets out from the conviction that God is one. Jesus, though the promised Messiah, 'made no other pretensions; referring all his extraordinary power to God, his Father'. To Peter, Jesus was '*a man approved of God*', while Paul declares that 'There is one God, and one mediator between God and man, the man Christ Jesus'—not 'the *God*, the *God-man*, or the *super-angelic being*, but simply *the man* Christ Jesus'.[72] With the passage of time 'the *Athanasian* doctrine of the Trinity' gave 'men more objects of divine homage than one', and 'It was

---

historical knowledge in the thought of Joseph Priestley', *Enlightenment and Dissent*, XIV, 1998, pp. 172-209.

68 Priestley, *An History of the Corruption of Christianity*, p. 480.

69 Ibid.

70 Ibid., p. 481. Cf. *A Free Address to Protestant Dissenters on the Subject of Church Discipline*, XXI, p. 375.

71 P. Schaff, *History of the Apostolic Church*, p. 257.

72 Priestley, *An History of the Corruption of Christianity*, p. 14.

impossible for the mind of man to conceive of *three* beings, or persons, as exactly alike....'[73] Turning to the doctrine of the atonement, Priestley argues that

> the doctrine of the *natural placability of the Divine Being*, and our ideas of the equity of his government, have been greatly debased by the gradual introduction of the modern doctrine of *atonement*, which represents the Divine Being as withholding his mercy from the truly penietent, till a full satisfaction be made to his justice; and for that purpose, as substituting his own innocent Son in the place of sinful men.[74]

Because sin is an offence against an infinite being, he continues, it is said to require infinite satisfaction which can be rendered only by an infinite person: hence the connection between soteriology and Christology. But this doctrine grossly misconceives 'the character and moral government of God', and is 'a departure from the primitive and genuine doctrine of Christianity'.[75] His own view is that 'Since...the great object of our Lord's mission was to teach the doctrine of a resurrection to a future immortal life, we see the necessity of his own death and resurrection as *a proof of this doctrine*.'[76] But the doctrine of the atonement as widely believed is 'a doctrine which has no foundation in reason, or in the Scriptures, and is indeed a modern thing'.[77] As for the doctrines of grace—election and predesination—they, as I have shown in chapter 3 above, are to Priestley 'doctrines disgraceful to Christianity'.[78]

But, to repeat, despite his serious objections to doctrinal corruptions, Priestley, in the wake of Bacon and Hartley, remains optimistic:

> The gross darkness of that *night* which has for many centuries obscured our holy religion, we may clearly see, is past; the *morning* is opening upon us; and we cannot doubt but that the light will increase, and extend itself more and more unto *the perfect day*. Happy are they who contribute to diffuse the pure light of this *everlasting gospel*.[79]

Indeed, Christianity has already begun to recover from its corrupted state and 'the reformation advances apace'.[80] With reference to the specific doctrine of atonement, he declares that 'It hath pleased Divine

---

73 Priestley, *A Free Address to Protestant Dissenters on the Subject of Church Discipline*, p. 375.

74 J. Priestley, *An History of the Corruption of Christianity*, p. 91.

75 Ibid., p. 92.

76 Ibid., p. 101.

77 Ibid., p. 154.

78 Ibid., p. 179.

79 Ibid., p. 4.

80 Ibid., p. 7.

Providence...to open the minds of men by easy degrees, and the detection of one falsehood prepares us for the detection of another, till, before we are aware of it, we find no trace left of the immense and seemingly well-compacted system.'[81]

More generally, while praising the Reformers for the great advance they made in rooting out the abuses and corruptions of a thousand years and more, Priestley contends that they cannot 'be supposed to have done more than a part...in this great and necessary work; and it behoves us, who come after them, not to keep the very ground which they occupied, but rather to be following their example, and advancing the work which they began'.[82] What sustains Priestley's optimism that all will come right in the end is his firm grasp of the doctrine of providence and his millennial hope. The latter is nowhere more clearly expressed than in his remarks upon the *Revelation* of John the Seer:

> at the next and proper coming of Christ, *they that are Christ's*, or his disciples, will rise, he will then enter upon his proper kingdom, and when the end of it shall be accomplished, he will resign this kingdom; and that this will take place at the general resurrection, viz. that of *all that dies in Adam*, which is in perfect agreement with the account here given by the apostle John.[83]

In all of this Priestley, no less than divines whose doctrinal position was substantially different from his own, rests upon the sufficiency of Scripture. But his interpretative focus is far narrower than that of others (though it does include the resurrection, miracles and the Second Coming—Priestley is no deist, and is stoutly opposed to deism[84]).

For an example of one who was no less opposed to doctrinal corruptions than Priestley, but who was committed to a broader and more traditional account of doctrine than he, let us turn to Robert Vaughan.[85] Following Congregational pastorates at Angel Street, Worcester (1819–25) and Kensington (1825–43), during the latter of which he

---

[81] Ibid., p. 153.

[82] J. Priestley, *A Sermon Preached December 31, 1780, at The New Meeting, in Birmingham, on Undertaking the Pastoral Office in that Place*, (1781), in his *The Theological and Miscellaneous Works,* XV, p. 38. Cf. his Birmingham sermon of 5 November 1785, *The Importance and Extent of Free Inquiry in Matters of Religion*, in *The Theological and Miscellaneous Works,* XV, p. 73.

[83] J. Priestley, *Notes on all the Books of Scripture for the Use of the Pulpit and Private Families*, (1804), in his *The Theological and Miscellaneous Works,* XIV, p. 504.

[84] See further ch. 3 above.

[85] For Vaughan see *ODNB*; Mander and Sell, eds., *Dictionary of Nineteenth-Century British Philosophers*; Anon., 'Dr. Robert Vaughan', *The Congregationalist*, VI, March 1877, pp. 129-148; William Urwick, *Nonconformity in Worcester*, London: Simpkin, 1897; Joseph Thompson, *Lancashire Independent College, 1843–1893*, Manchester: J. E. Cornish, 1893.

concurrently held the chair of Ancient and Modern History in the University of London from 1833–43, Vaughan became the first President and Professor of Theology at Lancashire Independent College (1843–57). There followed two further pastorates: Uxbridge (1857–60) and Torquay (1867–68), separated in time by a period of literary work in London. In 1834 Vaughan delivered the second annual Congregational Lecture under the title, *The Causes of the Corruption of Christianity*, and it is to the second, revised edition of this work that I here refer.

Vaughan sets out from a statement of what he regards as 'the revealed system of things which the term Christianity is employed to designate':

> The view of this system which first presents itself to an unprejudiced mind, is that of a Great Moral Remedy, adapted by Infinite Wisdom and Beneficence to the necessities of a sinful world. And whatever shall be found to alter or obscure the announcements of the gospel as to the moral state of the human race, or as to the nature of its own merciful provisions, we regard as constituting a corruption of the Christian doctrine.[86]

Which, specifically, are the doctrines which may not be 'mutilated'? Vaughan lists them, and at once we see that, as we might expect, his selection differs greatly from that of Priestley; we are also made aware of the authority on which Vaughan stands:

> The doctrine of the Trinity; the proper Deity of the Saviour; the reality and efficacy of his sacrifice as the medium of pardon to the guilty; the personality of the Holy Spirit, together with all his ordinary Influences in the regeneration and salvation of the soul,—these we view as the distinctive and essential truths of revelation. As before us in the Scripture, they are truths to which nothing may be added, and from which nothing may be taken.[87]

Vaughan is not concerned only that central doctrines remain inviolate. He is equally interested in the maintenance of the moral code enshrined in the gospel, and the church polity and style of worship enjoined in the New Testament; for these, no less than doctrines, are susceptible to corruption by human beings, and have in fact been corrupted. Not, indeed, that all is lost: 'we shall do well to remember that even the corruptions of Christianity have often been made to serve other than corrupt ends, by the wisdom and benevolence which can bring good out of evil'.[88]

Vaughan sets out from an enumeration of those tendencies in human nature which cause Christianity to be corrupted: a line of enquiry no

---

86 R. Vaughan, *The Causes of the Corruption of Christianity*, London: Jackson and Walford, 1852, p. 2.

87 Ibid.

88 Ibid., p. 3.

doubt urged upon him both by theological conviction and by interest in matters psychological which the Romantic movement's 'inward turn' in general stimulated. These tendencies, like doctrinal deviations, are to be judged in the light of 'the standard of human duty as presented in Scripture', and in relation to those differing historical contexts which render Christianity 'in its substance as enduring as the heavens, in its form a colouring as varied as the clouds'.[89] The corrupting tendencies of human nature are mental indolence, imbecile credulity, prejudice, and that presumptuousness which, as in 'the subtleties connected with the Arian, the Tritheistic, and Sabellian controversies' affects 'to be wise above what is written', and is curious regarding 'matters which must ever be too high for created intelligence'.[90]

Again, corruptions can result from an excess of imagination, or when the reason is unduly disturbed by feelings and fancies, as well as by an unhealthy physical condition. In this last respect Vaughan appears as an harbinger of present-day holistic medicine when he avers, 'In general, the nature of the physical system has a very perceptible influence on the inner man, especially in whatever connects itself with the feelings.' In illustration of this point he writes, 'It is not when drooping in his sick chamber that we should prefer consulting a friend as to the probability of success in some dangerous and laborious exercise. We should rather choose an interval of ease and health, as being much more conducive to a just estimate of difficulty and danger.'[91] Christianity has further been corrupted by misdirected appetites and passions, and by a worldliness which is content to 'leave the most pernicious evils in society wholly undisturbed, so long as they do not trespass on that little circle of decent selfishness in which these worshippers of quiet indulgence are content to pass their days, and to expect their elysium'.[92]

From a different direction come those corruptions which flow from undue preoccupation with the outward forms and manifestations of religion at the expense of the inner meaning; and from that vanity which affects to know better than Scripture and will not be guided by it. If the vain wish to appear important in the eyes of others, the proud wish to be important in their own estimation:

> the habit of mind now adverted to is in direct opposition to the spirit of the first preachers of the gospel; to the most explicit injunctions of Holy Writ, and to the natural tendency of the doctrine which it promulgates. There are lessons involved in this doctrine, with regard to the present state of the human understanding, and of the human heart, which must render a lowly docility under the teachings of inspiration,

---

89 Ibid., p. 8.
90 Ibid., p. 31, n.
91 Ibid., p. 44.
92 Ibid., p. 49.

> and the deepest self-abasement on account of our guilt and corruption, a reasonable service.[93]

As if recognizing that the catalogue of adverse natural tendencies which he has listed in his first two lectures may yield counter-productive despair, Vaughan concludes the second by cautioning us not to fall for the view that 'Christianity is not the remedy it claims to be, because we do not see it applied universally, and at once.'[94] Vaughan is optimistic regarding the eventual outcome:

> The extent of this triumph will be such as to embrace all nations; its duration the future only can determine; but when its last achievement on earth shall have been realized, eternity will remain to secure its more perfect development, and the larger communication of its blessings.[95]

Turning more directly to history, Vaughan argues that Christianity has been corrupted by misapprehensions of Judaism which have been imported into it. Among these are the transformation of the Lord's table into an altar, and the way in which 'The mediatory character sustained by the descendants of Aaron, was eagerly seized by the shrewd ambition of a prosperous clergy', an hierarchically organized order to vendors of 'those spiritual commodities, which they assumed the sole right of dispensing...'.[96] From Gentile philosophy came such corruptions as the merit of celibacy, penance and martyrdom 'as means of propitiating the Almighty, and washing away sin'.[97] Unfortunately, 'The Platonic doctrine of a separate state, where the spirits of the departed are purified, and on which the later doctrine of purgatory was founded, was approved by all the expositors of Christianity who were of the Alexandrian school, as was the custom of performing religious services at the tombs of the dead.'[98] From ancient paganism came the custom of treasuring relics, invoking the aid of the dead, and venerating shrines. Since none of these innovations could be vindicated by appeal to Scripture, 'a necessity was created for setting up some false authority in the place of the true'. To this authority the term 'CHURCH was applied. Such an authority, set up for such a purpose, would become the ready inlet to a multitude of similar delusions.'[99]

Vaughan proceeds to show how the innovations he repudiates have distorted Christian worship (incense, masses for the dead, and the like),

93 Ibid., p. 59.
94 Ibid., p. 61.
95 Ibid., p. 62.
96 Ibid., p. 117.
97 Ibid., p. 231.
98 Ibid., p. 231.
99 Ibid., p. 273.

and undermine New Testament church polity. Positively, according to Scripture, the Church is a voluntary assembly of saints—a holy community 'for whom Christ died'.[100] Negatively, it is not a State-Church establishment which can 'throw open the institute designed to be especially symbolic of the Christian fellowship, to the whole people of states and kingdoms'.[101] It is equally the case that, internally, the Church is not an hierarchical institution:

> A Christian church should know nothing of control, either from convocations or parliaments. Its statute-book is ever before it in the Scriptures, and is unerring and complete.[102]

As in the case of Priestley, it has not been my purpose to investigate Vaughan's scholarly reliability or to enter into dialogue with him. Rather, I have sought to show how these two divines, both relying upon the principle of the sole sufficiency of Scripture, both convinced that Christianity had been corrupted through time, and both Protestants, nevertheless adjudicated doctrinal and ecclesial change in the light of their own interpretations and experience, above all when specifying those doctrines presumed to represent the heart of the Christian Gospel.

What now of the Protestant-turned-Roman Catholic, John Henry Newman?[103] Roughly half-way between the publication of the first and second editions of Vaughan's Congregational Lecture, Newman's *An Essay on the Development of Christian Doctrine* (1845) appeared. It would seem that one general and one particular contextual factor stimulated Newman to take up his pen on this subject. In general terms he wished to counter the charges of doctrinal corruption which had been levelled by the likes of Priestley and Vaughan (though he does not mention these by name). His personal motive was to explain—to himself, possibly, as much as to others—how it was that he, who had been an Anglican evangelical willing to accuse the Roman Church of polytheism and idolatry, could now embrace Roman Catholicism with what were perceived, according to conviction, as its doctrinal accruals or excrescences.[104]

---

100 Ibid., p. 291.

101 Ibid., p. 292.

102 Ibid., p. 305.

103 Newman, too, has caused much ink to flow. See *ODNB*; Mander and Sell, eds., *Dictionary of Nineteenth-Century British Philosophers*; Ian Ker, *John Henry Newman: A Biography*, Oxford: Clarendon Press, 1988; Sheridan Gilley, *Newman and his Age*, London: Darton, Longman and Todd, 1990.

104 For a little more on Newman's context in relation to those of the Unitarian Martineau and the Baptist C. H. Spurgeon see Alan P. F. Sell, *Commemorations. Studies in Christian Thought and History*, Calgary: University of Calgary Press and Cardiff: University of Wales Press, (1993); reprinted Eugene, OR: Wipf & Stock, 1998, ch. 1. For

Intellectually, Newman's context was one in which, no less that Nevin and Schaff, he breathed the organic air. Where they conceived of the Church as an organism, Newman regarded the deposit of faith as such, and his *Essay* was designed to demonstrate the point.

Newman begins with a strong assertion of the objectivity of Christianity. No less fervently than Nevin, he stoutly denies that Christianity 'is to each man what each man thinks it to be, and nothing else...'.[105] He is equally opposed to the view that original Christianity has become so corrupt over the years that no existing denomination represents what was taught by Christ and his apostles. Such views imply that there is no historical continuity, and this needs to be demonstrated (we recall that the Protestants Nevin and Schaff were concurrently demonstrating the converse to their own satisfaction). The latter view is that of those like Priestley, Vaughan and the Campbells who 'fall back upon the Bible as the sole source of Revelation, and upon their own personal private judgment as the sole expounder of its doctrine'.[106] In view of the Mercersburg theology, and of other similar developments elsewhere in Protestant circles, Newman's judgment that the 'utter incongruity between Protestantism and historical Christianity is a plain fact'[107] is, if understandable, too sweeping, though it must be conceded that he, no less than Nevin and Schaff, was sorely tried by much of the Protestantism around him.

Newman is more than ready to concede that there have been, through its life of eighteen hundred years, 'certain apparent inconsistencies and alterations in [Christianity's] doctrine and its worship... [but] They are not sufficient to interfere with the general character and course of the religion...'.[108] What is required is 'a whole doctrine stated by a whole Church',[109] and as the articulation of doctrine is refined through discussion and the rebuttal of heresy, we find that

> the increase and expansion of the Christian Creed and Ritual, and the variations which have attended the process in the case of individual writers and Churches, are the necessary attendants on any philosophy or polity which takes possession of the intellect and heart, and has had any wide or extended dominion; that, from the nature of the human mind, time is necessary for the full comprehension and perfection of great ideas; and that the highest and most wonderful truths, though

---

the immediate context of the writing of the *Essay* see Ian Ker, *John Henry Newman*, pp. 298-301.

105 J. H. Newman, *An Essay on the Development of Christian Doctrine*, (1845), Westminster, MD: Christian Classics, 1968, p. 4.

106 Ibid., p. 6.

107 Ibid., p. 8.

108 Ibid., p. 9.

109 Ibid., p. 14.

> communicated to the world once for all by inspired teachers, could not be comprehended all at once by the recipients...[110]

The doctrine of development is the theoretical explanation of this process.

Newman fully understands that 'this process will not be a development [by which he must mean an acceptable development], unless the assemblage of aspects, which constitute its ultimate shape, really belongs to the idea from which they start';[111] and he does not discount the influence of the circumstances in which doctrinal discussion takes place. Furthermore, developments may be of five kinds:

> Taking the Incarnation as [Christianity's] central doctrine, the Episcopate, as taught by St. Ignatius, will be an instance of political development, the *Theotokos* of logical, the determination of the date of our Lord's birth of historical, the Holy Eucharist of moral, and the Athanasian Creed of metaphysical.[112]

Doctrinal developments are to be expected, Newman continues, because Christian teaching has to be interpreted in a variety of contexts, and also because 'When the nations were converted and offences abounded, then the Church came out to view, on the one hand as a temporal establishment [the very thing which Vaughan abominated], on the other as a remedial system...'.[113] Within the Bible itself there is doctrinal development, and hence we may 'fairly conclude that Christian doctrine admits of formal, legitimate, and true developments, that is, of developments contemplated by its Divine Author'.[114]

But how do we know which are the true developments? Newman contends that if, as he thinks is the case, 'the Christian doctrine, as originally taught, admits of true and important developments...this is a strong antecedent argument in favour of a provision in the Dispensation for putting a seal of authority upon those developments'.[115] Enter the Magisterium. To deny the need of such an official teaching authority on the ground that such a body would violate free-will and responsibility (a consideration which weighed heavily with Priestley) is 'to forget that there were infallible teachers in the first age, and heretics and schismatics in the ages subsequent'.[116]

Newman proceeds to explain that doctrine rolls into doctrine in mutually supportive ways. Thus, for example, 'From the doctrine of

---

110 Ibid., p. 30.
111 Ibid., p. 38.
112 Ibid., p. 54.
113 Ibid., p. 63.
114 Ibid., p. 74.
115 Ibid., p. 79.
116 Ibid., p. 83.

Mediation follow the Atonement, the Mass, the merits of Martyrs and Saints, their invocation and *cultus*.' Again, the Mass and the Real Presence are bound up with the veneration of Saints and their relics, and also with the intercessory power of Saints, which, in turn, is bound up with the Purgatorial State. The discomfort which Priestley and Vaughan would feel at this can readily be imagined—the 'following' may be temporal, but is it logical?—and we may suppose it would be reinforced by Newman's declaration, 'You must accept the whole or reject the whole; attenutation does but enfeeble, and amputation mutilate.'[117]

This, of course, is nothing more than a tacit appeal to authority. No adequate reason is offered as to why we must accept or reject the whole. Instead, a reference to 'the claims of sound logic' notwithstanding, we are offered a circular argument:

> It is a first strong point that, in an idea such as Christianity, developments cannot but be, and those surely divine, because it is divine; a second that, if so, they are those very ones which exist, because there are no others; and a third point is the fact that they are found just there, where true developments ought to be found,—namely, in the historic seats of Apostolic teaching and in the authoritative homes of immemorial tradition.[118]

Having regard to the fact, which Newman grants, of heretical formulations of doctrine, what are the criteria for judging that such and such a doctrinal development is worthy and legitimate? Newman answers:

> There is no corruption if [an idea] retains one and the same type, the same principles, the same organization; if its beginnings anticipate its subsequent phases, and its later phenomena protect and subserve its earlier; if it has a power of assimilation and revival, and a vigorous action from first to last.[119]

Newman proceeds to discuss his chosen tests in some detail, and I shall not follow him, but shall simply make two points. First, these tests constitute formidable hostages to fortune, for each is open to challenge—as James Orr drily remarked, 'The principles are excellent: by their help we might, I think, refute very successfully much that is advanced by Dr. Newman himself.'[120] None threw down the gauntlet with

---

117 Ibid., 94.

118 Ibid., p. 120.

119 Ibid., p. 171. For an interesting discussion of the tests see Thomas O'Loughlin, 'Newman, Vincent of Lerins and development', *Irish Theological Quarterly*, LVIII no. 2, 1991, pp. 146-166. See also A. Stephenson, 'Cardinal Newman and the development of doctrine', *Journal of Ecumenical Studies*, III, 1966, pp. 463-485.

120 J. Orr, *The Progress of Dogma*, London: James Clarke, [1901], p. 20.

more vigour than Orestes Augustus Brownson.[121] Whereas there is something neat about Newman's life in so far as by living sufficiently long he was able to spend forty-five years with Canterbury and forty-five with Rome, Brownson (1803–76) was a regularly rolling ecclesiastical-cum-secular stone. Raised among Congregationalists, he passed through Presbyterianism and Universalism and then, having lost his belief in divine revelation, he resigned from the ministry. After a while he embraced the Religion of Humanity, before returning to the ministry first as a freelance, then as a Unitarian, and finally, full circle, as a Congregationalist. In 1844 he was received into the Roman Catholic Church and, to judge by his critique of Newman's *Essay*, he partook fully of the zeal of the convert. In general his case is that Newman wrongly assumed that there had been doctrinal change, whereas in fact Catholic truth is unchanging and sure. Newman is led astray on this point because he fastens too much on the written word of Scripture, rather than perceiving that the whole truth was given to the Church regardless of the written word. In particular he finds Newman's seven tests wanting. To take one example: continuation through time applies to corruptions as much as to developments. Newman declares that the former are temporary but does not prove it and, in fact, Pelagianism, for example, has been with us since the garden of Eden.[122]

Of more relevance to present-day ecumenical debate are Newman's criteria regarding identity of type, principles and organization. A quotation from F. J. Powicke's exposition of Congregationalism will make the point:

> Our reverence for 'God in history' may easily induce the notion that all changes which can be called (in any sense) natural are normal. We may fail to see that changes are normal, are a true development, only so far as they at once conserve and expand the essential type or idea of that from which they start [Schleiermacher's point already noted]. Changes which involve a loss, or reversal, of the original idea are abnormal, however excellent the result may seem to be... [I]f you admit that the New Testament idea of the Church is a redeemed people, all kingly and priestly in functions, you must admit that the historic process which turned it into a society ruled and ministered to by a spiritual oligarchy of priestly office went wrong somehow; and if you still speak of the process as a true development you must show

121 For Brownson see *The Catholic Encyclopedia*, 1914, www.newadvent.org/cathen/03001a.htm

122 See O. A. Brownson, 'Newman's Development of Christian Doctrine', *Brownson's Quarterly Review*, July 1846. For Nevin's remarks on Brownson's position and on Newman's tests, see 'Early Christianity', January 1852, in Yrigoyen, Jr., and Bricker, eds., *Catholic and Reformed*, pp. 290-291. Newman's *Essay* did not have an entirely smooth passage in Rome. See Ian Ker, *John Henry Newman*, pp. 329-330.

> that the idea of the Church as a redeemed people is not really in the New Testament at all.[123]

As far as I am aware, Newman never rose to this challenge, expressed in more homely terms by Powicke's Congregational contemporary, J. D. Jones thus: 'The oak tree is a legitimate development of the acorn, but we cannot accept it as the legitimate development say of the potato.'[124]

Secondly, there is a whiff of the smoke-screen about Newman's tests, for we know (and Newman knows) that in the end it is the appeal to ecclesial authority which will carry the day. David Brown's observation on the *Essay* comes as no surprise. He writes, 'it is widely acknowledged that the argument of the work as a whole fares much better, in forcing the Church towards recognition of the fact of development rather than in offering any very precise conception of how this proceeds'[125]—or, I might add, of how worthy developments are to be judged and distinguished from unworthy ones.

It is only proper to point out that there is development in Newman's own thought. The fullest fruition is in his *An Essay in Aid of a Grammar of Assent* (1870). In contrast to inferential reasoning, the domain of which is restricted, Newman posits illative reasoning in which an act of judgment is central. This, frequently intuitional, mode of reasoning is employed in reaching conclusions on a wide variety of matters. The conclusions thus reached are compelling to the reasoner, but they also require to be justified if assent is to be unconditional, as Newman thinks it should be. Moreover, the process of justification is moral as well as

---

123 F. J. Powicke, 'The Congregational churches', in Selbie, ed., *Evangelical Christianity*, pp. 86-87. For an Anglican opinion see W. R. Inge, *The Platonic Tradition in English Religious Thought*, London: Longmans, Green, 1926, p. 112: 'The presuppositions upon which institutionalism rests—that Christ wished to found a hierarchical corporation, with a divinely guaranteed monopoly of certain spiritual benefits, and that this corporation was intended to be a universal Caesarean empire embracing the whole world, are doctrines which I cannot see the slightest reason for believing.' In passing I observe that J. W. Nevin is never more contentious than when describing the basis of Congregationalism as an 'unhistorical abstraction' of a rationalistic, democratic type. See 'Early Christianity', November 1851, in Yrigoyen, Jr., and Bricker, eds., *Catholic and Reformed*, pp. 232-233. No doubt Nevin was sorely tried by examples of wayward Congregationalism (which he, unfortunately, branded 'Puritanism'), but a Christian tradition should not be described only in terms of its deviant members. For an alternative view see Alan P. F. Sell, *Saints: Visible* [and hence not an unhistorical abstraction], *Orderly* [and hence not anarchic rabble] *and Catholic* [and hence not isolationist]*: The Congregational Idea of the Church*, Geneva: World Alliance of Reformed Churches and Allison Park, PA: Pickwick Publications, 1986.

124 Jones, 'The doctrine of development', p. 63.

125 D. Brown, '*Phronesis*, development and doctrinal definition', *International Journal for the Study of the Christian Church*, I no. 1, 2001, p. 72.

rational: the conscience is brought to bear upon the matter in hand, for as well as the rational judgment regarding the adequacy or otherwise of the evidence, the question whether one ought to commit oneself to a particular conclusion or course of action is raised.

There is much more which might be said about this.[126] But I introduce this further development of Newman's thought by way of tempering somewhat the strength of his commitment to the *Magisterium*. There is an ambiguity in his work, for on the one hand he can assert the position of the *Essay* with conviction; on the other, he can say, 'if I am obliged to bring religion into after-dinner toasts (which indeed does not seem quite the thing) I shall drink—to the Pope if you please—still, the conscience first, and to the Pope afterwards'.[127]

In this section I have introduced three divines, all of whom surveyed the course of Christianity from its infancy to their own time and came to dramatically different conclusions as to what had been going on as far as doctrine, worship and polity were concerned. Both Priestley and Vaughan deplored the corruption of an originally pure Gospel message, though they differed as to its precise terms, and both of them, while professing to rely upon the sole sufficiency of Scripture, brought their own presuppositions to bear upon its text. Newman, by contrast, regarded Christian truth, though given once for all, as a developing organism the reliability of which was ostensibly testable in accordance with his seven tests, but which was actually authorized by the Magisterium—albeit with a concession to the individual conscience in particular cases. In a word, whereas the appeal of Priestley and Vaughan is to Scripture (though with fairly clear 'imported' notions as to what it is reasonable to assent to), Newman's is to Scripture and Church Tradition in assumed partnership.

Interestingly, there lies behind the positions of both Priestley and Vaughan and Newman the conviction that the unalterable given—whether it be the Biblical witness (which needs to be recovered in restorationist fashion) or Church dogma (the full import of which is revealed only gradually over time)—is complete and unamendable. But Newman's attitude was markedly different from that of the Protestants, as the following statement makes clear:

---

[126] See further, M. Jamie Ferreira, *Doubt and Religious Commitment: The Role of the Will in Newman's Thought*, Oxford: Clarendon Press, 1980; David A. Pailin, *The Way to Faith: An Examination of Newman's Grammar of Assent as a Response to the Search for Certainty in Faith*, London: Epworth Press, 1969.

[127] J. H. Newman, *Letter Addressed to His Grace the Duke of Norfolk*, London: B. M. Pickering, 1875, p. 66. An effective way, no doubt, of ensuring delay in one's elevation to the position of cardinal. Pius IX, who was suspicious of Newman, died in 1878, whereupon, on 12 May, his successor, Leo XIII, promoted Newman.

> It is...sometimes said that the stream is clearest near the spring. Whatever use may fairly be made of this image, it does not apply to the history of philosophy or belief, which on the contrary are more equable, and purer, and stronger, when its bed has become deep, and broad, and full.[128]

As Ian Ker rightly remarked, 'It was one of Newman's deepest convictions that to cling to the literal letter of the past was to lose its essential spirit, and therefore to betray it.'[129] To Schaff, however, 'for all those who view not only biblical but also churchly Christianity as a complete, once and for all finished system and reject the concept of historical development, Rome is the proper, final home, whether they know and admit this or not.'[130] Of course, Newman did not wish to repudiate historical development, but rather to assert it. But whereas the Protestant restorationists had a biblical text before them, however they might use it, Newman's position was complicated by the fact that it was integral to his argument that the finished dogma once for all given was not completely to hand. As he remarked in 1868, 'the Apostles had the *fullness* of revealed knowledge, a fullness which they could as little realize for themselves, as the human mind, as such, can have all its thoughts present before it at once. They are elicited according to the occasion.'[131]

This raises the question how far the Apostles actually *had* the fullness of the revelation. However that may be, Nevin felt impelled to distinguish between Newman's idea of development which, by a look which is as backward as that of the biblical restorationists, is an arrested development, and the 'German', that is, post-Hegelian idea of it according to which we have 'a process carried forward, by the action of different forces, working separately to some extent, and so it may be even onesidedly and contradictorily for a time, towards a concrete result representing in full unity at last the true meaning and power of the whole'.[132] For his part, Schaff concluded that 'The true theory of development must be both conservative and progressive, and provide for what is good and valuable in all ages and divisions of Christendom.'[133] That this begs huge questions cannot be gainsaid, and any who doubt this need only consult

---

128 Newman, *An Essay on the Development of Christian Doctrine*, p. 40.

129 Ker, *John Henry Newman*, p. 441.

130 Penzel, *Philip Schaff*, p. 79, cf. p. 89; quoting P. Schaff, 'Gallerie der bedeutendsten jetzt lebenden Univeritätstheologen Deutschlands', *Der deutsche Kirchenfreund*, V, September 1852, p. 334. Cf. Nevin, 'Early Christianity', September 1851, in Yrigoyen, Jr., and Bricker, eds., *Catholic and Reformed*, pp. 196-198.

131 J. Derek Holmes, ed., *The Theological Papers of John Henry Newman on Biblical Inspiration and on Infallibility*, Oxford: Clarendon Press, 1979, p. 156.

132 Nevin, 'Early Christianity', January 1852, in Yrigoyen, Jr., and Bricker, eds., *Catholic and Reformed*, p. 294,

133 P. Schaff, *Theological Propaedeutic: A General Introduction to the Study of Theology*, New York: Charles Scribner's Sons, 1892, p. 241.

the history of the German Reformed Church in nineteenth-century America, where we find Bomberger increasingly convinced that Nevin and Schaff are attempting to lead the Church away from its Reformed roots in a Romeward direction, and warning thus:

> Development, progress may not be made a deceitful plea for radical revolution. To convert the Reformed Church into something manifestly subversive of Reformed principles, hostile to the Reformed life, must not be palmed off upon the world as development. Will men put thorns for grapes and thistles for figs, and ask us to admire the wondrous beauty of the development?[134]

Bomberger clamantly raises the question of the *locus* of authority once again, and returns us to the question from which I set out, namely that of the permissible degree of tolerance within the Church.[135] Whatever else may be said, it would seem that the fact of doctrinal change—at least change in the articulation of doctrine—contextually prompted as we have seen, and whatever the theory of development to account for it, argues the need for inner- and inter-ecclesial tolerance. This is necessary not only for the peace of the Church and the credibility of its witness, but also by way of acknowledging that there is mystery at the heart of the Christian faith: as the Puritan and other divines never ceased to remind us, while we may have a true apprehension of God we may not have a full comprehension of him.

What seems quite clear is that the history of the Church is littered with schisms and secessions resulting from the imposition of doctrinal formulae as tests of faith, particular understandings of church order as alone *bona fide*, and specific ethical postures as evidencing that 'godly walk' on which reception into church membership turns.[136] All of these can become legalistic principles of exclusion which deny the Gospel of God's grace.[137] Is there a way forward? I believe that there is, and I shall attempt briefly to outline a proposal in the concluding section of this chapter.

---

[134] J. H. A. Bomberger, 'First words', *The Reformed Church Monthly*, I no. 1, January 1868, p. 6.

[135] It is important to keep in mind the distinction between tolerance within the church and between the churches, and the toleration of religion. The former is a matter of Christian attitudes, the latter is a matter of the law.

[136] For a discussion of such sectarianisms see Sell, *Commemorations*, ch. 2, and *Aspects of Christian Integrity*, Calgary: University of Calgary Press and Louisville, KY: Westminster/John Knox Press, 1990; reprinted Eugene, OR: Wipf & Stock, 1998.

[137] See further ch. 11 below; and for the question of inclusivity, exclusivity and church discipline, ch. 12 below.

V

I set out from two sentences in the confession (1967) of The United Presbyterian Church in the United States of America:

> The one sufficient revelation of God is Jesus Christ, the Word of God incarnate, to whom the Holy Spirit bears unique and authoritative witness through the Holy Scriptures, which are received and obeyed as the word of God written. The Scriptures are not a witness among others, but the witness without parallel.[138]

While, against individualism, I should have welcomed the phrase 'by the Church' after the word 'obeyed', this is an otherwise adequate statement which endorses Powicke's earlier, rueful, remark, 'It has needed generations to persuade men that in Scripture the true Word of God is Christ; and that other voices there are only true so far as they blend harmoniously with His...'.[139] We are on the way to specifying our supreme authority, and to locating the criterion whereby we judge doctrinal change:

> Our final authority is our new Creator. The authority cannot, therefore, be either a Church or a Book—both of which are historically the products of such communion with God.... The only final authority for Christian faith is its Creator—God Himself acting on us in the Christian way of a new creation, *i.e.* God asserting His holy Self in Christ's historic and regenerative work, and in its perpetual energy in the soul.[140]

Positively, I should argue that what is witnessed to above all is the historic saving *act* of the God of all grace in the Cross and resurrection of Jesus Christ.[141] To this fact the apostles testified. 'I resolved', wrote Paul to the Christians in Corinth, that while I was with you I would not claim to know anything but Jesus Christ—Christ nailed to the cross.'[142] God's saving act is consistently at the heart of the apostolic Gospel, and for this reason Forsyth was so concerned to distinguish the Gospel from a doctrinal system or an evolutionary process. Indeed, 'The Gospel stands

---

138 *The Confession of 1967*, C.2, quoted by John Newton Thomas, 'The development of doctrine in Reformed theology', in *Reconsiderations. Roman Catholic/Presbyterian and Reformed Conversations 1966–67*, New York: World Horizons, 1967, p. 67.

139 F. J. Powicke, *The Cambridge Platonists: A Study*, London: J. M. Dent, 1926, p. 34.

140 Forsyth, *The Principle of Authority*, p. 53.

141 See further ch. 13 below.

142 1 Corinthians 2:2.

with the predominance of intervention, it falls with the predominance of evolution.'[143]

Under the subtle influences of post-Hegelian immanentism, evolutionary thought and the mid-nineteenth-century recovery of the Patristic emphasis upon the Incarnation, the Reformed theologian, Nevin, could sometimes omit the Cross and the atonement from his reckoning. Thus, for example, he informs us that the 'cardinal principle' of the Mercersburg theology is 'the fact of the Incarnation. ...Christ saves the world, not ultimately by what he teaches or by what he does, but by what he *is* in the constitution of his own person'.[144] Clearly, were Jesus not who he was, he could not do what he did; but what he did is of critical importance in any Christianity which claims to be in the line of the apostles. In fairness, however, it must be granted that elsewhere Nevin made good the soteriological omission.[145]

Negatively, important though doctrine be, and desirable though it be that Christian beliefs be clearly articulated, I should wish to argue that the Gospel is not a compendium of doctrines as such. Nevin knew this well:

> Christ...was not the founder simply of a religious school. ...Christianity is not a *doctrine*, to be taught or learned like a system of philosophy or a rule of moral conduct. ...Christianity...is a *life*, not only as revealed in Christ, but as continued in the church. It flows over from Christ to his people, always in this form. They do not simply bear his name, and acknowledge his doctrine. They are so united with him as to have part in the substance of his life itself.[146]

Newman also is well aware that 'Christianity is no theory of the study of the cloister';[147] but here he is thinking of Christianity's presence

---

143 P. T. Forsyth, 'The distinctive thing in Christian experience', *The Hibbert Journal*, VI no. 3, April 1908, p. 486. For a fuller discussion of history in relation to transcendence and immanence see Sell, *Confessing and Commending the Faith*, ch. 5.

144 J. W. Nevin, 'Letter to Dr. Henry Harbaugh', in Yrigoyen, Jr., and Bricker, eds., *Catholic and Reformed*, p. 408. For my attempt to bring Nevin and Forsyth into conversation upon such points as this see Sell, *Testimony and Tradition*, ch. 8. For the way in which some post-Hegelian idealists who were friendly disposed towards Christianity, or who were Christians themselves, played down the historical in favour of the idea—the dying and rising motif rather than the resurrection—in the writings of Edward Caird, for example, see Alan P. F. Sell, *Philosophical Idealism and Christian Belief*, Cardiff: University of Wales Press and New York: St Martin's Press, 1995, ch. 5. For a discussion of the way the problem arises in the thought of Caird's elder brother, John, see my *Defending and Declaring the Faith. Some Scottish Examples 1860–1920*, Exeter: Paternoster Press and Colorado Springs: Helmers & Howard, 1987, ch. 4.

145 See, for example, Nevin's *Vindication of the Revised Liturgy, Historical and Theological*, in Yrigoyen, Jr., and Bricker, eds., *Catholic and Reformed*, pp. 377, 379.

146 Nevin, *The Mystical Presence*, pp. 216, 222.

147 Newman, *An Essay on the Development of Christian Doctrine*, p. 3.

throughout the world. When he comes to discuss the faith itself it is undeniable that he characteristically thinks, as if an harbinger of some later philosophical idealists, that 'Christianity ... came into the world as an idea rather than an institution...'.[148] On this score O. C. Quick found Newman more modernist than the modernists themselves, for he 'treated Christianity itself from the human side as essentially a tremendous idea, living, growing, evolving itself in history, always being variously applied and elucidated in human thought and life.... Idea is opposed to fact as the basis of Christianity.'[149] Not surprisingly, Newman holds that 'the essence of all religion is authority and obedience...'.[150] I should myself have thought that the essence of Christianity is better summed up by the terms grace and gratitude. This is consistent with the fact that Christians are called by grace to be pilgrims on a way. As they proceed, so they will learn more of God's grace, of their need, and of the challenges of the Christian life.

This being the nature of the Christian life, God being who he is, the saints (that is, the church members) being also sinners, and contexts and challenges varying as they do through time, doctrines will be variously articulated and held with varying degrees of commitment and understanding. This is precisely what we should expect, and, to come full circle, it argues for tolerance within and between the churches. Where such tolerance is not to be found legalisms arise, often with sectarian consequences. Moreover, doctrinal tolerance would seem to be biblically warranted. Did not Paul remind the Corinthians that 'I fed you on milk and not on solid food, for which you were not yet ready'?[151] Or as I myself have dared to say, 'It is as unsatisfactory to serve Christ's babes the dregs of the latest theological fashion as it is to force-feed them on the hard rusks of five-point Calvinism.'[152] Thus, if all that a person can honestly say is, 'Jesus is my Master and I try to follow him', I do not retort, 'Go away, and come back when you have a decent Christology.' In other words, where individuals are concerned I am glad that 'the age-long prejudice that a man's mere opinions and beliefs must somehow involve the fate of his soul; that doctrinal heresy is the worst of crimes'[153] is receding.

But the Church may well wish to say more than the individual Christian can. And each church may properly invoke disciplinary procedures, if it

---

148 Ibid., p. 77.

149 O. C. Quick, *Liberalism, Modernism and Tradition*, London: Longmans, Green, 1922, pp. 27, 29.

150 Newman, *An Essay on the Development of Christian Doctrine*, p. 86.

151 1 Corinthians 3:2.

152 Sell, *Testimony and Tradition*, ch. 1.

153 Powicke, *The Cambridge Platonists*, p. 66.

so chooses, when its witness is being compromised. Thus, for example, the *Basis of Union* of The United Reformed Church:

> The United Reformed Church, believing that it is through the freedom of the Spirit that Jesus Christ holds his people in the fellowship of the one Body, shall uphold the rights of personal conviction. It shall be for the church, in safeguarding the substance of the faith and maintaining the unity of the fellowship, to determining when these rights are asserted to the injury of its unity and peace.[154]

I do not wish at this stage to proceed further into the area of church discipline.[155] Rather, I wish to conclude by stating four facts which have, I trust, been thrown into relief by this study. First, God's act of saving grace (which has been, and will be, variously interpreted), to which people are, by the Spirit enabled to respond, is *the* given, and it is prior to any doctrinal account of what has happened. Secondly, we must expect that formulations of doctrine will vary according to time and place. Hence, for example, the following declaration:

> The United Reformed Church, under the authority of Holy Scripture and in corporate responsibility to Jesus Christ its everliving head, acknowledges its duty to be open at all times to the leading of the Holy Spirit and therefore affirms its right to make such new declarations of its faith and for such purposes as may from time to time be required by obedience to the same Spirit.[156]

Thirdly, on the ground of the once-for-all saving act of sovereign grace, people are called into the fellowship of the Church, united as branches of the Vine and therefore related to all the other branches—with all that this entails concerning the ecumenical manifestation of that unity and the obligation to eschew sectarianism. Finally, as people of the Way, united with Christ and partaking of new life in him, believers are called to walk in the light in grateful response to God's grace.[157] In this last connection Question 86 of that most practical and pastoral of the Reformed catechisms, the *Heidelberg*, is very much to the point:

> Since we are redeemed from our sin and its wretched consequences by grace through Christ without any merit of our own, why must we do good works?
>
> Because just as Christ has redeemed us with his blood he also renews us through his Holy Spirit according to his own image, so that with our whole life we may show ourselves grateful to God for his goodness and that he may be glorified through us;

---

154 *The Basis of Union*, in *The Manual*, London: United Reformed Church, 1973, p. 12.

155 But see ch. 12 below.

156 *The Manual*, p. 14.

157 For Nevin on the new life see *The Mystical Presence*, pp. 162-166.

> and further, so that we ourselves may be assured of our faith by its fruits and by our reverent behaviour may win our neighbors to Christ.[158]

In Christian doctrine as in Christian ecclesial, ethical and personal life, 'The last authority of the redeemed is the Redeemer as such.'[159]

---

[158] *The Heidelberg Catechism*, (1563), Philadelphia: United Church Press, 1962, p. 87. See the illuminating article by Lee Barrett: 'A matter of passion: the Heidelberg Catechism's unique theological method', *The New Mercersburg Review*, XXXIII, Autumn 2003, pp. 18-35.

[159] Forsyth, *The Principle of Authority*, p. 250.

CHAPTER 7

The Perennial Peril of Pantheism

> England is being largely carried away by Rationalism and Pantheism; and, as I regard these apparently mutually exclusive *Weltanschauungen* as destructive of all higher life, I am anxious for the sake of my fellow-men, and for the sake of my Lord and Saviour Jesus Christ, to do what little I can to check their progress and to help those who are being fascinated by them.[1]

Thus wrote the Congregational divine, David Worthington Simon in 1908. I am here concerned with the second of his 'bogeymen', pantheism, and I shall shortly introduce two divines who, even as Simon wrote, were to the fore in rebutting it. First, however, we must take our bearings.

Any who may be tempted to think that ideas emerge as if from nowhere and later, as suddenly, vanish never to return, will be well advised to ponder the history of pantheism. From the Upanishads to Muhammad Iqbal, from the Greeks to the post-Hegelian absolute idealists, pantheism, whether more or less diluted, is detectable. It is not surprising that pantheism had a fresh lease of life in the sixty years from about 1860. During that period many, among them T. H. Green in England and John and Edward Caird in Scotland, turned in the direction of post-Hegelian idealism. They did this both in reaction against lingering eighteenth-century deism[2] and, more particularly, as a way of maintaining Christian ideas and ideals without the encumbrance of biblical history, on the details of which some biblical scholars—not to mention the boisterous battalions of atheists, positivists, agnostics and secularists—were casting doubt or pouring scorn. Again, many theologians and other religiously-inclined persons construed the theory of evolution as delineating the providential workings of the immanent Creator-God; while from the more technically doctrinal side, the revival of patristics at Oxford under

---

1 D. W. Simon, Letter to Dr. F. Lindner of Rostock, 14 March 1908, quoted by F. J. Powicke, *David Worthington Simon*, London: Hodder and Stoughton, 1912, pp. 287-88.

2 For some reflections on deism see ch. 4 above.

Benjamin Jowett renewed interest in the Incarnation and its temporal ramifications.[3]

Not the least of the problems in discussing pantheism is the elasticity and hospitability of the term. Theories deemed pantheistic are frequently seen on examination to manifest atheistic, deistic, polytheistic or theistic aspects. Confronted by this fact, Robert Flint, a contemporary of Simon, sought to bring a degree of order to the situation by pronouncing thus:

> Pantheism is the theory which regards all finite things as merely aspects, or modifications, or parts of one eternal and self-existent being; which views all material objects, and all particular minds, as necessarily derived from a single infinite substance. The one absolute substance—the one all-comprehensive being—it calls God.[4]

Flint goes on to explain that while the one substance may be conceived of in diverse ways, pantheism is always monistic and neccessarian. To it he opposes our knowledge of ourselves as self-conscious beings:

> In knowing ourselves as self-conscious and self-acting with a certainty far greater than any reasoning to the contrary can produce, we have a guarantee that the pantheism which includes fatalism is false,—and there is, properly speaking, no other pantheism.[5]

Here we have the stance typical of one raised in the tradition of Scottish common sense realism. Flint had imbibed this whilst a student at Glasgow University, where 'Moral Will' Fleming deviated but little from the views of Thomas Reid and Dugald Stewart. Although it was said of Fleming that he 'seems to have been a hodman amidst his brethren of the Scottish school',[6] Flint never succumbed to the idealism which his contemporary and Fleming's successor, Edward Caird, was to introduce to Glasgow. Rather, 'the Scottish standpoint diluted from Reid by lesser

---

[3] See further, Alan P. F. Sell, *Theology in Turmoil: The Roots, Course and Significance of the Conservative–Liberal Debate in Modern Theology*, (1986), Eugene, OR: Wipf & Stock, 1998, ch. 1, and *Philosophical Idealism and Christian Belief*, Cardiff: University of Wales Press and New York: St. Martin's Press, 1995, ch. 1.

[4] R. Flint, *Anti-Theistic Theories*, Edinburgh: William Blackwood, (1879), 6th edn 1899, p. 336. For Flint (1838–1910) see *ODNB*; Donald Macmillan, *The Life of Robert Flint, D.D., LL.D*, London: Hodder and Stoughton, 1914; Alan P. F. Sell, *Defending and Declaring the Faith. Some Scottish Examples 1860-1920*, Exeter: Paternoster Press and Colorado Springs: Helmers & Howard, 1987, ch. 3; Alan P. F. Sell with W. J. Mander, eds, *The Dictionary of Nineteenth-Century British Philosophers*, Bristol: Thoemmes Press, 2002.

[5] Flint, *Anti-Theistic Theories*, pp. 338-39.

[6] R. M. Wenley, quoted by Donald Macmillan, *The Life of Robert Flint*, p. 38. For Fleming (1792–1866) see Sell and Mander, eds, *The Dictionary of Nineteenth-Century British Philosophers*.

folk was impressed upon him as the sole outlook possible, and, be it said, he never shook himself free from it altogether'.[7]

On either side of the Atlantic two other divines shared this attitude: John L. Girardeau (1825–98),[8] an Old School Presbyterian who taught at Columbia Theological Seminary from 1876 to 1895; and James Iverach (1839–1922)[9] of the Free/United Free Church College, Aberdeen, from 1887 to 1922. Their papers on pantheism were published about a century ago, and I shall set out from these, supplementing their accounts from other sources, notably from Flint, as appropriate.

I

Girardeau's *Discussions of Philosophical Questions*, which was published in 1900, includes a paper on 'Objective idealism', the concluding paragraph of which sets the scene for the following essay on 'Pantheism', and confirms the author's commitment to realism:

> To the sacrifice of the doctrines of natural realism, and the creation of the material system, the theistic philosopher and the Christian theologian cannot quietly consent... They are essential alike to a true philosophy and a true theology.[10]

We shall see that this is the spindle upon which Girardeau's adverse criticisms of pantheism turn.

He begins by characterizing pantheism. 'The cardinal principle of pantheism', he declares, 'is, that there is but one substance. It is in the highest sense a monistic system.'[11] To this substance is given the name of God: 'God is everywhere, and everything is God.'[12] According to Spinozistic pantheism the one substance manifests itself in both spirit and matter; in the idealistic version it is construed exclusively as spirit; in the materialist, as matter. Though designated 'God', this one substance is impersonal, and it is not creative. Girardeau proceeds to expand upon these points.

---

[7] Wenley, quoted by Macmillan, *The Life of Robert Flint*, p. 39.

[8] For Girardeau see George A. Blackburn, ed., *The Life and Work of John L. Girardeau, Late Professor in the Presbyterian Theological Seminary, Columbia, S.C.*, Columbia, SC: State Company, 1916; C. N. Willborn, 'John L. Girardeau: Pastor to Slaves and Theologian of Causes', unpublished doctoral dissertation, Westminster Theological Seminary, Philadelphia, 2003.

[9] For Iverach see Sell, *Defending and Declaring the Faith*, ch. 6, and Sell and Mander, eds, *The Dictionary of Nineteenth-Century British Philosophers*.

[10] J. L. Girardeau, *Discussions of Philosophical Questions*, Richmond, VA: Presbyterian Committee of Publication, 1900, p. 166.

[11] Ibid., p. 167.

[12] Ibid.

Against the idea that there is but one substance he, like Flint, first pits 'the explicit testimony of consciousness. That testimony is, that the ego and the non-ego are different, though related, realities.'[13] We are obliged to infer from the mental phenomena of which we are conscious that there is a subject which they manifest, and to infer from the external phenomena presented to our consciousness that they too are substantive realities. Secondly, Girardeau argues that the incompatible qualities of spirit and matter cannot be reduced to one substance and, thirdly, that consciousness 'affirms the existence of finite substances, and the difference of one from another'.[14] His fourth contention is that pantheists are mistaken in holding that the universe is an evolution of the primordial substance, since contrasted and contradictory modes are produced. He grants that it is

> conceivable that contrasts, leading to ultimate unity, should characterize the government of a free intelligence, who is not only necessary substance, but elective cause; but the same is not predicable of a process enforced simply by impersonal necessity. The pantheist's Becoming is suicidal, his necessary substance the source of conflicting sources.[15]

So much for Girardeau's opening gambit. I shall introduce further points from his paper as we proceed. Now, however, we must see how Iverach sets about his chosen task of exposing the weaknesses of pantheism in his 1907 paper of that title.[16]

Iverach begins by analyzing the term 'pantheism':

> it may mean either (1) that the All is God, or else (2) that God is all... [I]t may signify (1) that the sum-total of particular existences is God, that the universe is the only real being: or (2) it may mean that God, the Absolute Being, is the only real being, that all finite being is only appearance, and is only illusion. Pantheism may thus be equivalent to a denial of God, or...a denial of the reality of the world. It may mean atheism or akosmism. In any event it means an absolute identification of God and other being. It either merges God in the universe, or the universe is merged in God.[17]

Following a brief account of the history of the phenomenon, Iverach observes that at the present time (1907) pantheism issues in either materialistic monism or objective idealism. Haeckel's naturalistic monism and Herbert Spencer's synthetic philosophy exemplify the former (and,

---

13 Ibid., p. 168.

14 Ibid., p. 171.

15 Ibid., p. 172.

16 J. Iverach, 'Pantheism', *The Expositor*, 7th series, III, 1907, i, pp. 493-507; IV.ii, pp. 20-35, 153-168.

17 Ibid., p. 494.

in face of strictly naturalistic principles, Haeckel ascribes divinity to Nature);[18] the latter is represented by post-Hegelian absolute idealism, which 'regards the universe as the experience of a single life, or the expression of an Absolute Self-consciousness'.[19]

Behind both of these modern varieties of pantheism lies the philosophy of Kant, for from his declaration that we can know phenomena only there has flowed modern agnosticism;[20] while from his transcendental principles there has, following a significant shift to be explained shortly, flowed absolute idealism. Kant's view is that there are universal and necessary categories of the understanding which enable us to experience objects as they are: 'Their implicit presence in experience in general, Kant calls their transcendental character, and the process by which they become explicit is shown in what he calls the transcendental deduction.'[21] The significant shift leading to absolute idealism resides in the fact that what was for Kant a critical philosophy concerning epistemological issues was transformed into a metaphysic in such a way that 'the subject–object unity is the rubric of explanation of all reality and of all experience'.[22] In this transformation, Fichte, Schelling and Hegel were prominent. From Kant's analysis of consciousness in general the idealists—illegitimately in Iverach's view—jumped to a single intelligence for which all things are. The world is the other of God, and the each is equally necessary to the other. We thus land in pantheism—however much such idealists as John and Edward Caird, Bradley, and McTaggart in Britain,[23] and Royce in America, protest against the label.[24] Iverach grants that Christians among the absolute idealists construe their position in terms of the immanence of God. Iverach's problem with this is that 'The Immanence of God may be

---

[18] Cf. A. E. Garvie's remark in 'Pantheism', in James Hastings, ed., *Encyclopaedia of Religion and Ethics*, Edinburgh: T. & T. Clark, 1917, IX p. 609(a): Spinoza 'clothes an intense piety in an altogether too scanty philosophical garment; [Haeckel] uses the word "God" only as a fig-leaf to hide the nakedness of his materialistic monism'.

[19] Iverach, 'Pantheism', p. 502.

[20] This can have a religious dimension, as when writers refer to the God beyond God: that is, to one deemed to be there but to be utterly unknowable by us. This position is in some respects reminiscent of that of the Pseudo-Dionysius and other mystics, for whom God was the Being beyond all things, about whom we could speak by saying only what he is not.

[21] Iverach, 'Pantheism', p. 23.

[22] Ibid., p. 22.

[23] For John Caird see Sell, *Defending and Declaring the Faith*, ch. 3; for Edward Caird and other British idealists who were Christians or inclined towards the faith, see Sell, *Philosophical Idealism and Christian Belief, passim.*

[24] For a brief account of the American situation see Bruce Kuklick, *A History of Philosophy in America 1720–2000*, Oxford: Clarendon Press, 2001, ch. 7.

stated in such a way as to obliterate all distinction between Him and the world.'[25]

Having presented the general stance of my two protagonists, we may proceed to particular critical points in sequence, categorizing them under the headings: philosophical, ethical, religious and theological.

II

Philosophical Criticisms

Girardeau finds it contradictory that on the one hand the primordial substance is said to be a necessary substance devoid of personality and elective freedom, whilst on the other hand its 'cosmical manifestations' with involve 'innumerable changes' are invincibly necessitated: 'A simply necessary substance which changes is a contradiction in terms.'[26] He anticipates the response that Spinoza spoke of a free necessary substance, and that by 'free' he meant 'spontaneous'. But, counters Girardeau, this necessary freedom cannot account for such changes as that from good to bad, of which we are conscious, for 'If a thing is necessarily good, it cannot become bad.'[27] Again it might be said that the primordial substance is a necessary and eternal cause. But this is self-contradictory, for 'A necessary and eternal cause supposes a necessary and eternal effect. As necessary and eternal it could not begin; as effect it must have begun.'[28] Finally, it might be contended that since theists uphold the necessity of the divine Being they are in the same position as the pantheists. Not so, for whereas the pantheist posits change in the necessary substance, the theist holds that 'as substance, God abides unchanged and unchangeable'.[29]

At a later point in his paper Girardeau advances a further argument against the transcendental philosophers, pantheists and absolutists, namely, that they 'deal with the measures of faith as if they were the measures of thought'.[30] He welcomes the way in which these philosophers affirm the infinite and refuse to be bound to the phenomenal realm: in a word, he applauds their ontological commitment. Unfortunately, however,

---

25 Iverach, 'Pantheism', p. 34.

26 Girardeau, 'Pantheism', p. 179. Cf. Flint, *Anti-Theistic Theories*, p. 427.

27 Girardeau, 'Pantheism', p. 180.

28 Ibid., p. 181.

29 Ibid., p. 182. I am, of course, aware that the question of the immutability or otherwise of God, like that of his proneness to suffering or otherwise, has received much attention from theologians in recent decades. I do not propose to challenge my two protagonists on neuralgic points such as this, but simply to set down their positions as clearly as I can with a view to determining what we may take from them by way of cautions wherever pantheism rears its head.

30 Ibid., p. 200.

they have committed the 'intellectual crime, of confounding the infinite with the finite, the indemonstrable with the demonstrable, the incomprehensible with the comprehensible'.[31] In particular, '*they treated faith-judgments as though they were concepts*'. Instead of accepting the infinite or Absolute as data of belief which are impervious to analysis, they construe them as analyzable data of thought. Furthermore, they are selective in ascribing infinity to the Absolute, but not causation and personality. Thereby they 'violated our mental nature' which thinks these things together.[32] Had they paid more heed to the history of philosophy they might have learned the folly of concentrating so fully upon one side of the idealist–empiricist divide. As it is, 'Having launched forth in search of the Absolute, without the compass of experience, they foundered in an ocean of mists without bottom and without shore.'[33] Their error was compounded by the fact that they affirmed

> as the last conclusion of philosophy, an absolute something, or, with Hegel, nothing, without consciousness or personality, and evolving, by the law of immanent necessity, into the matter and spirit of the universe: a climax of folly which the regulated genius of the Greek never reached.[34]

What particularly puzzled Iverach from the philosophical point of view was the way in which the absolute idealists so confidently assumed (for the position is not demonstrated) that a conscious self could be part of an all-inclusive self. It is, it must be admitted, a gigantic postulate. He invokes A. S. Pringle-Pattison in support:

> The unity of things (which is not denied) cannot be properly expressed by making it depend upon a unity of a Self in all thinkers; for the very characteristic of a self is this exclusiveness... I have a centre of my own, a will of my own, which no one shares with me or can share—a centre which I maintain even in my dealings with God Himself... Religion is a self-surrender of the human will to the divine. 'Our wills are ours to make them thine.' But this is *self*-surrender, a surrender which only self, only will can make.[35]

Iverach underscores the point: 'The quotation denies in terms the possibility of the assumption made by almost all the modern absolute idealists... No self is a part or an attribute of any other self. An absolute,

---

[31] Ibid., p. 202.

[32] Ibid., p. 204.

[33] Ibid., pp. 205-206.

[34] Ibid., p. 206.

[35] Iverach, 'Pantheism', pp. 162-63, quoting A. Seth (afterwards Pringle-Pattison), *Hegelianism and Personality*, Edinburgh: Blackwood, 1887, pp. 216-18 (though Iverach himself mistakenly cites pp. 227-29).

inclusive self-consciousness is unintelligible.'[36] Flint concurs and, with reference to the multiplicity of selves, he writes,

> pantheism, in order to adhere to its dogma of absolute unity, must contradict the testimony borne by the consciousness of all these beings. It is logically bound to affirm that each of them is under a delusion when he supposes himself to be truly a self or person. But what does this imply? Why, that from true persons, really distinct from all other beings—free, responsible, moral—it must reduce and degrade them to mere semblances; for with personality, their freedom of will, responsibility, duty, must likewise be sacrificed.[37]

However, if we are to do justice to the uniqueness of individual selves, we must do likewise in respect of 'the self-conscious Spirit from Whom all things are'.[38] Iverach therefore recommends that we seek a unity inclusive of God and of all other consciousnesses—a spiritual system in which all are mutually related and the integrity of all is preserved. But this is precisely what pantheism cannot do: 'Metaphysically, epistemologically, psychologically...we find it burdened with inadequate regard to truth and fact.'[39] Flint went further, contending that the pantheistic unity 'is a mere idol of the mind. Belief in it is intellectual idolatry. The hope of ever reaching it is consummate folly'.[40] Because pantheism is always in 'unstable equilibrium between theism and atheism' it is 'logically necessitated to elevate itself to the one or to descend to the other'.[41]

Ethical Criticisms

As we might expect, Girardeau's ethical critique of pantheism takes flight from our consciousness of being free moral agents, and from the conviction that electively free 'substances' must be personal: 'It is absurd to ascribe such freedom to impersonal substance.'[42] We are, in addition, conscious of moral qualities, and of the sense of moral duty with the necessary inference of moral responsibility. None of these factors can be accommodated within pantheism strictly conceived.

Iverach is in entire agreement. Convinced of the pantheizing tendencies of idealism, he quotes Royce to the effect that 'The very presence of ill in the temporal order is the condition of Perfection in the eternal order'; and Bradley as saying that 'The absolute is the richer for

---

36 Ibid., p. 163.

37 Flint, *Anti-Theistic Theories*, p. 433.

38 Iverach, 'Pantheism', p. 164.

39 Ibid., p. 164.

40 Flint, *Anti-Theistic Theories*, p. 414.

41 Ibid., pp. 376-7.

42 Girardeau, 'Pantheism,' p. 185.

every discord, and for all the diversity which it embraces.' He then declares,

> on the view of Pantheism...moral values vanish, and evil has its place in the Absolute. There can, on these terms, be no abiding distinction between good and evil, virtue and vice, right and wrong... Any philosophy which obliterates moral values, and which apologizes for ugliness, evil and sin, and makes these essential to the perfection of the eternal order, is under the necessity of revising its procedure, and of bringing its conclusions into something like harmony with the moral convictions and aspirations of mankind.[43]

Flint concurs:

> If evil be no less necessary or divine than good, evil must be but good in another way we are not skilled in, and neither God nor man can reasonably condemn it. If human personality and freedom are illusions, then must obligation, guilt and retribution be the absurdest fictions. In a word, from pantheistic premisses we can only legitimately infer that 'whatever is, is right,' or that 'might is right.'...[Pantheism] cannot allow that moral good and evil are in direct antagonism.[44]

We may summarize the perceived threats which pantheism poses to morality thus: we lose our selves, and with them our moral consciousness, as parts in the whole; and we obliterate moral distinctions in the onward and upward evolution of a necessitated process wherein, we are assured on no adequate grounds, all will come right in the end. The verdict of Ottley is not too harsh: 'It is characteristic of the Christian spirit frankly to recognize the natural world in its due subordination to personality, in its subserviency to ethical ends. An absolute idealism is not less alien to this standpoint than a crude materialism.'[45] Hence Forsyth's urgent demand, 'we must have a Dualism with a unity of Reconciliation, not a Monism with a unity of Identity as real in the sin and in the Saviour'.[46]

---

[43] Iverach, 'Pantheism', p. 165. His references are, J. Royce, *The World and the Individual*, New York: Macmillan, 2 vols., 1900–01, II, p. 385; F. H. Bradley, *Appearance and Reality*, London: Swan Sonneschein, 1893, p. 204. Cf. A. C. Ewing's dry remark in his *Idealism: A Critical Survey*, London: Methuen, 3rd edn, 1961, p. 409: 'it is difficult to see how perfection could be ascribed to a mind which really included in itself beings such as Nero or Caesar Borgia or, as far as that goes, myself'.

[44] Flint, *Anti-Theistic Theories*, pp. 396-97, 401; cf. pp. 398-99.

[45] R. L. Ottley, 'Christian ethics', in *Lux Mundi*, ed. Charles Gore, London: John Murray, (1889), 15th edn 1904, p. 349.

[46] P. T. Forsyth, 'Monism', a privately printed paper read to the London Society for the Study of Religion on 2 February 1909, p. 12.

The Religious Criticism

The argument that it is religiously inadequate is a key weapon in the armoury of those divines who oppose pantheism. On this ground Girardeau sets his face against the impersonal deity of pantheism and absolute idealism. As before, he launches forth from our consciousness of ourselves as personalities, and our inference, 'an indubitable faith-judgment', that God is personal too.[47] What he finds particularly odd is that pantheists frequently wish to claim that God comes to personal consciousness in humanity. But, counters Girardeau, this must mean that God originally possessed personality potentially, otherwise the claim is meaningless. But if the pantheist concede the claim, he has forsaken the doctrine of the impersonality of God.

Some pantheists then say that the impersonal substance passes through a process of Becoming; but this, chides Giradeau, 'is but an instance of that amazing circumgyratory process...by which the Absolute abdicates its crown in order to enjoy the pleasure of resuming it; by which it first 'steps down and out' in order to step up and in!'[48] He proceeds to argue that if the originally impersonal deity comes to personality in human beings, then humanity is God improved, for 'a being possessed of personality is greater than one destitute of it'.[49] The pantheistic argument is thus self-destroyingly absurd. His final argument on this matter is that 'If God comes to personal consciousness in man, he must have as many personal consciousnesses as there are men...for a personal humanity which is not individual would be contradictory of our fundamental conceptions.'[50] If this be denied, then it is accepted that human beings are distinct from God; and in that case pantheism, which asserts human–divine identity falls; and man, having personality, would be greater than God—'an absurdity [which] it would take the capacity of an absolutist speculator to swallow'.[51]

Somewhat more cautiously, Iverach is equally concerned to defend the distinct personality of God. All systems of idealism are, however, fatally flawed in that they are irreducibly anthropomorphic. They 'simply magnify the one self with which they are empirically acquainted, and as that self demands a not-self, and that subject demands an object, so the absolute self-consciousness is made into the likeness of the individual self'.[52] But on what grounds is it supposed that the only relation of God to the world is of a subject–object kind? Selves learn, receive, create, will,

---

47 Girardeau, 'Pantheism', p. 173.

48 Ibid., p. 175.

49 Ibid., p. 176.

50 Ibid., p. 177.

51 Ibid., p. 178.

52 Iverach, 'Pantheism', p. 157.

conceive ends and act. All of these aspects of God's personality are neglected in an idealistic intellectualism which recognizes God only as subject. By contrast,

> In Christian Theism the life of God was not a life of mere substance, nor a life as mere subject, nor a life as absolute, nor a life which can be adequately described by abstract predicates. It is the life of the Living God, not an abstract life, but a life of absolute fullness in which there is oneness and difference, in which there is the absolute realization of all perfection... God is Spirit, God is light, God is love, and in these three sayings there is more and truer philosophy than there is in all the speculations of all the idealistic schemers known to history.[53]

As Iverach elsewhere put it, 'To speak of the absolute and unconditioned as synonymous with God, is simply to alter the conception of God.'[54]

Once again, Flint is in full accord:

> Pantheism...would divest God of character: it denies to him self-consciousness, fatherly love, providential care, redeeming mercy: under the pretence of exalting Him above all categories of thought and existence it reduces Him to the level of dead things, of necessary processes, of abstract ideas, or even to the still lower level of the unknowable and non-existent; and it thereby leaves no room for that union with God in rational, pure, and holy love, which is the only basis, the grand distinction, the power, and the glory of true religion.[55]

It is not that Flint can see noting attractive in pantheism: 'It does well to insist on the omnipresence of God, and on the complete and ceaseless dependence of the universe on His power';[56] but the cost of these benefits is too great. W. P. Paterson likewise saw that 'pantheistic Mysticism is associated with a love of God which could become a veritable intoxication of the soul, but the general mass of mankind have found it beyond their power to love a God who, being impersonal, cannot know and love and truly care'.[57]

Positively, Iverach, proposes that if we take our cue from the New Testament,

> we shall no longer speak of God as absolute, and so on, but...we shall think of God as a determinate Being existing in relations, and these relations are abiding

---

53 Ibid., pp. 159-60.

54 J. Iverach, *Theism in the Light of Present Science and Philosophy*, London: Hodder and Stoughton, 1900, p. 307.

55 Flint, *Anti-Theistic Theories*, p. 387; cf. p. 395. See also pp. 393-94, where Flint quotes H. P. Liddon's verdict on pantheism in *The Divinity of our Lord and Saviour Jesus Christ*, London: Rivingtons, 1867, pp. 672-73.

56 Flint, *Anti-Theistic Theories*, p. 384.

57 W. P. Paterson, *The Nature of Religion*, London: Hodder and Stoughton, [1925], p. 376.

> distinctions within the circle of the divine life. God is not an abstract unity, nor an absolute and inclusive self-consciousness, God is a living, concrete, complex Being, and in the Godhead there are relations and activities always in relations and always in action. The relations within the Godhead come to our help and rescue us from the paralysis of thought wrought by the abstractions of metaphysics, and we are not compelled to think in terms of an abstract order, nor driven to the necessity of deriving a manifold universe from a simplicity in which there are no relations.[58]

With this we enter the territory of theology.

Theological Criticisms

The theological critics of pantheism tend to fasten upon three main areas of concern. First, they charge that pantheism unwarrantably obliterates the Creator-creature distinction apart from which worship is impossible, human experience is denied, and theology falls. Iverach readily grants that the pantheistic-idealistic philosophy of his day does not, like atheism, regard religion as a superstition; does not neglect it; and does not seek to transmute it into ethics. What seriously concerns him, however, is its tendency to state the immanence of God 'in such a way as to obliterate all distinction between Him and the world'.[59] This concern was widely shared by philosophers and theologians of many stripes,[60] with Pringle-Pattison warning that 'A purely immanental view of the divine is equivalent to a sheer Pantheism in which no distinction whatever is drawn between God and nature.'[61] In this connection Girardeau makes a direct appeal to the Bible as being entitled to the serious attention of pantheistically-inclined philosophers, for it 'utters itself in the sphere of ontology'. In particular, 'It declares the existence of a personal God, who is the creator of the world, and its providential preserver and ruler.'[62] This, of course, throws up the question of the authority of Scripture, and Girardeau fully recognizes this. He does not pursue the question in his paper on 'Pantheism', but contents himself with inviting the attention of pantheists to this significant witness.

In Iverach's opinion some of his Scottish compatriots were sailing too close to the wind on this matter. He was concerned that John Caird could

---

58 Iverach, *Theism in the Light of Present Science and Philosophy*, p. 307.

59 Iverach, 'Pantheism', p. 34.

60 See, for example, Liddon, *The Divinity of our Lord and Saviour Jesus Christ*, p. 674; Flint, *Anti-Theistic Theories*, p. 386; C. C. J. Webb, *Religion and Theism*, London: Allen & Unwin, 1934, pp. 135-36.

61 A. S. Pringle-Pattison, 'Immanence and transcendence', in *The Spirit*, ed., B. H. Streeter, London: Macmillan, 1928, p. 4.

62 Girardeau, 'Pantheism', p. 206.

say of idealism that it is simply 'Christianity theorized'.[63] Where God was concerned, Iverach stoutly repudiated the corollary of the idealistically blurred Creator-creature distinction, namely, that the world is as indispensable to God as God is to the world.[64] He reiterates the point a few lines later:

> it is absolutely necessary to insist on the distinction between God and the world, and while the world is dependent on God, God is not dependent on the world. The Christian conception of God insists that in him there is no becoming, in Him there is no realization of Himself... Now all idealistic, all pantheistic theories assume that God is in the process of realization, and that the evolution of the world is the evolution of God.[65]

The upshot is that

> the idealistic philosophy makes religion to be simply an aspect of itself, and does not leave us with a God into whose fellowship we may enter, in whose service we may find perfect freedom... We need a God who can speak to us, and if He cannot speak directly to us...the flower and fruit of religion will wither and die.[66]

Small wonder that Iverach could not tolerate the way in which, in his view, Edward Caird had 'calmly annexed' the sphere of revelation and made it part of the natural process.[67] Small wonder either that P. T. Forsyth pungently stated the obvious: 'a God conceived as above all things monistic and immanent to the world cannot reveal Himself, because He has no recipient Other.'[68]

But, secondly, this revelation of God occurs in history, and supremely in Christ; and this, according to the theological critics of pantheism, is a further factor which that world view is quite unable to accommodate. Iverach is convinced that under the pantheistic-idealistic regime

> Christianity is transformed beyond all recognition. Facts disappear, doctrines disappear, experience distinctively Christian is evaporated, and we are left with nothing save the ideas disembodie in the religion. History and Fact are merely scaffolding useful for the introduction of the Ideas, but as soon as the ideas are there the facts may usefully disappear.[69]

---

63 Iverach, 'Pantheism', p. 153, quoting J. Caird, *Encyclopaedia Britannica*, 9th edn, XVI, p. 102.

64 Iverach, 'Pantheism', p. 156.

65 Ibid.

66 Iverach, *Theism in the Light of Present Science and Philosophy*, p. 292.

67 See J. Iverach, 'Edward Caird,' *The Expository Times*, V, 1893–94, p. 205.

68 Forsyth, 'Monism', p. 8.

69 Iverach, 'Pantheism', p. 33.

The kind of ideas he had in mind were those promulgated by T. H. Green, who said that in John's gospel we have the 'final spiritual interpretation to the person of Christ, which has for ever taken it out of the region of history and of the doubts that surround all past events, to fix it in the purified conscience as the immanent God'.[70] Green elsewhere finds an inner contradiction in the Christian conception of faith, in that it concerns both 'a state of mind involving peace with God and love towards all men, and at the same time makes its object that historical work of Christ, of which our knowledge depends on evidence of uncertain origin and value'.[71] The inadequacy, in Green's view, of the history, facilitates the triumph of the ideas. Indeed, Iverach goes so far as to say that in Green's thought 'the historical Christ has vanished, and has been succeeded by the idea'.[72] In this connection the reminiscences of R. F. Horton, one of Green's students, are of interest:

> Never can I forget his expression when one day he found that I had a real and vivid faith in Christ. His own faith was philosophical and ethical; but Christ, as a Person, had been dissolved by criticism. 'You are very fortunate,' was his brief, intense comment.[73]

Again, when Horton was puzzling over whether he should remain in Oxford or take up the Congregational pastorate at Hampstead (which in due course he did), Green remarked, 'You are likely to much good here [in Oxford], because you believe, more than most of us, in the old doctrines.'[74]

To Iverach and to many others down the Christian ages, both the transcendence and the immanence of God must be upheld, and these are nowhere more clearly related or manifested in the Incarnation of Emmanuel, God with us—and with us in history.[75]

With this we come to the third main theological criticism of pantheism (though it is not one lodged by Girardeau or Iverach), namely, that by encouraging the transmogrification of Christianity into a set of *ideas*, those pantheists who are kindly disposed towards the faith cannot do justice to the decisive *act* at the Cross, whereby we are redeemed. They

---

70 T. H. Green, *Works of Thomas Hill Green*, ed. R. L. Nettleship, London: Longmans, Green, 3 vols. 1885–88, III, p. 242.

71 Ibid., II, p. 260.

72 J. Iverach, 'Professor Thomas Hill Green', *The Expository Times*, IV, 1892–93, p. 167.

73 Quoted in A. Peel and J. A. R. Marriott, *Robert Forman Horton*, London: Allen & Unwin, 1937, p. 75.

74 Ibid., p. 109.

75 For an attempt to wrestle with this intricate theme see Alan P. F. Sell, *Confessing and Commending the Faith: Historic Witness and Apologetic Method*, Cardiff: University of Wales Press, 2002, ch. 5.

thereby undercut the Gospel—as Kierkegaard made so clear in his dissent from Hegelianism.[76] We thus have Edward Caird's emphasis upon the centrality of the dying and rising motif in Christianity: 'It is the essential meaning of Christ's life and death that every one must die to himself in order to rise to the wider life of Christian love'[77]—to which the appropriate response is, No, it isn't, for Christ's death is an atoning one, not one designed simply to inspire self-effacing and self-powered altruism. Or again, Green's mode of expression is no less reductionist:

> A death unto life, a life out of death, must in some way be the essence of the divine nature, must be an act which though exhibited once for all in the crucifixion and resurrection of Christ was yet eternal—the act of God himself. For that very reason however it was one perpetually enacted and to be re-enacted by man...[78]

The atonement was the act of God in his Son; it is integrally related to the divine nature, but 'exhibited' is a weasel word in this context, for atonement was wrought once and for all at the Cross: we do not have there simply the representation of an eternal idea. Furthermore, Christians are called to follow Christ, not copy him; they live by his saving work, they do not re-enact it.

III

I am well aware that much intellectual water has flowed under the bridge since the anti-pantheistic protests of a century and more ago. In some circles panentheism has been in vogue, and process thought has taken manifold forms. I am also aware that some of the arguments of the divines who opposed pantheism are open to criticism, and I have not indulged in this. Rather, I have sought to bring out the main thrust of the anti-pantheist case, and in this I have been motivated not by antiquarian interests, but by the conviction that in varying guises pantheism, that most resilient of intellectual tendencies, is ever with us. It would take me too far afield to demonstrate this point. Suffice it to say, for example, that any Christian thinkers who at the present time seek intellectual rapprochement with those of other faiths, and those who go in quest of ecological theology—not to mention the many thoughtful Christian believers who stand bewildered before the 'Body Mind Spirit' sections of our major

---

76 See John Heywood Thomas, 'Kierkegaard's alternative metaphysical theology', *History of European Ideas*, XII no. 1, 1990, p. 61: 'Kierkegaard showed the fundamental flaw in Hegelian theology, its transformation of Christology into some abstract principle.'

77 E. Caird, *Lay Sermons and Addresses Delivered in the Hall of Balliol College, Oxford*, Glasgow: Maclehose, 1907, p. 273.

78 Green, *Works*, III, p. 233.

book chains—would do well to ponder the pertinence or otherwise of the critique of pantheism to some of the ideas they will encounter. In particular, they would do well to ask, How may we best articulate the idea of the personality of both God and human beings? Along which lines are moral values best upheld? How religiously satisfactory is pantheism's attenuated God? Why is it important to maintain the Creator-creature distinction? How may we give an account of the relations between immanence, transcendence and history which will preclude reductionist accounts of the Incarnation and the Atonement?

CHAPTER 8

Some Reformed Reflections on Spirituality

The delightful village of Cavendish, Suffolk, straddles a Roman road. From the point of view of English Dissent it is in 'martyr country', for John Copping and Elias Thacker (or Ffawker), were hanged at nearby Bury St. Edmunds on 4th and 5th June 1583 respectively.[1] Daniel Sutton, a former Rector of Cavendish, being unable to give his 'unfeigned assent and consent' to the *Book of Common Prayer* of the Church of England was, like nearly 2,000 others, ejected from his living under the Act of Uniformity of 1662.[2] It is just the kind of place to which Alexander James Grieve (1874–1952) might have been expected to remove when, after nearly forty years of training ministers in Bradford, Edinburgh and Manchester, he sought a sphere where he could 'try and practise a bit of it for myself'.[3] For Grieve was strongly rooted in, and deeply knowledgeable about, the history and principles of Dissent, above all the principle concerning the supreme and only headship of Christ over his Church (with its negative implications concerning the rights of monarch or parliament over worship and church order). On a wall in Cavendish United Reformed (formerly Congregational) Church a plaque bears the following inscription:

TO THE GLORY OF GOD
AND IN GRATEFUL MEMORY OF
ALEXANDER JAMES GRIEVE, M.A., D.D.
PRINCIPAL, LANCASHIRE INDEPENDENT COLLEGE,
1922–1943.
MINISTER, CAVENDISH CONGREGATIONAL CHURCH,
1943–1951.

---

1 See Albert Peel, 'Congregational martyrs at Bury St. Edmunds. How many?', *Congregational Historical Society Transactions*, XV no. 2, April 1946, pp. 64-67, and *The Noble Army of Congregational Martyrs*, London: Independent Press, 1948.

2 For Sutton (d. 1664) see A. G. Matthews, ed., *Calamy Revised*, (1934), Oxford: Clarendon Press, 1988, p. 470.

3 Quoted by Charles E. Surman [Grieve's son-in-law], *Alexander James Grieve, M.A., D.D., 1874–1952. A Biographical Sketch*, Manchester: Lancashire Independent College, 1953, p 53.

MISSIONARY, THEOLOGIAN, MINISTER.[4]

I set out from 'Sandy' Grieve not simply by way of marking the fiftieth anniversary of his death, but because he epitomized an earthed spirituality which believes that if 'a soft answer turneth away wrath', a witty one topples the presumptuous from their pedestals and the falsely pious from their perches. One example must suffice. Before the start of a united service the participating ministers were sharing the parts of the service between them. When asked what part he would take, an Anglo-Catholic replied, 'The Blessing, of course, must be mine, as I am the only *priest* present.' To which Grieve retorted, 'I shall be happy to serve in the Sacrament of the reading of the Word.'[5] It would be a great mistake to regard this as a flippant riposte: it is necessary not only to hear what Grieve was saying, but to see what he was doing. Negatively, Grieve was opposing sacerdotalism and its attendant sectarianism; he was identifying himself with the priesthood of all believers; and he was elevating the Word as that which, no less than the sacraments, by the Spirit brings the living Christ to the believing heart; and he was doing this in the presence of one who, presumably, regarded Nonconformists as peddling 'invalid' sacraments.[6] It is also entirely conceivable that Grieve was also cutting a pompous or self-important Christian down to size.

When I entered Lancashire Independent College in the year following Grieve's death his successor, W. Gordon Robinson,[7] was more than capable of maintaining the tradition of 'speaking the truth with wit'. One schooled in such an environment cannot but be more than a little underwhelmed by some of the antics which pass for expressions of spirituality in our time. For anyone with a sense of history, some of the incongruities are delightful. What a gulf exists, for example, between the self-mortification of a Peter Damian ('Since in spite of my longing I have not the opportunity of martyrdom, by riddling myself with blows I at least show how fervently I desire it'[8]) and those present-day pilgrims whose principal preoccupation seems to be whether or not Iona or Taizé

---

[4] For this church see T. J. Hosken, *History of Congregationalism and Memorials of the Churches of our Order in Suffolk*, Ipswich: W. E. Harrison, 1920, pp. 310-11; A. J. Grieve, 'Cavendish church, Suffolk', *Congregational Historical Society Transactions*, XV no. 1, May 1945, pp. 7-17, and XV, no. 2, April 1946, pp. 73-74.

[5] Recounted in Surman, *Alexander James Grieve,* p. 45.

[6] Cf. P. T. Forsyth, *Positive Preaching and the Modern Mind*, (1907), London: Independent Press, 1964, p. 4: 'The sacrament which gives value to all other sacraments is the Sacrament of the living Word.'

[7] For whom see *ODNB*.

[8] J. Leclerq, F. Vandenbroucke and L. Bouyer, eds., *A History of Christian Spirituality. II, The Spirituality of the Middle Ages*, London: Burns & Oates, 1968, p. 118 (*Epist*. VI, 27, J. P. Migne, *PL*, 144.416).

are furnished with *en suite* facilities. Again, how difficult it has sometimes been to strike the true note of holy joy, with some eighteenth-century Dutch pietists being convinced that gloominess is a sign of true piety, and some present-day charismatics quick to rebuke those who seem to them to be insufficiently jolly. In this connection some words of Kierkegaard are worth pondering:

> Christianity is certainly not melancholy; it is, on the contrary, glad tidings—for the melancholy; to the frivolous it is certainly not glad tidings, for it wishes first of all to make them serious.[9]

However it may have been in the past, it cannot be denied that, with courses here, retreats there; with secular book chains devoting ever-increasing amounts of shelf space to 'Body, Mind and Spirit'—with all that means in terms of self-help, yoga, the occult, astrology, witchcraft, earth goddesses, and numerous exotic spiritualities; and with Christian book shops purveying everything from free grace to feel good—the impression cannot be resisted that spirituality is big business. Insofar as the circumstances thus described witness to a genuine quest on the part of many for inner peace or contact with the divine (however conceived)—and 27 per cent of Britons describe themselves as 'spiritual'[10]—Christians would do well to read the signs of the times and to review their own 'programmatic provision' (if I have the jargon correctly). But when the objective is self-improvement egotistically construed, or the quest of ever more novel and exciting spiritual 'highs', one may be forgiven for raising a quizzical eyebrow.

It is against this background that I have set out to sketch the history of Reformed spirituality with a view to specifying its *differentia*. This causes me two problems. The first concerns the definition of 'spirituality'. In the sixteenth century a collective noun used of the clergy, the term came gradually to be used in contrast to things material and, later still, to designate the quest of those Christians who sought ever closer union with God by varying mixtures of prayer, participation in the means of grace, and the performance of spiritual exercises. As is well known, the term as such does not appear in the New Testament, though (to be brief) we do find there such prominent themes as life in the Spirit; the command to be holy; Paul's so-called Christ mysticism; the Johannine emphasis upon abiding in Christ; the heavenly Intercessor of the letter to the Hebrews; the call to conversion; regeneration by the Spirit; the doctrine of sanctification understood both as indicating the saints' separatedness

---

9 *The Journals of Kierkegaard 1834–1854*, ed. and trans. Alexander Dru, London: Collins Fontana, 1960, p. 129.

10 According to a poll carried out by Opinion Research Business in December 1999.

from the 'world' and their striving (against many downward pulls) after perfection; the challenge to bear the fruit of the Spirit—so one might go on. All of this suggests on the one hand that if we think of 'spirituality' narrowly in terms of technical manuals we shall have to admit that the Reformed have not been prolific contributors of these. On the other hand, the more we think in terms of the New Testament motifs just suggested the clearer it becomes that these are not ours in any exclusive sense. It will therefore be appropriate to think in terms of Christian spirituality as embracing the constituting and living of the Christian life, and to illustrate this by reference largely, though not exclusively, to Reformed sources.

The second problem I face is that Tom Schwanda, who originally invited me to undertake this task on behalf of the editorial board of the journal in which this chapter originally appeared,[11] has already done much of the work himself.[12] In particular he has properly argued that 'from its beginning the Reformed heritage has sought to be intentional about integrating the head and heart',[13] and has summoned Calvin and Jonathan Edwards to prove the point. He has also rightly emphasized the communal locus of Reformed spirituality, and has suggested how we may appropriate the insights of our heritage from the Bible, at the Lord's Supper, and in daily life. In fact, to add to the anatomical metaphors, we are here concerned with head, heart and hands (and feet as well, if we are in a mood to recall the 'godly walk' enjoined by our forebears—but some preachers like alliteration). The best I can do is to try to build a little upon what Mr. Schwanda has done, though with the proviso that the head-heart-hands scheme will be subject to modification as we proceed: this on the good Pauline principle that none of them may say to the others, 'I have no need of you' (1 Corinthians 12:21.).On the contrary, we shall find that almost as soon as we begin to think about any one of the three, the others will come into view.

I

In setting out from the head, we may first note that there is an ineradicable intellectual element in Christian spirituality as generally understood by the Reformed, among others. It is not a subjectivist wallow, a vague 'getting in touch with oneself'; still less is it a matter of attempting to bypass the mind in the interests of some sort of gnostic communion with an undifferentiated divine. There is a knowledge content here, as a long line of witnesses, some of them pre-Reformation,

---

11 *Reformed Review*, LVI no. 2, Winter 2002/2003, pp. 139-61.

12 See T. Schwanda, 'Closing the gap: recovering the experiential nature of Reformed spirituality', *Reformed Review*, XLIX no. 2, Winter 1995–96, pp. 109-125.

13 Ibid., p. 110.

will testify. To Paul, for example, the saints' peace with God and hope for the future are gifts consequent upon God's gracious atoning work at the Cross, about which salvific event the believer has knowledge which is confirmed as genuine by the Holy Spirit who floods the heart with God's love (Romans 5). For his part, Bonaventure held that that knowledge which is of Christ, and which issues in the love and service of God is the supreme kind of knowledge. To Calvin, piety was 'that reverence joined with love of God which the knowledge of God's benefits induces'.[14] In Christian spirituality we are concerned with the objective: a knowing that certain things are the case—that God is love, for example; this knowing is grounded in, and entails a rejoicing in, and a responding to, the fatherly God of sovereign grace known in Christ by the Spirit. This trinitarian mode of expression into which I have quite naturally fallen, was much earlier employed by the Anglican Jeremy Taylor (1613–67) who, his dislike of Presbyterians notwithstanding, is worth heeding on this matter:

> God is especially present, in the hearts of his people, by his Holy Spirit... For God reigns in the hearts of his servants: there is his kingdom. The power of grace hath subdued all his enemies; there is his power. They serve him night and day, and give him thanks and praise: that is his glory. This is the religion and worship of God in the temple. The temple itself is the heart of man; Christ is the High Priest, who from thence sends up the incense of prayers, and joins them to his own intercession, and presents all together to his Father; and the Holy Ghost, by his dwelling there, hath also consecrated it into a temple; and God dwells in our hearts by faith, and Christ by his Spirit, and the Spirit by his purities; so that we are also cabinets of the mysterious Trinity; and what is this short of heaven itself, but as infancy is short of manhood, and letters of words?[15]

To the point as far as they go, the communal implications of these words require to be underscored if an exclusively individualistic reading of them is to be forestalled, and we shall turn to spirituality *vis à vis* the Church in the next section. Not, indeed, that the communal should obliterate the personal, but the latter needs to be understood in the context of the former. Otherwise we may, for example, land in that exaggerated piety which seems to suppose that Christ died for me alone. The fact nevertheless remains that, as the Puritan Thomas Watson (c. 1620–86) put it—also in trinitarian terms—

> A Christian's heart is to be the presence-chamber of the blessed Trinity; and shall not holiness to the Lord be written upon it? Believers are children of God the

---

14 J. Calvin, *Institutes of the Christian Religion*, trans. Ford Lewis Battles, 2 vols, Philadelphia: Westminster Press, 1960, I.ii.1.

15 J. Taylor, *The Rule and Exercises of Holy Living and Holy Dying*, in *The Whole Works of the Right Rev. Jeremy Taylor, D.D.*, London: Ogle, Duncan, 1822, IV, p. 33.

> Father, members of God the Son, and temples of God the Holy Ghost; and shall they not be holy? Holiness is the badge and livery of God's people.[16]

It seems to me that the rejoicing in, and contemplation of, the grace of God in the Gospel is fundamental to Christian spirituality. But doctrine rolls into doctrine, and there is not a single doctrine which fails to conduce to spiritual growth when pondered devotionally by believers. This is not to say that every consideration of Christian doctrine will, or should necessarily, lead to such growth. It is perfectly in order for scholars to debate the intricacies of the Chalcedonian Formula, for example, in an academic environment where spiritual growth is not their immediate concern: even non-Christian scholars may do this. But when believers contemplate any aspect of Christian doctrine in a devotional spirit, their faith is strengthened. The head undergirds the heart.[17] Let me offer some examples.

First, the Christian teaching concerning the Last Things (so frequently avoided in pulpits—except at funerals, by which time it is rather late for the deceased), can have a profound effect upon the believer's daily demeanour. A. J. Grieve, clearly thinking that the Christians at Quinta Brook, Shropshire, had passed from the solemn to the morbid, was propelled into a piece of prophetic symbolism. The occasion was the funeral of a brilliant fourth-year student, Silvester Holland, who had died of meningitis:

> The pulpit desk had been draped in funeral black, and as he entered it the Doctor gathered up the drapings, put them behind him, and in a voice that trembled declared, 'Death is *swallowed up* in victory!'[18]

The related thought occurs that a half decent eschatology might persuade organists not to push in all the loud stops as a matter of course when they see the word 'death' coming at them along the line of a hymn—especially in that grand verse of godly defiance which comes in the middle of the metrical version of Psalm 23:

---

16 T. Watson, *A Divine Cordial*, (1663), Grand Rapids, MI: Sovereign Grace Publishers, 1971, pp. 79-80.

17 I may be pardoned for mentioning that it was primarily because of this conviction that I tried my hand at a trilogy under the general title, *Doctrine and Devotion*. The volumes are: *God Our Father*; *Christ Our Saviour*; *The Spirit Our Life*, Shippensburg, PA: Ragged Edge Press, 2000. The series was written for ministers and church members, in the hope of injecting content into devotions and warmth into doctrine. My subsidiary motive was the feeling that since much of what appears from the 'popular' religious press (self-help/charismatic excitements/fifty years up the Amazon with Joe Bloggs) is not apt to feed and frequently patronizes the saints, some of us ought to attempt to redress the balance.

18 Surman, *Alexander James Grieve*, p. 64.

Yea, though I walk through death's dark vale
Yet will I fear none ill
For Thou art with me...

Secondly, the doctrine of God the Holy Spirit is of special significance where spirituality is concerned. The Spirit both brings home the truth of the Word, and also enables the Christian's response of faith (that is, *fiducia*—trust). It is precisely this necessary enabling which precludes any boasting on the believer's part—as if faith were a 'work' humanly achieved (Ephesians 2:9). The Puritan Thomas Goodwin was quick to distinguish between the knowledge possessed by the worldling and that granted to the saints:

> Now all the knowledge that carnal men have of the gospel, is but by images received from the hearsay of it; but the knowledge which holy men have, is by the impress and image received from the thing itself made known unto them by the Holy Ghost.[19]

It must be emphasized that the knowledge of which I here speak is not simply matter for the intellect to feed upon. It is revivifying; it is granted in and with new life, one feature of which is that renewing of the mind of which Paul speaks. The source of this new life is that union with Christ of which Paul and Calvin make so much, and which was vigorously pressed in the nineteenth-century by the Mercersburg theologians. Of the believer, J. W. Nevin writes,

> In his regeneration, he is inwardly united to Christ, by the power of the Holy Ghost, and thus brought within the sphere of that 'law of the spirit of life', by which in the end the 'law of sin and death' is overpowered and destroyed in all them that believe. A divine seed is implanted in him, the germ of a new existence, which is destined gradually to grow and gather strength, till the whole man shall be at last fully transformed into its image. The new nature thus introduced is the nature of Christ...[20]

In commenting on these words Glenn Hewitt has said that 'Nevin rejected the idea that Christ simply subsumes the human personality. The believer continues to have a separate existence, but this existence is

---

[19] Thomas Goodwin, *The Works of Thomas Goodwin*, Edinburgh: James Nicol, 1861–66, IV, p. 297.

[20] J. W. Nevin, 'Catholic unity', in Philip Schaff, ed., *The Principle of Protestantism as Related to the Present State of the Church*, Chambersburg, PA: German Reformed Church, 1845, p. 195.

grounded in the life of Christ.'[21] That not everyone in Nevin's day thought that he had drawn the distinction clearly enough is evident from the writings of Nevin's opponent within the German Reformed Church, J. H. A. Bomberger. He detected pantheizing tendencies in the Romantic-organic-immanentist language of Mercersburg, and in an address to the World Presbyterian Alliance, he deemed it appropriate to point out that

> Christ is *not* our life in any pantheistic sense. Nay, the mystical union established between the regenerated soul and him is not even a hypostatical union of their two natures. Man is not deified by regeneration. In it men become Christians, but are not made Christs.[22]

A judicious referee would probably incline to the view that if the strongly Johannine Nevin, anxious to recover the heritage of catholic truth which he was convinced was obscured by both 'new measures' revivalism and the New England Unitarianism which he abominated (and which he unfortunately branded 'Puritanism'), was tempted to employ language incautiously; the enthusiastically Pauline Bomberger was sometimes too easily able to persuade himself that in Nevin's writings there was no smoke without fire. We seem to be in the realm of 'testing the spirits to see whether they are from God' (1 John 4:1)—a task impossible of achievement by the headless.

Intellectual discrimination is further required when we come to the Spirit's sanctifying work, to which I alluded at the outset. Many changes have been rung on this doctrine through the centuries, some of them mutually contradictory. Thus, at the end of the seventeenth century Jacob Verschoor was found teaching that the elect are guilt-free and that their faults incur no punishment: which undermines the ideas of going on to perfection and blunts the edge of the challenge to fight the good fight of faith.[23] On the other hand, Isaac Watts found it necessary to repudiate and

---

[21] G. Hewitt, 'Regeneration', in Sam Hamstra, Jr., and Arie J. Griffioen, eds, *Reformed Confessionalism in Nineteenth-Century America*, Lanham, MD: Scarecrow Press, 1995, p. 162.

[22] J. H. A. Bomberger, 'Regeneration', *Proceedings of the Second General Council of the World Prebyterian Alliance*, 1880, p. 552. See further, Alan P. F. Sell, *A Reformed, Evangelical, Catholic Theology. The Contribution of the World Alliance of Reformed Churches, 1875–1982*, (1991), Eugene, OR: Wipf and Stock, 1998, pp. 48-49. See further, Alan P. F. Sell, *Aspects of Christian* Integrity, (1990), Eugene, OR: Wipf and Stock, 1998, ch. 2, and *Commemorations. Studies in Christian Thought and History*, (1993), Eugene, OR: Wipf and Stock, 1998, ch. 10. For the underlying philosophical considerations see Alan P. F. Sell, *Philosophical Idealism and Christian Belief*, Cardiff: University of Wales Press and New York: St. Martin's Press, 1995. For further reflections on pantheism see ch. 7 above.

[23] I have no qualms about using biblical language from which more squeamish hymnal editors flinch because they tremble before pacifists of the more pugilistic sort.

encourage those whose position was tantamout to a denial of the Spirit's sanctifying grace:

> Suppose a *Christian* has most powerful Impressions made on the *Passion* of *Fear* by the tremendous Ideas of God's Majesty and his punishing Justice, and thence he concludes that the great God will pardon no wilful Sins, that he will forgive no repeated Iniquities, no Sins after Baptism and the Lord's Supper, or after Vows or solemn Ingagements, that he will have no Mercy upon Apostates, even tho' they turn to him by Repentance; this is yielding up Truth to the *Passion* of *Fear*, and an abuse of our religious Dread of the Majesty of God; for such an Opinion runs counter to the great Design of the Gospel, which assures us that *Christ came to save the chief of Sinners*, to remove the Guilt of wilful and repeated Sins, and to provide Forgiveness for some of the most profligate Rebels, even for all that renounce their Rebellion.[24]

But if some spoke as if sanctification were unnecessary and others implied that it was impossible, yet others seemed to think that it was all too easy, among them Sarah Taylor who, in the mid-eighteenth century 'was the chief instrument of propagating the infatuation of perfection and uninterrupted happiness and lawless liberty and vain conceit' among the Inghamite societies of the North of England.[25]

These historical illustrations lead us to the more general consideration that there is 'head work' to be done when seeking to derive benefit from the heritage of spiritual writing—not least that of judiciously balancing the perfectly proper devotional recourse to tradition against the temptation to mere intellectualist antiquarianism. An Anglican writer rightly warned that 'mere knowledge of spiritual states' can run 'far ahead of our own spiritual accomplishment, so that the soul honours God with correct spiritual patter while the heart strays far from him in a morass of unholy introspection or censoriousness'.[26] Thus cautioned, there is no reason not to explore the heritage of Christian spirituality in a thoughtful and disciplined way. Many have devoted much time to this, utilizing all possible occasions. Of the Puritan John Preston (1587–1628) it was said

---

The adjective 'good' sufficiently qualifies the noun 'fight'; and I am persuaded that we do well to retain the language and show the 'world' that it has not understood it yet. If we surrender the language we lose our opportunity of showing how Christianity turns values upside-down. And there *is* a war on against the 'principalities and powers'. The blessing of battleships is something else...

24 I. Watts, *Discourses of the Love of God and the Use and Abuse of the Passions in Religion*, (1729), reprinted Bristol: Thoemmes Press, 1999, pp. 217-18.

25 So William Batty, *Church History, Collected from the Memoirs and Journals of Mr. Ingham and the Labourers in Connection with Him*, John Rylands University Library of Manchester, MS MAM P11B, p. 90.

26 J. K. Byrom, 'Classics of mystical and ascetical theology', *Theology*, LXIII, February 1960, pp. 53-54.

that he used to read Aquinas at the barber's—one way of forestalling kindly enquiries about the state of his begonias, no doubt. But the context of the writings must ever be kept in view if our own spiritual experience is to have integrity. Precisely because of the way in which head and heart work together, we cannot simply take over everything we read and make it our own. The spirituality of Denys the Pseudo-Areopagite cannot easily be abstracted from his philosophical presuppositions and his angelology, both of which would cause most Reformed Christians a certain anxiety. Similarly with Marian devotions in the Roman Catholic Church: we do not share the undergirding theology. Moreover, the best spirituality is rooted in the living context, and in social terms our situation is far removed from that of some of our forebears. Thus we could not simply annexe the prayers which the eighteenth-century Presbyterian divine Samuel Bourn (1689–1754) of Coseley and Birmingham prepared for his young people, because they presuppose a strong belief in the orders of society and in the obligation of every person to remain within his or her station.[27] In all such cases, if rejection is not indicated, a work of translation—even of anabaptism—will be necessary; and this in order that our own spiritual growth will proceed with integrity.

But, to return more directly to doctrine: if we cannot always pray the prayers, or sing the hymns, of our forebears for the kinds of reasons described, we cannot build Christian experience on doctrines to which we cannot honestly assent. On this issue, and in face of a horde of theologians who at the present time seem to take every opportunity of indulging in anti-Enlightenment hysterics (whilst seeming in many cases to neglect both the careful reading of Enlightenment texts and the need to differentiate the several Enlightenments[28]), we may record the stand for intellectual integrity which many eighteenth-century divines took. Thus, against 'Popish' authoritarianisms, whether Roman or Reformed, the Presbyterian divine John Taylor of Norwich (1694–1761) entered his conscientious protest.[29] Again, in the course of his ordination charge to Job Orton at Shrewsbury on 18 September 1745, Samuel Bourn reminded Orton that

---

27 For this most entertaining divine and some of his contemporaries see Alan P. F. Sell, *Dissenting Thought and the Life of the Churches. Studies in an English Tradition*, Lewiston, NY: Edwin Mellen Press, 1990, ch. 7.

28 Lest this appear too cryptic: I have in mind that the English and Scottish Enlightenments were interestingly different at certain points, and neither was as anti-clerical as the French. See further, Alan P. F. Sell, *John Locke and the Eighteenth-Century Divines*, Cardiff: University of Wales Press, 1997, and ch. 3 above.

29 For Taylor see the chapter at n. 26 above; Alan P. F. Sell, *Dictionary of Eighteenth-Century British Philosophers*, Bristol: Thoemmes Press, 1999.

> Sincerity in searching after, and in professing religious Truth, or christian Honesty is, as to God, the only acceptable *Orthodoxy*; in any other Sense it is either precarious or impossible. In any other Sense, it signifies our Agreement to *Human Schemes*; which is only a topical and chronical Character, suited only to certain Places and Times; so that what is orthodox in one Church, or in one Age, is not so in another. But an upright Mind, a pure Conscience, a good and honest heart is the same in all Ages in all Places, in both Worlds.[30]

For his part, the Presbyterian divine Henry Grove (1684–1738) of the Taunton Dissenting Academy articulated the plea for Christian integrity with specific reference to the minister's calling as preacher of the Gospel in relation to the intellectual climate of the times:

> Ought not some consideration to be had of the prevailing genius and taste of the *Age* for rational knowledge, and freer enquiries? So that, allowing there have been times when a dogmatical way of asserting things without proving them, and raising the passions of people in a *mechanical*, rather than a *rational* way, answered the great ends of preaching better than any other method would have done (which I am far from believing) yet now that the state of things is very much altered, and great numbers are no longer to be treated as *children*, nor will be contented to have their understandings *amazed* and *dazzled*, instead of being *enlightened*, Ministers ought in *prudence* to change their way, as far as they can do it with a *good conscience*.[31]

Perhaps today more than ever we need integrity in matters spiritual and devotional. In this realm intellectual judgments are inevitable—or are we to be content with those who bundle Christian, Eastern and pagan insights together in syncretistic fashion? We by no means have to deny that the Spirit blows where he will; we may not seek to imprison him within the Church. But neither should we overlook the logical howlers we commit if we neglect the very different world views within which sometimes identical forms of words function,[32] or risk the reproach of those who find well-meaning attempts to annexe them in the name of a genial and general religiosity patronizing in the extreme.

---

30 S. Bourn, *A Charge delivered at the Ordination of the Reverend Mr. Job Orton; at Shrewsbury, September 18. 1745*, Birmingham: T. Warren, 1745, p. 41.

31 H. Grove, *Queries Proposed to the Consideration of all such as think it an Injury to Religion to shew the Reasonableness of it*, 1732, in *Henry Grove: Ethical and Theological Writings*, Bristol: Thoemmes Press, 2000, IV, p. 247. For Grove see my *Testimony and Tradition*, Aldershot: Ashgate, 2005, ch. 5; *Dissenting Thought*, ch. 6; *Dictionary of Eighteenth-Century British Philosophers*.

32 No doubt all of the characters in the parable of the Good Samaritan would have agreed that we must love our neighbour, but they differed significantly as to the definition of 'neighbour'.

II

While intellectual considerations cannot be excluded from spirituality, the Independent minister and hymn writer, Joseph Hart (1712–68) quite rightly declared that

> True religion's more than notion;
> Something must be known and felt.[33]

Undoubtedly, it is impossible believe the Gospel without feeling something: to respond lovingly to God's grace is something which engages the emotions. But the root of the experience is not in the human heart, but in the grace of God. As P. T. Forsyth said, 'Experience is the fruit of faith, or its medium, more than its ground.'[34] This is because 'The seat of revelation is in the cross, and not in the heart. The precious thing is something given, and not evolved.'[35] This idea may be applied in a number of directions, but let us focus upon assurance.

If a hymn like 'Blessed assurance, Jesus is mine' prompts us to fasten introspectively upon the possessive pronoun rather than upon the objective grace of God in the Gospel, we may find that when our feelings ebb, our *sense* of assurance ebbs too. Then, if we were to rely upon the strength of our feelings as the test of our faith, we should become needlessly alarmed, in the worst cases, neurotic. Against this peril Thomas Brooks (1608–80) wisely cautioned:

> To make sense and feeling the judges of our spiritual conditions, what is it but to make ourselves unhappy and miserable, righteous and unrighteous, saved and damned in one day, ay, in one hour, when sense and reason sit as judges upon the bench? Hath God made sense and feeling the judges of your condition? No. Why, then, will you?[36]

As Forsyth insisted, 'The real ground of our certitude...is the nature of the thing of which we are sure, rather than the nature of the experience in which we are sure.'[37]

---

[33] The first line of this hymn of 1759 is the not very elegant, 'Let us ask th'important question...' See David Denham's collection of hymns, *The Saint's Melody*, 1837, no. 502.

[34] P. T. Forsyth, *The Principle of Authority*, (1913), London: Independent Press, 1952, p. 331.

[35] P. T. Forsyth, *The Person and Place of Jesus Christ*, (1909), London: Independent Press, 1961, p. 193.

[36] T. Brooks, *Heaven on Earth. A Treatise on Christian Assurance*, (1654), London: Banner of Truth Trust, 1961, p. 109.

[37] Forsyth, *The Principle of Authority*, 52. See further, Sell, *The Spirit Our Life*, ch. 4, and *Confessing and Commending the Faith. Historic Witness and Apologetic Method*, Cardiff: University of Wales Press, 2002, pp. 47-350.

None of this is to deny that when William Cowper bids us sing, 'Oh! For a closer walk with God',[38] he expresses a perfectly legitimate Christian aspiration. In the same hymn he describes a common Christian experience which in no way implies the inadequacy of the One of whom we are assured:

Where is the blessedness I knew
 When first I saw the Lord?
Where is the soul-refreshing view
 Of Jesus, and his word?

The sense of bereftness is genuine, but it becomes the prompter of a quest, not a ground for denying God's availability and grace. Still less does it warrant the 'Stillness Doctrine' which the Moravian Philip Henry Molther propagated in the Fetter Lane Society in 1739. According to this, those who felt that they lacked assurance of salvation were to do nothing— no prayer, no Bible reading, no attendance at the means of grace—but simply to wait in quietness until they experienced full assurance.

The problem arises, and it is by no means unknown in Reformed circles, when introspection, the constant taking of one's spiritual temperature, becomes morbid, and when particular varieties of experience are sought as supposed guarantees of one's salvation. It is a further, sectarian, step to deny that those who do not manifest one's favoured experiential criteria are genuine Christians. We thus find numerous hymns which dwell upon our stuck-fastness in 'miry clay', and, with grave disrespect to a most useful member of the created order, our likeness to worms. Nor were some slow to see the pedagogical value of worms. Consider the following opening verse of hymn 313 in William Wileman's *Hymns for the Sunday School*, London: W. Wileman, 11th edn. (fifty-fifth thousand), 1900:

Death, in a thousand dreadful forms,
 Sweeps down our mortal, sinful race;
The grave, corruption, earth, and worms
 Shortly must be our dwelling-place.

Admittedly, the hymn goes on to admit the possibility that grace may intervene, but even so it is strong meat for little ones.[39]

---

38 *Olney Hymns*, London: W. Oliver, 1779, no. 3.

39 Cf. also some of the early Congregational church covenants. That of Cockermouth (1651), for example, begins, 'We poor worms, lost in Adam...do agree together to walk as a people whom the Lord hath chosen...' See Sell, *Dissenting Thought*, 6, and ch. 5 above.

Few have gone so far in this direction as those Strict and Particular Baptists (to which tradition Wileman belonged) who followed the teaching of the independent preacher, William Huntington, and whose magazine, *The Gospel Standard* (1835 onwards) also gave them their specific denominational name, the Gospel Standard Strict and Particular Baptists.[40] They looked for the evidence of 'spiritual exercises', they paid great attention to the interpretation of dreams, they assiduously recorded death-bed utterances (often at considerable length), and they loved sermons which took their allegorical flight from the Song of Songs.[41] Their tendency (in some cases more than a tendency) to make specific experiences normative for salvation is reminiscent of the position of that of Fridrich Adolph Lampe in eighteenth-century Holland.

As with assurance, so more generally: what rescues the Christian from undue introspection is a firm grasp of the objectivity of grace. This comes out, for example in one of Kierkegaard's prayers. He does not call himself a worm, but he knows the sinner's need of mercy and forgiveness. But the focus upon what God has first done at the Cross recontextualizes his feeling of worthlessness and gives him hope:

> Father in heaven! Hold not our sins up against us but hold us up against our sins, so that the thought of thee when it wakens in our soul, and each time it wakens, should not remind us of what we have committed but of what Thou didst forgive, not of how we went astray but of how Thou didst save us![42]

Or, as Forsyth memorably and crisply put it, 'Look to the Gospel and it will see to the experiences.'[43]

In all of this we are at a considerable remove—indeed, at the opposite pole—from that type of catholic spirituality which regards ecstatic union with God entailing personal extincton as the goal of the spiritual life, a condition to be achieved by mastery of techniques of devotion. But lest

---

[40] Their leaders were William Gadsby (1773–1844) and the erstwhile Anglican clergyman, J. C. Philpot (1802–69). Their opponents took their names from their journals: *The Earthen Vessel* (1845) and *The Christian's Pathway* (1896) (by their magazines ye shall know them). See further, Kenneth Dix, *Strict and Particular. English Strict and Particular Baptists in the Nineteenth-Century*, Didcot: Baptist Historical Society, 2001; Alan P. F. Sell, *The Great Debate. Calvinism, Arminianism and Salvation*, (1982), Eugene, OR: Wipf and Stock, 1998; Ian M. Randall, '"The tried people of God": Strict Baptist spirituality in inter-war England', *The Strict Baptist Historical Society Bulletin*, no. 24, 1997, pp. 16-33.

[41] For an attempt to get under the skin of a pastor of this type see Alan P. F. Sell, *Alfred Dye, Minister of the Gospel*, London: Fauconberg Press, 1974.

[42] Quoted in Anne Fremantle, *The Protestant Mystics*, New York: Mentor Books, 1964, p. 194.

[43] P. T. Forsyth, *Revelation Old and New*, London: Independent Press, 1962, p. 71.

we are tempted to thank God that we are not like others, we should do well to remember that Protestants too have had their ways of giving a 'worksy' flavour to their spiritual life, notwithstanding Luther's discovery that going through the disciplinary processes did not suffice. Consider William Batty's account of the Holy Club:

> Mr. Charles Wesley and Mr. Morgan began to meet together in Christ Church College in 1729; soon, Mr. John Wesley joined them. These were the first beginnings of the Methodists. Mr. Ingham became acquainted with the Messrs. Wesley in 1733. Their principles were to be good and do good; they fasted twice a week, prayed and examined themselves every hour, received the Sacrament every Sunday, visited the sick and prisoners, taught poor children to read and write, gave alms, and frequently met together to read the Scriptures, and to pray and exhort one another. They were then really concerned for their salvation, but being ignorant of God's righteousness they were going about to establish their own.[44]

Time and again those in the Puritan and Reformed traditions have been tempted to revert to a new legalism—for all that they have proclaimed about free grace—and they have sometimes done this even when considering the development of the spiritual life: 'It is a sin not to keep a diary of God's providences'; 'Unless you can give the time and place of your conversion you are not a born again believer'; and even, 'Unless you shun specific sins (*tacit*: which I myself abominate but am not particularly inclined to commit) you will come to a sticky end (or rather, a very hot one).' In face of such distortions which have been perpetrated in Protestant devotional literature down the years, we may feel inclined to adopt the attitude of Edmund Hoskyns who, for all his admirable Anglo-Catholic connections, nevertheless declared that he would glady exchange manuals of devotion for *The Farmer and Stockbreeder*.

Nothing more effectively counters individualism in spiritual matters than the realization that Christian life is life in community; that Christians are saints by calling; that to be engrafted by grace into the Vine, is necessarily to be related to all the branches. The church is called to be a nursery where saints are nurtured. Lest these sentiments seem commonplace to us, let us reflect that it was not ever thus. The Reformation did not only return the Bible to the people of God; it restored spirituality to them, in the sense that no longer was the active–contemplative distinction, hardened in the wake of Gregory the Great's position, maintained, with the monks having a head start as regards the latter.[45] Similarly, when in chapter 72 of his Rule Benedict

---

44 Batty, *Church History*, p. 1.

45 For Gregory's position see Leclerq, Vandenbroucke and Bouyer, eds., *A History of Christian Spirituality*, II, p. 10. Gregory regarded the contemplative life as open to all, not to monks only, albeit few of the laity attained to it. See p. 11 (cf. Gregory, *Mor.* XXXII.4).

emphasizes the fact that the context of sanctified living is the community, it is the monastic community that he has in mind. By contrast, Calvin was in no doubt that the sphere of sanctification is the Church.[46]

In keeping with the objective–subjective, head–heart balance with which we are here concerned, we should first remind ourselves that the Church's primary duty is that of the worship of God. As far as the Reformed tradition is concerned it is perhaps necessary to recall that what we are concerned with is the worship of the *Church*, amongst which *laos* the minister is to be found. In our history we have majored upon the prophetic role of the preacher—sometimes to the neglect of the Word enacted in the sacraments; and rarely, as in Mercersburg's attempt to redress the balance, the pendulum has swung in the direction of appearing to minimize the preaching of the Word.[47] I have elsewhere reflected upon worship in general,[48] but here I wish to make three points concerning ministers because they are the spiritual guides of the flock, and then to introduce brief reflections upon church discipline. In both cases I am prompted by the conviction that the spiritual health of churches is adversely affected if we do not take a properly theological view of these matters.

The first point concerning ministers is to do with their training. They need to be formed as well as informed, if they are to fulfil their primary obligation of leading the people of God to the throne of grace.[49] In this the example of their mentors is of the greatest importance. The words of William Jay (1769–1853), who served for sixty-two years at Argyle Congregational Church, Bath, might well be pondered by all charged with the joyful yet solemn duty of educating future ministers. He looked back upon his own training in the small Dissenting seminary which Cornelius Winter (b. 1741) conducted at Marlborough, and wrote,

---

46 See his *Commentaries* on John 13:18; 1 Cor. 12:13.

47 Thus, J. W. Nevin reiterates his passionately-held belief that the believer's union with Christ is a fact 'emphatically concentrated in the mystery of the Lord's Supper'. See his *The Mystical Presence*, Philadelphia, PA: United Church Press, 1956, p. 27. Cf. the remark of Howard Hageman, *Pulpit and Table*, Richmond, VA: John Knox Press, 1962, p. 97: 'Though [the Mercersburg theologians] were battling to restore the Table to a church which had come under the complete dominance of the pulpit, their failure to consider the Word indicates that they were still laboring under the scholastic idea of preaching as Biblical exposition and theological instruction. They had not recovered the Reformation idea of the Word itself mediating the presence of Christ, which was such an important element of early Reformed liturgics.' It must be confessed that one has on occasion sorely been tempted towards the rueful reflection that much would be gained if sermons today were *at least* biblically rooted and theologically informative.

48 See Alan P. F. Sell, *Testimony and Tradition: Studies in Reformed and Dissenting Thought*, Aldershot: Ashgate, 2005, ch. 13.

49 See further, ibid., ch. 1.

> [T]he preservation of spirituality is of great importance where the office is sacred: of this Mr. Winter never lost sight. He was always feeding and cherishing the piety, as well as promoting the literary improvement of those who were under his care. He constantly reminded them of the absolute necessity of personal religion; and endeavoured to keep alive a sense of their dependence on God, for the preservation and increase of their powers, and the success of their applications and exertions...it was impossible not to feel devoutly while near him: his presence was the very element of piety.[50]

What Jay calls 'the preservation of spirituality' is nowhere more important than in connection with the minister's pulpit proclamation. As Samuel Bourn cautioned Job Orton:

> [M]ake it appear to all Men, especially to *Believers*, who can see farther, and judge better than other Men, that the Gospel you preach to Others has rectified your own heart, and mended your own Life: This will convince them that *you* believe the Things which you seem so earnestly to recommend to *them*.[51]

Secondly, we may hope that ministers themselves are cognisant of their high vocation, their liturgical duties and their obligation to nurture the flock (though, unless my ears have deceived me, I have heard some of them refer to the ministry as a 'job'; I have heard talk of 'ministerial career patterns', and the like); but, especially perhaps in the West, it is well that church members themselves understand the minister's function. It would be a great point gained, for example—and it would probably obviate some cases of ministerial burnout—if churches remembered that the minister is not a master of ceremonies, a managing director (a pitfall into which they may be tempted to fall if some persist in describing themselves by the theological and verbal abomination, 'Senior Executive Pastor'), or one required to succumb to temptations analogous to those which Christ resisted, in order to fill up the empty pews. They, and the ministers themselves, should understand with Thomas Watson that 'The ministers of God are only the pipes and organs; it is the Spirit blowing in them, that effectually changes the heart.'[52] Perhaps an atrocity story which floats down the years from A. J. Grieve will suffice to make my point. He received a letter from the secretary of a vacant pastorate inviting him to send the names of three students who might be interested in the position. The secretary explained that he was also writing to three other college principals, and that when the church had heard all twelve candidates, a selection would be made. Grieve replied on a postcard, 'The

---

50 W. Jay, *Memoirs of the Life and Character of the late Rev. Cornelius Winter*, London: Williams and Smith, 1809, p. 256. For Jay see his *Autobiography*, eds. George Redford and John Angell James, (1854), London: Banner of Truth Trust, 1974.

51 Bourn, *A Charge*, p. 39.

52 Watson, *A Divine Cordial*, p. 78.

ministry is a calling not a horse race. No students will be coming from this college.'[53] An encouragement, surely, to all who are tempted to succumb uncritically to 'the corporate model'.

Thirdly, ministers need to be alive to the fact that it is not only that the spirituality of the past, being contextual, will sometimes chafe us like an ill-fitting shoe; it is also that what one might call monochrome present-day spirituality can have undesirable results. What I have in mind is the need for ministers to ensure that, having regard to their context, the church receives a balanced diet. I do not deny that there is a place for comforting the saints, and it may be that such a hymn as, 'Safe in the arms of Jesus', will serve this purpose well. But would it not verge upon the obscene if an affluent church were to be fed on an almost exclusive diet of such hymns? Ought not such a church to be stimulated to serve God in unstinting generosity to the needy? Is there not a difference between comforting and coddling the saints?[54] Do the affluent not insult the genuinely oppressed if we think that we are oppressed when our golf club subscription is increased?

All of which leads us to church discipline. This, though frequently misunderstood, properly concerns the Church as the sphere of corporate sanctification, of that growth of the saints to the end that they are equipped for mission. Traditionally the Reformed have not flinched from the realization that from time to time this may entail what one might call 'the policing of the saints'—and, no doubt, on occasion this was a sport too greatly enjoyed by the pious. But at their best they knew that it mattered whether the members were leading a godly walk; that Christ must not be dishonoured; that the wayward must be admonished and, as a last resort, suspended—though always with the hope that they might repent and be restored.[55] The end of church discipline, declared John Owen, is, 'with respect to the *church*, its purging and vindication—with respect the person *excommunicated*, his repentance, reformation and salvation…'.[56]

---

53 Grieve was famous for his postcards. When Sir John Stopford, FRS, was appointed Vice-Chancellor of the University of Manchester in 1934, he received a postcard inscribed thus: 'You'll do. A.J.G.'

54 The thought occurs that such a church ought not to feel comfortable singing 'Hear the pennies dropping' during the offertory, because it ought to be impossible to *hear* their offertory! They should be giving what the television wide boy, Arthur Daley, called 'folding money'.

55 See, for example, Calvin, *Institutes*, IV.xii.5.

56 J. Owen, *The True Nature of a Gospel Church*, in *The Works of John Owen*, ed. W. H. Goold (1850–53), London: Banner of Truth Trust, 1968, XVI, 171. See further, Alan P. F. Sell, *Church Discipline*, London: United Reformed Church, 1983. This pamphlet was published just before I left England for Geneva. Having written on this thorny subject, probably the only thing left to do was to leave the country.

Not the least important aspect of church discipline in those traditions whose ecclesiology turns upon the conviction that the Church comprises saints or, to use that sadly hi-jacked term, 'born again believers', is the discipline surrounding the reception of members. In the Reformed tradition children of the covenant are nurtured in the hope that they will one day make their profession of faith, and those who have not been baptized as infants are baptized on profession of faith, as in the baptist traditions. The question is, On what terms are they received? It is of great importance that they are adequately prepared for this step; that their grasp of God's grace in Christ is sincere (which is not the same as saying that they shall be competent to expound the full rage of Christian doctrine: babes in Christ must not be made to choke on systems—even five-point ones); and that, to use the old language, their lives 'adorn the Gospel'. As long ago as 1821 a Congregationalist ruefully wrote,

> No person used to be admitted into the church without being examined as to knowledge and experience publicly, before a considerable congregation; and, yet, it was scarcely ever known, that any person was deterred from offering himself for communion, on account of the strict mode of admission.[57]

By the time those words were written it had become commonplace for intending members simply to write (or to have a letter written for them) asking that their candidature be brought before the church. Down to our own time the nomination of the minister and the deacons or elders has sufficed in many places.[58]

That discipline in relation to the reception of church members has not been of concern in England alone is clear from the case of Isaac Chipman. He was a professor at what we now know as Acadia University—Baptist in origin. Following a meeting on 3 December 1836 he wrote in his diary:

> I was unavoidably impressed with the belief that we as a Church are not sufficiently cautious in receiving persons to our communion. What was said at the meeting seemed to imply that a *willingness to profess religion* was sufficient evidence of a change of heart. Day of calamity to the church of God, when anything is substituted for real, vital godliness! May the members of this Church have the word of Christ dwell in them richly, in all wisdom, and may they never lose sight of the absolute necessity of the Spirit's influence!'[59]

---

[57] *The London Christian Instructor, or Congregational Magazine*, IV, 1821, pp. 338-39.

[58] See further, Sell, *Commemorations*, ch. 14.

[59] J. M. Cramp, *Sketches of the History of Acadia College and Horton Collegiate Academy*, in *Memorials of Acadia College and Horton Academy for the Half-Century 1828–1878*, Montreal: Dawson, 1881, p. 46.

At a time of declining church rolls in the Western mainline churches it may sound like heresy even to pose the question, Have we made entry to the full privileges and responsibilities of the Church too easy? But given the way in which so many Western Christians are so thoroughly immersed in the culture around them, it is worth enquiring whether we sufficiently challenge those in our care and enquirers from without. To observers, do we seem more like passengers on a holiday cruise than pilgrims on the way of the Cross?

Quite apart from specific cases and occasions of church discipline, however, I wish to suggest that ministers and churches as wholes stand under the discipline of the Word and of the fellowship. With regard to the Word, nowhere are the relevant points more concisely yet comprehensively made than in the *Westminster Larger Catechism* of 1648. As to the ministers:

> They that are called to labour in the ministry of the word, are to preach sound doctrine, diligently, in season and out of season; plainly, not in the enticing words of man's wisdom, but in demonstration of the Spirit, and of power; faithfully, making known the whole counsel of God; wisely, applying themselves to the necessities and capacities of the hearers; zealously, with fervent love to God and the souls of the people; sincerely, aiming at his glory, and their conversion, edification, and salvation.

As to the hearers:

> It is required of those that hear the word preached, that they attend upon it with diligence, preparation, and prayer; examine what they hear by the scriptures; receive the truth with faith, love, meekness, and readiness of mind, as the word of God; meditate, and confer of it, and bring forth the fruit of it in their lives.[60]

The discipline of fellowship arises largely from the fact that the church, God's calling, is unlike no other organization. It is not based upon mutual interests of the ordinary sort (mercifully, we do not all have to like bee-keeping). Indeed, there are within the church people who have very little in common except that they have been called by grace. There are old and young, sick and well, clever and not so clever, rich and poor, pleasant and downright cussed. Yet all are to be loved (even if they cannot all easily be liked) for the Lord's sake. As Bernard Lord Manning told some Cambridge students:

> You say you love Christ's Church. Well, here it is: Tom, Dick, Harry, and the rest; a funny lot of lame ducks... They are not very good. But they have, in their own odd ways, heard Christ's call. They have trusted in Christ on His Cross. They have made a covenant with God, and so joined themselves in the saved society with Him. It is

[60] *Westminster Larger Catechism*, answers to Qs. 159, 160.

> little use your feeling mystical sympathy with St. Francis who is dead, with St. Somebody Else who never existed, with men of good will all over the world whom you are quite safe from meeting. If you do not love your brothers whom you have seen—Tom, Dick, Harry—you cannot, in fact, love those brothers (whom you call the Church) whom you have not seen.[61]

None knew better than that professional historian that he was there updating John Owen. Indeed, he proceeds immediately to quote his forebear in the faith: 'Let none, then, pretend that they love the brethren in general, and love the people of God, and love the saints, while their love is not fervently exercised towards those who are in the same church society with them.'[62]

As the saints together walk the road of sanctification and embark upon their mission they will from time to time be disciplined by circumstances. The writer to the Hebrews spelled out the nature of the Lord's loving discipline in the context of possible persecution (Hebrews 12:1-13). He goes so far as to say that those who are not under the Father's discipline are bastards. On such occasions the church recalls that God's pilgrim people are led through the valley of the shadow of death, not around it. And, by grace, their confidence is that

> By Thine unerring Spirit led,
> We shall not in the desert stray;
> We shall not full direction need,
> Nor miss our providential way;
> As far from danger as from fear,
> While love, almighty love, is near.[63]

But there is one thing more: the discipline of success. A 'successful' ministry can be dangerous (consider the book-keeping kind of evangelical preacher: 'I [*sic*] saved six more souls this week than during the corresponding week last year'); a 'successful' church can be at risk. The lukewarm church at Laodicea (Revelation 3:14-18) thought they had it made. They were rich; they had everything they needed (sizeable endowments; a minister for every conceivable sphere of work—and every one a DMin; three robed choirs; half a dozen handbell groups; their own page on the internet...?). To the risen Christ they were 'poor, blind and naked'.

---

[61] B. L. Manning, *Why Not Abandon the Church?* (1939), London: Independent Press, 1958, pp. 37-38.

[62] Ibid., pp. 38-39. Manning quotes from the sermon 'Gospel charity' in Owen's *Works*, IX, p. 262.

[63] From Charles Wesley's hymn, 'Captain of Israel's host...'

Those who have by grace given their hearts to the Lord; those who praise him in the sanctuary, who delight in the Word proclaimed and sacramentally enacted, and whose faith is nurtured in the fellowship of saints, they are a people equipped to serve. In Thomas Watson's pungent phrase, 'Grace, while it cures the heart, does not make the hand lame.'[64] So, thirdly and briefly, to 'hands'.

III

The spheres of Christian service, which begin in the household of faith, are as extensive as the world itself. It would be as impossible as it is unnecessary to exemplify them all, though prominent among them at the present time are crusades for justice, peace, and the right use of the earth's precious resources. Christians whose minds are being renewed are, it may be hoped, prominent in such movements, and characterized by gracious yet unwavering integrity where commercial, political or legal 'principalities and powers' need to be called to account.[65] But in every sphere Christians are called to walk the path of sanctification which, since the enabling grace we receive is *holy* love, is inseparable from righteousness. In all of this service, as Richard Baxter, the seventeenth century's Reformed pastor *par excellence* saw, the pre-eminent motive is gratitude for God's free and sovereign grace: 'Let Thankfulness to God

---

64 Watson, *A Divine Cordial*, p. 87.

65 To discuss the question how far local churches, or whole denominations, or entire Christian world communions, should seek a common mind on particular socio-political and economic issues, would take us too far afield. On the one hand, such affirmations may have a beneficial impact—as many would say that the 1982 'Resolution on racism and South Africa' of the World Alliance of Reformed Churches did. On the other hand, when highly politicized pressure groups within the Church press specific causes there is always the danger that an appropriately packed assembly may determine 'the common mind of the Church' which, in the aftermath of the vote, turns out on closer inspection to be repudiated by a large number—even a majority—of members in the total constituency. Again, attempts to preserve the Church's purity over against the allegedly godless world around by prohibiting formal churchly association with good causes may conduce to world-denying pietism. On this last point, see further James Henley Thornwell's statement, 'New York City Temperance Society Organized on Christian Principles', in *The Collected Writings of James Henley Thornwell*, ed. John B. Adger, Richmond, VA: Presbyterian Committee of Publication, 1871, vol. 4. Among the underlying questions are, Do specific denominations need to have a common mind on all issues, and if not on all, then on which ones? How far ought possible ecclesial rupture to be risked in seeking such a mind? By what criteria may it be determined that certain issues, for example, pacifism *versus* non-pacifism, need not be, and should not be, church dividing? See more generally, Sell, *Aspects of Christian Integrity*, pp. 68-71, and *A Reformed, Evangelical, Catholic Theology*, pp. 233-35.

thy Creator, Redeemer and Regenerator, be the very temperament of thy soul, and faithfully expressed by thy tongue and life.'[66]

It cannot be denied that from time to time, not least in Reformed circles, unbalanced Christian living has resulted from the ambiguity of 'world'. In one sense of the term, Christians are not to be conformed to the 'world'. This is when 'world' signifies apartness from, and hostility to, God. Thus Calvin exhorts us to 'separate ourselves from idolaters, and keep ourselves pure and uncontaminated from all the pollution which corrupts and vitiate the holy service of God'.[67] But in another sense of the term we are to go into all the 'world' (now construed geographically) with the Gospel. The ideas coalesce when we are exhorted to be in the world, but not of it; we are a colony, an outpost, of heaven: our true citizenship is there, but we are here *pro tem*. The opposite pitfalls clearly are that Christians will either withdraw from the world around into a pietistic, non-missionary huddle;[68] or that they will so identify with the 'world' *qua* culture around them, and become so consumed by activism, that their Good News cannot be heard even if it is articulated at all. The former type would do well to remember that from the fact that 'to pray is to work' we should not infer that we do not have to do anything in the world; the latter should appreciate how much is being asked of our often genial pagan neighbours if we expect them to guess the connection between what we do and what we believe; they should also consider how vulnerable Christians make themselves if they are too busy to nurture their devotional life. And both should understand that good works are not the means to the sanctified life, but the evidence of it.

---

[66] R. Baxter, *A Christian Directory*, 1673, I, iii.

[67] J. Calvin, *Sermons on the Epistle to the Ephesians*, London: Banner of Truth Trust, 1973, p. 577. The question how far support may be derived from Calvin for the view that 'Reformed spirituality has been characterized by its activism, both in family and church-centered religious life and in the world' (Charles Hambrick-Stowe, 'Piety', in Donald K. McKim, ed., *Encyclopedia of the Reformed Faith*, Louisville, KY: Westminster/John Knox, 1992, p. 278) has been queried by Richard C. Gamble, 'Calvin and sixteenth-century spirituality: comparison with the Anabaptists', *Calvin Theological Journal*, XXXI, November 1996, pp. 335-58. However that matter may finally be decided, in Calvin (following Paul) we have one root of the ecclesiology of Separatism and Anabaptism, for which see further ch. 1 above. For the same motive as referred to the monastic community see Peter Damian, *Apologeticum de contemptu saeculi*, ch. 27, Migne, *PL*, 145, 280.

[68] Hence Isaac Watts's prayer: 'Never let my Devotions break in upon any part of other necessary Duties which I owe to God or Man: The great God does not permit Sacrifice to stand in the Room of Works of Mercy, nor will he allow of Robbery for a Burnt-offering. Remember this, O my soul!' See his *Discourses of the Love of God and the Use and Abuse of the Passions in Religion*, (1729), reprinted Bristol: Thoemmes Press, 1999, p. 248.

IV

The degree to which our division of material into 'head, heart and hands' was little more than a methodological ploy will by now be patently obvious. They are inseparable. Few understood this more clearly than the nineteenth-century professor of Hebrew at the Free Church College, Edinburgh, John 'Rabbi' Duncan:

> Some persons preach only doctrine; that makes people all head, which is a monster. Some preach only experience; that makes people all heart, which is a monster too. Others preach only practice; that makes people all hands and feet, which is likewise a monster. But if you preach doctrine and experience and practice, by the blessing of God, you will have head, heart and hands, and feet—a perfect man in Christ Jesus.[69]

Where you have a church fellowship in which such people are growing together, you have a true nursery of saints, a beachhead for mission, and a light to the world around.

Spirituality as here conceived in its individual and corporate dimensions is, as A. J. Grieve might have said, a long way from wanton tree-hugging.

---

[69] William Knight, *Colloquia Peripatetica... Notes of Conversations with the late John Duncan, LL.D.*, Edinburgh: Oliphant, Anderson & Ferrier, 1907, p. 167. Cf. Grove, *Queries*, pp. 240-41.

CHAPTER 9

Reformed Theology in Britain in the Twentieth Century: A Bibliographical Survey

It is first necessary to comment upon the title of this paper. The term 'twentieth-century' will be stretched to include works published before or after that century, provided that the authors concerned published at least one work during it. The term 'Reformed' is used ecclesiastically to cover the writings of scholars who belonged, or belong, to one or other of the fifteen Reformed churches or unions currently to be found in the British Isles, or their predecessor bodies. This means both that some theologians whose position is far from Calvinistic, for example, will be included, and that those Anglican and Baptist authors who do subscribe to some form of Calvinism will not. Again, I shall not refer to those such as John Macquarrie who began Presbyterian and ended Anglican, and D. Martyn Lloyd-Jones the erstwhile Welsh Presbyterian who became something of an independent Calvinist guru, and whose acolytes (and possibly whose sermons) are scattered to the ends of the earth. By the term 'theology' is meant broadly systematic/historical theology with a glance towards philosophical theology, but not pastoral or moral theology—an exclusion necessitated purely by considerations of space. These considerations also dictate that 'a bibliographical survey' is the most that can reasonably be attempted, and even this will not be complete, for published books alone will be referred to, and not the considerable quantity of the century's articles, sermons and hymns. Even where books are in view, detailed discussion of particular authors or works is out of the question, and unless academic authors also contributed more popular works I shall not refer to the latter—under which rubric are excluded the writings of the elegant Nathaniel Micklem, the urbane Daniel T. Jenkins and the graciously pugilistic J. E. Lesslie Newbigin. Yet again, I shall not be able to name all of those, of whom Martin H. Cressey is a conspicuous example, who have trod the self-effacing path of making significant theological contributions to church union negotiations and ecumenical dialogues. Despite all the limitations, this bird's-eye view of a vast terrain may suffice to indicate something of the variety and range of theological work published approximately during the past century by those Britons whose ecclesiastical allegiance was or is to that Christian communion designated 'Reformed'.

It will make for order if we proceed geographically by region and chronologically by denomination and author. Where authors ended in united churches they are classified under those. Obituaries of the deceased scholars may normally be found in the year books of the churches to which they belonged. Dictionary articles have been written on a number of those listed here, and these generally refer to longer biographical and/or autobiographical studies where these exist. Reference works relevant in a number of cases are: *The Dictionary of Historical Theology* (2000); *Dictionary of Nineteenth-Century British Philosophers* (2002); *Dictionary of Scottish Church History and Theology* (1993); *Dictionary of Twentieth-Century British Philosophers* (2005); *The Dictionary of Welsh Biography* (1959); *Encyclopedia of the Reformed Faith* (1992); *The Oxford Dictionary of the Christian Church* (1997); *The Oxford Dictionary of National Biography* (2004); *The Scottish Congregational Ministry 1794–1993* (1993).

Scotland

N.B. Scots whose final position was in England are listed thereunder.

The Church of Scotland

(Constituted as we now know it in 1650; union with the United Free Church, 1929.)

As the twentieth century opened Robert Flint (1838–1910), Professor of Divinity at Edinburgh University, was at the height of his intellectual powers. Said to be the most learned man of his generation in Scotland, he published many sermons and addresses, a study of *Vico* (1882), and a critique of *Socialism* (1894) in which he welcomed the spirit of fraternity but feared the possibilities of revolution; but his major works are his *History of the Philosophy of History* (1893) and his apologetics trilogy: *Theism* (1877), *Anti-Theistic Theories* (1879) and *Agnosticism* (1903).

William Hastie (1842–1903), Professor of Divinity at Glasgow University wrote *The Theology of the Reformed Church in its Fundamental Principles*, which was published posthumously in 1904.

Henry Martyn Beckwith Reid (1856–1927), Hastie's successor in the Glasgow chair, wrote historical and popular works, and in his *Text-book of Dogmatics* (1919) he brought liberal sympathies to bear upon traditional Calvinism, upholding the penal substitutionary theory of the atonement on the one hand, whilst tending towards universalism on the other. The Bible, he held, was inerrant as regards its spiritual truth.

Alexander Martin (1857–1946), Principal of New College, Edinburgh, published his Cunningham Lectures, *The Finality of Jesus for Faith*, in 1933.

William Paterson Paterson (1860–1939), Professor of Systematic Theology at Aberdeen, and then of Divinity at Edinburgh, published an *Outline of the History of Dogmatic Theology* (1916), *The Rule of Faith* (1932), and his Gifford Lectures of 1924, *The Nature of Religion* (1925). Classical in Christology, he rejected penal substitution and was sympathetic to the witness of other faiths. His last book was on *Conversion* (1939).

To George Galloway (1861–1933), Principal and Professor of Divinity at the University of St. Andrews, we owe a number of works, theologically liberal in flavour, in which theological affirmations are discussed in relation to current intellectual trends. These are: *Studies in the Philosophy of Religion* (1904), his oft-reprinted work, *The Philosophy of Religion* (1914), *The Principles of Religious Development* (1909), *Theological Doctrines and Philosophical Thought* (1911), *The Idea of Immortality* (1919), *Religion and Modern Thought* (1922), and *Faith and Reason in Religion* (1927).

David Smith Cairns (1862–1946), raised in the United Presbyterian Church, became Professor of Apologetics and Dogmatics, and later Principal, in the United Free Church College, Aberdeen. A widely-read apologist, he published *Christianity in the Modern World* (1906), *The Reasonableness of the Christian Faith* (1918), *The Faith that Rebels* (1928), in which he argued that the universe is purposive and that it poses no ultimate threat to trustful human faith, and *The Riddle of the World* (1937). His son, David Cairns, compiled and published his father's *A System of Christian Doctrine* (1979).

Daniel Lamont (1869–1950) held the Chair of Apologetics at New College, Edinburgh, proceeding thence to the University Chair of Christian Ethics and Practical Theology. His major work is *Christ and the World of Thought* (1934).

Hugh Ross Mackintosh (1870–1936), Professor of Divinity at New College, Edinburgh, was one of Scotland's most distinguished theologians. He translated Ritschl's *Justification and Reconciliation* with A. B. Macaulay (1900); Loof's *Haeckel's Riddle of the Universe* (1903); and Schleiermacher's *The Christian Faith* with J. S. Stewart (1928). With A. C. Caldecott he published *Selections from the Literature of Theism* (1904), and in *Types of Modern Theology* (1937) he discussed writers from Schleiermacher to the early Barth. His constructive work is found in *Immortality and the Future* (1915), *Studies in Christian Truth* (1916), *The Originality of the Christian Message* (1920), *The Divine Initiative* (1921), *Some Aspects of Christian Belief* (1923), *The Christian Experience of Forgiveness* (1927), *The Christian Apprehension of God* (1929) and, above all, in his most learned work, *The Doctrine of the Person of Jesus Christ* (1912 and much reprinted), in which he espouses a mild kenoticism. He also published three volumes of sermons.

John Baillie (1886–1960), brother of Donald, was Professor of Divinity at Edinburgh University. In his early works, *The Roots of Religion in the Human Soul* (1926) and *The Interpretation of Religion* (1929), a Ritschlian emphasis is detectable, but this fades, partly under the influence of Karl Barth—though Baillie never became a decided Barthian: indeed, he became increasingly ill at ease with Barth's aversion to apologetics. Other works include, *Our Knowledge of God* (1956), *The Idea of Revelation in Recent Thought* (1956), and the Gifford Lectures (undelivered), *The Sense of the Presence of God* (1962), a gracious contribution to encounter theology which found more favour with the faithful than with such uncommitted analytical philosophers as Ronald W. Hepburn (see *Christianity and Paradox*, 1958).

Donald Macpherson Baillie (1887–1954), Professor of Systematic Theology at St. Andrews University, published *Faith in God and its Christian Consummation* (1927), *The Theology of the Sacraments* (1957), and two volumes of sermons. In his major work, *God Was in Christ* (1948), Baillie proposed that the paradox of grace as experienced by believers and epitomized by Paul's 'Not I, but Christ' constituted a fruitful point of departure for the discussion of the humanity and divinity of Christ.

Edgar Primrose Dickie (1897–1991), Professor of Divinity at St. Andrews University, wrote urbanely on *Spirit and Truth* (1935), *Revelation and Response* (1938), *God is Light* (1953), *The Unchanging Gospel* (1960), and *The Father Everlasting* (1964).

David Cairns (1904–92), Professor of Practical Theology at Aberdeen, translated many theological works from German, and published *The Image of God in Man* (1953), *A Gospel without Myth? Bultmann's Challenge to the Preacher* (1960), and *God Up There? A Study in Divine Transcendence* (1967).

Ian Henderson (1910–69) was Professor of Systematic Theology at Glasgow University. His theological works are a critique of Bultmann's thought, *Myth in the New Testament* (1952), and *Power Without Glory* (1967). The latter is, according to taste, either a tongue-in-cheek demonstration of ecumenism as fundamentally a power struggle, or a savage denunciation of all steps towards the manifestation of the Church's given unity.

John Kelman Sutherland Reid (1910–2002), Professor of Systematic Theology at Aberdeen University, translated and edited some works of Calvin, wrote on ecumenical affairs, and published *The Authority of Scripture* (1957), *Our Life in Christ* (1963), and *Christian Apologetics* (1967).

Norman Hamilton Galloway Robinson (1912–78), Professor of Divinity at St. Andrews University, published a series of works on theological ethics: *Faith and Duty* (1950), *The Claim of Morality* (1952),

Christ and Conscience (1956) and *The Groundwork of Christian Ethics* (1971).

Ronald Gregor Smith (1913–68), a professorial colleague of Henderson at Glasgow, was influenced by Hamann, Kierkegaard, Bultmann, Bonhoeffer and others in the direction of a secular theology, biblical in origin, entailing the freedom to live responsibly in God's world. He published *The New Man* (1956), *J. G. Hamann 1730–1788* (1960), *Secular Christianity* (1966), *The Free Man* (1969), and *The Doctrine of God* (1970).

Thomas Forsyth Torrance (b. 1913), brother of James and father of Iain, was Professor of Church History and afterwards of Christian Dogmatics at New College, Edinburgh. He is Scotland's most distinguished theologian of the second half of the twentieth century. He is widely known as a not uncritical follower of Barth, and as one who has devoted much thought to theology as a science analogous to general science in that it concerns a self-disclosing reality. Among his many works are *Theology in Reconstruction* (1965), *Theological Science* (1969), *Reality and Scientific Theology* (1965), *Space, Time and Incarnation* (1969), *God and Rationality* (1971), *Theology in Reconciliation* (1975), *Space, Time and Resurrection* (1976), *Christian Theology and Scientific Culture* (1981), *The Mediation of Christ* (1983), and *Reality and Scientific Culture* (1985). Other works reveal his strong trinitarian and Christological convictions, and these, together with his patristic interests, have equipped him to play a prominent part in Orthodox–Reformed dialogue.

John McIntyre (b. 1916), formerly Professor of Divinity at New College, Edinburgh, has published *On the Love of* God (1962), and a series of methodological reflections: *The Shape of Christology* (1957), *The Shape of Soteriology* (1992) and *The Shape of Pneumatology* (1997), as well as *Faith, Theology and Imagination* (1997).

Allan D. Galloway (b. 1920), formerly Professor of Divinity at Glasgow University, has published *The Cosmic Christ* (1951), *Faith in a Changing Culture* (1966), and a study of *Wolfhart Pannenberg* (1973).

James Bruce Torrance (1923–2003), formerly Professor of Systematic Theology at Aberdeen University, provoked a good deal of discussion following papers he has published on covenant theology. His Didsbury Lectures, *Worship, Community and the Triune God* were published in 1996.

Douglas William David Shaw (b. 1928), formerly Professor of Divinity at St. Andrews University, has published *Who Is God?* (1968) and *The Dissuaders: Three Explanations of Religion* (1968)—a study of Freud, Marx and Durkheim.

George M. Newlands (b. 1941), successor to Galloway at Glasgow, has published ethical studies, as well as *Hilary of Poitiers: A Study in*

Theological Method (1978), *A Theology of the Love of God* (1980), *The Church of God* (1984), *God in Christian Perspective* (1994), and *John and Donald Baillie: Transatlantic Theology* (2002).

Alasdair I. C. Heron (b. 1942), Professor of Christian Dogmatics at Erlangen University, has edited papers on the Trinity and the Westminster Confession, and in his own right has published *A Century of Protestant Theology* (1980), *The Holy Spirit* (1983) and *Table and Tradition* (1983).

Iain R. Torrance (b. 1949), son of Thomas F. Torrance and Professor of Theology at the University of Aberdeen, has written on ethics and worship, and has also published *Christology After Chalcedon: Severus of Antioch and Sergius the Monophysite* (1998).

David Alexander Syme Fergusson (b. 1956), Professor of Divinity at New College, Edinburgh, has published *Bultmann* (1992), *The Cosmos and the Creator* (1998), a pamphlet entitled, *John Macmurray, The Idea of the Personal* (1992), ethical discussions, *The Cosmos and Creation* (1998), and an edited volume on the brothers Baillie, *Christ, Church and Society* (1993).

Alan J. Torrance (b. 1956), son of James B. Torrance and Professor of Systematic Theology in the University of St. Andrews, has edited collections of papers, and has published a book whose theme is adequately indicated by its title: *Persons in Communion: An Essay in Trinitarian Description and Human Participation with Special Reference to Volume One of Karl Barth's Church Dogmatics* (1998).

The Congregational Union of Scotland (1812)

David Russell Scott (1870–1954), Professor of Systematic Theology and Biblical Languages and later Principal of the Theological Hall of Congregational Churches, wrote mainly on Old Testament themes, but also published *Christ, Sin and Redemption* (1926).

The Free Church of Scotland (1843, continuing)

Roderick Alexander Finlayson (1895–1989), Professor of Systematic Theology at the Free Church College, Edinburgh, published *The Cross in the Experience of Our Lord* (1955), *God's Light on Man's Destiny* (n.d.), and *The Story of Theology* (1963).

Wallace Nicholson (1903–84), *A Defence of Evangelical Theology* [1969].

Donald MacLeod (b. 1940), Principal and Professor of Systematic Theology at the Free Church College, Edinburgh, has published *Rome and Canterbury: A View from Geneva* (1989), *The Person of Christ* (1998), and *A Faith to Live By. Studies in Christian Doctrine* (1998).

The Free Presbyterian Church of Scotland (1893)

Donald Beaton (1872–1953), theological tutor of the Free Presbyterian Church, published a number of historical studies as well as *Some Foundation Truths of the Reformed Faith* (1938).

The United Free Church of Scotland (1900)

At various times James Iverach (1839–1922) held all but one of the chairs at the Free/United Free Church College, Aberdeen, as well as the Principalship. He published Bible handbooks, sermons, and a study of *Jonathan Edwards* (1884); but his main contributions were in epistemology, apologetics and the relations between theology and science: *Is God Knowable?* (1884), *The Truth of Christianity* (1896), *The Ethics of Evolution Examined* (1886), *Evolution and Christianity* (1894), *The Philosophy of Mr. Herbert Spencer Examined* (1884), *Descartes, Spinoza and the New Philosophy* (1904), and, most significantly, *Theism in the Light of Present Science and Philosophy* (1900).

James Orr (1844–1913), Professor of Church History at the United Presbyterian Hall, Edinburgh, became, at church union, Professor of Systematic Theology and Apologetics at the United Free Church College in Glasgow. He was an early and significant British critic of Ritschl: *The Ritschlian Theology and the Evangelical Faith* (1897); he (perhaps too schematically) traced *The Progress of Dogma* (1901), and he did not balk at treating such thorny issues as sin and the virgin birth of Christ. A robust supernaturalism characterizes all his writings. His greatest book is his first: *The Christian View of God and the World as Centring in the Incarnation* (1893). The Incarnation implies a high view of humanity, and while Christian truth is self-authenticating, fideism is averted by the strong appeal to truth as rational.

William Macallum Clow (1853–1930), Professor of Practical Training and Christian Ethics at Glasgow United Free Church College, published a number of works of which probably the best known is *The Cross in Christian Experience* (1908).

James Denney (1856–1917) was successively Professor of Systematic Theology, Professor of New Testament Language and Literature, and Principal of the Free Church/United Free Church College in Glasgow. He published biblical commentaries, wrote incisive letters which were subsequently published, and is widely known for his theological works: *Studies in Theology* (1894), *The Death of Christ* (1902), *The Atonement and the Modern Mind* (1903), and *The Christian Doctrine of Reconciliation* (1917). Eschewing speculation (and with it the approach of his teacher, the idealist philosopher, Edward Caird), Denney's work centres in the death and resurrection of Christ.

David William Forrest (1856–1918), Professor of Systematic Theology at Glasgow United Free Church College, published *The Christ of History and of Experience* (1897) and *The Authority of Christ* (1906). He advocated a subtle kenoticism, argued that the incarnation cannot be understood apart from the Cross, and elevated the believer's direct personal relationship with the historical Jesus into a touchstone of sound theology.

William Malcolm MacGregor (1861–1944), Professor of New Testament and then Principal of Glasgow United Free Church College, published works relating to his denomination and on preaching, and his Baird Lecture, *Christian Freedom* (1914).

Ireland

The Presbyterian Church of Ireland (1642)

John Thompson (b. 1922), formerly Professor of Systematic Theology at Union Theological College, Belfast, has written widely on Barth, and published *Christ in Perspective. Christological Perspectives in the Theology of Karl Barth* (1978), and *The Holy Spirit in the Theology of Karl Barth* (1991).

Stephen Nantlais Williams (b. 1952), successor to John Thompson, has published a pamphlet on *Faith and Certainty* (1994), and *Revelation and Reconciliation. A Window on Modernity* (1995).

Wales

N.B. A number of Welsh theologians on the ministerial roll of the Congregational Union/Church of England and Wales, or of the United Reformed Church, are listed under those headings as appropriate.

The Presbyterian Church of Wales

(Roots in the eighteenth century, first General Assembly 1864).

Huw Parri Owen (1926–96), Professor of Christian Doctrine at King's College, London, published the following works: *Revelation and Existence. A Study in the Theology of Rudolf Bultmann* (1957), *The Moral Argument for Christian Theism* (1964), *The Christian Knowledge of God* (1969), *Concepts of Deity* (1971), *W. R. Matthews, Philosopher and Theologian* (1976), and *Christian Theism. A Study in its Basic Principles* (1984).

England

The Congregational Union of England and Wales (1833) and The Congregational Church in England and Wales (1966–72)

David Worthington Simon (1830), successively Principal of Congregational colleges in Birmingham, Edinburgh and Bradford, translated a number of works from German, and published *The Bible an Outgrowth of Theocratic Life* (1886), *Reconciliation by Incarnation: The Reconciliation of God and Man by the Incarnation of the Divine Word* (1898), *The Redemption of Man* (1886, 2nd edn, revised, 1906).

Andrew Martin Fairbairn (1838–1912), Principal of Airedale College, Yorkshire, and then the first Principal of Mansfield College, Oxford, published on historical and philosophical subjects, his main theological works being *The Place of Christ in Modern Theology* (1893) and (its title notwithstanding), *The Philosophy of the Christian Religion* (1902).

James Muscutt Hodgson (1841–1923), Principal of the Edinburgh Congregational Theological Hall, published works with a strong experiential basis: *Philosophy and Faith: A Plea for Agnostic Belief* (1885), *Theologia Pectoris: Outlines of Religious Faith and Doctrine, Founded on Intuition and Experience* (1898), and *Religion—The Quest of the Ideal* (1911).

Peter Taylor Forsyth (1848–1921), Principal of Hackney College, published many books between 1897 and 1918. The title of the first, *The Holy Father and the Living Christ*, suggests that emphasis upon God's nature as gracious *holy* love, supremely *active* at the Cross, which diverted him from his earlier theological liberalism and was to pervade all his writings. These include *Positive Preaching and the Modern Mind* (1907), *The Cruciality of the Cross* (1909), *The Person and Place of Jesus Christ* (1909), *The Work of Christ* (1910), *Faith, Freedom and the Future* (1912), *The Principle of Authority* (1913) and his intensely practical theodicy written in time of war, *The Justification of God* (1916).

Walter Frederick Adeney (1849–1920), Principal of Lancashire Independent College, Manchester, published a substantial study of *The Greek and Eastern Churches* (1908), and was general editor of the celebrated *Century Bible*. He reflected upon the course of recent theology in *A Century's Progress in Religious Life and Thought* (1901)—the progress being deemed to consist in the escape from the artificial trammels of the Calvinist system; and also published *The Christian Conception of God* (1909) and *Faith Today* (1915).

Robert Mackintosh (1858–1933), Professor at Lancashire Independent College, published a number of works of which the most important are *Christ and the Jewish Law* (1886), *Essays Towards a New Theology* (1889), *From Comte to Benjamin Kidd* (1899), *Hegel and Hegelianism* (1903), *Christianity and Sin* (1913), *Albrecht Ritschl and His School* (1915), and *Historic Theories of Atonement* (1920).

Ebenezer Griffith-Jones (1860–1942), Principal of Yorkshire United Independent College, Bradford, published *The Ascent Through Christ* (1899), in which he elevated the principle of development. A quarter of a century later, in the aftermath of war and convinced that older writers had minimized the dire results which could accrue from human agency, he published *Providence—Divine and Human. A Study of the World Order in the Light of Modern Thought* (1925). In the midst of war his word of encouragement to serving personnel was entitled *Faith and Immortality* (1917): we are by nature immortal, and this life is probationary.

Alfred Ernest Garvie (1861–1945), Principal of New College, London, of Hackney and New College, London, and, finally, of the united College, published forty books on a remarkable number of topics at all levels of difficulty. The most significant are the work which made his name, *The Ritschlian Theology* (1899), and his trilogy, *The Christian Doctrine of the Godhead* (1925), *The Christian Ideal for Human Society* (1930), and *The Christian Belief in God* (1933).

William Boothby Selbie (1862–1944), the second Principal (and earlier, in 1886, the first student) of Mansfield College, Oxford, wrote popularly on biblical, historical, theological ethical and psychological topics, contributed a *Life* of Fairbairn (1914), and published a more substantial work, *Schleiermacher: A Historical and Critical Study* (1913).

Henry William Clark (1869–1949), a scholar-pastor who was bedridden for three years and incapacitated for a further six following a railway accident at the beginning of his ministry, published *The Philosophy of Christian Experience* (1906), *The Christian Method of Ethics* (1908), a *History of English Nonconformity from Wyclif to the Close of the Nineteenth Century* (1911, 1913), and *Liberal Orthodoxy* (1914). In *The Cross and the Eternal Order* (1941), he argued that the atonement sets humanity right with God, and sets God right with God.

Thomas Rees (1869–1926), Principal of Bala-Bangor Independent College, published *The Holy Spirit in Thought and Experience* (1915).

Robert Sleightholme Franks (1872–1964), Principal of Western College, Bristol, published some biblical studies, but made his name with his *History of the Doctrine of the Work of Christ* (1918). In his constructive work, the groundwork of which is seen in *The Metaphysical Justification of Religion* (1929), he set out from religious experience metaphysically justified. In his Dale Lectures on *The Atonement* (1933) he adopted an Abelardian approach to the doctrine, while in *The Doctrine of the Trinity* (1953) he maintained the immanent distinction of the Persons whilst setting his face against the social analogy on the ground that it represents the Godhead 'as though it were a company of human individuals'.

David Miall Edwards (1873–1941), Professor of Christian Doctrine and Philosophy of Religion at the Memorial College, Brecon, published articles and sermons as well as more substantial works in both Welsh and English: *Crefydd a Bywyd* (1915), *Crist a Gwaraeiddiad* (1921), *The Philosophy of Religion* (1924), *Christianity and Philosophy* (1932), and *Crefydd a Diwylliant* (1934).

Thomas Hywel Hughes (1875–1945), Principal and Professor of Systematic Theology at the Scottish Congregational College, published works on psychology, mysticism and pastoral theology, as well as a critical account of *The Atonement: Modern Theories of the Doctrine* (1949).

Cecil John Cadoux (1883–1947), Professor first at Yorkshire United Independent College and then at Mansfield College, was Congregationalism's most incisive and learned liberal evangelical scholar of his day. He wrote on New Testament themes, on church–state relations in the early centuries, on Congregationalism, and on pacifism, and published a massive work entitled, *Catholicism and Christianity. A Vindication of Progressive Protestantism* (1928). His theological stance is epitomized in *The Case for Evangelical Modernism. A Study of the Relation between Christian Faith and Traditional Theology*, (1938), and *The Message about the Cross* (1924).

Sydney Cave (1883–1953), Principal of New College, London, and student of Forsyth, published books in the fields of comparative religion, ethics and biblical studies, but emerged as a doctrinal critic and historian in *The Doctrine of the Person of Christ* (1925), *The Doctrine of the Work of Christ* (1937) and *The Christian Estimate of Man* (1944). His most systematic work is *The Doctrines of the Christian Faith* (1931).

The Presbyterian Church of England (1876)

James Oswald Dykes (1835–1912), Principal and Barbour Professor of Divinity in the Presbyterian Church of England Theological College, published a number of works, of which the most substantial was *The Divine Worker in Creation and Providence* (1909).

John Wood Oman (1860–1939), Professor of Systematic Theology and Apologetics and later Principal of Westminster College, Cambridge, published works on a variety of themes, of which the most significant are his personalistic treatments of *Grace and Personality* (1917), and *The Natural and the Supernatural* (1931).

The United Reformed Church (1972)

Henry Herbert Farmer (1892–1981) was Oman's student and successor at Westminster College, Cambridge, and then Norris-Hulse Professor of Divinity at Cambridge University. In addition to sermons and a book on preaching, he published *The World and God: A Study of Prayer,*

Providence and Miracle, (1935), *Towards Belief in God* (1943), *Revelation and Religion* (1954), and the posthumous work, *Reconciliation and Religion: Some Aspects of the Uniqueness of Christianity as a Reconciling Faith* (1998). Throughout he construes religious experience in terms of personal encounter.

Harry Francis Lovell Cocks (1894–1983), Forsyth's student and Franks's successor at Western College, Bristol, published *The Faith of a Protestant Christian* (1931), *The Nonconformist Conscience* (1943), *The Wondrous Cross* (1957), and *The Religious Life of Oliver Cromwell* (1960); he also gave the Drew Lecture on Immortality, *The Hope of Glory* (1955). His major work was *By Faith Alone* (1943) in which he argued that saving faith must be construed as presupposing natural faith, but as discontinuous with it—it is God's gift through his Word, Jesus Christ.

John Seldon Whale (1896–1997), Principal of Cheshunt College, Cambridge, expounded *The Christian Answer to the Problem of Evil* (1936), revealed his immersion in Reformation theology in *The Protestant Tradition* (1955), and his ecumenical commitment in *Christian Reunion: Historic Divisions Reconsidered* (1971). In his study of the atonement, *Victor and Victim* (1960) he related the doctrine to the Church and the sacraments, conceiving the resurrection hope as necessarily corporate. His oft-reprinted *Christian Doctrine* (1941) has deservedly achieved classic status.

Aubrey Vine (1900–73) served in pastoral charge and also, for a period, as Professor of Church History at Yorkshire United Independent College. He published *The Nestorian Churches* (1937) and *An Approach to Christology. An Interpretation and Development of Some Elements in the Metaphysic and Christology of Nestorius as a Way of Approach to an Orthodox Christology Compatible with Modern Thought* (1948).

Francis George Healey (1903–92), Farmer's successor at Westminster College, Cambridge, wrote on historical and linguistic themes, and published *Religion and Reality. The Theology of John Oman* (1965).

Hubert Cunliffe-Jones (1905–91), Professor of Theology at the University of Manchester and a not uncritical follower of Barth, published *The Holy Spirit* (1943), *The Authority of the Biblical Revelation* (1945), *Technology, Community and Church* (1961), two biblical commentaries, and *Christian Theology since 1600*, 1970. He edited *A History of Christian Doctrine* (1978) with assistance from Benjamin Drewery.

Charles Sim Duthie (1911–81), Principal first of the Scottish Congregational College and then of New College, London, published *God in His World* (1955) and *Outline of Christian Belief* (1968). He edited *Resurrection and Immortality. Aspects of Twentieth-Century Christian Belief* (1979), a collection of Drew Lectures on immortality.

Walter Alexander Whitehouse (1915–2003), formerly Professor of Theology at the University of Kent, brought scientific interests to bear upon theology, as is seen in his books, *Christian Faith and the Scientific Attitude* (1952) and *Order, Goodness, Glory* (1960). Considerably influenced by Barth, he published *The Authority of Grace. Essays in Response to Karl Barth* (ed. Ann Loades, 1981). He undertook translations from German, and contributed papers on natural law and eschatology to collections.

John Harwood Hick (b. 1922), formerly Professor at Birmingham University and Claremont Graduate School, California, has published widely upon philosophical and theological topics. His epistemological interests emerge in *Faith and Knowledge* (1957 etc.), and he has been at the centre of the discussion of religious faith as 'experiencing as'; in *Evil and the God of Love* (1966) he adopts an Irenaean stance; and with *God and the Universe of Faiths* (1973) he did much to advance the continuing debate on religious pluralism. Other works include *Philosophy of Religion* (1963), *Christianity at the Centre* (1969), *Death and Eternal Life* (1976), *The Myth of Christian Uniqueness* (1987), *An Interpretation of Religion: Human Responses to the Transcendent* (1989), *Disputed Questions in Theology and the Philosophy of Religion* (1993), *The Metaphor of God Incarnate* (1993), and *The Fifth Dimension. An Exploration of the Spiritual Realm* (1999).

John Heywood Thomas (b. 1926), formerly Professor of Theology at the University of Nottingham, brought the skills of analytical philosophy to bear upon Kierkegaard: *Subjectivity and Paradox* (1957), and Tillich: *Paul Tillich: An Appraisal* (1963). He has also published the introductory volume, *Paul Tillich* (1965), *Philosophy of Religion in Kierkegaard's Writings* (1995), and *Tillich* (2000).

Alan Philip Frederick Sell (b. 1935), who has held theological posts in England, Geneva, Canada and Wales, publishes on Christian (especially Reformed and Dissenting) thought, and on the relations between philosophy and theology. His trilogy on apologetic method comprises *Philosophical Idealism and Christian Belief* (1995), *John Locke and the Eighteenth-Century Divines* (1997) and *Confessing and Commending the Faith: Historic Witness and Apologetic Method* (2002). Other works of philosophical interest include *Philosophy, Dissent and Nonconformity 1689–1920* (2004) and *Mill on God: The Pervasiveness and Elusiveness of Mill's Religious Thought* (2004). In his trilogy, *Doctrine and Devotion* (2000), which follows a trinitarian line, he attempts a devotional systematics for ministers and church members. His ecumenical interests are seen, for example, in *A Reformed, Evangelical Catholic Theology. The Contribution of the World Alliance of Reformed Churches 1875–1982* (1991). He has published the following collections of papers: *Dissenting Thought and the Life of the Churches. Studies in an English Tradition* (1990); *Aspects of Christian* Integrity (1990); Commemorations*: Studies in Christian Thought and History* (1993);

Testimony and Tradition: Studies in Reformed and Dissenting Thought (2004); *Enlightenment, Ecumenism, Evangel: Theological Themes and Thinkers 1550–2000* (2005).

Colin Ewart Gunton (1941–2003), Professor of Christian Doctrine at King's College, London, wrote prolifically on theological questions, as the following titles will show: *Becoming and Being. The Doctrine of God in Charles Hartshorne and Karl Barth* (1978/2001), *Yesterday and Today. A Study of Continuities in Christology* (1983), *Enlightenment and Alienation. An Essay towards a Trinitarian Theology* (1985), *The Actuality of Atonement* (1988), *The Promise of Trinitarian Theology* (1991), *Christ and Creation* (1992), *The One, the Three and the Many. God, Creation and the Culture of Modernity* (1993), *A Brief Theology of Revelation* (1995), *Theology through the Theologians* (1996), *The Promise of Trinitarian Theology* (1997), *The Triune Creator. A Historical and Systematic Study* (1998), *Intellect and Action. Elucidations on Christian Theology and the Life of Faith* (2000), *Act and Being. Towards a Theology of the Divine Attributes* (2002), *The Christian Faith: An Introduction to Christian Doctrine* (2002), and *Father, Son and Holy Spirit. Toward a Fully Trinitarian Theology* (2003). A deeply committed church member, he published *Theology Through Preaching. Sermons for Brentwood* (2001).

David Raymond Peel (b. 1949), Principal of Northern College, Manchester, has published *Reforming Theology. Explorations in the Theological Traditions of the United Reformed Church* (2002).

Concluding Reflections

Although this catalogue of theological contributions has necessarily been a 'nuts and bolts' affair, it does at least indicate the range of topics treated by British Reformed theologians during the 'long' twentieth century. It also suggests that whereas at the beginning of that century the theology of the Cross was more prominent than perhaps it has been of late, the doctrine of creation is, for fairly obvious reasons, currently receiving a degree of attention which it was earlier denied. It further becomes clear that whereas a few writers, of whom John Hick is a conspicuous example, have raised the pressing question of religious pluralism, the theologians noted have not devoted themselves over much to feminism, liberation theology and that delightful 'catch-all', postmodernism.

Turning to particular contributions, and confining myself to the deceased: it would be difficult to find theologians more learned in their respective fields than Robert Flint and R. S. Franks. By contrast Fairbairn, though held in awe by some and (to use a favourite nineteenth-century noun) a 'worthy' indeed, seems rather to excel in depicting sweeping intellectual vistas than in marshalling close arguments. Few had as keen a mind as Denney, while Robert Mackintosh's wit was as sharp as his faith was simple. He, like Lovell Cocks, has been too quickly forgotten. Few succeeded as well as H. R. Mackintosh in holding together the detailed discussion of technical doctrinal questions and the realities of Christian life.

As for the more recently departed, it seems to me that thoughtful analysis of the theological underpinnings of Christian ethics of the kind offered by N. H. G. Robinson is all too rare in the British Reformed *corpus* (and, I suspect, not only there); while in the lucid and concise H. P. Owen we find the unusual combination of a Presbyterian deeply indebted to scholastic philosophy on the one hand, and capable of incisive criticisms of current theological trends of which he disapproves on the other.

If I were asked to nominate '*The* British Reformed theologian of the twentieth century', I should, on grounds of his depth and creativity (his unconventional method notwithstanding) opt for P. T. Forsyth. None penetrated more directly to the heart of the Gospel than he, and he well understood what a great deal of theology it takes to reform theology.

By way of an epilogue I should like to refer to one not hitherto mentioned for the very good reason that, of set purpose, he left no books and but a very few fugitive articles. George Phillips (1893–1967), nurtured among the Strict and Particular Baptists, became a liberal evangelical Congregationalist taught by Robert Mackintosh. He was far too self-effacing to think that a wider public would be interested in anything he might write, but, as Professor of Philosophy and Christian Doctrine, he made doctrine come alive in the classroom at Lancashire Independent College—more especially when we succeeded in the not very difficult task of diverting him from his notes. He would then sail away, comparing and contrasting doctrinal systems, and passing crisp but gracious judgments upon contemporary theologians, of which the harshest was 'He does seem to me to be rather over-enthusiastic about *Barth*!' Then, having realized that his extemporizing had left him in danger of not completing the course, he would leave the room with these words, 'I believe you know the drawer in which I keep my lecture notes....' Successive evenings of frantic typing would then ensue. The greatly loved and highly respected George Phillips may stand as a representative of many theological teachers who made a lasting impression whilst spilling very little ink.

CHAPTER 10

The Alliance in Dialogue, 1970–2002: Retrospect and Reflections

For more than thirty years the World Alliance of Reformed Churches has been involved in international bilateral dialogues with other Christian world communions.[1] This work, which has involved participants from many parts of the world, has been done at great cost in terms of time, money and human energy. It is entirely appropriate that in the interests of good stewardship of resources, and before taking further steps, we should pause and reflect upon the journey so far. But there is an even more important reason for taking stock: we need to thank God for the progress made in deepening relations with our friends of other Christian traditions, and we need honestly to appraise ourselves to see whether we have done all that we might to harvest the fruit of the dialogues to date. While we should be sufficiently realistic to understand that because of the diverse circumstances in which the Reformed family lives the results of dialogues will not be appropriated immediately or equally in all parts of the world, this should not become an excuse for wilful inertia.

The motivation in all of our conversations with other Christian world communions is the desire to manifest that unity in Christ into which God has, by grace, already called us, so that the Church truly becomes a sign of the ultimate reconciliation of all things ('the whole inhabited

---

[1] There was, in addition, a trilateral dialogue between Roman Catholics, Lutherans and Reformed on the specific question of *Theology of Marriage and the Problems of Mixed Marriages*, Geneva: WARC, 1976; and there is a series of multi-lateral 'Prague Conversations', initiated in 1986 and continuing, in the 'First, Radical and Second Reformations', For the latter see Milan Opocensky, ed., *Towards a Renewed Dialogue. The First and Second Reformations*, Geneva: WARC, 1996; M. Opocensky and Paraic Réamonn, *Justification and Sanctification in the Traditions of the Reformation*, Geneva: WARC, 1999. Conversations have also been held between representatives of the Alliance and the African Instituted Churches; see the news report, 'African Christians talk together', in *WARC Update*, XII no. 1, May 2002, p. 12. In this paper I focus on the international in the sense of 'global' (as distinct from regional—some of which are also international) bilateral conversations. I should like to say what a privilege it has been to be associated with a number of these over the years, and to thank Dr. Odair Pedroso Mateus for the invitation to offer some reflections upon this significant aspect of the Alliance's theological work.

earth'—not just the churches) in God. From the Reformation onwards, Christian unity has been sought by Reformed Christians. For example, Calvin declared that 'there is no other bond of Church unity than the fact that Christ, the Lord, has reconciled us with God the Father and has gathered us out of the dispersion into the communion of His body, that so we may grow together through His word and spirit into one heart and soul'.[2] However much our Reformed history has been blighted by inner-family secessions (a fact which makes our protestations of catholicity to our dialogue partners less than fully convincing), at our best we have understood that the Reformers did not set out to create new churches, but to reform the one Church of Christ according to the Word of God. Not surprisingly, therefore, the parent bodies of the Alliance, the World Presbyterian Alliance (1875) and the International Congregational Council (1891), made it clear from the outset that they were constituted for mutual fellowship and common witness, and that the creation of isolationist confession blocs was no part of their purpose. On the contrary, the Presbyterians declared that 'In forming this Alliance, the Presbyterian churches do not mean to change their fraternal relations with other Churches, but will be ready, as heretofore, to join with them in Christian fellowship, and in advancing the cause of the Redeemer, on the general principle maintained and taught in the Reformed Confessions that the Church of God on earth, though composed of many members, is one body in the communion of the Holy Ghost, of which body Christ is the Supreme Head and the Scriptures alone are the infallible law.'[3] Similarly, Christian unity was a prominent theme at the 1891 Congregational Council: 'It is not only fitting, it is imperative that this congress should affirm the relations of Congregational churches to all other Churches of Jesus Christ... From the beginning unity has been a distinctive note of Christianity...it is an article of every Christian creed, it enters...into every anticipation of the Christian millennium on earth, and of the Father's house in heaven.'[4]

In the light of such affirmations it is not surprising that during the Alliance's Executive Committee meeting held at Prague in 1956 John A Mackay felt able to call for a meeting, first held in the following year,

---

2 Letter of Calvin to Sadolet, quoted by G. W. Richards, *Proceedings of the World Presbyterian Alliance*, XIII, 1929, p. 291.

3 *Proceedings of the World Presbyterian Alliance*, I, 1877, p. 9.

4 *Proceedings of the International Congregational Council*, 1891, p. 245. See further, Alan P. F. Sell, *A Reformed, Evangelical, Catholic Theology. The Contribution of the World Alliance of Reformed Churches 1875–1982*, (1991), Eugene, OR: Wipf & Stock, 1998, pp. 112-30. For 'catholicity' in Alliance thought see pp. 104-111; see, more generally, Alan P. F. Sell, 'Reformed identity: a non-issue of catholic significance', (with responses by M. Eugene Osterhaven and others), *Reformed Review*, LIV no. 1, Autumn 2000, pp. 17-27.

which developed into the annual meeting of secretaries of Christian world communions.[5] In these gatherings the secretaries and other participants laid a foundation of personal relationships and mutual knowledge of the several communions on which the future dialogue programme could be built. A prominent spur towards bilateral dialogue came from the Second Vatican Council which prompted the Roman Catholic Church to reach out in conversation with other Christian families. Indeed the first phase of the Roman Catholic–Reformed dialogue ran from 1970 to 1977, while conversations co-sponsored with the Lutheran World Federation also began in 1970.[6] From that time to the present the Alliance has been a partner in international bilateral dialogues with eleven Christian world communions.

It cannot be said that the path of bilateral dialogue always runs smoothly. I do not here refer to the fact that on occasion commission members suffer stomach upsets in unfamiliar climes, or that there is a desire on the part of a few to travel to the dialogue venue by the most circuitious of routes. Rather, I am thinking of questions which have been raised concerning the ways in which dialogues are conducted. Let us address some of these at the outset.[7]

First, some have queried whether the Alliance's dialogue teams are adequately representative of the family as a whole and of particular categories within it. Clearly, the Alliance could not sponsor dialogue teams in excess of two hundred members, so that every member church had direct participation in the process of every dialogue: a measure of mutual trust is called for. As to 'the family as a whole', our Alliance turns upon the fact that in one way or another (whether by sixteenth-century origins or later missionary or revivalist activity) we find our roots in the Bible as recovered in a major wing of the European Reformation. But this leaves ample scope for variety. Whether we think in terms of liturgy, polity, attitudes towards classical confessions, ethical stances, there are considerable differences of theory and practice among us[8]—to such a degree that some of our dialogue partners have been known to wonder

---

5 See Marcel Pradervand, *A Century of Service. A History of the World Alliance of Reformed Churches 1875–1975*, Edinburgh: Saint Andrew Press, 1975, p. 202.

6 The strenuous efforts and kindly guidance of Richmond Smith, Theological Secretary during the first thirteen years of bilateral dialogue activity should not go unremarked.

7 I fear I have been around long enough to have said some of these things before: for example, in 'The role of bilateral dialogues within the one ecumenical movement', *The Ecumenical Review*, XLVI no. 4, October 1994, pp. 453-60.

8 See further, Alan P. F. Sell, 'The Reformed family today: some theological reflections', in Donald K. McKim, ed., *Major Themes in the Reformed Tradition*, Grand Rapids, MI: Eerdmans, 1992, pp. 433-41.

with whom, precisely, are they in dialogue?[9] When seeking members of a dialogue team we need to ensure that at least some of them are thoroughly conversant with these diverse tendencies. As to the representation of 'particular categories' within the family, Jane Dempsey Douglass, for example, has lamented the paucity of female membership of Alliance dialogue teams.[10] I have some reason to know that strenuous efforts have been made over the years of dialogue to rectify this, and it is easier said than done. One relevant consideration is the fact that a number of member churches (not all of them in the developing world) do not at present ordain women, still less entrust them with theological teaching. Indeed, some of our more prominent Western member churches have admitted women to the ministry only a few decades ago, and very few member churches, large or small, did so before 1917. My impression is that, happily, the situation is improving in many places, and that more and more member churches are, on the biblical grounds which Dr. Douglass specifies,[11] coming to understand that our oneness in the Christ who breaks down barriers (Galatians 3:28) entails the seeking of justice for all in the fellowship, in order that the gifts granted to all by God may be fully exercised.

Secondly, some have felt that the dialogue reports omit matters of importance. For example, Dr. Douglass regrets the absence of 'awareness of women or issues concerning women' from the dialogues with the Baptists and the Methodists, and this despite the fact that women were present at the Methodist–Reformed dialogue sessions.[12] This might be taken as implying either that the women participants in the latter dialogue failed in their duty, or that the men decided not to take pay heed to their contributions. Neither is the case. The point is that each dialogue has its

---

[9] There is a significant difference between the Alliance, a fellowship of Reformed churches each having its own confession(s) of faith—or not—and those Christian world communions which are structured in a more conciliar fashion. Not the least of these is the fact that the Alliance's recommendations come to its members with moral authority only. Karel Blei has wondered whether the time is ripe for the Alliance to transform itself into a more structured fellowship. See 'The WARC in bilateral dialogue. Introductory remarks', in H. S. Wilson, ed., *Bilateral Dialogues*, Geneva: WARC 1993, p. 15. This is a delicate matter indeed, for there are member churches who remain within the fold only because the Alliance is *not* a formal conciliar structure. It may not be irrelevant to recall on the one hand that in its very earliest days the World Presbyterian Alliance found it quite impossible to devise a confession of faith to which all its members would assent; while on the other hand the Alliance was able to discipline member churches over the issue of apartheid without being a tightly-structured conciliar body. See Sell, *A Reformed, Evangelical, Catholic Theology*, pp. 71-73, 233-35.

[10] See Jane Dempsey Douglass, 'Identifying the major theological issues in the dialogues…', in Wilson, ed., *Bilateral Dialogues*, p. 40.

[11] Ibid., p. 35.

[12] Ibid., p. 36.

own terms of reference, and that the Methodist–Reformed one sought to address the specific question, How far, if at all, should the traditional theological differences between Methodists and Reformed (notably those surrounding evangelical Arminianism and Calvinism) continue to be church-dividing?[13] By contrast, there is a substantial section on the ordination of women in the Anglican–Reformed report—as might have been expected given that 'ministry' was a prominent theme in the discussion.[14] Because of particular terms of reference we should expect that in any given dialogue there will be many live issues which will not be discussed. For the same reason we should expect both that some participants will be acknowledged experts on the technical issues concerned, while others will keep the participants anchored in reality by speaking from various regions concerning the relations of the dialogue partners at the grass roots. This, in turn, raises another representational point: the dialogue partners are not equal in size, and are unequally distributed around the world. While Roman Catholics are widely dispersed, there are many parts of the world where the Mennonites, the Disciples of Christ and the Oriental Orthodox, for example, are not to be found. It is important that at least some members of any dialogue team have personal knowledge of the other partner.

Thirdly, on a number of occasions it has happened that when the drafting of a final report is imminent one or more team members (almost invariably from the United States) will, sometimes to the puzzlement of participants whose first language is not English, raise the question of the language to be used in the report.[15] In so far as this is a plea that 'inclusive language' be employed where males and females are jointly being referred to my impression is that the point is widely taken. It does seem to me to be a requirement of the Gospel that we should not use language which might be taken as implying that we are ignoring half the human race. The less commonly agreed aspect of the problem relates to the language used of God. On the one hand there are those who feel that to use masculine personal pronouns when referring to God reinforces

---

13 See *Reformed and Methodists in Dialogue*, Geneva: WARC, 1988.

14 See *God's Reign and Our Unity*, London: SPCK and Edinburgh: Saint Andrew Press, 1984, pp. 62-65. Integrity prompted the comment that 'There is a substantial minority of Reformed Christians who do not accept women ministers. Even where there are women ministers there has been little serious consideration of the distinctive contribution that women might make in the ordained ministry' (pp. 62-63). The question of the ordination of women was raised, but not pursued, during the second phase of the Roman Catholic–Reformed dialogue. See *Towards a Common Understanding of the Church*, Geneva: WARC, 1991, p. 49. The question of ordination has yet to be broached in dialogues with the Orthodox and Oriental Orthodox Churches.

15 See, for example, the *Towards a Common Understanding of the Church*, p. iv n. 1.

patriarchy and tempts people into thinking (wrongly) that God is male. For the same reasons some of the same people substitute such formulations as 'Creator, Christ, Sustainer' for the traditional trinitarian language of Father, Son and Holy Spirit. On the other hand there are those who contend that especially at a time when New Age ideas and sundry gnosticisms are prevalent it is important that Christians use language which makes it clear that the Christian Godhead is (not male—or female but) personal; they feel that substitutions for Father, Son and Holy Spirit result in the loss of the idea of the inner-personal relations of the Trinity; and they resent what they perceive as the activities of an editorial 'thought police'—especially one which originates in a land which proclaims freedom of speech in its constitution. It would be foolish to pretend that full accord will swiftly or easily be reached across this divide but, once again, my impression is that in many circles there is greater willingness than hitherto to grant that neither side need treat the other as outcasts, that the sectarian spirit is to be shunned, that care should be taken not to ride roughshod over the sincerely-held, principled views of those with whom we may disagree, and that we should think more than twice before supposing that we can draw substantive theological conclusions from the grammatical conventions of particular languages.

Fourthly, there are those who urge that concern with bilateral dialogues somehow undermines, or needlessly duplicates, wider ecumenical work as undertaken by the World Council of Churches. This challenge has been addressed on numerous occasions over the years,[16] and the general conclusion seems to be that whereas the World Council is ideally placed to promote such multilateral studies as *Baptism, Eucharist and Ministry* with a view to seeing what degree of convergence or consensus obtains among its wide range of members, it cannot speak for its individual members on the ground, all of whom belong to one or other of the Christian world communions who, therefore, need to be in conversation with each other as well. In other words, the bilateral programmes of the several Christian world communions are complementary to, and are not in competition with, the activities of the World Council of Churches.

Lastly, there are those who contend that after all the effort the results have been few. It all depends on what one means by 'results'. I should like to address this issue through a consideration of 'form', 'content' and 'reception', and then offer some concluding reflections.

---

16 See, for example, Günther Gassmann, 'Nature and function of bilateral and multilateral dialogues and their interrelation', *Mid-Stream*, XXV no. 3, July 1986, pp. 299-308

Form

To a considerable degree the balance in the several reports between theological reflection and practical suggestions is directly related to the degree of historic and current proximity of the partners in dialogue. That is to say, the Reformed have closer historical and geographical links with some of their dialogue partners than with others. With their friends whose distinctive life originates in the European, Scottish and English Reformations—the Lutherans, the Anglicans, the Mennonites and the Baptists—they have so much in common that thoroughly practical recommendations for closer relations are feasible. The same applies to such later arrivals on the ecclesiastical scene as the Methodists and the Christian Church (Disciples of Christ): indeed, in some cases unions of various groupings of these six traditions have already occurred. Where the Roman Catholic Church is concerned, some of the Reformed may feel that they know that body only too well, and do not much care for it. Even the more tolerant among the Reformed cannot overlook the history of mutual recriminations—even condemnations. There is thus a need for the patient mutual exploration of issues on the part of these two communions with a view to better understanding, to the eventual reconciliation of memories, and, meanwhile, to such co-operation as may be possible. In the case of dialogue with the Orthodox Churches and the Oriental Orthodox many of the Reformed find themselves on a steep learning curve, for these traditions are not well known to them. (It also has to be said that the reverse is also true.) What assists here is that growth in mutual respect and trust which flows from the earnest consideration of such basic tenets of the faith as the Trinity and Christology. Where dialogue with the Pentecostals is concerned the Holy Spirit is naturally to the fore. Finally, the first dialogue session held between the Alliance and the Seventh-Day Adventists was an occasion for mutual sharing with a view to detecting the degree of common ground existing between parties both of whom had changed in attitude over the years and were now able to view each other with less suspicion than hitherto.

In the variety of circumstances thus described we have a key to explaining the diverse terms of reference of the several dialogues, and the fact that some reports contain more immediately applicable recommendations than others.[17]

Content

At the very least the dialogue reports provide a rich source of theological reflection upon a wide range of topics, and a number of them

---

[17] I suspect that there are points to be made about the varied psycho-dynamics of the several dialogues—but I forbear.

recommend steps which may be taken towards closer unity. I hope that the following review of the ever-growing library of documents, though necessarily selective, will demonstrate this claim. I begin with the reports of

Dialogues with our Nearer Neighbours

Following conversations in 1970 and 1975 between representatives of the **Lutheran World Federation and the Alliance**,[18] a full-scale international dialogue was inaugurated which produced the report, *Toward Closer Fellowship* (1989). Building on such regional findings as the *Leuenberg Agreement* (1973), the participants stated their common faith and urged their global constituencies 'to declare full communion with one another', understanding this to entail that the historic mutual condemnations no longer apply, that full pulpit and altar/table fellowship and the mutual recognition of ministers of the Word and sacrament be established, and that growth in unity through shared church life and mission be encouraged.[19] A third series of conversations was held between 1999 and 2001, the findings of which are in the report, *Called to Common Communion and Common Witness* (2002). The objectives were to follow up the suggestions made in1989, and to reflect upon the new situation created by the 'Joint Declaration on the Doctrine of Justification' signed by the Lutheran World Federation and the Roman Catholic Church in 1999.

In the **Anglican–Reformed** report, *God's Reign and Our Unity* (1984), the quest of unity is firmly set in the context of mission, and of the conviction that the unity of the Church cannot adequately be considered except in relation to the unity of humanity. The factors separating Anglicans and Reformed are discussed, the familiar themes of baptism, eucharist and ministry are rehearsed, with special reference to bishops and elders. The report contains pertinent questions for discussion, and among its nine recommendations is the following: 'We recommend that where churches of our two communions are committed to going forward to seek visible unity, a measure of *reciprocal* communion should be made possible; for communion is not only a sign of unity achieved, but also a means by which God brings it about.'[20]

On 5 March 1983 an historic service was held in Zurich Cathedral, attended by representatives of the Mennonite World Conference, the Baptist World Alliance and our Alliance, during which the Reformed

---

18 For the report of these see *Reformed World*, September 1975, pp. 314-20.

19 *Toward Closer Fellowship*, Geneva: Lutheran World Federation and WARC, 1989, p. 28.

20 *God's Reign and Our Unity*, 82. See further, Sell, *A Reformed, Evangelical, Catholic Theology*, pp. 137-42.

repudiated and regretted the historic condemnations they had uttered against the Anabaptists and sought the help of their erstwhile opponents in fostering reconciliation and renewed fellowship. There followed in 1984 a consultation in Strasbourg between representatives of the **Alliance and the Mennonite World Conference** which resulted in the document, *Mennonites and Reformed in Dialogue* (1986). Either side offers family portraits, the question of the historic condemnations of Anabaptists by the Reformed is addressed, and appendices concerning issues of peace and justice are included. A second phase of dialogue took place in Calgary in 1989. Here the traditionally 'neuralgic' questions of baptism, peace and the state were discussed in detail, with responses from members of other Christian traditions. In the recommendations the Reformed are challenged 'to revive and practise that understanding of the Church as God's covenant people, within which the integrity of infant baptism is actualized', while the Mennonites are challenged 'seriously to examine their attitude towards Christians baptized as infants who wish to exercise their church membership in a Mennonite church, in relation to the questions of the nature and mode of baptism, and in the light of the Gospel which has made us one.' Further recommendations urge reflection on the present state of just war theory and on 'Christian participation in the responsible use of coercive power'.[21]

The **Baptist–Reformed** dialogue of 1973–77 yielded a booklet entitled *Baptists and Reformed in Dialogue* (1984), which includes the dialogue report, the report of a group which evaluated the dialogue, a letter to the member churches of the Baptist World Alliance and the Alliance, some suggestions for further study and action, and some reflections of a Mennonite scholar. Among the topics discussed are Scripture, the nature of the Church (with special reference to wider councils and local autonomy), the Church's ministry and mission and, of course, baptism. As to the last, the participants wonder

> whether Christians of Reformed and Baptist convictions who are members in good standing of their churches could recognize one another as both occupying the position of those who have received and responded to the grace of God in baptism as this grace is understood in the New Testament. Such a mutual recognition could only arise from:

---

[21] Ross T. Bender and Alan P. F. Sell, eds., *Baptism, Peace and the State in the Reformed and Mennonite Traditions*, Waterloo, Ontario: Wilfrid Laurier University Press, 1991, p. 238. This phase of the dialogue represented a pioneering attempt to forward the Alliance's work by utilizing the resources of a university Institute for the Humanities—in this case, Calgary's. The two world bodies constituted their dialogue panels and covered the travel costs of their participants, while the Institute provided the physical facilities and organized funding from various quarters.

> (i) an agreed understanding that a complex of elements, including baptism with water in the name of the Trinity, public profession of faith and admission to the Lord's Supper, are all parts of the reception of and response to this grace of God;
>
> (ii) the acceptance (still problematic) that this complex of elements could find place in the life of any individual *either* contemporaneously in the act of believer's baptism, where profession of faith, water baptism and communion come together in time, or over a period of time, short or long, in which (infant) baptism, profession of faith (at 'confirmation' as it is often called), and admission to communion follow one another as separable stages in a process.[22]

As already mentioned, the **Reformed–Methodist** conversations, held in 1985 and 1987 with participants nominated by the World Methodist Council and the Alliance, focused upon those doctrinal points (grace and perfect salvation among them) which have traditionally kept the two traditions apart. The discussion of these took place in the context of the call to confess the Gospel today, and the conclusion clearly stated is that 'the classical doctrinal issues which we were asked to review ought not to be seen as obstacles to unity between Methodists and Reformed'.[23] In the light of this finding suggestions are made with a view to fostering closer relations on the ground.

In 1984 a preparatory meeting was held between representatives of the **Disciples Ecumenical Consultative Council and the Alliance**. Papers designed to introduce the families to one another were presented and topics for future consideration were noted.[24] In 1987 a full international dialogue session was held, and a report, *Towards Closer Fellowship* (1988), was published. The participants set down the faith which Reformed and Disciples share, and they pay particular attention to the nature of the Church, baptism and ministry. The paragraphs on baptism include one which is entirely in keeping with the aspiration expressed in the Baptist–Reformed report:

> the difference between infant and believers' baptism becomes less sharp when it is recognized that both forms of baptism embody God's own initiative in Christ and express a personal response of faith made within the believing community. Personal confession of faith normally takes place either at the time of baptism in the case of the believer, or at a later time by those who are baptized as infants.[25]

---

22 *Baptists and Reformed in Dialogue*, Geneva: WARC, 1984, pp. 19-20. See further, Sell, *A Reformed, Evangelical, Catholic Theology*, pp. 142-45.

23 *Reformed and Methodists in Dialogue*, Geneva: WARC, 1988, p. 14.

24 See Alan P. F. Sell, ed., *Reformed and Disciples of Christ in Dialogue*, Geneva: WARC, 1985.

25 *Towards Closer Fellowship*, Geneva: WARC, 1988, p. 11.

Having reviewed the topics assigned to them the participants conclude that 'On the basis of these discussions we believe there are no theological or ecclesiological issues which need to divide us as churches';[26] and they proceed to make a number of practical recommendations concerning the way forward.

Five international meetings were held between **Pentecostals and Reformed** between 1995 and 2000. The report has been published under the title, 'Word and Spirit, Church and world'.[27] The stated objectives are to foster mutual understanding and respect, to identify points of theological agreement, disagreement and convergence, and to explore possibilities of common witness. The participants heard and discussed papers on spirituality and biblical interpretation, the Holy Spirit and the Church, the Holy Spirit and mission in eschatological perspective, and the Holy Spirit, charisma, and the kingdom of God. The final report comprises elements from these papers and discussions. It becomes clear that while Pentecostals and Reformed take their stand on the Trinity, and understand the Church as being the creature of the Word and the Spirit—called to mission in, while not being of, the world—at certain points there are differences of emphasis. For example, some Pentecostals hold that the ability to speak in tongues is ultimately available to all believers, while many 'distinguish between speaking in tongues as a gift of the Holy Spirit (not available to all) and speaking in tongues as a sign or evidence (potentially available to all) that one has been baptized with the Holy Spirit (Acts 1:8, 2:1-4)'.[28] Again, dispensational theology has influenced many Pentecostals, and an emphasis upon the second coming of Christ is prominent among them. Some of them interpret reality dualistically: the Spirit over against the 'world', while others understand the Spirit as inviting Christians to engage in the reforming and transforming of society. The participants 'wish to encourage others in their respective communities to join in this mutual exploration'.[29]

Dialogues with More Distant Communions

Three phases of dialogue (1970–77, 1984–90 and 1998–2003) have so far been completed between the **Roman Catholic Secretariat for Promoting Christian Unity and the Alliance**. The findings of the first phase are in *The Presence of Christ in Church and World* (1977). The participants do not shirk their responsibility of articulating their disagreements over church order, the teaching authority of the Church and the eucharist; but some notable sentiments indicating convergence of

---

[26] Ibid., p. 14.

[27] *Reformed World*, L no, 3, September 2000, pp. 128-56.

[28] Ibid., p. 144.

[29] Ibid., p. 153.

views are also expressed. It is agreed that all who follow Christ have the task of witnessing corporately to the Gospel, and that 'the Church Catholic is really represented and exists in the local Church'.[30] It is further agreed that 'the Church has its authority to the extent that it listens to the Word Christ speaks to it ever afresh'.[31] But where the communication of what is heard is concerned there is a significant difference between the two parties: 'So far as instruction is concerned, for the Reformed it is the community as a whole which is responsible and which delegates qualified people; whereas for the Catholics there is a distinctive responsibility of the pastoral ministry: the latter is rooted in the believing community but does not derive its authority from an act of delegation on the part of the latter.[32] The agreed statement that 'The Christian who looks back on his own life will say that Christ was active in it, leading him to repentance, conversion, and faith, even before he was aware or made any conscious response',[33] seems to encapsulate the Pauline understanding of election, and to have implications for paedobaptism. As to Church and world: the sobering point is made that 'The Church exposes its fundamental orientations and controlling loyalties by the way it lives, no matter what it says to the contrary.'[34] In a paragraph advising that the localness and the catholicity of the Church be held together the important affirmation is made that 'It is only by participating in the local community that we share in the life of the universal Church.'[35] In the section on the eucharist the once-for-all-ness of Christ's sacrifice on the Cross is proclaimed, and it is agreed that the sacrament is 'a memorial of the Lord's death and resurrection, a source of loving communion with him in the power of the Spirit', and 'a source of the eschatological hope for his coming again'.[36]

In the report of the second phase of the Roman Catholic–Reformed dialogue Reformed and Roman Catholic reviews of relations in the period from the Reformation to the present day are presented. These point to the need for the reconciliation of memories (which entails dealing with mutual condemnations uttered in the past) as between the two

---

30 *The Presence of Christ in Church and World*, The Vatican: Secretariat for Promoting Christian Unity and Geneva: WARC, 1977, 8. See further Sell, *A Reformed, Evangelical, Catholic Theology*, pp. 132-37.

31 *The Presence of Christ in Church and World*, p. 10.

32 Ibid., p. 13. I think that Reformed communities recognize and ordain those whom God calls and equips, and whose sense of call is tested within the community. In other words, the above statement seems to elevate democracy at the expense of the divine initiative.

33 Ibid., p. 16.

34 Ibid., p. 19.

35 Ibid. Though there may, of course, be different understandings of 'local'.

36 Ibid., p. 27.

communions. The participants proceed to confess their shared faith, emphasizing the sole mediatorship of Christ, justification by grace through faith, and the inescapability of the Church as the community of the justified. The doctrine of the Church is then more closely examined, and the differences of emphasis which result from the Reformed emphasis upon the Church as *Creatura Verbi* and the Roman Catholic understanding of the Church as a sacrament are noted. It is suggested that these modes of expression may be seen as complementary. While the Roman Catholics believe that the Church 'subsists' in their communion, the question remains, 'to what degree they can recognize that the Church of Christ also exists in the Reformed churches'.[37] Another 'neuralgic' point, carried over from the first phase of the dialogue, is encapsulated in the question, 'Is the laying-on of hands [at ordination] a sending on a mission, a passing on of a power, or an incorporation into an order?'[38]

The third phase of the Roman Catholic–Reformed dialogue concerned the Church as a community of common witness to the kingdom of God. The nature of the kingdom of God and the Church as a sign of it in history were among the themes discussed. In addition case studies of the situation in South Africa and Northern Ireland were discussed in relation to the overall theme.

In 1977 Professor T. F. Torrance, acting on behalf of the Alliance, broached the possibility of **Orthodox–Reformed** conversations with the Ecumenical Patriarch Dimitrios I.[39] This resulted in meetings in 1979, 1981 and 1983 between the Alliance and the Patriarchate of Constantinople. The papers presented during these sessions concerned Orthodox–Reformed relations, and the doctrines of God, ecclesial authority and the Trinity.[40] Against the background of this promising beginning the Patriarchate of Constantinople invited all the autocephalous Orthodox churches to engage in official dialogue with the Alliance. The sessions began in 1998, and continue. The jointly agreed policy was to focus upon fundamental aspects of the Christian confession, and to date the result has been the publication of agreed statements on the Holy Trinity (accompanied by a common reflection on the doctrine) (1992) and on Christology (1994). The statement on the Trinity draws upon biblical and patristic sources, and in further explanation of it the participants underline the point that the statement turns upon the fact that

---

37 *Towards a Common Understanding of the Church*, p. 46.

38 Ibid., p. 49.

39 There had already been Reformed–Orthodox conversations in Romania (from 1964), the United States and Canada (1968) and Hungary (1972). See Lukas Vischer, 'Introduction' to *Agreed Statements from the Orthodox–Reformed Dialogue*, Geneva: WARC, 1998, p. 8.

40 The papers are published in T. F. Torrance, ed., *Theological Dialogue between Orthodox and Reformed Churches*, Edinburgh: Scottish Academic Press, 1985.

'it is only through God that God may be known'.[41] They also make it clear that 'The doctrine of the Holy Trinity expounded here is: One God, Three Persons, not Three Persons, One Nature.'[42] They claim that their statement

> cuts across mistaken polarized views of the doctrine of the Holy Trinity according to which Latin theology moves from the Oneness of God to the three Persons of the Father, the Son and the Holy Spirit, while Greek theology moves from the three Persons of the Father, the Son and the Holy Spirit to the Oneness of God. What is provided by the Agreed Statement of the Orthodox theologians of the East and the Reformed theologians of the West is pre-eminently a Statement on the Triunity of God as Trinity in Unity and Unity in Trinity.[43]

The statement on Christology focuses upon the affirmation in the Nicene Creed that 'it was "for us and our salvation" that the eternal Son of God became flesh, lived, died and rose again'.[44] It is suggested that while the Orthodox set out from the Mystery of the Incarnation understood as encompassing the entire saving economy proclaimed in the Bible, and the Reformed proceed from the scriptural witness to the life, death and resurrection of Jesus, the two approaches are not incompatible. Both sides 'agree that their teaching about Trinity and Incarnation reflects the encounter with the reality of God as revealed in Christ'.[45] The agent in this encounter is the Holy Spirit who, among other things 'brings about the communion of all believers both with the head of the Body of Christ and between themselves'.[46] In the wake of the significant agreements so far reached, discussions have been held since 1998 on the mystery, nature and membership of the Church; baptism, confirmation, chrismation and the apostolicity of the Church; and the holiness of the Church.

The dialogue between the **Alliance and the Oriental Orthodox Churches** began in 1992 and continues. Its objectives are to foster mutual understanding and fellowship between the two families. Christology is a central theme in this dialogue, and in an 'Agreed Statement on Christology' the Formula of Union of AD 433 is declared to be compatible with the Christological doctrines of both dialogue partners. Further,

> Both sides agree in rejecting the teaching which separates or divides the human nature, both soul and body in Christ, from His divine nature or reduces the union of the natures to the level of conjoining. Both sides also agree in rejecting the

---

41 *Agreed Statements*, p. 18.

42 Ibid.

43 Ibid., p. 20.

44 Ibid., p. 23.

45 Ibid., p. 21.

46 Ibid., p. 24.

teaching which confuses the human nature in Christ with the divine nature so that the former is absorbed in the latter and thus ceases to exist.

In offering this statement, we recognize the mystery of God's act in Christ and seek to express that we have shared the same authentic Christological faith in the one incarnate Lord.[47]

A number of other topics have been discussed, among them 'Holy Scripture and Tradition'. In this connection 'Both sides agreed on the normative function of Holy Scripture for the life of the Church... Holy Scripture and its correct interpretation, guided by Tradition, witnesses to the Word of God in our different contexts.'[48] As to mission, while the Reformed participants affirm that 'United by the Spirit to the risen Christ, our participation in the mission of the Triune God flows out in service and witness to the world',[49] their Oriental Orthodox colleagues declare that 'the Church, as the living Body of Christ, constantly called together and renewed by the Holy Spirit, worships the Triune God on behalf of all God's creation. This is mission in its totality.'[50] They do, however, proclaim the Word of God so as to 'bring about and foster the signs of the Rule of God in human history', and they believe that 'The Church's prayer and pastoral care, struggle for justice and search for communion are all vital expressions of her participation in the mission of Jesus Christ, her Lord and Saviour.'[51] Indeed, 'The ultimate form of the Church's mission is to carry the whole creation in all its brokenness and misery before the transforming presence of the Triune God in a perpetual act of praise and thanksgiving.'[52]

In 2001 the first dialogue session took place between the **Alliance and the General Conference of Seventh-Day Adventists**. The report includes a statement of the common ground between the two traditions. Among the points noted are acceptance of 'the Bible as the rule of faith and practice, the supreme witness to God's saving grace in Christ'; the Trinity; God's reconciling work in Christ: 'By the work of Christ God's holiness is honoured and our sins forgiven'; the calling of the Church to proclaim salvation and to work for 'healing, and deliverance from spiritual and economic poverty'. The participants affirm their belief that they 'stand in the succession of those who, through the ages, have faithfully proclaimed the Gospel of Christ'. For them the Lord's Supper

47 *Oriental Orthodox–Reformed Dialogue. The First Four Sessions*, Geneva: WARC, 1998, p. 52.

48 Ibid., p. 53.

49 Ibid., p. 54.

50 Ibid., p. 55.

51 Ibid.

52 Ibid.

is 'integral to the Church's worship and witness', and they acknowledge their debt to the Reformation's biblical emphases upon salvation by grace alone through faith alone in Christ alone.[53]

The report proceeds to tackle the mutual misunderstanding and suspicions which have hitherto marred their relationship. Among clarifications from the Adventist side are that their Church, organized in 1863, has never set dates for the second coming of Jesus; they understand the death of Christ on the cross as providing the once-for-all atonement for sins, and 'Their distinctive view of the high priestly ministry of Christ in the heavenly sanctuary teaches that he is applying the ongoing benefits of his atonement, not adding any value to it.' While Adventists highly prize the writings of Ellen G. White for their counsel, devotional content and biblical reflection, they 'hold firmly to the principle of *sola scriptura*'. Hence all other writings, including Ellen White's, are to be tested by the Bible. Adventists do not teach that they alone will be saved, and while they have been reluctant to engage in political activities designed to challenge societal structures, they 'have always been engaged in social betterment as part of their understanding of the Gospel'.

The Reformed participants were called upon to clarify their position regarding predestination. They replied that predestination is a religious term which is not to be elided with 'determinism', and that 'God's electing grace is not to be construed fatalistically, but in the context of God's undiscriminating love whereby *all* are called to salvation, to which call they make their own, enabled, response.' Along this line the sting can be drawn from the historic Calvinist–Arminian debates, it being understood that the former were seeking to honour God's sovereignty in salvation, the latter to uphold human responsibility before God. Adventist queries concerning the relative lack of interest among the Reformed in eschatology, and the over-emphasis on the part of some Reformed Christians on socio-ethical activities at the expense of Gospel proclamation, were also addressed.

The participants moved to a consideration of mission in relation to the world as it is. The issues of poverty, HIV/AIDS, violence, ecological destruction, religious freedom and gender biases were discussed, and the necessity of raised consciousness in relation to all of these matters was urged

It was recognized that this dialogue session was a learning process for both parties, and the desirability of further discussion on such topics as biblical interpretation, the Sabbath, church discipline and the meaning and significance of Christ's high priestly ministry was noted.

---

[53] The *Report of the International Theological Dialogue between the Seventh-day Adventist Church and the World Alliance of Reformed Churches*, 2002, is available on the internet: www.warc.ch/dt/erl1/22.html

Reception[54]

To begin at the most basic level, the fact must frankly be faced that there are practical difficulties in the way of the reception of dialogue findings. The reports are costly to produce and costly to mail. During my period as theological secretary of the Alliance I wrote two letters every year to general secretaries of member churches and deans or presidents of the nearly 400 theological colleges, seminaries and university faculties with which at that time we had connections. Once a year I wrote to the librarians of all such institutions. I reported on the Alliance's theological work, and normally whenever a dialogue report was to hand I enclosed it. But one cannot ensure that general secretaries will pass reports to the appropriate person, that deans or presidents will ensure that their professors of systematic theology will have access to the reports, or that librarians will actually catalogue and shelve them. (I fear I have visited a number of libraries to which I know I have sent materials only to find no trace of them.) More broadly, the nature of the Alliance is such that its members are under no obligation to receive, implement, or even read the findings of the panels which work on their behalf.

Over and above the practicalities there are contextual, theological and demographic factors which inhibit reception. There are, for example, representatives of some Alliance member churches who feel that bilateral dialogues are a 'Western' hobby far removed from their own concerns. (In fact it would be most encouraging if certain Western churches paid any attention at all to dialogue reports.) This concern has an historical and a practical aspect. To deal with the latter first: it is quite clear, and entirely understandable, that churches whose members live in life-or-death situations—and many do—should regard the digestion of dialogue reports as a luxury for which they have little time. The historical dimension comes to the fore when churches—especially in Africa, Asia and the Pacific—point out that the dialogues are concerned with the healing of divisions whose roots are in the West, and that these divisions have been imposed upon them by missionary endeavour. Thus, for example, during the Alliance's 1992 review of its dialogue programme African representatives 'felt that the dialogues presently going on within the context of WARC are inter-European. They are concerned with issues of theology and practice (praxis) which are not alive in Africa. They seem abstract and largely imposed.'[55] Thus, while they encourage their Western friends to sort these matters out, 'they feel that their agenda is

---

[54] For a variety of views of reception see *Ecumenical Trends*, XV no. 7, July–August 1986; see also L. Vischer, 'The process of "reception" in the ecumenical movement', *Mid-Stream*, XXIII no. 2, 1984, pp. 221-33.

[55] This comment was made before the dialogue with the African Instituted Churches began in 1998, but similar sentiments are expressed from various quarters.

quite different'.[56] A Westerner might, of course, be forgiven for muttering, 'What else could the missionaries do but take out what they had received?' But the more pertinent point is that on the very next page the African representatives declare that 'Traditional denominational distinctions were found to be standing in the way of bi-and/or multilateral "conversations" in Africa.'[57] To the extent that this is so, it would seem that the dialogues are, after all, relevant in Africa, for they have the goal of removing such obstacles. Above all, can we really say that the dialogues are of no relevance so long as, in all the countries of the world, the people of Christ are divided at the table of the Lord? However we have come by the divisions (and we have *all* inherited them from our Christian history, short or long), do they not need to be removed?

The phrase I have just used, 'all the countries of the world', underlines the point that there is more than one way of finding the dialogues irrelevant. There are Reformed Christians in many parts of the world who have a different understanding of the nature of the Church and hence of ecumenism. They emphasize and rejoice in the spiritual unity of the Church invisible and see no great urgency to address the disunity of the Church visible. But as John Whale once cheekily remarked, 'It would be an Irish result if the only discernible mark of the Church were its invisibility.'[58] Again, there are those who take to themselves the label 'conservative evangelical' for whom unity must be in the truth; and since they disagree with 'liberal' or 'ecumenical' Christians on specific doctrinal matters and/or on their understanding of Scripture, they co-operate (or not, as the case may be) only with those of like mind and see no point in bilateral dialogues. But what is the evangel which these Christians wish to conserve? It sometimes seems as if it is a rather individualistic piece of good news, namely, that God sent his Son to die on the Cross in order to save my soul. No doubt he did, but this as part of his sovereign purpose to call out one covenant *people* for his praise and service, uniting them to Christ and therefore to each other as branches of the Vine. If this is what God has done, then the actual disunity of his people is a challenge to be addressed, and bilateral dialogues constitute a sincere effort in this direction. Yet again, in some parts there is a more theologically diverse individualism which manifests itself in a variety of ways. Individuals, under the influence of consumerism, shop around for a church in which they feel 'comfortable' (baneful word!) regardless of theological considerations, while particular local churches and even denominations may be so well blessed with resources of various kinds that they feel no urgent need of fellowship with the wider family of

56 Wilson, ed., *Bilateral Dialogues*, p. 70.

57 Ibid., p. 71.

58 J. S. Whale, *Christian Doctrine*, London: Collins Fontana, 1957, p. 134.

Christians.[59] Perhaps the most straightforward reason for the lack of interest of some member churches in particular dialogues is that the dialogue partner is not present in their region. Even where both are present one partner may be much larger than the other, and this can have an inhibiting effect; and in some cases the partners may be on different sides in political conflicts.[60] In all of these ways, and many more, Reformed Christians may persuade themselves that they have no need of, or are not in a position to take advantage of, the findings of bilateral dialogues. I nevertheless believe that the reports of the bilateral dialogues contain a wealth of material the assimilation of which would make for the strengthening of the witness of Reformed churches in many places, and in some cases would stimulate the taking of practical steps towards closer relations with our friends of other communions. I should like to develop this point in a few

Concluding Reflections

I hope it has become clear, even from the highly selective survey that I have been able to present, that in the bilateral dialogue reports the Alliance and its diverse partners have covered a wide range of doctrinal and practical points. Quite apart from any results in terms of unity on the ground, there is a body of material here which should find its way into appropriate theological courses, not least those attended by Reformed candidates for ministry. Moreover this material should not be siphoned off into optional courses on ecumenism which are so frequently taken only by the 'converted', but should appear in general doctrine courses taken by the majority.

For the most part the reports are written clearly and with conviction: this is not bland 'committee theology'. Indeed, the integrity of the documents is shown not least by the fact that few punches are pulled, and continuing disagreements are honestly recorded. But the overall impression is that on many of the traditionally 'neuralgic' points convergence is apparent and in some cases consensus is reached. It is also quite remarkable, given the diversity of the dialogue teams, that there is such a high degree of consistency between the dialogue reports. It is true, as Karel Blei has shown, that some reports omit what others include (the eldership here, the idea of covenant there) when the topic under

---

[59] For a helpful brief study of individualism in one country see Dennis N. Voskuil, 'Individualism and evangelism in America', *Reformed Review* XLI no. 1, Autumn 1987, pp. 21-28.

[60] These points are noted in *Towards a Common Understanding of the Church*, p. 54.

consideration cried out for their inclusion,[61] but I have found very few cases of one report flatly contradicting another.

The fact must be faced that, for the reasons suggested above, too frequently the dialogue reports lie dormant. If it is odd that some Christians query the very idea of dialogue, it seems still odder that others, officially committed to the goal of manifesting the unity God has granted us all in Christ, do little to harvest the results of dialogue. I am here thinking particularly of the dialogues with our near neighbours. It is a matter for rejoicing that the dialogues with the Lutherans, Methodists and Disciples of Christ have declared that no theological obstacles to full communion exist. Yet on the ground, while some united churches have come into being, elsewhere there has been little movement, despite the fact that in an increasing number of places Reformed Christians already worship jointly with these partners at the local level. Whereas some churches have seized the opportunity of devising a church order in which both paedobaptism and believers' baptism are available as alternatives, it is particularly unfortunate that only twenty-two member churches of the Alliance and Baptist World Alliance responded to the Reformed–Baptist dialogue report in which that possibility was proposed for consideration.[62] All of which causes one to wonder whether a knowledgeable Reformed enthusiast could be found in every member church who would assume the role of monitoring the take-up of dialogue findings and sending feed-back to the Department of Theology in Geneva.

Concerning those whom history has given to be our near neighbours, some of whom are already united with us in some parts of the world,[63] it is not surprising that the dialogue reports concentrate upon particular 'neuralgic' issues—baptism, ministry and the like—and propose practical steps which might be taken to foster full union. This narrowing of concern occurs on the basis of a degree of familiarity with one another such that we do not have to expound the Trinity or Christology to each other. But where the more distant communions are concerned this fundamental theological work has been essential, and its fruit has been significant. But this leads me to express my view that, taking the dialogue reports as a whole, there is one fundamental doctrine in particular which, while it has been frequently alluded to, has not had detailed attention directed to it. I refer to the doctrine of the Christ's atoning work at the Cross. If convergence could be recorded—still better, if consensus could

---

61 Blei, 'The WARC in bilateral dialogue', pp. 7-9.

62 This may not be unconnected with the fact that the largest (and wealthiest) member of the BWA is the Southern Baptist Convention—a body which in recent years has not, to put it mildly, been to the fore in ecumenical endeavour.

63 So that it would have been embarrassing, to say the least, if the Reformed–Methodist report, for example, had concluded that the traditional doctrinal differences between Methodists and ourselves ought still to be church-dividing.

be reached on this issue between the Alliance and its dialogue partners—I suggest that this would place questions of ministry, sacraments and the like in proper perspective. As I have elsewhere asked, 'What are the ecclesiological implications of God's unmerited grace which has accepted even us.'[64] To begin to answer my own question: I believe that one implication would be that we would allow nothing to keep us from fellowship at the table of the Lord with all who by grace are in Christ—and anything which threatened to prevent such fellowship would immediately be perceived and repudiated as sectarian. In the words of the irenic John Howe (1630–1705), 'Without all controversy, the main inlet of all the distractions, confusions, and divisions of the Christian world hath been by adding other conditions of Church communion than Christ hath done.'[65] It is in the light of the reconciliation wrought on the Cross that we see our ecclesiological 'small print' for what it is.[66]

---

64 Sell, *A Reformed, Evangelical, Catholic Theology*, p. 240.

65 J. Howe, *The Works of John Howe, M.A., Sometime Fellow of Magdalen College, Oxon*, ed. Henry Rogers, London: The Religious Tract Society, 1862–63, V, p. 226.

66 Information concerning the ecumenical dialogues in which the World Alliance of Reformed Churches has been, or is, engaged may be found at www.warc.ch/dt. A bibliography by Odair Pedroso Mateus, the current Theological Secretary, concerning the Alliance and the ecumenical movement is shortly to appear.

CHAPTER 11

The Holy Spirit and Ecumenism: Some Catholic Ruminations of a Reformed Theologian

From time to time I have had occasion gently to remark that one of the advantages of the Reformed family is that it is not named after anyone.[1] The remote cause of the tradition is the Bible; the proximate cause is the activity of a galaxy of theologians among whom Calvin was prominent but by no means alone. Zwingli, Farel and many others, including John Owen in England, shaped the tradition in a variety of ways. Their overall objective was the reform of the one Church of Christ, and they managed to maintain a considerable degree of doctrinal family resemblance in their sixty or so confessions of faith—something much assisted by the amount of theological commuting across Europe which went on in those times.

Not least among earlier representatives of the Reformed family was Zacharias Ursinus (1534–83), the third generation Reformer who was largely responsible for the *Heidelberg Catechism* of 1563.[2] We may set out by noting the juxtaposition of topics in questions 53 and 54 of this the most pastorally framed work of its kind:

> Q. 53. What do you believe concerning the Holy Ghost?
>
> A. First, that He is co-eternal God with the Father and the Son. Secondly, that He is also given to me, makes me by a true faith partaker of Christ and all His benefits, comforts me, and shall abide with me forever.
>
> Q. 54. What do your believe concerning the Holy Catholic Church?
>
> A. That out of the whole human race, from the beginning of the world to its end, the Son of God, by His Spirit and Word, gathers, protects, and preserves for Himself in

---

1 It is not denied that some Anglicans and some Baptists espouse Reformed (generally Calvinistic) doctrine. Here, however, I have in mind those whose polity places them within the Presbyterian, Congregational and United folds. While not all Reformed churches are members of the World Alliance of Reformed Churches (Presbyterian and Congregational), 215 churches embracing some 75 million Christians are.

2 For Ursinus see Derk Visser, *Zacharias Ursinus, the Reluctant Reformer: His Life and Times*, New York, United Church Press, 1983.

> the unity of the true faith and unto everlasting life, a chosen community; and that I am, and forever shall remain, a living member of the same.[3]

These questions and answers on the Spirit and the Church appear in the section headed, 'God the Holy Ghost'. This arrangement of material makes it as clear as anything could that it is by the Spirit that believers are made, and that being made they are called into the fellowship of the Church which, far from being a human society of the ordinary sort, is a divine creation. It is, moreover, one: there is no suggestion that there is more than one Church.

There, in a nutshell, is the classical Reformed position on the relation between the Holy Spirit and ecumenism insofar as the latter concerns the Church. But we know that ecumenism concerns the whole inhabited earth. What is the relation of Church and Spirit to this? This is a question to which we shall return in due course.

In my own attempts at theologizing I have found it a good discipline to devise one-sentence statements of significant doctrinal points. Thus, on the Spirit and the Church I have written as follows:

> By God the Holy Spirit I mean the fatherly God of holy love whom we know in the victorious Christ of the Bible, as generously active in the world; as life-givingly active in us; as drawing out and enabling our response of faith, love and service; as uniting us to Christ and therefore to each other in his Church; as ever renewing and refining our life in the world; and as holding us in fellowship with himself eternally.[4]

> On the ground of the finished work of Christ the Son, the Father graciously and freely calls out by the Spirit a people for his praise and service; he enables their confession of Christ's lordship, and in drawing them to himself, he gives them to one another in a fellowship in which all barriers of race, sex, and class have been broken down; this people, whose membership encompasses heaven and earth, we call the church catholic.[5]

I submit that these affirmations, though clumsy, are at least trinitarian; that the Cross is foundational to them, and that the penultimate clause of the second is couched in terms which are influenced by our contemporary context, which is not that of old Heidelberg.

Though not, I trust, of an authoritarian disposition, I should be puzzled by any Christian who could not agree with me thus far. But if God the

---

3 See Thomas F. Torrance, ed., *The School of Faith. Catechisms of the Reformed Church*, London: James Clarke, 1959, p. 78.

4 Alan P. F. Sell, *The Spirit Our Life* [vol. 3 of my *Doctrine and Devotion* series], Shippensberg, PA, Ragged Edge Press, 2000, p. 1.

5 Alan P. F. Sell, 'Reformed identity: a non-issue of catholic significance', *Reformed Review*, LIV no. 1, Autumn 2000, p. 19.

Holy Spirit has done his Church-convoking work in the way proposed, I am still more puzzled by those who, by adding ecclesiastical, doctrinal or ethical small print to this Gospel after the fashion of the Galatian heretics, refuse full communion to their fellow Christians and fall into a sectarianism which divides what God in Christ has made one by the Spirit. I suggest that Christians and churchly bodies fall into sectarian mode when they say or imply, 'Unless or until you accept my/our formulation of major Christian doctrines (and I/we shall determine which the major ones are), and my/our church order, I/we cannot have full/any communion with you.' My thesis is that those who are, by God's free grace, united to Christ as branches of the vine, cannot but be united with one another; and if they are inhibited from manifesting this unity in any way—especially at the Lord's table (political and other circumstances being favourable)—something sectarian is going on. The question is not the quantitative one, 'How many doctrines, and which ones, must we all assent to before we can sit together at the Lord's table'?[6] It is, 'Has God the Holy Spirit called out one people for his praise and service'? If he has, then all who confess Christ as Lord and Saviour ought to find themselves around the Lord's table together.

Let me make it quite clear that in speaking as I do it is not my intention to convey the impression that I am behind my Reformed fortifications hurling brickbats at everyone else. On the contrary, although the Reformed have generally managed to regard one another as Christians and have not, except for church disciplinary purposes, excluded people from the Lord's table, no Christian world communion has been more adept at fostering inner-family sectarianism than they.[7] We have divided from one another over points of doctrine, some of them so infinitessimal that, for example, a Reformed resident of Grand Rapids once declared that to understand some of our divisions it is necessary to have been born within fifty miles of that fair city; we have divided over biblical interpretation, liturgy, life-style issues, political questions, and as a result of that overweening pride which delights in winning power struggles. In all of these ways we have given the lie to our profession of catholicity and to our testimony to what the Father by the Son through

---

6 As the pioneer English Reformed ecumenist, Richard Baxter declared in 1654, 'I knew how ticklish a Business the Enumeration of Fundmaentals was'. See *Reliquiae Baxterianae*, ed. M. Sylvester, 1696, II, p. 197, para. 51. See further, Alan P. F. Sell, *Commemorations. Studies in Christian Thought and History*, Calgary, University of Calgary Press and Cardiff: University of Wales Press, 1993; reprinted Eugene, OR: Wipf & Stock, 1998, ch. 2.

7 In our better-behaved moments we have been active in ecumenical endeavour. See, for example, Alan P. F. Sell, *A Reformed, Evangelical, Catholic Theology. The Contribution of the World Alliance of Reformed Churches, 1875–1982*, (1991), Eugene, OR, Wipf & Stock, 1998, ch. 4.

the Spirit has actually done. The Reformed family, at least as much as any other Christian communion, needs ever to live out the truth that it is through 'the secret energy of the Spirit' that 'we come to enjoy Christ and all his benefits'.[8] But let us examine, as even-handedly as possible, some particular aspects of the Spirit-ecumenism relationship.

I

To say that we discern the mind of God by the Spirit through the Scriptures within the fellowship (by which I mean those with us now, those around the world, and those gone before) is to articulate a characteristically Reformed sentiment. To admit that all too often we have driven wedges between these three, thereby promoting biblical fundamentalism on the one side and individualistic mysticisms on the other is simply to face facts. But at our best the Reformed have been able sincerely to answer the following questions in Calvin's *Geneva Catechism* of 1541:

> 301. M. Where do you find [God's] Word?
>
> C. It is comprised for us in the Holy Scriptures.
>
> 302. How are we to use it in order to profit by it?
>
> C. By receiving it with the full consent of our conscience, as truth come down from heaven, submitting ourselves to it in right obedience, loving it with a true affection by having it imprinted on our hearts, we may follow it entirely and conform ourselves to it.
>
> 303. M. Is this all within our own power?
>
> C. None of it; but God works them in us in this way by His Holy Spirit.
>
> 304. M. But are we not to take trouble and be diligent, and zealously strive by hearing and reading its teaching, as it is declared to us?
>
> C. Yes, indeed: first each one of us in particular ought to study it: and above all, we are frequently to attend the sermons in which this Word in expounded in the Assembly of the Christians.[9]

Admittedly Calvin, a child of his time, proceeds to elevate the minister as *the* expounder and interpreter of the Word—we are quite a long way,

---

8 J. Calvin, *Institutes of the Christian Religion*, trans. Ford Lewis Battles, 2 vols, Philadelphia: Westminster Press, 1960, III.i.1.

9 See Torrance, *The School of Faith*, pp. 52-53.

here, from free-ranging house groups; but the principle that hearing and receiving the Word of God is not an individualistic business but an ecclesial one is firmly established.

So determined is Calvin to underscore the fact that the Spirit does not speak contrary to, or argue with, the Scriptures, that he declares, 'We choke out the light of God's Spirit if we cut ourselves off from his Word.'[10] But just as the individual believer needs to hear and receive the Word, so does the Church. The Church does not control the Word; on the contrary, it is called out by the Spirit through the Word, and it ever stands under the mercy and judgment inherent in the Gospel of God's grace. This is the burden of Calvin's complaint against the Roman Church of his day, namely, that it believes that it cannot err even when it teaches what is apart from the Word.[11] He is equally opposed to those fanatical 'rascals' who think that they have direct communications from the Spirit apart from the Word. On the contrary, the Spirit does not have 'the task of inventing new and unheard-of revelations...but of sealing our minds with that very doctrine which is commended by the gospel'.[12] Calvin famously asserts that the Scriptures do not move or persuade us apart from the inner witness or testimony of the Holy Spirit.[13] Scholars have long debated what exactly Calvin meant by this. Was he simply a harbinger of John Wesley, who declared that 'the testimony of the Spirit is an inward impression on the soul, whereby the Spirit of God directly witnesses to my spirit, that I am a child of God...'?[14] Not altogether, for Calvin's focus is Christological: the Spirit witnesses to Christ, whereas Wesley's, as befits the expositor of Romans 8:16, 'The Spirit itself beareth witness with our spirit, that we are the children of God', is anthropological. Calvin cites Paul (2 Cor. 3:6) in support of his view that the letter of Scripture 'is dead, and the law of the Lord slays its readers where it is both cut off from Christ's grace...and, leaving the heart untouched, sounds in the ears alone. But if through the Spirit it is really branded upon hearts, if it shows forth Christ, it is the word of life...'.[15] With regard to this new life P. T. Forsyth wrote,

---

10 J. Calvin, *Treatises Against the Anabaptists and Against the Libertines*, trans. B. J. Farley, Grand Rapids, MI: Eerdmans, 1982, p. 56. See further, I. John Hesselink, *Governed and Guided by the Spirit. A key issue in Calvin's doctrine of the Holy Spirit*, in Heiko A. Oberman, *et al.*, (eds.), *Reformiertes Erbe. Festschrift für Gottfiried W. Locher zu seinem 80. Geburtstag*, Zurich, Theologischer Verlag, 1992, pp. 161-71.

11 Calvin, *Institutes*, IV.viii.13.

12 Ibid., I.ix.1.

13 Cf. ibid., I.vii.4, and many other places.

14 J. Wesley, *Sermons on Several Occasions*, (1944), London, Epworth Press, 1946, p. 115.

15 Calvin, *Institutes*, I.ix.3.

> We are raised from our death of sin not simply by the preaching of Christ's resurrection, but by the same action of the same Spirit that raised Christ from the dead... The old gospel, preached with spirit, makes an impression; when preached with the Holy Spirit it makes regeneration.[16]

So we come to our first set of mirror images, which seem to manipulate the Spirit and annexe the Word with implicitly if not explicitly sectarian consequences. Consider first John Henry Newman in Roman Catholic mode. He invites us to sing:

> And I hold in veneration
>   For the sake of [Christ] alone,
> Holy Church as His creation,
>   And her teachings as his own.

Behind these words lie convictions concerning the Magisterium, and, notwithstanding that Vatican II documents, teach that the Spirit through the Word gives the Church what it must say, the Irish Jesuit Robert Nash can still say that *the* teacher is the Catholic Church, and that God 'promises that His Holy Spirit will be with her, endorsing her words'.[17] We have already noted Calvin's objection to the implicit sectarianism of the idea that the Church is above the Spirit, or that God's truth is in any sense controlled, by the Church.

For a Protestant mirror image we may turn to those conservative evangelicals who also seem to have a firm handle on the truth of God. One of them, Bruce Nicholls, was deeply disturbed at the 1975 Nairobi Assembly of the World Council of Churches. He felt that the 'loss of the authority of Scripture as normative produced a hermeneutical crisis'; that 'The cultural context rather than the biblical message dominated the addresses of all the plenary speakers' with the exception of that by Bishop Arias; and he insisted that 'The New Testament teaches that unity is always unity in truth and faithfulness to the apostolic witness. It warns against the spirit of anti-Christ and denounces false doctrines.'[18] The problem here is that while it sounds fine to speak of unity in the truth (and I am not at all opposed to clarity of doctrinal statement), we should never forget that we are saved by God's sovereign grace, not by commitment to our little accounts of it. Christianity is a religion, a Way, more than it is any system—least of all mine. It is a Way on which all

---

16 P. T. Forsyth, *Faith, Freedom and the Future*, (1912), London, Independent Press, 1955, pp. 30, 33. Cf. Sell, *The Spirit Our Life*, pp. 9-10.

17 R. Nash, *The Sunday Press*, Dublin, 8 February 1981. Cf. Sell, *Commemorations*, pp. 8-14.

18 B. Nicholls, 'Nairobi 1975: a crisis of faith for the WCC', *Themelios*, I no. 3, Summer 1976, pp. 67, 69.

those who confess Christ as Lord and Saviour are fellow pilgrims. All of which is to say that while our primary, given unity and identity are in Christ who is, indeed, the Truth, our doctrinal accounts of what this comes to are fallible and open to correction as we gather in fellowship under the Word, seeking the guidance of the Spirit. I therefore see warning lights when so able a Reformed thinker as Richard Mouw writes of doctrinal formulations, 'the interpretations...must be agreed upon before we can begin to talk about "our unity in Christ"'.[19] Similarly, Donald MacLean of the Free Church of Scotland argued that 'Unity in the faith', by which he meant doctrinal accord, 'is the essence of real unity.'[20] What then so frequently happens is that Christian groups elevate their favoured formulae into terms of fellowship. If we do this we have, once more, taken the sectarian route. The most conservative Christian cannot be unaware of the fact that there are, for example, absolute inerrantists who get into sundry intellectual contortions as they endeavour to show that everything the Bible asserts—its apparent history no less than its apparent science—is to be literally construed; and relative inerrantists who affirm only that the Bible is inerrant respecting its major doctrinal claims (and then further sub-divide over which doctrinal claims are *really* the major ones). Nor can it be denied that these issues have been church-dividing. I cannot resist the conclusion that those conservative evangelicals (and I am well aware of the slipperiness of all such labels[21]) who withhold themselves from ecumenical affairs on the ground that unity is in the truth and we do not all agree on it, have elevated their chosen interpretations above that *evangel* at whose heart is the *fact* that those who have been constrained by the Spirit to confess the Lordship of Christ are already one—whether they like it or not.[22] Furthermore, such persons seem to have forgotten that they are dominically obliged to manifest their unity in Christ, and to love as they have been loved—starting with those in the household of faith. If they reply, 'But *x*, *y* and *z* are not truly of the household of faith, or are only, as it were, "below stairs" in the household of faith', then they have become a sectarian mirror image of Christians from whom they normally regard themselves as widely separated. For my part, I find myself on the

---

19 R. J. Mouw, 'Rethinking ecumenism', *The Reformed Journal*, XXXIII no. 9, September 1983, p. 2.

20 D. MacLean, quoted by G. N. M. Collins, *Donald MacLean, D.D.*, Edinburgh, Lindsay, 1944, p. 62.

21 See Alan P. F. Sell, *Theology in Turmoil. The Roots, Course and Significance of the Conservative–Liberal Debate in Modern Theology*, (1986), Eugene, OR, Wipf & Stock, 1998.

22 I am well aware that for egalitarian reasons some Christians do not like such 'Lordship' language. But our Lord takes a towel and does slave's work (John 13). Moreover, we shall be hard put to explain to the 'world' that it has not understood what true lordship is if we forsake the term. See further Sell, *Commemorations*, p. 371 n. 87.

side of the seventeenth-century Reformed ecumenist *par excellence*, Richard Baxter who, in the sixth of ten 'directions' prefixed to his book, *The Saint's Everlasting Rest*, wrote,

> He that is not a son of peace is not a son of God. All other sins destroy the Church consequentially; but Division and Separations demolish it directly... Many Doctrinal differences must be tolerated in a Church: And why? But for Unitie and Peace?[23]

None of which is to deny that Bruce Nicholls rightly sounds a warning note concerning the way in which context can come to dominate doctrinal content: and with this I come to my third mirror image. The theologian Leanne Van Dyk describes a meeting of theological educators thus:

> We were reflecting on the now familiar fact that, for some people, the doctrine of the atonement seems like very bad news—that God would, for the sake of the world, require the death of a beloved Son. This deep biblical paradox of the cross is profoundly repugnant to some. Yet it is just as profoundly liberating to others. And it's not always easy to predict what the response will be. Some privileged, educated women theologians in North America, for instance, recoil against traditionally stated atonement theories. Yet, they have not been the victims of horrendous social crises such as war, famine, torture or displacement. Women theologians in Uganda, however, report that traditionally stated atonement theories are deeply liberating. Such language, for them, is good news. Here is just one example of the thoroughly contextual nature of theological language.

It is not very helpful, then, for one context to say to another context, 'Your way of stating this central Christian claim is not right. My way of stating it is right.' Instead, it is helpful to realize that the same statement of a doctrine can be damaging in one context and liberating in another...[24]

Leanne Van Dyk is clearly not over impressed by the pontificatings of some women theologians who, as we might put it, sit at ease in the Ivy League. But she is too gentle with them in leaving the relativistic impression that since we all have differing contexts the language we use is appropriate provided that it reflects that diversity. But this is to risk elevating the particular context above the biblical content. I have heard theologians say, and I have read their statements to the effect, that 'We cannot have dealings with a God who is a child-batterer.' It is difficult not to believe that here context too uncritically prevails. While it cannot be

---

[23] R. Baxter, *The Saint's Everlasting Rest: or, a Treatise of the Blessed State of the Saints in their Enjoyment of God in Glory, etc.*, London: Rob. White, 1650.

[24] L. Van Dyk, *Growing Up Theologically* (Theology and Worship Occasional Paper, 15), Louisville, Presbyterian Church (USA), 2002, p. 5.

denied that grotesque atonement theories are still propagated by some preachers (not least on American television), a half educated radical theologian would know sufficient Latin to understand that to be radical (*radix*) is to go to the root; and in this case the root is 2 Corinthians 5:19: '*God* was *in Christ* reconciling the world to himself.' Whatever else that means, it is perverse to suppose that it means that a wrathful Father batters his obedient, innocent Son. It is sad that some break fellowship with the rest of us on the ground of their contextually prejudiced readings of Scripture. It is not falsely pious arrogance to say that they need the mutual corrections of ecclesial fellowship, and it is not altogether cheeky to suggest that the rest of us need to have them where we can see them.[25]

So much for the need to hold together Spirit, Word and fellowship, and for the sectarian pitfalls into which Christians of many different stripes may tumble if they privatize the faith and elevate their own favoured stances into terms of fellowship.

II

In the light of the position now outlined let us look more directly at the ecclesiastical aspects of the Spirit-Church relationship. The Church comprises those who are 'saints by calling' (Rom. 1:7). In addressing his call God the Holy Spirit uses means, normally the preaching of the Word. As the Congregational *Savoy Declaration of the Institution of Churches, and the Order appointed in them by Jesus Christ* (1658) has it:

> Those thus called (through the Ministery of the Word by his Spirit) he commandeth to walk together in particular Societies or Churches, for their mutual edification, and the due performance of that publique Worship, which he requireth of them in this world.[26]

With regard to this preaching of the Word, that wisest and pithiest of Puritans, Thomas Watson, rightly pointed out that 'The ministers of God are only the pipes and organs; it is the Spirit blowing in them, that effectually changes the heart.'[27] The saints are those who are accounted right before God by grace through faith, they partake of new life in

---

[25] It is not inconceivable that some may quite mistakenly, in *ad hominem* fashion, find me 'anti-women' in view of the above remarks. What I *am*, of course, is *pro* expository integrity. For some further remarks on the current propensity on the part of some for devising new sectarianisms on the basis of theological methods or ethical stances, see Sell, *Commemorations*, pp. 49-57.

[26] Appended to A. G. Matthews, ed., *The Savoy Declaration of Faith and Order 1658*, London, Independent Press, 1959, p. 121.

[27] T. Watson, *A Divine Cordial*, (1663), Grand Rapids, MI: Sovereign Grace Union, 1971, p. 78.

Christ, and they are both sanctified now, in the sense of being 'separated unto the Lord', and on the path to entire sanctification—a path from which they frequently stray owing to what the writer to the Hebrews calls 'the sin which doth so easily beset us' (Heb. 12:1).

But, to repeat, God's gracious call is not to individualism, but into a household of faith, a body with many limbs, a covenant people. The fellowship of the Church worldwide and eternal is entered locally. One cannot be a Christian 'in general': to be a Christian is to be of the visible company of Christ somewhere, and there is no other way of belonging to the Church catholic and eternal. As John Owen remarked in the seventeenth century,

> Let none...pretend that they love the brethren in general, and love the people of God, and love the saints, while their love is not fervently exercised towards those who are in the same church society with them. Christ...will try your love at the last day by your deportment in that church wherein you are.[28]

The initiative in the call to sainthood is always God's, for the Church is a divine creation. We neither create it nor 'join' it unaided. Only by the gracious prompting and drawing of God the Holy Spirit are we enabled to climb down from our prideful thrones and rendered willing. Our response to God's gracious approach, though genuinely ours, is a product of the new life granted to us; it is not the condition of it. All who by grace live this life comprise the Church catholic.

If all of this is true, our manifold sectarianisms, many of which take the form of denominational small print which we add to the terms of the Gospel, are utterly out of place and immediately under judgment. As the Puritan Presbyterian/Independent[29] John Howe declared long ago in his reply to Edward Stillingfleet's 'Sermon on Schism', 'Without all controversy the main inlet of all the distractions, confusions, and divisions of the Christian world hath been by adding other conditions of Church communion than Christ hath done.'[30] Consider the following examples.

In view of the careful New Testament case which my revered teacher, T. W. Manson made against the Anglican Kenneth Kirk's view of apostolic succession, it ought no longer to be possible to claim that the

---

28 J. Owen, 'Sermon XXI', *Gospel charity*, in *The Works of John Owen*, William H. Goold, ed., (1850–53), reprinted London, Banner of Truth Trust, 1968, IX, p. 262.

29 This awkward labelling reminds us of the fluidity of pre-nineteenth-century ecclesial tendencies, institutionalized 'denominations' as we know them being creatures of the last two hundred years only.

30 Henry Rogers, ed., *The Works of John Howe*, London, 1862–23, V, p. 226. Stillingfleet was the bishop of Worcester who pursued John Locke on a number of issues. See Alan P. F. Sell, *John Locke and the Eighteenth-Century Divines*, Cardiff, University of Wales Press, 1997.

apostles handed on the kind of authority which Kirk's theory of ordination required to bear it out.[31] Similarly, in the wake of many historical studies which have drawn attention to the murkiness which envelops certain aspects of the linear theory of apostolic succession, and the admission of many that the alleged imparting of *potestas* to the ordained is a notion unknown before medieval times, it ought to be difficult to sustain those positions on ministry and sacraments which exclude some who are in Christ from the Lord's table, and which deny to their own kind the opportunity of accepting the *Lord's* invitation to his table in places where the minister's ordination is deemed—blasphemy of blasphemies—irregular or invalid. Bernard Lord Manning's words in *Essays in Orthodox Dissent* (required reading for all ecumenists) thunder down the years:

> The grace of God...needs no legal machinery to protect it... The Supper of the Lord is either celebrated or not celebrated. The Body and the Blood of Christ are spiritually received or they are not received. We simply do not know what an irregular or an invalid sacrament is. We do not deal in percentages with the grace of God... When we can botanise about the Burning Bush, either it has ceased to burn or it has been consumed...[32]

Hence the reply of John Howe, who had been ordained by Presbyterians during the Interregnum, to his friend Seth Ward, Bishop of Exeter:

> Why, pray Sir, said the Bishop to him, what hurt is there in being twice Ordain'd? Hurt, my Lord, says Mr. Howe; the thought is shocking; it hurts my Understanding; it is an absurdity: For nothing cane have two Beginnings. I am sure, said he, I am a Minister of Christ...and I can't begin again to be a Minister.[33]

Had Howe been trained under twentieth-century analytical philosophers, he would have designated 're-ordination', like 're-baptism' and 'unicorn', a non-instantiated concept. Yet despite the fact that the so-called ecumenical century is now behind us, the offending positions are

---

[31] See K. Kirk, ed., *The Apostolic Ministry*, London, Hodder and Stoughton, 1946, p. 40; T. W. Manson, *The Church's Ministry*, London, Hodder and Stoughton, 1948, ch. 2; Alan P. F. Sell, *Aspects of Christian Integrity*, (1990), Eugene, OR, Wipf & Stock, 1998, pp. 93-97.

[32] B. L. Manning, *Essays in Orthodox Dissent*, (1939), London, Independent Press, 1953, pp. 114, 116-17. Concerning 'irregularity': it is not, of course, denied that principles of church order govern the conduct of the Lord's Supper in Reformed churches among others. Manning is opposed to those who, in sectarian fashion, question the sacramental practice of *others* on the ground that it falls outside the critics' own approved procedures.

[33] Edmund Calamy, *Memoirs of the Life of the Late Rev. Mr. John Howe, M.A.*, 1724, p. 39.

still maintained; they divide the saints at the Lord's table; they cause heartache on all sides to those who by God's sovereign grace have been called out by the Spirit to be his one Church. Above all, they repudiate significant aspects of the gracious work of God's Spirit.

Two memories of mine may further illuminate the point. First, although for some years now the Church of England has welcomed to the Lord's table persons of good standing from other Christian traditions (though not all Anglicans will move in the opposite direction, notwithstanding the fact, as I understand it, that there is no canon law preventing it), in the early years of my ministry it was not so. Once a year the Anglicans would say, 'Because the Week of Prayer for Christian Unity is approaching, and because the bishop approves, we can arrange a joint service of holy communion, provided that it takes place on our premises and we conduct it.' I quite understood the kindly spirit in which this sort of thing was said, but I nonetheless found it offensive on the ground that it is not for the Church of England to decide when the Lord's Supper can be ecumenical, because it always is.

My second memory concerns the second phase of the international Roman Catholic–Reformed dialogue, which it was my privilege and pleasure to serve. It was the custom, during every dialogue session for the Roman Catholics to celebrate Mass, and for the Reformed to organize a service of Word and Sacrament. Our Roman Catholic colleagues would attend our service, but not share in the sacrament. On one occasion our preacher, one of the participating Reformed theologians, took as his text Paul's words, 'Because there is one loaf, we, though many, are one body; for it is one loaf of which we all partake' (1 Cor. 10:17). He announced the text, looked directly at the Roman Catholic participants, and began his sermon with the words, 'But we don't, do we?' It was a painful experience all round. The fact that we do not partake together is a denial of our catholicity and a slight upon what God the Holy Spirit has done in calling out his one Church.[34]

---

[34] One way of describing what I am attempting in this chapter is to say that I am advocating an exercise in lateral thinking on the part of Christians. I have lost count of the number of times in ecumenical discussion when the stumbling block has been the plea, 'Until we agree on what is happening at the Lord's Supper, and who [apart from Christ] is entitled to preside at it, it would be dishonest to advocate inter-communion.' This, anthropocentrically, places the emphasis upon our understanding as supplying the criterion for discerning what we may responsibly do. (And is it not passing strange that sometimes those who have most to say about the *mysteries* of the faith seem to know exactly what is, or is not, happening at the Lord's table?) My recommendation is that we start somewhere else—in fact, from what God in Christ has already done by the Spirit. He has called out *one* Church comprising all in heaven and on earth who are 'in Christ'. To be engrafted into the Vine by God's grace is to be related to all the other members (whether we like it or not). This being so, the desire to honour what God has done by

But lest the mistaken impression be gained that those only who take the label 'catholic' to themselves have work to do in this connection, let me remind you of those Strict and Particular Baptists, who require believer's baptism as a term of fellowship, and who fence the Lord's table against those who have not received it. As Donald MacLeod of the Free Church of Scotland has written, 'To practise close communion or to insist that those who join us from other churches must do so as novices is in effect to excommunicate the rest of Christendom.'[35] Here, as elsewhere, mirror images are in view once more.

Again, there is more than a tendency in some Pentecostal/charismatic circles to make the capacity for speaking in tongues the sign of true Christian status. This attitude is based upon the view that Spirit-baptism is a second blessing distinct from conversion, whereas the teaching of Paul is that 'In the one Spirit we were all brought into the one body by baptism' (1 Cor. 12:13). It is not, of course, denied that some traditional local churches of many denominations manifest little of the power and joy of the Spirit. Old William Jay, who ministered for sixty-two years at Argyle Congregational Church, Bath, was right: 'To deny the influences of the Spirit is to relax the energy of the Gospel, and turn the church into a valley of dry bones.'[36] Nevertheless, as Hugo Meynell has pointed out, 'The corruptions of institutions, like the poor, are always with us; so are the ingredients for a romantic but superficial pneumatology.'[37] But it is a false step, in our enthusiasm for things pneumatic, to divide along charismatic lines what God *by the Spirit* has made one.

The notorious claim in the Vatican text, *Dominus Iesus*, that 'the ecclesial communities which have not preserved the valid [there is that word again!] Episcopate and the genuine integral substance of the Eucharistic mystery are not Churches in the proper sense',[38] is among the more recent examples of that sectarian spirit which denies, or seeks to modify, the work of God's free Spirit. I have written on this matter elsewhere,[39] and I here content myself with pronouncing my verdict on this sorry episode: a significant ecumenical step forward would be taken

---

gathering in fellowship at the Lord's table should take precedence over our limited grasp of what happens during the sacrament. The same motive should judge any propensity on the part of Christians to fence the table in sectarian ways.

35 D. MacLeod, 'Christian unity and evangelical succession', *The Monthly Record of the Free Church of Scotland*, May 1978, p. 92.

36 George Redford and John Angell James, eds, *The Autobiography of William Jay*, (1854), Edinburgh, Banner of Truth Trust, 1974, p. 86.

37 H. Meynell, 'Two directions for pneumatology', *The Irish Theological Quarterly*, XLIX no. 3, 1982, p. 172.

38 *Dominus Iesus*, The Vatican Office of the Doctrine of the Faith, 2000, para. 17.

39 See Alan P. F. Sell, *Testimony and Tradition: Studies in Reformed and Dissenting Thought*, Aldershot: Ashgate, 2005, ch. 13.

if the Pope and his theological advisers could bring themselves even to consider the possibility that in their hands the Church's true catholicity may be under threat, and that there are biblically appropriate ways of manifesting the unity which God has given in Christ by the Spirit which do not require any to embrace the sectarianism of others.[40] All that is required is the joyful recognition of what the gracious God has done for us all in the Cross-Resurrection, and the celebration of this together at the table of the Lord. To the degree that our theory prohibits such celebration we need, in the light of Scripture, to modify or reject it. Failure at this point communicates itself to others as arrogance, and protestations to the effect that despite our lack of episcopacy we of the Reformed family, for example, 'are, by Baptism, incorporated in Christ and thus are in a certain communion, albeit imperfect, with the Church' however well-intentioned, come across as patronizing nonsense (or invite the slang response, big deal!), for to be 'incorporated in Christ'[41] by God's sovereign grace is precisely and exclusively what suffices for full Christian fellowship. Accordingly, the sooner the ecclesiastical obstacles to such fellowship are removed, the better. If my language seems strong at this point it is not primarily because many of my own tradition feel hurt, despair or irritation on reading the offending paragraph in an official document of one of our dialogue partners. It is because the qualification in the last phrase quoted seems to minimize what God the Holy Spirit has done in calling out his Church. We may not deal in percentages of the grace of God.

In the light of the discussion so far I should like to utter three cautionary words. First, if, as I argued earlier, the Church, while it proclaims the Word, cannot control the Word, neither can it control or command the Spirit:

> the Church must continually confess her recognition that the Holy Spirit cannot be domesticated or kept within prescribed channels. It is ecclesiastical self-idolatry to regard the Holy Spirit as the essential substance of the Church, submerged in and identified without residue with the Church actual. The Church is ever tempted to make God, in effect, a *deus ex machina*, a piece of impressive stage-property, ready to her hand in the wings to lend colour to the action. The Church of the Spirit always has her east-window open to new light, new calls, from the living Word; a Church which holds herself open to be continually reformed.[42]

Secondly, and similarly, while it is true that Christ is the *one* Lord of the one Church (something which in my tradition, for example, entails a

---

40 Cf. n. 34 above.

41 *Dominus Iesus*, para. 17.

42 Glynmor John, 'The doctrine of the Holy Spirit in our ecclesiology', *The Congregational Quarterly*, XXXIV no. 1, January 1956, pp. 15-16.

witness against church–state establishment);[43] and while it is true that the risen and ascended Lord is, by the Spirit, alive in the midst of his people, Christ is not to be identified with the Church which is his body. To put it otherwise, while the Church is called to be about its Lord's business in the world, it is inaccurate to regard it as an extension or continuation of the Incarnation, as many Christians—not least the Reformed Christians of the Mercersburg tradition—do.[44] Even the pioneer Congregational ecumenist, A. E. Garvie, slipped up at this point. Most of what he says is entirely to the point, but note the sentence I have italicized:

> The Church (the ideal and the actual, the total community and the local congregation) is essentially one because Christ is one, because the Father Whom He brings to men, and to Whom He brings men as His children, is one, because the Spirit Whom He imparts to all, united to Himself by faith, is one. The unity of the Church is no less of its essence than of the essence of God Himself. *As the body of Christ the Church continues His incarnation in the world*; it is His voice, hands, feet, to fulfil God's redemptive purpose in Him. As the Church is the community (*koinonia*) of the Holy Spirit, not only is the Holy Spirit 'the common possession' of all believers, but they are thereby made one in the fellowship of the Spirit.[45]

Had P. T. Forsyth not been in his grave for eight years when Garvie wrote the offending sentence we may confidently suspect that the fur would have flown between him and his colleague. For concerning the Church Forsyth thundered: 'That which owes itself to a rebirth cannot be the prolongation of the ever sinless.'[46] No doubt we may, and frequently do, speak of the Church as called to continue Christ's work in the world. But we cannot replicate his saving work, and we are not sinless as he was. As the German Reformed theologian J. H. A. Bomberger insisted, by regeneration we 'become Christians, but we are not made Christs.'[47]

Thirdly, we cannot rest content with the view of those—some of them Reformed, and some of them from that branch of the Reformed family whose ecclesiology turns on the concept of the *visible* saints[48]—who suppose that since the Church invisible is already one, we need not concern ourselves over much with the disunity of the Church visible. In

---

43 See, for example, Sell, *Testimony and Tradition*, ch. 11.

44 See, for example, ibid., ch. 8.

45 A. E. Garvie, 'The Free Churches in England', in James Marchant, ed., *The Reunion of Christendom*, London, Cassell, 1929, pp. 132-33.

46 P. T. Forsyth, *The Church and the Sacraments*, (1917), London, Independent Press, 1947, p. 83.

47 J. H. A. Bomberger, 'Regeneration', *Proceedings of the Second General Council of the Presbyterian Alliance*, Philadelphia, 1880, p. 552.

48 See Alan P. F. Sell, *Saints: Visible, Orderly and Catholic: The Congregational Idea of the Church*, Geneva, World Alliance of Reformed Churches, and Allison Park, PA: Pickwick Publications, 1986.

the teasing words of John Whale, 'it would be an Irish result if the only discernible mark of the Church were its invisibility'.[49] There is a way of glorying in the fact that we are 'All one in Christ Jesus' which feels no distress at the divided table, and sees no need to confront the challenge of manifesting the Church's unity 'that the world may believe...' (John 17).

III

As I remarked at the outset, no consideration of the Holy Spirit and ecumenism would be complete without some consideraton of the Spirit in relation to 'the whole inhabited earth'. As far as I know there is widespread acceptance among Christians of the following view expressed in the Congregational *Declaration of Faith* of 1967. Concerning the Holy Spirit it is affirmed that

> His gracious presence is not confined to the Church; for even when the Spirit is not understood in relation to Jesus Christ, where his presence is undiscerned, where his very existence is denied, there too God works perpetually in the Holy Spirit to enlarge the possibilities of human life and to open the way for faith and sonship.[50]

Nor would Calvin have us forget 'those most excellent benefits of the divine Spirit, which he distributes to whomever he wills, for the common good of mankind'.[51]

Before, however, we become too excited by Reformed generosity on this point, let us not overlook the fact that there are tendencies pulling in the opposite direction among some Reformed authors. On another day and in another place Calvin himself declared that 'Scripture teaches that none but the elect are led by the Spirit of God'.[52] Again, in our own time G. S. Hendry argued that 'the witness of the New Testament to the gift of the Spirit is soteriological and eschatological in character; when the attempt is made to fit it into the framework of a conception that is cosmological and anthropological in character, it almost certainly loses something of its distinctiveness'.[53] I do not see why this should be the case. If we wish to claim, as Hendry and others do, that the Spirit's primary work is to witness to the Father's atoning work in the

---

49 J. S. Whale, *Christian Doctrine*, (1941), London, Collins Fontana, 1957, p. 134.

50 *Declaration of Faith*, London, Congregational Church in England and Wales, 1967, p. 21.

51 Calvin, *Institutes*, II.ii.16.

52 J. Calvin, *The Eternal Predestination of God*, trans. J. K. S. Reid, London: James Clarke, 1961, p. 134.

53 G. S. Hendry, *The Holy Spirit in Christian Theology*, London, SCM Press, 1961, p. 16.

Incarnation, Cross and Resurrection; and if we are properly wary of any reductionism which would construe the Spirit as the spirit of the age, or even of our better selves, we are not thereby prohibited from affirming that the Holy Spirit is active in other ways in the world, and certainly beyond the Church. On the contrary, if we wish to say that the Godhead is immanent in the created order, it is difficult to see how this could be so if the third person were somehow abstracted from the situation. Indeed, Moltmann contends that God's 'creative Spirit is the dynamic of the universe and the power that creates community [presumably in principle, and where it actually happens] in the widening, differentiating network of the living'.[54] But in whatever he does, the Spirit bears witness to Christ and forwards his work, as Richard Baxter came belatedly to see:

> I more sensibly perceive that the Spirit is the great witness of Christ and Christianity in the world. And though the folly of fanatics tempted me long to overlook the strength of this testimony of the Spirit, while they place it in a certain internal assertion or enthusiastic inspiration, yet now I see that the Holy Ghost in another manner is the witness to Christ and his agent in the world.[55]

Among the many ecumenical implications of this is that there is not only anthropological-epistemological common ground as between Christians and others, since all are created in the *imago dei*;[56] there is the pneumatological consideration that all are in some way accessible to, and reached by, the Spirit. This cannot but influence the approach of Christians to people of other faiths and of no faith, though no false immanentism should be fostered which would blur the Creator-creature distinction and construe the Spirit's work in terms of genial intellectual accord rather than dramatic rescue on the ground of Christ's atoning work;[57] and no well-meaning but debatable notion such as Rahner's concerning 'anonymous Christians' should blur the distinction of eternal significance between those who are 'in Christ' and those who, variously on grounds of personal integrity or by reason of wilfulness, are not. Atheists and sincere members of other faith communities will feel patronized rather than impressed by what they may well perceive as our desire to annexe them to Christianity. At the same time, Christians should

---

54 J. Moltmann, *The Spirit of Life: A Universal Affirmation*, London, SCM Press, 1992, p. 227; my parenthesis.

55 R. Baxter, *Autobiography*, abridged from *Reliquiae Baxterianae* (1696), London, Dent, 1931, p. 110.

56 See further, Alan P. F. Sell, *Confessing and Commending the Faith. Historic Witness and Apologetic Method*, Cardiff, University of Wales Press, 2002, ch. 2.

57 For the way in which Christian philosophical idealists were, among other things, inclined to blur the Creator-creature distinction, see Alan P. F. Sell, *Philosophical Idealism and Christian Belief*, Cardiff: University of Wales Press and New York: St. Martin's Press, 1995.

ponder carefully those words and stories of Jesus which warn that, come the *eschaton*, the 'religious' will be astounded to discover who is in heaven—and who is not.

But it is one thing to think in terms of the Spirit's relation to non-Christian human beings; it is another to think of him in relation to animals and inanimate objects. Is it more than a literary flourish when Paul speaks of the eager longing of the groaning and travailing created order for deliverance? Can we give any real content to John the Seer's notion of a new *earth*? No doubt such ideas may prompt us in the direction of good stewardship of the created order, and of this there is a dire need. But what exactly is the Spirit doing directly in and through animals and inanimate creation? I see no option but godly agnosticism at this point, for as Hendrikus Berkhof said, 'While we know the mode of God's concern for man, we do not know the mode of his concern for nature.'[58] Since, however, everything we know about God suggests that he loves all that he has made, it is a justified, and not simply a pious, hope that for the whole created order it will be well.

In the meantime, while we may have every confidence that, as the old hymn has it, 'God is working his purpose out As year suceeds to year', we should remember our calling to be his co-workers, not his impediments; and whether we think in terms of the *ecclesia*, or of the human family at large, or of the entire created order, we should do well to ponder one of the most sobering injunctions in the whole of Scripture: 'Do not grieve the Holy Spirit of God.'[59]

---

58 H. Berkhof, *Christian Faith*, Grand Rapids, MI: Eerdmans, 1986, p. 536.

59 Ephesians 4:30.

CHAPTER 12

Nicknames, Labels and Slogans in Christian History and Thought

'I do not fight with chimney sweepers', wrote John Wesley of Augustus Toplady: 'He is too dirty a writer for me to meddle with; I should only foul my fingers... I leave him to Mr. Sellon. He cannot be in better hands.'[1] It would appear that Sellon, the baker turned Wesleyan preacher rose to the occasion. According to Toplady's list, which he submits 'for the Reader's amusement', Sellon branded him

> A Flaming Calvinist.
> A Dragon.
> An Hooter.
> A Venemous Slanderer.
> A Persecutor, possessing the same butcherly spirit that was in Bishop Gardiner; yea, ten times more.
> A Perfectionist.
> A malapert Boy, severely scratching and gnawing with venomous nails.
> A Papist.
> A Socinian.
> A Mahometan.
> The greatest Bigot that ever existed, without one grain of candour, benevolence, forbearance, moderation, good-will, or charity.
> A wild Beast of impatience and lion-like fury.
> A Materialist; that is, an Atheist.

On all of which Toplady, not without justification, remarks, 'A goodly string of appellations! And not a little extraordinary, that they should all centre in one and the same man!'[2]

Not, indeed, that nicknames were confined to individuals: religious groups were also subject to this form of branding, which could betoken anything from gentle teasing through mild disdain to utter abhorrence. With the passage of time some such nicknames carry no pejorative

---

[1] Quoted by Luke Tyerman, *The Life and Times of the Rev. John Wesley*, London, 1872, III, p. 83.

[2] *The Complete Works of Augustus M. Toplady, B.A. Late Vicar of Broad Hembury, Devon*, London: J. Cornish, 1869, p. 50.

connotations whatsoever. Thus, according to George Fox, it was Justice Gervase Bennet of Derby 'that first called us Quakers because we bid them tremble at the word of God'.[3] According to other accounts the nickname derived from the charismatic quakings of the Quakers themselves. In the 1740s the tailor James Wardley and his wife Jane, former Quakers, left the now more quietist Friends, had a vision of Christ's Second Coming and the defeat of the Antichrist, and began shaking during religious exercises in Bolton and Manchester. They were derided as 'Shakers' but they cheerfully accepted the name, and bear it to this day. The Welsh Jumpers, who originated in the heady days of Calvinistic Methodist revival and whose energetic antics were defended by William Williams of Pantycelyn reached the point of exhaustion rather sooner.[4] Less well known are the Dependent Brethren of the Sussex-Surrey borders, who, it is said, were nicknamed 'the Cokelers', because of their preference for drinking cocoa rather than beer at meals between their services. They are a communitarian body who sing their own hymns and, in addition to their meeting-house and dwellings, some of their communities have a shop in which their members are employed.[5] Most famous and most widespread of all are the Methodists, whose name was originally bestowed by other students upon the members of the Holy Club—including the Wesley brothers—at Oxford University on account of the methodical devotions in which they shared. The group was also called Sacramentarians, Enthusiasts, Supererogation Men, the Reforming Club and The Godly Club.[6]

While some nicknames have, with the passage of time, become respectable designations, many other labels, not originally humourous or

---

3 *The Journal of George Fox*, ed. John L. Nickalls, London: Religious Society of Friends, 1975, p. 58.

4 For brief sketches of the Shakers and Jumpers, and marked disapproval of the latter, see John Evans, *A Sketch of the Denominations of the Christian World; With a Persuasive to Religious Moderation*, London: J. & E. Hodson, 12th edn 1811, pp. 211-41 and 181-86 respectively. For Evans (1767–1827), a Baptist minister, see *ODNB*; *The Dictionary of Welsh Biography down to 1940*, London: The Honourable Society of Cymmrodorion, 1959.

5 Their main centre is at Loxwood whither John Sirgood (1820–85), an erstwhile preacher among the Plumstead Peculiars, went in 1850, pushing his wife, so it is said, from Essex to Loxwood in a wheelbarrow. In 1972 I began to seek access to the records of the Dependent Brethren, but my request was denied, possibly because they had been displeased by more popular treatments of their way of life and beliefs. Some years later Roger Homan fared better. See his 'The Society of Dependents: a case study in the rise and fall of rural Peculiars', *Sussex Archaeological Collections*, CIX, 1981, pp. 195-204. The story of the Plumstead Peculiars has been told by Mark Sorrell, *The Peculiar People*, Exeter: Paternoster Press, 1979.

6 So Henry D. Rack, *Reasonable Enthusiast. John Wesley and the Rise of Methodism*, London: Epworth Press, 1989, p. 84. A third edition appeared in 2003.

pejorative, are to be found in Christian history and thought. As a general rule these labels should be regarded with a certain caution, for we frequently find that on closer inspection considerable variety is to be found among those who wear the same label; and even that some of them may in some respects have views more similar to those of other parties than to some members of their own.[7] Some of these labels refer to the doctrinal banners under which groups of Christians travelled. For example, the Alexandrians, among whom Cyril was prominent, emphasized the divinity of Christ, over against the Antiochenes, whose ranks included Theodore of Mopsuestia, John Chrysostom and Nestorius, who elevated Christ's humanity. Again, the Franciscans all regard themselves as followers of Francis of Assisi, but a close perusal of their writings reveals a number of different theological emphases, so that some present-day Franciscan scholars lament what they perceive as the decline of the vernacular theology of Francis himself into a version of scholasticism, with the result that the Franciscan life and the Franciscan intellectual tradition are disjoined.[8]

As for my own tradition, the Reformed, it is diverse culturally, theologically, liturgically and in terms of polity, having Reformed, Presbyterian, Congregational and United components. In terms of this large communion, many are Reformed in terms of their ecclesiastical allegiance who would not easily think of themselves as sons or daughters of Calvin, John Owen or Karl Barth (nor were they in entire accord).[9]

---

[7] This is not, of course, a phenomenon unique to religion and theology. The Parliamentary Conservative Party includes Thatcherite monetarists and 'one nation' Tories; the Labour Party Members of Parliament comprise a few who are close to Marxism, a number who think of themselves as 'Old Labour', and a sizeable group who find it appropriate, or useful, to think of themselves as 'New Labour'. On some issues the last named are closer to the 'one nation' Tories than the latter are to the hard-line Thatcherites. Similar points could be made regarding such labels as 'Enlightenment' and 'Romantic', while in philosophy we may speak of right-wing and left-wing Hegelians, and those philosophical idealists most sympathetic to Christianity, or actually Christians, displayed considerable variety among themselves, as I sought to show in *Philosophical Idealism and Christian Belief*, Cardiff: University of Wales Press and New York: St. Martin's Press, 1995.

[8] See, for example, Ilia Delio, 'The Franciscan intellectual tradition: contemporary concerns', in Elise Saggau, ed., *The Franciscan Intellectual Tradition*, St. Bonaventure, NY: Franciscan Institute, 2002, p. 5. On vernacular theology see Dominic Monti, 'Francis as a vernacular theologian: a like to the Franciscan intellectual tradition', in Saggau, ed., *The Franciscan Intellectual Tradition*, ch. 2; Bernard McGinn, *The Flowering of Mysticism: Men and Women in the New Mysticism—1200–1350*, New York: Crossroad, 1998.

[9] See further, Alan P. F. Sell, *Testimony and Tradition. Studies in Reformed and Dissenting Thought*, Aldershot: Ashgate, 2005, ch. 10, and 'The Reformed family today:

With reference to Roman Catholic catechetics Diane Tomkinson has remarked, 'There is energy in discovering that Catholic theology is more than Thomas Aquinas, the Baltimore Catechism, or "Jesus loves you; draw a picture."'[10] For my tradition one might readily substitute 'Calvin' or 'Barth', and 'Westminster'; and those of other traditions may similarly amuse themselves. Theological fecundity expressed in manifold ways is precisely what we should expect given, on the one hand, a living Word and an ever-active Holy Spirit, and, on the other, human originality, perversity and the wilful refusal to hear.[11]

A particular cluster of more than ordinarily slippery theological labels began to come into prominence in the late nineteenth century, and they are still in use today. As in other cases, they sometimes obscure more than they reveal. I refer to the terms 'conservative' and 'liberal' both of which could be, though the latter was not always, attached to the further term 'evangelical'. These terms came into vogue in an intellectual climate fertilized by the higher criticism of the Bible, the increasing prominence of the Oxford Movement, and the Protestant suspicion—even in some cases hostility—to both. The supernatural was in many quarters under a cloud, the evolutionary-progressive theme was in vogue; some were disenchanted, more were optimistic; while from outside the churches came sometimes vociferous critiques in the name of secularism, naturalism and agnosticism. Since I have dealt with these terms at some length elsewhere,[12] I shall here be brief to the point of blunt. In broad terms the conservative evangelicals were most cautious regarding the 'assured results' of biblical criticism—indeed, some repudiated the critical method altogether, and they emphasized Christ's substitutionary death upon the Cross.[13] The liberal evangelicals sought to couch the Gospel in terms open to exegetical advances and to the thought-world of their day, frequently espousing the moral influence theory of the atonement. The out-and-out liberals offloaded doctrines deemed antiquated to the extent that they were charged by their opponents of

---

some theological reflections', in Donald K. McKim, ed., *Major Themes in the Reformed Tradition*, Grand Rapids, MI: Eerdmans, 1992, pp. 433-41.

10 D. Tomkinson, 'Why pursue a doctorate in Franciscan studies today?', in Saggau, ed., *The Franciscan Intellectual tradition*, p. 87.

11 For considerations respecting the possible limits to be imposed upon such fecundity see ch. 6 above.

12 See Alan P. F. Sell, *Theology in Turmoil. The Roots, Course and Significance of the Conservative–Liberal Debate in Modern Theology*, (1986), Eugene, OR: Wipf & Stock, 1998, ch. 5.

13 There is much more to conservative evangelicalism than this, of course: modes of worship, methods of evangelism, varieties of spirituality are all involved. See further, David Bebbington, *Evangelicalism in Modern Britain. A History from the 1730s to the 1980s*, London: Unwin Hyman, 1989. But doctrine is at the core.

purveying a reduced Gospel if a Gospel at all. In all of this the titles alternatively accorded to Jesus were frequently indicative of general theological positions: the first Christian, Master, Elder Brother, Saviour.[14]

To complicate matters further, it was quite possible for an Anglo-Catholic slum priest to be liturgically conservative, biblically liberal, homiletically evangelical and socially radical. In opposition to liberalism and to such sects as Mormonism there arose 'fundamentalism', which took its name from *The Fundamentals*, a series of pamphlets published by Lyman Stewart between the years 1910–15. Not, indeed, that fundamentalism is all of a piece. Generally holding to a more or less strict understanding of biblical inerrancy, fundamentalists could, and can, vary doctrinally from hyper-Calvinism through Arminianism holiness emphases and charismatic interests to the wilder reaches of prophecy and millenarianism. Fundamentalist excesses were not the least important factor in the development of a neo-evangelical critique of the phenomenon. Of this critique Edward J. Carnell's book, *The Case for Orthodox Theology* (1957), is an early and typical example.

But if nicknames and labels are variously amusing or problematic, slogans catch the ear, and are proclaimed with a view to mustering followers and on occasion, in our own time, to 'packing' church assemblies with the 'true believers' when specific issues are under review. In a word, slogans can become tools of politicized Christians. In a less sensational way they become part of the frequently unargued currency of religious or theological discourse. When this happens they, like labels, can obscure more than they reveal. In what follows I propose to examine in some detail three slogans (each of which spawns what one might call satellite slogans) before which a good deal of obeisance has been done in the past forty years. The first two may be considered as a pair by way of revealing interesting differences between them: 'The Church must take its agenda from the world' and 'All theology must be contextual'; the third is 'Inclusivity is good, exclusivity is bad.'

I

One of the fashionable slogans in the popular Christian literature of the 1960s proclaimed that 'The Church must take its agenda from the world.' One of a number of influential theologians to whom those taking this line were indebted was Paul Tillich. While it is true, and to Tillich's credit, that he was more attentive to the 'world's' questions than most of his professional colleagues, the full import of his position was not always

14 An interesting variety of understandings of theological liberalism on the part of present-day 'liberal' theologians may be found in Mark D. Chapman, ed., *The Future of Liberal Theology*, Aldershot: Ashgate, 2002.

grasped by the popularizers of that time; in fact they seriously neglected his critique of those manifestations of older liberal theology which had sought to take Christianity's agenda from the world, and which was roundly denounced by P. T. Forsyth for so doing: 'We must, of course, go some way to meet the world, but when we do meet we must do more than greet.'[15] In a word, they caught hold of only half of Tillich. A glance at Tillich's method of correlation will make the point.

Though holding that the created order is revelatory of God, Tillich denies that the content of the faith can be produced, or prescribed, by the surrounding culture. There is, in Tillich's writings, no capitulation to, or total absorption by, culture. On the contrary, he is convinced that the ultimate questions thrown up by humanity's existential situation derive from alienation from God, the consequences of which are anxiety and loneliness. These questions cannot be answered apart from God's revealed message. Accordingly, his method of correlation represents his attempt to 'correlate the questions implied in the situation with the answers implied in the message'.[16]

Tillich is the first to grant that this is by no means a novel method: 'As method', he writes, 'it is as old as theology. We have not...invented a new method.[17] The mutual oscillation between the Gospel and the changing contexts in which it must be proclaimed has been the stuff of apologetics (and mission) from New Testament times until today. But Tillich emphasizes more than many the need to hear and respond to the world's questions, not because the message as given was deficient in content—his system 'does not derive the answers from the questions as a self-defying apologetic theology does'[18]—but in order that it would engage people where they were. Although Tillich's writing is replete with the modern language of existentialism and informed by contemporary psycho-analytical interests, there is nevertheless a perennial concern in his approach, which is classically exemplified by Augustine's assertion, 'Thou hast created us unto Thyself, and our heart finds no rest until it rests in Thee.'[19]

---

15 P. T. Forsyth, *Positive Preaching and the Modern Mind*, (1907), London: Independent Press, 1964, p. 89.

16 P. Tillich, *Systematic Theology*, Chicago: University of Chicago Press, 1951, I, p. 8.

17 Ibid., II, 1957, p. 16.

18 Ibid., I, p. 8.

19 *The Confessions of Saint Augustine*, trans. C. Bigg, London: Methuen, (1897), 13th edn, 1951, p. 33. Allen O. Miller and Donald E. Arthur recall that when a pastor asked Tillich if he were a liberal or neo-orthodox he replied, 'Neither of these labels are particularly relevant or helpful. I am an Augustinian.' See their diagrammatic *Paul Tillich's Systematic Theology*, published by request of The North American Paul Tillich Society, 1979, unpaginated.

Tillich thus thinks in terms of a kerygmatic theology which articulates the 'unchangeable truth of the message (kerygma) over against the changing demands of the situation'[20]; and of an apologetic or 'answering' theology which 'answers the questions implied in the "situation" in the power of the eternal message and with the means provided by the situation whose questions it answers'.[21] But (and here the popularizers referred to above are not entirely without excuse) a number of Tillich's critics have urged that revelation does more than answer our human questions: 'No amount of protesting that the content of the theological answer is given in revelation can remove the offence of regarding theology as having merely the value of providing us with the answers to *our* questions instead of being the light that lightens our feet so that even the question is given.'[22] Kenneth Hamilton bluntly concurred: 'This is to put the gospel in the position of a prisoner in the power of an inquisitor.'[23] It seems to me, though I cannot stay to argue the case here,[24] that this deficiency results from Tillich's (idealist[25]) conviction that philosophy and theology concern the same subject matter, namely, ultimate reality. This has the effect of playing down the unique content of revelation, and of subordinating theology to ontological analysis in the line of Husserl and Heidegger. I further think that we do well to remember the cautionary word of J. P. Clayton: 'Despite what he sometimes says, Tillich is not in fact setting out a theory of relations between, say, philosophy and theology generally: he is intent only on correlating certain sorts of philosophical questions with certain sorts of theological answers.'[26] There is the further question: Is Tillich's range of human questions comprehensive enough? What changes, if any, would have to have been made to his system if 'moral shock' regarding sin and guilt were given attention equal to, or greater than, than the 'ontic shock' which preoccupies him? However these much-debated questions are to be

---

20 Tillich, *Systematic Theology*, I, p. 4.

21 Ibid., p. 6. Cf. I, pp. 31, 60-66; and II, pp. 13-16. For some incisive criticisms of Tillich's method see John Heywood Thomas, *Paul Tillich: An Appraisal*, London: SCM Press, 1963, ch. 1.

22 J. Heywood Thomas, *Paul Tillich*, London: Lutterworth, 1965, p. 9.

23 K. Hamilton, *The System and the Gospel. A Critique of Paul Tillich*, London: SCM Press, 1963, p. 121; cf. p. 130. Cf. Jerry H. Gill, 'Paul Tillich's religious epistemology', *Religious Studies*, III, 1967–68, p. 478.

24 I have attempted a slightly fuller account in Alan P. F. Sell, *The Philosophy of Religion 1875–1980*, (1988), Bristol: Thoemmes Press, 1996, pp. 170-75.

25 Tillich wrote, 'I am an idealist if idealism means the assertion of the identity of thinking and being as the principle of truth.' See his *The Interpretation of History*, New York: Scribners, 1936, p. 60.

26 J. P. Clayton, *The Concept of Correlation: Paul Tillich and the Possibility of a Mediating Theology*, Berlin: W. de Gruyter, 1980, p. 179.

answered, Tillich's method throws into relief the importance of relating the given revelation to the world's questions, the 'vertical' dimension to the 'horizontal'. As we turn now to our second, related, slogan, 'All theology must be contextual', we shall see that this challenge is answerable in quite a different way.

II

On the face of it the slogan 'All theology must be contextual' is an unexceptionable claim. Indeed, it seems to be stating the obvious to say that theological discourse must be rooted in, and adjusted to a context. The way in which Christian doctrines have been articulated has changed with the passing centuries as new cultures have been reached with the Gospel and as fresh challenges have been thrown up by the socio-intellectual environment.[27] But when many today speak of contextual theology they mean rather more than this. They are not simply concerned with the expressing of received doctrines in diverse circumstances; rather, they understand that in some way the *content* to be articulated is given by the context in which its recipients live.

From one point of view this is entirely acceptable. If I say that the context of theological reflection is the Trinity, then context and the content are given together. But contextual theologians mean something else. They regard what one might broadly call the surrounding circumstances, whether intellectual, socio-political or environmental as providing not only a fresh perspective, or as demanding revised doctrinal articulation, but as supplying fresh ingredients or emphases to theology. In some cases the experience of blacks, or of women, or of the poor becomes the lens through which the whole of theology is to be viewed. In opposition to this it is alleged that this amounts to the privileging of one kind of experience over others; and it is not even the case that the experience of all blacks, all women, all of the poor is identical. We have, therefore, so the complaint goes, an ideological rather than an empirical understanding of 'experience' as being that of the underdog: the further slogan concerning 'God's preferential option for the poor' comes to mind, and in its train come the demons of imperialism, capitalism, patriarchalism, and sinful systems in general.

I have deliberately depicted the situation in provocative—even, some might think, inflammatory—terms by way of making the point that if such allegations can be made then some, perversely, will feel justified in paying no further heed to the claims of blacks, women, the poor and,

---

27 See further ch. 6 above. For some historical illustrations of the point see Alan P. F. Sell, *Confessing and Commending the Faith. Historic Witness and Apologetic Method*, Cardiff: University of Wales Press, 2002, pp. 47-60, 84-85.

indeed, any other classes of oppressed persons. Their cause will be shelved and consciences will be salved on the grounds that the case is badly put, the claims exaggerated, the arguments insufficiently discriminating. What follows is an attempt carefully to analyse the slogan under review in relation to one prominent contextual theology (or, rather, one prominent class of contextual theologies—for they are not identical), Latin American liberation theology. This attempt is inspired by the conviction that we fail Christ if we do not heed the cry of the marginalized and the oppressed. In this connection John S. Pobee writes,

> Given the task of proclaiming the Christ-event as the good news in a particular context, Christian theology may not start simply from a body of church doctrines, lest it become insensitive to the situation around it... Its point of departure should be the specific social relations, the hopes and fears of people—the particular context into which the gospel must enter.[28]

The general accusation we need to have in mind as we approach one variety of liberation theology is that some or all of its proponents run the risk of elevating empirical contextual realities and concerns above the Gospel message in a way analogous to Tillich's tendency to elevate ontological considerations above moral ones. Among the questions to be raised are: How, and by whom, is fidelity to context to be determined? What is the analysis of 'context'? It might be thought advisable to place the analysis of 'context' first, but I think that when we have seen what the liberation theologians do, and how their theological method derives from and follows their practice, we shall be in a better position to reach some conclusions on this question.

First, it is essential that I briefly indicate the historical background to liberation theology; only then shall we begin to appreciate the motives and objectives of the liberation theologians. A number of writers, among them Leonardo Boff,[29] have depicted colonial domination from the sixteenth century onwards as the shared experience of the Latin American nations. Millions of Indians were killed; African slaves were imported; and

> In return for political servitude, the Church was given the right to arbitrate the social mores of colonial society and to inculcate the 'heathen' with a Spanish Catholicism still rigidly bound to the Middle Ages.[30]

---

[28] J. S. Pobee, 'Theology, contextual', in N. Lossky, *et al.*, eds, *Dictionary of the Ecumenical Movement*, Geneva: World Council of Churches, 2002, p. 1108.

[29] See L. Boff, *A New Evangelization: Perspective of the Oppressed*, Petropolis: Vozes, 1990.

[30] Penny Lernoux, 'The long path to Puebla', in John Eagleson and Philip Scharper, eds, *Puebla and Beyond*, Maryknoll, NY: Orbis Books, 1979, p. 3.

In the wake of the demise of colonialism have come economic imperialism, military dictatorships and foreign debt. Voices of protest began to be heard among state university students, first in Argentina at the beginning of the twentieth century, and soon in other Latin American countries. There thus developed an educated middle class which was ready to struggle for the rights of the poor and marginalized people, and irked by the restrictive attitudes of Church and state.[31] Their attitudes to such matters as popular religiosity, however, did not endear them to the poor, and it became clear that the culture gap could be bridged only if the intellectuals learned from the people at the grassroots. As recently as 1982, Orlando Costas could still call Latin America an oppressed continent, whose cry is 'for liberation from cultural domination, economic exploitation, military repression, social marginalization, and political imperialism; it is a cry for fairness in international trade and the establishment of a social order that promotes human dignity, respects democratic institutions, and guarantees an equitable distribution of wealth'.[32] There is also a cry from Latin America that the truth of this situation be exposed, not hidden by 'sophisticated, dominant (Western) social sciences'. To this must be added the cry for theological truth: 'the Word of God...has been hidden in the barrels of imported theologies from Europe and North America'.[33] So much for the background.

The sources of liberation theology are manifold and, as we shall see, the published products of it are neither monolithic nor intellectually static. Although Protestant theologians have contributed valuably and not always uncritically to liberation theology, the initial impetus came from the Roman Catholic Church, some of whose theologians were influenced by the such writers as Maurice Blondel, whose book *L'Action* (1893) was seminal in its discussion of the mutual relations of knowledge and action; the anti-Nazi protest of Henri De Lubac; and by the worker-priest movement in France, among whose intellectual leaders was Marie-Dominique Chenu.[34] Again, encyclicals on social concerns had been emanating from Rome since 1891, albeit the liberation theologians faulted them for not going far enough in denunciation of the domination of the poor by capitalist structures;[35] and it is not without significance that in 1968, three years after the Second Vatican Council ended, a landmark conference took place in Medellín, Colombia, on the subject 'The Church

31 See further, Juan Luis Segundo, 'The shift within Latin American theology', *Journal of Theology for Southern Africa*, no. 52, September 1985, pp. 17-29.

32 O. Costas, *Christ Outside the Gate*, New York: Orbis, 1982, pp. 104-105.

33 Ibid., p. 105.

34 See Gerard O'Hanlon, 'The Jesuits and modern theology—Rahner, von Balthasar and liberation theology', *Irish Theological Quarterly*, LVIII no. 1, 1992, pp. 24-45.

35 See, for example, G. Guttiérrez, 'The poor in the Church', in Norbert Greinacher and Alois Müller, eds, *The Poor and the Church*, New York: Seabury Press, 1977, p. 14.

in the present-day transformation of Latin America in the light of the Council.' This was followed by what, in retrospect, can only be described as a priceless example of godly subterfuge. An Episcopal Conference was held at Puebla, Mexico, in 1979. It was under the control of conservative bishops whose objective was to turn the theological clock back. The leading Latin American theologians—Guttiérrez, Segundo, Boff, Assmann, Sobrino, Comblin and others—were excluded from the conference. They were, however, invited by progressive bishops to occupy a convent close to the conference venue, and this they did. Banned from the conference precincts, the bishops went to them, discussed the proceedings as they unfolded, and brought drafts from the exiles into the conference debate, with the result that the feared denunciation of liberation theology was forestalled.

As to a secular influence upon the movement, Karl Marx, on whom some of the first generation of liberation theologians in particular depended quite heavily for their social analysis, was 'white, western and bourgeois;'[36] he did not have much time for the underdog; and the pedigree of his thought is Hegel out of the Enlightenment by the British Library.[37] For all that, some liberation theologians, Sergio Arce Martinez of Cuba among them, embraced Marx's socio-economic views to the extent of advocating revolution; others, including Hugo Assman, made no bones about proclaiming, 'I am a Marxist and I can't see the reality of Latin America in any other category';[38] many were open to Marxist insights whilst being alive to the important distinctions between Christianity and Marxism. Thus Guttiérrez writes that 'it is to a large extent due to Marxism's influence that theological thought, searching for its own sources, has begun to reflect on the meaning of the transformation of this world and the action of man in history.'[39]

It almost goes without saying that some well-heeled Christians who moved in capitalist circles used Marxism as a stick with which to beat the liberation theologians. 'In its essence', writes one, 'liberation theology is

---

36 The allusion is to Guttiérrez's observation that 'The history of Christianity has...been written by white, western, bourgeois hands.' See 'Two theological perspectives: liberation theology and progressivist theology', in Sergio Torres and Virginia Fabella, eds, *The Emergent Gospel: Theology from the Underside of History*, London: Geoffrey Chapman, 1978, p. 248.

37 The influence of such European political theologians as Metz and Moltmann should not be overlooked. For Guttiérrez's assessment of the positions of Moltmann and Metz see, for example, his *A Theology of Liberation*, (1971), Maryknoll, NY: Orbis Books, 1973, pp. 116-18 and 220-25 respectively.

38 H. Assmann in a contribution to a plenary discussion reported in *Risk*, IX no. 2, 1973, p. 59.

39 G. Guttiérrez, *A Theology of Liberation. History, Politics, Salvation*, (1971), trans. and eds. Caridad Inda and John Eagleson, Maryknoll, NY: Orbis Books, 1973, p. 9.

Marxist thought disguised as Christianity...[it] represents a genuine threat to Christian civilisation'.[40] Somewhat more soberly, a Scottish missionary wondered whether liberation theology 'is ultimately not merely a functionalist theology for a Marxist society'.[41] That even more exalted voices could be a little shrill is evident from the fact that in its 1984 *Instruction on Certain Aspects of the 'Theology of Liberation* the Vatican's Sacred Congregation for the Doctrine of the Faith opined that 'the ideological core borrowed from Marxism...exercises the function of a *determining principle*'.[42] In fairness, however, it must be noted that just two years later, from the same source there came *Instruction on Christian Freedom and Liberation*—a more temperately-worded document to which I shall refer again shortly. As for a mainline Protestant response, the General Assembly Mission Board of the Presbyterian Church in the United States adverted to

> liberation theology's perplexing use of Marxist theory not only to analyze and repudiate capitalism, but also to opt for the socialist alternative as a structure more akin to the demands of God's kingdom. The actual socialist societies we know about are uniformly authoritarian, if not totalitarian, with a consequent loss of basic democratic freedoms...[43]

As if to take this point and redress the balance, Helder Camara argued that it will not suffice to brand as communist those who expose 'the materialistic roots of capitalism' and urge that 'the growing gap between the developed and the underdeveloped nations, not communism, is today's most serious social problem'.[44]

From both the Roman Catholic and Protestant wings of liberation theology have flowed remarks critical of Marxism. Thus, for example, the Jesuit, Juan Luis Segundo, points out that Marxists and Christians will differ over what precisely opting for the poor and marginalized entails: 'I think the critical dividing line in connection with means is whether or not we must manipulate human masses and turn them into tools before we

---

40 Dave Breese, 'Will we succumb to liberation theology?', *Christian Irishman*, October 1987, pp. 10, 13.

41 G. Stewart McIntosh, 'The liberation of theology: an evangelical response to theologies of liberation in the mid-eighties', *Bulletin* of the International Council for the Promotion of Christian Higher Education, no. 3, Summer 1986, p. 25.

42 *Instruction on Certain Aspects of the 'Theology of Liberation'*, Vatican City: Sacred Congregation for the Doctrine of the Faith, 1984, p. 20.

43 *What is Liberation Theology?* Atlanta, GA: General Assembly Mission Board, Presbyterian Church in the United States, 1980, pp. 37-8. The monograph was prepared by Jorge Lara-Braud.

44 H. Camara, 'The Church and modern Latin America', in *Between Honesty and Hope: Documents from and about the Church in Latin America*, trans. John Drury, Maryknoll, NY: Orbis Books, 1970, p. 35.

can raise their consciousness.'[45] For his part, although he can speak of the 'common engagement' on the part of Marxists and Christians 'in the creation of a new society', the Methodist José Míguez Bonino faults Marxist anthropology, which makes no adequate allowance for the spiritual dimension of the quest for liberation.[46] He underlines the point thus: 'the ultimate horizons of the Christian and Marxist ethos are radically different—they see the source and the power of solidarity love in mutually exclusive ways'.[47] Not surprisingly, he has elsewhere affirmed '*the priority of grace*...the specific nature and quality of the "good news" in Christ's message'.[48]

In the light of the examples cited, I am content to endorse Deane William Ferm's judgment:

> In simplistic terms, if by Marxism one means: 1. State ownership and complete state control of the economy; 2. The overthrow of the present non-socialist government by force; 3. An atheistic world view—then one is hard put to single out any Third World liberation theologian who advocates any one of these points. But all of them agree that the present terribly unequal distribution of wealth, property and power is unchristian.[49]

Let Leonardo and Clodovis Boff speak for themselves: 'by no means is Marxism the moving force, basis, or inspiration of the theology of

---

45 J. L. Segundo, *The Liberation of Theology*, trans. John Drury, Dublin: Gill and Macmillan, 1977, p. 88; cf. pp. 57-62. Elsewhere Segundo criticizes Marxism and especially the concept of violence. See his *A Theology for a New Humanity*, trans. John Drury, Dublin: Gill and Macmillan, 1980, V, pp. 96-101; 121. The influence of Teilhard de Chardin's evolutionary worldview is evident in Segundo's work. On the one hand this no doubt helps to inform his critique of Marxism; on the other hand it prevents a radical contrast with Marxism as regards the final outcome, for to Teilhard the universe is Christified and the Church is self-consciously so. (See *A Theology for a New Humanity*, I, pp. 120-24; II, 82-86; V, *passim*). See my reviews of Segundo in *Philosophical Studies* (Dublin), XXVI, n.d., pp. 302-305; XXVIII, 1981, pp. 270-73. See further John W. Cooper, 'Teilhard, Marx and the worldview of prominent liberation theologians', *Calvin Theological Quarterly*, XXIV no. 2, November 1989, pp. 241-62.

46 See J. Míguez Bonino, *Doing Theology in a Revolutionary Situation*, Philadephia, PA: Fortress Press, 1975, p.130. For his criticisms of Marxism see his *Christians and Marxists: The Mutual Challenge to Revolution*, Grand Rapids, MI: Eerdmans, 1976. At the same time he considers that the socio-analytic tools offered by Marxism are 'indispensable for revolutionary change', *Christians and Marxists*, p. 8. See also René Coste, *Marxist Analysis and Christian Faith*, Maryknoll, NY: Orbis Books, 1985.

47 Míguez Bonino, *Christians and Marxists*, p. 119.

48 Míguez Bonino, 'Historical praxis and Christian identity', in Rosino Gibellini, ed., *Frontiers of Theology in Latin America*, London: SCM Press, 1975, p. 265.

49 D. W. Ferm, 'Third World liberation theology: What's it all about?', *Irish Theological Quarterly*, LI no. 4, 1985, p. 315.

liberation. Christian faith is. It is the Gospel that is the determining qualifier of the theology of liberation... When Marxism is used at all, it is used only *partially* and *instrumentally*.'[50]

Of particular importance in the development of liberation theology was the advent of the Base Church Communities. According to the Brazillian theologian, Antonio Gouvêa Mendonça,

> Historically, the impetus for Base Church Communities is due to a reaction to the amazing growth of the Pentecostals. The Catholic hierarchy decided to give lay people the task of evangelism, and these communities grew out of meetings of lay people to determine their message and strategy. The Base Church Communities have three distinctive features: they are linked to parishes; they devote themselves to Bible study; and they are loyal to the Church... The absence of a biblical tradition among Catholics left the way open for the Base Church Communities... Bible study is done in close connection with everyday problems, which results in a high level of political awareness within them.[51]

As a result of such fresh acquaintance with the gospel, 'the poor are beginning to see in it a paradigm for social transformation hardly compatible with the oppression and classism they were conditioned to accept in the past'.[52] In the dramatic words of Enrique Dussel, 'this "kidnapping" of the "kidnapped" Bible is the originating act and the condition that makes possible a "theology *by* the people."'[53]

In the light of this biblically-inspired reflection, and convinced that Christ came with a message to the poor, that poverty was endemic in Latin American society, and that it was neither necessary nor justifiable, liberation theologians subjected their society to close scrutiny. They concluded that the socio-economic systems which held people in subservience must be challenged and changed. This entailed political activity which set the perpetrators against the prevailing 'powers', the rich, the oppressors: 'To be with the oppressed is to be against the oppressor.'[54] As is well known, the liberation movement became increasingly influential, though at the cost of swelling the 'white-robed army of martyrs'.

---

50 Leonardo Boff and Clodovis Boff, *Liberation Theology: From Confrontation to Dialogue*, San Francisco, CA: Harper and Row, 1986, p. 22.

51 A. G. Mendonça, 'Christology and ecclesiology in a world of oppression', *Reformed World*, XL no. 1, March 1988, pp. 878-79.

52 Curt Cadorette, 'Basic Christian Communities: their social role and missiological promise', *Missiology*. XV no. 2, April 1987, p. 23.

53 E. Dussel, 'Theology by the people', *Ministerial Formation*, no. 31, Geneva: World Council of Churches, September 1985, p. 6. See also this author's indispensable work, *A History of the Church in Latin America*, (1971), trans. Alan Neely, Grand Rapids, MI: Eerdmans, 1981.

54 Guttiérrez, *A Theology of Liberation*, p. 301.

The theological reflection which derives from active solidarity with the poor, does not set out to answer the intellectual doubts of western post-Enlightenment people, but to speak good news to the poor and marginalized, and to work with them for the rectification of society. To put it otherwise, they are not in the first place concerned with secularized non-believers, but rather with those who, despite living in 'Christian' societies in which the Church has traditionally been on the side of the rich and powerful, are deemed to be non-persons. This is not, in the first place, a matter of theory; it is a matter of *praxis*, of 'acting truthfully' amidst the poor. Theological reflection on the basis of such action follows. More globally, according to the analysis of Guttiérrez, the socio-economic system which advantaged the western bourgeousie 'brought only new forms of oppression and exploitation to the peoples of Latin America'.[55] When due account is taken of this tragic fact the claim of liberation theologians that one cannot consistently claim to be saved and at the same time be unconcerned about rampant injustice in the world becomes intelligible. To love one's neighbours is to oppose the systems which dehumanize them.

Against this background I shall now examine three themes, 'the Exodus', 'the poor' and 'liberation', in an attempt to discover the bearing of the context upon the theological articulation in Latin American liberation theology. There can be no question that the Exodus was a very prominent motif in the writings of many of the first generation of liberation theologians, nor is its force spent in their successors. The story of the rescue of the oppressed and their progress to the promised land is deeply rooted in the psyche of many oppressed peoples—the spirituals of the American slaves come at once to mind. The charge has been levelled, however, that liberation theologians think too much in terms of political liberation, at the expense of salvation from sin. The complaint is that the context of oppression exercises undue control of the biblical text and leads to a reduction in the full-orbed message of the Gospel. Hence the remark of the Congregation for the Doctrine of the Faith: 'Man's sin, that is to say his breaking away from God, is the radical reason for the tragedies which mark the history of freedom. In order to understand this, many of our contemporaries must first rediscover a sense of sin.'[56] In passing I would note that this can be a morbid quest indeed, and that most people do not experience a sense of sin until they have heard the Gospel of grace. That is to say, it is when we see what God in Christ has done, and why it was necessary, that we begin to see who we are, who God is, and what the distance between us is. Remember Zacchaeus. Nevertheless from the same source comes the following:

---

[55] Guttiérrez, 'Two theological perspectives', p. 237.

[56] *Instruction on Christian Freedom and Liberation*, p. 21.

> The exodus, in fact, is the fundamental event in the formation of the chosen people. It represents freedom from foreign domination and from slavery. One will note that the specific significance of the event comes from its purpose, for this liberation is ordered to the foundation of the people of God and the Covenant cult celebrated at Sinai. That is why the liberation of the Exodus cannot be reduced to a liberation which is principally or exclusively political in nature.[57]

It seems to me that the generality of first generation liberation theologians agree that there is more to liberation than political liberation. Their point is, however, that there is no genuine liberation of persons which does not have a socio-political dimension, and that where the oppressed are concerned it is necessary to be for them and against the oppressors. Further, they are not unaware of the tragedy of sin, committed to unrelieved 'horizontalism', or blind to the Exodus-covenant link. On the contrary, the most prominent early liberation theologian, Guttiérrez, deals specifically with all these matters within a few pages in his seminal work, *A Theology of Liberation.* He sets out from creation as the work of the Saviour God who, in a political act, sets his people free from 'despoilation and misery', and, through Moses, leads them towards the promised land. Indeed, 'The God of Exodus is the God of history and of political liberation more than he is the God of nature.'[58] I feel that the 'more than' is unhelpful here: I should have preferred 'just as', for creation is the theatre of God's saving activity. But there can be no quarrel with Guttiérrez's main point: 'The Covenant and the liberation from Egypt were different aspects of the same movement....'[59] Christ's redemptive, re-creative work is part of this same movement, he continues, and this work 'is presented simultaneously as a liberation from sin and from all its consequences: despoilation, injustice, hatred'.[60] Since the Exodus from Egypt meant freedom from a monarchical rule, social praxis is now 'desacralized', and human beings must work to transform the world:

> The Exodus experience is paradigmatic...it structures our faith in the gift of the Father's love. In Christ and through the Spirit, men are becoming one in the very heart of history, as they confront and struggle against all that divides and opposes them. But the true agents of this quest for unity are those who today are oppressed (economically, politically, culturally) and struggle to become free.[61]

I shall turn to 'the poor' shortly; but first I wish to say a little more concerning the charge that the liberation theologians think too much in

---

57 *Instruction on Certain Aspects of the 'Theology of Liberation'*, p. 9.

58 Guttiérrez, *A Theology of Liberation*, p. 157.

59 Ibid.

60 Ibid., p. 158.

61 Ibid., p. 159.

'horizontal'-political terms and not enough in 'vertical' terms,[62] and then to introduce a further criticism which has been levelled against them.

First, it is quite clear from a careful reading of his work, and especially of his book, *The Power of the Poor in History* (1983), that Guttiérrez thinks that there is a balance to be redressed. No doubt he brings social sin and structural transformation to the fore, but if some feel that this reduces the Gospel to a programme of socio-political reform,

> He insists...that Christian theology is threatened by reductionism at both ends. Traditional theologians are tempted to reduce the meaning of salvation to a 'spiritual' realm above history, to reduce the message of the Gospel to matters of personal holiness, and to reduce the action of God in history to a narrow verticalism that neglects the incarnational aspect of human mediation. Guttiérrez stands against one reductionism as much as the other.[63]

Almost a century ago, long before the liberation theologians hove into view, A. E. Garvie struck the balance which, I believe, most of them wish to maintain: 'Man's self-sacrifice for the good of society has sometimes been so insisted on as to obscure God's self-sacrifice on behalf of man, in which alone is a motive potent enough for the moral task to which man is called.'[64]

Secondly, liberation theologians have been accused of paying insufficient attention to Christ's resurrection and the hope deriving therefrom. If I understand the situation aright, it would seem that the first generation of liberation theologians, with a triumphalist Church behind them, were reluctant to move too quickly to a theology of glory until the way of the Cross had been fully accepted and the plight of the oppressed addressed. What seems clear, however, is that in the writings of some liberation theologians, among whom Jon Sobrino is prominent, greater emphasis is placed upon the New Testament, the historical Jesus as being on the side of the oppressed, and the resurrection hope than upon the Exodus motif.[65]

Turning now to 'the poor' we find that the idea that God has a preferential option for the poor was articulated at the Puebla Conference,

---

62 For Guttiérrez's stout defence against this claim see his 'Liberation praxis and Christian faith', in Gibellini, ed., *Frontiers of Theology in Latin America*, pp. 28-30.

63 So Gregory Baum, 'Guttiérrez and the Catholic tradition', *The Ecumenist*, XXI no. 6, September–October 1983, p. 82.

64 A. E. Garvie, 'The limits of doctrinal restatement', *Proceedings of the Third International Congregational Council*, London: Congregational Union of England and Wales, 1908, p. 94.

65 See J. Sobrino, *Christology at the Crossroads: A Latin American Approach*, Maryknoll, NY: Orbis Books, 1978; *The True Church and the Poor*, Maryknoll, NY: Orbis Books, 1984; *The Principle of Mercy: Taking the Crucified People from the Cross*, Maryknoll, NY: Orbis Books, 1994.

and it is not difficult to see in the slogan the hand of those theologians who were excluded from the conference sessions. This preferential option entails an hermeneutical recommendation to the effect that theology should be written from the vantage point of the poor; and a challenge to active solidarity with the poor. That God has this preferential option is an inference drawn from Scripture rather than a directly stated fact; but the liberation theologians deem it to be a legitimate inference.

The slogan, 'God's preferential option for the poor', sent many a biblical scholar to their Bibles to examine the concept of 'the poor' therein. A considerable number of word studies were published,[66] and it seems to me that the vast majority of them endorse the position taken by Guttiérrez,[67] namely, that the biblical 'poor' are to be found in two main classes. First there are the 'poor in spirit' of whom the Beatitudes speak. These are the ones who know their need of God; they are open to him and teachable (meek) by him. Secondly, there are the economically disadvantaged, the oppressed, the outcasts, whose cause was taken up by God in the Exodus, in the legislation of Leviticus and Deuteronomy, by the prophets in their denunciations of injustice, and by Jesus in his ministry to the least and the lowest. Guttiérrez, however, adds what is for him an important rider: spiritual poverty 'is above all total availability to the Lord'. Nevertheless, 'Its relationship to the use or ownership of economic goods is inescapable, but secondary and partial.'[68]

Some found a tendency on the part of liberation theologians to messianize the poor, to overlook the fact that they, no less than everyone else, are sinners and that the Gospel is for rich and poor alike,[69] and even to leave the impression that liberation is a human work. In fact, 'All liberation and salvation is through [Jesus Christ] and his work, even when that is hidden and unacknowledged.'[70] As Ronald Sider has said,

---

66 The following is a very small sample: Richard J. Coggins, 'The Old Testament and the poor', *Expository Times*, XC, 1987–88, pp. 11-14; Sue Gillingham, 'The poor in the Psalms', *Expository Times*, C, 1988–89, pp. 15-19; James M. Dawsey, 'The biblical authority of the poor', *Expository Times*, CI, 1999–90, pp. 295-8; R. T. France, 'Liberation in the New Testament', *Evangelical Quarterly*, LVIII no. 1, January 1986, pp. 3-23; Hans Kvalbein, 'Jesus and the poor: two texts and a tentative conclusion', *Themelios*, XII no. 3, April 1987, pp. 80-87.

67 See Guttiérrez, *A Theology of Liberation*, pp. 291-302.

68 Ibid., p. 299.

69 As Ronald Sider has pointed out, in the preferential option for the poor God seems 'biased only in contrast with our sinful unconcern. It is only when we take our perverse preference for the successful and wealthy as natural and normative that God's concern appears biased'. In Daniel S. Schipani, *Freedom and Discipleship. Liberation Theology in Anabaptist Perspective*, Maryknoll, NY: Orbis Books, 1989, p. 98.

70 *What is Liberation Theology?* p. 37.

> Knowing God involves much more than seeking justice for the oppressed—although it does not involve less. People enter into a right relationship with God and enter the church not by caring for the poor but by confessing their sins and accepting Jesus Christ as Lord and Saviour.[71]

But this raises the question of the analysis of 'liberation' *vis à vis* 'salvation', and to this I now turn.

A fairly common complaint against the liberation theologians was that they equated social reform with salvation and reduced the Gospel to a political programme. That this challenge emanated not only from politically and theologically conservative capitalists but also from authoritative commentators is evidenced by John Pobee's comment on contextual theology in general:

> Contextualization has become a slogan of third-world theology, referring to a kind of theology which starts from the problems of the community and attempts to formulate the Christian message accordingly. Contextual theology thus not unexpectedly often reads like a programme, a crusade rather than a gospel.[72]

There is no smoke without fire. Thus, for example, on the one hand the black theologian, Joseph A. Johnson, Jr., fully grasps the soteriological and eschatological significance of the life and work of Jesus, and quotes J. K. Mozley with approval: 'There is in the New Testament no speculative Christology divorced from the gospel of the Savior and the salvation he brings.'[73] On the other hand, his constructive focus is entirely upon Jesus' earthly ministry to the poor and needy: 'Liberation was the aim and goal of the life of Jesus in the world. Liberation expresses the essential thrust of his ministry. The stage of his ministry was the streets.'[74] We seem here to stop short of the Cross, and the question is whether 'liberation' as thus understood accommodates all that Jesus did in the world.

This question lies behind Schubert Ogden's concern that liberation theology is more an ethic than a theology, and that in it liberation understood as emancipation is an inadequate substitute for redemption.[75] While it is true that the emphasis of many liberation theologians is, understandably enough in view of the dire circumstances they are called

---

71 Sider, *Freedom and Discipleship*, p. 98.

72 Pobee, 'Theology, contextual', p. 1108.

73 J. A. Johnson, Jr., 'Jesus the liberator', in James J. Gardiner and J. Deotis Roberts, Sr., eds., *Quest for a Black Theology*, Philadelphia: United Church Press, 1971, p. 106, quoting J. K. Mozley, 'Jesus in relation to believing man', *Interpretation*, XI, January 1958, p. 11.

74 Johnson, Jr., 'Jesus the liberator', p. 110.

75 See Schubert M. Ogden, *Faith and Freedom: Toward a Theology of Liberation*, Nashville, TN: Abingdon, 1979, pp. 36-37.

upon to address, upon emancipation rather than individual sin, they by no means overlook individual salvation. What they insist upon, however, is that the saved should enlist in the crusade against injustice and stand alongside the oppressed—and why not? For his part, Guttiérrez is convinced that the changing of hearts and the changing of structures are complementary:

> Both aspects...are interdependent and complementary because they are grounded on a common unity. The view that a structural transformation will automatically produce different human beings is no more and no less 'mechanistic' than the view that a 'personal change of heart' will automatically lead to a transformation of society. Any such mechanistic views are naïve and unrealistic.[76]

This is compatible with his view that

> Sin demands a radical liberation, which necessarily includes liberation of a political nature. Only by participating aggressively and effectively in the historical process of liberation can we point a finger at the basic alienation that underlies every partial form of alienation. The radical liberation called for by sin is a gift from Christ. Through his death and resurrection he redeemed us from sin and all its consequences.[77]

I should like at this point to shine a warning light upon the concept of sinful structures about which some liberation theologians wax lyrical. We do well to remember that structures cannot repent; people can; and the complacent should not be able to hide behind 'structures', claiming them as the cause of their inactivity on behalf of the oppressed. Not without reason did Helder Camara observe that 'if people's minds and hearts are not changed radically, then any structural reforms, no matter how basic, will remain paper reforms of no real effect'.[78]

Before taking the next step in this discussion I shall set down in order quotations from the Congregationalist A. E. Garvie, a liberation theologian and the Congregation for the Doctrine of the Faith:

> In some advocates of social reform as the first task of the church need and suffering seem to demand more attention, and to excite more compassion, than sin. The emphasis must be kept where the gospel puts it, on man's sin and on God's sacrifice.[79]

> Christ the Savior liberates man from sin, which is the ultimate root of all disruption of friendship and of all injustice and oppression. Christ makes man truly free, that

---

76 Guttiérrez, 'Liberation praxis and Christian faith', p. 11.

77 Ibid., p. 21.

78 Camara, *Between Honesty and Hope*, p. 53.

79 Garvie, 'The limits of doctrinal restatement', p. 94.

> is to say, he enables man to live in communion with him; and this is the basis for all human brotherhood.[80]
>
> Through his Cross and Resurrection, Christ has brought about our Redemption, which is liberation in the strongest sense of the word, since it has freed us from the most radical evil, namely sin and the power of death... The salvific dimension of liberation cannot be reduced to the socio-ethical dimension, which is a consequence of it. By restoring man's true freedom, the radical liberation brought about by Christ assigns him to a task...[81]

Far from elevating a socio-political programme above, or regarding it as an alternative to, the Gospel, it seems to me that these three voices are singing from the same hymn sheet, so to speak. With reference to the two tables of the Law, Calvin declared,

> I recognize that piety toward God comes before love of our brothers; therefore to observe the first table is more precious before God than to observe the second. But since God is invisible, our piety cannot be seen by our fellow men... He therefore presents Himself to us in our brothers, and in their persons demands from us what we owe to Him... It is certainly wrong to separate the love of God from the love of man.[82]

One of the strengths of liberation theology is its anti-docetic thrust. Christ is at work in history, and the saved are working there for, and with, him, sustained by an eschatological hope. In the opinion of the Brazilian Presbyterian, A. G. Mendonça, this emphasis was much needed in Latin America, for the Roman Catholic Church had traditionally presented a dead Christ to the people, the Protestants, a 'living but remote Christ. Neither has presented the living Christ of the gospels proclaiming the kingdom in the midst of mankind.'[83] For the Protestants, conversion to Christ was construed as conversion out of the world to a Christ high in the heavens. He concludes,

> It is thus possible to sum up all Latin American Christology as docetic: the great human dimensions of the life of Christ and the profound meaning of his death and resurrection recede before the instrumental role he plays in this Christology.[84]

By contrast, 'the great discovery of Latin American theology has been the Christ of the gospels, i.e. the post-prophetic Christ before his death and resurrection'.[85]

---

80 Guttiérrez, *A Theology of Liberation*, p. 37.

81 *Instruction on Freedom and Liberation*, pp. 5, 42.

82 J. Calvin, *The Epistles of Paul the Apostle to the Galatians, etc.*, trans. T. H. L. Parker, eds, Edinburgh: Oliver and Boyd, 1965, on Gal. 5:13-14.

83 Mendonça, 'Christology and ecclesiology in a world of oppression', p. 869.

84 Ibid., p. 872.

From this anti-docetic protest others than Latin Americans may learn; for the reminder from José Míguez Bonino that 'In the Bible there is no divine activity that does not have some bearing on human history'[86] they may be grateful; but from exclusive concentration upon the ministry of Jesus up to the Cross they should be weaned. For there is no redemption, no hope, no final victory, short of that. Nor is there the motivation for the liberating work to which the Church is called, for what is required is not the example of a teacher from long ago, but a living Lord who comes in the power of the Spirit.

But this invocation of trinitarian language brings me full circle to the hint I dropped at the beginning of this discussion of contextual theology, and it raises once again the question, What is the context of Christian theology?

The question of the analysis of 'context' is by no means straightforward. According to some responsible liberation theologians it would seem that the first phase of that theology encountered problems because of an inadequate appraisal of the diverse contexts within Latin America within which it was to be developed. As early as 1985 Juan Luis Segundo was speaking of a shift in liberation theology which had begun to appear in the 1970s, and which made it appropriate to think in terms of two co-existing liberation theologies. In the earlier type the concern was to bring orthodoxy into relation with orthopraxis, and this movement, as I noted earlier, grew out of the insights of the educated middle classes in the several Latin American nations. Segundo argues, however, that it failed to reach to the oppressed who were the primary object of its concern:

> the common people had neither understood nor welcomed anything from the first theology of liberation, and had actually reacted against its criticism of the supposed oppressive elements of popular [Roman Catholic] religion. They resisted the new pastoral trends trying to correct it.... [I]f theologians were still to be the 'organic intellectuals' of the common people...they were obliged to learn how oppressed people lived their faith.[87]

The 'second' liberation theology has accordingly sought to pay much more attention to the great variety of cultural traditions, some of them very ancient, whose members have a proper concern for the survival of their heritages. In the fifteenth anniversary edition of *A Theology of Liberation* Guttiérrez observes that earlier liberation theory 'is now an inadequate tool, because it does not take sufficient account of the internal

---

85 Ibid., p. 877.

86 Míguez Bonino, 'Historical praxis and Christian identity', p. 266.

87 J. L. Segundo, 'The shift within Latin American theology', *Journal of Theology for Southern Africa*, no. 52, September 1985, p. 23.

dynamics of each country or of the vast dimensions of the world of the poor'.[88] Among the fruits of this reappraisal are fresh treatments of ecclesiology as it relates to the poor. Indeed, Segundo cites Sobrino as one who regards the poor as the *locus* of an ecclesiology in which one becomes 'the other'.[89]

Assuming that Segundo's analysis is accurate, it would seem that for all their good intentions the first wave of liberation theologians failed to engage adequately with those for whom they wished most urgently to speak. To the extent that this is true it by no means justifies the abandonment of the legitimate theological insights to which they were led in reflecting upon the situation of the oppressed. But it does clamantly raise the question of the inculturation and not merely the announcement of the Gospel. Paul's attempt at contextualization in Athens was not conspicuously successful. In which connection the words of P. T. Forsyth come to mind:

> It is a curious thing, but it is possible for a movement or a church to be very evangelical on the extensive scale but not evangelical at all on the intensive. That is to say it is Low Church. It spreads its gospel over the face of the earth, but not into the thought and temper of the age. It covers, but it does not leaven. It does not recreate the age's habit of mind, or affect at all its culture, while it is tremendously earnest and enterprising in gathering converts in from the whole world. That is why missions, which owe so much to Low Church, are losing their staying power. They spread the Word rapidly—but so thin that it cracks.[90]

There is the further risk that by inadequately analysing 'context' we may land in parochialism, or even in sectarianism. Samuel Amirtham has rightly said that 'The test of theology in any context is its faithfulness to the gospel in that context'; but when he immediately adds, 'There is no extra-territorial accountability',[91] parochialism looms and concern mounts. Taking Amirtham's statement at face value it would seem that the theologian's accountability before God and to the apostolic witness of the Christian ages is overlooked. And, again, what is the 'context'? In one sense nobody but myself lives in my context. That is to say, my experience, though shared with others, is in important ways unique to me, as are my thoughts, capacities and sins. In a broader sense I seem to live in more than one context. I mingle in gatherings of theologians,

---

88 G. Guttiérrez, *A Theology of Liberation*, Maryknoll, NY: Orbis Books, 1988 edn, p. xxiv.

89 Ibid., pp. 28-29. Segundo proceeds to note the influence of Levinas on such liberation theologians as Enrique Dussel and Juan Carlos Scanone.

90 P. T. Forsyth, *Faith, Freedom and the Future*, (1912), London: Independent Press, 1955, pp. 93-94.

91 S. Amirtham, 'Theological education in Europe', *Ecumenical Press Service*, 21 January 1986.

philosophers and historians; I belong to a local church; I live among people who do none of these things, some of whom belong to other nationalities and faiths. In my travels I find myself in a variety of different cultural and socio-political contexts. I could belong to a range of interest groups which meet in my locality, but I do not. In other words, my context is circumscribed to some extent by what I choose not to do—because life is short, time is limited, and I am not well suited to origami.

But if it is difficult to define my context, it is even more difficult to constrict it. During the week beginning 25 July 2004, as I was writing this paper, I watched a television news broadcast including the following items: the plight of thirty million Bangladeshis driven from their homes by devastating floods; the starving thousands in the Darfur region of the Sudan and people fleeing therefrom into camps in neighbouring Chad; and the murder of innocents in Iraq. Are not these part of my context? Of particular interest was a report in which we first learned that the inhabitants of the Maldives Islands in the Indian Ocean will in due course have to be evacuated because of their low-lying territory and rising sea levels, and then we were immediately shown an enormous glacier in Greenland which, as a result of global warming, has shrunk by three to four metres in the past three months. Such meltings into the sea contribute to the problems of the Maldives Islands thousands of miles away. This news bulletin was full of parables illustrative of John Donne's line,

> No man is an *Island*, entire of it self...

When to all of this we add the ongoing challenge of an economic order which is unfairly weighted against nations in the developing world, whose own leaders and officials are not always as scrupulous as they might be, it becomes quite clear that however we define our personal, local or regional contexts, they are inextricably interwoven into the fabric of the global context. Imagine, therefore, my concern when an Asian theologian declared, with no regret whatsoever but as a simple statement of fact, that the time is coming when he and I will not be able to speak to each other because he is Asian and I am Western and our contexts are so different. I believe that we have a Gospel for the world, and that in a threatened and dangerous world it is of the greatest importance that Christians keep their channels of communication open so that prayers may be realistic, governments be challenged and aid be given. The context into which the good news comes is a continuum at one end of which is the individual Christian, at the other, the whole of humanity.

It is unfortunately the case that the kind of parochialism which I am concerned to counter can afflict theological method. It comes across, crudely, as the assertion that 'You cannot understand/speak to/witness to me because you are not economically oppressed/black/a woman.' It is evident that no individual can have experienced every conceivable aspect of the human lot, and we do not expect our prison chaplains to have served criminal sentences in order that they may more effectively minister to prisoners. In many circumstances an imaginative sympathy is all that we can muster, and we are not blameworthy for that, nor paralyzed by it.

But then some take a further step and say, 'The only legitimate theology is done in our way, by looking through our experiential lens.'[92] We thus have the paradox that contextual theologies which are supposed to critique the imposition of theological imperialisms from elsewhere themselves become imperialistic in attitude. They privilege a particular form of human experience in an elitist way, making it the sole norm of biblical or theological interpretation. If this leads to the 'unchurching' of others who do theology differently the sectarian spirit is at work, and of this J. W. Nevin said,

> The liberty of the sect consists at last, in thinking its particular notions, shouting its shibboleths and passwords, dancing its religious hornpipes, and reading the Bible only through its theological goggles. These restrictions, at the same time, are so many wires, that lead back at last into the hands of a few leading spirits, enabling them to wield a true hierarchical despotism over all who are thus brought within their power.[93]

At the very least theological sectarians deprive themselves of the support and challenge of those who are outside their group but within the Christian family. The dry observation of Robert Mackintosh comes to mind: 'Persons, who herd in corners with those who share their prejudices, are apt to take the whisperings of a coterie for the verdict of "the civilised world", or even of the Almighty.'[94] More recently, Gabriel Fackre has explained that where tribalist attitudes prevail

---

[92] J. M. Dawsey has found that this can happen in respect of the Bible reading done in the Base Church Communities, as when it is believed that 'only the poor, or the person who approaches the text from the perspective of the poor, can understand. Otherwise, scripture speaks in riddles. But if we are not careful, such a hermeneutic takes away scripture's mysterious power to convert the reticent hearer. We must remember that the Word of God is more than a message to the oppressed; it is also power that changes the hearts and minds of people who oppress.' See 'The biblical authority of the poor', p. 298.

[93] J. W. Nevin, 'The sect system', (1849), reprinted in Charles Yrigoyen, Jr., and George H. Bricker, eds, *Catholic and Reformed. Selected Writings of John Williamson Nevin*, Pittsburgh, PA: Pickwick Press, 1978, p. 144.

[94] R. Mackintosh, *The Obsoleteness of the Westminster Confession of Faith*, p. 52; bound with his *Essays Towards a New Theology*, Glasgow: Maclehose, 1889.

> relationships with outsiders can only be polemical or calls to conversion. No *conversation* is conceivable, for that would undercut the assumption of privileged loci. Where imperial tribalism reigns, the theological forum, or the church, begins to look like an armed camp. The city of Beirut replaces the city of God. *Beirutization* is the end.[95]

It is increasingly being recognized by liberation theologians and contextual theologians generally that in fact we do not come intellectually innocent to any particular context: 'An observation is always preceded by a particular interest, a question or a problem—in short, by something theoretical.'[96] If we are Christian we come as Christians bearing good news. We cannot set on one side the claim that there are universal truths; and in fact the liberation theologians have not done so. Even when some of the earlier ones denied that there were such truths, they nevertheless assumed the contrary with their conviction that God addresses people through the Bible. Raúl Vidales makes no bones about it: 'By the law of the Incarnation, the whole cosmic and historical process has been penetrated by the Christ-happening.'[97] The Asian contextual theologian, Shoki Coe, concurs: 'I believe that the incarnation is the divine form of contextualization.... As the catholicity of the gospel is given through the Word becoming flesh, so our task should be through our responsive contextualization, taking our own concrete, local contexts seriously.'[98] But, to repeat, this should not be done in such a way that our context becomes our cabbage patch. The Incarnation—indeed, the work of the triune God—is prior to anything we do, and it alone provides the all-sufficient, overarching context for all our Christian living and witness. There is that in the Gospel which addresses our deepest needs and judges our most perverse parochialisms. As so often, Forsyth put it in a nutshell: 'We must all preach *to* our age, but woe to us if it is our age we preach, and only hold up the mirror to the time.'[99] There is, in fact, an inclusivity in the Gospel which breaks down barriers, transcends localities and cultures, calls out the one Church, and meets our deepest need of salvation. But if the Gospel is in this way inclusive, ought not the Church

---

95 Gabriel Fackre, 'Evangelical catholicity today', *The New Mercersburg Review*, VIII, Autumn 1990, p. 43. For further reflections on this point see Alan P. F. Sell, *Aspects of Christian Integrity*, (1990), Eugene, OR: Wipf & Stock, 1998, pp. 12-14, and *Commemorations. Studies in Christian Thought and History*, (1993), Eugene, OR: Wipf & Stock, 1998, ch. 2. In *Systematic Theology*, I, p. 60, Tillich declares that 'Methodological imperialism is as dangerous as political imperialism.'

96 Karl Popper, *Objective Knowledge*, Oxford: Clarendon Press, 1972, p. 342.

97 R. Vidales, 'Methodological issues in liberation theology', in Gibellini, ed., *Frontiers Theology in Latin America*, p. 56.

98 Quoted by Pieter N. Holtrop *et al.*, 'Witnessing together in context', *Reformed World*, XLV no. 4, December 1995, p. 162.

99 Forsyth, *Positive Preaching and the Modern Mind*, p. 5.

to be also? With this I come to the third slogan on which I wish to comment.

III

It is not at all surprising that in open-minded circles in Western society inclusivity is regularly proclaimed as a virtue, the frequent vagueness of its definition notwithstanding. The post-Enlightenment spread in open societies of ideas concerning human dignity and human rights, together with increased migration of peoples around the world has fostered a spirit of tolerance and made it less easy or appropriate to ostracize others on grounds of race, creed or political persuasion. This, coupled with a genial individualism which allows others to 'do their own thing' provided that it does not 'frighten the horses', has facilitated neighbourliness in pluralistic communities, and fostered relativism where truth is concerned and a *laissez-faire* attitude in some quarters to questions of moral discipline.

It seems quite widely agreed that where the Church is concerned inclusivity is good, exclusivity is bad. 'Sooner or later', declares the Reverend Donald Horsfield, echoing nineteenth-century secularists, 'all religions will have to stop making exclusive claims for their own understanding of God and truth.'[100] In connection with the debate on homosexuality, a group of twenty-three Roman Catholic priests in Chicago affirm that the 'Catholic church is most catholic when it is inclusive and embracing, and least reflective of the Gospel of Jesus when it is exclusive and rigid'.[101] On the other hand P. T. Forsyth thundered, 'a Christianity which would exclude none has no power to include the world'.[102] Since it is always advisable to subject alleged truisms to close scrutiny before jumping on passing band wagons, I shall proceed with caution, illustrating my discussion from the fields of doctrine, church polity, ethics and worship. I shall suggest that blanket denunciations of exclusivity and uncritical commendations of inclusivity are uncalled for, that it is sometimes difficult to assign meaning to some inclusivist locutions, and that neither exclusivists nor inclusivists are innocent of sectarian tendencies. I turn first to a doctrine.

Increasingly since the Reformation, the doctrine of predestination has been the target of inclusivists who accuse others, notably Calvinists, of adhering to, and advocating, an immoral doctrine which unwarrantably excludes large numbers of people from heaven—not least those who were

100 D. Horsfield, letter to *Reform*, December 2003, p. 9.

101 Quoted by John M. Buchanan, 'Couples', *The Christian Century*, 27 January 2004, p. 3.

102 P. T. Forsyth, *The Work of Christ*, (1910), London: Independent Press, 1958, p. 62.

born before Christ, or outside the reach of Christianity, and hence were or are unable to be converted to it. While, given some ways in which the doctrine was and still is proclaimed, such accusations are understandable, it must be said that some reactions verge upon the hysterical. A writer on Catholic spirituality was unusually zealous in casting the first brick: 'For Salesians the point of departure is God's love, for Calvinists it is God's hatred.'[103] More temperately, the Cambridge Platonists, the liberal Presbyterians of eighteenth-century England, and the English Congregationalists were among those who properly rejected some versions of predestinarian doctrine as dishonouring to God.[104] Tiptoeing gingerly into this doctrinal thicket, I shall first sketch the biblical basis of the doctrine, then discuss some unwarranted inferences from it, and finally set forth the good news contained in it.

Having ransacked the relevant biblical commentaries, especially those on *Romans* from Sanday and Headlam through Dodd to Cranfield and beyond, I have some confidence in making the following summary claims:

> The theme of election runs through both the Old and the New Testaments. In the former it principally concerns the people of God, Israel, who were chosen not because of their righteousness or prestige, but simply because God loved them (Deuteronomy 7:7; 23:5). In the latter election refers both to the people of God, the Church, and to individuals who are called out of 'the world' to Christ himself, and into fellowship with those who are 'in Christ', the Church.
>
> The call is not to privilege but to service. God's saving grace is to be made known to the ends of the earth. Before the question, Why are these called for this purpose but not those? we must remain agnostic: it is not for us to probe the workings of the divine mind (Romans 9:20, 22; 11:33-36).
>
> Although the initiative in calling lies exclusively with God, secondary causes are by no means effaced: persons are fully responsible for their obedience or disobedience, and God is not the author of sin.
>
> In Jesus Christ, the elect One, God's saving purposes are brought to bear upon individuals in the most direct way: they were chosen in Christ before the foundation of the world (Ephesians 1:4); in this life they are called by the living Lord who said, 'You did not choose me, I chose you' (John 15:16); their final destiny, which entails the restoration of the defaced image of God to conformity to Christ, is determined by their relationship to him; and in their present condition, no matter how tempestuous it may be, they are secure, for by Christ's death and resurrection death and the grave are vanquished (Romans 8:28-39). This is all of grace, 'not for

---

103 Francis Vincent, 'The spirituality of Saint Francis of Sales', in Jean Gautier, ed., *Some Schools of Catholic Spirituality*, (1953), trans. Kathryn Sullivan, Paris: Desclee Company, 1959, p. 254.

104 See chs 1 and 5 above.

any merit of ours but for his own purpose and of his own grace, granted to us in Christ Jesus from all eternity' (II Timothy 1:9).

In Romans 9–11 Paul, a Jew by birth and upbringing, and one who had formerly persecuted the infant Church, seeks to explain why so many of his own people have refused God's Messiah. While salvation is solely by God's grace, the Jews alone are culpable for their refusal of the Gospel. Whereas it is by God's predestinating will that all such are passed by, they alone are responsible for their unbelief. However, their defection has opened the way of salvation to the Gentiles, and Paul's conviction is that eventually the faithful of the old Israel, of which a remnant already survives within the Church,[105] will be grafted into the new. God has by no means rejected his ancient people, and their fall was far from final (Romans 11:1, 11).

God's gracious purpose is to show mercy to all, and election and reprobation are not equal options. The former, a matter of God's prevenient, unmerited, grace, is not contingent upon divinely forseen faith or good works on the part of individuals; the latter concerns his justice in face of human obduracy. Sin pays a wage: death; God freely gives eternal life in union with Christ (Romans 6:23). There is thus 'not a shadow of justification for the blasphemous doctrine that God creates some men solely to be destroyed for His greater glory.'[106]

The doctrine of predestination, like the warning parables in the gospels, prevents us from affirming that all will be saved. We have no grounds for assigning numbers to the saved or the damned. We may not set limits upon the grace of the God who does not will that any should perish (II Peter 3:9). The gospels make it clear that the 'religious' will have some surprises when they discover who are finally saved (Matthew 25:37-40)—and who are not (Luke 16:19-31); and they caution all to be on the alert, for 'the Son of Man will come at the time you least expect him' (Luke 12:40). In the meantime we are to bring forth the fruit of good deeds (Ephesians 2:10).

Although I have attempted to set down the principle points concisely and positively, this is by no means to say that the underlying mystery of the relations between divine sovereignty and human freedom has been fully penetrated. It has puzzled Christians through the ages,[107] not least

---

[105] Cf. Anders Nygren, *Commentary on Romans*, London: SCM Press, 1952, p. 393: 'A "remnant" is not just a group of separate individuals, taken out of a people doomed to overthrow; it is itself the chosen people, it is Israel *in nuce*. It is the seed which, after the winter, will bear the harvest.'

[106] George Caird, 'Expository problems: predestination—Romans ix-xi', *Expository Times*, LXVIII no. 11, August 1957, p. 326.

[107] For some early reflections on early aspects of the history see Alan P. F. Sell, 'Augustine *versus* Pelagius: A cautionary tale of perennial importance', *Calvin Theological Journal*, XII no. 2, November 1977, pp. 117-43; 'Augustinian and Pelagian variations from Cassian to Luther', *Theologia Evangelica*, XI nos. 2 and 3,

Howel Harris the Welsh evangelist, who recorded the following in his diary on 5 December 1741:

> Discoursed on Rom. 5:1, to near 9. Surely the Lord did come down here, many wept bitterly. I could not preach now in the same universal manner as I did when in London, though I have no guilt for any word I said then. I was then called 1. To incite the unawakened. 2. To moderate the predestinarians. 3. To remove the prejudice of the universalists, and to pave the way for an union. [Perhaps not surprisingly, he immediately adds] Slept with great uneasiness. Conflict.[108]

But if we shall ever fail to plumb the depths of this teaching, we can at least, in the light of the summary statements made above, do two things: we can reject some inferences which are unwarrantably drawn from the doctrine, and we can restate the good news to be found in it.

The first unwarranted inference is that the elect comprise only a few. Although there is no biblical ground for this view, it has been promulgated by enemies and friends of the doctrine alike. The former frequently contrast the few saved with the many damned and, since all of this was allegedly determined before the birth of anyone, they urge this as a reason for doubting God's love: he does what no upright human being would do. The latter state the 'fewness' of the saved as a fact. Calvin declares that election confers salvation 'on a few'.[109] In a sermon delivered in 1648 the Puritan William Bridge advised his hearers that while 'there is a certain number of elect persons, who are but few comparatively...this is in no way prejudicial to the existence or growth of your comfort';[110] and a twentieth-century Christian woman of hyper-Calvinistic persuasion said to her minister, 'How good God is! He has damned nearly all my friends, but he has saved me.'[111] The fact is, as the inhabitants of Dante's Paradise realised, that

> we, who see God,
> Do not yet know who all the elect are.[112]

July–September 1978, pp. 79-100; The *Great Debate: Calvinism, Arminianism and Salvation*, (1982), Eugene, OR: Wipf & Stock, 1998, ch. 1.

108 *Howell Harris's Visits to Pembrokeshire*, transcribed by Tom Beynon, Aberystwyth: Cambrian News Press, 1966, p. 66; cf. p. 20.

109 J. Calvin, *Institutes of the Christian Religion*, ed. J. T. McNeill, trans. Ford Lewis Battles, 2 vols, Philadelphia: Westminster Press, 1960, III.xxiii.1.

110 W. Bridge, *A Lifting Up for the Downcast*, London: Banner of Truth Trust, 1961, p. 250.

111 Quoted by E. J. Poole-Connor, *Evangelicalism in England*, Worthing: Henry E. Walter, (1951), new edn, 1956, p. 116 n.

112 Dante Alighieri, *The Divine Comedy*, III.xx.134-35. Trans. by C. H. Sisson, Oxford: Oxford University Press, 1998. Cf. The Second Helvetic Confession, X, in Arthur

God's intention, we may say, is inclusive; exclusion is the consequence of the obdurate, rebellious, abuse of human freedom, and that is as God would have it too.

The second unwarranted inference is that the fate of the reprobate is sealed by God's inscrutable will from eternity. Augustine, Luther and Calvin were united in the belief that God had decreed that some people were predestined to salvation. But Calvin, Zanchius, Beza and others, brought logic, and their understanding of the requirements of Scripture, to bear and concluded that the reprobate also were in their predestined state. Hence the doctrine of double predestination. It must be admitted that Calvin spoke only very gingerly about predestination at all: the one who is carefree in this matter will not satisfy his curiosity, and 'will enter a labyrinth from which he can find no exit';[113] it is by no means the foundation-stone of his doctrine; and he was especially reticent concerning the fate of the wicked, referring their destiny to the will of God than which there is nothing higher.[114]

The Calvinistic understanding of the decree of reprobation launched many an eighteenth-century writer into polemical mode. 'The grosser pagans contented themselves with divinizing lust, incest and adultery', declared the convert to Roman Catholicism, Chevalier Ramsey, 'but the predestinarian doctors have divinized cruelty, wrath, fury, vengeance, and all the blackest vices.'[115] More coolly, the Unitarian Joseph Priestley, and others, entered their protest in the eighteenth century:

> That by any arbitrary decree of God, independent of the good dispositions and good works of men, some should be predestinated to eternal life, while others are doomed to eternal damnation, is a doctrine far from being favoured by the Scriptures, and is so contrary to all idea of equity in the Divine government, that it must be rejected at any rate.[116]

Calvin, of course, has his reply to complaints of this kind. He restates the charge thus: 'Why from the beginning did God predestine some to death who, since they did not yet exist, could not yet have deserved the judgment of death?'[117] He brands the idea that people 'perish by the hidden judgment of God beyond their deserts' as 'false' and 'a foul

---

C. Cochrane, *Reformed Confessions of the 16th Century*, Philadelphia, PA: Westminster Press, 1966.

113 See Calvin, *Institutes*, III.xxi.1.

114 Ibid., III.xxiii.2.

115 David Hume, *Essays, Moral, Political and Literary*, eds T. H. Green and T. H. Grose, London: Longmans, Green, 1875, II, p. 356, quoting C. Ramsay, *Philosophical Principles and Revealed Religion*, Glasgow, 1748–49, II, p. 401.

116 J. Priestley, *The Theological and Miscellaneous Works of Joseph Priestley*, ed. J. T. Rutt, (1817–32), Bristol: Thoemmes Press, 1999, XIII p. 446.

117 Calvin, *Institutes*, III.xxiii.3.

sacrilege',[118] and rebukes such opponents for overlooking the fact of human corruption.[119] Perpetuating a line of thought which flows down from Augustine,[120] Calvin insists that in view of sin God would have been justified in condemning the entire human race to death. Despite Calvin's best efforts, however, the moral objection to the unbiblical notion that a God of all grace would decree the reprobation of specific individuals from eternity was not removed. On the contrary, it continued to be the subject of intense debate and even, in the hands of Robert Burns, of satire:

> O Thou that in the heaven dost dwell!
> Who, as it pleases best Thysel',
> Sends ane to heaven and ten to hell
> A' for Thy glory;
> And no for any guid or ill
> They've done before Thee.[121]

The doctrine of double predestination flowed down through many Reformed confessions and catechisms—not least the *Canons of Dort* and the *Westminster Larger Catechism*—though the doctrine is not present in that most pastoral catechism, the *Heidelberg*. As far as the English-speaking Reformed world is concerned, it achieved classic status in chapter three of the *Westminster Confession*, two sections of which I now quote:

> VI. As God hath appointed the elect unto glory, so hath he, by the eternal and most free purpose of his will, foreordained all the means thereunto. Wherefore they who are elected being fallen in Adam, are redeemed by Christ; are effectually called unto faith in Christ by his Spirit working in due season; are justified, adopted, sanctified, and kept by his power through faith unto salvation. Neither are any other redeemed by Christ, effectually called, justified, adopted, sanctified, and saved, but the elect only.
>
> VII. The rest of mankind, God was pleased, according to the unsearchable counsel of his own will, whereby he extendeth or witholdeth mercy as he pleaseth, for the glory of his sovereign power over his creatures, to pass by, and to ordain them to dishonour and wrath for their sin, to the praise of his glorious justice.

As for twentieth-century products of this kind, the *New Confession* (1972) of the Presbyterian Church in the Republic of Korea is most unusual in devoting a paragraph to predestination.[122]

---

118 J. Calvin, *Concerning the Eternal Predestination of God*, trans. J. K. S. Reid, London: James Clarke, 1961, IX.7.

119 Calvin, *Institutes*, III.xxiii.3.

120 See Augustine, *On the Gift of Perseverance*, VIII.17.

121 R. Burns, 'Holy Willie's Prayer'.

Not least because of the contribution of Karl Barth, fresh attention has been paid to the place of Christ in election and reprobation. According to Barth, Christ is the elect One, in whom humanity at large is chosen. In his death for all Christ became reprobate, and by his death all are reconciled to God. Adverse critics of Barth claim that this places him on the brink of universalism,[123] and some allege, against his own denials, that he fell in. It may fairly be said that his mode of expression does on occasion make it appear that the salvation of all is effected eternally, regardless of any human response in history to God's grace; but then Barth introduces the complication that on grounds of God's freedom, he cannot assert that all will in fact be saved, and hence he is not an universalist.[124] This seems at the very least to make salvation something arbitrarily applied—either before time began or at the eschaton—and it is a high price to pay for the insight that sinful human beings can never escape from God, and are never beyond his grace.[125] It is, moreover, difficult to understand how those who are elect in Christ (in Barth's sense) may not be saved at the last. Their salvation seems to be less than sure because Barth does not wish to be a universalist. It is all very puzzling.[126]

---

[122] Reprinted in Lukas Vischer, ed., *Reformed Witness Today. A Collection of Confessions and Statements of Faith Issued by Reformed Churches*, Bern: Evangelische Arbeitsstelle Oekumene Schweiz, 1982, p. 74. It would seem that in mainstream Reformed circles it has proved easier to shelve double predestination than to attend to it, either because the confessionally strict remnant would rebel against change, or because of widespread unconcern for doctrine (to speak of doctrinal laxity would presuppose that people knew what the doctrines were and sat loose to them; I am not sure that today they always know what they are).

[123] See the challenge of Emil Brunner, *The Christian Doctrine of God*, trans. Olive Wyon, London: Lutterworth, 1949, p. 348. Brunner rebukes Barth for holding that 'Since Jesus Christ has taken the condemnation of sin upon Himself, "rejection *cannot* again become the portion of man."'

[124] K. Barth, *Church Dogmatics*, trans. and ed. G. W. Bromiley and T.F. Torrance, 14 vols, Edinburgh: T. & T. Clark, 1936–77, IV/3, p. 477: 'Even though theological consistency might seem to lead our thoughts and utterances most clearly in this direction, we must not arrogate to ourselves that which can be given and received only as a free gift.'

[125] Barth, *Church Dogmatics*, II/2, p. 317: '[man] can certainly flee from God (he does so); but he cannot escape Him'. The literature for and against Barth is vast. For a lucid exposition of his thought on the matters under review see John Thompson, *Christ in Perspective in the Theology of Karl Barth*, Edinburgh: Saint Andrew Press, 1978. For a gracious adverse criticism see Colin Brown, *Karl Barth and the Christian Message*, London: Tyndale Press, 1967.

[126] For evidence that I am not alone in my puzzlement see Oliver Crisp, 'On Barth's denial of universalism', *Themelios*, XXIX no. 1, Autumn 2003, pp. 18-29.

Nevertheless, in so far as Barth construed election Christocentrically, I am sure that he was right.[127] Indeed, his complaint against Calvin is that 'in the last analysis he separates God and Jesus Christ'.[128] This is not entirely fair, however, for Calvin's discussion of predestination falls under the heading of 'The way we receive the grace of Christ' and he knows full well that those who are adopted by grace as sons and daughters of God 'have been chosen not in themselves but in his Christ [Eph. 1:4]'.[129] But it is as if Calvin does not follow this thought through at the crucial point. For when focusing upon the decrees in detail he so elevates God's inscrutable will as to suggest that it is as inscrutable to Christ as it is to us—that is to say, that the Son, although a person of the Trinity, has at best limited involvement at the point of the eternal determinations regarding human beings; and this despite the fact that Calvin does not wish God to be regarded as a tyrannical despot.[130] In a word, we seem to hear more of sovereign will than of sovereign grace, and '*God's unmotivated or secret will, used as the master-key*—always works for the disintegration both of theology and of faith.'[131]

In this connection J. K. S. Reid's discussion is illuminating:

> If Christ is given his rightful place in the determining counsels of God, it is impossible to maintain a parity of relation [of the two decrees]. He came on His own testimony to 'seek and to save that which was lost'; and in the strictest sense we may say that in His coming God pledges His preference for one of the decrees over the other.[132]

Not, indeed, that despite the divine preference we may not opt for unbelief. As to whether any will finally 'contract out', Reid says we cannot pronounce upon this with any certainty. He concludes,

> if evil were explicable, then it would be rational; and if it were rational, it would have parity of relation to God with the good. This would be once again to stand

---

[127] It is interesting to note that whereas in chapter 3 of the Westminster Confession, double predestination is taught and there is but a brief passing reference to election in Christ, in chapter 8 of the Scottish Confession of 1560 the Christological reference is paramount, the reprobate are mentioned once in passing, but there is no decree of reprobation.

[128] K. Barth, *Church Dogmatics*, II/2, p. 111.

[129] Calvin, *Institutes*, III.xxiv.5. See further, R. A. Muller, *Christ and the Decree*, Durham NC: Labyrinth Press, 1986.

[130] Calvin, *Institutes*, III.xxiv.5.

[131] Robert Mackintosh, *Historic Theories of Atonement with Comments*, London: Hodder and Stoughton, 1920, p. 155.

[132] J. K. S. Reid, Introduction to Calvin's *Concerning the Eternal Predestination of God*, p. 42.

> where Calvin's doctrine lands us, but not, I think, where Christians ought to stand.[133]

Robert Mackintosh, that self-styled 'refugee' from high confessional Calvinism, was more forthright:

> Calvinism, in its naked reality, is anything but Christian.... The essential features of Christianity are summed up in the revelation of God as moral character, not in His revelation as infinite power....
>
> [I]n Christ, the character of God comes to meet us with forgiveness for our sin, because God is God and Father, and with the pledge of victory over evil for all who deny themselves and follow Christ. If we commit ourselves to his power it will never fail us.
>
> Belief in God as our Father, and in Christ as Saviour of the world, is Christian faith. Whatever obscures this is leaven of the Scribes and Pharisees.[134]

Elsewhere Mackintosh complained of the *Westminster Shorter Catechism* that in it 'we never read that God so *loved* the *world*—only that He *chose* to save the *elect*'.[135]

P. T. Forsyth stated the matter with sufficient clarity, in a manner consonant with the main thrust of the Bible as set down above, and I invoke him to bring this part of my discussion to a conclusion:

> The lost are lost by refusing [the] gospel in their mysterious and incalculable freedom.... The self-determining power of the individual is part of the ordered predestination of God, and of the necessity felt by His love to endow man with a freedom like His own if he expected man to respond to His own. Only a fatalistic predestination, not a personal, excludes such freedom.[136]

The third unwarrantable inference which has been, and sometimes still is, drawn from the doctrine of predestination is that antinomianism may properly be entertained. In its crudest form this is the protest: Since I am of the elect, God's law is, for me, annulled, and as my good works could not have saved me, so my future evil deeds will not prejudice my final state, which is eternally guaranteed. This view runs counter to biblical injunctions concerning the bearing of the good fruit of the Spirit, and it

---

133 Reid, Introduction, p. 44.

134 Mackintosh, *Essays Towards a New Theology*, p. 475. For Mackintosh's life and theological pilgrimage see Alan P. F. Sell, *Robert Mackintosh: Theologian of Integrity*, Bern: Peter Lang, 1977.

135 Robert Mackintosh,, 'The religion of "The Shorter Catechism"', *The Holborn Review*, January 1927, p. 21.

136 P. T. Forsyth, *The Principle of Authority*, (1913), London: Independent Press, 1952, p. 357.

was trounced by Paul as presuming on the grace of God: 'Shall we persist in sin, so that there may be all the more grace? Certainly not! We died to sin, how can we live in it any longer?' (Romans 6:1-2). On the contrary, believers should, like the psalmist of old, love God's law, for, like the One who enacts it, it is holy (Romans 7:12).[137]

The fourth unwarrantable inference is that because the elect alone are saved there is no point in engaging in missionary work since the saved are saved whether others venture into foreign parts or not; and it is wrong to proclaim that Christ died for all. Along the former line some sought to inhibit the modern missionary movement, while those who disallow the 'free offer' of the Gospel in preaching are reduced to construing 'the world' in 'God so loved the world' (John 3:16) as meaning not everyone, but 'Jews and Gentiles alike'. In either case we have an exclusivist perversion of the biblical witness. The first chapter of the *Second Helvetic Confession* (1566) contains a rousing call to proclaim the Gospel to all who will listen (the external call of the Gospel), without denying the crucial importance of the inward illumination of the Holy Spirit. Even Tobias Crisp, the high Calvinist accused of (theoretical) antinomianism, found it possible to say to his congregation, 'Beloved, will you starve in a cook's shop, as they say? Is there such plenty in Christ, and will you perish for hunger?'[138] The *London* Confession of the Particular Baptists (1644) was clear on the propriety of the free offer of the Gospel,[139] while to the Congregational *Savoy Declaration of Faith* (1658), which largely follows the *Westminster Confession*, was added a new chapter 'Of the Gospel, and of the extent of the grace thereof.'[140]

The final unwarranted inference drawn from the concept of predestination is that which equates election with philosophical necessity. Considerable mischief has been done by this unfortunate assimilation, which has persuaded some that the God of Calvinism is Stoic fate or an oriental despot, and that Christianity according to Calvinism is necessarily and unacceptably exclusive. In polemical mood against Erasmus, Luther came near to warranting the charge:

---

137 For a discussion of post-Reformation antinomianism see Sell, *The Great Debate*, pp. 42-52.

138 T. Crisp, *Christ's Pre-eminence*, reprinted Sheffield: Zoar Publications, c.1974, pp. 13-14. For further discussion of this point, and for the continuation of the anti-free offer line among the Gospel Standard Baptists see Sell, *The Great Debate*, pp. 52-57, 93-94, 133-34, 135, and *Theology in Turmoil*, pp. 137-39, 187-88; Kenneth Dix, *Strict and Particular. English Strict and Particular Baptists in the Nineteenth Century*, Didcot: Baptist Historical Society, 2001.

139 *The London Confession*, (1644), ch. XXV, in William L. Lumpkin, *Baptist Confessions of Faith*, Valley Forge, PA: Judson Press, rev. edn 1969, p. 163.

140 *Savoy Declaration of Faith*, (1658), ch. XX, in *The Savoy Declaration of Faith and Order*, ed. Albert Peel, London: Independent Press, 1959, pp. 101-102.

> This...is...essentially necessary and wholesome for Christians to know: that God foreknows nothing by contingency, but that He sees, purposes, and does all things according to His immutable, eternal, and infallible will. By this thunderbolt, 'Free-will' is thrown prostrate, and utterly dashed to pieces.[141]

Luther wishes there were some better term than 'necessity', which suggests compulsion and what is contrary to will, for will is free; but God's will, he repeats, is 'immutable and infallible'.[142]

Calvin seeks to refine the position. He agrees that what God decrees cannot fail to come to pass, but he wishes to distinguish the doctrine of predestination from necessarian fate. As well as the divine necessity of the supernatural order there is in the natural order both necessity (cause and effect, for example) and contingency. Were it otherwise human beings could not be accountable for their sin; but they are, for they sin 'not by extrinsic impulse but by the spontaneous inclination of the heart, knowingly and voluntarily'.[143]

But the term 'necessity' stuck to Calvinism, especially in anti-Calvinistic tracts. Interestingly, among those anxious to distinguish determinism from Calvinism was Joseph Priestley, but that was because he was a determinist in philosophy, and would have been horrified if anyone thought that he had any love of double predestination. He writes:

> the essential difference between the two schemes is this: the Necessarian believes that his own dispositions and actions are the necessary and sole means of his present and future happiness; so that in the most proper sense of the words, it depends entirely upon *himself* whether he be virtuous or vicious, happy or miserable... As far as any system of faith can induce men to cultivate virtuous principles and habits, this doctrine of necessity must do it.
>
> On the other hand, I do not see what motive a Calvinist can have to give any attention to his moral conduct. So long as he is unregenerate, all his thoughts, words and actions are necessarily sinful, and in the act of *regeneration* he is altogether passive. On this account the most consistent Calvinists never address any exhortations to sinners, considering them as *dead in trespasses and sins*, and therefore that there would be as much sense and propriety in speaking to the dead as to them. On the other hand, if a man be in the happy number of the *elect*, he is sure that God will...work upon him his miraculous work of *saving and sanctifying grace*. Though he should be ever so wicked immediately before this divine and *effectual*

---

141 M. Luther, *On the Bondage of the Will*, Grand Rapids, MI: Associated Publishers, n.d., p. 18.

142 Ibid., p. 19.

143 Calvin, *Concerning the Eternal Predestination of God*, p. 116.

> *calling*, it makes nothing against him.... If any system of speculative principles can operate as an axe at the root of all virtue and goodness, it is this.[144]

In view two of our previously-mentioned unwarrantable inferences from predestination, it is interesting that Priestley should find Calvinists consistent in refusing the free offer of the Gospel, and encouraged in antinomianism. Neither stance is essential to Calvinism, as we have seen. As to necessity, Calvinists no less than Priestley can allow for moral responsibility: indeed, the doctrine of reprobation in particular positively requires it. But I do not wish to pursue Priestley further. My purpose was to show that an opponent of Calvinism could be as eager to distinguish between Calvinism and philosophical determinism as Calvinists are well advised to be.

For an example of a Calvinist who was keen to maintain the distinction, I introduce William Cunningham who, in a very perceptive paper, makes good the following claims:

> 1st, There is nothing in the Calvinistic system of theology, or in the Westminster Confession of Faith, which *precludes* men from holding the doctrine of philosophical necessity. 2d, There is nothing in the Calvinistic system of theology, or in the Westminster Confession, which *requires* men to hold the doctrine of philosophical necessity.[145]

He proceeds to argue that while Calvinist doctrines 'establish necessity and exclude liberty in some sense', they do not do this in such a way as to remove the liberty of second causes.[146] For this reason,

> We are not prepared to concur in [the] identification of the philosophical doctrine of necessity with the theological doctrine of predestination.... Predestination implies that the end or result is certain, and that adequate provision has been made for bringing it about. But it does not indicate anything as to what must be the nature of this provision in regard to the different classes of events which are taking place under God's government, including the volitions of rational and responsible beings.[147]

The upshot is that neither doctrine can directly be inferred from the other. He grants that in philosophy most Calvinists have been necessarians, but some have been libertarians. There is no problem here,

---

144 Priestley, *The Theological and Miscellaneous Works of Joseph Priestley*, III, pp. 534-35.

145 W. Cunningham, *The Reformers and the Theology of the Reformation*, (1862), London: Banner of Truth Trust, 1967, p. 482.

146 Ibid., p. 494. He quotes Calvin in support of this view, p. 498.

147 Ibid., pp. 508-509.

for the biblical and theological doctrine of predestination is untouched by either standpoint.

My view is that Cunningham is correct in distinguishing the theological from the philosophical doctrines. I should go further and suggest that predestination is best understood as a doctrine rooted in the Bible and confirmed by Christian experience. The doctrine comes to be articulated retrospectively, as it were. To put it bluntly, the most famous New Testament statement of it grows out of Paul's realization that he had not reached his destination as a Christian believer under his own steam. The eternal purposes of God were behind it all. He may have thought that he had chosen Christ, but Christ had chosen him. At this point I find the words of Norman Snaith helpful: 'the idea of a human choice is the language of the newly converted, but the certainty of the divine choice is the language of the sanctified'.[148]

With this I come to the good news in predestination. The doctrine speaks above all of the sovereignty of God's *grace* (not the absoluteness of his will), which calls, converts and keeps:[149] 'We must put God's free grace first—far before our free thought or action.'[150] When we can do nothing, God does everything.[151] Let us be guided by the Congregationalist shipwright of Bideford, John Kent (1766–1843), whose robust hymn of 1827 is sadly missing from all current mainline hymnals known to me:

> Sovereign grace o'er sin abounding!
>   Ransomed souls the tidings swell;
> 'Tis a deep that knows no sounding;
> Who its breadth or length can tell?
>   On its glories,
> Let my soul for ever dwell.

Here is the ground of the Christian's confidence, and the source of solace in time of trial. 'It is well to fall back, every now and then, in sheer weariness, upon the great truth of predestination', declared C. H. Spurgeon: 'It is a bed for some men's idleness; to us, it should be a couch for our refreshment. After all, God's will is done.'[152]

---

148 N. Snaith, 'Chosen', in Alan Richardson, ed., *A Theological Word Book of the Bible*, London: SCM Press, 1956, p. 67.

149 John Whale draws out one ecclesiological implication of this when he says that this doctrine is 'Fatal to all papal, hierarchical and sacerdotal pretensions...'. See *The Protestant Tradition*, Cambridge: Cambridge University Press, 1959, p. 144.

150 Forsyth, *The Principle of Authority*, p. 255.

151 This is precisely the good news to which paedobaptism bears witness.

152 C. H. Spurgeon, *An All-Round Ministry*, (1900), London: Banner of Truth Trust, 1960, p. 84.

> My every need he richly will supply;
> Nor will his mercy ever let me die;
> In him there dwells a treasure all divine,
> And matchless grace has made that treasure mine.
> (William Gadsby, 1773–1844)

Not indeed that the comfort of God is for individual believers alone. The entire communion of saints is called and sustained by grace and lives in hope: 'the Son of God, by His Spirit and Word, gathers, protects, and preserves for Himself in the unity of the true faith and unto everlasting life, a chosen community...'.[153]

Finally, this doctrine is a stimulus to that gratitude which is expressed in holy living and humble service. The Puritan, Thomas Watson, was as pungent and as practical as ever:

> Some boast of their high calling, but they lie idly at anchor. Religion does not seal warrants to idleness. Christians must not be slothful. Idleness is the devil's bath; a slothful person becomes a prey to every temptation. Grace, while it cures the heart, does not make the hand lame. He who is called of God, as he works for heaven, so he works in his trade.[154]

The predominant theme in all of this is sovereign, gracious, electing, *inclusive* love.

IV

How inclusive should the empirical church be? That this is a pressing question is illustrated by some remarks of P. Mark Achtemeier:

> 'Inclusiveness' as an abstract concept has frequently been lifted up as the pre-eminent foundation of the church's unity. Because this concept is an abstraction, what began as a relatively innocuous synonym for the catholicity of the church has drifted in directions leading to a thoroughgoing religious individualism and relativism. The 'inclusiveness' of the mainline Protestant churches is now in danger of becoming a completely elastic concept, embracing and affirming every private and idiosyncratic belief system, regardless of whether it stands in any discernible continuity with historic Christian, much less Reformed, faith.[155]

---

153 *The Heidelberg Catechism*, A54.

154 T. Watson, *A Divine Cordial*, (1663), Grand Rapids, MI: Sovereign Grace Publishers, 1971, p. 87.

155 P. Mark Achtemeier, 'The *Union with Christ* doctrine in renewal: Movements of the Presbyterian Church (USA)', in William M. Alston, Jr. and Michael Welker, eds, *Reformed Theology: Identity and Ecuemnicity*, Grand Rapids, MI: Eerdmans, 2003, p. 343.

We shall do well first to define 'Church'. It seems beyond doubt that in the New Testament the Church comprises the saints, the believers, the called and committed ones and their children, all of whom are within God's covenant. More technically, we might say that the Church comprises the regenerate, and we might regret that that concept, when de-Latinized, has become the slogan of a particular brand of 'born again Christians'. R. W. Dale, though his specific reference was to Congregationalism, no doubt thought that he was stating the obvious when he declared, 'The members of a Christian Church should be Christians.'[156] The Christian family is inclusive of all ages, races and abilities, and each should be able to play his or her part in its ministry and mission. In this sense, the Church is to be distinguished from the Sunday congregations, which might include unbaptized children, unprofessed adherents and visitors who belong to other faiths or no faith at all—all of whom should be welcomed. In what follows I have in mind the Church as defined, not the congregation, and my references will be especially to the traditions of Old Dissent.[157]

Questions of inclusion and exclusion have frequently arisen in connection with church discipline, and it should be noted that the Dissenting traditions differ among themselves over the disciplinary process. Thus, for example, whereas the Westminster Assembly's *Form of Presbyterial Church-Government* allows that wider assemblies 'have some power to dispense church-censures', local discipline is for the most part the responsibility of the ruling elders of particular congregations.[158] In Baptist and Congregational circles the local church as a whole was more prominent, as Article XLII of the Baptists' *London Confession* (1644) makes plain:

> Christ has likewise given power to his whole Church to receive in and cast out, by way of Excommunication, any member; and this power is given to every particular

---

[156] R. W. Dale, *Essays and Addresses*, London: Hodder and Stoughton, 1889, p. 184. This is not, of course, to say that God is somehow the Church's exclusive property. His providence is over all, his Spirit everywhere active: we may not exclude him from any part of the created order. See further remarks in Alan P. F. Sell, *Confessing and Commending the Faith. Christian Witness and Apologetic Method*, Cardiff: University of Wales Press, 2002, pp. 361-63.

[157] Discipline among the Quakers is a fascinating study. For some references to this see ch. 2 above. See also Robert Barclay, *A Treatise on Christian Discipline; or The Anarchy of the Ranters and other Libertines, the Hierarchy of the Romanists, and other Pretended Churches, Equally Refused and Refuted, in a Two-fold Apology for the Church and People of God Called in Derision Quakers*, 1676.

[158] *The Form of Presbyerial Church-Government and of the Ordination of Ministers*, in *The Subordinate Standards and Other Authoritative Documents of the Free Church Of Scotland*, Edinburgh: Free Church of Scotland, 1933, pp. 310-11. Cf. *The Westminster Confession of Faith*, ch. XXX.

> Congregation, and not one particular person, either member or Officer, but the whole.[159]

However, the Congregational *Savoy Declaration of the Institution of Churches* (1658) recommends that private offences be treated privately in the first instance; public offences and private ones not repented of, be brought before the whole church, which must consent to any excommunication.[160]

The term 'excommunication' notwithstanding, it is noteworthy that in both Baptist and Congregational church books there is a reluctance to use it. Rather, offenders are frequently 'withdrawn from' lest their poison spread through the body. We may suppose that many ministers, like their Scottish Presbyterian counterpart, Robert Murray M'Cheyne (1813–43), shrank from their disciplinary duties but, like him, persisted with them because

> two keys are committed to us by Christ, the one the key of doctrine, by means of which we unlock the treasures of the Bible, the other the key of discipline, by which we open or shut the way to the sealing ordinances of the faith. Both are Christ's gift, and neither is to be resigned without sin.[161]

As for the Presbyterians of Old Dissent: being quite unable to establish presbyterial structures in the wake of the Act of Uniformity of 1662, they had in many cases become *de facto* independent churches by the eighteenth century, though without the Independent polity as represented by Church Meeting—the ultimate disciplinary organ in Baptist and Congregational circles. Thus by 1732, in a letter reporting an enquiry into the state of Dissent, a writer (almost certainly not a Presbyterian) could say,

> The Presbyterians very rarely if ever as a church, enquire into the conduct or behaviour of their members, and it is a thing almost as seldom known that they discharge any of them either for heresy or disorderly walking, and if at any time anything of this kind is acted, it is done by the pastor only or by the managers or committee, which terms are made use of in the room of deacons, and for want of proper discipline immoral persons are continued in their societies.[162]

---

159 *The First London Confession*, (1644), p. 168.

160 *The Savoy Declaration of Faith and Order*, p. 125.

161 Andrew A. Bonar, *The Life of Robert Murray M'Cheyne*, (1844), London: Banner of Truth Trust, 1962, p. 88.

162 The Letter is dated 24 February 1731/32. It is at Dr Williams's Library, London, MS (RNC) 38.18. It is discussed by Roger Thomas, 'The Difference between Congregational and Presbyterian in the chapel-building age', in *Studies in the Puritan*

The Church is supposed to be a disciplined body, honouring God and equipped for his mission in the world. As Dale drily remarked, 'It would be very strange if a Society were instituted merely to preserve the purity of its own membership and a regular succession of efficient officers.'[163] In particular, the Church is under the discipline of the Word, revealed in the Bible and savingly active in Jesus Christ, to whom the Scriptures witness. Both ministers and members are under the discipline of the Word, as the *Westminster Larger Catechism* (Q and A 159, 160) rightly insists. In a narrower sense church discipline concerns the steps taken to ensure that the Church lives up to its high calling. In this connection it must be granted that the 'policing of some saints' can be enjoyed too much by others: for example, a prurient interest in cases of moral laxity was always a possibility in days before the Sunday tabloids and the *National Enquirer*. But this does not afford grounds for dispensing with discipline altogether. Indeed, some of the classical Reformed statements introduce discipline as the third mark, or note, of the Church, alongside the faithful preaching of the Word and the right administration of the sacraments. The marks do not define the Church, but they show us where it is. *The Common Confession of Faith* (1967) of the Council of Churches in Indonesia is one of the few twentieth-century confessions to mention discipline: 'Church Discipline has as its aims that Christians who have gone astray may return to the way of truth, and that the holiness of the congregation may be protected.'[164] The Congregational *Declaration* of 1967 tiptoes gently and rather vaguely in the direction of discipline when it observes that the challenge to be a holy people

> calls for disciplines within the Church's life, that members may be strengthened when they must offer resistance or make renunciations in face of evil, and the half-hearted may be encouraged to commit themselves more deeply to the standards God expects from his Church.[165]

Here we have the tested and the half-hearted, but where are the positively naughty?

Although fully conceding that church discipline in the sense now under review can be badly mishandled, the positive intention of it should be emphasized. The primary objective is that Christ, the Head of the Church, be not dishonoured by immoral or hypocritical behaviour

Tradition, A joint Supplement of the Congregational and Presbyterian Historical Societies, December 1964, pp. 28-40. The above quotation is from p. 37.

163 Ibid., p. 142.

164 Vischer, ed., *Reformed Witness Today*, p. 37.

165 *A Declaration of Faith*, London: Congregational Church in England and Wales, 1967, p. 33.

(Romans 2:23). The second is that weaker brothers and sisters be not harmed, on which matter John Knox was as blunt as he was graphic:

> as it would be a work both uncharitable and cruel to join together in one bed persons infected with pestilent and other contagious and infected sores, with tender children or such as were sound, so it is no less cruelty to suffer among the flock of Christ such obstinate rebels...for 'a little leaven corrupteth the whole mass.'[166]

The third objective is that the erring brother or sister repent and be restored to fellowship (2 Thessalonians 3:14; 1 Corinthians 5:5; Matthew 18:15; 2 Corinthians 2:6-8; Galatians 6:1).[167] John Owen declared that 'The *nature and end*' of church discipline is '*corrective*, not *vindictive*,—for healing, not destruction...'.[168] In addition, the motive of not being conformed to the world has sometimes been operative, as when the Quakers Joseph Pike and his cousin Samuel Randall dispensed with their 'fine veneered and garnished cases of drawers, tables, stands, cabinets, escritoires, etc.';[169] while William Sprague was convinced that '*The toleration of gross offences in the church*, is...a serious hindrance to a revival of religion.'[170]

It is of supreme importance that two principles be kept firmly in mind. First, church discipline is discipline under the Gospel. This implies that both legalism and antinomianism are ruled out. Christianity is neither a new set of rules, nor an inducement to free-wheeling license. Secondly, the will of the Lord of the Church is paramount and this should sincerely be sought. 'The right and arbitrament is the Lords, not the servant's', declared Tertullian.[171] In his wake came Robert Browne the Separatist: 'by his discipline and government [Christ] hath over us, he is our king... So if we sever Christ and his discipline, rule, and government, what is he but an Idol Christ?'[172]

---

166 J. Knox, *Order of Excommunication*, in *The Works of John Knox*, ed. David Laing, Edinburgh: James Thin, 1895, VI, pp. 447-70.

167 For church discipline in the New Testament see, for example, Eduard Schweizer, *Church Order in the New Testament*, (1959), London: SCM Press, 1961.

168 J. Owen, *The True Nature of a Gospel Church*, in *The Works of John Owen*, ed. William H. Goold, (1850–53), London: Banner of Truth Trust, 1968, XVI, p. 171.

169 Quoted from Pike's *Life* by W. C. Braithwaite, *The Second Period of Quakerism*, Cambridge: Cambridge University Press, 2nd edn, 1969, p. 507.

170 W. Sprague, *Lectures on Revivals*, (1832), Edinburgh: Banner of Truth Trust, 1959, p. 73.

171 Tertullian, *De Pudicita*, XXI.

172 R. Browne, *An Answere to Master Cartwright His Letter*, (1585?), in A. Peel and Leland H. Carlson, eds., *The Writings of Robert Harrison and Robert Browne*, London: Allen & Unwin, 1953, p. 461.

Questions of inclusion and exclusion arise especially in connection with the confirmation or reception of church members, doctrine, and morals. Let us consider each of these in turn.

Although the number and names of the elect are known to God alone, the Church is intended as a visible sign and foretaste of God's kingdom in the world. The saints are earthed; and the only way to be a member of the Church catholic is to be a member of the church local. One cannot be a Christian 'in general' and this fact in itself entails a measure of discipline:[173]

> You say you love Christ's Church. Well, here it is: Tom, Dick, Harry, and the rest; a funny lot of lame ducks... They are not very good. But they have, in their own odd ways, heard Christ's call. They have trusted in Christ on His Cross. It is little use your feeling mystical sympathy with St. Francis who is dead, with St. Somebody Else who never existed, with men of good will all over the world whom you are quite safe from meeting. If you do not love your brothers whom you have seen...you cannot, in fact, love those brothers (whom you call the Church) whom you have not seen.[174]

Thus Bernard Lord Manning, the Congregationalist historian, who went on to point out that in the remark quoted he was simply updating John Owen:

> Let none pretend...that they love the brethren in general, and love the people of God, and love the saints, while their love is not fervently exercised towards those who are in the same church with them. Christ hath given it you for a trial: he will try your love at the last day by your deportment in that church wherein you are.[175]

But what are the criteria for the confirmation or reception of members? Traditionally, these have concerned a profession of faith in Christ as Saviour and Lord and evidence of a 'godly walk'. In this matter the addition of locally devised 'small print' can lead in the direction of new Galatian heresies, that is to say, of the imposition of 'new circumcisions' whether doctrinal or ethical: You must be a Calvinist, or a teetotaller, to belong to this church. No doubt a good case can be made for both of

---

173 I have developed this theme in a number of places. See, for example, *Saints: Visible, Orderly and Catholic. The Congregational Idea of the Church*, Geneva: World Alliance of Reformed Churches and Allison Park, PA: Pickwick Publications, 1986; *Commemorations*, ch. 13; *Testimony and Tradition*, ch. 11. It is, I believe, biblically and theologically defensible. In the English political context it gained a new lease of life with the Separatists and their Congregational and Baptist successors. See ch. 1 above.

174 Bernard Lord Manning, *Why not Abandon the Church?* (1939), London: Independent Press, 1958, pp. 37-38.

175 *The Works of John Owen*, ed. William H. Goold, (1850–53), London: Banner of Truth Trust, 1968, IX, p. 262.

these positions, but endorsement of them should not be elevated into terms of church membership, for they would then take equal place with, if not precedence over, confession of faith in Christ as Saviour and Lord as *the* term of membership, and would reduce the church to a theological party or a specific social crusade. But let us not judge churches on the basis of their more idiosyncratic ways.

In general it is true to say that, traditionally, great care was taken over the reception of church members.[176] Inclusion among the visible saints was by no means automatic. The primary criteria, to repeat, were a credible confession of faith in Christ supported by a 'godly walk.' Thus in the 1670s the church at Bedford, under the pastoral care of John Bunyan, recorded their practice thus:

> The principle upon which they thus entered into fellowship with one another, and upon which they did afterwards receive those that were added to their body and fellowship, was *faith in Christ and Holiness of life*, without respect to this or that circumstance or opinion in outward and circumstantiall things. By which meanes grace and faith was incouraged, Love and Amity maintained, disputings and occasion to janglings and unprofitable questions avoyded, and many that were weake in the faith confirmed in the blessing of eternall life.[177]

As to the procedure adopted, Stephen Ford's *Epistle to the Church of Christ in Chippin-Norton* [*sic*] (1657) is instructive:

> That when any persons are desirous to joyne themselves to the church; the said persons should first make known their desires to the Pastor or Elders... That is the Pastor or Elder be satisfyed...(he) is to propose the said persons to the Church at their next meeting. That all the members...are upon Scripture grounds to be satisfyed in the fitnesse and worthiness of the person to be admitted; & also to give their free consent... That such persons as through modesty, or want of the gift of utterance, cannot by word of mouth declare the dealings of God with them to the

---

176 I use the term 'reception of members' in preference to 'confirmation', since it is what one finds in the first centuries of Dissenting church life. In Dissenting circles the latter term has come into use (and not yet universally—in some cases because it is what the Church of England does!) only under the influence of the twentieth-century ecumenical movement. In common parlance people would speak of 'making members' on candidates' profession of faith. In fact, however, they were already within the covenant, and baptism, whether of infants or believers, witnessed to this. Thus candidates were members being received, or 'admitted' to the full privileges of church membership, including attendance at the Lord's table and, in Baptist and Congregational churches, attendance at Church Meeting.

177 Quoted by R. H. Coats, *John Bunyan*, London: SCM Press, 1927, p. 54. Bunyan and his church never made believer baptism by immersion a term of church membership. A number of churches in the Bedford area adopted a similar position and to this day Bunyan Meeting, Bedford, and other churches, continue in Bunyan's line on this matter.

> satisfaction of the Church, that then the said persons have liberty to give satisfaction to the Church in writing, or otherwise.[178]

If local churches took the reception of members seriously, there is a good deal of evidence to suggest that those seeking reception were likewise very much in earnest. John Pye Smith, for example, agonized over the matter for months. Some time after making his personal covenant with God, we find him writing on 23 September 1791:

> I am this week to confer with Mr. Brewer about that *serious duty*, Church fellowship. O may the Lord preserve me from all *rash*, hasty proceedings! May he give me his blessing! I would commit this, and all my ways, to the hands of my faithful and compassionate Redeemer. O mould my spirit at thy will. Amen and amen.[179]

Not until 21 November 1792 did he write to the church in these terms:

> If it shall seem good to this Church of Christ to admit me into communion with them in divine ordinances, I solemnly call upon, and earnestly intreat every individual to deal faithfully with me; to warn, advise, reprove, and in every respect to watch for my soul, as we shall assuredly give an account to the Great Head of His body, the Church.[180]

Pye Smith was duly received, and went on to become a distinguished minister. Interestingly, he became the first pastor of Clapton Park Congregational Church, and its first Minute Book, in his hand, records the reception of a member on 2 July 1807 thus:

> Elizabeth Whitwell, one of the children of this church, gave a satisfactory account of her hope towards God and her experience of personal religion, which was corroborated by pleasing testimonies to the Christian propriety of her habitual deportment. She was, therefore, unanimously advanced to the full enjoyment of all the privileges of church-communion.[181]

It would seem from an anonymous observation of 1821 that in some quarters at least standards were slipping:

---

[178] Quoted by K. W. H. Howard, ed., *The Axminster Ecclesiastica 1660–1698*, (1874), Sheffield: Gospel Tidings Publications, p. 240.

[179] John Medway, *Memoirs of the Life and Writings of John Pye Smith, D.D., LL.D., F.R.S., F.G.S., Late Theological Tutor of The Old College, Homerton*, London: Jackson and Walford, 1853, p. 21.

[180] Ibid., p. 23.

[181] Quoted by Albert Peel, 'A Congregational church's first pastorate', *Transactions of the Congregational Historical Society*, X no. 5, April 1929, p. 237. Peel's second pastorate was at Clapton Park, 1922-34.

> No person used to be admitted into the church without being examined as to knowledge and experience publicly, before a considerable congregation; and, yet, it was scarcely ever known, that any person was deterred from offering himself as a candidate for communion, on account of the strict mode of admission.[182]

Two decades later, the prominent Dr Robert Vaughan, took a somewhat less rigorous view:

> That the church should have some ground on which to believe that the persons desirous of being admitted to membership with it are pious persons is manifest; but it is left to the great law of Christian benevolence and sympathy to suggest, that the manner in which such knowledge may be obtained, so as to expose the feeling of the candidate to the least possible cost, is that which should in each case be adopted.... Even the practice of requiring candidates to make their appearance at the church-meeting at the time when their names are approved, though very seemly and good in itself, I would rather we should be understood to recommend than to enforce.... While resolved not to open the doors of the church to the worldly, we should be careful that we do not close them against Christians.[183]

There can be no doubt that the kind of testimony expected when one 'gave in one's experience' at Church Meeting caused some prospective members considerable distress, and in some cases there may have been undue psychological pressure to deliver the 'right kind' of testimony. During the months when he was in turmoil over whether to proceed to reception, Pye Smith wrote, 'I was firmly persuaded that I could never have real religion unless I experienced far greater degrees of terror than I had yet known.'[184] In a word, to use the 'language of Canaan' of those times, he needed to feel more 'worm-like' and to have struggled longer in the 'miry clay' before being rescued by the Saviour. A similar well-documented case is that of the rumbustious Joseph Parker (1830–1902) of London's City Temple. Having been raised in a climate of evangelical testimonies, Parker the teenager feared that his sins were not sufficiently serious and therefore that his repentance would not be sufficiently telling: 'So I stood outside the gate, crying bitter tears, because I had not sinned

---

182 *The London Christian Instructor, or Congregational Magazine*, IV, 1821, pp. 338-39.

183 R. Vaughan, *Congregationalism: or, the Polity of Independent Churches, Viewed in Relation to the State and Tendencies of Modern Society*, 2nd edn., London, 1842, pp. 197-200. Not even Vaughan would have endorsed a much more recent, hopefully apocryphal, view of the matter: a candidate for reception as a member was advised, 'Just have a word with the minister on the golf course—but make sure he wins!' Vaughan's remark calls to mind the earlier one of Richard Baxter: 'I am not so narrow in my principles of Church communion as once I was... I am not for narrowing the Church more than Christ himself alloweth us, nor for robbing him of any of his flock.' See *The Autobiography of Richard Baxter* (abridged), London: Dent, 1931, p. 116.

184 Medway, *Memoirs of the Life and Writings of John Pye Smith*, p. 22.

according to the magnitude and quality of another man's transgression.'[185] (We should not, of course, conclude that testimonies couched in stereotypical language are, by that fact, necessarily insincere. The problem arises when candidates for reception as members *seek* what they regard as qualifying experiences of specific, approved, kinds, and worry if they do not receive them.)

A concern to the Baptists of Abingdon was that some were being baptized as believers but not being received as members.[186] They were visited and instructed to join a church in their locality.[187] In some churches members, on being received, were asked to sign the local church covenant. Some covenants, like that of the Worcester church (1687) were strongly doctrinal. At Worcester the doctrine of the Trinity was staunchly advocated—a prime example of contextual theology, given incipient Socinianism in the area. In 1767, David Bradberry declared that he would accept the call to Ramsgate only if the church members agreed to eight solidly Calvinistic articles of faith, together with a ninth eschewing smuggling (more contextual theology). The church finally agreed, but in the following year the ninth clause was deleted because it had spawned hypocrisy and deception among the saints.[188]

All of which leads us from inclusion to exclusion. However disciplined a church may be in receiving members, the fact remains that the saints are also sinners. What is to be made of this in cultures and contexts which proclaim inclusivity as a virtue and exclusivity as a vice? Those of such a mind-set will regard 'suspension from communion' and, still more, 'excommunication' as disasters to be avoided at all costs; yet it is arguable that occasions may arise, and in fact do arise, when, in the interests of honouring God and maintaining the peace and integrity of the church, such actions may regretfully be required. Those charged to deal with such awesome matters would do well to remember that for all the rebukes and reprimands delivered by Paul to recalcitrant Christians and churches, 'he never loses sight of the Ideal; for him a Church is

---

185 Quoted by Albert Dawson, *Joseph Parker, D.D. His Life and Ministry*, London: Partridge, 1901, p. 22.

186 I understand that this still happens in some Baptist circles.

187 See Kenneth Dix, 'Baptists in fellowship, 1630–1660', *Strict Baptist Historical Society Bulletin*, no. 16, 1989, p. 11.

188 For the Worcester covenant see John Noake, *Worcester Sects: or A History of the Roman Catholics & Dissenters of Worcester*, London, 1861, pp. 111-14. For Ramsgate see Alan G. Hurd, *These Three Hundred Years*, Ramsgate: W. H. Bligh, [1962], p. 4. For Congregational covenants see Alan P. F. Sell, *Dissenting Thought and the Life of the Churches. Studies in a Christian Tradition*, Lewiston, NY: Edwin Mellen Press, 19990, ch. 1.

always a society of men who have received the Holy Ghost, and entered into the Kingdom of Heaven'.[189]

Traditionally, the main grounds for the suspension or excommunication (withdrawing from) members were doctrinal and moral. I shall present a few cases to illustrate each in turn.

It would seem from the records and writings I have consulted that the candidate's experience and way of life were the paramount criteria of reception, but in many places catechizing preceded and followed reception,[190] with the result that doctrinal considerations were never very far away. They were, indeed, on occasion the cause (or in some cases the pretext) for secession, and some ministers found to their cost just how sensitive the doctrinal antennae of some members of their flocks could be. There was widespread agreement that agreement in doctrine was an important ingredient in the cement that held churches together, as Priestley made plain to the congregation gathered in New Meeting, Birmingham, in 1782:

> Since Christianity, like any other religion, consists of *doctrines* which all Christians believe, and those who are not Christians do not believe, it is evident that no person can be a proper member of a Christian society who is not a Christian in principle. Though, therefore, a *Heathen* or a *Mahomentan*, a *Deist* or an *Atheist*, should, for any particular reason, choose to attend the worship of this place, and contribute to the support of it, you could not consider him as a proper member of your society. You meet here as *Christians*, and therefore cannot consider any other than a Christian as one of your body.[191]

Of course, Priestley's reference to doctrines which all Christians believe begs a huge, pamphlet-engendering, question. His beliefs were not on all fours with those of John Wesley, for example. While Priestley could have made Wesley's words his own—'a catholic spirit is not *speculative* latitudinarianism. It is not indifference to all opinions: this is the spawn of hell, not the offspring of heaven'[192]—his tally of believable doctrines differed significantly from that of Wesley. All of which afforded plenty of scope for church discipline of the excluding or 'withdrawing' kind.

---

[189] Dale, *Essays and Addresses*, p. 122. Dale further points out, pp. 134-39, that Jesus's parable of the wheat and the tares (Matthew 13:24-43) in no way constitutes a prohibition of proper church discipline; for the wheat and tares grow together in the world, not in the Church. Hence there is no reference to the disciplined separation from wrongdoers within the Church prior to the *eschaton*.

[190] Richard Baxter was especially committed to this aspect of ministry. See Sell, *Testimony and Tradition*, ch. 3.

[191] Priestley, *The Theological and Miscellaneous Works of Joseph Priestley*, XV, p. 59.

[192] J. Wesley, *Sermons on Several Occasions*, Sermon XXXIV, 'Catholic spirit', London: Epworth Press, 1946, p. 453.

Early in the eighteenth century, in the Northern Baptist Association, three members were removed from the roll because they had adopted Quaker views.[193] For more than fifty years the Particular Baptists of Arnesby excommunicated both members who married unbelievers and those who were married in the parish church.[194] In the 1740s William Prys was reported to a Welsh Calvinistic Methodist Association for spreading antinomian doctrine:

> he asserted that he had not sinned for some time, and that there *was* no sin either in his understanding, his will, or his conscience, and because he clung stubbornly to these views, he was expelled, and the Societies were warned to beware of his heresies, and the brethren to avoid his society. 'After long discussion and prayer,' says the report, 'and with great solemnity, we turned him out, while our hearts were overwhelmed with love to his soul and jealousy for the glory of God, and full of fear and anxiety for the safety of the flock.[195]

In 1809 Jacob Martell arrived at the Congregational church in Heathfield, Sussex, as co-pastor with George Gilbert. However, according to John Press, within a year Martell 'embraced the Sentiment of Adult Baptism by Immersion and was ejected'.[196] In 1810 the church declared that Baptists who requested the privilege might become occasional communicants, but they were 'not to have a Voice in the affairs of the Church'.[197] By contrast, in the following year the church at Clapton Park received as members former Baptist deacon, Thomas Pilby Burford, and his wife, Elizabeth, as members. The relevant resolution contains nine careful clauses, of which the fifth is the crucial one:

> That the difference of sentiment between us and Mr. And Mrs. Burford, as to the right of the infant seed of God's people to the ordinances of church-membership and baptism (though the affirmative of that question is considered by us as a scriptural doctrine and an important privilege), yet cannot, on solid and scriptural grounds, be made a bar to the communion of saints.[198]

---

193 See Stephen Copson, *English Baptist Records 3. Association Life of the Particular Baptists of Northern England 1699–1732*, Didcot: Baptist Historical Society, 1991, p. 69.

194 So Peter Naylor, *Picking up a Pin for the Lord. English Particular Baptists from 1688 to the Early Nineteenth Century*, London: Grace Publications, 1992, p. 54.

195 William Williams, *Welsh Calvinistic Methodism. A Historical Sketch of the Presbyterian Church of Wales*, London: Presbyterian Church of England, 2nd edn, 1884, p. 58.

196 Quoted by N. Caplan, 'Free will or election: conflict in a Sussex church, 1778', *Journal of the United Reformed Church History Society*, I no. 5, May 1975, p. 151.

197 Ibid.

198 Quoted by Peel, 'A Congregational church's first pastorate', p. 239.

In the following clause, and in return for this 'forebearance', the saints

> confidently rely on a correspondent disposition in Mr. And Mrs. Burford, and that they will candidly avoid the introduction of discussions on the question of baptism as what, under these circumstances, could not contribute to godly edifying and holy love.[199]

Precisely the same attitude was adopted by R. W. Dale of Carrs Lane Church in the staunchly Nonconformist town of Birmingham, twenty of whose mayors in a period of forty years in the nineteenth-century were Unitarians, and whose ministerial inheritance included Samuel Bourn and Joseph Priestley. Dale explained in a letter of 6 February 1885 to T. C. Finlayson that he would be willing to receive a Unitarian as a church member on the ground that a person may have the faith that saves whilst denying the divinity of Christ.[200] This was consistent with what Dale had written in his celebrated *Manual of Congregational Principles*:

> A Christian society which imposes any other condition of membership than faith in Christ is a sect, and not, in the highest sense of the term, a Christian church. It is a private Christian club. It receives persons into membership, not because they are the brethren of Christ, but because they are the brethren of Christ professing certain religious opinions or observing certain religious practices.... It is a society not for all Christians, but for a particular description of Christians. It is a sect—not a Church.[201]

This, while it rightly warns against the imposition of new 'Galatian heresies', does not really answer the question concerning the proclamation of the church as a community of faith. As I have said elsewhere, there are 'babes in Christ' who are not yet ready for strong doctrinal meat; there are members whose commitment to Christ is not in doubt, but their opinions on certain doctrinal matters are distinctly odd, even heterodox; and none of us will gain entry to heaven by the 'work' of reciting a doctrinally sound confession of faith to which we sincerely assent. But, as D. W. Simon observed, it is one thing for a church member to hold heterodox opinions, it is another for him or her to propagate them within the fellowship:

> Suppose...that an individual member of an individual Church notoriously and plainly not only entertains, but actually propagated Unitarianism, *i.e.*, in other words, gives himself up to active dishonesty, are [the church members] to do

---

199 Ibid.

200 See A. W. W. Dale, *The Life of R. W. Dale of Birmingham*, London: Hodder and Stoughton, 1899, pp. 344-45.

201 R. W. Dale, *A Manual of Congregational Principles*, London: Hodder and Stoughton, 1884, p. 50.

> nothing but protest? It seems to me that duty to Christ, themselves, and the erring brother, requires, first, admonition, then formal separation, either of him from the Association, or of the Association from him, *i.e.*, disfellowshipping. But you can't do this unless a certain body of doctrine is a constitutive factor of Congregationalism...[202]

With Dale's general view, and with Simon's qualification, I have considerable sympathy. 'Galatian' sectarianism is to be avoided; the 'faith once delivered is to be upheld'. There is a faith commonly agreed amongst the saints, and this should be respected or, after due consultation, amended. I shall have more to say about this in the final section of this chaper. For the present I offer an autobiographical reminiscence by way of showing that there is more than one way to handle doctrinal divergence.

I was present at a service in North Street Congregational Church, Guildford, in the late 1940s. In the absence of the minister the service was conducted by John P. Stephens, a small, puckish man of considerable intelligence and keen wit. The theme of his sermon was fidelity to the faith once delivered to the saints. Clearly possessed of knowledge gained in advance, at one point the proceedings went as follows:

> It is remarkable the strange beliefs that some quite intelligent people will fall for. I have even heard that in this district there are those who have succumbed to British Israelite doctrine. [Pause; palpable silence; shocked expression on face]. Have I dropped a brick? [Pause; peering intently around the congregation]. Did it hit anyone?[203]

A delightful example of the 'softly softly' method of church discipline.

In Baptist and Congregational church books moral cases greatly outnumber doctrinal ones. For all his abhorrence of legalism and sectarianism, Dale rightly insisted that 'the right to "excommunicate" the irreligious appears to be essential to the very existence of the

---

[202] F. J. Powicke, *David Worthington Simon*, London: Hodder and Stoughton, 1912, pp. 230-31.

[203] I quote from memory—but it is hard to forget. For Stephens (1884–1953) see the obituary in *The Congregational Year Book*, London: Congregational Union of England and Wales, 1955, pp. 525-26, which confirms, p. 526, that 'His sermons were thoughtful and deep, illustrated most aptly, in delivery fresh and lively, and progressive in outlook.' In a different context, Albert Peel showed himself able to pour a little wit over doctrinal strife. With reference to the Modern Free Churchmen's Union, whose base of activity was at the Blackheath Congregational Church, London, and to Nathaniel Micklem of Mansfield College, Oxford, he wrote: 'So far as I see them, most Congregationalists are not disposed to wander with the wizards on the Blackheath, not do they propose to fall down and worship the dogmatic image which Nathaniel the principal has set up.' *Inevitable Congregationalism*, London: Independent Press, 1937, p. 113.

Church'.[204] At their best the saints knew that they must not take cases of moral discipline with anything other than due seriousness; they also knew that a primary objective was the repentance and restoration of the offender. Richard Baxter has left us an account of his careful procedure in such matters:

> I do, if it be secret, make the fault at first no more public than the owner made it, but secretly admonish him to repent and reform. If it be public, or if he repent not, and reform not, I admonish before two or three, and then call him to our meeting (where the representative church, *viz*. 2 presbyters, 4 deacons and 24 delegates meet once a month for such work) and there endeavour his humiliation and reformation. If he declare not repentance there, or if he do but return again to the sin, I do in the face of the congregation mention his crime, and our proceedings, and again with all seriousness and compassion there summon him to repentance: and if he refuse I desire the congregation to join in earnest prayer for him. This I do once or twice or thrice as prudence shall direct, considering the quality of the sin and sinner and the measure of the scandal. If yet he hear not the church, I do, from certain texts recited, require them to avoid him, and no more.[205]

The practice of the Presbyterian, Philip Henry, was similar to that of Baxter, though in cases of scandal 'he suspended them from the ordinance of the Lord's Supper till they gave some tokens of their repentance and reformation'.[206]

Jenkin John of Margam fell foul of his fellow Baptists at Ilston, Wales, in March 1653. His offence was that despite an earlier warning he insisted on 'kneeling after the corrupt fashion of the world when he came into a public parish house to hear a sermon'. For this he was delivered to Satan (that is, excommunicated).[207] It clearly was not safe to sail too close to the Anglican wind. In 1671 Richard Deane was dismissed from the roll of the Independent Church, Bedford, because he had left the cause and been 'bishopt' (confirmed) in the Church of England.[208]

The Congregationalists at Axminster kept careful records of some disciplinary cases. In the 1670s Robert Bull stole a sheep from a neighbour and, when challenged, denied the offence. He was brought

---

[204] Dale, *Essays and Addresses*, p. 134.

[205] Dr Williams's Library, London, MS 2:256; quoted by Geoffrey F. Nuttall, *Richard Baxter*, London: Nelson, 1965, p. 60.

[206] J. B. Williams, *The Life of the Rev. Philip Henry, A.M. with Funeral Sermons for Mr. And Mrs. Henry, by the Rev. Matthew Henry, V.D.M.*, (1688), Edinburgh: Banner of Truth Trust, 1974, p. 196.

[207] Ilston Church Book, p. 36, quoted by B. R. White, 'John Miles and the structures of the Calvinistic Baptist mission to South Wales', in Mansel John, ed., *Welsh Baptist Studies*, Cardiff: South Wales Baptist College, 1976, p. 49.

[208] H. G. Tibbutt, ed., *The Minutes of the First Independent Church (now Bunyan Meeting) at Bedford, 1656–1766*, Bedford: Bedfordshire Historical Society, 1976, p. 64.

before the church, and the pastor preached on Joshua 7:25, concerning the stoning of an offender. Perhaps not surprisingly, 'it was a day of trembling of soul, trouble and heaviness indeed to many'. When called upon to acknowledge his sin and repentance, Bull remained silent. This brought a further exhortation from the pastor, who ended with a word to the congregation:

> Brethren, know your duty, to admonish him, and call upon him to repentance; know your duty, to abstain from affectionate communion with him till he doth repent, but still to pray for him and put on bowels for him. The Lord give a blessing to this institution of His for the saving benefit of the whole body.[209]

The proceedings concluded with the renewing of the covenant.

Between c.1669 and 1698 Axminster members were disciplined for lying, stealing, fraud, drunkenness, disorderly walking, enthusiasm, evil relationship, immodesty and adultery.[210] Such cases are so regular in the literature that it is something of a relief to learn of Joseph Harrison, from whom the General Baptist Church at Speldhurst, Kent, withdrew in August 1694 because he sold 'cow dung mixed with graese and tare to ye Coachman to greese ye Coach Wheels they being altogether ignorant of any such matter as cow dung neither did he for such a mixture make any abatement of his usual price'.[211] At about the same time Brother Campion was called before the Congregational church at Rothwell, Northamptonshire, for 'proferring love to a Sister, when engaged to another'. The same church acted against dancing, card-playing, other games and secular songs.[212] Despite the fact that, unlike the Baptist and Congregationalists, the northern followers of Benjamin Ingham did not have Church Meeting in their polity, they were not inhibited from exercising discipline: 'John and Margaret Dugdale to come with their child to ye meeting; if they can declare themselves clear of the charge of fornication, ye child is then to be baptized.'[213]

T. M. Bassett has provided a lengthy list of sins for which Welsh Baptists were disciplined as the nineteenth century approached:

---

209 Howard, *The Axminster Ecclesiastica*, pp. 52-55.

210 Ibid., pp. 242-3.

211 Quoted by Geoffrey F. Nuttall, 'The Speldhurst Church Book', *Journal of the United Reformed Church History Society*, VI no. 8, May 2001, p. 562.

212 See John Taylor, 'The survival of the Church Meeting', *Transactions of the Congregational Historical Society*, XXI no. 2, December 1971, p. 33.

213 'Church history, collected from the Memoirs and Journals of Mr. Ingham and the labourers in connection with him', p. 63. John Rylands University Library of Manchester MS MAM P11B, quoted by H. M. Pickles, *Benjamin Ingham, Preacher amongst the Dales of Yorkshire, the Forests of Lancashire, and the Fells of Cumbria*, Coventry: privately published, 1995, p. 103.

> wandering to listen to Methodist preachers...; selling beer without a license; stealing wreckage from the sea; selling barley contrary to the statute and custom of the market; and breaking a hiring contract.... The Industrial Revolution brought its own catalogue of sins—striking a haulier with a sprag and so forth.[214]

With the nineteenth century there came the Bible Christians, pioneers in the matter of women preachers, but not unwilling to discipline them. Thus a Conference minute of 1825:

> Q. Are our preaching women so plain in dress as formerly?
> A. Some are not.
> Q. What can be done to prevent this evil?
> A. Let them be admonished, and if they will not reform, let them travel no longer.[215]

On occasion ministers used church discipline to their own advantage. Thus Samuel Newton, of the Old Meeting, Norwich,

> wearing a full-bottomed wig, and accustomed to smoke a pipe on the way to worship—ruled his flock with rather high-handed notions of clerical authority.... [W]hen he received a memorial complaining of certain things in his ecclesiastical administration, he proposed and accomplished the excision of the memorialists from the roll of membership.[216]

If Newton rid himself of his trouble-makers, the bulk of the Bible Christian denomination withdrew *en bloc* from their leader, William O'Bryan in 1827. He had become increasingly autocratic, and had brought trumped-up charges against his younger co-worker, James Thorne. There ensured a struggle to ensure that the Conference should be the organ of government. This being achieved, O'Bryan repaired to Canada, where he became a greatly appreciated evangelist and was 'held in honour and reverence'.[217]

Sufficient has been said to suggest that in matters of church membership, both inclusion and exclusion are too important and too pastorally delicate to make blanket sloganizing appropriate. Nor are the issues of concern only to the individuals involved. The honour of God and the peace of the church are at stake and, as Calvin said,

---

214 T. M. Bassett, *The Welsh Baptists*, Swansea: Ilston House, 1977, p. 79.

215 Quoted by Richard Pyke, *The Early Bible Christians*, London: Epworth Press, 1941, p. 30. Cf. Thomas Shaw, *The Bible Christians 1815–1907*, London: Epworth Press, 1965, p. 110.

216 John Stoughton, *Reminiscences of Congregationalism Fifty Years Ago*, London: Hodder and Stoughton, 1881, pp. 6-7.

217 Pyke, *The Early Bible Christians*, pp. 43-45.

> all who desire to remove discipline or to hinder its restoration—whether they do this deliberately or out of ignorance—are surely contributing to the ultimate dissolution of the church.[218]

No doubt this would be regarded as a hard saying in more wantonly inclusive, 'feel-good' circles at the present time. This simply serves to underline its importance.

V

I turn now to a widely discussed ethical issue which concerns inclusion and exclusion, and has implications for the Christian understanding of both marriage, the ministry, church discipline and the wider society: the place of homosexuals[219] in the Church. The World Alliance of Reformed Churches has been seeking information on the views of its member churches on the matter: indeed, on whether they have discussed the subject at all. A task force has reported that there is 'clarity among us that discussion of sexual orientation cannot be avoided in the future',[220]

---

[218] Calvin, *Institutes*, IV.xii.1. For the development of Calvin's ideas on discipline see Richard R. De Ridder, 'John Calvin's views on discipline: A comparison of the *Institution* of 1536 and the *Institutes* of 1559', *Calvin Theological Journal*, XXI no. 2, November 1986, pp. 223-30.

[219] I use 'homosexual' to cover males and females. When I wish to refer exclusively to female homosexuality I shall use the term 'lesbian'. I am aware that many lesbians regard their stance as a product of the drive for sexual equality in society at large; that for some of them the emphasis falls upon relationships rather than upon sexual activity as such; and that they regard their anti-sexism platform as analogous to anti-racism and anti-classism platforms, for example. In a word, they oppose the marginalization and oppression of peoples on account of who they are. See, for example, Mary Hunt, 'Lovingly lesbian: toward a feminist theology of friendship', in J. B. Nelson and S. P. Longfellow, eds, *Sexuality and the Sacred*, Louisville, KY: Westminster/John Knox, 1994, p. 172. To some of these, though not, by their own account, to all lesbians, homosexual no less than heterosexual males are part of the problem. I do not think we should appear to marginalize those lesbians who, while not being sexually attracted to men have nothing particular against them, and who live their lives in what may be called a non-ideological way. I shall not pursue these important points further here, for my purpose is simply to suggest that however homosexuals understand themselves and their objectives, they should not be excluded from the Church simply because they are homosexuals. As a small indication of the rapid influence which the debate on human sexuality has had we may note that the *Popular Oxford Dictionary* (1978) defines 'gay' first as 'light-hearted, sportive, mirthful, etc.' and, subsequently records 'gay' as slang synonymous with 'homosexual'. *The Pocket Oxford English Dictionary* (1996) gives the first definition as '(especially of a man) homosexual', and subsequently brands 'light-hearted and carefree' as 'dated'.

[220] Jane Dempsey Douglass, 'Encouraging civil conversations on gays and lesbians', *WARC Update*, XIV no. 1, May 2004, p. 8.

though no reason is offered for this view. Indeed, given that out of some 220 member churches who were approached on the matter, only thirty-five replied and of these fifteen said they were discussing 'homosexual orientation' and twenty that they were not, it would seem that the member churches of the Alliance are not at present unduly eager for such discussion. It does not, of course, follow from this that the matter should not be broached; on the contrary, in view of the turmoil caused in some churches which have addressed the issue, there is something to be said for cool reflection upon the method and manner of conducting conversations on this issue before the occasions arise. What would be unfortunate would be any sense that those European and North American churches which have been to the fore in considering homosexuality were 'imperialistically' telling member churches in the rest of the world that they ought to be discussing this issue, when they may not wish, or be ready, to.

Homosexuality has been discussed in a number of Western churches at least since the 1970s. The main issues may be encapsulated in the following questions: Ought we to distinguish between homosexuals as such and homosexuals who practise same-sex intercourse? Are homosexuals to be included within the membership of the Church? Are homosexuals to be included within the ordained ministry? The following illustrations, many of which demonstrate the liveliness of the issue in 1988, may provide something of the flavour of the debate.

In August 1988, at the end of an arduous debate[221] on marriage and human sexuality in the Thirty-second General Council of the United Church of Canada, Anne Squire, the outgoing moderator said, 'For me, what is at stake is whether we as a church will be an inclusive or exclusive body.'[222] The basis for the discussion had been a report entitled, *Toward a Christian Understanding of Sexual Orientation, Lifestyles and Ministry.* In the event it became clear that the report as it stood was unacceptable to the Council as a whole, and therefore it was deemed to be an 'historic document' only. The Council endorsed the importance of Christian marriage and family life as traditionally understood; it admitted that it was not of one mind on homosexuality (the part of the report which most interested the media) but it was able to resolve as follows:

---

221 For a report of the debate see *The United Church Observer*, ns LII no. 4, October 1988, pp. 13-20. See also articles written from a variety of standpoints by members of the United Church of Canada in *Touchstone*, VII no. 2, May 1989. For a collection of conservative Reformed responses to *Homophilia*, a report of 1981 published by the Reformed Churches in the Netherlands (GKN), see *The Reformed Ecumenical Synod Theological Forum*, XII nos. 2 and 3, February 1985.

222 Gordon Legge, 'Church leader pleads for tolerance', *The Calgary Herald*, 19 August 1988, p. A15.

> That all persons regardless of their sexual orientation, who profess faith in Jesus Christ and obedience to Him, are welcome to be or become full members of the Church.
>
> All members of the Church are eligible to be considered for Ordered Ministry.
>
> All Christian people are called to a lifestyle patterned on obedience to Jesus Christ.
>
> That all congregations, presbyteries, and conferences covenant to work out the implications of sexual orientation and lifestyles in light of the Holy Scriptures according to their responsibilities as stated in The Manual.[223]

Homosexuals, like heterosexual church members, may thus be 'considered' for the ordered ministry, but the Council did not in its resolution distinguish between homosexuals who were sexually active and those who were not; and this placed responsibility upon local judicatories and congregations upon whom the actual calling of ministers devolves.[224] Within two months some presbyteries resolved not to accept practising homosexuals as candidates for ordination.[225] To cite one example of a local church's concern: on 6 November 1988 the Board of Hillhurst United Church, Calgary, brought a 'Statement of position and response' which rejected the Council's decision 'to declare that all persons, regardless of their sexual orientation are welcome to be or to become full members of the United Church of Canada, unless the term sexual orientation is defined so as not to include unrepentent [*sic*] homosexual practise'.[226]

---

223 From a circular of 24 August 1988 headed 'Actions of the 32nd General Council', p. 3.

224 The Reverend Anne Squire further remarked, 'The question is also whether we can close our eyes to the kind of suspicion that is already wrecking the careers of all suspected gays and lesbians, which in essence means all single candidates and indeed all single members of the order of ministry.' See Legge, 'Church leader pleads for tolerance', p. A15. Leaving on one side the question whether the Christian ministry is best regarded as a 'career', it seems to me that while it is right that homosexuals should be accepted for who they are, it is sad if heterosexual single people are suspected of being who they are not. Some of the argumentation on both sides of the debate was less than rigorous. For example, in the course of arguing for the acceptance of homosexuals into the ministry on grounds of justice, the Reverend Ella Taylor-Walsh asked, 'Is it fair to judge someone if you have never been made to walk where that person must walk?' See 'Church takes sides on gays', *The Calgary Herald*, 20 August 1988, p. G9. It is difficult to resist the feeling that here a type of sentimentality has taken over which, if applied to society at large, would lead to anarchy.

225 See Gordon Legge, 'Church council votes against gays', *The CalgaryHerald*, 28 October 1988, p. A20.

226 Final draft approved by the Official Board of Hillhurst United Church, Calgary.

Other Canadian denominations had less difficulty in coming out against the ordination of sexually active homosexuals. The Atlantic Baptist Convention resolved not to ordain 'known, practising homosexuals';[227] a report of the Presbyterian Church of Canada distinguished between homosexuality and homosexual practice, and concluded thus:

> Our society wishes to present us with two alternatives, either to share in the homophobic cruelty so widely practised in our culture, or to accede to the antinomian ethical indifference which often passes for wisdom in our time. For us the task is to proclaim a middle way, to point sinners both heterosexual and homosexual to the grace and mercy of Jesus Christ and to declare before all his unconditional demand for holiness. Perhaps our word can be that of our master, 'Neither do we condemn you; go, and sin no more.'[228]

In 1988 the bishops of the Evangelical Lutheran Church in America declared that

> Persons of homosexual orientation who seek to be ordained or who are already ordained will be expected to refrain from homosexual practice.... Just as heterosexual sex outside of marriage comes under discipline, so will homosexual practice. There is no way we condone marriage between homosexuals.[229]

In the same year the United Methodist Church (USA) reaffirmed the ineligibility of practising homosexuals for ordination.[230]

Ten years on union talks between the Mennonite Church, the General Conference Mennonite Church and the Canadian Mennonite Church ran into choppy water when it was reported that at least five area conferences of the Mennonite Church would withdraw from the discussions if non-celibate homosexuals were accepted as church members.[231]

---

227 'Atlantic Baptists veto gay clergy', *The Calgary Herald*, 27 August 1988.

228 *Acts and Proceedings of the General Assembly of the Presbyterian Church of Canada*, 1985, pp. 238ff.

229 'Lutherans say homosexual pastors must be celibate', *Canadian Churchman*, May 1988, p. 7,

230 *Canadian Churchman*, September 1988, p. 2.

231 www.religioustolerance.org/hom_men.htm This position was reaffirmed on 2 July 2004 by 259 votes to 255. See *The Christian Century*, 27 July 2004, p. 16. This is not the place to pursue the matter, but a majority of four votes on this neuralgic issue does call into question the habit into which many of the Reformed have fallen, namely, that of thinking that their polity is democratic (an anachronistic notion indeed where Calvin or John Owen are concerned). It is Christocratic: the will of Christ and unanimity in him is the objective. If votes are to be taken it is crucial that there be a mechanism for 'interpreting' results which do not nearly approach unanimity; otherwise what a General Assembly deems to be 'the mind of the Church' may well be repudiated by large parts of the constituency, to the embarrassment of all.

Homosexuality has been on the agenda of the Presbyterian Church USA since 1976. In 1997 the following amendment to the *Book of Order* was agreed:

> Those who are called to office in the church are to lead a life in obedience to Scripture and in conformity to the historic confessional standards of the church. Among these standards is the requirement to live either in fidelity within the covenant of marriage between a man and a woman...,[232] or chastity in singleness. Persons refusing to repent of any self-acknowledged practice which the confessions call sin shall not be ordained and/or installed as deacons, elders or ministers of the Word and Sacrament.[233]

The general drift of the official positions described is that marriage is between two persons of the opposite sex; it is monogamous; that the unmarried, whether homosexual or heterosexual are to be chaste; and that such homosexuals are to be welcomed by the Church and eligible for its ministry.[234]

The question underlying all of the debates is, On the basis of which authority are answers to be sought? Here Christians will regularly opt for the Bible which, on this issue, can sadly be wielded as a party weapon on both sides of the argument; and Church tradition, particular social contexts and reason may also be invoked as deemed appropriate. I cannot here discuss all the biblical texts which may be thought to be relevant to marriage and sexuality, though I would commend the Church of England's discussion document, *Some Issues in Human Sexuality. A Guide to the Debate* (2003) for its thoroughness and sensitivity. I stand neither with those who regard the Bible as a catalogue of ethical prescriptions, nor with those who think that ethical determinations may be made by exclusive reference to current cultural attitudes and assumptions. The Bible, I believe, gives clear direction on ethical issues, but not specific directions on many of the matters on which we today have to make judgments; moreover some of the ethical judgments passed in Scripture apply to life before Christ's fulfilment (not abolition) of the Law (a point which concerns both prescribed ritual and such matters as the killing of witches), and Christians must be guided ethically by reference to God's supreme revelation in his Son. With these provisos, and having examined

---

232 Thus, for example, the *Westminster Confession*, XXIV.1: 'Marriage is to be between one man and one woman: neither is it lawful for any man to have more than one wife, nor for any woman to have more than one husband at the same time.'

233 www.psusa.org/101/101-homosexual.htm

234 I use the term 'chaste' (as some of the Church resolutions do) rather than 'celibate' since the latter, according to the dictionary, means the 'unmarried state' and in some Christian circles this is regarded as a divine calling; whereas the adjective 'chaste' means 'abstaining from unlawful or immoral, or from all, sexual intercourse'.

the texts as far as I am able, I concur with those who hold the following positions:

(a) Both the Old and New Testaments are united in their denunciation of sexual perversions of various kinds.[235]

(b) Those for whom homosexuality is (for whatever reason) a given orientation for which they are nonculpable, and to whom the inclination towards homosexual practice may in some sense (to be discussed below) be deemed 'natural' are not within the purview of either Testament.

(c) The sex act, biologically considered, is never an end in itself. In principle reproduction is one of its objectives, but where this is not realistic because of age, or is prevented by the use of contraceptives, the context is nevertheless relational in that the whole person is involved in self-giving to another. It concerns the 'one flesh' instituted by God in marriage.

(d) '[T]he majority of scholars still hold that in Romans 1.26-27 St Paul rejects all forms of homosexual practice, both gay and lesbian, as sinful.'[236]

(e) 'There is...in Scripture an evolving convergence on the ideal of lifelong, monogamous, heterosexual union as the setting intended by God for the proper development of men and women as sexual beings. Sexual activity of any kind outside marriage comes to be seen as sinful, and homosexual practice as especially dishonourable. It is also recognised that God may call some to celibacy for particular service in his cause. Only by living within these boundaries are Christians to achieve that holiness which is pleasing to God.'[237]

(f) The Bible has considerably more to say concerning self-righteousness and other widespread sins (to some of which the godly are not entirely immune) than about homosexuality.

I now wish to comment further on some of these points. First, are homosexual acts natural or unnatural? Thomas Aquinas stands at the head of a long line of argument to the effect that moral acts are in accord with right reason; that the end of the sex act is procreation; that procreation results only from heterosexual unions, and hence homosexual acts, because procreation is ruled out, are against nature, unnatural. This line flows down, for example, to the official Roman Catholic statement that 'homosexual acts are intrinsically disordered and

---

[235] For examples of scholars who read the same biblical texts in different ways see Ian K. Duffield, 'The clear teaching of the Bible? A contribution to the debate about homosexuality and the Church of England', *Expository Times*, XV no. 4, January 2004, pp.109-15; Ron Cassidy, 'The clear teaching of the Bible on homosexual practice: A response to Ian K. Duffield', *Expository Times*, XV no. 9, June 2004, pp. 298-301.

[236] *Some Issues in Human Sexuality. A Guide to the Debate*, London: Church House Publishing, 2003, p. 136.

[237] *Some Issues in Human Sexuality*, p. 168, quoting *Issues in Human Sexuality*, 1991, p. 18.

can in no case be approved of'.[238] It seems to me that this case is weakened by the emphasis upon procreation which, as indicated above, need not—indeed, in practice cannot—always be the goal of sexual union, though it should in principle be so, I believe. The primary objective is relational, the expression of the 'one flesh' which God creates in marriage. Hence one may consistently query aspects of the natural law argument whilst refusing to approve of homosexual acts. On the other hand, the Dutch Bishops' Catholic Council for Church and Society declared that 'There is a growing insight that homosexual behaviour can be a natural expression of constitutional or irreversible homosexual orientation.'[239] In less sophisticated public debate I have heard people say, 'But some people are born lefthanded, and we don't denounce them: why should we denounce homosexuals for acting in accordance with who they are?' But it matters enormously whether lefthanded persons uses their left hands to hold pens or point guns. That is to say, both homosexuals and heterosexuals (except perhaps in pathological cases) may choose how to express their sexuality. If we were to say that they have no option but 'doing what comes naturally', we should in fact be demeaning them by denying their status as free agents, treating them as automata, and adopting a mechanistic, dehumanizing, view of them. As a Roman Catholic writer reminds us, 'We do not act sexually by automation as animals do when biologically triggered.'[240] Both homosexuals and heterosexuals can choose whether to be faithful in long-term relationships, or chaste, or celibate, or promiscuous. In the words of a Methodist Working Party, 'Persons cannot be held responsible for their sexual orientation, heterosexual, bisexual, or homosexual, although they are responsible for the way they behave.'[241]

Secondly, are homosexual acts sinful? There are those who say that homosexuality as such is part of the disorder wrought upon God's good creation by sin. This is not to say that homosexual persons are *by that fact* sinners—on the contrary, they are in this respect nonculpable; in other respects they are no more sinners than anyone else. What is intended is that homosexual orientation witnesses to an 'out-of-sortsness' in nature and humanity of which sin is deemed to be the cause. Homosexual orientation (as distinct from homosexual acts) witnesses to

---

[238] *Sexual Ethics: A Declaration by the Sacred Congregation*, Vatican City, 1975, p. 11.

[239] *Homosexual People in Society*, Mt. Rainer, MD: New Ways Ministry, 1980, p. 18. See further, Robert Nugent, 'Homosexuality and Magisterial teaching', *Irish Theological Quarterly*, LIII no. 1, 1987, pp. 66-74.

[240] Dennis O'Brien, 'Reservations about gay marriage. A more perfect union', *The Christian Century*, 27 January 2004, p. 28.

[241] *A Christian Understanding of Human Sexuality*, in the Conference Agenda of the Division of Social Responsibility, 1980, London: Methodist Church, p. 9.

the brokenness of God's world, not to the wilfulness of specific individuals within it.[242] In this connection the following cautionary word is important: 'Self-righteousness on the part of heterosexual people will be avoided more easily if it is remembered that such human orientations as racism and economic elitism equally manifest the same complex, yet powerful, condition of sinfulness.'[243]

More recently the question of homosexual marriage/civil union has been raised—again notably in North America. Among the questions raised are the following: Is the concept of homosexual marriage/civil union theologically viable? Would the legal implications of homosexual marriage/civil union disadvantage (in relation, for example, to inheritance tax) unmarried same-sex heterosexuals who on grounds of friendship and possibly of finance share property and possessions? It is clear from these questions that whereas the questions, Who may be a church member? and Who may be ordained?, primarily concern the fellowship of the churches, the present set of questions concern the wider social implications of the Gospel and the public witness of the Church.

It is perhaps well at this point to take a step backwards in order to remind ourselves of the Christian understanding of marriage. I do not speak of the understanding of Christian marriage because I hold that the main thrust of what has traditionally been taught by the Church concerning marriage concerns God's will for marriage as such, not simply for Christian marriage (an anachronistic concept indeed *vis à vis* the days of Genesis). Echoing words from Genesis, Jesus reminded those who set out to test him that

> in the beginning, at the creation, 'God made them male and female.' 'That is why a man leaves his father and mother, and is united to his wife, and the two become one flesh.' It follows that they are no longer two individuals: they are one flesh.'[244]

I therefore stand in the long line of those who regard marriage as an order of creation.[245]

---

242 See *Homosexuality and the Church: A Position Paper Adopted by the 119th General Assembly*, Atlanta, GA: Presbyterian Church in the United States, 1979, p. 5.

243 Ibid.

244 Mark 10:6-8.

245 Don Browning has declared that 'this form of argumentation does not convert easily into discourse that can stand up in the give and take of public discourse'. This need not, of course, inhibit us from making the attempt. Later, as a self-styled liberal theologian, he admits that 'since Protestant liberalism disregards both Catholic naturalism on family formation and the classical Protestant orders or spheres-of-creation argument, it has no way of discerning the central regularities of life that a just and loving "committed relation" should nurture and organise.' See his paper, 'World family trends', in Robin Gill, ed., *The Cambridge Companion to Christian Ethics*, Cambridge: Cambridge University Press, 2001, pp. 250, 255.

It follows that there is an inescapably public testimony to be made concerning marriage: it is not simply a matter between two individuals. A public witness to the nature of God's created order and societal intentions is being made when the Church marries couples or discusses such issues as marriage, sex and the family:[246]

> Christianity tends to see most things that the world regards as private, as intensely public. For us, sex is not a private matter. Sex is a public responsibility, intertwined with politics, something to be engaged in for the common good, not merely for individual satisfaction.[247]

For this reason, and also because it seems to sit loose to God's 'one flesh' creation, I cannot accept Rowan Williams's suggestion that if mutual joy and delight rather than procreation are primary in sexual relations, there are no theological grounds for restricting these to heterosexuals.[248] To repeat, procreation is not the exclusive end of sexual relations, but the expression of the 'one flesh' creation is; and I cannot find any sanction in the Bible or Church tradition for the view that God makes 'one flesh' of two homosexuals (which is not to say that such persons cannot have long-term, deep, stable relationships: clearly many of them do). Moreover, I consider that, in addition to the above Markan quotation, I have Genesis 1–2, the teaching of Jesus in Matthew 19:1-12 and Paul's discussion in 1 Corinthians 7:1-40 on my side.

Positively,

> We believe that marriage is a good gift of God. The covenant of wife and husband to serve one another faithfully is intended to reflect the faithfulness of God. God gives us the gift of sexual union to be the sign of that mutual and lasting covenant and a means whereby we may share in creating new life....[249]

In the light of the biblical and confessional witness concerning marriage, where are we to stand on the question of homosexual marriage? Two news items on one page of *The Christian Century* may represent the poles of opinion. According to the first, on 20 May 2004 at Arlington Street Unitarian Church, Boston, 'three clergypersons married 48 [homosexual] couples at 20-minute intervals between 9 a.m. and 9 p.m.'.

---

[246] Hence at the marriage service of my wife and myself Hubert Cunliffe-Jones, standing about six inches in front of us, thundered, 'You are getting married for the good of society.'

[247] William H. Willimon, *Pastor: The Theology and Practice of Ordained Ministry*, Nashville, TN: Abingdon, 2002, p. 107.

[248] R. Williams, *The Body's Grace*, London: Lesbian and Gay Christian Movement, 2003, p. 10. I say 'suggestion' because Williams writes tentatively here.

[249] *A Declaration of Faith* (1975) of the Presbyterian Church in the United States, in *Reformed Witness Today*, p. 236.

By contrast, the new Roman Catholic bishop of Worcester, Massachusetts, stated that 'It must be pointed out that Catholics, especially public officials, who willingly and with approval facilitate the legal sanctioning of same-sex unions are involving themselves in cooperation with evil.'[250] My own view is that given that in heterosexual marriage God does that which creates an ontological reality ('one flesh') which is not present in homosexual relationships, the use of the term 'marriage' in relation to the latter is inappropriate. This is not to deny that there may well be a case for civil arrangements which acknowledge that those who are in long-term same-sex partnerships,[251] whether homosexual or heterosexual (for we should not encourage discrimination in either direction), ought to benefit from inheritance tax legislation, for example, in the same way that married couples do. We should also note that according to Adrian Thatcher, who has paid particular attention to these issues, 'lesbian women and gay men sometimes wish to commit themselves to each other in a life-long union, though they would not necessarily want to define this in terms of marriage'.[252]

On the basis of my understanding of the Christian Gospel and of the nature of marriage, I conclude that homosexuals and heterosexuals alike are to be welcomed within the Church, and are eligible for baptism, confirmation and all the privileges of the Christian fellowship. All alike are eligible to become candidates for the ordained ministry. All alike are under responsibility to maintain the peace of the Church and to promote its teaching. Church members who engage in same-sex intercourse are freely placing themselves in a position from which they cannot without

---

250 *The Christian Century*, 15 June 2004, p. 14.

251 On 20 June 2003 the United Church of Canada commended the Federal Government of Canada for undertaking to draft legislation which would recognize same-sex civil unions. I wish that some of those who are rightly concerned that homosexuals receive justice and are not discriminated against were as concerned to treat justly those who disagree with their position on same sex marriage. Marvin M. Ellison, who writes as a liberal Christian, takes his stand on justice, but can yet contend that those who uphold the traditional view of marriage make gender difference the core structure of marriage. I have been at some pains to point out that basic to the structure of marriage are the will and the activity of God. Moreover, *pace* Ellison, I am no supporter of a social hierarchy based upon patriarchalism. The issue is sufficiently important to warrant something other than straw man arguments. See Ellison's *Same Sex Marriage? A Christian Ethical Analysis*, Cleveland, OH: Pilgrim Press, 2004. I have heard such arguments as the following: 'You do not support same sex marriage because you are homophobic.' 'You support the traditional view of marriage because you favour the subservience of women.' Such *non sequitur* arguments would not be acceptable in a first year philosophy essay. But when they occur in ostensibly serious discussions, as on occasion they do, one writing a paper on labelling finds it difficult to hold the term 'balderdash' at bay.

252 A. Thatcher, 'Marriage guidance', *The Times Higher Education Supplement*, 3 December 1993, p. 19.

hypocrisy teach the Church's understanding of marriage or witness to marriage as the sole locus of sexual expression; and heterosexuals who find sexual gratification outside of marriage, whether adulterers or not, freely place themselves in the same position. Both parties are in a situation analogous to those who, in a trinitarian Church, embrace Unitarian views and wish to proclaim them. Such persons may not be ordained, or if they are already ordained they should be graciously disciplined; for the minister is in these respects a public person who is not appointed to peddle his or her own ethical or doctrinal preferences, but to proclaim the Church's teaching. If he or she cannot do this, the first task is to work for change through the appropriate channels, and if change does not come, to consider one's position. It is ideologically selfish and pastorally inept to proceed as if change has occurred when it has not. As with predestination, so with homosexuals: all may be included in the family of the Church; some, under Gospel discipline, may exclude themselves. In both cases the primary thing is what God the Lord has graciously done. 'Fidelity within marriage, chastity outside of marriage' is the all-too-tarnished ideal. It is also a slogan I see no theological grounds for repudiating.

VI

I come finally, and briefly, to one further area of discussion surrounding the concepts of inclusiveness and exclusiveness: language, and in particular trinitarian language in relation to public worship.[253] The debate on this issue is increasingly widespread, perspectivally diverse, and occasionally explosive. It is a debate in which my work has from time to time involved me, in academic and church circles in a variety of cultures around the world. Because of the sensitivity of the issue, those, like myself, who wish to query some of the claims and arguments advanced by promoters of linguistic change are frequently moved to set out from a disclaimer. Let me at once say, therefore, that I have nothing against women; like many others I agonize over the pernicious and continuing oppression of people on account of their sex, race and social background; and although, like Paul, I have no grounds for boasting, let me also say that through travelling, speaking and writing, I have sought to raise the profile of women in the Reformed churches of the world.

In this last connection I have, for example, encouraged some churches which do not at present ordain women to the ministry, or in some cases to the eldership, to review their position in the light of the Gospel. In the course of doing this I have discovered that in some cultures talk of

---

[253] In what follows, and with the editor's permission, I expand a short article which appeared in *Reform*, May, 2004, pp. 20-21, entitled, 'I bind unto myself.'

women's rights is a dissuasive, and that there is the greatest degree of receptivity to the ordination of women when the matter is presented in what I take to be the strongest possible theological way. Thus: if the sovereign God of all grace and mercy calls out one people by his Spirit through the Word; and if in that called community the barriers between male and female, bond and free are broken down; and if God should then determine to call this man or this woman to be his ministers, on what conceivable grounds may we deny God's right to issue such a call? This is one of the cases where, as it seems to me, the churches are (all too slowly) catching up with the Gospel.

Another instance of catching up concerns inclusive language where the reference is to males and females together. I have come to believe that on such occasions it is consistent with the Gospel that we should not use language which excludes half of the human race. At the same time, I do not damn all earlier writers as sexist when, for example, they used 'mankind' for the whole of humanity. They were working within the linguistic conventions of their day, and everyone knew what they meant and so, if we are honest, do we. In every generation there are things which, from the point of view of later generations, those living in it did not 'see'. Accordingly, a little humility will incline us to wonder in which connections people two hundred years hence will be tempted to regard us as having been benighted. We may be sure that there will be such criticisms, but we, as children of our time, are not aware of the issues which will prompt them.

The most problematic area concerns the language appropriately to be used of the Godhead. First, there are those who do not believe that masculine personal pronouns should be used of God, for this is to suggest that God is male, a man. As I write, Mary Daly's slogan of 1974, 'Since God is male, the male is God',[254] celebrates its thirtieth anniversary. To think thus would, of course, be idolatry, since God is above sexuality; and to deny that one is an idolater is by no means to endorse the domination of women by men. But then some writers contend that because the Greek *sophia* is a feminine noun[255] it refers to the feminine side of God. But the phrase 'female side of God' is, strictly, meaningless: God is above sexuality; he has neither a male nor a female side. That *sophia* is in the feminine gender is a convention of the Greek language, and we should be very careful before we construct arguments which proceed from the grammatical conventions of particular languages to substantive theological claims.

---

[254] M. Daly, 'The qualitative leap beyond patriarchal religion', *Quest*, I, 1974, p. 21.

[255] In the Old Testament 'wisdom' is feminine on thirty-six occasions, but masculine on seven occasions. So John W. Cooper, *Our Father in Heaven. Christian Faith and Inclusive Language for God*, Grand Rapids, MI: Baker Books, 1998, p. 110.

It is unfortunate that some feminist writers resort to special pleading. They invoke grammar and sexuality in such a way as to force their argument on the unsuspecting. Margrethe B. J. Brown is at fault here—and in an *a priori* way too:

> Would a God who, in spite of the wealth of the Biblical language, in our more recent times has been referred to only as a male Father or Lord ever bind HIMself in a covenant to a people who contained in their midst as partners anyone who was not also male?[256]

No theologian of whom I am aware contends that God is a male.

It will be evident that my practice is to use masculine personal pronouns when referring to God. I do this because, especially at a time of rampant gnosticism and pantheism, I deem it important that Christians make plain that the Godhead is personal. To this end I need personal pronouns. I cannot bring myself to refer to God using the neuter 'it' as a few writers do; if I were to begin to use feminine pronouns in the interests of balance, somebody somewhere may think that I have now decided that God is a woman—which I have not; and any talk of such balancing is crypto-idolatry. It follows that I cannot assign meaning to requests that we use inclusive language when referring to God. Because God is neither male nor female conventions regarding inclusive language in the human context (logically) cannot apply to him. That would be to sanction the grotesque double idolatry that God is both a male and a female.[257]

In order to avoid using pronouns, some writers simply repeat the term 'God': 'God sent God's son into God's world to save God's people from their sins.' This makes for stylistic awkwardness, not to say boredom, but, more importantly, it again does not make God's personal nature explicit, for 'God' might, for example, refer to that 'certain Something' in which many people profess to believe when confronted by opinion pollsters. As for the barbarous coinage, 'Godself', I concur with Hook and Kimel:

> *Godself* most naturally reads as a noun denoting some sort of divine substance. In the sentence, 'God gives Godself to humanity in Jesus Christ,' the immediate sense is that God gives something to us which is not identical to his person. *Godself* will

---

256 M. B. J. Brown, 'The challenge to male chauvinist exclusivism in Church and society', in Allen O. Miller, *A Covenant Challenge to Our Broken World*, Atlanta, GA: Carribean and North American Area Council of the World Alliance of Reformed Churches, 1982, p. 229.

257 Cf. Roland M. Frye, 'Language for God and feminist language', in Alvin F. Kimel, Jr., ed., *Speaking the Christian God. The Holy Trinity and the Language of Feminism*, Grand Rapids, MI: Eerdmans, 1992, p. 25.

> not be heard—indeed, cannot be heard—as reflexively referring to the antecedent *God.*[258]

More serious still is the debate surrounding the threefold name, Father, Son and Holy Spirit.[259] It would be quite wrong to suppose that all feminists oppose this formula. But some feminists, distressed by what they perceive as biblical and ecclesiastical patriarchalism, do not use, and do not wish others to hear in worship, the threefold name because of its reference to God as 'Father'.[260] They argue that the biblical world was, and the ecclesiastical world still is, patriarchal, and that as a result of this women have been demoted and oppressed. There is, however, a considerable body of biblical evidence[261] and scholarly literature to show that the Semitic cultures around Israel, and the Hellenistic culture surrounding the early Church were replete with 'female' deities, societal patriarchalism notwithstanding. We might almost say that the biblical use of 'Father' went in face of much of the culture of the time and, as I shall suggest shortly, this can only be because that is how God had made himself known to his people. Moreover, against patriarchy, Jesus enjoined his disciples, 'Do not call any man on earth "father", for you have one Father, and he is in heaven' (Matthew 23:9). As Ted Peters has rightly recommended, 'We must operate with the assumption that metaphors such as "our Father in heaven" coming from the mouth of Jesus are closer to the original revelation of God than are our current ethical agendas.'[262]

As P. T. Forsyth put it, echoing a long line of exposition—especially Franciscan:

> The New Testament name and idea of God is no simply 'Our Father', but 'the God and Father of our Lord Jesus Christ.' And Christ's own prayer was 'Holy Father.' That was Christ's central thought of God, and he knew God as he is.[263]

---

258 Donald D. Hook and Alvin F. Kimel, Jr., 'The pronouns of deity: a theolinguistic critique of feminist proposals', *Scottish Journal of Theology*, XLVI, 1993, p. 317.

259 See Donald G. Bloesch, *The Battle for the Trinity*, Ann Arbor, MI: Servant Books, 1985.

260 Some writers also object to 'Son', not because they deny that Jesus was male, but because they disapprove of the masculine emphasis in the formula. This, it seems to me, puts the Incarnation at risk.

261 1 Kings 11:1-8; 15:13; Jeremiah 7:17-19; 44:15-17; Acts 19.

262 T. Peters, 'On adding divine mothers to the Bible', *Currents in Theology and Mission*, XIII no. 5, October 1986, p. 283.

263 P. T. Forsyth, *God the Holy Father*, (1897), London: Independent Press, 1957, p. 3. Cf. Elise Saggau, ed., *The Franciscan Intellectual Tradition*, p. 35. Janet Martin Soskice notes that 'The modest 11 designations of God as father in the Old Testament

This point notwithstanding, many feminists wish to substitute other terms for 'Father, Son and Spirit' in the trinitarian formula. A popular choice is, 'Creator, Redeemer, Sustainer'. These, however, are functional terms which do not express all that the three persons do, and in the liturgy the idea that one can be blessed not by persons but by what have been jocularly called items from God's job description is ludicrous. More importantly, the alternative formula loses the inner-personal relations of the Godhead thereby obscuring the important point that the Godhead is intimately involved in all the actions of the persons. When this idea is lost, modalism—even tritheism—threatens.

Underlying this debate is the distinction between metaphor, simile and analogy. If a psalmist says that God is a rock or a fortress, we are in the realm of metaphor, for God is not literally either of these things. Many metaphors are used of God in the Bible, some of which are feminine. We should do well to use a wider range of these than we have traditionally done in our worship and private devotions. We might also wish to use such a simile as 'God loves us *like* a (good) mother'. But in the trinitarian formula, 'Father' is more like (but not exactly like) an analogy. There is a claimed basis of identity between the Father of all and human fatherhood (in a way there is not between God and a rock), but there are profound differences too. God is absolute in holiness, human fathers are not; human fathers are male, God is not. But why, it might be asked, may we not construct an analogy using 'Mother'? Here we come finally to the authority of the biblical revelation confirmed in the experience of Christians through the ages.

There can be no question that Jesus, who knew the Father as no other, taught us to address God as Father. The early Christians did not cast around for images which they might appropriately use of God. They spoke of God as he had shown himself to be; and as he has shown himself, so he is. While it is true, as the Puritans and their predecessors never tired of insisting, that while we may have a true apprehension of God we may not have a full comprehension of him, we are not altogether in the dark. We may see only what Paul called 'puzzling reflections in a mirror' (1 Corinthians 13:12), but they are reflections of the truth. This is why the analogy from the divine to the human fatherhood is odd as analogies go: it is not something we project on the basis of our human experience of fatherhood: that would be to risk blurring of the Creator-creature distinction; rather, the human fatherhood is a pale reflection of the divine Fatherhood. Because God has revealed himself in this way, in orthodox Christianity 'Father' when used of God denotes an ontological

contrast sharply with the 170 times Jesus designates God as father in the very much shorter New Testament.' See her paper, 'Can feminists call God "Father"?' in Kimel, Jr., ed., *Speaking the Christian God*, p. 90.

reality, 'mother' remains an instructive simile. God lets us know who he is; otherwise we should not know him at all. In the covenant with Israel and in the Incarnation of the Son the Father reveals his active, inclusive holy love. Geoffrey Wainwright has well said that 'the trinitarian name of God is *given* to us with Jesus's address to "Abba, Father," his self-understanding and career as "the Son," and his promise of the Holy Spirit'.[264] We are not, therefore, in the position of those who, in an anthropocentric way, are called upon to cast around for what they hope will be appropriate metaphors to use in our God-talk.

Undeniably, the term 'Trinity' is not used in the Bible: that is why John Taylor and other eighteenth-century Arians would not accept the term.[265] It may fairly be argued, however, that the concept is there. It is equally clear that the final formulation on the doctrine of the Trinity was a long time in coming. It occurred as early Christians reflected upon the way in which they had been drawn to the Father through the Son by the prompting of the Spirit; and as the experience was articulated in the face of those who stood for different (that is, 'heretical') accounts of Christian teaching. It is my belief that the New Testament contains more than enough clues to justify trinitarian doctrine, and that that doctrine is confirmed by the experience of Christians through the ages.

By contrast, 'when we change what the Bible does say to what we think it should say, it becomes a dummy for our own thought—and no dummy exercises authority over the ventriloquist'.[266] Why, then, are some feminists so eager (according to taste) to revise/modify/repudiate/devastate trinitarian language? As Isabel Carter Heyward informs us, giving the game away: 'I am re-imaging humanity, God, and Jesus in order to speak my truth'[267]—a breathtakingly bold undertaking indeed. But this is what some feminists attempt to do. Why do they make the attempt? One of their number may answer for them:

> Inclusive language is born of the struggle of those who are linguistically invisible as they come to the recognition that their invisibility reflects and perpetuates the exclusivist bias of the institutions of their society.[268]

---

264 G. Wainwright, 'Trinitarian worship', in Kimel, Jr., ed., *Speaking the Christian God*, p. 218.

265 See above ch. 3.

266 Paul S. Minear, 'Changes in metaphor produce changes in thought', *Presbyterian Outlook*, 19-26 December 1983, quoted by R. M. Frye, 'Language for God and feminist language', p. 33.

267 I. C. Heyward, *The Redemption of God: A Theology of Mutual Relation*, Lanham, MD: University Press of America, 1982, p. 14.

268 Susan Brooks Thistlethwaite, 'Inclusive language and linguistic blindness', *Theology Today*, XLIII no. 4, January 1987, p. 534.

In other words, their starting-point is the malign experience of women in a male-dominated society, and this (after Feuerbach, perhaps) they project onto God. This leads them to read the Bible through their specific experiential lens; their experience is elevated into the interpretative norm, and this in turn can propel them towards an angular censoring of others on the basis that 'Included in feminist consciousness are some fundamental convictions so basic and so important that contradictory assertions cannot be accepted without violence being done to their very understanding and valuations'.[269] Margaret Farley describes this as a 'minimal claim'.

While it is true that no one comes to the Bible presuppositionally 'neat', as it were, the danger here is that instead of standing under the Word, readers treat the Bible as if it were Locke's 'nose of wax':

> [S]ystems, the inventions of men, are turned into so many opposite gospels; and nothing is truth in each sect, but what suits with them. So that the scripture serves but, like a nose of wax, to be turned and bent, just as may fit the contrary orthodoxies of different societies.[270]

Along this route some reached their heretical justification of the sin of apartheid;[271] others drew forth the determined response of the *Barmen Declaration* of 1934:

> We reject the false doctrine, as though the Church were permitted to abandon the form of its message and order to its own pleasure or to the changes in prevailing ideological and political convictions....
>
> We reject the false doctrine, as though the Church in human arrogance could place the Word and work of the Lord in the service of any arbitrarily chosen desires, purposes, and plans.[272]

---

[269] Margaret Farley, 'Feminist consciousness and the interpretation of Scripture', in Letty Russell, ed., *Feminist Interpretation of the Bible*, Philadelphia, PA: Westminster, 1985, p. 44.

[270] J. Locke, *A Second Vindication of the Reasonableness of Christianity*, in *The Works of John Locke in Ten Volumes*, London: W. Otridge *et al*, 11th edn, 1812, VII, p. 295. See further Alan P. F. Sell, *John Locke and the Eighteenth-Century Divines*, Cardiff: University of Wales Press, 1997, ch. 3.

[271] For a biblically-grounded response to which see the 'Resolution on racism and South Africa', in Edmond Perret, ed., *Proceedings of the 21st General Council of the World Alliance of Reformed Churches*, Geneva: WARC, 1983, pp. 176-80. For a discussion of this see Alan P. F. Sell, *A Reformed, Evangelical, Catholic Theology. The Contribution of the World Alliance of Reformed Churches 1875–1980*, (1991), Eugene, OR: Wipf & Stock, 1998, pp. 232-35.

[272] *The Theological Declaration of Barmen, 1934*, in Arthur C. Cochrane, ed., *Reformed Confessions of the 16th Century*, pp. 335-36.

Few have begged the question as clearly as Sallie McFague, who denies that there is any 'gender-neutral language *if we take ourselves as the model for talk about God*, because we are sexual beings'.[273]

A further step is taken when worship takes on the character of a 'party' activity in which nothing other than the approved formulae are tolerated. We thus have a mirror image of those fundamentalists who doubt one's 'soundness' if they do not hear their favoured 'language of Canaan' in worship.[274] In this connection Gabriel Fackre's account of behind the scenes activity at a Christian conference is disturbing:

> Members of the Boston Feminist Dialogue group caucused during the meeting and organized a protest over the use of some less-than-inclusive language in one of the worship services, announcing that its group and supporters would stand in silent witness whenever such took place again.[275]

It seems to me that to approach worship in such a 'looking for trouble' spirit betrays a less than appropriately devotional attitude; and to announce that one intends to act thus simply puts all other worshippers on edge in a quite unwarrantable way.[276] As Kathryn Greene-McCreight

---

273 S. McFague, *Models of God: Theology for an Ecological, Nuclear Age*, Philadelphia, PA: Fortress Press, 1987, p. 98. My italics.

274 Some post-Christian feminists think in terms of a mother goddess who gives birth to the world. This implies the identity of the goddess with creation. Here the Creator-creature distinction is removed and pantheism is the result. For pantheism in relation to Christian claims see ch. 7 above.

275 G. Fackre, *The Christian Story. A Pastoral Systematics. II. Autority: Scripture in the Church for the World*, Grand Rapids, MI: Eerdmans, 1987, p. 34.

276 I am deeply distressed by some examples of a lack of Christian sensitivity which I have encountered where fundamentalist attitudes of various kinds are in vogue. I recall the headline of a Christian bulletin which proclaimed: 'The women of Europe have spoken.' On closer inspection it turned out that these 'women of Europe' were about twenty feminists almost entirely under the age of forty. I gently pointed out to the editor of the bulletin that my mother was also a 'woman of Europe', and that her views were significantly different from those reported; moreover, that my mother was in the most numerous class of persons in most western European mainline congregations, namely, elderly women. I was met with blank incomprehension that anyone might be interested in what such antediluvians might think. Again, in a remote African village my wife and I met a group of Christian women who were greatly disturbed by a visitation of feminists a few days earlier: 'They told us that we should be feeling oppressed by our men. We could not make them understand that in our village we do not feel oppressed by our men. We feel oppressed by hunger and poverty, and so do our men.' It is difficult to banish the term 'cultural imperialism' from one's mind; but at the very least such a refusal to listen is not the most apt way of advancing one's cause.

has remarked, 'When sexuality replaces soul and politics replaces praise, we have a thin gruel.'[277]

But this brings me to the ethics and the church disciplinary implications of the matter. Time would fail to tell of the re-writing of hymns—not in such a way as to remove archaic language, but on feminist-ideological grounds. I shall simply illustrate my argument by reference to the trinitarian blessing in the name of God, Father, Son and Holy Spirit. I have noticed in my own Church and elsewhere that some who lead worship are reluctant to use this blessing. They do not wish the people in the pews to hear about the Father and the Son, hence the attempted modifications noted earlier. What is frequently overlooked is the fact that those who lead Christian worship in trinitarian churches do not do so as private persons, choosing their favourite biblical passages and hymns and making their personal prayers. They are public—even priestly—persons, whose awesome responsibility is to lead the prayers and praises of the people and, at the end of worship, to bless them in God's name.

To give a specific example: The first sentence of 'The faith of the United Reformed Church' crisply situates that Church in the catholic faith of the ages and invokes the threefold name: 'The United Reformed Church confesses the faith of the Church Catholic in one God, Father, Son and Holy Spirit.'[278] It is also the case that the document quite rightly affirms the United Reformed Church's 'duty to be open at all times to the leading of the Holy Spirit and therefore affirms its right to make such new declarations of its faith' in obedience to the Spirit.[279]

Writing as a member of this Church, it seems to me that unless and until it becomes 'commonly agreed among us' that we should no longer use the threefold name in worship (which conclusion would, for good or ill, place us outside the mainstream of historic Christianity), those who lead our worship are morally obliged to retain and use the formula. The Unitarian, Joseph Priestley, saw the point. He informed the inhabitants of Northumberland, Pennsylvania, that he could not worship with them because their devotions were 'altogether Trinitarian, *as they ought to be while you are Trinitarians*'.[280] I am by no means arguing that the traditional blessing is the only one which may appropriately be used; but I do think that it is the one which we should least willingly surrender.

---

277 K. Greene-McCreight, 'Feminist theology and a generous orthodoxy', *Scottish Journal of Theology*, LVII no. 1, 2004, p. 108.

278 Percy W. Bush, ed., *Manual*, London: United Reformed Church in England and Wales, 1973, p. 12.

279 Ibid., p. 14.

280 Priestley, *Theological and Miscellaneous Works*, XXV, p. 143; my italics.

If worship leaders' personal conscientious convictions will not permit the use of the trinitarian blessing[281] they ought first to seek to change the mind of the Church. If this fails, they may need to consider their position. I am not pleading for heresy trials. Rather, I am seeking to recognize the need to honour the consciences of both worship leaders and church members, and to uphold the integrity of both. If we were to diminish the matter to the language of rights, we could say that worship leaders have a right to a quiet conscience, and church members of trinitarian churches have a right to trinitarian worship. If they are consistently denied this, and if as a result pastoral relations break down, disciplinary procedures may need to be invoked. Thomas Belsham (1750–1829) took a more appropriate way. In 1781 he left the Congregational pastorate at Angel Street, Worcester, and became a tutor at the Dissenting academy at Daventry. Whilst there he embraced Unitarian views, honourably resigned his post in 1789, and removed to the academy which the Rational Dissenters established at Hackney, London. I believe that his action exemplified both personal integrity and implied his acknowledgement that those desiring a trinitarian framework for their Christian life and worship, which he could no longer in conscience supply, ought not to be denied it.

For my part, I am happy to join the Canadian Presbyterians in affirming that

> with the one church universal
> we believe in one God, eternal Trinity,
> Father, Son and Holy Spirit,
> three in one,
> one in three,
> equal in power and glory.
> God is the Father to whom we come,
> the Son through whom we come,
> the Spirit by whom we come.[282]

That Christian confession is not a matter of the lips alone, none knew better than the Puritans, of whom Thomas Watson is typical:

> A Christian's heart is to be the presence-chamber of the blessed Trinity; and shall not holiness to the Lord be written upon it? Believers are children of God the

---

[281] I find that some seem to think that any threefold pattern of words is trinitarian. The name of the chain of shoe shops, Freeman, Hardy and Willis, is threefold, but it is not trinitarian.

[282] *Living Faith. A Statement of Christian Belief*, Winfield, BC: Wood Lake Books, 1984, pp. 5-6.

> Father, members of God the Son, and temples of God the Holy Ghost; and shall they not be holy? Holiness is the badge and livery of God's people.[283]

VII

It would seem that nicknames, labels and slogans are endemic in Christian theology and life. Although they may variously amuse or wound those to whom they are applied, nicknames are the least serious, for they either lose currency with the passage of time or they become respectable. Labels are more important. Their very slipperiness requires that they be subjected to close scrutiny lest important distinctions between persons and movements classified under the same heading be overlooked.

Perhaps slogans are most important of all, for they become rallying cries of parties, and in certain circumstances those who own them exercise considerable influence.[284] I have concentrated upon three such slogans. In order to illustrate the first, 'The Church must take its agenda from the world', I discussed Tillich's method. I then turned to a particular way, or variety of ways, of doing this as represented by the liberation theologians of Latin America, with a view to analyzing the slogan, 'All theology must be contextual'. It became clear that the term is elastic, referring as it can to my specific situation, that of my kind, and the trinitarian parameters within which all Christian theology should be articulated. If this last is overlooked, parochial sectarianism threatens. Finally, I discussed the slogan 'Inclusiveness is good, exclusiveness is bad'. I argued that such a blanket slogan is unhelpful, and I illustrated the senses in which the Church may be variously inclusive or exclusive by reference to doctrine, morals, the wider-than-ecclesiastical issue of homosexuality, and the language of worship. When inclusivism becomes so open-ended that things of importance drop out, we have lost the Gospel and weakened the Church. When exclusivism turns sectarian, we have lost the Gospel and betrayed the Church. As the Preacher might have said, 'There is a time to be inclusive and a time to be exclusive'. There are also ways of adopting either of these attitudes which challenge our pastoral skills, especially in relation to church discipline.

Despite the risks, I thought it would be appropriate to end this lengthy chapter with a literary flourish by hazarding a slogan of my own. On analogy with the famous slogan of World War II, 'Careless talk costs lives', I thought of 'Careless theological talk costs the Gospel'. It will not quite serve the purpose, however, for, as we have seen, the suppression of

---

283 Watson, *A Divine Cordial*, pp. 79-80.

284 I think, for example, of the highly politicized, and sometimes well funded, pressure groups which endeavour to sway opinion in some church assemblies.

theological talk, whether wilful or principled, can be equally damaging to Christian proclamation.

CHAPTER 13

May We Still Glory in the Cross?

> The Cross is absolutely central to the Gospel and without the Cross there is no Gospel left at all. The good news of the Christian faith centres in the proclamation that God in Christ dealt seriously with sin and made an ethical forgiveness possible.[1]

Thus spoke J. D. Jones in the course of his sermon delivered in 1920 at the Fourth International Congregational Council. But what are we to understand by 'Cross'? Clearly, in Christian discourse the term signifies more than a gallows, and more than a crucifixion—of which there were many in those days. Paul could not have 'gloried' in these, and nor could any right-minded person; yet Paul famously declared, 'God forbid that I should boast of anything but the cross of our Lord Jesus Christ, through which the world is crucified to me and I to the world!'[2]

Such 'boasting' or 'glorying' was possible only because in Christian usage 'Cross' becomes a multi-dimensional term. It was so for Paul and other New Testament writers, and it has been so throughout the Christian ages, differences of emphasis notwithstanding. Thus, for example, John of Damascus (c.655–c.750) writes:

> Every action, therefore, and performance of miracles by Christ are most great and divine and marvellous: but the most marvellous of all is His precious Cross. For no other thing has subdued death, expiated the sin of the first parent, despoiled Hades, bestowed the resurrection, granted the power to us of contemning the present and even death itself, prepared the return to our former blessedness, opened the gates of Paradise, given our nature a seat at the right hand of God, and made us the children

---

1 J. D. Jones, 'The doctrine of development', the Council Sermon (on John 16:14), *Proceedings of the Fourth International Congregational Council*, 1920, New York: National Council of the Congregational Churches of the United States, 1921, p. 62. Jones spoke during a period of heightened activity in the field of soteriology. For a discussion of some of the contributors to this see Thomas Hywel Hughes, *The Atonement. Modern Theories of the Doctrine*, London: Allen & Unwin, 1949.

2 Galatians 6:14.

> and heirs of God, save the cross of our Lord Jesus Christ. For by the Cross all things have been made right.[3]

For a twentieth-century example we may turn to one who was pre-eminently a theologian of the Cross, P. T. Forsyth. I have elsewhere sought to show that to him 'Cross' encompassed

> a cluster of convictions: God's fatherly love as holy and victorious; grace as judgment; Christ as having wrought once and for all at Calvary an atonement for the race, by virtue of which penitent sinners receive new life in the Spirit, are engrafted into the Church, and are in fellowship with God and the communion of saints eternally. For all of this, at least, 'Cross' is shorthand in Forsyth.... In making the umbrella term 'Cross' central and determinative for Christology and all else, Forsyth sounded notes which must never be absent from the score of Christian theology.[4]

It seems to me that both Paul, John of Damascus and Forsyth, albeit in different accents, have sought to hold together things which belong together.[5] In this they are by no means alone, though in the writings of some theologians[6] and, as we shall see, in some forms of Christian religious expression, the Cross has been treated almost in isolation from the Incarnation—and, indeed, from the resurrection—and *vice versa*. Notwithstanding this, it is true to say that a long line of witnesses would endorse the view that

> the Christian Gospel is a Gospel because it consists of credenda, facts of faith, given objectively, if not in Scripture as a whole, yet in and through the historical Person—Jesus Christ; that from these the Church has always derived its Evangelical witness and experience.[7]

---

3 John of Damascus, *Exposition of the Orthodox Faith*, IV.xi, trans. S. D. F. Salmond, (A Select Library of Post-Nicene Fathers of the Christian Church, IX), Oxford: James Parker, 1899, p. 80. The comprehensiveness of the passage quoted inclines me to think that Hastings Rashdall's adverse criticism of John is somewhat one-sided. See Rashdall's *The Idea of Atonement in Christian Theology*, London: Macmillan, 1920, pp. 316-320.

4 See Alan P. F. Sell, *Testimony and Tradition. Studies in Reformed and Dissenting Thought*, Aldershot: Ashgate, 2005, ch. 7.

5 Accordingly, I use the upper case 'C' in 'Cross' by way of underlining the fact that I am employing the word as an umbrella term; I am not speaking only of a gallows or a crucifixion.

6 For example, in *The Shape of Soteriology*, Edinburgh: T. & T. Clark, 1992, p. 44, John McIntyre writes, 'It is a false abstraction to separate crucifixion from resurrection as Aulén does, almost in neglect of Scripture.'

7 F. J. Powicke, *David Worthington Simon*, London: Hodder and Stoughton, 1912, p. 221.

I cannot in one chapter discuss the full range of topics opened up by the term 'Cross'.[8] My concern is rather with an impression I have (it is no more than that, and I have not brought the sociologist's tools to bear upon the matter) that in some Christian circles (certain American television programmes come to mind) the Cross is heavily emphasized, in at least some of its significations, in ways which call to mind the adjective 'grotesque'; whereas in some mainline Christian circles the Cross does not feature as centrally as, I believe, it ought to do in current theological writing and Christian worship. That the latter impression not exclusive to myself is shown by the remark of Derek Tidball, the principal of a highly respected evangelical theological institution,[9] who writes,

> in recent days, there are signs that all is not what it was. The cross no longer seems to occupy the central place in evangelical theology, preaching and spirituality that it once did. Trinity, creation, incarnation, resurrection and the Spirit are nudging it down the evangelical agenda. ... Evangelical preaching of the cross might justifiably be accused of having often been too narrow.... But in so far as these moves are a denial of our evangelical heritage they are to be rejected.[10]

From the many factors which may discourage theologians and others from emphasizing the Cross I shall select a few for discussion. The issues to be raised merit book-length treatments, and such they have quite frequently received. But there is something to be said for a check-list of things to be borne in mind by those who ponder and proclaim Christian centralities. Moreover, I shall be able to show that some aspects of the ensuing discussion relate to topics treated elsewhere in this volume, and thus this short chapter will serve as a conclusion to the whole.

I

There are many reasons why theologians and preachers may feel reluctant to focus upon the Cross. I turn first to the inhibiting effect of statements of traditional atonement theory which may be deemed one-sided or otherwise inadequate. It is not unfair to say that all of the traditional theories may be pushed in untoward directions. Thus, while the ransom theory preserves the important insight that our redemption is

---

[8] I have, however, attempted to deal with some of them in *Christ Our Saviour*, Shippensburg, PA: Ragged Edge Press, 2000, chs. 2-5. This is the second volume of my 'Doctrine and Devotion' trilogy, a 'devotional systematics' for ministers and church members.

[9] The London School of Theology, by British standards a large institution which is related to Brunel University.

[10] D. J. Tidball, 'The Cross of Christ. The defining centre of evangelicalism', *LBC Review*, London Bible College, n.d., p. 2.

costly work,[11] it takes an unfortunate turn when writers, pondering the question, To whom was the ransom paid? answer, 'The devil'; for the latter has no rights (assuming his existence as an entity over against God). Again, Anselm's view of Christ's work as satisfying God's outraged honour, though couched in quantitative terms, does remind us that in view of humanity's sinfulness, God's holiness must be vindicated even as his mercy is actively displayed. Yet again, the penal substitutionary theory of the atonement, though too frequently couched in terms which suppose the punishment of the innocent, obedient Son, contains within an insight which must never be lost, namely, that in a crucial sense Christ stood where we should have stood, and did for us what we could never have done for ourselves. As for the moral influence theory, classically articulated by Abelard and favoured by many, not least those on the liberal wing of theology, the example of Christ is powerful and does evoke in many a response of commitment; but on its own it is more aesthetic than realistic: it underestimates what needed to be done at the Cross to break the power of sin and death and reconcile sinners to God.

It may be appropriate to add some flesh to the bones thus swiftly exposed. I wish to say, first, that any view of the work of Christ which proceeds as if a wedge may be driven between the Father and the Son should be eschewed. It is not that the angry Father required the death of his Son before he could be gracious and merciful: though I have fairly frequently heard that very doctrine proclaimed on television. On the contrary, 'God's Fatherhood is not the result, but the cause of the Cross of Christ'[12]—so A. E. Garvie. Or, as Garvie's older contemporary expressed it in what I have sometimes called the single most important sentence in the whole of twentieth-century theology, 'The atonement did not procure grace, it flowed from grace.'[13] These witnesses have Calvin and many others behind them:

> we do not suggest that God was ever inimical or angry toward [Christ]. How could he be angry toward his beloved Son, 'in whom his heart reposed'? How could Christ by

---

[11] Cf. H. F. Lovell Cocks, *The Wondrous Cross*, London: Independent Press, 1957, p. 50: 'The forgiveness that is freely offered is costly indeed. The Cross of Christ is the revelation of its infinite price.' There is more in Lovell Cocks's eighty pages than in many a longer and heavier (if not weightier) tome. For this unduly neglected theologian see Alan P. F. Sell, *Commemorations. Studies in Christian Thought and History*, (1993), Eugene, OR: Wipf & Stock, 1998, ch. 12; *ODNB*.

[12] A. E. Garvie, *A Guide to Preachers*, London: Hodder and Stoughton, 1906, p. 145.

[13] P. T. Forsyth, *The Cruciality of the Cross*, (1909), London: Independent Press, 1957, p. 41; cf. his *The Work of Christ*, (1910), London: Independent Press, 1958, p. 180.

> his intercession appease the Father toward others, if he himself were hateful to God?... Indeed, 'because he first loved us', he afterward reconciles us to himself.[14]

Few set the matter more concisely in its trinitarian context than Forsyth's pupil, H. F. Lovell Cocks:

> The ugly gap between the stern Father and the merciful Son, which seems to open as we listen to some expositions of the Atonement, is not to be found in the New Testament. There Christ and the Father are at one. Christ the Son has come to do the Father's will and to give His life a ransom for many. God in His love has pity upon the sin-stricken world, and in Jesus Christ His incarnate Son He has visited and redeemed His people. This is our starting-point as we set ourselves to try to understand something of the depth and glory of Christ's saving work. We begin, as we must, with the unity of Father, Son and Spirit in that divine love by which we are redeemed. The Atonement is the work of the triune God.[15]

A current variant of the 'Father *versus* the Son' approach may be found in the writings of some, though by no means all, feminist and womanist theologians. I have alluded to this elsewhere,[16] but the misunderstanding into which these writers have, in my opinion, fallen is sufficiently important to warrant brief mention here. The womanist theologian, Dolores Williams, writes,

> If God, the Father, intended the death on the cross of Jesus, his innocent son, then child abuse by fathers might not be taken as seriously as it need be in Christian societies. Rather, the social tendency might be to ignore the need to enforce stringent measures against child abusers because the religion fosters the belief that God, the Father, was in some ways in agreement with the death of Jesus.[17]

This is a relatively restrained way of making the point: some writers do not hesitate to call God a 'child batterer'. Williams goes on to refer to 'the cannibalistic insinuations' of the eucharist:

> The question that always comes to my mind is whether this emphasis upon dying-sacrifice has implications for women's oppression. Since many women are conditioned to sacrifice 'all' for their family's well-being, I wonder if this 'sacred sacrifice', achieved through brutalization of Jesus' body, can encourage battered

---

14 J. Calvin, *Institutes of the Christian Religion*, ed. John T. McNeil, trans. Ford Lewis Battles, 2 vols, Philadelphia: Westminster Press, 1960, II.xvi.11,3.

15 Lovell Cocks, *The Wondrous Cross*, p. 7.

16 See ch. 11 above.

17 D. Williams, 'Humans brutalizing humans: necessary images in the Christian religion?', *Quarterly Newsletter* of the Women's Theological Center, IX no. 1, March 1991, p. 1.

> women to stay in battering situations, thereby sacrificing themselves to some 'higher purpose' like family unity?[18]

It would, of course, be tragic if some women were to think in this way, and it is quite conceivable to me that some may in fact think thus. If so, whether we think of battered children or women, the point needs to be made that to construe doctrines or liturgical moments through dire human experiences is to adopt something akin to a Feuerbachian method of projection; it is to elevate the experiences to the status of interpretative norms, thereby running the risk that the given revelation will be manipulated rather than heeded. We should take care lest we adopt positions which imply the dividing of the work of God the holy Trinity, and overlook Paul's grand claim that '*God* was *in Christ* reconciling the world to himself' (2 Corinthians 5:19).[19]

Secondly, we should set our face against any suggestion that God needed to punish his Son because someone had to bear the punishment of sin, and if we ourselves are to be spared, the punishment must fall on the innocent Son. Robert Mackintosh's hostility towards this view glowers through the language he uses in criticizing the *Westminster Shorter Catechism*:

> We are faced by an angry God; and His anger is 'due' to us for sin. Yet this angry God will lift his curse from off us—on terms. He will accept a composition. He is prepared to bargain.[20]

Mackintosh elsewhere rammed the point home: 'The necessity for Atonement can neither be diabolic and undivine, nor yet legal and only half divine.'[21]

---

18 Ibid., p. 2.

19 John McIntyre's helpful analysis of soteriological models in *The Shape of Soteriology* is a useful foil to some of the more distorted current accounts of the atonement; and for the biblical roots of the matter Vincent Taylor's trilogy is of continuing assistance: *Jesus and His Sacrifice. A Study of the Passion-Sayings in the Gospels*, London: Macmillan, 1937; *The Atonement in New Testament Teaching*, London: Epworth Press, 1940; *Forgiveness and Reconciliation. A Study in New Testament Theology*, London: Macmillan, 1941. According to Gabriel Fackre, writing in 1993, there were some in the United Church of Christ (USA) who were advocating the elimination of the Cross as that Church's central symbol 'since it entails an atonement in which God the Father abuses his son, Jesus, and adding insult to injury, glorifies suffering, teaching victims to be subservient to their oppressors'. He adds, 'These charges are such departures from Christian teaching, based on caricatures of classical belief, that they will gain little headway.' But they were levelled. See Fackre's *Theology and Culture Newsletter*, no. 33, Advent 1993.

20 R. Mackintosh, 'The religion of the "Shorter Catechism"', *The Holborn Review*, January 1927, p. 23.

The moral thus far is that we should resist theories which are more forensic than personal. At the same time, we should not forget that

> The juristic aspect is a real element in Christ's death. It has a moral core; and we cannot discard it without discarding the moral order of the world as one revelation of that irrefragable holiness of God which must be expressed in judgment and confessed from its midst.[22]

This is not a return to the perverse view that the innocent Son was punished. Rather, it is to assert that as our representative, Jesus Christ paid to the full the penalty of our sinful refusal to honour God's law, to obey his will and to receive his grace.[23] He was utterly obedient to his holy Father and utterly identified with us in our plight—the most intensely painful position which anyone could willingly occupy.[24] As an exponent of Franciscan spirituality has well said,

> Christ is not the victim of a sanguinary prosecution, which takes delight in torturing One who is innocent in place of those who are guilty. He is the friend who offers Himself spontaneously, out of love for Father and children, to draw His guilty loved ones from the abyss where they have hurled themselves and to ransom them at whatever cost to Himself.[25]

James Denney may round off this part of our discussion:

> while the agony and the Passion were not penal in the sense of coming upon Jesus through a bad conscience, or making Him the personal object of divine wrath, they were penal in the sense that in that dark hour he had to realise to the full the divine reaction against sin in the race in which He was incorporated, and that without

---

21 R. Mackintosh, *Historic Theories of Atonement*, London: Hodder and Stoughton, 1920, p. 20. For Mackintosh—yet another neglected theologian—see Alan P. F. Sell, *Robert Mackintosh: Theoogian of Integrity*, Bern: Peter Lang, 1977; *ODNB*.

22 Forsyth, *The Work of Christ*, p. 228.

23 See further ibid., pp. 156-165. It is to the credit of the eighteenth-century Arian divines that they lodged a moral objection to the ideas that the Father was over against the Son, and that the Son had to be punished. See further ch. 3 above. The deist, Thomas Paine, spoke of 'the outrage offered to the moral justice of God by supposing him to make the innocent suffer for the guilty, and the loose morality and low contrivance of supposing him to change himself into the shape of a man in order to make an excuse to himself for not executing his supposed sentence on Adam.' See *The Age of Reason*, (1794, 1796), London: Watts, 1938, p. 35. John McLeod Campbell, albeit in a different key, was no less opposed to the notion that Christ was punished. See *The Nature of the Atonement*, (1865), London: Macmillan, 2nd edn., 1867.

24 See further, A. E. Garvie, 'The restatement of the Gospel for to-day', *The Expositor*, 7th series, IV, 1907, p. 403.

25 Valentin Breton, 'Franciscan spirituality', in Jean Gautier, ed., *Some Schools of Catholic Spirituality*, Paris: Desclee, trans. Kathryn Sullivan, 1959, pp. 61-62.

> doing to the uttermost He could not have been the Redeemer of that race from sin, or the Reconciler of sinful men to God.[26]

Thirdly, implicit in what has already been said is the view that to understand Christ's saving work in purely exemplary terms is inadequate. The divine purpose at the Cross is not simply to move us, still less to encourage us to replicate Christ's sacrifice. This is *the* point at which we cannot follow him; he alone is Saviour:

> The Cross is not the place where humanity rises to the peak of its capacity for self-sacrifice to offer the best it has to its Creator. It is the place where God offers His best to us, all undeserving as we are, and where the sinless Son of God identified Himself with sinners even to the point of being numbered with the transgressors and dying the death of the accursed.[27]

It follows that 'The real objectivity of the atonement is not that it was made to God, but by God.'[28]

Fourthly, it further follows that if at the Cross the holy God acted in the Son for our salvation, then it will not suffice to construe the Cross as simply a parabolic visual aid designed to show the lengths to which God goes in suffering for us. In an address given to a conference of The Modern Churchpeople's Union in February 2003, Paul Badham claimed that in current theology it is frequently held that

> God was 'wholly present' in Jesus' suffering on the cross and that this illustrates the way in which God always shares in and is present in the darkest afflictions of humanity. This was the view held by all the leading modernists who saw the death of Christ as a parable of the way God suffers for us.[29]

It cannot be denied that the Cross does show this. But if that were all it did we should have not so much the God of pity, but a pitiable God who is alongside us in our plight and no more able to do anything about it than we ourselves are. I find no real evangel here. The case is similar if Jesus is regarded as the noblest martyr who ever lived—another way in which some liberal writers have portrayed him. But

---

26 J. Denney, *The Christian Doctrine of Reconciliation*, London: Hodder and Stoughton, 1917, p. 273.

27 Lovell Cocks, *The Wondrous Cross*, p. 59. Cf. Lovell Cocks's teacher, P. T. Forsyth: 'It was not human nature offering its very best to God. It was God offering His very best to man.' *The Work of Christ*, p. 24.

28 Forsyth, *The Work of Christ*, p. 92.

29 The address may be found on the website of The Modern Churchpeople's Union: www.modchurchunion.org/

> If the Cross was a mere martyrdom, and ended all, it really upset all. It did not overcome the world. It solved nothing. Nay, it aggravated everything. The best of men met the worst of fates and succumbed, and God said nothing and did nothing... [T]he Cross alone is no solution without the solution for the Cross itself, the Resurrection, and all its train beyond Christ's death.[30]

We have a Gospel when we understand that at the Cross God in Christ did not merely *show* us something about his love, or our need, or both, but *acted* once-for-all for the salvation of the world by vanquishing sin and death and all that could keep us from him.[31]

The sixth reason why some may feel inhibited from paying much attention to the Cross is that they have become less than content with excessive devotional attention to the wounds of Christ. This can tend to direct a worshipper's attention too much to the crucifixion and too little to the Cross, to revert to the distinction I drew earlier. The atmosphere is solemn, sometimes to the point of morbidity. Moreover, the emphasis upon things physical can obscure both the deeper, spiritual, agony suffered by Jesus, and the fact that he went voluntarily and purposefully (not languidly) to his death, in obedience to his Father and with a view to completing his earthly mission:

> Christ never merely accepted His fate; He willed it. He went to death as a king. It was the supreme exercise of His royal self-disposal... And when we obscure that, when we pity where we should worship, melt where we should kneel, or kneel where we should rise to newness of life, it is no wonder if faith become a mere affectation, or a mere ethical ritual of conduct, and cease to be the absolute committal of ourselves to communion with Him for ever.[32]

My seventh observation is that at the polar opposite to 'the wounds' stands that Christian triumphalism so deplored—with good reason—in these politically correct times. Douglas John Hall is among those who have brought searching criticism to bear upon the ecclesiastical triumphalism which has marred Christianity's witness from Constantine onwards.[33] As an English Dissenter, I am, so to speak, constitutionally disinclined towards ecclesial Constantinianism[34] (though I should have to

---

30 P. T. Forsyth, *The Justification of God*, (1917), London: Independent Press, 1957, p. 215.

31 I have investigated this confession and discussed the related questions of transcendence, immanence and history in *Confessing and Commending the Faith. Historic Witness and Apologetic Method*, Cardiff: University of Wales Press, 2002, chs. 2 and 5.

32 Forsyth, *The Cruciality of the Cross*, p. 38.

33 D. J. Hall, *The Cross in Our Context: Jesus and the Suffering World*, Minneapolis: Fortress Press, 2003.

34 See Alan Sell, *Testimony and Tradition*, ch. 11.

grant that it is easier to see when traditions other than one's own have become infected with the virus). Colin Gunton has well said,

> For much of its history the church has failed to allow its mind to be reproportioned to correspond to the truth of the kind of victory of which the New Testament speaks. It will not escape the demonism of power in which it has culpably shared unless it associates itself with the manner of the conquest of evil by Jesus on the cross.[35]

In the course of making their anti-Constantinian case, some Christians repudiate the concept of Lordship as being hierarchical and as conducing to Christian triumphalism. What needs to be remembered is that Jesus was first called Lord over against the Caesars of this world; that his Lordship is that of one who takes a towel and does slave's work by washing his friends' feet; that to a large extent the Gospel concerns the condescension of this Lord; and that he, and no one else—and no ideology either—can claim our absolute loyalty. Moreover, if by overlooking the way in which the Gospel forces us to rebaptize certain concepts we simply discard them, we shall not be able to tell 'the world' that it has not understood them yet.

The anti-triumphalist attitude sometimes surfaces in the context of dialogue with people of other faiths. Whether on grounds of politeness, or because they deplore Christian Constantinianism and do not wish to replicate it, some Christians will, as it were, pull their punches in such debate. They rightly perceive that the dialogue room is not a mission hall; but if they feel unable to witness to their deepest convictions the integrity of the dialogue is called into question. It sometimes happens that members of other faiths are not as reticent in stating their position as some Christians are. They can also be very quick to perceive the contradiction into which some more liberal Christians fall when they affirm the pluralistic nature of society whilst at the same time seeking 'a common genus or common genera under which to subsume the world-faiths'.[36] This activity can appear as imperialistic as anything alleged (not always justly) against early representatives of the modern missionary movement.

But the main point is well taken: the Cross does not legitimate Christian triumphalism. On the contrary,

> Gethsemane and the cry from the cross, 'My God, my God, why hast thou forsaken me!' are the end of all attempts to misinterpret the Gospel as the message of the

---

[35] C. E. Gunton, '*Christus Victor* revisited. A study in metaphor and the transformation of meaning', *Journal of Theological Studies*, n.s. XXXVI pt. 1, April 1985, p. 144.

[36] McIntyre, *The Shape of Christology*, p. 56.

> triumphant epiphany of a saviour-god after the manner of ancient mystery religions or the epic of a religious hero.[37]

Quite so; but if the Church may not embrace triumphalism, a Church which does not proclaim Christ's triumph and rejoice in it has, it would seem, lost the Gospel. The *Study Catechism* adopted by the Presbyterian Church USA in 1998 declares that

> No one else will ever be God incarnate. No one else will ever die for the sins of the world. Only Jesus Christ is such a person, only he could do such a work, and he in fact has done it.

George Hunsinger comments on this passage thus: 'Christians make large claims about Jesus Christ, but not about themselves.'[38] (Well, this is what they do when they are behaving themselves, and it is what they ought to do at all times.) The *Declaration of Faith* of the Congregational Church in England and Wales underlines the point: The 'redeeming grace of God is triumphantly present in the life, the death, the resurrection and the reign of Jesus Christ'.[39] For this reason the 7,000 who have not bowed the knee to the oppressive ideological baalim will continue to sing John Bowring's lines with joy:

> In the cross of Christ I glory
> Towering o'er the wrecks of time;
> All the light of sacred story
> Gathers round its head sublime.

Finally some, perhaps appalled by more grotesque versions of atonement doctrine and preaching, make the prophetic witness for social justice their principal theme. Undeniably, this note needs to be struck. Indeed, the pursuit of social justice would be legitimate on humanitarian grounds alone even if it were not sanctioned by eighth-century BC prophets and Jesus himself. But where this becomes the supreme theme a balance needs to be redressed. As long ago as 1920 Robert Mackintosh declared,

---

37 Herman Sasse, 'On the theology of the Cross', *Reformed Theological Review*, XXXI, September–December 1972, p. 84. Cf. Forsyth, *The Work of Christ*, p. 150.

38 G. Hunsinger, 'Social witness in generous orthodoxy: The new Presbyterian Study Catechism', in Wallace M. Alston, Jr. and Michael Welker, eds, *Reformed Theology: Identity and Ecumenicity*, Grand Rapids: Eerdmans, 2003, p. 316.

39 *A Declaration of Faith*, London: Independent Press, 1967, p. 16.

> To-day we hear not indeed too much but disproportionately much about the evil of social injustice. Christ speaks to us of deeper things; and yet the redeeming of social wrongs is a plain part of His programme.[40]

He further cautioned that

> A Christ who has no functions except Addisonian essays and gentle moral suasion, is not a Christ. The death of such a Christ has no appreciable meaning, and He will have no appreciable meaning to us when we are on our deathbeds.[41]

It may be that some of those driven towards social justice concerns are repelled by the exclusively individualistic manner in which Christ's atoning work has been construed. To suppose that 'Christ died for me' is the whole of the Gospel is arrogance indeed. To bask in such knowledge to the extent of hibernating with the Saviour is, theoretically, to disregard the cosmic scope of his work and, practically, to decline that call to mission and service of neighbour the response to which is integral to, and a sign of, gratitude towards and commitment to the Saviour.

It must, however, be admitted, that some Christians who are rightly concerned with social justice issues are inclined to overlook the fact that 'We shall never get permanent justice done to human nature till we are concerned before that about having justice done to God.'[42]

Having now noted some of the reasons why some may feel reluctant to write or preach about the Cross, I must now pursue two themes in somewhat more detail. The first, triggered by Forsyth's words as just quoted, concerns God's justice and mercy in relation to sinful humanity; the second has to do with the Incarnation in relation to the Atonement, or Christ's person in relation to his work.

II

In the course of his 2003 address to the Modern Churchpeople's Union, to which I have already referred, Paul Badham observed that the idea of hell has largely receded from view in Christian thinking. Not, indeed, that this is a recent occurrence. In 1920 some were speaking of 'a hell frozen over or turned to innocuous ashes'.[43] As A. E. Garvie noted a century ago,

---

40 Mackintosh, *Historic Theories of Atonement*, p. 312.

41 Mackintosh, 'The fact of the Atonement', *Expository Times*, XVI, 1902–03, p. 347.

42 P. T. Forsyth, *Faith, Freedom and the Future*, (1912), London: Independent Press, 1955, p. 38.

43 Quoted by John Horsch, *Modern Religious Liberalism*, Chicago: The Bible Institute Colportage Association, 1920, pp. 127-28. See further, Alan P. F. Sell, *Theology in Turmoil. The Roots, Course and Significance of the Conservative–Liberal Debate in Modern Theology*, (1986), Eugene, OR: Wipf & Stock, 1998, chs. 5 and 6.

> As the conception of God's Fatherhood received fuller recognition, this theory that the limited and temporal transgressions of ignorant and imperfect men were visited with inexhaustible and unceasing torments became an outrage, not only inconsistent with, but even a blasphemy on, the truth about God.[44]

This, thought Garvie, was an understandable reaction against hell-fire preaching of the more grotesque sort ('Where will you be tomorrow morning if you wake up and find yourselves dead?', enquired the apoplectic evangelist of his jittery audience), but he elsewhere made it clear that the reaction could go too far: 'For persistent defiance of grace there can be only Divine Judgment.'[45]

That not all have achieved due balance in these matters is evidenced from a number of quarters. For example, it is interesting to note that some of the preachers who made most of the individual's need to flee from the wrath to come so emphasized God's anger and the hearer's requirement to 'decide for Christ' that the Cross and God's atoning work received short shrift. Of the evangelist C. G. Finney, who majored on God's wrath, it has been said that 'he never seemed to understand, all his life, that unbelievers can be won to faith as much...by the preaching of God's *love*, as by threats of damnation and the presentation of God as wrathful and threatening'.[46] At crucial points in his writings he 'mentioned nothing of the atonement of Christ as the basis of reconciliation of humanity to God and the foundation of the believer's confidence for salvation...'.[47]

From a quite different context, Ron Selleck writes[48] (with comments from Sydney Cave, Lovell Cocks and myself in square brackets),

> Since 'sin' is a human construction, why can't it be redefined or the consequences modified by a majority (or a consensus)? [Sin is a state of rebellion against a holy, loving God, and 'It is because of Calvary, not because of Eden, that we are compelled to judge gravely of human sin.'[49]] Isn't what we really need to do simply

---

More recently, Michael Watts has argued, somewhat one-sidedly in the opinion of some, that the numerical decline of English Nonconformity is attributable to the decline of hell as a prominently-proclaimed doctrine. See his *Why Did the English Stop Going to Church?* London: Dr. Williams's Trust, 1995.

44 Garvie, *A Guide to Preachers*, p. 123.

45 Garvie, 'Fifty years' retrospect', *Congregational Quarterly*, VII, 1929, p. 22.

46 Keith J. Hardman, *Charles Grandison Finney 1792–1875, Revivalist and Reformer*, Syracuse, NY: Syracuse University Press, 1987, p. 100.

47 Ibid., p. 346; cf. pp. 237-38.

48 R. Selleck, 'Comments', *Quaker Religious Thought*, XXI no. 4, Spring 1986, p. 47.

49 Sydney Cave, *The Christian Estimate of Man*, London: Duckworth, 1944, p. 228. Cf. his *The Doctrine of the Work of Christ*, London: University of London Press, 1937, p. 234.

to persuade people to walk in the right direction? [If only we could; if only they would. Paul knew what he ought to do...] We know that 'evil' is only the product of poor environment, and many of us are working diligently to improve that. [Victorian evolutionary optimism *redivivus*.] Really, sin is simply 'missing the mark.' [Sin 'is very much more than the sum total of all the separate sins. It is the disease of which they are symptoms.'[50]] And many of us try conscientiously to heed the example of Jesus and listen intently to our inner promptings. [Where is the enabling Spirit? How reliable are our inner promptings, and whence do they come?] Why this arcane puzzle of the Atonement? [It is a puzzle only to those who do not see that God's holy love needs to be vindicated, our sins need to be forgiven, and our and the world's relationship with God needs to be restored: in short, that something needs to be done, not simply taught or exemplified.]

From a quite different direction come the attitudes of those who imbibe and propagate 'feel-good' Christianity. They, too, can fail to do justice to God's atoning grace. If some of the devotions which focus on the wounds of Christ can leave us, as it were, with a perpetual Easter Saturday, some of the jollier expressions of resurrection cosiness seem to deprive us of Good Friday. If some old-time evangelists majored on sin, wrath, guilt and judgment, some 'feel-good' preachers shun such terms as off-putting to the (sometimes well-heeled and well-placed) congregations whom they cocoon with comforts of various kinds. No doubt some may feel that I am being unduly judgmental here; but it is as odd as it is disconcerting to note how easily the Cross can be side-stepped both by those who emphasize the divine wrath and those who bask in the joy of the Lord.

I side with those—Paul, Luther, Calvin, McLeod Campbell, Forsyth and many others—who underline the truth that the first word of the Gospel is grace. Preachers who offer fifty-five minutes of sin and five minutes of good news have the balance wrong, as do those who never challenge their hearers with God's righteousness. God is the God of all grace; but his love is holy love. His righteousness goes out against sin and his mercy endures for ever. Nor is it only preachers who may need to adjust their sights. Consider the following two quotations: in the course of an exposition of the thought of Duns Scotus, Mary Beth Ingham writes,

The God of Scotus is the God of Francis, a God so generous he throws everything away out of love.... Our categories of soteriology must change from those of justice to those of generosity.[51]

Again, from a Mennonite fold comes the bold assertion that

[50] Lovell Cocks, *The Wondrous Cross*, p. 30.

[51] M. B. Ingham, 'John Duns Scotus: retrieving a medieval thinker for contemporary theology', in Elise Saggau, ed., *The Franciscan Intellectual Tradition*, St. Bonaventure, NY: The Franciscan Institute, 2002, p. 95.

> The cross is the victory of agape over penal vengeance, and not the admission that in the end love must recognize the moral right of such vengeance as 'justice.'[52]

If in the former question a wedge is wrongly driven between justice and love, in the latter, justice is tendentiously construed as penal vengeance. As I understand it, what triumphs at the Cross is holy love, sovereign grace, righteous mercy, and these may not be disjoined: 'God's love is the radiance of His righteousness; God's justice is the sternness of His love.'[53] Moreover, 'The seeking, saving love of God which we see *is* the divine judgment on our sin. And a more radical, more devastating condemnation could not be conceived.'[54] For 'Love is not holy without judgment'.[55]

I invoke a theologian and a preacher to conclude this point. James Denney writes,

> It is because divine necessities have had homage done to them by Christ, that the way is open for sinners to return to God through Him. When they are forgiven, it is...by a love the very nature of which is that it does absolute homage to the whole being and self-revelation of God, and especially to the inexorable reactions of the divine nature against sin.[56]

In more homely fashion, William Jay (1769–1853), who ministered at Argyle [Congregational] Chapel, Bath, for sixty-two years, declared,

> I think no man can rationally hope for pardon unless he can see a way in which God can do it *as God*, and be '*faithful* and *just* to forgive us our sins, and to cleanse us from all unrighteousness.' Such a scheme is the Gospel; it reveals a free, rich,

---

52 C. Norman Kraus, 'Interpreting the Atonement in the Anabaptist-Mennonite tradition', *Mennonite Quarterly Review*, LXVI no. 3, July 1992, p. 308. Cf. J. Denny Weaver, *The Nonviolent Atonement*, Grand Rapids: Eerdmans, 2001.

53 Robert Mackintosh, *Essays Towards a New Theology*, Glasgow: Maclehose, 1889, p. 426. For an attempt to hold mercy and justice together see Alan P. F. Sell, *God Our Father*, Shippensburg, PA: Ragged Edge Press, 2000, ch. 3. Cf. Colin E. Gunton, *The Actuality of Atonement. A Study of Metaphor, Rationality and the Christian Tradition*, Edinburgh: T. & T. Clark, 1988, p. 101: 'The Christian church still stands or falls by whether it proclaims and lives by the Gospel of the liberating grace of God, or whether its life degenerates into some form of self-salvation. For that reason, the doctrine of the atonement must continue to be at the heart of Christian theology, and the metaphor of the justice of God at the heart of the doctrine of the atonement, if Christianity's orientation to the action of God in re-establishing free human life is to be maintained and articulated.' For Gunton's understanding of metaphor see ibid. ch. 2.

54 Lovell Cocks, *The Wondrous Cross*, p. 56.

55 Forsyth, *The Work of Christ*, p. 85.

56 Denney, *The Christian Doctrine of Reconciliation*, p. 235. Cf. his *The Second Epistle to the Corinthians*, London: Hodder and Stoughton, 1916, p. 212.

righteous salvation through Jesus Christ, 'set forth to be a propitiation, through faith in his blood.' Hence it answers its name: it is good news, glad tidings.[57]

III

Probably the most intellectually sophisticated way of getting out of balance matters which should be held together is that of those down the ages who have majored on either the Atonement or the Incarnation to the neglect of the other. The tendency to elevate the Incarnation at the expense of the Atonement is long-standing, and it is to some extent understandable. For example, when early theologians were called upon to enter the lists against gnosticism, docetism, Arianism and other views deemed unorthodox discussion of the person of Christ assumed prominence. Thus, for example, Irenaeus famously declared that God's salvific purpose is focused in 'our Lord Jesus Christ, who did, through His transcendent love, become what we are, that He might bring us to be even what He is Himself'.[58] However, as John McIntyre reminds us, Irenaeus also said more than this: 'Redeeming us by his blood, in accordance with his reasonable nature, he gave himself a ransom for those who had been led into captivity.'[59] Nevertheless, it cannot be denied that while the early theologians by no means repudiated the Cross, their intellectual context prompted their thoughts more towards the Incarnation than towards the Atonement.[60]

Again, in the period following the Evangelical Revival with its strong emphasis upon the Atonement, salvation and conversion, the turn, under the influence of Benjamin Jowett, to patristics at Oxford in the mid-nineteenth century inclined many Anglican scholars in the direction of Christology and an Incarnational theology, the immanentist thrust of which seemed to accord well with the evolutionary thought of the times.[61] When to this is added the contribution of those more sceptical biblical critics who threatened the historical roots of the faith,[62] we can see why some of the Christian post-Hegelian idealists, Edward Caird and T. H. Green among them, transmuted the Gospel into a set of universal ideas

---

57 George Redford and John Angell James, eds, *The Autobiography of William Jay*, (1854), Edinburgh: Banner of Truth Trust, 1974, p. 85.

58 Irenaeus, *Adversus Haereses,* V, Preface, in *The Writings of Irenaeus* (Ante-Nicene Christian Library) trans. Alexander Roberts and W. H. Rambaut, Edinburgh: T. & T. Clark, 1869.

59 McIntyre, *The Shape of Soteriology*, p. 4, quoting *Adversus Haereses*, V.1.1.

60 See further Sell, *Confessing and Commending the Faith*, pp. 47-52.

61 For some observations upon evolution as a theme see Sell, *Theology in Turmoil*, ch. 3.

62 See further ibid., *Theology in Turmoil*, ch. 2.

untouchable by adverse historical criticism or blistering exposition. Thus, for example, for Caird the resurrection of Jesus became a parable of the way in which we (and even the natural order, as that liturgical invention of the period, the modern Harvest Festival, made plain) die and rise to life.[63] As for Green,

> He refuses to recognise that sin is an abnormal condition requiring exceptional remedies. Indeed, for so good a man, Mr. Green had a singularly dull sense of sin. No awakened conscience could tolerate the doctrine that 'forgiveness *is the moral act of putting off the old man.*'[64]

It was at the height of immanentist Incarnationalism that P. T. Forsyth protested that the Incarnation,

> central as many find it, has no such centrality as the principle of atoning forgiveness. The doctrine of the Incarnation did not create the Church; it grew up (very quickly) in the Church out of the doctrine of the cross which did create it—in so far as that can be said of any doctrine, and not rather the act and power which the doctrine tries to state.[65]

This, it might be thought, is just what we should have expected Forsyth to say. But before dismissing it out of hand, let us reflect upon the concerns expressed by the Anglican scholar, Michael Ramsey, in his perceptive study of the period in question. While recognizing the way in which Incarnational theology has 'enabled genuine contact between supernatural religion and contemporary culture',[66] he uttered some warning notes: the Incarnation could be construed as a principle

---

[63] See further Alan P. F. Sell, *Philosophical Idealism and Christian Belief*, Cardiff: University of Wales Press and New York: St. Martin's Press, 1995, ch. 5, and *Theology in Turmoil*, ch. 1. J. H. Muirhead recalls the impact of Hegelian idealism at the grassroots. The Rev. John Wellwood 'carried his Hegelianism into the pulpit to the confusion and dispersal of his congregation'. On innocently asking the beadle why this decline should have occurred he was informed, 'Ye are aye talking of contradictories and the unity of contradictories and nane of us ken what contradictories are, and what is more, we dinna care. And ye are aye preaching agin the existence of the Deevil. Noo we're just a'thinking that Christianity wi'oot the Deevil is no worth a damn.' See J. H. Muirhead, *Reflections by a Journeyman in Philosophy*, London: Allen & Unwin, p. 60 and n.

[64] Mackintosh, *Essays Towards a New Theology*, p. 125.

[65] Forsyth, *The Cruciality of the Cross*, p. 50, n.1. In this footnote (a rarity in Forsyth) he goes on to say that 'The Church of the papacy and the mass was reformable; but a Church that renounced universally its atoning redemption would not be reformable. It would be extinct....'

[66] Even P. T. Forsyth wryly conceded that 'Were there no other alternative, Bishop Gore's gospel would make many put up, for the time at least, with his view of the ministry.' See *The Principle of Authority*, (1915), London: Independent Press, 1952, p. 224.

explanatory of the world in such a way that the terminus is far removed from 'the sort of faith which, seeing no hope for a world sin-racked and frustrated, throws itself empty on the Cross of Christ and knows that the world *cannot* be explained until it has been radically changed'. He further observed that Incarnationalism could yield 'a sort of rationalism', and could entail the neglect of biblical themes 'which "Incarnation" alone does not convey'.[67] As I understand it, our redemption and that of the world is not a matter of a metaphysical divine–human union, but of a once-for-all dramatic act of moral rescue by the triune God of sovereign grace who, as immanent in the world, is uncomfortably close (Isaiah 6), and as transcendent over it is abundantly able to save.[68] Taken to its extreme, the immanentist view would seem to place us in an ongoing process which, by bypassing the Cross, renders our union with God automatic, not moral. In a word, the peril of pantheism looms before us.[69]

I by no means deny that Christ can do what he does only because he is who he is, namely, the divine–human Son of God. Were he not divine he could not be our Saviour, for God alone can save; were he not human he could not represent and save us. The Incarnation is logically prior to the Atonement. But I should argue, indeed, have argued, that it is through Christ's saving work that we, not to mention the Church of the ages, come to see who he is. Who is it that can forgive sins? Who alone can save? Thus we come to Christology via soteriology, and we understand what Denney meant when he declared that 'the rationale of the incarnation is in the atonement'.[70]

---

[67] A. M. Ramsey, *From Gore to Temple*, London: Longmans, 1960, p. 28. The separation of what should belong together comes out in W. R. Inge's remark that 'The Christ-mysticism which is at the heart of [Paul's] personal faith is seen to be far more important for an understanding of his Christianity than his arguments about justification by faith and vicarious atonement.' See *The Platonic Tradition in English Religious Thought*, London: Longmans, Green, 1926, p. 30. Cf. Robert Franks's criticism of H. A. Hodges, *The Pattern of Atonement*, London: SCM Press, 1955, in *The Congregational Quarterly*, XXXIII no. 4, October 1955, p. 367.

[68] See further Sell, *Confessing and Commending the Faith*, ch. 5.

[69] See further ch. 7 above. For the way in which process theology can foster a Christology grounded in cosmology rather than in soteriology see Ray S. Anderson, 'The Incarnation of God in feminist theology', in Alvin F. Kimel, Jr., ed., *Speaking the Christian God. The Holy Trinity and the Challenge of Feminism*, Grand Rapids: Eerdmans, 1992, pp. 301-303.

[70] Denney, *The Christian Doctrine of Reconciliation*, p. 65.Sydney Cave concurs: 'It is through our experience of Christ's work that we learn the meaning of His person.' See *The Doctrines of the Christian Faith*, p. 194. I have developed this theme in *Aspects of Christian Integrity*, (1991), Eugene, OR: Wipf & Stock, 1998, ch. 2, and it informs the method of *Christ Our Saviour*. At this point I may seem to have placed myself in the position of disagreeing with T. F. Torrance. He speaks of 'our persistent Protestant attempt to interpret Christ solely through His works', and continues, 'When you start off

Again, I by no means deny that Christ's death is set within the context of his birth, life, ministry and, indeed, of his continuing high priestly work on our behalf.[71] We may not divide the death from the life, the sacrifice at Calvary from all that went before in terms of Jesus' teaching and actions and the reactions they provoked, both positive and negative:

> To preach only the atonement, the death apart from the life, or only the person of Christ, the life apart from the death, or only the teaching of Christ, His words apart from His life, may be all equally one-sided, and extreme to falsity.[72]

It nevertheless seems to me that it is the light of the Cross, understood as an umbrella term, that all else is to be construed.

IV

The large claim I have just made may, to some small extent, be supported by reference to preceding papers in this book. With the Cross as our point of reference we may challenge

---

from the saving work of Christ...and from what He means to you in your experience, Christ Himself tends to disappear behind His benefits, so that a doctrine of the person of Christ is determined by the value-judgments you pass on Him.' See his 'Cheap and costly grace', *Baptist Quarterly*, XXII, April 1968, p. 295, reprinted in his *God and Rationality*, London: Oxford University Press, 1971, ch. 3. I shall in a moment affirm that Christ is not to be interpreted *solely* through his works. Further, I regard myself as standing for an objective doctrine of the Atonement, and hence what is done at the Cross is done regardless of what I feel about it. Nevertheless, I think that it is hard to deny that as early Christians pondered the question, What has been done?, the issue of Christ's person was clamantly raised: Who, then, must he be? It is not without significance that the title 'Lord' came to be applied to Jesus Christ largely after the Resurrection. I am also aware of medieval contention that on grounds of his love and his desire to be with his children, God would have become incarnate even if Adam and Eve had not sinned. This view was advanced prominently by Duns Scotus (*Ordinatio*, III. D.7, q.3). While I believe that in all conceivable circumstances God would remain holy love, I decline to speculate upon what would have happened had things been quite otherwise than they are.

71 Cf. Forsyth, *The Work of Christ*, pp. 153-54.

72 Forsyth, *The Cruciality of the Cross*, p. 42. Cf. Mackintosh, *Historic Theories of Atonement*, p. 3. It must be said, however, that some of Forsyth's contemporaries did not feel that he followed his own advice sufficiently closely: he so focused upon the Cross as to downplay the earthly ministry of Jesus. See, for example, A. S. Peake, *Recollections and Appreciations*, ed. W. F. Howard, London: Epworth Press, 1938, p. 193; A. E. Garvie, 'Placarding the Cross: the theology of P. T. Forsyth', *Congregational Quarterly*, XXI, October 1943, p. 352. There is justice in the charge. But in Forsyth's defence it may be suggested that in elevating the Cross he drove to the heart of the Gospel in a way he thought absolutely necessary in the theological climate of his time. It will be evident that I believe that, no matter how we may wish to supplement it, the main thrust of his message is of continuing importance.

any method of biblical interpretation which overlooks or denies the fact that the Bible witnesses, above all, to God's saving act in Christ, in the light of which all else is to be viewed;[73]

any individualism which obscures the fact that the Word of God is most readily discerned by the Spirit through the Bible within the fellowship;[74]

any attempt to replace the Cross with any authority whether intellectual, ecclesiastical,[75] or civil;[76]

doctrinal developments which obscure the universal call of the Gospel[77] and yield demeaning views of God;[78]

deism[79] and docetism;[80]

pantheism and pantheizing tendencies which blur the Creator-creature distinction and cannot deal adequately with history or sin;[81]

ecclesiastical sectarianism which obscures the fact that on account of the once-for-all saving act and the call of the Holy Spirit Christians are already one body in Christ, and hence they should manifest this unity, supremely at the Lord's table;[82]

grace-less church discipline;[83]

ecclesiastical triumphalism;[84]

esoteric spiritualities which fail to engage with the world;[85]

any tendency in contextual theologies to elevate particular human experiences into interpretative norms for the whole of theology.[86]

I believe that all of these points are important, for they concern the Gospel we proclaim, the theological method we embrace and the

---

73 See above chs. 1, 6, 12.

74 See above chs. 2, 3.

75 See above ch. 1.

76 See above ch. 2.

77 See above ch. 6.

78 See above, chs. 3, 5, 13.

79 See above ch. 4.

80 See above ch. 12.

81 See above, chs. 1, 7 and the brief remarks on immanentism in this chapter.

82 See above, chs. 10, 11.

83 See above chs. 6, 12.

84 This chapter.

85 See above, ch. 8.

86 See above, ch. 12 and this chapter.

ecumenical stances we adopt. But although these questions of content and method remind us that while Christianity is personal it is not private, it is personal. In the final resort—rather, in the first place—what matters is not 'theological system but theological footing, not an ordered knowledge of divine procedure but an experienced certainty of divine redemption'.[87] In other words, Christianity is not in the first instance an intellectual exercise, a theory, a policy; it is a Way. Our feet have been set on this Way by the call of God the Holy Spirit, and on the ground of the Son's finished work at the Cross.[88] To reproduce a quotation I used in chapter 6 above:

> Christ...was not the founder simply of a religious school.... Christianity is not a *doctrine*, to be taught or learned like a system of philosophy or a rule of moral conduct.... Christianity...is a *life*, not only as revealed in Christ, but as continued in the church. It flows over from Christ to his people, always in this form. They do not simply bear his name and acknowledge his doctrine. They are so united with him as to have part in the substance of his life itself.[89]

Not the least of the consolations afforded by the fact of union with Christ is that 'Even after the dogmatists have spoken their last and worst word, God remains wonderful.'[90]

It may be that in some Christian circles the lack of emphasis upon the Cross is as nothing compared with the scant attention paid in some places to the consequences of Christ's work in the lives of believers. More than forty years ago Hugh T. Kerr detected something of the sort in the theology of the day and in the Reformed circles in which he moved. He recalled the thorough treatment given by Calvin in his *Institutes* Book III to the *ordo salutis*:

---

87 Forsyth, *Faith, Freedom and the Future*, p. 139.

88 For an attempt to expound this line of thought see Alan P. F. Sell, *The Spirit Our Life*, Shippensburg, PA: Ragged Edge Press, 2000. Cf. A. E. Garvie, 'The limits of doctrinal restatement', *Proceedings of the Third International Congregational Council*, London: Congregational Union of England and Wales, 1908, p. 92: 'If forgiveness through atonement be the essential of Evangelical Christianity; then, even as it is historical in affirming the fact of the atonement in the death and rising again of Jesus Christ, so must it be *experimental* in interpreting the fact of forgiveness in the individual life. It is only as the forgiveness is appropriated that the atonement can be appreciated.' See also P. Mark Achtemeier, 'The *Union with Christ* doctrine in renewal: movements of the Presbyterian Church (USA)', in Wallace M. Alston, Jr. and Michael Welker, eds., *Reformed Theology. Identity and Ecumenicity*, pp. 339-40.

89 J. W. Nevin, *The Mystical Presence*, (1846), Philadelphia: United Church Press, 1966, pp. 216, 222. Nevin here echoes Calvin, *Institutes*, III.i.1 and III.11.10. For Karl Barth's substantial discussion of union with Christ see *The Doctrine of Reconciliation* (*Church Dogmatics* IV.iii.2), trans. G. W. Bromiley, Edinburgh: T. & T. Clark, 1962, pp. 481-680.

90 Mackintosh, 'The fact of the atonement', p. 347.

> Behind the Reformed covenant schema, the dialectic of God's sovereign initiative and man's responsibility, bristling doctrines (calling, justification, adoption, election, faith, repentance, sanctification, witness and mission) detail the nature and content of Christian life.
>
> Modern thinkers such as Barth, Brunner, Niebuhr, Tillich, Bultmann, have almost nothing to say about or to contribute towards a theology of the third article of the Creed.... Preaching on the Christian life tends to be moralistic, hortatory, voluntaristic, prudential, energistic....
>
> The crucial Christian claim that the sinner can be saved, that the old man can be reborn,[91] that a new creation in Christ is a possibility, that life-death-rebirth is as much the paradigm of Christian life as the person of Jesus Christ himself—all this is strangely muted in our Reformed theology, preaching, worship and witness.[92]

It would not surprise me to learn that some of the Reformed today, and even perhaps some in traditions other than the Reformed, feel that the cap still fits. To the extent that it does, I wonder whether this has to do with attitudes towards the doctrine of the Holy Spirit, for the Spirit is the agent of our union with Christ and our growth in grace? It used to be said, on the evidence of the paucity of theological works produced, that the Holy Spirit was the least contemplated person of the Trinity. In more theologically sophisticated circles much has been done in recent years to redress the balance, but in popular Christianity it may be that so much that is excitable and sometimes banal has been attributed to, and written about, the Spirit that his more solid work is neglected.[93] However that may be, the fact remains that

> It is the Spirit who brings divine and human nature together in the hypostatic union and mediates between them. It is the Spirit who empowers and makes possible the obedience of the Son in and through His human nature. It is the Spirit who joins us to the Son, thereby effecting our sanctification and our justification. And it is the Spirit who 'glorifies' believers by glorifying the Son in eternity.[94]

---

[91] One of our present misfortunes is the way in which the term 'born again' has been hijacked by a certain type of 'born again believer'. As a result many Christians distance themselves from the term. But, since ecclesiology turns upon it, it would be disastrous if they were to overlook the concept.

[92] H. T. Kerr, 'Building the Reformed image', *The Reformed and Presbyterian World*, XXVII no. 7, September 1963, pp. 307-308.

[93] Some have had much to say to me about tongues and healings, but scarcely anything about the Spirit and the Word, the Spirit and the Church, the Spirit and the World, still less about the Holy Spirit in relation to the triune Godhead.

[94] Bruce L. McCormack, 'For us and our salvation. Incarnation and Atonement in the Reformed tradition', *Studies in Reformed Theology and History*, I no. 2, Spring 1993, p. 36.

Lest, against the author's intention, this be construed exclusively in individualistic terms, as if the Christian life were a solitary pilgrimage, I invoke William Manson, whose words will remind us that we are called to be a saved *people*: 'We are...on firm ground when we assert that in the two things, the Cross of Christ and the transcendent principle of the Holy Spirit, there lie the distinctive marks of the new life of Christianity and the foundations on which the Christian Church is built.'[95]

Sustained by these truths, we take our place in the communion of saints (some of whom have been my mentors and conversation partners in this book) and walk the victorious way of the Cross. Fortified by hope, through circumstances happy and sad, 'we are being trained and disciplined for the true felicity of heaven and the blessedness that never cloys'.[96] And as we go we may feel led to make some such words as Calvin's our own:

> I embrace the grace which [God] has offered me in our Lord Jesus Christ, and accept the merits of his suffering and dying that through him all my sins are buried; and I humbly beg him to wash me and cleanse me with the blood of our great Redeemer, as it was shed for all poor sinners so that I, when I appear before his face, may bear his likeness.[97]

---

95 W. Manson, *The Way of the Cross*, London: Hodder and Stoughton, 1958, p. 25.

96 Lovell Cocks, *The Wondrous Cross*, p. 55.

97 From Calvin's 'Last Will', *The Letters of John Calvin*, Edinburgh: Banner of Truth Trust, 1980, p. 29.

Index of Persons

Abelard, Peter, 380
Achtemeier, P. Mark, 338, 397
Acworth, Richard, 4, 37
Adeney, Walter F., 161, 253
Adger, John B., 242
Ainsworth, Mr., 52
Aldham, Thomas, 58
Alline, Henry, 145
Alston, Wallace M., 338, 387, 397
Ames, William, 148
Amirtham, Samuel, 321
Amory, Thomas, 88, 105
Anderson, Ray S., 394
Andrewes, Lancelot, 5
Anne, Queen, 73
Anselm, 147, 380
Arias, Bishop, 286
Aristotle, 36, 116
Arminius, Jacobus, 5
Armour, Leslie, 35
Arthur, Donald E., 304
Assmann, Hugo, 309
Augustine, 13, 47, 146, 329, 330
Aulén, G., 378
Ayer, A. J., 111
Ayre, Justice, 56

Bacon, Francis, 19-20, 21, 115-6, 174, 180, 186
Badham, Paul, 384, 388
Bagshaw, William, 49, 51
Baillie, Donald M., 248
Baillie, John, 248
Barber, Joseph, 142
Barbour, Hugh, 63
Barclay, Robert, 17-19, 28, 40, 47, 48, 64, 65, 123, 172, 339
Barrett, Lee, 204
Barrow, Henry, 3, 4, 31-2, 35, 182
Barth, Karl, xiii, 161, 162, 247, 248, 249, 252, 259, 301, 302, 331-2, 398
Bassett, T. M., 353-4
Bateman, Phebe (see Gratton, Phebe)
Battles, F. L., 147, 225, 284
Batty, William, 229, 235
Baum, Gregory, 315
Baur, F. C., 177
Baxter, Richard, 1, 4, 15, 16, 22, 30, 35, 38, 39, 43, 55, 63, 65, 124-5, 126, 141, 152, 242-3, 283, 288, 297, 346, 348, 352
Beals, Corey, 63, 67
Beaton, David, 251
Bebbington, David, 302
Bedford, R. D., 117
Begg, Alexander, 155
Belsham, Thomas, 374
Bender, Ross T., 268
Benedict, 235-6
Bennet, Gervase, 17, 300
Bentley, Richard, 126-7
Berkhof, Hendrikus, 298
Beverley, James, 145
Beynon, Tom, 131
Beza, T., 329
Bibby, Reginald, 109
Biddle, J. C., 125-6
Billingsley, John, 48-9
Bishop, Mary, 131
Blackburn, George A., 207
Blei, Karel, 263, 279
Bloesch, Donald G., 36-7, 368
Blondel, Maurice, 308
Blount, Charles, 117-18, 120, 126, 127, 142
Bold, Samuel, 125
Boff, Clodovis, 311, 312
Boff, Leonardo, 307, 309, 311, 312
Bolingbroke, Henry St J., 128, 131, 135
Bolton, R., 155
Bomberger, J. H. A., 176, 199, 228, 295

Bonar, Andrew A., 340
Bonaventure, 225
Bonhoeffer, D., 249
Borgia, Caesar (Cesare), 213
Bourn, Samuel, xiii, 88, 89-90, 92, 95, 102, 105, 147, 148, 230-1, 237, 350
Bouyer, L., 222, 235
Bowden, H. W., 177
Bowder, John, 123
Bowring, John, 387
Brachlow, Stephen, 32, 33
Brackney, William H., 104
Bradberry, David, 347
Bradbury, Thomas, 73, 79-80, 150
Bradley, F. H., 177, 209, 212, 213
Braithwaite, W. C., 46, 342
Brandon, S. G. F., xv
Breed, William P., 182
Breese, Dave, 310
Brentall, John M., 49, 51
Breton, V., 383
Brewer, Jehoiada, 345
Bricker, George H., 174, 175, 177, 195, 198, 201, 323
Bridge, William, 328
Briggs, John H. Y., 104
Brine, John, 150
Bromiley, G. W., 331, 397
Brooks, Thomas, 232
Brown, Colin, 331
Brown, David, 130, 196
Brown, J. Baldwin, 161
Brown, Margrethe J., 367
Browne, Robert, 3, 4, 32, 182, 342
Browning, Don, 362
Brownson, O. A., 195
Bruce, John, 77
Brunner, Emil, 331, 398
Buchanan, John M., 325
Budge, Frances A., 47
Bull, Robert, 352-3
Bullinger, H., 148
Bultmann, Rudolf, xiii, 248, 249, 398
Bunyan, John, 47, 50, 344
Burford, Elizabeth, 349-50
Burford, T. P., 349-50
Burke, Edmund, 131, 132
Burnet, Gilbert, 6
Burns, Robert (poet), 330
Burns, Robert (1789-1869), 161
Bush, Percy W., 373
Butler, Joseph, 85, 125, 129-30, 140-1
Byrne, Peter, 113, 117
Byrom, J. K., 229

Cadorette, Kurt, 312
Cadoux, C. J., 66, 255
Caird, Edward, 201, 205, 206, 209, 219, 251, 392
Caird, George, 327
Caird, John, 201, 209, 216-17
Cairns, David, 247, 248
Cairns, David S., 247
Calamy, Edmund, 291
Caldecott, A. C., 247
Calvin, John, 13, 94, 147, 148, 156, 224, 225, 227, 238, 243, 261, 281, 284, 285, 296, 302, 319, 328, 329, 330, 332-3, 335, 355, 358, 380-1, 390, 397, 399
Camara, Helder, 310, 318
Cameron, Nigel M. deS., 149
Campbell, Alexander, 178, 179-81, 192
Campbell, John McLeod, 107, 161, 383, 390
Campbell, Thomas, 178, 179, 192
Campion, Mr., 353
Canovan, Margaret, 109, 169, 184
Caplan, N., 349
Carlson, Leland H., 31, 32, 342
Carnell, E. J., 303
Carre, H., 132
Casey, Michael, 178
Cassidy, Ron, 360
Cave, Alfred, 11
Cave, Sydney, 255, 389, 394
Chandler, Samuel, 80-1
Chapman, Humphry, 53
Chapman, John, 124
Chapman, Mark D., 303
Chenu, Marie-Dominique, 308
Chillingworth, William, 5

Chipman, Isaac, 239
Chryssides, George, 173
Chubb, Thomas, 112, 113, 122-3, 131
Clark, Henry W., 11-12, 13, 21, 28-9, 31, 40, 254
Clarke, Robert, 52
Clarke, Samuel, 89, 91, 113-14, 126, 141
Clayton, J. P., 305
Clipsham, E. F., 111
Clow, W. M., 251
Coates, R. H., 344
Cocceius, J., 148
Cochrane, Arthur C., 328-9, 371
Cocks, H. F. Lovell, 158, 162, 256, 259, 380, 381, 384, 389, 390, 391, 399
Coe, Shoki, 324
Coggins, Richard J., 316
Coleridge, S. T., 35, 107
Colie, Rosalie, 25
Collins, Anthony, 112, 115, 119-20, 125, 126, 130, 131, 142
Collins, G. N. M., 287
Collinson, Patrick, 32
Collyer, Martha, 2
Comblin, J., 309
Conder, E. R., 159, 160, 164-5
Conway, Anne F., 17
Cooper, Anthony Ashley, 112, 135
Cooper, John W., 311, 366
Copping, John, 221
Copson, Stephen, 349
Costas, Orlando, 308
Coste, R., 311
Cowper, William, 233
Cornish, William, 88, 105
Cramp, 239
Cranfield, C. E. B., 326
Cressey, Martin H., 245
Crisp, Oliver, 331
Crisp, Tobias, 334
Crocker, Robert, 17
Cromwell, Oliver, 9
Cudworth, Damaris, 3
Cudworth, Ralph, 2, 3, 5, 6, 8, 9, 10, 15, 17, 19, 20, 21, 22, 23, 27, 29-30, 37, 38
Culverwel, Nathaniel, 3, 5, 8, 14-15, 24, 25, 26, 27, 48
Cunliffe, Christopher, 130
Cunliffe-Jones, Hubert, 66, 256, 263
Cunningham, William, 159, 336-7
Cupitt, Don, 143
Cyprian, 55
Cyril of Alexandria, 301

Dale, A. W. W., 350
Dale, George, 56-7
Dale, R. W., 146, 155, 157, 158, 159-60, 339, 341, 348, 350-1, 352
Dalrymple, David, 74
Daly, Mary, 366
Daniel, S. H., 118
Dante Alighieri, 328
Davidson, Edward, H., 111
Davidson, Thomas, 55, 59
Davies, James, 153-4
David, John W., 22
Dawsey, James M., 316, 323
Dawson, Albert, 347
Deane, Richard, 352
DeBie, Linden J., 174
Dekker, Eef, 147
Delio, Ilia, 301
De Lubac, H., 308
Denham, David, 232
Denney, James, 251, 259, 383-4, 391, 394
De Ridder, Richard R., 355
Descartes, R., 21-2, 23, 27, 37
Dickie, E. P., 248
Dimitrios I, 272
Dionysius the Pseudo-Areopagite, 209, 230
DiPuccio, William, 174
Dix, Kenneth, 234, 334, 347
Dixon, Philip, 91
Dockery, David S., 78. 111
Dodd, C. H., 326
Doddridge, Philip, 101, 124, 154
Dodwell, Henry (the Younger), 123-4, 131

Donne, John, 322
Douglass, Jane D., 263, 355
Drewery, Benjamin, 256
Dru, Alexander, 223
Drury, John, 311
Dudrey, Russ, 180
Duff, Archibald, 155-6
Duff, Archibald (Professor), 155
Duffield, Ian K., 360
Dugdale, John, 353
Dugdale, Margaret, 353
Duhamel, Jean-Baptiste, 13
Duncan, John, 244
Duns Scotus, J., 390, 395
Durkheim, E., 249
Dussel, Enrique, 312, 321
Duthie, C. S., 256
Duthie, Robert, 156
Dye, Alfred, xiii
Dykes, J. O., 255

Eagleson, John, 309
Eddy, G. T., 87, 148
Edwards, D. Miall, 254-5
Edwards, John, 91
Edwards, Jonathan, 99, 111, 152, 224
Edwards, Samuel, 111
Ella, George, 78, 97
Ellis, George, 56
Ellis, John, 82-3
Ellison, Marvin M., 364
English, John C., 5, 35
Erasmus, D., 118, 334
Erskine, Thomas, of Linlathen, 87, 107, 161
Evans, Caleb, 76-7, 104
Evans, John, 300
Evans, Thomas, 46
Evans, William, 46
Ewing, A. C., 213
Excell, E. O., 146

Fabella, Virginia, 309
Fabend, F. H., 158
Fackre, Gabriel, 323-4, 372, 382
Fairbairn, A. M., 112, 161, 253, 254, 258
Farel, G., 281
Farley, B. J., 285
Farley, Margaret, 371
Farmer, H. H., 160, 255
Farney, Widow, 54
Fawcett, Benjamin, 101
Fell, John, 83-4
Fergusson, D. A. S., 250
Ferm, D. W., 311
Fern, Rev. Mr., 57
Ferreira, M. Jamie, 197
Ffallowfield, William, 63
Fichte, J. G., 209
Ficino, Marsilio, 13
Fiddes, Paul S., 104
Finlayson, R.A., 250
Finlayson, T. C., 350
Finney, Charles, G., 156, 174, 389
Fitzpatrick, Martin, 88, 183-4
Fleming, William, 206
Flint, Robert, 114, 206, 208, 212, 213, 215, 246, 258
Ford, James, 48
Ford, Stephen, 344
Forrest, D. W., 252
Forsyth, P. T., xii, 12, 86, 107, 157, 162, 166, 200, 201, 204, 213, 217, 222, 232, 234, 253, 259, 285-6, 295, 321, 324, 325, 333, 337, 368, 378, 380, 384, 385, 388, 390, 391, 393, 395
Foskett, Bernard, 104
Fowler, Edward, 6
Fowler, John, 50
Fox, George, 17, 18, 40, 47, 49, 300
France, R. T., 316
Francis of Assisi, 301
Franklin, Benjamin, 132
Franks, R. S., 254, 258, 394
Fremantle, Anne, 234
Freud, S., 249
Fruchtman, Jack, Jr., 111
Frye, Roland M., 367, 370
Fuller, Andrew, ch. 4, 150, 151

Gabbey, Alan, 22
Gadsby, William, 234, 338
Gale, Theophilus, 36
Galloway, A. D., 249

Galloway, George, 247
Gamble, Richard C., 243
Garrison, W. E., 178
Garvie, A. E., 161-2, 209, 254, 295, 315, 318, 380, 383, 388-9, 395, 397
Gassmann, G., 265
Gautier, Jean, 326, 383
Gay, Peter, 109
Gee, Henry, 49
George, Timothy, 78, 111
Gibbon, Edward, 135
Gibbons, Thomas, 82
Gibellini, R., 311, 315
Gibson, William, 62
Gilbert, George, 349
Gill, Jerry, H., 305
Gill, John, 71, 78-9, 88, 92-3, 94-5, 97-8, 99-100, 102-3, 105, 106, 150
Gill, Robin, 362
Gilley, Sheridan, 198
Gillingham, Sue, 316
Gilpin, W. Clark, 179
Girardeau, John L., 207-8, 210, 212, 214, 216, 218
Goldie, Mark, 72
Gomarus, F., 148
Goodwin, John, 8
Goodwin, Thomas, 227
Goold, William H., 43, 238, 290, 342, 343
Gordon, Alexander, 3, 49, 92
Gore, Charles, 213, 393
Grant, John W., 68
Gratton, Ann, 53
Gratton, John, ch. 2, 171
Gratton, John (b. 1670), 53
Gratton, Joseph, 53
Gratton, Josiah, 53
Gratton, Phebe, 53, 68
Green, T. H., 201, 205, 218, 219, 392, 393
Greene, Robert A., 14
Greene-McCreight, Kathryn, 372
Greenwood, John, 3, 4, 31, 32
Gregory the Great, 235
Greinacher, Norbert, 308
Grieve, A. J., 41-2, 221-2, 226, 237-8, 244
Griffioen, Arie J., 174, 228
Griffith-Jones, E., 254
Groshart, A. B., 40
Grotius, Hugo, 74, 120, 152
Grove, Henry, xiii, 71, 74, 75, 81, 88, 89, 90, 95-6, 103, 105, 231, 244
Grubb, Edward, 18, 38, 172
Gunton, Colin E., 72, 258, 386, 391
Guttiérrez, G., 308, 309, 312, 313, 314, 315, 316, 318, 319, 320, 321
Guyse, John, 104
Gysi, L., 21

Haaknonssen, Knud, 82, 109
Hadfield, Thomas, 77, 80, 81
Haeckel, Ernst, 209
Hageman, Howard, 236
Hague, William, 64
Hales, John, 5, 74, 117
Hall, Douglas John, 385
Hall, Spencer T., 46, 47, 63
Halley, Robert, 156
Halyburton, Thomas, 127
Hambrick-Stowe, Charles, 243
Hamilton, Kenneth, 305
Hamilton, Richard Winter, 153
Hamann, J. G., 249
Hamstra, Sam, Jr., 174, 228
Hardman, Keith J., 389
Hardy, William John, 49
Harris, Howel, 131, 328
Harris, Solomon, 131
Harrison, Joseph, 353
Hart, Joseph, 156
Haskoll, Farnham, 74
Hartley, David, 186
Hastie, William, 246
Hastings, James, 74
Hayden, Roger, 104
Haydock, Roger, 63
Haykin, Michael A. G., 78, 112
Headlam, A. C., 326
Healey, F. G., 256
Hedley, Douglas, 35
Hegel, G. W. F., 209

Heidegger, M., 305
Helm, Paul, 148
Henderson, Ian, 248
Hendry, G. S., 296
Henry, Philip, 352
Hepburn, Ronald W., 248
Herbert of Cherbury, 117, 127, 132
Heron, Alasdair I. C., 149, 250
Herrick, Jim, 143
Hesselink, I. John, 285
Hewitt, Glenn, 227, 228
Heyward, Isabel Carter, 370
Heywood Thomas, John, xvi, 219, 257, 305
Hick, John H., 257, 258
Hill, Andrew M., 173
Hill, Christopher, 64
Hill, Harry E., 154, 155
Hill, Thomas, 80
Hill, Thomas Wright, 101
Hoadly, Benjamin, 89, 126
Hobbes, Thomas, 8, 15, 20, 21, 30, 113, 116
Hodge, A. A., 163
Hodge, Charles, 163
Hodges, H. A., 394
Hodgson, J. M., 253
Holland, Silvester, 226
Holmes, J. Derek, 198
Holtrop, Pieter N., 324
Homan, Roger, 300
Hook, Donald D., 368
Hopkins, Mark, 158
Horrocks, Don, 87
Horsch, John, 388
Horsfield, Donald, 325
Horton, George, 52
Horton, R. F., 218
Hosken, T. J., 222
Hoskyns, Edmund, 235
Howard, K. W. H., 345, 353
Howard, W. F., 395
Howe, John, 152, 174, 280, 290, 291
Hoyles, John, 24
Hubbard, John, 104
Hughes, Richard T., 180
Hughes, T. Hywel, 255, 377
Humbleton, Ralph, 52
Hume, David, 39, 113, 135, 140, 329
Hunsinger, George, 387
Hunsworth, George, 101
Hunt, Mary, 355
Hunter, Henry, 83
Huntington, William, 234
Hurd, A. G., 347
Husserl, E., 305
Hussey, Joseph, 150
Hutchinson, Ann, 31
Hutton, Sarah, 15, 17

Ignatius of Antioch, 193
Inda, Cariad, 309
Inge, W. R., 18, 21, 116, 172, 196, 394
Ingham, Benjamin, 235, 353
Ingham, Mary Beth, 390
Iqbal, Muhammad, 205
Irenaeus, 39
Iverach, James, 207-9, 210, 211, 212-13, 214-17, 218, 251

Jackson, John, 52
Jackson, S. M., 114
Jackson, T., 131
James II, 57
James, John Angell, 155, 170, 237, 293, 392
James, William, 67
Jay, William, 155, 236-7, 293, 391-2
Jenkins, Daniel T., 162, 245
Jephson, Julie, 158
John Chrysostom, 301
John, Glynmor, 294
John, Jenkin, 352
John, Mansel, 352
John of Damascus, 377-8
John the gaoler's son, 57
Johns, H. V. D., 155
Johnson, Charlotte, 23
Johnson, J. A., Jr., 317
Johnson, Mark D., 68, 158
Jollie, Timothy, 79
Jones, David, 131
Jones, Griffith, 131

Jones, J. A., 78, 83
Jones, J. D., 162, 170-1, 196, 377
Jones, R. Tudur, 3
Jowett, Benjamin, 206, 392

Kant, I., 39, 88, 209
Kaye, Elaine, 1
Keith, George, 19, 47, 62
Kendall, R. T., 148
Kennedy, Ludovic, 142-3
Kent, John, 337
Ker, Ian, 191, 192, 195, 198
Kerr, Hugh T., 397-8
Kierkegaard, S, xvi, 219, 223, 234, 249
Kimel, Alvin F., Jr., 367, 368, 369, 370, 394
King, Mr., 52
Kirk, Kenneth, 290-1
Knight, William, 244
Knox, John, 342
Kraus, C. Norman, 391
Kuklick, Bruce, 209
Kvalbein, Hans, 316

Lamont, Donald, 247
Lamont, William, 64
Lampe, F. A., 234
Lara-Braud, Jorge, 310
Lash, Nicholas, 167
Latham, Ebenezer, 80, 81
Laud, William, 5
Law, William, 85-6, 129, 130
Lawson, Christopher, 54-5
Lechler, G. V., 114
Leclerq, J., 222, 235
Legge, Gordon, 356
Leland, John, 113, 123, 124, 125, 128
Lennon, Thomas M., 22
Leo XIII, 197
Lernoux, P., 307
Leslie, Charles, 115
Levinas, E., 321
Lewis, W., 145
Lichfield, Bishop of (John Hacket), 54
Liddon, H. P., 215
Lidgett, John Scott, 157
Linder, F., 205
Lindsey, Theophilus, 184
Livingstone, David, 168
Livingstone, Patrick, 64
Lloyd-Jones, D. Martyn, 245
Loades, Ann, 257
Locke, John, 23-4, 24-5, 26, 36, 71, 82, 85, 91, 106, 115, 119, 125, 126, 180, 371
Longfellow, S. P., 355
Lowman, Moses, 124
Lumpkin, W. L., 334
Luther, Martin, 26, 33, 106, 235, 329, 334-5, 390
Lynch, T. T., 158

McAinish, Beverley, 67
Macaulay, A. B., 247
M'Cheyne, R. M., 340
McCormack, Brule L., 398
MacFadyen, D., 42
McFague, Sallie, 372
McGinn, Bernard, 301
McGonigle, H. B., 97
McGrath, Alister E., 70-1, 114.
MacGregor, W. M., 252
Machen, J. G., 163
McIntosh, G. Stewart, 310
Mackennal, Alexander, 33, 42
McKim, Donald K., 243, 262, 302
MacKinnon, Donald M., 71-2
MacKinnon, F. I., 4, 38
Mackintosh, H. R., 247, 259
Mackintosh, Robert, 68-9, 112, 154, 156-7, 161, 253, 259, 323, 332, 333, 382, 387-8, 391, 393, 395, 397
McIntyre, John, 249, 378, 382, 386, 392
McLachlan, H. John, 184
MacLean, Donald, 287
MacLeod, Donald, 149, 250, 293
Macmillan, Donald, 206, 207
McMillon, Lynn A., 178
McNeill, John T., 147
Macquarrie, John, 246
McTaggart, J. M. E., 209

McWilliams, David B., 149
Malebranche, Nicholas, 3, 4, 14, 24, 30, 37
Mander, W. J., 172-3, 187, 198, 206, 207
Manners, Emily, 47
Manning, Bernard Lord, 162, 168-9, 240-1, 291, 343
Manning, James, 101-2
Manson, T. W., xv, 290-1, 399
Manuel, Frank E., 113
Marchant, James, 295
Marriott, J. A. R., 218
Marsh, Jophn, 162
Martell, Jacob, 349
Martin, Alexander, 246
Martineau, James, 21, 22, 172, 191
Martinez, Sergio Arce, 309
Marx, Karl, 249, 309
Masland, Hugh, 56
Mason, John, 84-5
Mateus, Odair Pedroso, 260, 280
Matthews, A. G., 42-3, 49, 57, 221, 289
Matthews, Charles, 155
Matthews, James, 154
Maudlin, F. L., 78
Maurice, F. D., 107, 161
Maurice, Matthias, 150, 151
Medway, John, 345
Meller, Robert, 57
Mellone, S. H., 173
Mendonça, A. G., 312, 319
Metz, Johann B., 309
Meynell, Hugo, 293
Micklem, Nathaniel, 162, 245, 351
Míguez Bonino, J., 311, 320
Mill, John Stuart, xiii, 9, 140
Miller, Allen O., 304, 367
Miller, Perry, 154
Miller, William F., 58
Milton, John, 147
Minear, Paul S., 370
Mintz, Samuel I., 21
Mitchell, Basil, 130
Molesworth, William, 116
Molther, P. H., 233
Moltmann, Jürgen, 297
Monti, Dominic, 301
Moody, Barry, 145
Moon, Norman, 76, 104
Moore, John, 113
Moore, Rosemary, 67
More, Henry, 2, 3, 9, 10, 13, 14, 15, 17, 19, 20, 21, 22, 23, 27, 33, 39
Morgan, Thomas, 112, 123, 131, 135
Morgan, William, 235
Mouw, Richard, 287
Mozley, J. K., 317
Muggleton, Ludovic, 52, 64-5
Muirhead, J. H., 16, 22-3, 38, 172, 393
Müller, Alois, 308
Muller, Richard A., 149, 332
Murch, Jerom, 101

Nash, Robert, 286
Naylor, James, 28, 49
Naylor, Peter, 349
Neander, J. A. W., 175
Neely, Alan, 312
Nelson, J. B., 355
Nero, 213
Nestorius, 301
Nettles, Tom J., 112
Nettleship, R. L., 218
Newton, Isaac, 73, 133
Nevin, J. W., 174-6, 179, 180, 192, 196, 198, 199, 201, 203, 227-8, 236, 323, 397
Newbigin, J. E. Lesslie, 245
Newlands, George M., 249-50
Newman, J. H., 183, 191-8, 201-2, 286
Newton, Samuel, 354
Nicholas, John M., 22
Nicholls, Bruce, 286, 288
Nichols, J. H., 174
Nicholson, Wallace, 250
Nickalls, John L., 17, 300
Nidditch, Peter H., 25
Niebuhr, Reinhold, 398
Nightingale, Benjamin, 145
Noake, John, 347

Norris, John, 2, 3-4, 7, 9, 10, 12, 13-14, 15, 16, 18, 19, 20, 21, 22-3, 24, 30, 31, 33, 34, 35, 37-8, 39, 42, 85
Notcutt, John, 81-2
Nugent, Robert, 361
Nuttall, Geoffrey F., 40, 43, 64, 353
Nygren, Anders, 327

Oberman, Heiko A., 285
O'Brien, Dennis, 361
O'Bryan, William, 354
Ogden, Schubert, 317
Ogden, Uzal, 126
O'Hanlon, Gerard, 308
Oldfield, John, 49, 51
O'Loughlin, Thomas, 194
Oman, John W., 255
Opocensky, Milan, 260
Origen, 14
Orr, James, 194, 251
Orton, Job, 230, 237
Osterhaven, M. Eugene, 261
Ottley, R. L., 213
Owen, H. P., 252, 259
Owen, John, 17, 43, 163, 238, 241, 290, 301, 342, 343, 358
Owen, Josiah, 130

Pailin, David A., 117, 197
Paine, Thomas, ch. 4, 383
Palmer, Elihu, 126
Parker, Joseph, 346-7
Parry, K. L., 1
Passmore, John, 8, 9, 20, 21, 22, 30
Paterson, W. P., 141-2, 215, 217
[Patrick, Simon], 10
Payne, George, 155-6, 163
Peake, A. S., 395
Peel, Albert, 9, 44, 68, 109, 153, 154, 218, 221, 334, 342, 345, 349, 351
Peel, David R., 258
Penelhum, Terence M., 130
Penn, William, 56
Penzel, Klaus, 176, 177, 198
Perkins, William, 148
Perret, Edmond, 371
Peter Damian, 222, 243
Peters, Ted, 368
Pfizenmaier, T. C., 91
Phillips, George, 259
Philp, Mark, 111
Pickles, H. M., 353
Picton, J. Allanson, 68
Pike, Joseph, 342
Philpot, J. C., 234
Pius IX, 197
Plato, 10, 11, 21, 25, 36, 45
Plotinus, 7, 8, 10, 11, 13
Pobee, John S., 307, 317
Pocock, J. G. A., 72
Poole-Connor, E. J., 328
Popper, Karl, 324
Porritt, Arthur, 171
Porter, Roy, 72-3
Powicke, F. J., xi, ch. 1, 50, 55, 68, 92, 108, 109, 156, 164, 182, 195, 196, 200, 205, 351, 378
Powicke, F. M., xi, 2
Powicke, W. A., 2
Pradervand, Marcel, 262
Press, John, 349
Preston, John, 229-30
Preston, Ronald H., xv
Price, E. J., 162
Price, John V., 183
Price, Richard, xiii, 101
Priestley, Joseph, xi, 71, 75-6, 77, 86-7, 89, 90, 94, 96, 99-100, 102, 103, 106, 109, 158, 183-7, 191, 192, 194, 197, 329, 335-6, 348, 350, 373
Pringle-Pattison, A. S., 211, 216
Proclus, 10, 13
Prys, William, 349
Pufendorf, Samuel, 74
Punshon, John, 18-19, 40, 59, 67, 172
Pyke, Richard, 354
Pyle, Andrew, 15

Quick, O. C., 202

Rack, Henry D., 300
Rahner, Karl, 297

Rambaut, W. H., 392
Ramsey, A. M., 393-4
Ramus, Peter, 147
Ramsey, Chevalier, 329
Randall, Ian M., 234
Randall, Samuel, 342
Rauch, F. A., 174, 177
Rawlinson, A. E. J., 41
Réamonn, P., 260
Reay, Barry, 64
Rashdall, Hastings, 378
Redford, George, 153, 237, 293, 392
Redwood, J. A., 118
Rees, Thomas, 254
Reeve, John, 52, 64, 65
Reid, H. M. B., 246
Reid, J. K. S., 248, 332
Reid, Thomas, 206
Richards, G. W., 261
Richardson, Alan, 337
Ridgley, Thomas, 93, 150-1, 155, 163
Ritschl, A., 247, 251
Rix, Samuel, 145
Roberts, Alexander, 392
Roberts, Arthur O., 63, 172
Roberts, J. D., Sr., 14
Robertson, F. W., 161
Robinson, John, 3, 4, 32, 33, 182
Robinson, N. H. G., 248-9, 259
Robinson, W. Gordon, 222
Rogers, G. A. J., 17. 23
Rogers, Henry, 290
Rollock, Robert, 148
Rolston, Holmes, III, 148
Rooker, James, 82
Rousseau, J-J., 161
Rowley, H. H., xv
Royce, Josiah, 209, 212, 213
Rupp, E. Gordon, xv, 112
Rush, David, 66
Russell, Bertrand, 183
Russell, Letty, 371
Rutt, J. T., xi, 75, 183, 329

Sacheverell, Henry, 73
Sadolet, J., 261
Saggau, Elise, 301, 368, 390
Sailor, Danton B., 21
Salmond, S. D. F., 378
Sanday, W., 326
Sasse, H., 386-7
Saunders, Alan, 82
Saveson, J. E., 21, 22
Scanfield, John, 63
Scanone, J. C., 321
Schaff, Philip, 114, 174, 176-8, 179, 192, 198, 199, 227
Scheick, William J., 111
Schelling, F. W. J. von, 177, 209
Schipani, Daniel S., 316
Schleiermacher, F. D. E., 176, 247
Schofield, Robert E., 183
Schwanda, Tom, 224
Schweizer, E., 342
Scott, David Russell, 250
Scott, James, 104, 105
Segundo, Juan Luis, 308, 309, 310, 311, 320, 321
Selbie, W. B., 18, 44m 172, 196, 254
Sell, Alan P. F., Preface, 3, 5, 9, 14, 17, 23-4, 28, 31, 34, 36, 38, 39, 47, 49, 57, 68, 71, 73, 74, 75, 77-8, 81, 83, 86, 87, 91, 92, 93, 94, 99, 101, 104, 108, 111, 115, 117, 125, 130, 140, 143, 148, 149, 150, 153, 156, 157-8, 159, 162, 163, 164, 168, 170, 172-3, 176, 177, 187, 191, 196, 199, 201, 202, 206, 207, 209, 218, 228, 230, 232, 233, 234, 236, 238, 239, 242, 257-8, 261, 262, 263, 267, 268, 269, 271, 280, 282, 283, 286, 287, 289, 290, 295, 297, 301, 302, 305, 306, 324, 327-8, 333, 334, 339, 343, 347, 371, 378, 379, 380, 383. 388, 388, 389, 391, 392, 393, 394, 397
Sell, Karen, xvi
Sell-Maestro, Hugo, xvi
Selleck, Ron, 389
Sellon, Walter, 299
Servetus, Michael, 166
Seth, A., (see Pringle-Pattison, A. S.)

Shaftesbury (see Cooper, Anthony Ashley)
Shaw, Charles Gray, 74
Shaw, D. W. D., 249
Shaw, Thomas, 354
Short, John, 162
Shriver, George H., 177
Sibbes, Richard, 40
Sider, Ronald, 316, 317
Simon, D. W., 1, 2, 27, 68, 109, 156, 164, 205, 253, 350-1
Sirgood, John, 300
Sisson, C. H., 328
Smith, John, 3, 6-7, 8, 11, 12-13, 15, 16, 20, 22, 23, 25, 27, 29, 30, 35, 38-9
Smith, John Pye, 152, 345
Smith, Leonard, 173
Smith, Richmond, 262
Smith, Rodney 'Gypsy', 146
Smith, R. G., 249
Smithson, Isaac, 103
Snaith, Norman, 337
Sobrino, Jon, 309, 315, 321
Socrates, 119
Soskice, Janet Martin, 368-9
Spearritt, Placid, 11
Spencer, Herbert, 177
Spinoza, Benedict de, 37, 209, 210
Sprague, William, 342
Spurgeon, C. H., 160, 191, 337
Squire, Anne, 356
Stanley, Brian, 111
Staudenbaur, C. A., 12
Stek, John H., 149
Stepelvich, Lawrence S., 176
Stephen, Leslie, 112, 113, 130
Stephens, John, 183
Stephens, J. P., 351
Stephenson, A., 194
Sterry, Peter, 3, 5, 6, 31, 37
Stewart, Dugald, 206
Stewart, J. S., 247
Stewart, Lyman, 303
Stillingfleet, Edward, 290
Stoddard, Solomon, 154
Stone, Barton W., 180
Stopford, John, 238
Stoughton, John, 152, 153, 354
Streeter, B. H., 41, 216
Sullivan, Kathryn, 326, 383
Sullivan, Robert E., 113, 118
Surman, Charles E., 42, 221, 222, 226
Sutton, Daniel, 222
Swaine, Stephen A., 76
Sweet, W. W., 178
Swinton, John, 65
Sykes, John, 54
Sykes, Samuel, 54
Sylvester, M., 283

Talbot, Nellie, 146
Tallack, William, 28
Taylor, Abraham, 150
Taylor, Jeremy, 35, 225
Taylor, John, xiii, 87, 90, 93-4, 98-9, 103-4, 147-8, 230, 370
Taylor, John (20–21 century), 353
Taylor, Vincent, 382
Teich, M., 73
Teilhard de Chardin, 311
Telford, John, 131
Tertullian, 55, 342
Thacker, Elias, 221
Thatcher, Adrian, 364
Theodore of Mopsuestia, 301
Thistlethwaite, Susan Brooks, 370
Thomas, Aquinas, 13, 230, 302, 360
Thomas, G. Michael, 148
Thomas, Roger, 92, 340
Thomas, J. N., 200
Thompson, Bard, 176
Thompson, David M., 178
Thompson, John, 252, 331
Thompson, Joseph, 187
Thorne, James, 354
Thornwell, James Henley, 242
Tibbutt, H. G., 352
Tidball, Derek J., 379
Tillich, Paul, xiii, xvi, 143, 303-6, 307, 324, 375, 398
Tindal, Matthew, 112, 113, 115, 121-2, 123, 124, 126, 128, 129, 131, 135

Toland, John, 112, 117, 118, 125, 126, 131
Tomkinson, Dianne, 302
Toothill, Jonathan, 104
Toplady, A. M., 158, 159, 161, 299
Torrance, Alan, 250
Torrance, Iain, 249, 250
Torrance, James B., 149, 163, 249
Torrance, T. F., 249, 272, 282, 284, 331, 394-5
Torres, Sergio, 309
Towgood, Micaijah, 101-2
Trelawney, Harry, 84
Trites, Allison, 143
Trost, Theodore L., 177
Tuck, Richard, 74
Tuckney, Anthony, 6, 8, 25-6
Tulloch, John, 6, 20, 21, 24, 29, 34, 40
Turnbull, Joseph, 153
Turner, George Lyon, 52
Tyerman, Luke, 299

Ursinus, Z., 148, 281
Urwick, William, 187

Van Asselt, Willem J., 147
Vandenbroucke, F., 222, 235
Van Dyk, Leanne, 288
Vane, Harry, 31
Vaughan, Robert, 183, 187-91, 192, 194, 197, 346
Verschoor, Jacob, 228
Vidales, R., 324
Vienne, J. M., 17
Vincent, Francis, 326
Vine, Aubrey, 256
Vischer, Lukas, 272, 331, 341
Visser, Derk, 281
Voltaire (Françoise Marie Arouet), 135
Voskuil, Dennis N., 278

Wadsworth, Kenneth W., 105
Wainwright, Arthur W., 26
Wainwright, Geoffrey, 370
Walker, D. P., 117
Walker, Williston, 154
Warburton, William, 130
Ward, Seth, 291
Wardlaw, Ralph, 152, 163
Wardley, James, 300
Wardley, Jane, 300
Warfield, B. B., 163
Waterland, Daniel, 130
Watson, Philip, 26
Watson, Thomas, 225-6, 237, 242, 289, 338, 374, 375
Watts, George, 57
Watts, Isaac, 127-8, 145, 228-9, 243
Watts, M. R., 57, 389
Weaver, J. Denny, 391
Webb, C. C. J., 34, 216
Webster, C., 22
Weddle, David, 99
Welker, Michael, 338, 387, 397
Wells, Algernon, 153
Wellwood, John, 393
Wenley, R. M., 206, 207
Wesley, Charles, 235, 241, 300
Wesley, John, 6, 35, 71, 72, 94, 96-8, 99, 102, 108, 131, 141, 156, 235, 285, 299, 300, 348
Whale, John S., 162, 256, 277, 296, 337
Whichcote, Benjamin, 3, 5, 6, 8, 10, 11, 12, 13, 14, 15, 17, 20, 25-6, 27, 29, 30, 33-4, 116
Whiston, William, 120, 126
White, B. R., 32, 352
White, Ellen G., 275
Whitefield, George, 102
Whitehouse, W. A., 162, 256-7
Whitwell, Elizabeth, 345
Wileman, William, 145-6, 233-4
Willborn, C. N., 207
Willen, Diane, 32
William of Ockham, 147
Williams, Dolores, 381-2
Williams, Edward, 151-2
Williams, J. B., 352
Williams, Rowan, 363
Williams, Stephen N., 252
Williams, William, 300
Willimon, William H., 363
Wilson, H. S., 263, 277

Wilson, John, 52
Wilson, John M., 150
Wilson, Rev. Mr., 57
Wilson, Walter, 78, 79, 93
Wilson, William, 55-6
Winter, Cornelius, 236-7
Witherow, Thomas, 181-2
Withers, John, 101-2
Witsius, H., 148
Wollaston, William, 112
Wolrich/Woolrich, Thomas, 62, 63
Woodrow, Woody, 180
Woolrich, Humphry, 63
Woolston, Thomas, 112, 120, 121, 142
Wright, Thomas, 156
Wykes, David L., 73

Yolton, John, 183
Yrigoyen, Charles, Jr., 174. 175, 177, 195, 196, 198, 201, 323

Zagorin, P., 72
Zanchius, J., 329
Zarka, Y. C., 17
Zwingli, Ulrich, 281

General Index

Aberdeen, 58
Aberdeen University, 247, 248, 249, 250
Acadia University, 239
Abingdon, 347
Act of Uniformity, 49, 221, 340
adoptionism, 56
Africa, 276, 277
African Instituted Churches, 260, 276
agnosticism/agnostics, 66, 110, 159, 173, 205, 209
Airedale Independent College, 253
Alexandria, 166
Alnwick, 1
America, 132, 158, 166, 199, 362
Anabaptists, 51, 52, 53, 59-60, 61, 243
Anglicans (see also Church of England), 85, 112, 113, 120, 130, 183, 222, 229, 235, 245, 264, 266, 267, 292, 303, 352
antinomians, 30-1, 154, 333-4
apologetics, 120, 125, 141, 143, 246, 248, 251, 257
Argentina, 308
Arianism/Arians, 81, 87, 93, 94, 101, 108, 113, 120, 122, 131, 147, 172, 181, 189, 370, 383, 392
Arminianism/Arminians, 5, 6, 71, 72, 75, 94, 96, 97, 101, 103, 130, 145, 150, 156, 264, 275, 303
Arnesby, 349
Ashford in the Water, 50
Asia, 296
atheism/atheists, 66, 73, 110, 113, 114, 116, 131, 133, 142, 173, 205, 206, 212, 216, 311, 348
Athens, 321
Atlantic Baptist Convention, 358
atonement (see Cross)
Attercliffe [Congregational] Academy, 79
authority, 44, 85, 119, 132, 143, 157, 163, 183, 188, 190, 193-4, 197, 200, 202, 204, 263, 272, 286, 291, 359, 369, 396
Axminster, 352-3

Bakewell, 52, 55
Bala-Bangor Independent College, 254
baptism, 52-3, 55, 59-62, 108, 157, 185, 229, 267, 268-9, 273, 279, 294, 344, 349, 364
Baptism, Eucharist and Ministry, 265
Baptist Missionary Society, 111, 150
Baptists, 76, 84, 105, 145, 151, 164, 191, 239, 245, 263, 266, 340, 343, 344, 347, 351, 352, 353, 358
- General Baptists, 353
- Gospel Standard Baptists, 234
- Particular Baptists, 149, 334, 349
- Southern Baptist Convention, 279
- Strict and Particular Baptists, 259, 293

Baptist World Alliance, 267, 268, 279
Base Church Communities, 312, 323
Basis of Union, 203
Baslow, 65
Bath, 155, 236, 293
Bedford, 344, 352
Bible, 6, 25-8, 36, 39, 40, 42, 43, 44, 49, 50, 52, 55, 56, 63, 64, 65, 66, 68, 76, 78, 79, 80, 81, 83, 86, 87, 88, 89, 90, 92, 94, 97, 98, 100, 106, 107, 116, 118, 119-20, 122, 123, 130, 132-3, 134-5, 136, 137, 138, 139, 141, 142-3, 130, 132-3, 134-5, 136, 137, 138, 139, 141, 142-3, 147-8, 163, 166, 167, 172, 175, 178, 179, 180, 181, 186, 187, 188, 189, 190, 191, 192, 193, 195, 197, 200, 216, 222, 224, 233, 235, 240, 261, 268, 273, 274, 275,

281, 282, 284, 285, 286, 287, 289, 294, 296, 312, 320, 323, 324, 329, 337, 340, 341, 359-60, 363, 369, 371, 396
Bideford, 337
Birmingham, 76, 102, 148, 155, 230, 348, 350
Birmingham riots, 73
Birmingham University, 257
Blackheath, 351
Blackwell-Ditch, 52
Bolton, 300
Bonsall, 47
Boston, 363, 372
Bournemouth, 170
Bradford, 164, 221
British Reformed theology, ch. 9
Burton, 123
Bury St. Edmunds, 221

Calgary, 268, 357
Calvinism/Calvinists, 5, 6, 8-9, 10, 15, 34, 43, 71, 72, 75, 76, 77, 78, 80, 82, 83, 94, 97, 101, 103, 104, 111, 127, 130, 131, ch. 5, 171, 202, 245, 246, 253, 264, 275, 303, 325, 326, 328, 333, 334, 335-6, 343, 347
Calvinistic Methodism (see also Presbyterian Church of Wales), 300, 349
Cambridge, 150, 168
Cambridge colleges, 3, 5
Cambridge Platonists, ch. 1, 54, 116, 117, 326
Cambridge University, 3, 89, 240, 255
Canada, 257, 354, 358, 364
Carmarthen, 131
Catechisms
- *Geneva Catechism*, 284
- *Heidelberg Catechism*, 203-4, 281-2, 330
- *Study Catechism*, 387
- *Westminster Larger Catechism*, 150, 240, 330, 341
- *Westminster Shorter Catechism*, 333, 382
Catholic Council for Church and Society, 361
catholicity, 261, 271, 282, 290, 294, 324, 343, 373
Cavendish, 221
Chalcedonian Formula, 226
Cheshire, 69
Cheshunt College, Cambridge, 256
Chesterfield, 47, 49, 51, 64, 81
Chicago, 325
Chipping Norton, 344-5
Christology (see also Incarnation), 69, 118, 123, 172, 181, 185-6, 188, 201, 202, 247, 249, 266, 273, 279, 285, 301, 317, 392, 394
Church
- covenants, 34, 68, 108, 157, 347
- discipline, 62-3, 199, 203-4, 238-42, 275, 339-55, 373, 396
- doctrine of, 4, 9, 31-5, 41-5, 59-61, 68, 107-9, 158, 176-7, 178, 179, 181, 182, 184, 195-6, ch. 10, 282-3, 290, 295-6, 339, 350
- establishments, 136, 191, 295
- Meeting, 145, 156, 157, 340, 344, 346, 353
- membership, 199, 239, 342-51, 356, 362, 364
Church of England, 3, 6, 31, 33, 53, 55, 60, 98, 115, 181, 221, 292, 352
Church Order Group, 162
Civil War, 73
Clapton Park, 345
Claremont Graduate School, 257
Cockermouth, 144, 146
Colombia, 308
common sense philosophy, 174, 178, 180, 206
confessions, creeds and declarations, 89-90. 148, 163, 181, 261, 263, 282, 398
- *A Declaration of Faith*, 363
- *Barmen Declaration*, 371
- *Canons of Dort*, 363
- *Common Confession of Faith, The*, 341
- *Declaration and Address*, 178

- *Declaration of Faith*, 152-4, 296, 341, 387
- *London Confession*, 334
- *Nicene Creed*, 273
- *Savoy Declaration of Faith and Order*, 149, 153, 163, 289, 334, 340
- *Second London Confession*, 149
- *Westminster Confession of Faith*, 148-9, 150, 164, 250, 330, 359

Congregation for the Doctrine of the Faith, 319
Congregational Theological Hall, Edinburgh, 250, 253, 255, 256
Congregationalism/Congregationalists, 1, 2, 9, 11, 41-4, 48, 51, 59, 68, 77, 81-2, 84, 93, 104, 108, 112, 123, ch. 5, 170, 171, 172, 182, 183, 187, 195, 196, 205, 218, 221, 232, 233, 236, 239, 255, 259, 281, 289, 290, 295, 296, 301, 318, 326, 334, 337, 339, 340, 341, 343, 344, 345, 347, 349, 351, 352, 353, 374
- Congregational Church in England and Wales, 173, 253-5, 387
- Congregational Union of England and Wales, 152-3, 156, 158, 173, 253-5, 351
- Congregational Union of Scotland, 250

Constantinianism, 385-6
consumerism, 277
contextual theology, 173, 174, 288, 305-25, 375, 396
conversion, 108, 157, 271
Coseley, 148, 230
covenant theology (see federal theology)
Creator-creature distinction, 216-17, 220, 297, 369, 396
Cross, 65, 99-101, 118, 127, 131, 133-4, 139, 141, 152, 186, 188, 194, 200, 201, 218-19, 220, 234, 246, 251, 252, 253, 254, 256, 274, 277, 279, 280, 282, 288-9, 294, 297, 302, 315, 318-19, 333, ch. 13
Daventry Academy, 374
Declaration of Indulgence, 50
deism, 71, 87, 103, ch. 4, 187, 205, 206, 348, 383, 396
Denton, 145
Dependent Brethren, 300
Derby, 56, 57, 58, 300
Derbyshire, 47, 54, 55
determinism, 158-9, 161, 206, 275, 335
development of doctrine, ch. 6, 396
dialogues (see also ecumenism) 45, 166-7, 249, ch. 10, 386
Disciples of Christ, 173, 178-9, 180, 182, 266, 269, 279
dispensationalism, 270
docetism, 319-20, 396
Dominus Iesus, 293
Dutch Reformed Church in America, 158

ecumenism, 67, 166-7, 174, 179, 248, 257, ch. 10, ch. 11, 397
Edinburgh, 221
Edinburgh University, 246, 247, 248
election (see predestination)
England, 36, 132, 154, 205, 239, 253-8, 257, 282, 326
Enlightenment, 67, ch. 3, 88, 101, 106, 107, 109, 110, 117, 157, 163, 171, 173, 230, 309, 323
enthusiasm, 17, 123
Epicureans, 113-14
Erlangen University, 250
ethics, 249, 250, 373-4
Evangelical Lutheran Church in America, 358
Evangelical Revival, 72, 83, 106, 108, 157, 159, 392
evolutionary thought, 159, 201, 205
exclusivity, 325-75
Exodus, 313-14
experience, 232-4, 257, 306, 323, 371, 382, 396
Exton (or Elton), 54

Farnsfield, 68
federal theology, 148-50, 249

feminism/feminists, 141, 288-9, 367-72, 381, 394
Fetter Lane Society, 233
Findern Academy, 80
Finneyism, 174
Five Mile Act, 49
Form of Presbyterial Church Government, 339
Formula of Union, 273
France, 132
Franciscans, 301, 368, 383
Fraserburgh, 155
Free Church College, Edinburgh, 244, 250
French Revolution, 132, 161
Frome, 123

General Conference of Seventh Day Adventists, 274
Geneva, 238, 257, 279
German Reformed Church, 146, 176, 199, 228, 295
God
- attributes of, 124, 142, 160
- authority of, 157
- death of, 141
- existence of, 78-84, 140
- Fatherhood of, 157, 165, 172-3, 185, 389
- immanence of, 114, 209-10, 216, 218, 220, 385, 394
- nature of, 215-16
- omnipresence of, 215
- righteousness of, 390-2
- transcendence of, 114, 218, 220, 385, 394
Glasgow University, 2, 206, 246, 248, 249
Grand Rapids, 283
Greenland, 322
Greenock, 12
Guildford, 351

Hackney Congregational College, 11, 253
Hackney [Unitarian] Academy, 374
Hampstead, 218
Hatherlow, 1
Haverhill, 154
Heaton Moor, 1
Heckmondwike Academy, 104
higher criticism, 86, 159, 302
Highlow, 56
Holy Club, 235
Holy Spirit, 17, 31, 39, 40, 42, 46, 49, 53-4, 55, 60, 63-4, 66, 68, 94, 99, 123, 124, 127, 141, 150, 163, 165, 166, 170, 171, 173, 179, 181, 188, 203, 222, 223, 225, 227-9, 237, 240, 261, 266, 270, 273, 274, 282-6, 287, 289, 290, 292, 293, 294, 295, 296, 297, 298, 302, 314, 320, 334, 339, 348, 379, 381, 390, 396, 397, 398, 399
Homerton Academy, 83, 104
homiletic practice (see also preaching), 102-4
homosexuality, 325, 355-65, 375
Hoxton Independent Academy, 142
humanists, 173
humanity, doctrine of, ch. 5, 285, 297, 389

idealism, 174, 202-2, 205, 206, 207, 208, 209, 210-13, 214, 215, 217-18, 297, 305, 392-3
immortality, 114, 137, 185, 186, 254, 256
Incarnation (see also Christology), 193, 201, 206, 218, 220, 251, 252, 273, 297, 324, 370, 379, 387, 388, 392-4
inclusive language, 264-5, 365-75
inclusivity, 325-75
Independents (see Congregationalists)
individualism, 34, 35, 36, 67, 68, 99, 107, 108, 109, 157-8, 174, 175, 200, 235, 277, 278, 284, 285, 290, 325, 388, 396, 399
Indonesia, 341
International Congregational Council, 170, 182, 261, 377
Iona, 222
Ireland, 36, 58, 159, 252

Jesuits, 73, 286

Jews, 115, 139, 140, 142, 327
Jumpers, 300

Kendal, 57
Kensington, 187
Kent, 353
Kent University, 256
Kettering, 111
Kidderminster, 101, 124

labels, 300-3, 375
Lancashire Independent College, 1, 188, 221, 222, 259, 253
Latin America, 307-25, 375
Latitudinarians, 6, 117, 129
Leicester Conference, 67-8
Leicestershire, 52
liberation theology, 307-25
libertarianism, 159, 336
Llanddowror, 131
London, 53, 57, 64, 152, 346, 351
London University, 2, 168, 188, 252, 258
Lord's Supper, 62, 176, 185, 224, 229, 236, 267, 271, 274, 277, 283, 291, 292-3, 352, 396
Loxwood, 300
Lutherans, 260, 262, 266, 267, 279, 358
Lutheran World Federation, 267

Maldives, 322
Manchester, 1, 221, 300
Manchester University, 256
Mansfield College, 1, 2, 253, 254, 255, 351
Marlborough, 236
marriage, 359, 361, 362-3, 364-5
Marxism, 309-12
materialism, 20-1, 109, 213
Matlock, 55
Medellín, 308
Memorial College, Brecon, 254
Mennonites, 264, 266, 267-8, 35
- Canadian Mennonite Church, 358
- General Conference Mennonite Church, 358
- Mennonite Church, 358
Mennonite World Conference, 267, 268
Mercersburg theology, 173, 174-8, 180, 181, 192, 201, 227, 236, 295
Methodists, 153, 157, 159, 235, 263-4, 266, 269, 279, 300, 311, 358, 361
- Bible Christians, 354
- United Methodist Church, 358
Mexico, 309
ministers, 236-8, 284
ministry, 267, 268, 269, 271, 279, 280, 393
miracles, 118, 120-1, 123, 142, 185
Modern Churchpeople's Union, 384, 388
Modern Freechurchmen's Union, 351
monasticism, 243
monism, 206, 207, 208, 217
Monyash, 50, 52, 54, 55, 56, 59, 68
moral influence, 380, 384-5
morality, 28-31, 38, 94-8, 107, 114, 123, 130, 133, 136-7, 139, 142, 157, 188, 212-13, 383
Moravians, 233
Mormonism, 303
Muslims, 169

naturalism, 67, 208-9
natural religion, 113, 114, 115, 117-18, 121-2, 123, 124, 126, 127, 129, 129-30, 136, 141
natural rights, 74
natural theology, 78-84, 106
New College, Edinburgh, 246, 247, 249, 250
New College, London, 254, 255, 256
nicknames, 299, 300, 275
Nonconformity, 389
Norfolk, 145, 151
Northamptonshire, 353
Northern Baptist Association, 349
Northern College, Manchester, 258
Northumberland, PA, 373
Norwich, 87, 354
Nottinghamshire, 69
Nottingham University, 257

ordination, (see also women, ordination of), 272, 291, 356, 357, 358, 362, 364, 365
ordination confessions, 76-7, 79-84
Oriental Orthodox, 264, 266, 273-4
original sin, 98-9, 104, 106
Orthodox Churches, 266, 272-3
Oswestry, 151
Over Haddon, 53
Oxford Movement, 302
Oxford University, 2, 3, 84, 205, 218, 300, 392

Pacific, 276
pantheism, 24, 36-8, 39, 114, ch. 7, 228, 394, 396
Pantycelyn, 300
Patriarchate of Constantinople, 272
Pattowhill, 52
peace, 268
Peckham, 80, 81
penal substitution, 380
Pentecostals, 266, 270, 312
personalism, 255
pluralism, 257, 386
Plymouth Brethren, 180
poor, 306, 308, 312-13, 315-17
positivism, 67, 110, 141, 159, 205
Prague, 261
preaching (see also homiletic method), 236, 286, 289
predestination, 5, 6, 8-9, 34, 48, 79, 94-8, 106, 150-1, 152, 155-7, 158-9, 161, 162, 163, 185, 275, 325-8, 365
Presbyterian Church of England Theological College, 255
Presbyterianism/Presbyterians, 28, 48, 49, 50, 51, 60, 71, 77, 80, 81, 82, 84, 87, 98, 101, 104, 123, 130, 150, 159, 164, 172, 181-2, 195, 225, 230, 231, 245, 259, 281, 290, 301, 326, 340, 352, 358
- Church of Scotland, 246-50
- Free Church of Scotland, 161, 250, 293
- Free Presbyterian Church of Scotland, 251
- Presbyterian Church in the Republic of Korea, 330
- Presbyterian Church in the United States, 310
- Presbyterian Church of Canada, 358, 374
- Presbyterian Church of England, 255
- Presbyterian Church of Ireland, 252
- Presbyterian Church of Wales (see also Calvinistic Methodists), 252
- Presbyterian Church USA, 359, 363, 387
- United Free Church of Scotland, 246, 251-2
- United Presbyterian Church in the USA, 200
priesthood of all believers, 106
Princeton Theological Seminary, 163
prophecy, 120, 142
Protestant scholasticism, 6-8
Puebla, 309
Puritans, ch. 1, 147, 199, 369, 374

Quakers, 2, 6, 17-19, 28, 31, 35-6, 39, 40, ch. 2, 123, 171-2, 300, 349
Quinta Brook, 226

racism, 242
ransom, 380, 392
rationalism, 205
realism, 207
reason, 10, 11, 12-25, 29, 40, 54, 71, 75-6, 82, 84, 85-7, 89, 106, 115, 116-19, 121, 123-4, 125, 126 127-8, 129, 133
Reformation, 76, 90, 106-7, 173, 175, 177, 224, 235, 256, 261, 266, 271, 275
Reformed tradition, 63, 67, 158, 176, 224, 235, 236, ch. 10, ch. 11, 301
Religion of Humanity, 195
Religious Society of Friends (see Quakers)
restorationists, 173, 175, 178-181, 184, 197, 198

revelation, 28, 64, 71, 75-6, 79, 80, 84, 87, 89, 115, 116, 117-18, 121, 122, 123, 125, 126, 127-8, 129, 132-3, 140, 141, 180, 192, 198, 217, 305, 333, 382
revivalism, 174-5, 228
right of private judgment, 26, 72, 74, 75, 76-7, 84, 88, 106-7, 175
Roman Catholics, 6, 26, 36, 57, 73, 75, 102, 115, 116, 147, 167, 183, 191, 195, 198, 230, 260, 262, 264, 266, 267, 270-2, 285, 286, 292, 302, 307, 308, 310, 312, 319, 320, 325, 326, 329, 361, 364
Romanticism, 108, 174, 180, 189
Ross-on-Wye, 151
Rostock, 205
Rostock University, 2
Rotherham, 151
Rothwell, 353

Sabellianism, 189
Sabbath, 275
Sacheverell riots, 73
sacraments (see also baptism; Lord's Supper), 61-2, 63, 79, 184, 222, 236, 256, 280, 291, 341
St. Andrews University, 127, 247, 248, 249, 250
Salesians, 326
Salisbury, 112
sanctification, 229, 238, 241, 242, 243, 290, 398
Sandemanianism, 112
satisfaction, 380
Schism Bill, 73
science, 249, 251
scientific method, 73-4, 115-16, 133
Scotland, 36, 58, 104, 166, 205, 246-52
Second Conventicle Act, 53
Secretariat for Promoting Christian Unity, 270
sectarianism, 33, 67, 199, 202, 203, 222, 280, 283, 286, 287, 289, 290, 291-2, 293, 323-4, 325, 351, 396
secularism, 205, 325
Sedbergh, 57
Separatists, 2-4, 31-9, 41-4, 51, 59, 62, 181, 182, 243, 342, 343
Seventh Day Adventists, 266, 274-5
Shakers, 300
Shropshire, 226
sin, 389-90
slogans, 303-76
Social Gospel, 157
social justice, 387-8
Socinianism/Socinians, 82, 111, 112, 153, 164, 172
Soham, 111
Somerset, 123
Speldhurst, 353
spirituality, 67, 105, 106, 136, ch. 8, 383, 396
Spring Hill College, 1, 2
Staffordshire, 57
state, 268
Stockport, 1
Strasbourg, 268
subscription, 89-90
Suffolk, 221
Surrey, 300
Sussex, 300, 349
Synod of Dort, 5

Taizé, 222
Taunton Academy, 74, 231
Thaxted, 83
The Modern Question, 150-1
theological ethics, 248
Tideswell, 47, 49
tithes, 55-6
tolerance, 199, 202, 288
Toleration Act, 73, 115
Torquay, 188
Totteridge/Whetstone, 154
Tradition, 166, 167, 274
Trinity, 11, 59, 60, 79, 84, 91-4, 106, 147, 148, 163-4, 173, 181, 185, 188, 225-6, 249, 250, 257, 265, 266, 270, 272-3, 274, 279, 282, 306, 332, 347, 365-9, 370, 373-5, 379, 381, 382, 398
tritheism, 189
triumphalism, 385-6, 396

Union Theological College, Belfast, 252
Unitarianism/Unitarians, 71, 72, 73, 75, 94, 102, 115, 158, 164, 172-3, 183, 191, 195, 228, 329, 350, 363, 365, 373
United Church of Canada, 356-7, 364
United Church of Christ, 382
United Free Church College, Aberdeen, 247, 250
United Free Church College, Glasgow, 252-2
United Reformed Church, 203, 221, 255-8, 373
Upanishads, 205
universalism, 112, 195, 246, 328, 331
Uxbridge, 188

Vatican II, 167, 262, 286, 308

Wales, 36, 159, 252, 257
Western College, Bristol, 254, 256
Westminster Assembly, 339
Westminster College, Cambridge, 255, 256
Whitehough, 57, 62
Winebrennerism, 174
Woking, 12
womanists, 381-2
women, 288-9, 306, 354, 364
- ordination of, 263, 264
Worcester, 187, 347, 374
Worcester, Massachusetts, 364
World Alliance of Reformed Churches, 242, ch. 10, 281, 355-6
World Council of Churches, 265, 286
World Presbyterian Alliance, 228, 261, 263
World War I, 162
World War II, 169, 375
Worplesdon, 146

Yorkshire United Independent College, 164, 254, 255, 256

Zurich, 267

Studies in Christian History and Thought

(All titles uniform with this volume)
Dates in bold are of projected publication

David Bebbington
Holiness in Nineteenth-Century England
David Bebbington stresses the relationship of movements of spirituality to changes in their cultural setting, especially the legacies of the Enlightenment and Romanticism. He shows that these broad shifts in ideological mood had a profound effect on the ways in which piety was conceptualized and practised. Holiness was intimately bound up with the spirit of the age.
2000 / 0-85364-981-2 / viii + 98pp

J. William Black
Reformation Pastors
Richard Baxter and the Ideal of the Reformed Pastor
This work examines Richard Baxter's *Gildas Salvianus, The Reformed Pastor* (1656) and explores each aspect of his pastoral strategy in light of his own concern for 'reformation' and in the broader context of Edwardian, Elizabethan and early Stuart pastoral ideals and practice.
2003 / 1-84227-190-3 / xxii + 308pp

James Bruce
Prophecy, Miracles, Angels, *and* Heavenly Light?
The Eschatology, Pneumatology and Missiology of Adomnán's Life of Columba
This book surveys approaches to the marvellous in hagiography, providing the first critique of Plummer's hypothesis of Irish saga origin. It then analyses the uniquely systematized phenomena in the *Life of Columba* from Adomnán's seventh-century theological perspective, identifying the coming of the eschatological Kingdom as the key to understanding.
2004 / 1-84227-227-6 / xviii + 286pp

Colin J. Bulley
The Priesthood of Some Believers
Developments from the General to the Special Priesthood in the Christian Literature of the First Three Centuries
The first in-depth treatment of early Christian texts on the priesthood of all believers shows that the developing priesthood of the ordained related closely to the division between laity and clergy and had deleterious effects on the practice of the general priesthood.
2000 / 1-84227-034-6 / xii + 336pp

July 2005

Anthony R. Cross (ed.)

Ecumenism and History

Studies in Honour of John H.Y. Briggs

This collection of essays examines the inter-relationships between the two fields in which Professor Briggs has contributed so much: history—particularly Baptist and Nonconformist—and the ecumenical movement. With contributions from colleagues and former research students from Britain, Europe and North America, *Ecumenism and History* provides wide-ranging studies in important aspects of Christian history, theology and ecumenical studies.

2002 / 1-84227-135-0 / xx + 362pp

Maggi Dawn

Confessions of an Inquiring Spirit

Form as Constitutive of Meaning in S.T. Coleridge's Theological Writing

This study of Coleridge's *Confessions* focuses on its confessional, epistolary and fragmentary form, suggesting that attention to these features significantly affects its interpretation. Bringing a close study of these three literary forms, the author suggests ways in which they nuance the text with particular understandings of the Trinity, and of a kenotic christology. Some parallels are drawn between Romantic and postmodern dilemmas concerning the authority of the biblical text.

***2006** / 1-84227-255-1 / approx. 224 pp*

Ruth Gouldbourne

The Flesh and the Feminine

Gender and Theology in the Writings of Caspar Schwenckfeld

Caspar Schwenckfeld and his movement exemplify one of the radical communities of the sixteenth century. Challenging theological and liturgical norms, they also found themselves challenging social and particularly gender assumptions. In this book, the issues of the relationship between radical theology and the understanding of gender are considered.

***2005** / 1-84227-048-6 / approx. 304pp*

Crawford Gribben

Puritan Millennialism

Literature and Theology, 1550–1682

Puritan Millennialism surveys the growth, impact and eventual decline of puritan millennialism throughout England, Scotland and Ireland, arguing that it was much more diverse than has frequently been suggested. This Paternoster edition is revised and extended from the original 2000 text.

***2007** / 1-84227-372-8 / approx. 320pp*

Galen K. Johnson

Prisoner of Conscience

John Bunyan on Self, Community and Christian Faith

This is an interdisciplinary study of John Bunyan's understanding of conscience across his autobiographical, theological and fictional writings, investigating whether conscience always deserves fidelity, and how Bunyan's view of conscience affects his relationship both to modern Western individualism and historic Christianity.

2003 / 1-84227-223-3 / xvi + 236pp

R.T. Kendall

Calvin and English Calvinism to 1649

The author's thesis is that those who formed the Westminster Confession of Faith, which is regarded as Calvinism, in fact departed from John Calvin on two points: (1) the extent of the atonement and (2) the ground of assurance of salvation.

1997 / 0-85364-827-1 / xii + 264pp

Timothy Larsen

Friends of Religious Equality

Nonconformist Politics in Mid-Victorian England

During the middle decades of the nineteenth century the English Nonconformist community developed a coherent political philosophy of its own, of which a central tenet was the principle of religious equality (in contrast to the stereotype of Evangelical Dissenters). The Dissenting community fought for the civil rights of Roman Catholics, non-Christians and even atheists on an issue of principle which had its flowering in the enthusiastic and undivided support which Nonconformity gave to the campaign for Jewish emancipation. This reissued study examines the political efforts and ideas of English Nonconformists during the period, covering the whole range of national issues raised, from state education to the Crimean War. It offers a case study of a theologically conservative group defending religious pluralism in the civic sphere, showing that the concept of religious equality was a grand vision at the centre of the political philosophy of the Dissenters.

2007 */ 1-84227-402-3 / x + 300pp*

July 2005

Byung-Ho Moon

Christ the Mediator of the Law

Calvin's Christological Understanding of the Law as the Rule of Living and Life-Giving

This book explores the coherence between Christology and soteriology in Calvin's theology of the law, examining its intellectual origins and his position on the concept and extent of Christ's mediation of the law. A comparative study between Calvin and contemporary Reformers—Luther, Bucer, Melancthon and Bullinger—and his opponent Michael Servetus is made for the purpose of pointing out the unique feature of Calvin's Christological understanding of the law.

***2005** / 1-84227-318-3 / approx. 370pp*

John Eifion Morgan-Wynne

Holy Spirit and Religious Experience in Christian Writings, c.AD 90–200

This study examines how far Christians in the third to fifth generations (c.AD 90–200) attributed their sense of encounter with the divine presence, their sense of illumination in the truth or guidance in decision-making, and their sense of ethical empowerment to the activity of the Holy Spirit in their lives.

***2005** / 1-84227-319-1 / approx. 350pp*

James I. Packer

The Redemption and Restoration of Man in the Thought of Richard Baxter

James I. Packer provides a full and sympathetic exposition of Richard Baxter's doctrine of humanity, created and fallen; its redemption by Christ Jesus; and its restoration in the image of God through the obedience of faith by the power of the Holy Spirit.

2002 / 1-84227-147-4 / 432pp

July 2005

Andrew Partington,

Church and State

The Contribution of the Church of England Bishops to the House of Lords during the Thatcher Years

In *Church and State*, Andrew Partington argues that the contribution of the Church of England bishops to the House of Lords during the Thatcher years was overwhelmingly critical of the government; failed to have a significant influence in the public realm; was inefficient, being undertaken by a minority of those eligible to sit on the Bench of Bishops; and was insufficiently moral and spiritual in its content to be distinctive. On the basis of this, and the likely reduction of the number of places available for Church of England bishops in a fully reformed Second Chamber, the author argues for an evolution in the Church of England's approach to the service of its bishops in the House of Lords. He proposes the Church of England works to overcome the genuine obstacles which hinder busy diocesan bishops from contributing to the debates of the House of Lords and to its life more informally.

***2005** / 1-84227-334-5 / approx. 324pp*

Michael Pasquarello III

God's Ploughman

Hugh Latimer: A 'Preaching Life' (1490–1555)

This construction of a 'preaching life' situates Hugh Latimer within the larger religious, political and intellectual world of late medieval England. Neither biography, intellectual history, nor analysis of discrete sermon texts, this book is a work of homiletic history which draws from the details of Latimer's milieu to construct an interpretive framework for the preaching performances that formed the core of his identity as a religious reformer. Its goal is to illumine the practical wisdom embodied in the content, form and style of Latimer's preaching, and to recapture a sense of its overarching purpose, movement, and transforming force during the reform of sixteenth-century England.

***2006** / 1-84227-336-1 / approx. 250pp*

Alan P.F. Sell

Enlightenment, Ecumenism, Evangel

Theological Themes and Thinkers 1550–2000

This book consists of papers in which such interlocking topics as the Enlightenment, the problem of authority, the development of doctrine, spirituality, ecumenism, theological method and the heart of the gospel are discussed. Issues of significance to the church at large are explored with special reference to writers from the Reformed and Dissenting traditions.

2005 / 1-84227-330-2 / xviii + 422pp

July 2005

Alan P.F. Sell

Hinterland Theology

Some Reformed and Dissenting Adjustments

Many books have been written on theology's 'giants' and significant trends, but what of those lesser-known writers who adjusted to them? In this book some hinterland theologians of the British Reformed and Dissenting traditions, who followed in the wake of toleration, the Evangelical Revival, the rise of modern biblical criticism and Karl Barth, are allowed to have their say. They include Thomas Ridgley, Ralph Wardlaw, T.V. Tymms and N.H.G. Robinson.

***2006** / 1-84227-331-0 / approx. 350pp*

Alan P.F. Sell and Anthony R. Cross (eds)

Protestant Nonconformity in the Twentieth Century

In this collection of essays scholars representative of a number of Nonconformist traditions reflect thematically on Nonconformists' life and witness during the twentieth century. Among the subjects reviewed are biblical studies, theology, worship, evangelism and spirituality, and ecumenism. Over and above its immediate interest, this collection provides a marker to future scholars and others wishing to know how some of their forebears assessed Nonconformity's contribution to a variety of fields during the century leading up to Christianity's third millennium.

2003 / 1-84227-221-7 / x + 398pp

Mark Smith

Religion in Industrial Society

Oldham and Saddleworth 1740–1865

This book analyses the way British churches sought to meet the challenge of industrialization and urbanization during the period 1740–1865. Working from a case-study of Oldham and Saddleworth, Mark Smith challenges the received view that the Anglican Church in the eighteenth century was characterized by complacency and inertia, and reveals Anglicanism's vigorous and creative response to the new conditions. He reassesses the significance of the centrally directed church reforms of the mid-nineteenth century, and emphasizes the importance of local energy and enthusiasm. Charting the growth of denominational pluralism in Oldham and Saddleworth, Dr Smith compares the strengths and weaknesses of the various Anglican and Nonconformist approaches to promoting church growth. He also demonstrates the extent to which all the churches participated in a common culture shaped by the influence of evangelicalism, and shows that active co-operation between the churches rather than denominational conflict dominated. This revised and updated edition of Dr Smith's challenging and original study makes an important contribution both to the social history of religion and to urban studies.

***2006** / 1-84227-335-3 / approx. 300pp*

Martin Sutherland
Peace, Toleration and Decay
The Ecclesiology of Later Stuart Dissent

This fresh analysis brings to light the complexity and fragility of the later Stuart Nonconformist consensus. Recent findings on wider seventeenth-century thought are incorporated into a new picture of the dynamics of Dissent and the roots of evangelicalism.

2003 / 1-84227-152-0 / xxii + 216pp

G. Michael Thomas
The Extent of the Atonement
A Dilemma for Reformed Theology from Calvin to the Consensus

A study of the way Reformed theology addressed the question, 'Did Christ die for all, or for the elect only?', commencing with John Calvin, and including debates with Lutheranism, the Synod of Dort and the teaching of Moïse Amyraut.

1997 / 0-85364-828-X / x + 278pp

David M. Thompson
Baptism, Church and Society in Britain from the Evangelical Revival to *Baptism, Eucharist and Ministry*

The theology and practice of baptism have not received the attention they deserve. How important is faith? What does baptismal regeneration mean? Is baptism a bond of unity between Christians? This book discusses the theology of baptism and popular belief and practice in England and Wales from the Evangelical Revival to the publication of the World Council of Churches' consensus statement on *Baptism, Eucharist and Ministry* (1982).

***2005** / 1-84227-393-0 / approx. 224pp*

Mark D. Thompson
A Sure Ground on Which to Stand
The Relation of Authority and Interpretive Method of Luther's Approach to Scripture

The best interpreter of Luther is Luther himself. Unfortunately many modern studies have superimposed contemporary agendas upon this sixteenth-century Reformer's writings. This fresh study examines Luther's own words to find an explanation for his robust confidence in the Scriptures, a confidence that generated the famous 'stand' at Worms in 1521.

2004 / 1-84227-145-8 / xvi + 322pp

Carl R. Trueman and R.S. Clark (eds)

Protestant Scholasticism

Essays in Reassessment

Traditionally Protestant theology, between Luther's early reforming career and the dawn of the Enlightenment, has been seen in terms of decline and fall into the wastelands of rationalism and scholastic speculation. In this volume a number of scholars question such an interpretation. The editors argue that the development of post-Reformation Protestantism can only be understood when a proper historical model of doctrinal change is adopted. This historical concern underlies the subsequent studies of theologians such as Calvin, Beza, Olevian, Baxter, and the two Turrentini. The result is a significantly different reading of the development of Protestant Orthodoxy, one which both challenges the older scholarly interpretations and clichés about the relationship of Protestantism to, among other things, scholasticism and rationalism, and which demonstrates the fruitfulness of the new, historical approach.

1999 / 0-85364-853-0 / xx + 344pp

Shawn D. Wright

Our Sovereign Refuge

The Pastoral Theology of Theodore Beza

Our Sovereign Refuge is a study of the pastoral theology of the Protestant reformer who inherited the mantle of leadership in the Reformed church from John Calvin. Countering a common view of Beza as supremely a 'scholastic' theologian who deviated from Calvin's biblical focus, Wright uncovers a new portrait. He was not a cold and rigid academic theologian obsessed with probing the eternal decrees of God. Rather, by placing him in his pastoral context and by noting his concerns in his pastoral and biblical treatises, Wright shows that Beza was fundamentally a committed Christian who was troubled by the vicissitudes of life in the second half of the sixteenth century. He believed that the biblical truth of the supreme sovereignty of God alone could support Christians on their earthly pilgrimage to heaven. This pastoral and personal portrait forms the heart of Wright's argument.

2004 / 1-84227-252-7 / xviii + 308pp

Paternoster
9 Holdom Avenue,
Bletchley,
Milton Keynes MK1 1QR,
United Kingdom
Web: www.authenticmedia.co.uk/paternoster

July 2005